W9-BFF-372

The Complete Guide to America's National Parks

The Official Visitor's Guide of the National Park Foundation

Comprehensive Information on all 367 National Park Areas

1994-1995 Edition

Published by:
National Park Foundation

1101 17th St., NW, Suite 1102
Washington, DC 20036

Distributed by:
Fodor's Travel Publications, Inc.
A Random House Company

201 East 50th Street
New York, NY 10022

The Complete Guide to America's National Parks

1994-1995 Edition

EDITOR	Jane Bangley McQueen
PROJECT MANAGER	Charles O. Hyman
BOOK DESIGN, COVER DESIGN & MAP ART	Kevin Osborn, Research & Design; Arlington, Virginia
EDITORIAL ASSISTANT	Shari L. Yoder
RESEARCH ASSISTANCE	Research assistance provided by the National Park Service: Office of Public Inquiries; Division of Park Planning and Protection; and Harpers Ferry Center Publications Division.
PHOTOGRAPHY CREDITS	Cover photograph of Glacier National Park in Montana by Tom Algire. Cover background photograph of clouds by Fred J. Maroon. All other photographs courtesy of the National Park Service: Photographic Collection, Harpers Ferry Center; Wind Cave National Park; Mammoth Cave National Park; and Samoa National Park. Photographs by - Richard Frear, M. Woodbridge Williams, Cecil W. Stoughton, Fred Mang, Jr., John M. Kauffmann, Bryan Harry, Douglas Faulkner, W.S. Keller, Fred R. Bell, Cliff McAdams, Thomas C. Gray and Ernest Braun.
DONATIONS	Cover and color section paper donated by **Potlatch Corporation**. Text paper partially donated by **Westvaco**.

Library of Congress Catalog Card No. 93-86476

ISBN: 0-679-02676-2

Copyright, ©, 1994 National Park Foundation.

Printed in the United States of America on recycled paper.

All rights reserved. No part of this book may be reproduced in any form without the express written permission of the National Park Foundation.

 Printed on Recycled Paper.

Message from the President

Dear Visitor

The National Park Foundation is proud to present the revised and newly designed *Complete Guide to America's National Parks*. Use this Eighth Edition to plan trips and learn more about our nation's amazing array of National Park Areas.

Thumb through the *Guide* and you'll see 367 diverse National Park Service sites that have been set aside to protect our natural, historical and cultural heritage. The *Guide* is the only book that provides information on all of these national treasures, including Trails and Rivers.

Take your *Guide* along on any trip as a reference to find National Park sites wherever you are - sites like the George Washington Carver National Monument in Missouri or the Saint-Gaudens National Historic Site in New Hampshire. These sites add so much to our cultural and historical knowledge, and yet many people don't even know they exist. A 20-page color section of photographs in the *Guide* provide a sample of the sites' wildlife and majestic scenery.

Other features that you'll find only in the *Guide* are the **Regional Touring Maps**, helping you plan car trips between sites; the **Peak Visitation** section, telling you when areas are crowded; **Special Interest Parks**, providing easy reference to sites of particular cultural and historical significance; and **Climatables**^{tm}, weather charts for 40 National Park Areas.

What really makes the *Guide* stand out from the crowd, though, is that by buying this book, you're helping to support the National Parks. For more than 25 years, the National Park Foundation has been the official private foundation of the National Park Service. Donations of money, land, buildings and artifacts are channeled by the Foundation into the National Parks to support education, interpretation and preservation programs.

To find out more about how to contribute to the National Parks or how to order more *Guides*, write to the National Park Foundation, Department CG, 1101 17th St., NW, Suite 1102, Washington, DC 20036.

I hope you enjoy your *Guide* and your National Parks.

Alan A. Rubin
President
National Park Foundation

NATIONAL PARK FOUNDATION

Officers and Board Members of the National Park Foundation

CHAIRMAN

The Honorable Bruce Babbitt
Secretary of the Interior
Washington, DC

VICE CHAIRMAN

Mr. James R. Harvey
Chairman, Transamerica Corporation
San Francisco, California

SECRETARY

The Honorable Roger G. Kennedy
Director, National Park Service
Washington, DC

TREASURER

Mr. E. William Cole, Jr.
Administrator/CEO, Trans-Alaska Pipeline Liability Fund
Arlington, Virginia

PRESIDENT

Mr. Alan A. Rubin
Washington, DC

COUNSEL

The Honorable Leonard L. Silverstein
Silverstein and Mullens
Washington, DC

MEMBERS OF THE BOARD

Mr. Linden S. Blue
Vice Chairman, General Atomics
San Diego, California

The Honorable Peter M. Flanigan
Managing Director, Dillon, Read & Co., Inc.
New York, New York

The Honorable John Gavin
Chairman, The Century Council
Los Angeles, California

Mr. Walter A. Haas, Jr.
Honorary Chairman of the Board, Levi Strauss & Co.
San Francisco, California

The Honorable Marian S. Heiskell
Director, The New York Times Company
New York, New York

Mr. John E. Jacob
President and CEO, National Urban League
New York, New York

Mr. Donald M. Kendall
Chairman, PepsiCo Foundation
Purchase, New York

Mr. Homer L. Luther, Jr.
Private Investor
Houston, Texas

Mr. Jack A. MacAllister
Chairman Emeritus, U S West, Inc.
Englewood, California

Mr. Richard B. Madden
Chairman and CEO, Potlatch Corporation
San Francisco, California

Mr. Robert H. Malott
Chairman, Executive Committee, FMC Corporation
Chicago, Illinois

Mr. Morton H. Meyerson
Chairman & CEO, Perot Systems Corporation
Dallas, Texas

Ms. Nancy Clark Reynolds
Senior Consultant, The Wexler Group
Santa Fe, New Mexico

The Honorable Donald Rumsfeld
Chairman & CEO, General Instrument Corporation
Chicago, Illinois

Mr. Charles R. Schwab
Chairman & CEO, The Charles Schwab Corporation
San Francisco, California

The Honorable Ed E. Williams III
Partner, Baker, Worthington, Crossley, Stansberry & Woolf
Johnson City, Tennessee

Mr. Robert E. Wycoff
President Emeritus, Atlantic Richfield Company
Los Angeles, California

Table of Contents

Introduction

Using the Guide

The 1994-1995 Eighth Edition of *The Complete Guide to America's National Parks*, sales of which support the National Parks, makes the information you need for your trip easy to find. Each site is listed in alphabetical order by state. Refer to the appropriate heading for information on camping and lodging, visitor activities, accessibility, etc.

Information for each site has been submitted for review by the site's staff and checked again for accuracy by the National Park Foundation.

There are separate chapters on National Scenic and National Historic Trails, the National Rivers and National Wild and Scenic Rivers, Regional Tours, Peak Visitation and Special Interest Parks.

These graphic symbols will indicate sites that are a:

National Park, National Preserve,

National Memorial,

National Monument,

National Battlefield, National Battlefield Park, National Battlefield Site, National Military Park,

National Historic Site, National Historical Park,

National Recreation Area, National Seashore, National Lakeshore,

National River, National Wild and Scenic River,

National Scenic Trail and National Historic Trail.

Every effort has been made to provide accurate information, but the National Park Foundation assumes no responsibility for inconvenience, delay or damage caused by any inaccuracy or omission. Information on campgrounds and other facilities has been included for the convenience of readers. No endorsement should be inferred.

Maps

Each section begins with a state map indicating sites as well as major roads and helpful locators such as cities or rivers. There are city maps for Washington, DC; Boston, MA; New York, NY; Philadelphia, PA; and San Francisco, CA. Seven maps in the Regional Tours chapter will help you plan trips between sites that are within an easy drive of each other. A 2-page trails map highlights the 14 National Scenic and National Historic Trails under National Park Service management.

The maps in this book are not detailed road maps.

Entrance Fees

National Park entrance fees are included, but are subject to change. The **Golden Eagle Pass** is an annual entrance permit issued for $25, which is honored at all Federal recreation areas that charge fees. The National Park Service affiliated areas do not accept the pass and are noted in the Guide. Beginning in 1994, Golden Eagle Passes will be valid for 1 year from the date of purchase and may be obtained from Federal agencies as well as businesses, nonprofit groups and other organizations authorized by the Secretary of the Interior and the Secretary of the Department of Agriculture.

The **Golden Age Passport** is available for people 62 years old and older for a one-time fee of $10. Persons with disabilities who are eligible for Federal benefits may obtain the **Golden Access Passport**.

For more information on the entrance permits, contact the National Park Service in Washington, DC, at 202-208-4747 or any of the NPS regional offices.

Climatables ᵗᵐ

Climatables ᵗᵐ begin on page 476 and are compilations of official National Oceanic and Atmospheric Administration weather data from individual National Weather Service offices, cooperative observation stations and from publications on the National Climatic Data Center. They do not represent a forecast, but do indicate the type and range of past weather conditions. A metric conversion chart provided by the National Weather Service is featured on page 475.

The Climatables were compiled by Lowell Krawitz Associates of Philadelphia, PA.

Access for Persons With Disabilities

The Guide includes information on accessible attractions and facilities within sites. The National Park Service is a leader in developing accessible recreation and interpretation for people with disabilities, but much remains to be done.

The National Park Foundation and the National Park Service are working together to improve accessibility to sites through the *Easy Access Park Challenge*, a program that matches community-based volunteers with local Parks to complete access projects.

Order the Easy Access National Parks video by sending $19.95 plus $3 for postage and handling in a check or money order payable to: National Park Foundation - Video, 1101 17th St., NW, Suite 1102, Washington, DC 20036.

The half-hour video features opportunities for people with disabilities, seniors and families with young children at 9 National Park sites. Proceeds support the *Easy Access Park Challenge*.

Regional Tours

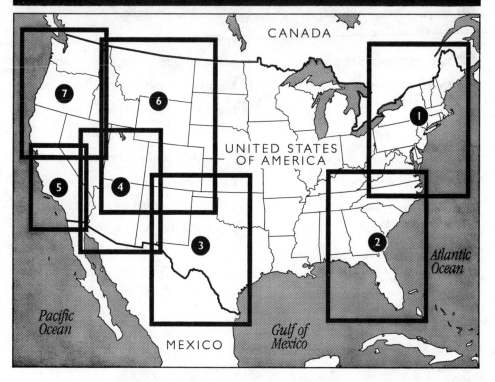

The following maps of 7 regions in the Continental United States with National Park areas indicated will help visitors plan car trips between sites in different states. The sites included are within a day's drive of each other.

1 Regional Map #1

2 Regional Map #2

3 Regional Map #3

4 Regional Map #4

5 Regional Map #5

6 Regional Map #6

7 Regional Map #7

Regional Tour Map #1

1 Acadia National Park

2 Alleghany Portage Railroad National Historic Site

3 Antietam National Battlefield

4 Appomattox Courthouse National Historical Park

5 Cape Cod National Seashore

6 Cape Hatteras National Seashore

7 Catoctin Mountain Park

8 Chesapeake & Ohio Canal National Historical Park

9 Eisenhower National Historic Site

10 Eleanor Roosevelt National Historic Site

11 Fort Raleigh National Historic Site

12 Fort Necessity National Battlefield

13 Fredericksburg and Spotsylvania County Battlefields Memorial NMP

14 Friendship Hill National Historic Site

15 George Washington Memorial Parkway

16 Gettysburg National Military Park

17 Harpers Ferry National Historical Park

18 Home of Franklin D. Roosevelt National Historic Site

19 Johnstown Flood National Memorial

20 Lowell National Historical Park

21 Manassas National Battlefield Park

22 Martin Van Buren National Historic Site

23 Minute Man National Historical Park

24 Monocacy National Battlefield

25 Prince William Forest Park

26 Roger Williams National Memorial

27 Saint-Gaudens National Historic Site

28 Salem Maritime National Historic Site

29 Saugus Iron Works National Historic Site

30 Shenandoah National Park

31 Touro Synagogue National Historic Site

32 Vanderbilt Mansion National Historic Site

33 Weir Farm National Historic Site

34 Wolf Trap Farm Park for the Performing Arts

35 Wright Brothers National Memorial

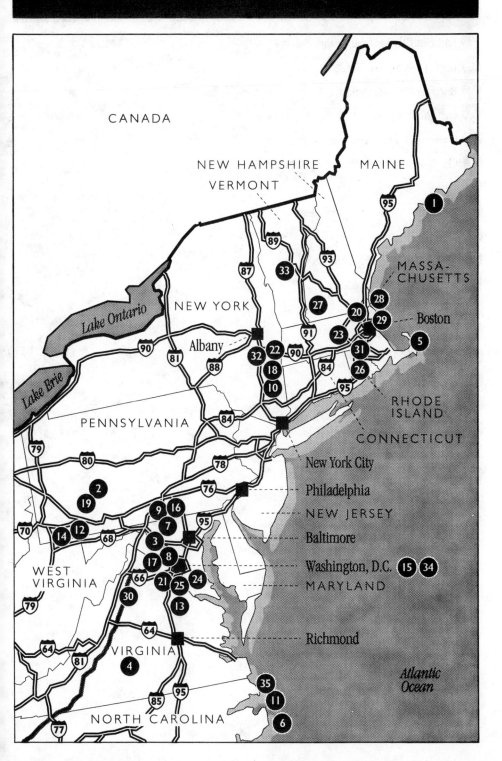

1. Andersonville National Historic Site
2. Big Cypress National Preserve
3. Biscayne National Park
4. Carl Sandburg Home National Historic Site
5. Castillo de San Marcos National Monument
6. Chattahoochee River National Recreation Area
7. Cowpens National Battlefield
8. Cumberland Island National Seashore
9. Everglades National Park
10. Fort Matanzas National Monument
11. Fort Caroline National Memorial
12. Fort Frederica National Monument
13. Fort Pulaski National Monument
14. Great Smoky Mountains National Park
15. Jimmy Carter National Historic Site
16. Kennesaw Mountain National Battlefield Park
17. Kings Mountain National Military Park
18. Martin Luther King Jr. National Historic Site
19. Ninety Six National Historic Site
20. Russel Cave National Monument
21. Timucuan Ecological and Historic Preserve
22. Tuskegee Institute National Historic Site

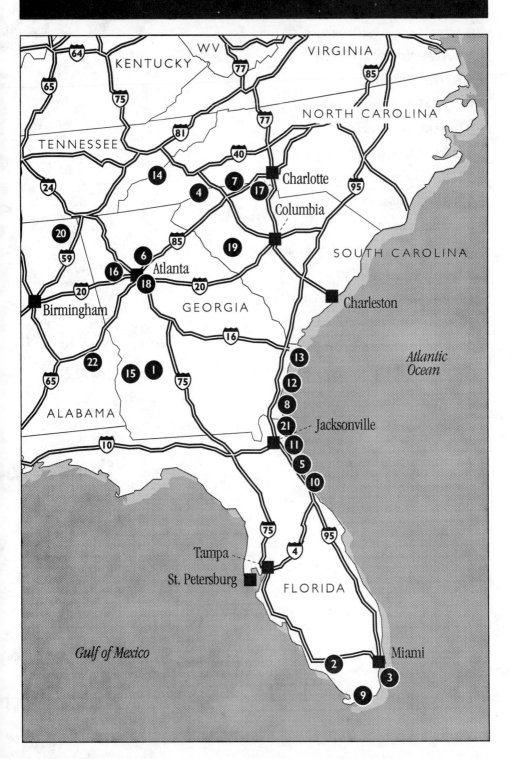

1 Amistad National Recreation Area

2 Bandalier National Monument

3 Big Bend National Park

4 Capulin Volcano National Monument

5 Carlsbad Caverns National Park

6 Chamizal National Memorial

7 El Malpais National Monument

8 Fort Union National Monument

9 Guadalupe Mountains National Park

10 Lyndon B. Johnson National Historical Park

11 Padre Island National Seashore

12 Palo Alto Battlefield National Historical Park

13 Petroglyph National Monument

14 San Antonio Missions National Historical Park

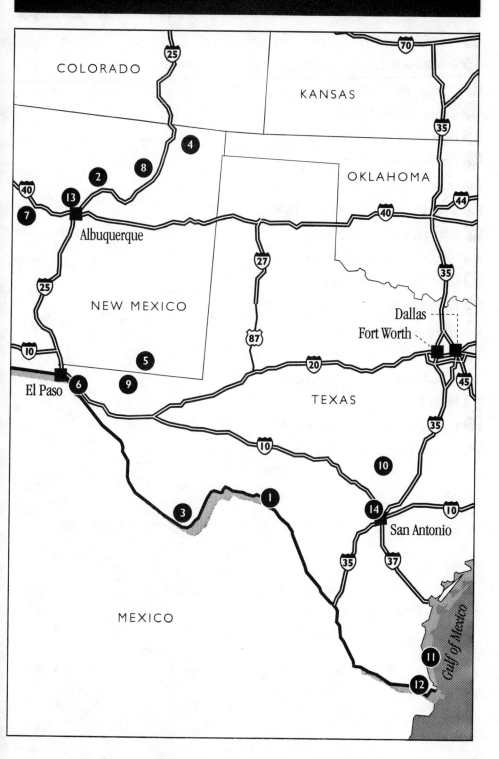

1. Arches National Park
2. Aztec Ruins National Monument
3. Bryce Canyon National Park
4. Canyon de Chelly National Monument
5. Canyonlands National Park
6. Capitol Reef National Park
7. Cedar Breaks National Monument
8. Chaco Culture National Historical Park
9. Curecanti National Recreation Area
10. Glen Canyon National Recreation Area
11. Grand Canyon National Park
12. Hovenweep National Monument
13. Lake Mead National Recreation Area
14. Mesa Verde National Park
15. Natural Bridges National Monument
16. Navajo National Monument
17. Pipe Spring National Monument
18. Rainbow Bridge National Monument

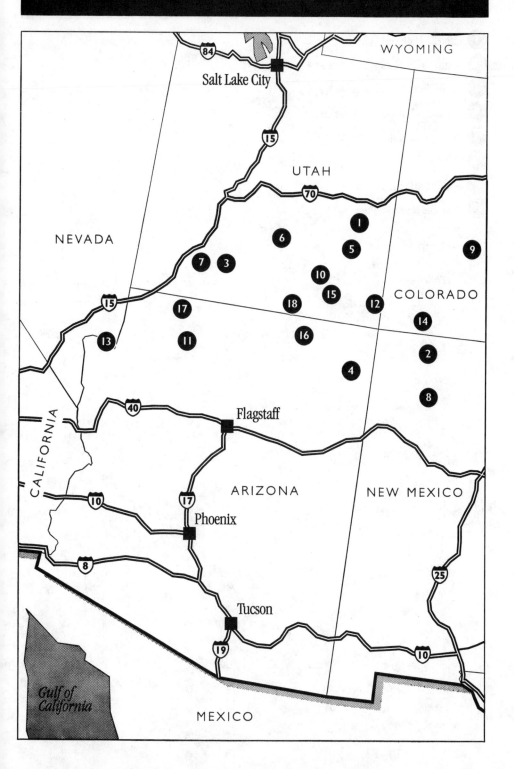

Regional Tour Map #5

1. Cabrillo National Monument
2. Death Valley National Monument
3. Devils Postpile National Monument
4. Pinnacles National Monument
5. Point Reyes National Seashore
6. Santa Monica Mountains National Recreation Area
7. Sequoia and Kings Canyon National Park
8. Yosemite National Park

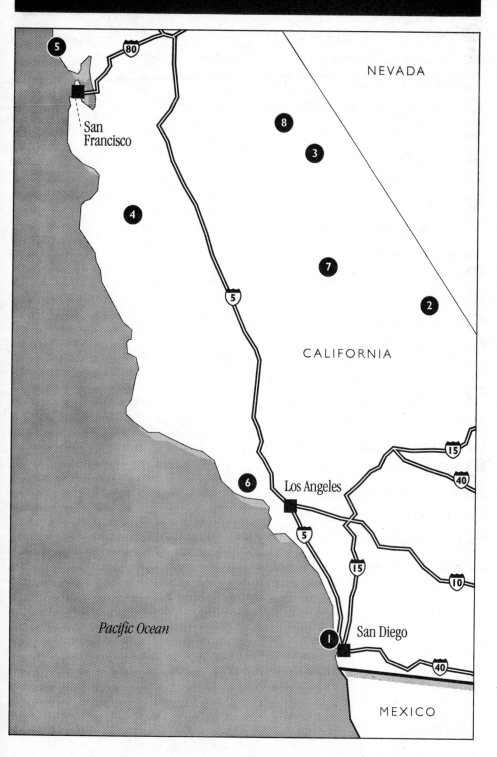

Regional Tour Map #6

1. Agate Fossil Beds National Monument
2. Badlands National Park
3. Big Hole National Battlefield
4. Bighorn Canyon National Recreation Area
5. City of Rocks National Reserve
6. Craters of the Moon National Monument
7. Fort Union Trading Post National Historic Site
8. Fort Laramie National Historic Site
9. Fossil Butte National Monument
10. Glacier National Park
11. Golden Spike National Historic Site
12. Grand Teton National Park
13. Grant-Kohrs Ranch National Historic Site
14. Hagerman Fossil Beds National Monument
15. Jewel Cave National Monument
16. John D. Rockefeller, Jr. Memorial Parkway
17. Knife River Indian Villages National Historic Site
18. Little Bighorn Battlefield National Monument
19. Mount Rushmore National Memorial
20. Scotts Bluff National Monument
21. Theodore Roosevelt National Park
22. Wind Cave National Park
23. Yellowstone National Park

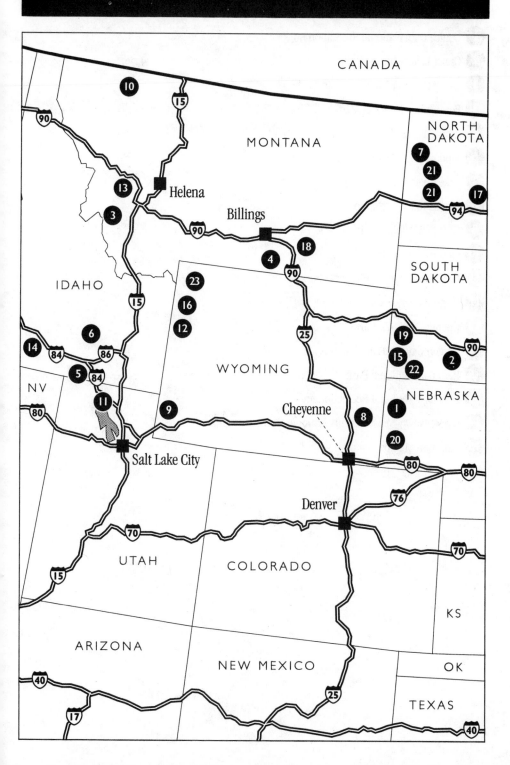

1. Coulee Dam National Recreation Area
2. Crater Lake National Park
3. Fort Vancouver National Historic Site
4. Fort Clatsop National Memorial
5. John Day Fossil Beds National Monument
6. Klondike Gold Rush National Historical Park
7. Lake Chelan National Recreation Area
8. Lassen Volcanic National Park
9. Lava Beds National Monument
10. Mount Rainier National Park
11. Nez Perce National Historical Park
12. North Cascades National Park
13. Olympic National Park
14. Oregon Caves National Monument
15. Redwoods National Park
16. Ross Lake National Recreation Area
17. Whiskeytown-Shasta-Trinity National Recreation Area
18. Whitman Mission National Historic Site

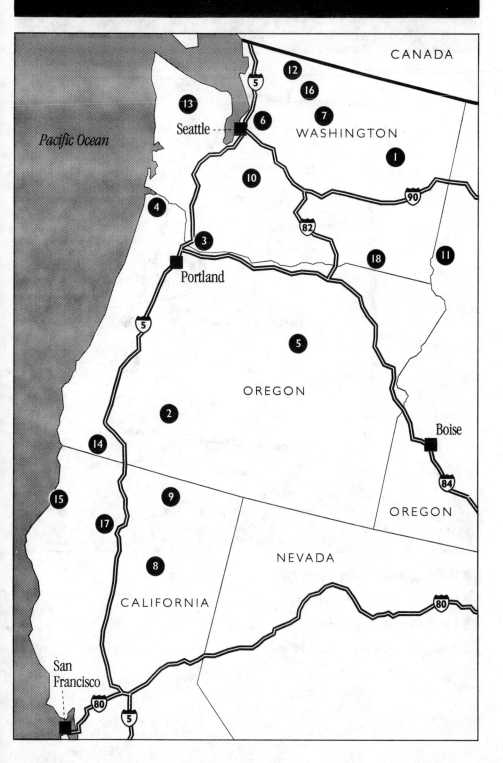

Alabama

1 Horseshoe Bend National Military Park

2 Little River Canyon National Preserve

3 Russell Cave National Monument

4 Tuskegee Institute National Historic Site

Horseshoe Bend National Military Park
Daviston, Alabama

The Battle of Horseshoe Bend on March 27, 1814, between nearly 3,000 Tennessee frontier troops led by Andrew Jackson and close to 1,000 Creek Indians led by Chief Menawa ended the Creek Indian War. It also broke the tribe's power in the Southeast and added Creek lands comprising three-fifths of the present Alabama and one-fifth of Georgia to the United States.

MAILING ADDRESS

Horseshoe Bend National Military Park, Superintendent, Rt. 1 - Box 103, Daviston, AL 36256 **Telephone:** 205-234-7111

DIRECTIONS

Horseshoe Bend National Military Park is on Alabama Highway 49, 12 miles (19.3 km) north of Dadeville, and 18 miles (29 km) east of Alexander City via Alabama Highway 22 to New Site.

VISITOR ACTIVITIES

• Museum with military artifacts, diorama and electric map about the battle. • Exhibits about Creek Indian life. Ten-minute slide program: "The Creek War and the Battle of Horseshoe Bend." • Flintlock musket or rifle demonstrations offered when staffing permits. • Monthly special interpretive programs. • Facilities include a 3-mile (4.8 km) auto tour of the battlefield, 2-mile (3.2 km) and 3-mile (4.8 km) hiking trails through the Park and battlefield, 2 picnic areas and a boat ramp. • Park grounds are open daily from 9 a.m. to 5 p.m., except Dec. 25.

PERMITS, FEES & LIMITATIONS

• Permits and fees are required for special uses. • Vehicles are allowed only on paved roads. • Pets must be on a leash.

ACCESSIBILITY

Visitor Center/Museum is accessible.

CAMPING & LODGING

• Nearest camping facilities are located at Wind Creek State Park, 6 miles (9.6 km) south of Alexander City. Additional campgrounds are available at Talladega National Forest and Mount Cheaha State Park, 50 miles (80.6 km) north on Alabama Highway 49. • Lodging is available in Alexander City in Dadeville.

FOOD & SUPPLIES

Food and supplies are available in both Alexander City and Dadeville.

FIRST AID/ HOSPITAL

• First Aid is provided by the park rangers. • Hospitals are located in Dadeville and Alexander City.

GENERAL INFORMATION

For your safety - Be careful of dangerous snakes, poison ivy and biting fire ants.

Alabama

Little River Canyon National Preserve

DeKalb County and Cherokee County, Alabama

Little River Canyon National Preserve was established on Oct. 21, 1992 to protect 35 miles (56.5 km) of the Little River flowing atop Lookout Mountain in northeastern Alabama. The Preserve contains one of the most extensive canyon systems of the Cumberland Plateau, provides a habitat for a unique assemblage of plants and animals, and contains outstanding scenic vistas and world class white water for boaters. It is also the deepest canyon in Alabama.

MAILING ADDRESS

Little River Canyon National Preserve, PO Box 45, Fort Payne, AL 35967
Telephone: 205-997-9239

VISITOR ACTIVITIES

Visitor services and facilities are not yet offered by the National Park Service. Planning is underway for the acquisition of lands currently owned by the State of Alabama, the Alabama Power Co., and Cherokee County, AL.

Russell Cave National Monument

Bridgeport, Alabama

An almost continuous archaeological record of human habitation from at least 7000 BC to about 1650 AD - Early Archaic to Mississippian cultural periods - is displayed in Russell Cave.

MAILING ADDRESS

Russell Cave National Monument, Route 1, Box 175, Bridgeport, AL 35740
Telephone: 205-495-2672

DIRECTIONS

The Monument is best approached by US 72 to Bridgeport, AL. Turn north on County Road 75 to the community of Mount Carmel, then turn right on County Road 98 to the Monument entrance. The distance from Bridgeport to the Monument is 8 miles (12.9 km) on paved road.

VISITOR ACTIVITIES

• Interpretive films and slide programs are available upon request in the Monument's audio-visual room. A slide program is shown in the cave shelter area. • Interpretive exhibits and talks, demonstrations of ancient Indian life and guided tours of the cave shelter or groups. • Visitor facilities include hiking trails and restrooms. • The Monument is open daily from 8 a.m. to 5 p.m. except for Dec. 25.

PERMITS, FEES & LIMITATIONS

No fees.

ACCESSIBILITY

Parking and restrooms are accessible. Audiovisual programs and printed cave program texts are available for the hearing impaired.

CAMPING & LODGING	• Nearby lodging is in Kimball, TN, at the junction of US 72 and I-24, 18 miles (29 km); and at Bridgeport, AL, 7 miles (11.2 km).
FOOD & SUPPLIES	• No food or supplies are available in the Monument. • Numerous stores are within 20 miles (32.2 km).
FIRST AID/ HOSPITAL	• First aid is available in the Monument. • The nearest hospital is on US 72 between Bridgeport and Stevenson, AL, 10 miles (16.1 km).
GENERAL INFORMATION	Summers are hot and humid. Winters are relatively mild.

Tuskegee Institute National Historic Site

Tuskegee, Alabama

In a post-Reconstruction era marked by growing segregation and disenfranchisement of African Americans, Booker T. Washington established Tuskegee Institute with the goal of training teachers and developing occupational skills to equip students for jobs in the trades and agriculture.

MAILING ADDRESS	Tuskegee Institute National Historic Site, P.O. Drawer 10, Tuskegee, AL 36087-0010 **Telephone: 205-727-6390**
DIRECTIONS	The Site is on Old Montgomery Road and is adjacent to the City of Tuskegee, AL. From I-85, exit onto AL 81 South, turn right at the intersection of 81 and Old Montgomery Road. Follow the signs to the Visitor Center located in the Carver Museum.
VISITOR ACTIVITIES	• Facilities include the Carver Museum and The Oaks, a restored home. • Informal interpretive talks at the Carver Museum, formal tours at The Oaks and special activities intermittently throughout the year.
PERMITS, FEES & LIMITATIONS	None.
ACCESSIBILITY	The museum is accessible. Parking is available behind The Oaks.
CAMPING & LODGING	Overnight accommodations are available on I-85 and Notasula Highway, 5 miles (8 km), from the Site and at the Kellogg Conference Center at I-994 on the Tuskegee University Campus.
FOOD & SUPPLIES	Supplies are available on the Tuskegee University Campus or in downtown Tuskegee, Kellogg Conference Center on I-994.
FIRST AID/ HOSPITAL	• First aid is available within the Site • The nearest hospital is at the East Alabama Medical Center in Opelika, AL, 25 miles (40.3 km) north.
GENERAL INFORMATION	• For your safety - Be especially careful on old walkways and steps. Natural areas have steep slopes, poisonous or spiny vegetation, and insects that sting or bite. • Pedestrians have the right of way on campus roads.

Alaska

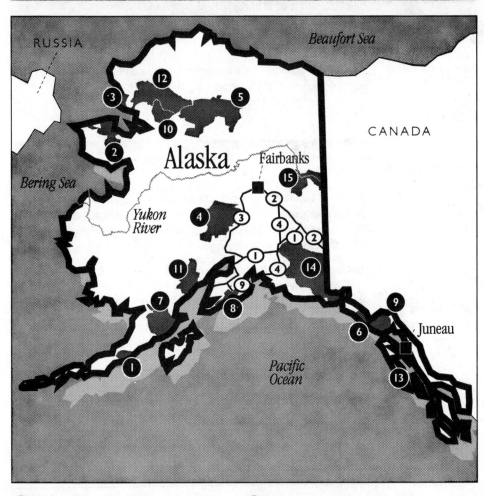

1	Aniakchak National Monument and Preserve	**8**	Kenai Fjords National Park
2	Bering Land Bridge National Preserve	**9**	Klondike Gold Rush National Historical Park
3	Cape Krusenstern National Monument	**10**	Kobuk Valley National Park
4	Denali National Park and Preserve	**11**	Lake Clark National Park and Preserve
5	Gates of the Arctic National Park and Preserve	**12**	Noatak National Preserve
6	Glacier Bay National Park and Preserve	**13**	Sitka National Historical Park
7	Katmai National Park and Preserve	**14**	Wrangell-St. Elias National Park and Preserve
		15	Yukon-Charley Rivers National Preserve

Alaska

Aniakchak National Monument and Preserve

Alaska   See Climatable No. 2

The volcanic Aniakchak Caldera created by the collapse of the central part of a volcano that covers 30 square miles (48.3 km) and is 6 miles (9.6 km) wide includes Surprise Lake, heated by hot springs, which cascades through a 1,500-foot (457.2 m) rift in the crater wall.

MAILING ADDRESS

Aniakchak National Monument and Preserve, Box 7, King Salmon, AK 99613-0007 **Telephone: 907-246-3305**

DIRECTIONS

Reeve Aleutian Airways, Inc., has scheduled flights between Anchorage and Port Heiden Airfield. From Port Heiden Airfield, the Monument is a 10-mile (16.1 km) walk over difficult terrain. Charter flights are also available into the Monument. Mark Air and Peninsula Airways all have twice daily flights from Anchorage to King Salmon. From King Salmon, charter airplanes are available.

VISITOR ACTIVITIES

• Wildlife watching, primitive camping, float trips and fishing. • There are no visitor facilities. • Information on backcountry trails is available from the Alaska Regional Office of the National Park Service or Superintendent, Katmai National Park and Preserve in King Salmon.

PERMITS, FEES & LIMITATIONS

• No fees. • An Alaska fishing license, available in Anchorage and King Salmon, is required.

CAMPING & LODGING

• Primitive camping only is available. • Other overnight accommodations are available in King Salmon, 150 miles (241.9 km).

FOOD & SUPPLIES

All food and supplies should be obtained in King Salmon or Anchorage.

FIRST AID/ HOSPITAL

• First aid is not available in the Monument. • The nearest hospitals are in Kodiak and Dillingham.

GENERAL INFORMATION

• Visitors to the area should have wool clothing, rubber boots and good rain gear. • Bring all food if camping and be sure that tents can withstand bad weather conditions. • The caldera is subject to violent wind storms.

Bering Land Bridge National Preserve

Alaska   See Climatable No. 3

Bering Land Bridge National Preserve commemorates the prehistoric journey of people into the Americas from Asia over a continuous land bridge that stretched between Siberia and Alaska at least 13,000 years ago.

MAILING ADDRESS

Bering Land Bridge National Preserve, Box 220, Nome, AK 99762-0220 **Telephone: 907-443-2522**

DIRECTIONS

The Preserve is quite isolated. No roads lead to the area, and airports at Nome and Kotzebue that handle jets are rather distant from the Preserve's boundaries. Nonetheless, Nome and Kotzebue are the immediate points from which to fly into the Preserve or to native villages in close proximity to the boundaries. Round-trip air fare from Anchorage to either Kotzebue or Nome is $580. It is possible to charter flights out of Nome and Kotzebue into Serpentine Hot Springs and onto beaches of the Preserve. Charter fares run about $200 per hour.

VISITOR ACTIVITIES

• Wilderness hiking and camping, photography, fishing, river floating, boating, canoeing, walking, wildlife and wildflower watching. • Information on backcountry hiking is available from the Superintendent's office. • Part of the attraction of the Preserve is the lifestyle of Eskimos from the neighboring villages, including their reindeer herds, and arts and crafts. • The Preserve never closes.

PERMITS, FEES & LIMITATIONS

• No fees. • Alaska fishing license, available locally, is required.

CAMPING & LODGING

• Primitive camping only - no reservations. • Lodging is available at the intermediate points of Nome and Kotzebue. Room reservations are suggested because touring groups book much of the touring space. Rooms average about $85 per day.

FOOD & SUPPLIES

• Certain items - food, clothing, beverages and some gear - may be purchased from merchants in Nome and Kotzebue, but supplies in village stores are generally limited. • Meals are served in Nome and Kotzebue.

FIRST AID/ HOSPITAL

• First aid is not available in the Preserve. • The nearest hospitals are in Nome and Kotzebue.

GENERAL INFORMATION

• Transportation costs for goods and services in "bush" Alaska raise prices considerably in such places as Nome and Kotzebue. **Visitors planning to stay in the Preserve should arrive self-sufficient.** • Most visitors come into the area between mid-June and mid-September when the temperatures average in the mid-40s°F, along the coast and mid-60s°F, inland. During the ice-free periods along the coasts (late May to late October), cloudy skies prevail, fog occurs, daily temperatures remain fairly constant in the long hours of daylight, and the relative humidity is high. • There is some driftwood along the beaches, but inland wood is scarce and should be used chiefly for cooking. • Visitors should possess skills, talents and stamina to survive some difficult conditions. • Bring only the essentials - good tents with rain flies, sleeping bags and pads, insect repellents and head nets, cooking and eating utensils, first aid items, maps, knife, food, warm clothing and rain gear, calf-high boots with water proof lowers, fishing tackle, extra socks, and possibly some camera equipment. • In parties of 2 or more it is advisable to always travel with others in the Preserve.

Cape Krusenstern National Monument

Northwest Alaska, north of the Arctic Circle   See Climatable No. 3

Treeless Cape Krusenstern National Monument is a coastal plain dotted with lagoons and backed by gently rolling limestone hills. Visitors experience extraordinary views of bluffs and 114 beach ridges that record 6,000 years of prehistoric human use of the coastline.

MAILING ADDRESS

Superintendent, Northwest Alaska Areas, Cape Krusenstern National Monument, National Park Service, P.O. Box 1029, Kotzebue, AK 99752 **Telephone:** 907-442-3760/3890

DIRECTIONS

The Monument is 26 miles (41.9 km) north of the Arctic Circle. There are no roads or rail service. General access is via scheduled air service from Fairbanks or Anchorage to Kotzebue and then air taxi to nearby villages. Summer access to and through the Monument includes motorized and non-motorized watercraft, aircraft, and by foot. Winter access includes snowmobiles, aircraft and by foot.

VISITOR ACTIVITIES

• There are **no National Park Service developments**, services, campgrounds or trails in the Monument. • There is kayaking along the coast and through the lagoons. • Primitive camping, backcountry hiking, beach walking, general wildlife observation, and photography. • Local residents still pursue hunting, fishing, trapping and other subsistence activities due to special provisions of legislation establishing the Monument. • The Monument is always open to the general public. • The Kotzebue Public Lands Information Center is an interagency information center located in Kotzebue. The Center is open from 8 a.m. to 5:30 p.m., Monday through Friday and for longer hours during the summer.

PERMITS, FEES & LIMITATIONS

• No fees. • Alaska hunting and fishing licenses, available in Anchorage or Kotzebue, are required.

ACCESSIBILITY

The Kotzebue Public Lands Information Center is accessible.

CAMPING & LODGING

• Tundra and river bars are often used for primitive camping. • Lodging is available year-round in Kotzebue.

FOOD & SUPPLIES

Supplies are available in Kotzebue.

FIRST AID/ HOSPITAL

• First aid is not available in the Monument. • The nearest hospital is in Kotzebue.

GENERAL INFORMATION

• Rugged terrain is subject to harsh weather, high winds, rain and snow. • Guard against hypothermia, giardia lamblia, wild animals, mosquitoes and biting flies. • Please do not interfere with subsistence camps, fishnets or other equipment. • Respect property and privacy.

Alaska

Denali National Park and Preserve

Denali Park, Alaska   See Climatable No. 4

Denali National Park and Preserve exemplifies Alaska's character as one of the world's last great frontiers for wilderness adventure. It contains 6 million acres, including the Mount McKinley massif, and wildlife that includes caribou, moose and grizzly bears.

MAILING ADDRESS

Superintendent, Denali National Park and Preserve, PO Box 9, Denali Park, AK 99755 Telephone: 907-683-2294

DIRECTIONS

The Park/Preserve is 238 miles (383.8 km) north of Anchorage and 126 miles (203.2 km) south of Fairbanks on Alaska Highway 3. Buses run regularly from both cities in the summer. The Alaska Railroad provides passenger and freight service to the Park/Preserve that takes 8 hours from Anchorage and 4 hours from Fairbanks. For information, write to Alaska Railroad, Traffic Division, PO Box 7-2111, Anchorage, AK 99510.

VISITOR ACTIVITIES

• Wildlife watching, interpretive talks and walks, hiking, backcountry use, fishing, dog sledding and cross-country skiing. • Stop at the Visitor Access Center for bus coupons, backcountry permits, books, maps, etc. • Visitor facilities and the shuttle bus are available from late May through mid-September. • During winter, the Park/Preserve road is closed beyond Headquarters.

PERMITS, FEES & LIMITATIONS

• The entrance fee is $3 per person or $5 per family. • Camping and backcountry use require permits, available at the Visitor Access Center. • Private vehicles are not permitted beyond the Savage River. A free shuttle bus provides access. • All permits and bus coupons are on a first-come, first-served basis. • Snowmobiles are prohibited.

ACCESSIBILITY

The Visitor Access Center, the shuttle, the wildlife tour, 5 of the 7 campgrounds, ARA Denali Park Hotels, Headquarters and the Eielson Visitor Center are accessible. TTY available. A pamphlet on services and facilities is available.

CAMPING & LODGING

• Camping is available on a first-come, first-served basis for $12 a night with registration at the Visitor Access Center. Marino Campground is available for walk-in, tent campers only for $3 a night with self-registration. Riley Creek, Savage River and Teklanika campgrounds are accessible by vehicle. Sanctuary Igloo and Wonder Lake campgrounds are accessible by shuttle bus. • Hotel accommodations are available by writing ARA Outdoor World, Ltd., 825 W. 8th Ave., #240, Anchorage, AK 99501, phone 907-276-7234.

FOOD & SUPPLIES

Basic supplies and groceries are obtainable at a small store near the hotel or in Healy, 12 miles (19.3 km) north.

FIRST AID/ HOSPITAL

• A clinic with a physician's assistant is in Healy. • The closest hospitals and doctors are in Fairbanks.

GENERAL INFORMATION

• During the peak season, 2-day waits are normal for obtaining bus coupons, camp sites and backcountry permits. • Few trails exist. Most hiking is cross-country. • Stop at the Visitor Access Center for information about safety in bear country. • Gasoline and food services are not available in the Park/Preserve interior.

Gates of the Arctic National Park and Preserve

Central and Western Brooks Range, Alaska   See Climatable No. 3

The 8 million acres of Gates of the Arctic National Park comprise a vast tundra wilderness containing 7 designated wild rivers and many lakes and rivers yet unnamed. Broad glacial valleys contrast with the rugged peaks of the Brooks Range. Here, 200 miles (322.5 km) northwest of Fairbanks, is habitat that is vital to the arctic caribou, grizzly bear, sheep, moose, wolves and raptors.

MAILING ADDRESS

Gates of the Arctic National Park and Preserve, PO Box 74680, Fairbanks, AK 99707-4680 **Telephone:** 907-456-0281

DIRECTIONS

Most visitors fly via scheduled flights from Fairbanks to Bettles (about $100 one-way) and then charter small aircraft in Bettles for flights into the Park ($200-$400 per hour). Charter flights can also begin in Fairbanks (air time is generally paid to and from the destination). Scheduled flights from Fairbanks and Bettles to Anaktuvuk Pass (within Park boundaries) are available daily. Write to the Park for a list of licensed air taxi operators.

VISITOR ACTIVITIES

• Hiking, backpacking, rock and mountain climbing, river running, limited fishing, wildlife watching, cross-country skiing and dogsledding. • **No development or facilities** in the Park. • No vehicle access. • No developed hiking trails. • Visitor information available at Park offices in Fairbanks and Bettles. • Air taxi, outfitter and guide services are available from licensed commercial operators - write to the Park for a list of services and providers.

PERMITS, FEES & LIMITATIONS

• No fees or permits for private parties. • Commercial operators must obtain a commercial use license. • Group size limited to 10 people for river trips and 7 people for backpacking trips. • Write for information about other low impact camping requirements and bear safety information.

ACCESSIBILITY

Bettles Ranger Station is accessible and includes accessible restrooms.

CAMPING & LODGING

• Backcountry camping is allowed throughout the Park. • A few small private lodges are located within or adjacent to the Park. • Limited lodging is available in Bettles, Anaktuvuk Pass and Coldfoot.

FOOD & SUPPLIES

Limited supplies are available in Bettles and Anaktuvuk Pass.

FIRST AID/ HOSPITAL

• There are no medical services in the Park. • Small clinics are located in Bettles and Anaktuvuk Pass. • The nearest hospital is in Fairbanks.

GENERAL INFORMATION

• This area is extremely remote. **Visitors must come prepared to be self-sufficient.** • Equipment and clothing should be appropriate for extended travel in rugged backcountry. Clothing should include enough layers, even during the summer, to provide warmth in sub-freezing temperatures. Rain gear is essential. • Extra food should be carried to allow for delays in air taxi service, which can occur in bad weather. • Visitors should be competent at backpacking, camping and survival skills. Winter travel requires special skills and hardiness and should only be undertaken after careful planning and preparation. • Freezing temperatures can occur at any time. August is often rainy. • Mosquitos usually come out in mid-June and begin to disappear by early August. Carry good mosquito repellent and a head net.

Glacier Bay National Park and Preserve

Gustavus, Alaska   See Climatable No. 5

Great tidewater glaciers, a dramatic range of plant communities - from rocky terrain recently covered by ice to lush temperate rain forest - and a large variety of animals - including brown and black bear, mountain goats, whales, seals and eagles - can be found within the Park and Preserve.

MAILING ADDRESS

Glacier Bay National Park and Preserve, Superintendent, P.O. Box 140, Gustavus, AK 99826-0140 **Telephone:** 907-697-2230

DIRECTIONS

The Park is located at the northwest end of the Alexander Archipelago in southeastern Alaska. There are no roads to the Park, and access is by various types of commercial transport, including regularly scheduled and charter air services, cruise ships, charter boats and private boats.

VISITOR ACTIVITIES

• Glacier viewing, boating, camping, backcountry hiking, kayaking, fishing, wildlife- and bird-watching, interpretive talks, hikes and exhibits. • Visitor facilities are open from mid-May to mid-September. • A tour boat makes daily cruises from the lodge to the glaciers.

PERMITS, FEES & LIMITATIONS

• No entrance fee. • Fees for concession-operated and commercial transportation to tidewater glaciers. • Alaska license is required for fishing. • Permits are required for private boaters from June 1 to Aug. 31.

ACCESSIBILITY

Lodge has 2 accessible rooms, ramp and elevator. Restrooms are accessible. One section of the forest trail is accessible via a boardwalk. An access guide is available upon request by writing to the Park.

CAMPING & LODGING

• A campground is available at Bartlett Cove on a first-come, first-served basis. • Backcountry camping and hiking are accessible by boat or plane. • Camper orientation and bear resistant canisters are musts. • Bring all food and supplies. • For lodging reservations, write to Glacier Bay Lodge, Glacier Bay National Park and Preserve, Gustavus, AK 99826 during the operating season, and Glacier Bay Lodge, Inc., 520 Pike St., Suite 1610, Seattle, WA 98101, 800-451-5952, for the remainder of the year. • Lodging is also available in Gustavus. A brochure is available by writing to Gustavus Visitors Association, PO Box 167, Gustavus, AK 99826.

FOOD & SUPPLIES

• Meals are served at Glacier Bay Lodge during the season. • There is a small grocery store in Gustavus, 10 miles (16.1 km) from Park Headquarters. • There are restaurants in Gustavus.

FIRST AID/ HOSPITAL

• First aid is available at Park Headquarters. • The nearest hospital is in Juneau, 100 miles (161.2 km) by air.

Katmai National Park and Preserve

Alaska   See Climatable No. 1

Since Katmai was declared a national monument in 1918 to preserve the living laboratory of its cataclysmic 1912 volcanic eruption, most of the surface geothermal features have cooled and the protection of brown bears has emerged as an equally compelling mission.

MAILING ADDRESS

Superintendent, Katmai National Park and Preserve, PO Box 7, King Salmon, AK 99613 **Telephone:** 907-246-3305

DIRECTIONS

Katmai is 290 air miles (467.7 km) southwest of Anchorage. Daily commercial flights connect Anchorage with King Salmon. Travel from King Salmon to Brooks Camp is by float plane. Travel to other sections of the Park is by charter aircraft. Visitor information is available at Brooks Camp Visitor Center, Park Headquarters or the King Salmon Visitor Center in King Salmon.

VISITOR ACTIVITIES

• Hiking, backpacking, wildlife- and bird-watching, angling, camping, boating, mountain climbing, kayaking, canoeing, photography, sightseeing bus tour, interpretive talks, guided walks and exhibits. • Visitor services at Brooks Camp are open from early June through mid-September and include a Visitor Center, bookstore, auditorium, cabins, lodge, dining room, camper store, campground, canoe and kayak rental, guided fishing, white gas and bear-viewing platforms.

PERMITS, FEES & LIMITATIONS

• No fees. • Backcountry permits are optional, but are recommended and are available at Brooks Camp Visitor Center or Park Headquarters in King Salmon.

ACCESSIBILITY

Trail surfaces are all dirt, but most at Brooks Camp are accessible. Bear-viewing platform includes challenge level ramp.

CAMPING & LODGING

• Overnight camping at Brooks Camp is free but usually requires an advance reservation. • No camping within 5 miles (8 km) of Brooks Camp except at Brooks Campground. • Accommodations, meals and guide services are available through the main Park concessioner, Katmailand, Inc., 4700 Aircraft Drive, Suite 2, Anchorage, AK 99502, phone 907-243-5448 or 1-800-544-0551. • Cabins are available at Brooks Camp and Grosvenor Lake. • There are other private operators that provide air taxi, guiding and nearby lodging. Write to the Park for a list.

FOOD & SUPPLIES

• Camping supplies and groceries should be obtained before visiting the Park. • Limited freeze-dried foods and stove fuel are available.

FIRST AID/ HOSPITAL

• Limited first aid is available in the Park. • The nearest hospital is in Anchorage. • There is a clinic in nearby Naknek, and a doctor is on duty during the summer.

GENERAL INFORMATION

• Day hikers should have sturdy hiking boots with good support, good rain gear and warm clothing. Come prepared for sunshine and stormy weather with high winds. • Insect repellent and/or a head net are recommended. • Katmai is a wildlife sanctuary. Keep your distance from wildlife. At Brooks Camp, maintain at least 50 yards (55 m) from individual bears and 100 yards (109 m) from sows with young. • Make noises while walking or hiking.

Kenai Fjords National Park

Seward, Alaska   See Climatable No. 2

The Kenai Fjords are coastal mountain fjords whose placid seascapes reflect scenic icebound landscapes. Their salt spray mixes with mountain mists in Kenai Fjords National Park, which boasts an icefield wilderness, waterfalls in canyons, and a coastline where thousands of seabirds and mammals raise their young each year.

MAILING ADDRESS

Kenai Fjords National Park, Box 1727, Seward, AK 99664-1727 **Telephone:** 907-224-3175

DIRECTIONS

Seward is located 127 miles (204.8 km) from Anchorage. The Visitor Center is located in Seward. Exit Glacier is the only area of the Park accessible by car or RVs on an 8.5-mile (13.7 km) gravel road.

VISITOR ACTIVITIES

• Fishing, sailing, sea kayaking, hiking, skiing, snowmobiling, dog sledding, snow shoeing, visiting a glacier, wildlife-watching, sightseeing and charter boats. • The Visitor Center in Seward is open from 8 a.m. to 7 p.m. daily from May to September and Monday through Friday the rest of the year. • Evening programs, films and a regularly scheduled Park slide show are offered. • There is a Ranger Station at Exit Glacier.

PERMITS, FEES & LIMITATIONS	No fees.
ACCESSIBILITY	All public use cabins are accessible to some degree. A 1.5-mile (2.4 km) paved trail leads to a view of Exit Glacier and a nature display.
CAMPING & LODGING	• A 10-site, no-fee campground is at Exit Glacier - tents only. • There are 2 public-use cabins at Aialik Bay, 2 at Nuka Bay and 1 at Exit Glacier for winter use only. • Fees and reservations are required.
FOOD & SUPPLIES	Supplies are available in Seward.
FIRST AID/ HOSPITAL	First aid and a hospital are available in Seward.
GENERAL INFORMATION	• Nights are cool along the coast. • Heavy rainfall can be expected. • Appropriate clothing and rain gear are essential.

Klondike Gold Rush National Historical Park

Skagway, Alaska and Seattle, Washington

In August 1896, George Washington Carmack and his two Native American companions, Skookum Jim and Tagish Charlie, found gold in a tributary of the Klondike River in Canada's Yukon Territory. They had no idea that they would set off one of the greatest gold rushes in history, which created the Alaskan tent and shack towns of Skagway and Dyea.

MAILING ADDRESS	Klondike Gold Rush National Historical Park, PO Box 517, Skagway, AK 99840 *or* Superintendent, Klondike Gold Rush National Historical Park, 117 South Main St., Seattle, WA 98104. **Telephone:** AK: 907-983-2921 WA: 206-553-7220
DIRECTIONS	Access to Skagway is by auto, plane, bus, cruise ship, or by State of Alaska ferry. For further information, contact your travel agent or the City of Skagway, Box 415, Skagway, AK 99840. The City of Skagway Visitor Center is located in the Arctic Brotherhood Building on the west side of Broadway, South of the alley between Second and Third Avenue. The National Park Service Visitor Center is located at 2nd and Broadway. The Seattle Visitor Center is at 117 South Main St., in the Pioneer Square area.
VISITOR ACTIVITIES	• Skagway: Wildlife-watching, camping, foot, bus and chartered aircraft tours. Information on films, displays, interpretive programs and guided walks available at Skagway Visitor Center. • Seattle: Interpretive displays, films, special tours and other events. • The Seattle Visitor Center is open

from 9 a.m. to 7 p.m. in summer with shorter hours during the off-season. The Skagway Visitor Center is open from 8 a.m. to 6 p.m., daily from mid-May to September. Contact Park offices for other times.

PERMITS, FEES & LIMITATIONS

• No fees or permits. • Vehicles are restricted to designated roadways.

FOOD & SUPPLIES

• In Alaska, no reservations are available for primitive campsites. • There are other overnight accommodations in the Park and in Seattle and Skagway.

CAMPING & LODGING

• Meals are not served in the Park, but are available nearby. • Food and supplies are obtainable in the Park. • Supplies are also available in Seattle, 2 blocks north, and in Alaska in the Skagway Historic District.

FIRST AID/ HOSPITAL

• First aid is available in the Park. • The nearest hospital is in Seattle, 1 mile (1.6 km) away for Skagway; Whitehorse, 112 miles (180.6 km); and Juneau 90 airmiles (145.1 km).

GENERAL INFORMATION

• In Alaska, the 33-mile (53.2 km) Chilkoot Trail is accessible only on foot. You must be properly outfitted before embarking on a hike over the Chilkoot Trail. • Weather conditions may change rapidly from hour to hour, especially in the summit area. You must be prepared for cold temperatures, snow or rain, fog, and travel through swampy areas and snow fields. • Proper equipment includes warm clothing (preferably wool), sturdy rain gear (not plastic), a tent with waterproof fly, camp stove and adequate fuel (there is no wood in the summit area and campfires are not allowed at all in the Canadian portion), good hiking boots, adequate food plus emergency rations and a first-aid kit. • Current trail information is available at the Visitor Center in Skagway or the Area Superintendent, Yukon National Historic Sites, Canadian Parks Service, 205-300 Main St., Whitehorse Yukon, YIA 2B5, phone 403-667-3910. • Hiking the trail north from Dyea is recommended because it is the historic route. Traveling the trail in reverse is not recommended because descending the steep summit scree, the "Gold Stairs" of the gold rush days, is dangerous.

FOR YOUR SAFETY

• Be alert for symptoms of hypothermia, a lowering of body temperature that results in uncontrollable shivering, disorientation, weariness, and possibly death. • Never feed wild animals. Make noise when you hike, announcing your presence, since bears are most dangerous when startled or cornered. • Keep your campsite and equipment clean. Food should be sealed in airtight containers and hung from trees so that animals will not be attracted by the food odors. • You are advised not to take pets on the Chilkoot Trail. • Customs and Immigration laws require that anyone traveling to Canada must report to Canadian Customs. Canadian Customs Offices are located in Fraser, B.C., and Whitehorse, YT. Anyone proceeding to Skagway from Canada must report to U.S. Customs and Immigration authorities in Skagway.

Kobuk Valley National Park

Northwest Alaska, north of the Arctic Circle   See Climatable No. 3

Kobuk Valley National Park is enclosed by the Baird and Waring mountains. It includes the central section of the Kobuk River, the 25-square-mile (40.3 km) Great Kobuk Sand Dunes, and the Little Kobuk and Hunt River sand dunes which were created by the grinding action of ancient glaciers and carried by wind to the valley.

MAILING ADDRESS

Kobuk Valley National Park, National Park Service, PO Box 1029, Kotzebue, AK 99752 **Telephone: 907-442-3760/-3890**

DIRECTIONS

The Park is about 26 miles (41.9 km) north of the Arctic Circle. There are no roads or rail service. General access is via scheduled air service from Fairbanks or Anchorage to Kotzebue and then air taxi from Kotzebue to nearby villages. Summer access to and through the Park includes motorized and non-motorized watercraft, aircraft and by foot. Winter access includes snowmobiles, aircraft, and by foot.

VISITOR ACTIVITIES

• There are **no National Park Service developments**, services, campgrounds or trails. • Motorboats, kayaks, canoes and rafts are used on the rivers for a variety of water activities. • There are opportunities for primitive camping, backcountry hiking, general wildlife observation and photography. • Local residents still pursue hunting, fishing, trapping and other subsistence activities due to special provisions of legislation establishing the Park. • The Park is open all year to the general public. • The Kotzebue Public Lands Information Center is an interagency information center located in Kotzebue that is open from **8 a.m. to 5 p.m.**, Monday through Friday and for longer hours during the summer.

PERMITS, FEES & LIMITATIONS

• No fees. • Alaska hunting and fishing licenses, available in Anchorage or Kotzebue, are required. • There are no roads and no trails.

ACCESSIBILITY

Interagency Kotzebue Public Lands Information Center is accessible.

CAMPING & LODGING

• Tundra and river bars are often used for primitive camping. • Seasonal, overnight lodging is available in the villages of Ambler and Kiana. • Lodging is available year-round in Kotzebue.

FOOD & SUPPLIES

Food and supplies are available in the nearby villages of Ambler and Kiana and the city of Kotzebue.

FIRST AID/ HOSPITAL

• First aid is not available in the Park, but is available in the villages of Ambler and Kiana. • The nearest hospital is in Kotzebue.

GENERAL INFORMATION

• Rugged terrain is subject to harsh weather, high winds, rain and snow. • Guard against hypothermia, giardia lamblia, wild animals, mosquitos and biting flies. • Please do not interfere with subsistence camps, fishnets or other equipment. • Respect property and privacy.

Lake Clark National Park and Preserve

Southwest of Anchorage, Alaska. West side of Cook Inlet.

A composite of ecosystems that are representative of many diverse regions in Alaska, Lake Clark National Park and Preserve is where the mountains of the Alaska and Aleutian Ranges join. The active volcanoes of Iliamna and Redoubt also vent steam and rise more than 10,000 feet (3,048 m) in the Park, and rivers cascade dramatically to the sea through forests.

MAILING ADDRESS

Lake Clark National Park and Preserve, 4230 University Drive, Suite 311, Anchorage, AK 99508 **Telephone:** 907-271-3751 *or* Field Headquarters: General Delivery, Port Alsworth, AK 99653 **Telephone:** 907-781-2218

DIRECTIONS

Most visitors charter an aircraft from Anchorage to the Lake Clark area for $180 an hour depending on the weight load, number of passengers, and type of aircraft. Charter is also available from the Kenai area. Most places in the Park and Preserve are within 1 1/2 hours flight time from Anchorage. There is commercial air service available from Anchorage to Iliamna, costing about $160-$210 round trip. Points within the Park and Preserve from Iliamna are visited via air charter, at the same cost per hour as Anchorage's air charter services. Lake Clark Area has a "seat fare" service from Merrill to Port Alsworth.

VISITOR ACTIVITIES

• Hiking, wildlife, bird watching, fishing, hunting, boating, river trips, primitive camping, photography, and mountaineering. • Boat rental, fishing tackle, guide services on the coast shores of Lake Clark, and lodging and Guide Services at Silver Salmon Coast. • Information on backcountry hiking can be obtained from Park Field Headquarters. • The Park and Preserve is always open.

PERMITS, FEES & LIMITATIONS

• No fees or permits required for noncommercial users. • Alaska fishing licenses are required and are available in Anchorage and at Port Alsworth. • Voluntary registration with field headquarters is advised for safety and statistics.

ACCESSIBILITY

No accessible accommodations.

CAMPING & LODGING

• Primitive camping in the Park. • Limited lodging is available within the Park boundaries along the shores of Lake Clark, at Port Alsworth and in the interior areas through private/commercial operators. • Other lodging is available through commercial and air charter services in Anchorage and Kenai. • Lodging ranges from primitive cabins to modern lodges with plumbing.

FOOD & SUPPLIES

• Meals are served in the Park, but generally for guests at lodging facilities. • Food and supplies are obtainable in the Park on a minimal or seasonal basis at Port Alsworth and at nearby Nondalton and Iliamna.

FIRST AID/ HOSPITAL

• First aid is available in the Park on a limited basis. • There is a clinic in Iliamna. • The nearest hospitals are in Kenai and Anchorage.

GENERAL INFORMATION

• Most visitors arrive between mid-June and early September when high temperatures average between 60°F and 75°F with an occasional 80°F day in the interior. Coastline areas are cooler with temperatures between 50°F and 65°F. Wind and rainfall are present on the coastal areas, with mostly sunny and milder temperatures in the interior. Weather is quite variable in the interior. Strong winds are occasional. Snow is possible at higher elevations at any time. • Insects may be numerous and precautions should be taken by using adequate tents for camping on open river and lake bars. Carrying an ample supply of insect repellent and head nets is suggested. • Plan on wearing clothing that will protect from the extremes of possible freezing temperatures, wet weather, and warm sunny days.

Noatak National Preserve

Northwest Alaska, north of the Arctic Circle   See Climatable No. 3

O ne of North America's largest mountain-ringed river basins with an intact, unaltered ecosystem, the Noatak National Preserve features some of the Arctic's finest arrays of plants and animals and superlative wilderness float-trip opportunities.

MAILING ADDRESS

Noatak National Preserve, Superintendent, Northwest Alaska Areas, National Park Service, PO Box 1029, Kotzebue, AK 99752 **Telephone:** 907-442-3760/-3890

DIRECTIONS

The Preserve is 26 miles (41.9 km) north of the Arctic Circle. There are no roads or rail service. General access is via scheduled air service from Fairbanks or Anchorage to Kotzebue and then air taxi to nearby villages. Summer access to and through the Preserve includes motorized and non-motorized watercraft, aircraft and by foot.

VISITOR ACTIVITIES

• There are no National Park Service developments, services, campgrounds, or trails in the Preserve. • Motorboats, kayaks, canoes, rafts are used on the rivers for a variety of water activities. • Primitive camping, backcountry hiking, general wildlife observation and photography. • Sport hunting/fishing permitted. • Local residents still pursue hunting, fishing, trapping and other subsistence activities due to special provisions of legislation establishing the Preserve. • The Preserve is open all year to the general public. • The Kotzebue Public Lands Information Center is an interagency information center located in Kotzebue that is open from 8 a.m. to 5 p.m., Monday through Friday, and for longer hours during the summer.

PERMITS, FEES & LIMITATIONS

• No fees. • Alaska hunting/fishing licenses, available in Anchorage or Kotzebue, are required.

ACCESSIBILITY

Interagency Kotzebue Public Lands Information Center is accessible.

CAMPING & LODGING

• Tundra and river bars are often used for primitive camping. • Lodging is available year-round in the city of Kotzebue.

FOOD & SUPPLIES

Food and supplies are available in Kotzebue.

FIRST AID/ HOSPITAL

• First aid is not available within the Preserve. • First aid and a hospital are available in Kotzebue.

GENERAL INFORMATION

• Rugged terrain is subject to harsh weather, high winds, rain and snow. • Guard against hypothermia, giardia lamblia, wild animals, mosquitoes and biting flies. • Please do not interfere with subsistence camps, fishnets or other equipment. • Respect property and privacy.

Sitka National Historical Park

Sitka, Alaska   See Climatable No. 5

Cultural and political hub of Russian America in the early 19th Century and part of America's Old West after 1867, Sitka possesses a colorful history as an area where Russian fur traders, Aleut hunters and Tlingit workers lived a peaceful, but rough existence.

MAILING ADDRESS

Superintendent, Sitka National Historical Park, PO Box 738, Sitka, AK 99835 **Telephone: 907-747-6281**

DIRECTIONS

The Park Visitor Center and main Park grounds are located one-quarter mile (.4 km) from the central business area of Sitka. The Russian Bishop's House is located in the historic section of Sitka.

VISITOR ACTIVITIES

• The Visitor Center contains exhibits of the Tlingit Indian culture, slide and movie programs on the area's history and the Southeast Alaska Indian Cultural Center where native artists demonstrate wood carving, basketry, weaving, and silver carving. • Visitor Center facilities include telephones, restrooms and a bookstore. • The Visitor Center is open daily from 8 a.m. to 5 p.m., during the winter and 8 a.m. to 6 p.m., in the summer. • The Park grounds contain 1.5 miles (2.4 km) of hiking trails through the temperate rain forest and offer opportunities for picnicking and bird-watching. • Totem poles line the Park's Totem Trail. • During August and September, salmon spawn in the Indian River, which flows through the Park. • The Russian Bishop's House contains a museum on Russian America, exhibits, and historic furnishings in the upstairs and Chapel. • The Bishop's House is open daily from 8:30 a.m. to 5 p.m., in summer and by reservation in the winter.

PERMITS, FEES & LIMITATIONS

No entrance fees.

Alaska

ACCESSIBILITY

The Visitor Center, most Park trails and the ground floor of the Russian Bishop's House are accessible.

CAMPING & LODGING

Overnight accommodations are available in Sitka and the surrounding area.

FOOD & SUPPLIES

Food and supplies are available in Sitka.

FIRST AID/ HOSPITAL

A hospital is located in Sitka.

Wrangell-St. Elias National Park and Preserve

Alaska   See Climatable No. 2

The quantity and scale of everything at Wrangell-St. Elias National Park and Preserve is enormous with peak after peak, including 9 of the 16 highest peaks in the United States, glacier after glacier, and many braided rivers and streams.

MAILING ADDRESS

Wrangell-St. Elias National Park and Preserve, PO Box 29, Glennallen, AK 99588 **Telephone:** 907-822-5234

DIRECTIONS

Access into the central portion of the Park by road is available from the community of Chitina. Take the state maintained Chitina-McCarthy Road, which is passable by conventional vehicle with good clearance during the summer months. It extends 61 miles (98.3 km) up the Chitina River Valley following the historic route of the Copper River and Northwestern Railroad to the Kennicott River. Road access into the northern section of the Park/Preserve is from Slana (on the Tok cutoff). Follow a state-maintained route passable by conventional vehicle that extends some 45 miles (72.5 km) into the abandoned mining community of Nabesna. Access to the remaining portions is by air. Charter air service is available from the Gulkana and Tok airports at varying costs with an average round-trip from Gulkana to McCarthy costing about $700 a plane with 3 people and gear. Glennallen is some 200 miles (322.5 km) by paved highway from Anchorage and is reached by regularly scheduled bus service (seasonal). Air access to the southern coastal sections, including the beaches, is available from Yakutat, Cordova and Valdez.

VISITOR ACTIVITIES

• Backpacking, lake fishing, river rafting, cross-country skiing, mountain climbing, hiking and air tours. • Surface transportation is available between McCarthy and Kennecott, 5 miles (8 km). • Hiking trails are primitive. • The Park/Preserve never closes.

PERMITS, FEES & LIMITATIONS

• No entrance fees. • Alaska fishing licenses are required and are available in surrounding communities.

CAMPING & LODGING
• Camping is available. • There are scattered remote cabins located throughout the region that accommodate backcountry parties. • Standard accommodations are available in motels and cabins in and around the communities of Chitina and Glennallen, on the Glenn and Richardson highways, and along the Tok cutoff. • There are state campgrounds at Liberty Creek near Chitina and along the major highways.

FOOD & SUPPLIES
There is a supermarket in Glennallen, and limited supplies are available in McCarthy.

FIRST AID/ HOSPITAL
• First aid is not available in the Park. • The nearest clinic is in Glennallen.

GENERAL INFORMATION
• Good rain gear and wool clothing are a must. • Road conditions can change on very short notice making roads impassable to all but 4-wheel-drive vehicles. • All visitors to the backcountry must be self-sufficient and carry enough food to cover unexpected delays in air service.

Yukon-Charley Rivers National Preserve
Alaska

A xis of the region, the silt-laden Yukon River flows through a great geologic fault. It is joined along the way by other crystal rivers, including the Charley, and offers spectacular unspoiled wilderness scenery.

MAILING ADDRESS
Superintendent, Yukon-Charley Rivers National Preserve, PO Box 167, Eagle, AK 99738 **Telephone: 907-547-2233**

DIRECTIONS
Eagle and Circle are the gateway cities to the Preserve. Take either the Taylor Highway to Eagle (the highway connects with the Alaska Highway at Tetlin Junction near Tok, AK) or the Steese Highway from Fairbanks to Circle. There are scheduled flights from Fairbanks to both Eagle and Circle.

VISITOR ACTIVITIES
• Wildlife and bird watching, river floating, hiking, photography, backcountry, picnicking, kayaking and canoeing. • Facilities include a Visitor Center in Eagle. • Backcountry information can be obtained from the Superintendent's office in Eagle. Topographic maps are available from the Alaska National History Association outlet in the Visitor Center; there is also a small reference library for visitor use. • The Preserve never closes, but the Visitor Center and other offices close for Thanksgiving, Dec. 25 and Jan. 1.

PERMITS, FEES & LIMITATIONS
• No fees. • Alaska fishing and hunting licenses, available at local sporting goods stores, are required. • There are no roads in the Preserve.

CAMPING & LODGING
• No reservations are necessary at Eagle and Circle campgrounds.
• A 6-passenger houseboat is available for rent/charter out of Eagle. • One public-use cabin is available on a first-come, first-served basis at Slavens

Roadhouse. Other cabins may be available. Check at the Eagle
Superintendent's office for current information. • Other overnight accommodations are available in Circle Hot Springs or along the Alaska Highway
and in Eagle and Circle.

FOOD & SUPPLIES

Food and supplies are available in Eagle and Circle.

FIRST AID/ HOSPITAL

• First aid is not available in the Preserve. • The nearest hospital is in
Fairbanks, 180 air miles (290.3 km).

GENERAL INFORMATION

• Carry clothing for all seasons in the summer. Wear layered clothing.
Tennis shoes are practical for river travel, but additional footwear will be
needed. Extra socks and rain gear are essential. • Bring all necessary food
and camping gear. • Plan to protect your food from bears. • Insects are
numerous and irritating from early summer to early August. To avoid some
of the irritation, most travelers camp on bars and open shorelines where
winds are most likely to prevail. • Yukon River currents are strong, swift and
deceptive. The Charley River and other floatable side streams are subject to
rapid rises in water levels from up-river thunderstorms.

Arizona

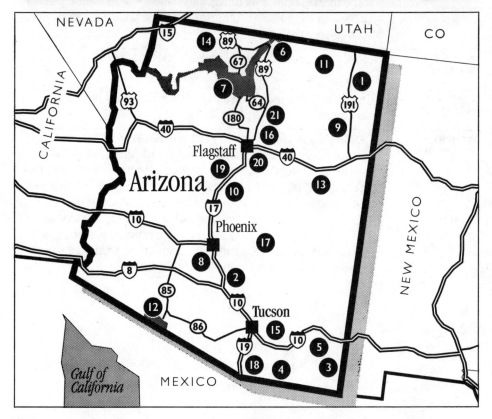

1	Canyon De Chelly National Monument	**12**	Organ Pipe Cactus National Monument
2	Casa Grande National Monument	**13**	Petrified Forest National Park
3	Chiricahua National Monument	**14**	Pipe Spring National Monument
4	Coronado National Memorial	**15**	Saguaro National Monument
5	Fort Bowie National Historic Site	**16**	Sunset Crater National Monument
6	Glen Canyon National Recreation Area	**17**	Tonto National Monument
7	Grand Canyon National Park	**18**	Tumacacori National Monument
8	Hohokam Pima National Monument	**19**	Tuzigoot National Monument
9	Hubbell Trading Post National Historic Site	**20**	Walnut Canyon National Monument
10	Montezuma Castle National Monument	**21**	Wupatki National Monument
11	Navajo National Monument		

Arizona

Canyon de Chelly National Monument

Chinle, Arizona

With its beautiful, steep-walled canyons and numerous prehistoric Indian dwelling ruins nestled below towering cliffs or perched on high ledges, Canyon de Chelly National Monument offers visitors the chance to learn about Southwestern Indian history from the earliest Basketmakers to the Navajos who still live in the area.

MAILING ADDRESS

Superintendent, Canyon de Chelly National Monument, PO Box 588, Chinle, AZ 86503 **Telephone:** 602-674-5500/5501

DIRECTIONS

The Visitor Center is 3 miles (4.8 km) from Rt. 191 in Chinle. From Gallup, NM, follow routes 666 and 264 to 191, 99 miles (159.6 km) to Chinle. From Grand Canyon, AZ, take Rts. 64, 89, 160 and 264 to 191, 270 miles (435.4 km). From Holbrook-Petrified Forest, take I-40 to 191. From Kayenta, take Rts. 160 and 59 to 191, 82 miles (132.2 km). From Mesa Verde, take Rts. 789 and 160 to 191, 158 miles (254.8 km). From Monument Valley, take Rts. 163 and 160 to 191, 128 miles (206.4 km). From Page-Lake Powell, take Rts. 98, 160 and 59 to 191, 208 miles (335.4 km). From Tuba City, take Rts. 160 and 59 to 191, 176 miles (283.8 km).

VISITOR ACTIVITIES

• Auto tours, hiking, pictograph viewing, interpretive exhibits and talks, horseback riding (by prior arrangement), picnicking and photography.
• Concession jeep tours are available from Thunderbird Lodge, PO Box 548, Chinle, AZ 86503, phone 602-674-5841/5842. • Facilities include hiking and auto trails, parking, restrooms, exhibits, concession canyon trips and horse rentals. • The Visitor Center is open daily from **8 a.m. to 5 p.m.**, October to April; and **8 a.m. to 6 p.m.**, May to September. • The inner canyons are impassable in winter and at certain other times of the year.

PERMITS, FEES & LIMITATIONS

• **No entrance fee.** • A tribal fishing permit is required. • Hiking within the canyon requires a Park Service permit and an authorized Navajo guide, except along the 2.5-mile (4 km) White House Ruins Trail. One guide may take up to 15 people for $10 per hour. • To drive on the canyon bottom, a 4-wheel drive vehicle, a Park Service permit and an authorized Navajo guide are required. The fee is $10 an hour for 1 vehicle, $5 an hour for each additional vehicle with a 5-vehicle limit per guide. • Autos should use paved roads only.

ACCESSIBILITY

Some overlook areas are accessible as well as some areas of Thunderbird Lodge.

CAMPING & LODGING

• Camp sites are available at no charge on a first-come, first-served basis year-round. Reservations for group sites of 15 or more people can be made by contacting the Monument. No reservations are accepted for RV groups.

• Backcountry camping is allowed with an authorized guide. • Lodging is available at Thunderbird Lodge. Make reservations in advance by writing Thunderbird Lodge, Box 548, Chinle, AZ 86503, or calling 602-674-5841/5842. • Other overnight accommodations are available in Window Rock, AZ, 66 miles (106.4 km); Monument Valley, 128 miles (206.4 km); and Gallup, NM, 99 miles (159.6 km).

FOOD & SUPPLIES

• Meals are served at Thunderbird Lodge, but no food or supplies are available in the Monument. • Food and supplies are available nearby.

FIRST AID/ HOSPITAL

• First aid is available in the Monument. • The nearest hospital is Chinle Hospital, 3 miles (4.8 km). Other hospitals are in Gallup and in Ganado, AZ, 36 miles (58 km).

GENERAL INFORMATION

For your safety - Quicksand, deep dry sand, cliffs, loose rocks and flash floods make the canyons hazardous.

Casa Grande Ruins National Monument

Coolidge, Arizona

A mong the 60 prehistoric Indian sites at Casa Grande Ruins National Monument, the 4-story earthen building built about 650 years ago that gives the Monument its name is the most prominent and most perplexing. Its purpose in the widespread civilization that once flourished in the Gila Valley has never been determined.

MAILING ADDRESS

Casa Grande Ruins National Monument, Superintendent, 1100 Ruins Drive, Coolidge, AZ 85228 **Telephone:** 602-723-3172

DIRECTIONS

The Monument is in North Coolidge on AZ 87 about halfway between Phoenix and Tucson.

VISITOR ACTIVITIES

• Interpretive talks and exhibits, walking tours and picnicking. • A 400-yard (365.7 m) round trip self-guiding walking trail leads through the Ruins area. • Facilities include parking and restrooms at the Visitor Center, drinking water and a picnic area. • The Monument is open from 7 **a.m.** to 6 p.m. year-round.

PERMITS, FEES & LIMITATIONS

The entrance fee is $1 per person.

ACCESSIBILITY

The Ruins are accessible.

CAMPING & LODGING

Overnight accommodations are available in Coolidge, AZ 87; Florence, AZ 287, 12 miles (19.3 km) east; and Casa Grande, AZ 287, 22 miles (35.4 km) southwest.

FOOD & SUPPLIES

Supplies are available in Coolidge.

FIRST AID/ HOSPITAL

• First aid is available in the Monument or nearby in Coolidge. • The nearest hospital is in Florence.

GENERAL INFORMATION

• The most comfortable time for visiting is between early October and early May. • Beware of the cactus. • Intense heat can cause varying degrees of discomfort. • Be cautious of poisonous snakes, centipedes and scorpions. • The Casa Grande and other ruins were set aside under the Federal Lands Office on June 22, 1892, and as a National Monument in 1918.

Chiricahua National Monument

Willcox, Arizona

Known as the "Land of the Standing-Up Rocks" by the Chiricahua Apaches, this northwest corner of the Chiricahua Mountains harbors towering rock spires, massive stone columns and huge balanced rocks as well as many plants and animals of the Southwest. In addition, there are a number of Mexican species even though Mexico is 50 miles (80.6 km) to the south.

MAILING ADDRESS

Chiricahua National Monument, Superintendent, Dos Cabezas Route, Box 6500, Willcox, AZ 85646 **Telephone:** 602-824-3560

DIRECTIONS

Take I-10 to Willcox and get off at Exit 340 (Highway 186). Follow the signs and take Highway 186 to Highway 181, which leads to the Monument.

VISITOR ACTIVITIES

• Hiking, picnicking, auto tours, bird-watching, interpretive exhibits and activities at the Visitor Center. • Tours of the historical Faraway Ranch.

PERMITS, FEES & LIMITATIONS

The entrance fee is $4.

ACCESSIBILITY

The Visitor Center, Faraway Ranch and Massai Point are accessible.

CAMPING & LODGING

• Twenty-six camp sites are located one-half mile (.8 km) from the Visitor Center. Sites are available for $6 a night. • There are restrictions on RVs more than 26 feet (7.9 m) long. • Overflow camping is available on nearby National Forest lands. • No backcountry camping is allowed within the Monument, but it is permitted in nearby National Forests. • Various lodgings are available in Willcox, 45 minutes away, Tombstone or Bisbee, 1 1/2 hours away.

FOOD & SUPPLIES

• No gas or food is available in the Monument. • Willcox contains all amenities, including gas. • A small store is located 4 miles (6.4 km) from the entrance station. • Groceries and restaurants are also located at Sunizona.

FIRST AID/ HOSPITAL

• First aid is available in the Monument. • The nearest hospital is in Willcox.

GENERAL INFORMATION

For your safety - Be alert for rattlesnakes during warm weather. The scenic road is winding and dangerous. Be aware of fallen rocks and ice in winter.

Coronado National Memorial

Hereford, Arizona

Coronado National Memorial is in oak woodlands on the Mexican border. It commemorates the first major exploration of the American Southwest led by Vasquez de Coronado in search of the fabled Cities of Cibola.

MAILING ADDRESS

Superintendent, Coronado National Memorial, 4101 East Montezuma Canyon Road, Hereford, AZ 85615 **Telephone:** 602-366-5515

DIRECTIONS

The Visitor Center is 22 miles (35.4 km) south of Sierra Vista and 30 miles (48.3 km) west of Bisbee in Montezuma Canyon, 5 miles (8 km) off of AZ 92.

VISITOR ACTIVITIES

• Hands-on cultural and natural history exhibits, videos, bookstore, hiking trails, scenic overlook, picnic area and cave. • The Visitor Center is open from 8 a.m. to 5 p.m. daily except Thanksgiving, Dec. 25 and Jan. 1. • The Memorial is open from dawn to dusk all year.

PERMITS, FEES & LIMITATIONS

• No fees. • A permit, obtainable at the Visitor Center, is required to enter the cave. • Vehicles and bicycles are restricted to designated roads. • No pets are allowed on the trails. • Vehicles longer than 24 feet (7.3 m) are not permitted beyond the Visitor Center/picnic area.

ACCESSIBILITY

The Visitor Center, picnic area and restrooms are accessible.

CAMPING & LODGING

• Camping is available in nearby Forest Service areas. • Lodging is available in Sierra Vista and Bisbee.

FOOD & SUPPLIES

Food and supplies are available in Sierra Vista and Bisbee.

FIRST AID/ HOSPITAL

The nearest hospital is in Sierra Vista.

GENERAL INFORMATION

• Bring flashlights to use in the cave. • Carry water while hiking.

Fort Bowie National Historic Site

Bowie, Arizona

The spring located at Apache Pass was a dependable source of water, which attracted a long procession of Native Americans, emigrants, prospectors and soldiers based at Fort Bowie. Fort Bowie was the headquarters of military operations against the Chiricahua Apaches for control of the region.

Arizona

MAILING ADDRESS

Superintendent, Fort Bowie National Historic Site, PO Box 158, Bowie, AZ 85605 Telephone: 602-847-2500

DIRECTIONS

There is no road to the ruins proper. A 1.5-mile (2.4 km) foot trail that begins midway in Apache Pass provides access to the ruins. The trailhead is accessible from either the town of Willcox, on I-10, 22 miles (35.4 km) south on AZ 186 to the graded road leading east into Apache Pass; or from the town of Bowie, also on I-10, 12 miles (19.3 km) south on a graded dirt road that bears into Apache Pass.

VISITOR ACTIVITIES

• Hiking on the foot trail to the ruins, a 1.5-mile (2.4 km) alternate return trail and a 3-mile (4.8 km) primitive trail along the Butterfield Overland Stage Road. • Picnicking, interpretive exhibits and talks, wildlife- and bird-watching and photography. • The Site is open from sunrise to sunset. • The Visitor Center is open from 8 a.m. to 5 p.m. daily except Dec. 25. • Visitor facilities include a bookstore, restrooms, picnic areas and water. • Special events are scheduled throughout the year. Write or call for more information.

PERMITS, FEES & LIMITATIONS

• No fees. • All historic and natural features and historic artifacts are protected. • No metal detectors, digging tools, guns, or wheeled vehicles are permitted. • Hunting is prohibited. • Please do not climb on the fort's fragile walls and mounds.

ACCESSIBILITY

The fort ruins and Visitor Center are accessible, but advance notice is required. Write or call to make arrangements or for further information.

CAMPING & LODGING

• Lodging is available in Willcox, 30 miles (48.3 km) via AZ 186; or Bowie, 13 miles (20.9 km) via Apache Pass Road. • Camping is available at Chiricahua National Monument, 22 miles (35.4 km) south of Fort Bowie on AZ 186.

FOOD & SUPPLIES

Food and supplies are available in Fort Bowie or Willcox.

FIRST AID/ HOSPITAL

• First aid is available at the Visitor Center. • The nearest hospital is in Willcox.

GENERAL INFORMATION

• Water is available at the Fort. The summer hiker should carry a canteen since temperatures may climb above 100°F. • Summer storms occur suddenly and briefly flood the washes. Wait out high water. • Be alert for rattlesnakes.

Glen Canyon National Recreation Area
Page, Arizona

Glen Canyon National Recreation Area provides a dramatic example of the combination of one of nature's most inspiring settings, nearly one million acres of desert-and-canyon country, and one of man's most ambitious projects, the Glen Canyon Dam on the Colorado River that formed Lake Powell.

MAILING ADDRESS

Glen Canyon National Recreation Area, PO Box 1507, Page, AZ 86040
Telephone: 602-645-8200

DIRECTIONS

The Recreation Area Headquarters is at 691 Scenic View Drive on US 89. There is a Visitor Center by Glen Canyon Dam, 2 miles (3.2 km) from Page on US 89. Bullfrog Visitor Center is on Hwy. 276 on the approach to the lake at Bullfrog, UT.

VISITOR ACTIVITIES

• Swimming, boating, fishing, water skiing, hunting, driving, hiking, dam tours, photography, interpretive exhibits and picnicking. • Facilities include restrooms, marinas, launching ramps, beaches, boat rentals and tours, and picnic areas. • Nearly 90 percent of the area is wilderness backcountry. Write for information. • An all-day or half day cruise takes boaters to Rainbow Bridge National Monument.

PERMITS, FEES & LIMITATIONS

• No entrance fee. • Fishing permits are available at sporting goods stores in Page or at the Area's marina. • Drive only on designated roads. • Boaters should be familiar with boating regulations - a pamphlet is available at the Visitor Center.

ACCESSIBILITY

The visitor centers at Bullfrog and Wahweap are accessible. The lodging accommodations are also accessible.

CAMPING & LODGING

• Camping is on a first-come, first-served basis for $7 a night. • Lodging is available at Wahweap, Bullfrog, Hite and Halls Crossing. • RV hookups are available at Wahweap, Bullfrog and Halls Crossing. • Houseboats are available at Wahweap, Bullfrog, Halls Crossing and Hite. • Write: Reservations, Del Webb Recreational Properties, Box 29040, Phoenix, AZ 85038 or call 1-800-528-6154 (in Arizona, call 1-800-352-6508). • Other overnight accommodations are available in Page.

FOOD & SUPPLIES

• Food and supplies are available at Wahweap, Bullfrog, Halls Crossing, Dangling Rope and Hite. • Meals are served at Wahweap and Bullfrog.

FIRST AID/ HOSPITAL

• First aid is available at Dangling Rope Marina and Ranger stations at Wahweap, Bullfrog, Halls Crossing and Hite. • The nearest hospital is in Page, 6.5 miles (10.4 km) from Wahweap; The Samaritan Health Clinic is in Bullfrog. There's a clinic in Green River and another hospital in Grand Junction, CO.

Arizona

Grand Canyon National Park

Northern Arizona   See Climatable No. 6

Grand Canyon National Park is awesome in its depth, about 1 mile (1.6 km), and mind-boggling in its extent, 277 miles (446.7 km) counting all of the Colorado River's twists and turns. The process that has taken millions of years to create this wonder of nature continues with the moving water.

MAILING ADDRESS

Grand Canyon National Park, PO Box 129, Grand Canyon, AZ 86023
Telephone: 602-638-7888

DIRECTIONS

There are 3 areas in the Park - The South Rim, the North Rim (open from about mid-May to late October) and the Inner Canyon. The South Rim Visitor Center is 6 miles (9.6 km) north of the South Entrance Station in Grand Canyon Village, 60 miles (96.7 km) north of Williams, 57 miles (91.9 km) west of Cameron, on AZ 64, and 78 miles (125.8 km) from Flagstaff via AZ 180. The North Rim Ranger Station and developed area is on State Hwy. 67, 45 miles (72.5 km) south of Jacob Lake (at the intersection with Hwy. 89).

VISITOR ACTIVITIES

• Interpretive exhibits, guided and self-guiding tours, picnicking, backcountry hiking, horseback riding (outside the Park only, on the South Rim), white water rafting, kayaking, fishing, biking, bus tours, mule trips and river tours. • Facilities include picnic areas, hiking trails, bus, taxi, religious services, post office, bank, backpacking equipment rentals and air tours outside the Park. • For information about interpretive activities, phone 602-638-7888. • The 3 areas of the Park have different facilities, activities and even different climates. The South Rim never closes, but the North Rim is closed in the winter.

PERMITS, FEES & LIMITATIONS

• There is a $10 entrance fee. • Permits are required for stock use and river running. • Fishing licenses and trout stamps are available at Babbitt's Store in Grand Canyon Village. • Vehicles are restricted to established roads.

ACCESSIBILITY

Accessibility varies from facility to facility. An Accessibility Guide is available at the Park Visitor Center or by mail. There is accessible parking, and wheelchairs are free at the Visitor Center. Some West Rim and Village shuttle buses are equipped with lifts and ramps.

CAMPING & LODGING

• Desert View Campground fees are $8. There's a $10 fee at Mather Campground; $8 fee at North Rim Campground. • No reservations are required for Desert View, which is closed in winter. Reservations are taken for Mather Campground (South Rim) between March 1 and Dec. 1. North Rim Campground is open from mid-May to late October. • For reservations, contact MISTIX at 1-800-365-2267 or at PO Box 85705, San Diego, CA 92186-5705. • Backcountry camping reservations and permits are required and are issued by mail or are available in person. Contact Backcountry Office, Grand Canyon National Park, PO Box 129, Grand Canyon, AZ 86023 or phone 602-638-7888. • Other overnight accommodations within the Park include: Bright Angel Lodge, El Tovar Hotel, Kachina Lodge, Thunderbird Lodge, Maswick Lodge and Yavapai Lodge on the South Rim. For reservations, phone 602-638-2401. The Grand Lodge is on the North Rim. For reservations, phone 801-586-7686. • Accommodations outside of the Park are available in Tusayan, Cameron, Gray Mountain, Flagstaff, Williams, Kaibab Lake, Jacob Lake, Fredonia, Marble Canyon and Page, AZ; and Kanab, UT.

FOOD & SUPPLIES

• Meals are served at North Rim, Grand Canyon Village, Desert View, Phantom Ranch and Tusayan. • Food and supplies are available in the Grand Canyon Village, Desert View, and the North Rim. • Food and supplies are also available in Tusayan, 1 mile (1.6 km) south of the Park.

FIRST AID/ HOSPITAL

• First aid is available at the Information Desk in Grand Lodge (North Rim) or at the Grand Canyon Clinic on Center Road between the South Entrance Station and Grand Canyon Village. Dial 911 in an emergency. • The nearest hospital for the South Rim is in Flagstaff, I-40 and AZ 180. Williams has a daytime clinic. • The hospital nearest to the North Rim is in Kanab, UT, via UT 89, 81 miles (130.6 km).

GENERAL INFORMATION

• For recorded information about weather and road conditions, phone 602-638-7888. • **For your safety** - Do not climb in the canyon. Most of the rock is too crumbly. Avoid overexertion. • The South Rim averages 7,000 feet (2,133.6 m) and the North Rim more than 8,000 feet (2,438.4 m) in elevation. Cardiac and respiratory patients should be careful. • Temperatures within the Inner Canyon can reach extremes. Take plenty of water and food, dress for the weather and know your physical limitations. • Be careful near the canyon rim.

Hohokam Pima National Monument

Sacaton, Arizona

The Monument is not open to the public. The Monument will preserve the Snaketown archeological site, which contains the remains of a large Hohokam Indian village occupied between 300 and 1100 AD. The Monument was authorized by Congress on Oct. 21, 1972, but it has not yet been established. The area remains closed to the public.

MAILING ADDRESS

Superintendent, Hohokam Pima National Monument, c/o Casa Grande Ruins National Monument, PO Box 518, Coolidge, AZ 85228 **Telephone:** 602-723-3172

Hubbell Trading Post National Historic Site
Ganado, Arizona

The dean of the traders to the Navaho was John Lorenzo Hubbell, who operated Hubbell Trading Post on the reservation from the late 1800s into the 1900s. He was not only the Navajos' merchant, but also their trusted guide and teacher who translated and wrote letters, settled quarrels, explained government policy and cared for the sick.

MAILING ADDRESS

Superintendent, Hubbell Trading Post National Historic Site, PO Box 150, Ganado, AZ 86505 **Telephone:** 602-755-3475/3477

DIRECTIONS

The Site is on the Navajo Indian Reservation, 1 mile (1.6 km) west of Ganado and 55 miles (88.7 km) northwest of Gallup, NM. Follow AZ 264 (Navajo Route 3) from the east and west, take US 191 from the north and south.

VISITOR ACTIVITIES

• Walking tours, exhibits, weaving and silversmithing demonstrations, picnicking, tours of the Hubbell home, trading operation and craft demonstrations. • Facilities include parking and restrooms at the Visitor Center and a picnic area. • The Site is open daily from 8 a.m. to 5 p.m., with hours extended until 6 p.m., in the summer. The Site is closed Thanksgiving, Dec. 25 and Jan. 1.

PERMITS, FEES & LIMITATIONS

• No entrance fee. • Off-road vehicle travel is prohibited.

ACCESSIBILITY

Parking and restrooms are accessible. Portable wheelchair ramps are available.

CAMPING & LODGING

Accommodations are available in Chinle, 37 miles (59.6 km) north on US 191; Window Rock, 28 miles (45.1 km) east on AZ 264; Chambers, 38 miles (61.2 km) south on US 191; and Second Mesa, 67 miles (108 km) west on AZ 264.

FOOD & SUPPLIES

• Groceries are available in the Site. • There is a restaurant in Ganado. • Food and supplies are also available in Chinle and Window Rock.

FIRST AID/ HOSPITAL

• First aid is available in the Site. • The nearest hospital is in Ganado.

GENERAL INFORMATION

For your safety - Be cautious when walking around the grounds; watch for burrs and bits of metal that have been left over the years. Often the floors are uneven in the buildings, and there is usually a step between rooms.

Montezuma Castle National Monument
Camp Verde, Arizona

The Sinagua Indians inhabited the foothills and plateau beyond the Verde Valley until about 1125 when they moved into the valley and began constructing large pueblos such as Montezuma Castle. The Castle is a 20-room dwelling that stands in a cliff recess 100 feet (30.4 m) above the valley.

MAILING ADDRESS
Superintendent, Montezuma Castle National Monument, PO Box 219, Camp Verde, AZ 86322 Telephone: 602-567-3322

DIRECTIONS
The Visitor Center is 2.5 miles (4 km) off Interstate 17 and 5 miles (8 km) north of Camp Verde.

VISITOR ACTIVITIES
• Self-guiding walking tour, exhibits, picnicking and photography. • Facilities include restrooms, picnic areas, interpretive trails and a museum.

PERMITS, FEES & LIMITATIONS
The entrance fee is $2 (16 and under and 62 and over enter free).

ACCESSIBILITY
Montezuma Castle, restrooms, the Visitor Center and trails are accessible. At Montezuma Well, the picnic area but not the trail is accessible.

CAMPING & LODGING
Lodging and camping are available in nearby communities.

FOOD & SUPPLIES
Food and supplies are available in Camp Verde.

FIRST AID/ HOSPITAL
• First aid is available in the Monument or nearby in Camp Verde.
• The nearest hospital is in Cottonwood, 20 miles (32.2 km).

GENERAL INFORMATION
Visitors may wish to explore other nearby monuments, including Tuzigoot, Walnut Canyon, Wupatki and Sunset Crater (see listings in this book). Nearby points of interest also include Fort Verde and Jerome state historical parks.

Navajo National Monument
Northeastern, Arizona

The ruins of villages left behind by the Kayenta Anasazi Indians about 1300 AD are preserved in Navajo National Monument. They tell the story of farmers who were able to overcome for half a century the area's scarce rainfall to grow crops, build houses and raise families.

MAILING ADDRESS
Navajo National Monument, HC71, Box 3, Tonalea, AZ 86044
Telephone: 602-672-2366/2367

DIRECTIONS

Follow US 160 at Black Mesa, 50 miles (80.6 km) northeast of Tuba City, 22 miles (35.4 km) southwest of Kayenta. Turn north on SR 564, travel 9 miles (14.5 km) to the Visitor Center.

VISITOR ACTIVITIES

• Interpretive exhibits and short overlook trails, guided tours during summers and picnicking. • Access to the Ruins is through guided tours only. • Sandal Trail is a 1-mile (1.6 km) round-trip overlook trail from which visitors can view the Betatakin Ruin. • Reservations accepted up to 2 months in advance for Keet Seel tours. • Tickets for Betatakin are available the day of tour.

PERMITS, FEES & LIMITATIONS

No fees.

ACCESSIBILITY

Tours are not accessible. The Sandal Trail is minimally accessible. The Visitor Center, restrooms and one camp site are accessible.

CAMPING & LODGING

• The campground has 30 sites available with no fee. Trailers up to 25 feet (7.6 m) in length can be accommodated. • Group campsites and overflow campsites are available. • Lodging is available in Kayenta, Tuba City and Page.

FOOD & SUPPLIES

Food and supplies are available in nearby communities.

FIRST AID/ HOSPITAL

• Basic first aid is available at the Visitor Center. • The nearest hospitals are in Flagstaff and Page.

GENERAL INFORMATION

• Betatakin Ruins tours, which can accommodate no more than 24 people, are 5 miles (8 km) round trip involving a climb down and back up a 700-foot (213.4 m) steep incline taking 5 to 6 hours. • Ruins may be entered only with a Ranger. • Keet Seel is open from Memorial Day through Labor Day to 20 people per day. The tour is 16 miles (25.8 km) round trip by reservation only for a day, overnight or horseback trip.

Organ Pipe Cactus National Monument

Ajo, Arizona

Organ Pipe Cactus National Monument exhibits an extraordinary collection of plants and animals of the Sonoran Desert, including the organ pipe cactus, a large cactus rarely found in the United States. There are also other creatures that have adapted themselves to the region's extreme temperatures, intense sunlight and infrequent rainfall.

MAILING ADDRESS

Superintendent, Organ Pipe Cactus National Monument, Rt. 1, Box 100, Ajo, AZ 85321 **Telephone:** 602-387-6849

DIRECTIONS

From the north: follow AZ 85 through Ajo and Why. The Monument is 22 miles (35.4 km) south of Why. From the east: follow AZ 86 to Why, then turn south on AZ 85. From the west: follow I-8 to Gila Bend or I-10 to Buckeye, then turn south on AZ 85. From Mexico: drive on Mexico Route 2 to Sonoyta, then north to Lukeville.

VISITOR ACTIVITIES

• Scenic drives, hiking, backpacking, mountain biking, photography, wildlife and bird watching, picnicking and self-guided nature walks. • The Visitor Center, open daily from 8 a.m. to 5 p.m., offers a slide program on the Sonoran Desert region, museum exhibits and a bookstore. • Other facilities include picnic areas, a mail drop, trails, restrooms and telephones (credit card accessible only).

PERMITS, FEES & LIMITATIONS

• The entrance fee is $4. • There is a 35-foot (10.7 m) limit for RVs in the campground and a 25-foot (7.6 m) limit on RV scenic drives.

ACCESSIBILITY

The Visitor Center, parking area and restrooms are accessible. The audiovisual programs have volume control, captioned slide programs and listening devices. There are accessible campsites, and the scenic drives have accessible restrooms.

CAMPING & LODGING

• Camping is on a first-come, first-served basis for $8 a night with no reservations, except for the Group Campground (call or write the Superintendent). Tent and RV sites are available. • A permit, available at the Visitor Center, is required for the primitive campground and for backcountry camping. • Other overnight accommodations are available in Lukeville, 5 miles (8 km) south; Why, 22 miles (35.4 km) north; and Ajo, 34 miles (54.8 km) north.

FOOD & SUPPLIES

Food and supplies are available in Lukeville, Why and Ajo.

FIRST AID/ HOSPITAL

• First aid is available in the Monument. • The nearest hospitals are in Phoenix and Tucson, 145 miles (233.8 km).

GENERAL INFORMATION

• Sonoran Desert plants and animals, found nowhere else in the United States, are protected throughout Arizona. • The Monument was established by Presidential Proclamation on April 13, 1937. • As a Biosphere Reserve, it is an almost pristine example of the Sonoran Desert. • Beware of the cactus and some dangerous wildlife. There are 6 varieties of rattlesnakes as well as gila monsters and scorpions. These animals play an important part in the ecology of the desert and should not be harmed. • Visitors should be prepared for desert walking. A hat, sunscreen, comfortable and sturdy clothing and shoes, and a flashlight are necessary. • Carry enough drinking water, 1 gallon (4 l), per person per day.

Petrified Forest National Park

Northeastern, Arizona

About 225 million years ago, tall, stately pine-like trees grew at the headwaters of streams that crossed a vast floodplain. When they fell they were washed into the floodplain and were covered by a blanket of deposits and eventually preserved as petrified wood in an area that is today a dry tableland.

MAILING ADDRESS
Superintendent, Petrified Forest National Park, PO Box 2217, Petrified Forest National Park, AZ 86028 **Telephone:** 602-524-6228

DIRECTIONS
The Painted Desert entrance is on I-40, 25 miles (40.3 km) east of Holbrook, AZ. The Rainbow Forest entrance is on US 180, 19 miles (30.6 km) southeast of Holbrook.

VISITOR ACTIVITIES
• Self-guiding auto tours, photography, walking trails and wilderness hiking, summer interpretive talks, picnicking and sightseeing. • Orientation film at the Visitor Center and exhibits at the museum. • The Park is open daily from **8 a.m. to 5 p.m.** except Dec. 25 and Jan. 1 (extended hours are possible in the summer).

PERMITS, FEES & LIMITATIONS
• The **entrance fee** is $5 per vehicle or $3 per person. • A free wilderness backpacking permit is available. • Federal Law prohibits removal of any petrified wood or other natural, cultural object. Heavy fines are levied against violators.

ACCESSIBILITY
All major facilities, including concessions, are accessible. A detailed guide is available describing floor conditions, steps, curbs, etc.

CAMPING & LODGING
• Wilderness backcountry camping with a free permit only. • Lodging is available in Holbrook or Winslow, AZ, and in Gallup, NM.

FOOD & SUPPLIES
• Painted Desert Oasis offers meals, and Rainbow Forest Curios offers snacks and sandwiches. • The gas station at the Oasis carries basic food supplies. • Additional food and supplies are available in Holbrook.

FIRST AID/ HOSPITAL
• There are EMTs in the Park and an ambulance service in Holbrook. • The nearest hospitals are in Winslow, AZ, or in Gallup, NM.

GENERAL INFORMATION
• Park elevations range from 5,100 (1,554 m) to 6,235 feet (1,900 m). Beware of over exertion in the high altitude. • Carry sufficient water and notify Park personnel of any extended hikes.

Pipe Spring National Monument

Moccasin, Arizona

Pipe Spring National Monument is a memorial to the early cattle ranches and cowboys of the vast, trackless grassland that stretched to the Rocky Mountains. This land provided ample feed for the Texas long-horns that would supply the growing demand for beef in the East.

MAILING ADDRESS	Superintendent, Pipe Spring National Monument, HC 65, Box 5, Fredonia, AZ 86022 **Telephone:** 602-643-7105
DIRECTIONS	Pipe Spring is 14 miles (22.5 km) west of Fredonia. Follow US 89A via AZ 389. From I-15, UT 9 and 17 connect with UT 59 at Hurricane, UT, where a paved road leads to the Monument.
VISITOR ACTIVITIES	• Walking tours, self-guiding tours around the fort, conducted tours, exhibits, and visual interpretation. • The Monument is open daily from 8 a.m. to 4:30 p.m. except for Thanksgiving, Dec. 25 and Jan. 1. The historic buildings close at 4 p.m. The Visitor Center is open until 4:30 p.m.
PERMITS, FEES & LIMITATIONS	• The entrance fee is $2 a person age 17 through 62. • Vehicles must park in the lot at the Visitor Center.
ACCESSIBILITY	There is limited accessibility to the Visitor Center, the grounds and inside the Fort.
CAMPING & LODGING	Overnight accommodations are available in Kanab, 21 miles (33.8 km) east on US 89; or in Fredonia.
FOOD & SUPPLIES	Food and supplies are obtainable in Kanab or Fredonia.
FIRST AID/ HOSPITAL	• First aid is available in the Monument or in Fredonia. • The nearest hospital is in Kanab.
GENERAL INFORMATION	• Be especially careful of the steep, narrow stairways and low doorways in the buildings. • Watch children around ponds and livestock.

Saguaro National Monument

Tucson, Arizona

The saguaro cactus has been described as the supreme symbol of the American Southwest with its variety of odd, all-too-human shapes. It is also known as the monarch of the Sonoran Desert, a desert that far surpasses other North American deserts in lushness and variety of life despite its heat and dryness.

Arizona

MAILING ADDRESS	Superintendent, Saguaro National Monument, 3693 South Old Spanish Trail, Tucson, AZ 85730-5699 **Telephone:** 602-296-8516
DIRECTIONS	The Visitor Center and Park Headquarters in the Rincon Mountain District are on Old Spanish Trail at Freeman Road, 2 miles (3.2 km) east of the Tucson City limits. The Red Hills Visitor Center in the Tucson Mountain-District is on Kinney Road, 2 miles (3.2 km) west of the Arizona-Sonora Desert Museum.
VISITOR ACTIVITIES	• Wildlife and bird watching, hiking, picnicking, photography, wilderness backcountry camping and hiking (Rincon Mt. District only), horseback riding, bicycling and scenic driving. • Rincon Mt. District is open from 7 a.m. to 7 p.m., April to October, and from 7 a.m. to 5 p.m. from November to March. Tucson Mt. District is open all year, and Red Hills Visitor Center is open daily from 8 a.m. to 5 p.m. • Both District visitor centers offer audiovisual programs, exhibits, nature walks and scheduled seasonal programs. • Facilities include picnic areas and hiking trails in both districts.
PERMITS, FEES & LIMITATIONS	• There is a $4 per vehicle and $2 per person **entrance fee** at Rincon Mt. District. There is no fee at Tucson Mt. District. • Frequent visitors may purchase a Saguaro National Monument Pass for $10. • Permits from the Visitor Center are required for camping in Rincon Mt. Wilderness Area. • No off-road vehicles are allowed.
ACCESSIBILITY	Visitor centers and restrooms are accessible. There are modified latrines at some picnic areas and a captioned audiovisual program for the hearing-impaired. Check at visitor centers for accessible hiking trails.
CAMPING & LODGING	• Backcountry camping only in the Rincon Mt. District. • Overnight accommodations are available in Downtown Tucson, 16 miles (25.8 km) west of the Rincon Mt. District and 15 miles (24.1 km) east of the Tucson Mt. District along I-10, and at Gilbet Ray Campground, 2 miles (3.2 km) from the Red Hills Visitor Center.
FOOD & SUPPLIES	• Meals are available nearby. • Food and supplies are available in Tucson.
FIRST AID/ HOSPITAL	• First aid is available in both districts. • The nearest hospital to the Rincon Mt. District is St. Joseph's, 10 miles (16.1 km) west via Broadway at Wilmot and 5th Street. The nearest hospital to the Tucson Mt. District is St. Mary's, 16.5 miles (26.6 km) east on the corner of St. Mary's and Silverbell.
GENERAL INFORMATION	On the way to Tucson Mt. District, visit the adjacent Arizona-Sonora Desert Museum and see a presentation of living plants and animals of the desert in simulated natural habitats.

Sunset Crater National Monument

Flagstaff, Arizona

Sunset Crater appeared in the winter of 1064-65 when molten rock sprayed out of a crack in the ground high into the air, solidified quickly and fell to earth as large bombs or smaller cinders. A 1,000-foot (304.8 m) cone was built up around the vent over the next 100 years as periodic eruptions continued.

MAILING ADDRESS
Superintendent, Sunset Crater National Monument, 2717 N. Steves Blvd., #3, Flagstaff, AZ 86004 **Telephone:** 602-556-7042 (Park), 602-556-7134 (Headquarters)

DIRECTIONS
Drive north of Flagstaff on US Hwy. 89, 13 miles (20.9 km). Turn right on the Sunset Crater-Wupatki Loop Road and continue 2 miles (3.2 km) to the Visitor Center.

VISITOR ACTIVITIES
• Naturalist activities, campfire programs in the summer, exhibits and picnicking. • Facilities include information and drinking water at the Visitor Center, picnic areas and restrooms. • The Monument is open daily from 8 a.m. to 5 p.m. except for Dec. 25.

PERMITS, FEES & LIMITATIONS
• The entrance fee is $4 in summer only. • Vehicles should stay on the roads due to soft shoulders.

CAMPING & LODGING
• Camp sites are available on a first-come, first-served basis at a US Forest Service campground next to the Sunset Crater Visitor Center. A nightly fee is charged. The camping season runs from late May to mid-October. • Other overnight accommodations are available in Flagstaff.

FOOD & SUPPLIES
Food and supplies are available in Flagstaff.

FIRST AID/ HOSPITAL
• First aid is available in the Monument. • The nearest hospital is in Flagstaff.

GENERAL INFORMATION
• Sunset Crater is an interesting stop before the Grand Canyon. Wupatki National Monument (see listing in this book) is 20 miles (32.2 km) from Sunset Crater. Both monuments are located on a scenic 35-mile (56.4 km) loop. • The most prominent hazards are deep, narrow earth cracks, razor-sharp lava and unstable backcountry ruins. • Do not walk on pre-historic walls or disturb plants, animals, or geological and archaeological features. • Sunset Crater is closed to hiking, but other nearby craters may be climbed.

Tonto National Monument

Roosevelt, Arizona

The well-preserved cliff dwellings at Tonto National Monument were occupied during the 13th and 14th centuries by Salado Indians who farmed in the Salt River Valley.

MAILING ADDRESS
Tonto National Monument, HC02, Box 4602, Roosevelt, AZ 85545
Telephone: 602-467-2241

DIRECTIONS
From Phoenix, go east on Apache Trail (Hwy. 88) to the Monument. Turn north on Hwy. 87 to Hwy. 188 to 88 to the Monument. Take Hwy. 60 east to Hwy. 88 to Roosevelt Lake.

VISITOR ACTIVITIES
• Hiking, museum, slide shows, picnicking, photography and interpretive talks. • Facilities include a Visitor Center, restrooms and information. • The Monument is open daily from 8 a.m. to 5 p.m., except Dec. 25.

PERMITS, FEES & LIMITATIONS
The entrance fee is $4 per privately owned vehicle and $2 per person for commercial vehicles and motorcycles.

ACCESSIBILITY
Restrooms, the Visitor Center and the Museum are accessible. Hiking trails are not accessible.

CAMPING & LODGING
Overnight accommodations are available 7 miles (11.2 km) east at Roosevelt Lodge and 2 miles (3.2 km) west at Roosevelt Marina with RV spaces, a general store and fast food.

FOOD & SUPPLIES
Food and supplies are available at the Spring Creek store, 7 miles (11.2 km) east, and at the Roosevelt Marina store and the Roosevelt Lodge.

FIRST AID/ HOSPITAL
• The Gila County Sheriff's aid station is 2 miles (3.2 km) west of the Monument. • The Cobra Valley Hospital is 30 miles (48.3 km) south.

GENERAL INFORMATION
• The summers are hot and arid between May and July, and hot and humid from late July through September. • The fall and winter climate is mild and pleasant. • Average rainfall is between 15 to 20 inches (38.1-50.8 cm). • There is snow in higher elevations. • Carry water.

Tumacacori National Monument

Tumacacori, Arizona

The ruins of a historic Spanish Catholic mission building stand near the site first visited in 1691 by Father Eusebio Francisco Kino, a German-educated Italian Jesuit. Later, the building was a northern outpost of a mission chain constructed by Franciscan priests during the late 1700s on sites established by the Jesuits.

MAILING ADDRESS

Superintendent, Tumacacori National Historical Park, PO Box 67, Tumacacori, AZ 85640 **Telephone:** 602-398-2341

DIRECTIONS

Tumacacori is 45 miles (72.5 km) south of Tucson on I-19 and 18 miles (29 km) north of Nogales and the Mexican border.

VISITOR ACTIVITIES

• Interpretive exhibits, self-guiding walks, living history demonstrations and picnicking. • Facilities include parking and a picnic area. • The Park is open daily from 8 a.m. to 5 p.m., except Thanksgiving and Dec. 25. • A fiesta is held the first Sunday in December, featuring an outdoor Mariachi Mass, continuous entertainment, and craft and native food sales.

PERMITS, FEES & LIMITATIONS

The entrance fee is $2 per person.

ACCESSIBILITY

The parking area, museum, restrooms and trails are accessible.

CAMPING & LODGING

Overnight accommodations are available in Tucson; Nogales; Rio Rico, 8 miles (12.9 km); Tumacacori, 3 miles (4.8 km), and Tubac, 3 miles (4.8 km).

FOOD & SUPPLIES

Food and supplies are available in Tucson, Nogales and Carmen, 1 mile (1.6 km).

FIRST AID/ HOSPITAL

• First aid is available in the Park. • The nearest hospital is in Nogales.

Tuzigoot National Monument

Clarkdale, Arizona

Tuzigoot (Apache for "crooked water") is the remnant of a Sinaguan Indian village built between 1125 and 1400 AD. It was originally 2 stories high in places with 77 ground-floor rooms occupied by farmers and fine artisans.

MAILING ADDRESS

Superintendent, Tuzigoot National Monument, PO Box 219, Camp Verde, AZ 86322 **Telephone:** 602-634-5564

DIRECTIONS

The Monument is off of Broadway Street, 3 miles (4.8 km) west of Cottonwood or 2 miles (3.2 km) east of Clarkdale.

VISITOR ACTIVITIES

• Self-guiding walking tour and exhibits. • The Monument is closed Dec. 25.

PERMITS, FEES & LIMITATIONS

The entrance fee is $2 per person (16 and under and 62 and over admitted free).

ACCESSIBILITY

The Visitor Center and restrooms are accessible. The trail and ruins are not accessible.

CAMPING & LODGING

Overnight accommodations are available in nearby communities.

FOOD & SUPPLIES

Food and supplies are available in Cottonwood.

FIRST AID/ HOSPITAL

The nearest hospital is in Cottonwood.

GENERAL INFORMATION

Twenty-seven miles (43.5 km) from Tuzigoot on a good road off of US 89A is Montezuma Castle National Monument (see listing in this book). If continuing north on US 89A to Flagstaff, other national monuments include: Walnut Canyon, Wupatki and Sunset Crater (see listings in this book).

Walnut Canyon National Monument

Flagstaff, Arizona

Cliff dwellings at Walnut Canyon National Monument were built in shallow caves between 1125 and 1250 AD by Pueblo Indians known today as the Sinagua - Spanish for without water. They farmed and hunted in the area for almost 150 years before abandoning their homes for unknown reasons.

MAILING ADDRESS

Superintendent, Walnut Canyon National Monument, Walnut Canyon Road, Flagstaff, AZ 86004-9705 **Telephone:** 602-526-3367

DIRECTIONS

The entrance road to Walnut Canyon is a 2.8-mile (4.5 km) highway connecting with I-40, 7.5 miles (12 km) east of Flagstaff.

VISITOR ACTIVITIES

• Interpretive exhibits, hiking and interpretive walks in the summer.
• Facilities include parking, a museum, a picnic area and hiking trails.
• The Monument is open daily from 7 **a.m.** to 6 **p.m.** from Memorial Day through Labor Day; and 8 **a.m.** to 5 **p.m.** the rest of the year except Dec. 25.

PERMITS, FEES & LIMITATIONS

• The **entrance fee** is $2 per person or $4 per car. • Vehicles are restricted to designated roads. • It is prohibited to leave designated trails.

ACCESSIBILITY

Parking, restrooms and the Rim Trail are accessible.

CAMPING & LODGING

Overnight accommodations are available in Flagstaff and Winslow and along major highways.

FOOD & SUPPLIES

Food and supplies are available in Flagstaff.

FIRST AID/ HOSPITAL

• First aid is available in the Monument. • The nearest hospital is in Flagstaff.

GENERAL INFORMATION

Those with heart ailments or other physical conditions should realize that the Island Trail includes a 185-foot (56.3 m) climb at an altitude of nearly 7,000 feet (2,134 m). These conditions can tax the heart and lungs.

Wupatki National Monument

Flagstaff, Arizona

When the Sinagua Indians moved to the Wupatki basin in the early 12th century, they found the native materials ideal for construction of freestanding masonry dwellings. Made from slabs of sandstone, limestone and basalt with a clay-based mortar, these dwellings were inhabited until about 1225 AD.

MAILING ADDRESS

Superintendent, Wupatki National Monument, 2717 N. Steves Blvd., Suite #3, Flagstaff, AZ 86004 **Telephone:** 602-556-7040, Monument; 602-556-7134, Headquarters

DIRECTIONS

The Visitor Center is on the 35-mile (56.4 km) loop road that connects Wupatki with Sunset Crater Volcano National Monument. Drive 15 miles (24.1 km) north of Flagstaff on Highway 89, then east on the loop road (F5545) 22 miles (35.4 km) to the Wupatki Visitor Center.

VISITOR ACTIVITIES

Interpretive talks and exhibits, hiking, walking, auto tours, photography and self-guiding trails to the Nalakihu-Citadel Ruins, the Wupatki Ruin, the Wukoki Ruin, the Lomaki Ruin and the Doney Crater.

PERMITS, FEES & LIMITATIONS

• The entrance fee is $4 per vehicle or $2 for bicycles and walk-ins. • All vehicles are restricted to designated roads. • Backcountry hiking is allowed by permit only. Permits are available at the Visitor Center. • No overnight use is allowed.

ACCESSIBILITY

The Wupatki Ruins, the Visitor Center and most ruin trails are accessible.

CAMPING & LODGING

• Lodging is available in Flagstaff, 37 miles (59.6 km); and in Grey Mountain, 22 miles (35.4 km). • A US Forest Service campground across from the Sunset Crater Visitor Center is available on a first-come, first-served basis from late May until mid-October.

FOOD & SUPPLIES

Food and supplies are available nearby.

FIRST AID/ HOSPITAL

• First aid is available at the Visitor Center. • The nearest hospital is in Flagstaff.

GENERAL INFORMATION

Carry water and wear sturdy shoes when hiking off of the main road. Wupatki is primarily a desert environment.

Arkansas

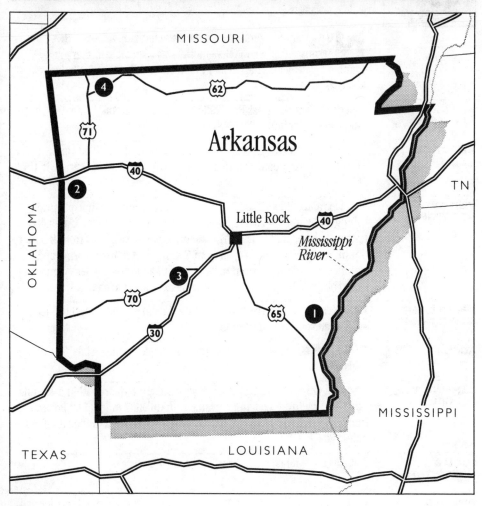

1 Arkansas Post National Memorial

2 Fort Smith National Historic Site

3 Hot Springs National Park

4 Pea Ridge National Military Park

Arkansas

Arkansas Post National Memorial
Gillett, Arkansas

Now a tranquil, rural spot on the ever-changing Arkansas River, the Arkansas Post National Memorial was a strategic military and commercial center on the frontier that is often called the "Birthplace of Arkansas."

MAILING ADDRESS
Superintendent, Arkansas Post National Memorial, Route 1, Box 16, Gillett, AR 72055 Telephone: 501-548-2207

DIRECTIONS
The Memorial is on AR 169, 7 miles (11.2 km) south of Gillett via US 165 (The Great River Road) and 18 miles (29 km) northeast of Dumas via US 165.

VISITOR ACTIVITIES
• Indoor and outdoor exhibits, audiovisual program, walking, picnicking, fishing and biking. • Facilities include a Visitor Center, a picnic area, restrooms and paved trails. • The Visitor Center is open daily from 8 a.m. to 5 p.m. • The Memorial is open from 7 a.m. to dark in the spring and summer, and from 8 a.m. to dark in the fall and winter. • The Memorial is closed on Dec. 25 and other holidays that are subject to change.

PERMITS, FEES & LIMITATIONS
• No fees. • An Arkansas fishing license is required and is available locally. • Off-road vehicle use is prohibited.

ACCESSIBILITY
The Visitor Center, parking areas and picnic areas are accessible. The hiking trails are paved.

CAMPING & LODGING
• Several Corps of Engineer and private campgrounds are within a 30-mile (48.3 km) radius. • Lodging is available in Gillett, 7 miles (11.2 km); Dumas, 18 miles (29 km); DeWitt, 20 miles (32.2 km); and Pine Bluff, 50 miles (80.6 km).

FOOD & SUPPLIES
Supplies are available in Dumas, DeWitt or Gillett.

FIRST AID/ HOSPITAL
• First aid is available in the Memorial. • The nearest hospitals are located in Dumas and DeWitt.

GENERAL INFORMATION
• Watch for snakes, ticks and poison ivy while walking the trails. Watch your step and stay on the trails. • The best time to visit the Memorial is September through May due to the extreme heat, humidity and insects in summer.

Arkansas

Fort Smith National Historic Site

Fort Smith, Arkansas

Fort Smith National Historic Site embraces the remains of 2 frontier forts and the Federal Court for the Western District of Arkansas. The site commemorates a significant phase of America's westward expansion and 80 turbulent years in the history of Federal Indian policy.

MAILING ADDRESS

Superintendent, Fort Smith National Historic Site, PO Box 1406, Fort Smith, AR 72902 **Telephone:** 501-783-3961

DIRECTIONS

The Site is in downtown Fort Smith. Take Garrison Avenue (US 64) and turn south on 4th Street, turn right on Parker Avenue. A Visitor Center is in the Old Barracks Building.

VISITOR ACTIVITIES

• Interpretive exhibits and walks. • Facilities include a parking lot and restrooms at the Visitor Center. • The Site is open daily from 9 a.m. to 5 p.m., except Thanksgiving, Dec. 25. and Jan. 1.

PERMITS, FEES & LIMITATIONS

There is a $2 entrance fee for adults. Entrance is free for children 16 and under and adults 62 and older.

ACCESSIBILITY

The parking lot and trails are mostly accessible. Wheelchair lifts are available in the Visitor Center. Restrooms are accessible.

CAMPING & LODGING

Lodging is available in Fort Smith.

FOOD & SUPPLIES

Food and supplies are obtainable in Fort Smith.

FIRST AID/ HOSPITAL

• First aid is available in the Site. • The nearest hospital is in Sparks on South I Street, 1 mile (1.6 km) from the Site.

GENERAL INFORMATION

• Summer is hot and humid. Winter is generally mild and humid. Strong winds occur often in the spring. • The Old Fort Museum is a nearby point of interest.

Hot Springs National Park

Hot Springs, Arkansas   See Climatable No. 7

People first stumbled on the hot springs of Hot Springs National Park perhaps 10,000 years ago, and have used them for bathing and drinking ever since. The heyday was in the 1920s when monumental bathhouses were built to cater to crowds of health seekers.

MAILING ADDRESS

Superintendent, Hot Springs National Park, PO Box 1860, Hot Springs, AR 71902 **Telephone:** 501-321-1433

DIRECTIONS

Take US 70, US 270 or AR 7. The Visitor Center is located in the middle of magnolia-lined Bathhouse Row on AR 7.

VISITOR ACTIVITIES

• The Fordyce Bathhouse Visitor Center, offers an introductory movie, a bathing video, exhibits, 24 furnished rooms and a bookstore. • Thermal Features Tours, campfire programs, two picnic grounds, Hot Springs Mountain Observation Tower, and thermal water bathing on Bathhouse Row (and at several hotels).

PERMITS, FEES & LIMITATIONS

• Fee schedule is available for commercially operated bathhouses. • Hot Springs Mountain Drive is restricted to vehicles less than 32 feet (9.75 m). • Pull-out space in front of the Visitor Center is limited to loading and unloading. Buses have priority.

ACCESSIBILITY

Most facilities and programs are accessible. An accessibility bulletin is available.

CAMPING & LODGING

• Gulpha Gorge Campground is alongside the creek on the east side of the Park and features 42 sites. The fee is $6 a night with self-registration on a first-come, first-served basis. There are no hookups or showers. There is an adjacent picnic area, amphitheater and hiking trails. • Abundant lodging is available in Hot Springs.

FOOD & SUPPLIES

Food and supplies are available in Hot Springs.

FIRST AID/ HOSPITAL

There are two hospitals located in Hot Springs.

GENERAL INFORMATION

The city, a separate entity from the Park, uses the name Hot Springs National Park from the historic designation of the railroad depot by that name. For city information, call 1-800-SPA-CITY.

Pea Ridge National Military Park

North of Rogers, Arkansas

The control of Missouri was a prime objective of both Union and Confederate forces during the first year of the Civil War. It was one of the reasons for the clash at Pea Ridge in March 1862 that ended with Missouri in Union hands.

MAILING ADDRESS

Pea Ridge National Military Park, Highway 62 E, Pea Ridge, AR 72751
Telephone: 501-451-8122

DIRECTIONS

The Park is 10 miles (16.1 km) north of Rogers, AR, on Highway 62.

VISITOR ACTIVITIES

• Civil War Museum exhibits, 12-minute slide program and self-guided auto tour. • The Visitor Center is open daily from 8 a.m. to 5 p.m.

Arkansas

• Elkhorn Tavern is open from 10 a.m. to 4 p.m., May through October.
• The Park is closed Thanksgiving, Dec. 25 and Jan. 1.• There is a 10-mile (16.1 km) hiking trail and an 11-mile (17.7 km) horse trail. • Ranger talks on the battle are available depending on visitation and staffing.

PERMITS, FEES & LIMITATIONS

• There is a $2 **entrance fee** for adults ages 17 to 61. Children under 16 and adults 62 and older enter free.

ACCESSIBILITY

Most Visitor Center activities are fully accessible. Some help may be needed for restrooms. Elkhorn Tavern is not accessible.

CAMPING & LODGING

Camping is available at nearby Beaver Lake, operated by the Army Corps of Engineers.

FOOD & SUPPLIES

There are family restaurants, convenience stores and gasoline along the highway within 3 miles (4.8 km) of the Park.

FIRST AID/ HOSPITAL

• First aid is available in the Park. • The nearest hospital is in Rogers.

California

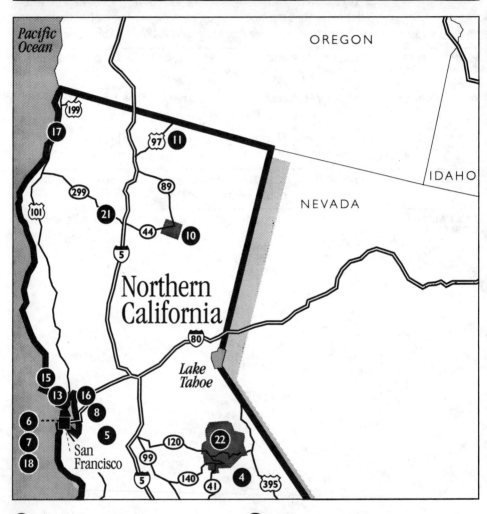

1	Cabrillo National Monument	**8**	John Muir National Historic Site
2	Channel Islands National Park	**9**	Joshua Tree National Monument
3	Death Valley National Monument	**10**	Lassen Volcanic National Park
4	Devils Postpile National Monument	**11**	Lava Beds National Monument
5	Eugene O'Neill National Historic Site	**12**	Manzanar National Historic Site
6	Fort Point National Historic Site	**13**	Muir Woods National Monument
7	Golden Gate National Recreation Area	**14**	Pinnacles National Monument

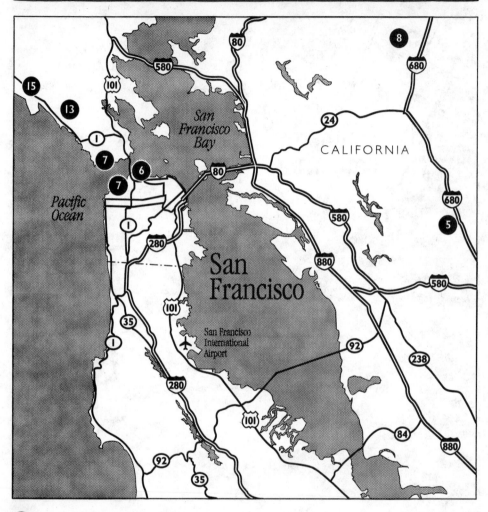

5　Eugene O'Neill National Historic Site

6　Fort Point National Historic Site

7　Golden Gate National Recreation Area

8　John Muir National Historic Site

13　Muir Woods National Monument

15　Point Reyes National Seashore

Cabrillo National Monument

San Diego, California

Cabrillo National Monument in San Diego commemorates Juan Rodriguez Cabrillo's epic voyage of discovery along the California coast 50 years after Columbus landed in the New World. It marks the site of Cabrillo's first landing.

MAILING ADDRESS

Superintendent, Cabrillo National Monument, PO Box 6670, San Diego, CA 92116 **Telephone:** 619-557-5450

DIRECTIONS

Follow Rosecrans Street (Rt. 209) to Canon Street. Turn right on Canon and follow Catalina Boulevard. Turn left on Catalina and proceed through the US Navy gate past Fort Rosecrans National Cemetery to the Monument.

VISITOR ACTIVITIES

• Hiking, bird watching, whale watching, tide pools, interpretive exhibits, guided walks, self-guided tours, lighthouse tours, audiovisual programs and photography. • The Monument hours are **9 a.m. to 5:15 p.m.**, daily.

PERMITS, FEES & LIMITATIONS

• The **entrance fee** is $4 per vehicle or $2 per person for a 7-day pass. There is no fee for children under 17 years old or US residents older than 62.
• Vehicles and bicycles are restricted to paved roads and parking areas.

ACCESSIBILITY

An access guide is available at the Visitor Center. The Visitor Center, restrooms, museum, bookstore, auditorium, whale overlook shelter and statue area are accessible. Vehicle access to the Lighthouse area is permitted by special pass obtainable at the Visitor Center.

CAMPING & LODGING

Overnight accommodations are available in San Diego and include a commercial bread and breakfast on Point Loma.

FOOD & SUPPLIES

Supplies are available within 6 miles (9.6 km) on Point Loma.

FIRST AID/ HOSPITAL

• First aid is available in the Monument. • The nearest hospital is on Point Loma.

Channel Islands National Park

Ventura, California   See Climatable No. 8

Isolation from the mainland plus the mingling of warm and cold water currents in the Santa Barbara Channel adds to the unique character of the Channel Islands. Five of these islands and their surrounding 6 nautical miles (9.6 km) of ocean comprise Channel Islands National Park and National Marine Sanctuary. Great numbers of plants, animals and marine life abound in the Park.

California

MAILING ADDRESS	Superintendent, Channel Islands National Park, 1901 Spinnaker Drive, Ventura, CA 93001 **Telephone: 805-658-5700**
DIRECTIONS	South bound on US Highway 101, take Seaward off ramp in Ventura, then take Harbor Boulevard south to Spinnaker Drive. Turn right and proceed to the Visitor Center at the end of the drive. North bound on US Highway 101, take Victoria off ramp in Ventura and follow the Channel Islands signs.
VISITOR ACTIVITIES	• Hiking, camping, exhibits, audiovisual programs, scuba diving, picnicking, wildlife and bird watching, fishing, snorkeling, swimming, kayaking and boating. • The Visitor Center is open daily, except Thanksgiving, Dec. 25 and Jan. 1, from 8 a.m. to 5 p.m., with extended hours in the summer.
PERMITS, FEES & LIMITATIONS	• No entrance fees. • Permits required for camping and island landing on Santa Rosa and San Miguel islands.
ACCESSIBILITY	The Visitor Center, located at the Park Headquarters, is fully accessible.
CAMPING & LODGING	• Camping is available on Anacapa, Santa Barbara and Santa Rosa islands year-round. Camping on San Miguel Island is seasonal. Call Park for more information on availability. All camping is backcountry, and campers must supply their own water, stove, food and equipment. • No fires or pets are permitted.
FOOD & SUPPLIES	Supplies are available in Ventura and Oxnard.
FIRST AID/ HOSPITAL	• First aid is available in the Park. • The nearest hospital is in Ventura, 4 miles (6.4 km) from headquarters and 18 miles (29 km) from Anacapa.
GENERAL INFORMATION	• Access to the islands is obtainable from the Park concessionaires. Contact Islands Packer's boat service at 805-642-1393. For Santa Rosa Island only, contact Channel Islands Aviation for day trips and camping at 805-987-1301. • Bring warm clothing because nights are cool.

Death Valley National Monument

Death Valley, California

D espite the harshness and severity of Death Valley National Monument, more than 900 kinds of plants live within the park. Visitors can find spectacular wildflower displays, snow-covered peaks, beautiful sand dunes and abandoned mines in the hottest spot in North America.

MAILING ADDRESS	Superintendent, Death Valley National Monument, Death Valley, CA 92328 Telephone: 619-786-2331
DIRECTIONS	Take US 395 and connect with Rts. 190 and 136 or by an unnumbered county road from Trona, CA, to the Monument. Take US 95 and connect

with NV 267, 374 and 373 to the Monument. I-15 passes southeast of the Monument and connects with Rt. 127 to the Monument.

VISITOR ACTIVITIES

• Driving, hiking, jeep riding, camping, photography, biking, interpretive exhibits, guided tours, picnicking, backcountry and horseback riding. • Facilities include a Visitor Center, hiking trails, parking, restrooms, picnic areas, a post office and bicycle rentals. • With elevations from more than 11,000 feet (3,352.8 m) to less than 300 feet (91.4 m) below sea level, activities vary with the seasons.

PERMITS, FEES & LIMITATIONS

• The vehicle entrance fee is $5 for 7 days. • Tickets are sold on a first-come, first-served basis for tours of Scotty's Castle - $6 for adults, $3 for children 6 to 11 years old and adults 62 and older, children under 6 enter for free. Tours are limited to 19 people at a time. • Vehicles of all kinds are restricted to designated roads.

ACCESSIBILITY

Furnace Creek area has the most accessible services and facilities. Access limited in other areas due to severe desert environment and age of facilities.

CAMPING & LODGING

• There are 9 campgrounds with more than 1,500 sites. Different locations and elevations are open during different times of the year and are available on a first-come, first-served basis. Reservations are accepted for Furnace Creek Campground and for group sites at Texas Spring Campground from October through April. Call 1-800-365-2267. Fees are $8 a night at Furnace Creek and $40 a night for group sites. • Backcountry camping is allowed. Information and voluntary registration available at the Visitor Center.

FOOD & SUPPLIES

Food and supplies are available at Furnace Creek and Stovepipe Wells campgrounds, Scotty's Castle and in Lone Pine, Trona, Beatty, Pahrump and Shoshone.

FIRST AID/ HOSPITAL

• Ranger medics and ambulance provide emergency first aid only. • Air and ground ambulance service is available for transport to area hospitals in Las Vegas, NV; Tonopah, NV; and Lone Pine, CA.

GENERAL INFORMATION

The harsh environment, lack of water and distance between facilities make desert travel hazardous at times.

Devils Postpile National Monument

Mammoth Lakes, California

A long the picturesque Middle Fork of the San Joaquin River lies the 800-acre Devils Postpile National Monument with one of the world's finest examples of columnar-jointed basalt and the 101 foot (30.8 m) Rainbow Falls.

MAILING ADDRESS	Superintendent, Devils Postpile National Monument, PO Box 501, Mammoth Lakes, CA 93546 **Telephone:** 619-934-2289 summer and fall, 209-565-3341 winter and spring
DIRECTIONS	Follow a 10-mile (16.1 km) drive to Minaret Summit from US 395 on SR 203, then travel 7 miles (11.2 km) on a paved mountain road with turnouts.
VISITOR ACTIVITIES	• Guided walks, picnicking, evening campfire programs and fishing. • Hiking trips north or south along the John Muir Trail and west on the King Creek Trail. There are also several short trails in and around the Monument. • Facilities include restrooms near the Ranger Station, a picnic area and shuttle bus. • The Monument is open from about mid-June through October.
PERMITS, FEES & LIMITATIONS	• No entrance fee. • A California fishing license, available locally for a fee, is required. • Use of vehicles is restricted in mid-day during the heavy-use season when visitors are required to use a shuttle bus to reach the Monument.
ACCESSIBILITY	Access is very limited.
CAMPING & LODGING	• There are 21 camp sites available on a first-come, first-served basis for $8 a night with a 14-day limit. • Other overnight accommodations are available in Mammoth Lakes, 14 miles (22.5 km); and Reds Meadow, 1.5 miles (2.4 km).
FOOD & SUPPLIES	Food and supplies, while not available in the Monument, are available in Mammoth Lakes and Reds Meadow.
FIRST AID/ HOSPITAL	• First aid is available in the Monument. • The nearest hospital is in Mammoth Lakes.
GENERAL INFORMATION	For your safety - Bears inhabit the Monument. Proper food storage is required by Federal Law. Stay on the designated trails. Stand back when viewing features from the edges of cliffs or gorges. Footing is hazardous.

Eugene O'Neill National Historic Site

Danville, California

Of all the places Eugene O'Neill, one of America's greatest playwrights, called home during his restless life, Tao House was the one that held him the longest and provided the refuge where he wrote his last plays.

MAILING ADDRESS	Superintendent, Eugene O'Neill National Historic Site, PO Box 280, Danville, CA 94526 **Telephone:** 510-838-0249
DIRECTIONS	About 35 miles (56.4 km) east of San Francisco, the Site is located in Danville, CA, off of I-680.

VISITOR ACTIVITIES
Ranger led tours and self-guided tours are available Wednesday through Sunday at 10 a.m. and 12:30 p.m. Reservations can be made by writing or calling the Site.

PERMITS, FEES & LIMITATIONS
• No fees or permits. • Access to the Site is available only through reserved programs. Call for more information.

ACCESSIBILITY
The Site is accessible with the exception of the second floor and pool area. The shuttle van has no wheelchair lift. Call to make arrangements.

CAMPING & LODGING
Lodging is available in Danville.

FOOD & SUPPLIES
Food and supplies are available in Danville.

FIRST AID/ HOSPITAL
• First aid is available at the Site. • The nearest hospital is in Walnut Creek, 10 miles (16.1 km) from Danville.

Fort Point National Historic Site

San Francisco, California

Situated beneath the Golden Gate Bridge, Fort Point is a classic example of the mid-19th century coastal fortifications built by the U.S. Corps of Engineers. It symbolizes the commercial and strategic military importance of San Francisco.

MAILING ADDRESS
District Ranger, Fort Point National Historic Site, PO Box 29333, Presidio of San Francisco, CA 94129 **Telephone:** 415-556-1693

DIRECTIONS
Fort Point is located under the southern end of the Golden Gate Bridge. Turn off of Hwy. 101 at the bridge and turn left onto Lincoln Boulevard. The Site is one-third of a mile (.5 km) away.

VISITOR ACTIVITIES
• Ranger-led, audio cassette and self-guided tours are available. • Visitors are encouraged to take part in the interpretive exhibits, a 17-minute laser-disc show and the cannon drills. • The park is open Wednesday through Sunday, 10 a.m. to 5 p.m., except Thanksgiving, Dec. 25 and Jan. 1. • Candlelight tours are available during the winter. • Visitor facilities include a bookstore, picnic areas, restrooms, a fishing pier, short hiking trails and a bike path.

PERMITS, FEES & LIMITATIONS
• No entrance fee. • All programs are free with the exception of the audio tour. Audio tours are $2.50 for adults and $1 for children 12 and under.

ACCESSIBILITY
All first-floor exhibits, theater, bookstore, restrooms and drinking fountain are accessible. A close-captioned video is available for the hearing-impaired.

CAMPING & LODGING
A large selection of accommodations are available in the San Francisco area.

FOOD & SUPPLIES

• Coffee, hot chocolate and hot apple cider are sold in the Visitor Center. No food is available at the Site. • Food and supplies are available in the San Francisco area.

FIRST AID/ HOSPITAL

Several medical and emergency facilities, including the California Pacific Medical Center, St. Mary's Hospital and U.C.S.F. Mount Zion Hospital, are nearby.

GENERAL INFORMATION

Visitors should dress warmly regardless of the weather elsewhere in the Bay Area. Cold weather along with fog and wind are common at Fort Point.

Golden Gate National Recreation Area

San Francisco, California

Golden Gate National Recreation Area wraps around San Francisco's northern and western edge offering a series of scenic, historic, urban and natural features - including the entrance to the city's harbor at Golden Gate.

MAILING ADDRESS

General Superintendent, Golden Gate National Recreation Area, Building 201, Fort Mason, San Francisco, CA 94123 **Telephone:** 415-556-0560

DIRECTIONS

The Recreation Area follows San Francisco's northern and western shoreline. These areas are accessible by the Municipal Railway (MUNI) bus system and by car. Ferries provide service to Alcatraz. Across the Golden Gate Bridge in Marin County, follow any of the various access roads off of Hwy. 101, including Alexander Avenue, Shoreline Highway and Sir Francis Drake Boulevard to the Recreation area. MUNI serves Rodeo Beach in Marin on Sundays. Visitor information is available at Fort Mason, the Cliff House, Ft. Point, The National Maritime Museum, Rodeo Beach and Muir Woods.

VISITOR ACTIVITIES

• Alcatraz tours, picnicking, fishing, swimming, short walks and sightseeing, hiking and cultural programs at the Fort Mason Center. • Facilities include picnic sites, fishing piers, beaches, restrooms and parking. • Most of the Recreation Area is open all day, all year. Hours for individual facilities vary, but the most common hours of operation are **10 a.m. to 5 p.m.**

PERMITS, FEES & LIMITATIONS

• The Hyde Street Pier **entrance fee** is $3 for adults, children under 12 admitted free. • The Alcatraz ferry fee is $5.50. • The audio tour fee is $3. • No off-road vehicles allowed.

CAMPING & LODGING

• American Youth Hostels offer overnight accommodations in the Marin Headlands area of the Recreation Area and at Fort Mason. Hike-in and group camping is available in the Marin Headlands area. • The San Francisco area offers a wide variety of overnight accommodations.

FOOD & SUPPLIES

Food and supplies are available in the surrounding urban community.

California

FIRST AID/ HOSPITAL	• First aid is available at most Visitor Centers and in the surrounding community. • Nearby hospitals include Letterman and San Francisco General Hospital.
GENERAL INFORMATION	The Presidio of San Francisco is a 1,440-acre US Army base that will become part of the Golden Gate National Recreation Area in September 1995. It contains a unique 200-year history of continuous occupation and use that is reflected in the buildings, grounds and artifacts, and includes some of the best military architecture in the country. Its urban parkland includes one of the oldest golf courses on the West Coast, 21 listed rare plant species and San Francisco's last free-flowing stream.

John Muir National Historic Site

Martinez, California

This 8.8-acre park preserves John Muir's residence and a small part of his fruit ranch. John Muir, the champion of American wilderness, successfully established preservation as a national land policy and lived here from 1890 until his death in 1914.

MAILING ADDRESS	John Muir National Historic Site, 4202 Alhambra Ave., Martinez, CA 94553 Telephone: 510-228-8860
DIRECTIONS	The site is at the foot of the off ramp of the Alhambra Avenue Exit off Hwy. 4, 10 miles (16.1 km) east of I-80, 5 miles (8 km) west of Rt. 680.
VISITOR ACTIVITIES	• Guided and self-guided tours are available. • A film about Muir's life and philosophy is shown hourly. • Picnicking. • Daily guided tours are at 2 p.m. Special guided tours are available for groups of 10 or more. Please notify park 2 weeks in advance for reservations. Self-guided tours are available from 10 a.m. to 4:30 p.m., Wednesday through Sunday. • The Site is closed Monday and Tuesday and open Wednesday through Sunday from 10 a.m. to 4:30 p.m., except Thanksgiving, Dec. 25 and Jan. 1. The Mt. Wanda Natural area is open the same hours as the Muir House.
PERMITS, FEES & LIMITATIONS	The entrance fee is $2 for adults. Children under 16 and adults over 62 free.
ACCESSIBILITY	There is 1 accessible parking space, the restrooms in the Visitor Center are accessible, and there is an easy access trail to house, and ramps to Adobe and Carriage House. There is a wheelchair lift to the first floor of the house. Electric cart rides are available from the Visitor Center to the Muir House.
CAMPING & LODGING	Several motels are nearby.
FOOD & SUPPLIES	Food and supplies are available in Martinez.

FIRST AID/ HOSPITAL

The nearest hospital is in Martinez, 1 mile (1.6 km).

Joshua Tree National Monument

Twentynine Palms, California

Two deserts come together at Joshua Tree National Monument and encompass some of the most interesting geologic displays found in California's deserts. The lower Colorado Desert in the eastern half with its abundant creosotebush joins with the slightly higher Mojave Desert and its extensive stands of the Joshua tree to form the Monument.

MAILING ADDRESS

Superintendent, Joshua Tree National Monument, 74485 National Monument Drive, Twentynine Palms, CA 92277 **Telephone:** 619-367-7511

DIRECTIONS

The Monument is 140 miles (225.8 km) east of Los Angeles. From the west, take I-10 (US 60) and Twentynine Palms Highway (Hwy. 62) to the west entrance at the town of Joshua Tree and the north entrance at the town of Twentynine Palms. The Cottonwood Spring (south) entrance is 25 miles (40.3 km) east of Indio, CA, via I-10 (US 60).

VISITOR ACTIVITIES

• Hiking, interpretive walks and talks, picnicking, wildlife watching and camping. • Facilities include picnic tables, fireplaces and restrooms. • The Monument is always open. • The Visitor Center is open daily from **8 a.m. to 5 p.m.**, except Dec. 25. • Guided tours are available in the spring and fall only.

PERMITS, FEES & LIMITATIONS

• The **entrance fee** is $5 for 7 days. • Backcountry use is available through self-registration. Contact the Monument or inquire at the Visitor Center. • Vehicles are restricted to established roads.

ACCESSIBILITY

Cottonwood, Black Rock and Jumbo Rocks campgrounds, and the Cup Rock Nature Trail and Twentynine Palms Oasis Nature Trail are accessible.

CAMPING & LODGING

• Six of the 8 campgrounds are available free on a first-come, first-served basis. There is an $8 fee per night at Cottonwood Campground and a $10 fee per night at Black Rock Campground. Reservations for Black Rock Campground are available through MISTIX. • All campgrounds are open year-round. • Campers must bring their own water and firewood. • There are 3 group camping sites available by reservation. • Lodging is available in Twentynine Palms, 3 miles (4.8 km) from the north entrance; in Joshua Tree, 5 miles (8 km) from the west entrance; and in Yucca Valley, 11 miles (17.7 km) from the west park entrance.

FOOD & SUPPLIES

Food and supplies are available in Twentynine Palms, Joshua Tree and Yucca Valley.

FIRST AID/ HOSPITAL

• First aid is available in the Monument. • The nearest hospital is in Joshua Tree.

GENERAL INFORMATION

- When hiking, biking or driving in the Monument during hot weather, drink at least 1 gallon (4 l) of water per day. • Stay clear of mine shafts.
- Beware of rattlesnakes. Be prepared for wide fluctuations in temperature.

Lassen Volcanic National Park

Mineral, California   See Climatable No. 10

In May 1914, Lassen Peak erupted, beginning a 7-year cycle of sporadic volcanic outbursts that profoundly altered the surrounding landscape. The Park features great lava pinnacles, huge mountains created by lava flows, jagged craters and steaming sulphur vents.

MAILING ADDRESS

Superintendent, Lassen Volcanic National Park, PO Box 100, Mineral, CA 96063-0100 **Telephone:** 916-595-4444

DIRECTIONS

From the north and the south take Highway 89; or from the east and the west follow Rts. 36 and 44. Rt. 36 is to the south of the park, and Rt. 44 is to the north. Redding is 48 miles (77.4 km) west of the park on Rt. 44. Bus access is available daily, expect Sundays and holidays via the Mt. Lassen Motor Transit in Mineral and Red Bluff.

VISITOR ACTIVITIES

- Interpretive programs, nature walks, hiking, self-guided auto tours, cross-country and downhill skiing, picnicking, boating, backpacking, swimming and winter sports. • Facilities include hiking trails, picnic areas, boat ramp and ski trails, tows and equipment rental. • Motorized boats are not allowed on any Park waters. • The Park is always open. • Trans-park Road is closed during winter. • Restrooms only open during summer except for the Chalet restroom, which is open most of the year.

PERMITS, FEES & LIMITATIONS

- The vehicle entrance fee is $5. • Wilderness permits are required for overnight stays in the backcountry. Permits are available at Park Headquarters and all Ranger Stations. Request permits at least 2 weeks in advance.

ACCESSIBILITY

Most of the Park's facilities are accessible, including the Visitor Center, restrooms and Indian Ways Program and amphitheater (with assistance) at Manzanita Lake; the campsite, restrooms and picnic area (with assistance) at Summit Lake; the information station and campground restrooms at the Southwest Entrance; the campsite and restrooms at Butte Lake; the restrooms at Park Headquarters; and the portable restrooms (with assistance) at Bumpass Hill, Lassen Peak and the Lupine picnic area.

CAMPING & LODGING

- There are 4 campgrounds located along Lassen Trans-park Road. The campground fee is $6 to $8 a camp site, depending on the facilities. • Group campgrounds are also available, reservations must be made in advance.
- Call 916-595-4444 for information on lodging. • Call the Susanville oper-

ator and ask for Drakesbad Toll Station No. 2 for information on the Drakesbad Guest Ranch. • Other overnight accommodations are available in Mineral, 10 miles (16.1 km) south; and in Hat Creek, 14 miles (22.5 km) north.

FOOD & SUPPLIES

• Food and supplies are available at Manzanita Lake Campground.
• Supplies are also obtainable in Mineral, 10 miles (16.1 km) south; in Old Station, 15 miles (24.1 km) northeast; and in Shingletown, 17 miles (27.4 km) northwest.

FIRST AID/ HOSPITAL

• First aid is available in the Park. • The nearest hospital is located in Chester on Rt. 36, 35 miles (56.4 km) from the south end of the park. The hospital in Burney is located on Rt. 44, 45 miles (72.5 km) west of the north end of the park.

GENERAL INFORMATION

• For your safety – Stay on established trails at all times around hot springs or steaming areas. • Keep small children under strict control to avoid burns or accidents. Ground crusts that appear to be safe may be dangerously thin. • Hot lunches and ski-rental equipment and accessories are available on weekends and holidays. • Ski lifts are operated 3 days a week. • The terrain and snow conditions are usually excellent for cross-country skiing. For safety reasons, Park Rangers should be notified of all trips.

Lava Beds National Monument

Tulelake, California

Lava Beds National Monument's history is full of volcanic activity that has resulted in cinder cones, shield volcanoes and nearly 200 lava tube caves. Also significant to the history of the area is the Modoc War of 1872 when Modoc Indians fought to remain in their native land.

MAILING ADDRESS

Superintendent, Lava Beds National Monument, PO Box 867, Tulelake, CA 96134 **Telephone: 916-667-2282**

DIRECTIONS

The Monument Visitor Center is 30 miles (48.3 km) from Tulelake and 58 miles (93.5 km) from Klamath Falls, OR, off of Rt. 139.

VISITOR ACTIVITIES

• Walking, picnicking, interpretive talks, campfire programs, cave exploration, bird and animal watching. • Facilities include picnic areas, drinking water and restrooms. • The Visitor Center is open daily, except Thanksgiving and Dec. 25, from **8 a.m. to 5 p.m.**, with hours extended to **6 p.m.** in the summer.

PERMITS, FEES & LIMITATIONS

• The entrance fee is $4. • Vehicles are restricted to maintained roads. • Hunting, gathering specimens and collecting souvenirs are prohibited.

ACCESSIBILITY

The Visitor Center, its restrooms, and the Fleener Chimneys picnic area are accessible. An accessible site at the campground is reserved until 4 p.m. There are guidebooks and program scripts for the hearing impaired. There are guidebooks for assistants and tours of the historic area for the seeing impaired.

CAMPING & LODGING

• Camping is on a first-come, first-served basis for $6 a night at a 40-unit campground near the Visitor Center. Sites are suitable for tents, pickup campers and small trailers. The sites have water and restrooms. From Oct. 15 through May 15, water must be carried from the Monument Headquarters. • Backcountry information is available by writing or calling the Monument or from the Visitor Center. • Lodging is available in Tulelake, Klamath Falls and Merrill, OR.

FOOD & SUPPLIES

Food and supplies are available in Tulelake and Klamath Falls.

FIRST AID/ HOSPITAL

• First aid is available in the Monument or in Tulelake. • The nearest hospital is in Klamath Falls.

GENERAL INFORMATION

For your safety - Potential hazards in lava tubes are low ceilings, steep trails and stairways, and uneven footing. Carry more than 1 light source. Wear protective headgear. Notify a Ranger before exploring caves other than those listed in the brochure or if you plan to use your own lighting equipment. Rattlesnakes are found throughout the Monument. Children should be cautioned not to put their hands and feet in places they cannot see.

Manzanar National Historic Site

Independence, California

Manzanar National Historic Site preserves 1 of the 10 World War II relocation camps where Japanese-American citizens and aliens were interned from 1942 through 1945 by the U.S. Government. It also contains Native American campsites and the remains of an early 1900s agricultural community.

MAILING ADDRESS

Superintendent, Death Valley National Monument, Death Valley, CA 92328 Telephone: 619-786-2331

DIRECTIONS

The Site is along side Hwy. 395 in the Owens Valley, Inyo County, CA, between the towns of Independence, 5 miles (8 km) north, and Lone Pine, 2 miles (3.2 km) south.

VISITOR ACTIVITIES

• The Site was established in March 1992, and has **no facilities or staff.**
• Initial funds for staffing and development are planned for 1994, including acquisition of the 550-acre tract that held most of the camp buildings.
• Day-time visits are possible.

PERMITS, FEES & LIMITATIONS	• No permits or fees. • Land is privately owned.
ACCESSIBILITY	Primitive roads and trails, cut by ditches, trees and underbrush make accessibility difficult.
CAMPING & LODGING	Facilities and information available in Lone Pine, CA, 12 miles (19.3 km) south of the Site, and Independence, CA, 5 miles (8 km) north of the Site.
FOOD & SUPPLIES	Food and supplies are available in Lone Pine and Independence.
FIRST AID/ HOSPITAL	Medical facilities are available in Lone Pine and Independence.
GENERAL INFORMATION	• Archaeological sites and architectural remains dot the Site as well as 3 extant camp-era buildings. • The Eastern California Museum in Independence has exhibits that relate the story of Manzanar.

Muir Woods National Monument

Mill Valley, California

Muir Woods National Monument's 295 acres of old-growth redwood forest was donated to the Federal government by Congressman William Kent and his wife Elizabeth Thacher Kent. The area was named at Kent's request for the conservationist John Muir.

MAILING ADDRESS	Site Manager, Muir Woods National Monument, Mill Valley, CA 94941 **Telephone:** 415-388-2595
DIRECTIONS	The Monument is 17 miles (27.4 km) north of San Francisco. Take US 101 and CA 1. Tour van service is available from downtown San Francisco.
VISITOR ACTIVITIES	• Facilities include the Visitor Center, parking and restrooms. • There are trailside markers, signs and exhibits for walking and hiking. • Six miles (9.6 km) of trails join those of other public lands. • Jr. Ranger Discovery packs are available for families to use while visiting. • The Monument is open daily from 8 a.m. to sunset.
PERMITS, FEES & LIMITATIONS	• No permits or fees. • Motorized equipment, horses or bicycles are not permitted. • No picnicking or dogs allowed at the Monument.
ACCESSIBILITY	All facilities and main park trails are accessible. Parking, restrooms, telephones and most special programs are also accessible.
CAMPING & LODGING	Overnight accommodations are available in Mill Valley, 4 miles (6.4 km) from the Monument.
FOOD & SUPPLIES	Snacks are available at the concession shop near the Visitor Center.

FIRST AID/ HOSPITAL

• First aid is available in the Monument. • The nearest hospital is in San Rafael, 12 miles (19.3 km).

GENERAL INFORMATION

• The Monument is very crowded during summer months. Winter and spring visits are recommended. • Weather is often cool and wet, jackets are advisable. • Stay on trails, which become slippery when wet. • Do not pick berries, roots or mushrooms.

Pinnacles National Monument

Paicines, California

The spires and crags that inspired the name Pinnacles are part of the remains of an ancient volcano that helps to tell the story of the San Andreas Rift Zone and the forces of erosion. The area as a whole preserves the plants and animals of a chaparral community.

MAILING ADDRESS

Superintendent, Pinnacles National Monument, Paicines, CA 95042
Telephone: 408-389-4485

DIRECTIONS

The Monument is separated into an east and west district with visitor facilities located in both districts. Monument Headquarters and the Bear Gulch Visitor Center are on the east side of the Monument via CA 25 and Highway 146 from Hollister. The Chaparral Ranger Station and campground are on the west side via CA 146 from Soledad. The road from Soledad to West Pinnacles is steep and narrow. Visitors driving large campers and towing trailers should use extreme caution. There is no road connecting the east and west sides of the Monument.

VISITOR ACTIVITIES

• Hiking, climbing and picnicking. • Evening talks during spring and fall weekends. • Wildlife, wildflower and bird watching. • Facilities include picnic areas, drinking water, restrooms, self-guided trails and hiking trails. • Trails vary in length and difficulty. • For more information, inquire at the Visitor Center. • The Monument never closes.

PERMITS, FEES & LIMITATIONS

• Vehicle entrance fee is $4. • Motor vehicles and mountain bikes are not allowed on any of the trails. • Pets are not allowed on the trails.

CAMPING & LODGING

• Campsites are available on a first-come, first-served basis for individuals for $10 per night. Take Hwy. 101, 11 miles (17.7 km) east from turnoff at Soledad to west side Chapparal Campground. Organized groups are permitted from June 1 to Jan. 31. Requests for reservations must be received by mail or telephone 7 days prior to arrival date. Reservations for group sites can be made by calling 408-389-4526. Picnic tables, fireplaces, water and chemical toilets are provided. • No backcountry camping allowed.
• Pinnacles Campground, Inc., a private campground, is adjacent to the Monument's east boundary on CA 146 and offers individual and group

camp sites with tables, grills and modern restrooms. Also offers showers, a camper store, gas pump, swimming pool, recreation vehicle utility hookups and an amphitheater. The campground operates on a first-come, first-served basis. Reservations are required for groups of 10 or more. For more information, call 408-389-4462 or write 2400 Highway 146, Paicines, CA 95043.
• Other overnight accommodations are available in Soledad, Hollister and King City.

FOOD & SUPPLIES

Food and supplies are available at stores at Pinnacles Campground and in Paicines, 23 miles (37 km) to the north.

FIRST AID/ HOSPITAL

• First aid is available in the Monument. • The nearest hospitals are located in Hollister and King City.

GENERAL INFORMATION

• Fall and spring are the busiest seasons. • Summer daytime temperatures can exceed 100°F. • Caves have low ceilings and slippery rocks. Use flashlights. • Only experienced climbers and persons under competent leadership should attempt rock climbs in the Monument. • Stay on regular, designated trails to avoid unstable rock faces and poison oak. • Be aware of rattlesnakes in the spring and fall. • Only drink water from hydrants and fountains on the Monument's water supply. • Carry water.

Point Reyes National Seashore

Point Reyes Station, California

The Point Reyes Peninsula rides high on the eastern edge of the Pacific plate - 1 of the 6 great plates forming most of the Earth's crust - and is a land where there are many miles of beaches in addition to Douglas-fir and Bishop pine forests. Deer may graze on the same rocks where sea lions bask in the sun.

MAILING ADDRESS

Superintendent, Point Reyes National Seashore, Point Reyes Station, CA 94956 **Telephone:** 415-663-8522

DIRECTIONS

The Seashore is 1 hour or 40 to 45 miles (64.5 to 72.5 km) north of San Francisco via US 101 and Sir Francis Drake Boulevard or via US 1 near Mill Valley.

VISITOR ACTIVITIES

• Hiking, biking, picnicking, guided tours, surf fishing, horseback riding, bird watching. • Visitor facilities include hiking trails, horse trails, picnic areas, 3 Visitor Centers and self-guiding trails. • The Bear Valley Trailhead is the gateway to more than 140 miles (225.8 km) of trails. The 4.1-mile (6.6 km) Bear Valley Trail is the most popular, winding through grassy meadows and forests to the sea. • The Seashore is always open, but some facilities are closed on Dec. 25. The Visitor Center is generally open from 9 a.m. to 5 p.m.

PERMITS, FEES & LIMITATIONS

• No entrance fee. • All motor vehicles are restricted to developed, paved roads and parking areas. • Pets limited to developed picnic areas and North and South Beaches. • No camping allowed on beaches.

ACCESSIBILITY

The Bear Valley Visitor Center has accessible exhibits, listening device and close-captioned film. The Earthquake Trail is a one-half mile (.8 km) paved loop. Some large print handouts are available.

CAMPING & LODGING

• Free camping permits for 4 hike-in campgrounds are available at the Bear Valley Visitor Center. Call 415-663-1092, Monday through Friday, 9 a.m. to noon for reservations up to 60 days in advance. • Lodging is available nearby in the towns of Olema, Inverness and Point Reyes Station. • There is drive-in camping at Olema Ranch and Samuel P. Taylor State Park.

FOOD & SUPPLIES

Food and supplies are available in Olema, Inverness and Point Reyes Station.

FIRST AID/ HOSPITAL

• First aid is available in the Seashore or in Point Reyes Station. • The nearest hospitals are in San Rafael or Petaluma, both 20 miles (32.2 km) away.

GENERAL INFORMATION

• For your safety - Pounding surf and rip currents make some Point Reyes beaches too dangerous for swimming, surfing or wading. • Steep cliffs crumble, so don't walk near edges. • Ticks carrying Lyme disease are found, take precautions. • Check at visitor centers for up-to-date information.

Port Chicago Naval Magazine National Memorial

Concord, California

Affiliated area. The Memorial is located at the site of the worst state side World War II-related catastrophe. On July 17, 1944, as ships were being loaded with munitions to supply the Pacific Theater, a nighttime explosion took 320 lives, injured another 390, destroyed 2 ships and an ammunition loading pier and caused severe damage to buildings in the nearby town of Port Chicago. The explosion and its aftermath became a turning point both for race relations in the Navy and increased safety in munitions loading.

MAILING ADDRESS

Commanding Officer, Attention: Public Affairs Officer, Concord Naval Weapons Station, 10 Delta St., Concord, CA 94520-5100
Telephone: 415-744-3968

DIRECTIONS

The Memorial is located on the waterfront of the Concord Naval Weapons Station, an active ordinance transshipment facility. The Memorial is 4 miles (6.4 km) from the station's main gate in a controlled-access area. Visits begin at the main gate where visitors must register and receive passes. The main gate is located 1 mile (1.6 km) north of the intersection of Hwy. 4 and Port Chicago Highway. Take I-680 north to Hwy. 242 north to Concord and follow signs to the Naval Weapons Station.

VISITOR ACTIVITIES

• A visitor brochure is provided. • Tour guides are knowledgeable about the history of Port Chicago and the explosion. • There is a Port Chicago museum and a memorial chapel in the Base Headquarters vicinity. • The tours take about an hour.

PERMITS, FEES & LIMITATIONS

• There is no fee. • Visits are granted only by the Concord Naval Weapons Station Commanding Officer. All visits will be escorted by the Navy. • Foreign nationals are not allowed on the station. • Private vehicles may be used to reach the Memorial when a visiting group consists of less than 4 persons. Larger groups must be transported by either commercial or government van or bus. • Visits may be scheduled by writing to the Memorial or phoning 510-246-5450. Groups of more than 7 should make requests at least 30 days in advance and smaller groups at least 7 days in advance in order to evaluate safety conditions. • Visits on shorter notice will be considered on a case-by-case basis.

ACCESSIBILITY

Base Headquarters and the Memorial site are accessible.

CAMPING & LODGING

Overnight accommodations are available in nearby communities.

FOOD & SUPPLIES

Food and supplies are available in nearby communities.

FIRST AID/ HOSPITAL

Full medical services are available in Concord.

GENERAL INFORMATION

Access is not available without advance reservation for the tours.

Redwood National Park

Crescent City, California   See Climatable No. 11

From sea level to 3,100 feet (944.8 m) in the Coast Range, a mild, moist climate assures Redwood National Park an abundant diversity of wildlife, adding to the attraction of the Redwood trees, examples of the world's tallest living things.

MAILING ADDRESS

Superintendent, Redwood National Park, 1111 Second St., Crescent City, CA 95531 Telephone: 707-464-6101

DIRECTIONS

From the north and south follow US Hwy. 101 and from the east follow US Hwy. 199. Information centers are in Hiouchi, Crescent City and Orick.

California

VISITOR ACTIVITIES

• Hiking, backpacking, bird, elk and whale watching, photography, horseback riding and picnicking. • Interpretive talks, tidepool walks and guided kayak programs. • Facilities include 3 information centers, bookstore, telephones, restrooms, hiking trails, exhibits and picnic areas at a number of locations, including Enderts Beach Road, Lagoon Creek and state parks.
• The Redwood Information Center is open year-round, except Dec. 25 and Jan. 1.

PERMITS, FEES & LIMITATIONS

• No entrance fee. • Free permits are required for backcountry camping and for vehicle access to Tall Trees Grove trailhead. • No dogs are permitted on the trails. • Fishing licenses may be purchased at hardware and tackle shops. • Trailers should not be taken off of the main roads due to weather, general road conditions and steep grades.

ACCESSIBILITY

An Access Guide is available at the information centers, which are accessible. Some trails are accessible. Wayside exhibits are viewable from autos. Accessible restrooms are available at Lady Bird Johnson Grove, Lost Man Creek Picnic Area, Requa Road, Lagoon Creek Picnic Area and Redwood Creek Trailhead.

CAMPING & LODGING

• Camp sites are available in 3 California state parks - Jedediah Smith Redwoods, el Norte Coast Redwoods and Prairie Creek Redwoods. Reservations in summer are available through MISTIX at 1-800-444-7275.
• There are 4 backcountry camps in the Park. • More campgrounds are located in Six Rivers, Klamath and Trinity national forests. • Abundant private lodging is available in the surrounding area.

FOOD & SUPPLIES

Food and supplies are available in Crescent City, Eureka, Klamath and Orick.

FIRST AID/ HOSPITAL

• First aid is available in the Park. • Sutter Coast Hospital is in Crescent City. Mad River Hospital is 35 miles (56.4 km) south of the Park's south end.

GENERAL INFORMATION

• US Hwy. 101 traverses 40 miles (64.5 km) through the Park. • The Park is a World Heritage Site and part of the California Coast Ranges Biosphere Reserve.

San Francisco Maritime National Historical Park

San Francisco, California

San Francisco Maritime National Historical Park preserves the ships from the period that shaped the development of America's Pacific Coast. The Park offers a museum, exhibits of tools, crafts and photographs, and historic ship tours.

California

MAILING ADDRESS	Superintendent, San Francisco Maritime National Historical Park, Hyde Street Pier, Fisherman's Wharf, San Francisco, CA 94123 **Telephone:** 415-556-3002
DIRECTIONS	The Park is located on San Francisco Bay at the west end of Fisherman's Wharf between Hyde and Polk streets. Public transportation to the Wharf area is recommended.
VISITOR ACTIVITIES	• Board and visit exhibits on an 1886 square-rigged ship, an 1895 sailing schooner, an 1890 steam ferryboat and an 1891 scow schooner. • Tours are available on a 1907 steam tug and a 1915 steam schooner. • A paddle tug and numerous smaller boats are also preserved. • Traditional sailor crafts and music activities daily, including small boat building. • The museum, open daily from 10 a.m. to 5 p.m., features 2 floors of exhibits, models and art. • There are unique photo opportunities of the Golden Gate Bridge and the city. • The picnic area has a view of the bay and offers opportunities to view marine life. • There is a maritime bookstore and the Maritime Library with a public reading room and research facilities, including access to reprints of 250,000 historic photographs. • Write for a quarterly calendar listing special events, lectures, exhibits, workshops and concerts.
PERMITS, FEES & LIMITATIONS	• Entrance to the museum and Maritime Library is free. • Hyde Street Pier entrance fees are $3 for adults; $1 for children ages 12-17 and free entrance for children under 12 and for seniors.
ACCESSIBILITY	The museum first floor and the library are accessible. The vessels are accessible to varying degrees, dependent on tide levels.
CAMPING & LODGING	Budget world-class hotels are within walking distance of the Park.
FOOD & SUPPLIES	Fast food and gourmet dining is within walking distance.
FIRST AID/ HOSPITAL	Many hospitals and other care facilities are available in San Francisco.
GENERAL INFORMATION	• The Hyde Street Pier is open daily from 10 a.m. to 6 p.m., May 16 to Sept. 15; 9:30 a.m. to 5 p.m., Sept. 16 to May 15. • Call 415-556-9870 for library hours. • Parking is scarce, but the Park is well served by public transportation. The Hyde Street Cable Car line stops in the Park, and numerous bus lines link the area with the Bay Area's light rail system, BART. • The Park is a great place to explore after a walk through Fisherman's Wharf.

California

Santa Monica Mountains National Recreation Area

Agoura Hills, California

The Santa Monica Mountains rise above Los Angeles, widen to meet the curve of Santa Monica Bay and reach their highest peaks facing the ocean, forming a beautiful and multi-faceted land. The scenic, natural and cultural resources of the Santa Monica Mountains are enhanced as urban development continues.

MAILING ADDRESS

Santa Monica Mountains National Recreation Area, 30401 Agoura Road, Suite 100, Agoura Hills, CA 91302 **Telephone:** 818-597-9192

DIRECTIONS

The Recreation Area is bordered by US 101 on the north side and by the Pacific Coast Highway on the south. Access is available via the many roads that cross the mountains between those 2 major highways.

VISITOR ACTIVITIES

• Bird watching, hiking, mountain bicycling, horseback riding, nature walks, festivals, campfire programs and picnicking activities are available.
• All activities are offered year-round, except for the summer concerts in the park and silent films under the stars programs.

PERMITS, FEES & LIMITATIONS

No permits or fees.

ACCESSIBILITY

Many sites are accessible to some degree, but please call to confirm.

CAMPING & LODGING

• Camping is available throughout the state parks within the boundaries.
• Happy Hollow Campground is run by the National Park Service at the Circle X Ranch site. The fee is $6 per night, and no RVs are permitted - only tents. Twenty-three sites are available on a first-come, first-served basis.
• Hundreds of hotels and motels are located within a short distance.

FOOD & SUPPLIES

All food and supplies are available in the surrounding urban area.

FIRST AID/ HOSPITAL

There are many major hospitals in the surrounding area.

Sequoia and Kings Canyon National Parks

Three Rivers, California   See Climatable No. 12

Big trees, high peaks and deep canyons in North America's longest single continuous mountain range are a few of the superlatives used to describe Sequoia and Kings Canyon National Parks. The 2 parks contain giant sequoia trees standing in cathedral-like forests, dry foothills covered with low-growing chaparral and 6 peaks more than 14,000 feet (4,267 m) in elevation.

California

MAILING ADDRESS	Superintendent, Sequoia and Kings Canyon National Parks, Three Rivers, CA 93271 **Telephone:** 209-565-3341
DIRECTIONS	Proceed east on CA 198 from CA 99 to the south entrance of Sequoia Park. To reach Kings Canyon Park, go east on CA 180 from CA 99 to the entrance. Generals Highway connects CA 198 and 180 and passes through Sequoia Park to the Grant Grove area, Kings Canyon Park.
VISITOR ACTIVITIES	• Sightseeing, photography, camping, 700 miles (1,129 km) of hiking trails, fishing, Nordic and downhill skiing, horseback riding, exhibits, campfire programs and guided nature walks are all available. • The Parks are open all year. • Some activities are closed during the winter snow period.
PERMITS, FEES & LIMITATIONS	• The **entrance fee** is $5. An annual pass is also available for $15. • Permits for wilderness use, including wilderness camping, are obtainable at Park Headquarters or at any Visitor Center. • Fishing licenses are available from local stores. • All vehicles are restricted to the developed roadways. No vehicles are permitted on the trails. • There is a 50-foot (15.2 m) limit on vehicles traveling Generals Highway between Hospital Rock and Giant Forest. • Trailers are restricted to specific campgrounds.
ACCESSIBILITY	Visitor Centers, campgrounds, restrooms, several paved trails, modified fountains, picnic tables and telephones are fully accessible. Most campgrounds and picnic areas have at least one accessible camp site. A chart is also available that indicates the curb cuts, steep grades and surface limitations.
CAMPING & LODGING	• Campgrounds are available on a first-come, first-served basis with the exception of the Lodgepole Campground where reservations are required. Reservations may be made at 1-800-365-2267 with Visa or MasterCard. Reservations at Lodgepole are available from Memorial Day to Labor Day and can be made no more than 8 weeks in advance of the day of visit. • During the regular season, nightly lodging fees for Lodgepole are $12; for South Fork and Mineral King, $5; and for all the other campgrounds, $10. • For cabin reservations, contact Sequoia and Kings Canyon Guest Services, Sequoia National Park, CA 93262. Telephone: 209-561-3314. • Overnight accommodations are available in Fresno, CA, 55 miles (88.7 km) from Grant Grove; Three Rivers, CA, 22 miles (35.4 km) from Giant Forest; and Visalia, CA, 55 miles (88.7 km) from Giant Forest.
FOOD & SUPPLIES	• Meals are served in the Parks. • Food and supplies are available at Giant Forest, Lodgepole, Grant Grove and Cedar Grove. • Food and supplies are available outside the Parks in Three Rivers, Visalia and Fresno.
FIRST AID/ HOSPITAL	The closest hospital to Kings Canyon National Park is in Fresno, CA, 55 miles (88.7 km) from Grant Grove. The closest hospital to Sequoia National Park is located in Exeter, CA, 46 miles (74.1 km) from Giant Forest.

GENERAL INFORMATION

For your safety - Many park roads are steep and curvy. Drive slowly, keep to the right and use lower gears to avoid overheating the brakes and transmissions. Drowning is the leading cause of fatalities. Use extreme caution around rivers, especially in the spring and early summer when they are swift, deep and very cold.

Lightning is dangerous on exposed peaks. Injuries from falling are best prevented by staying away from steep places, wearing proper footgear and hiking in the company of others. Respiratory or circulatory problems may be aggravated at higher elevations. Bears and other wildlife, though sometimes tame in appearance, are wild and can be dangerous. Regulations that prohibit feeding or aggravating animals are enforced for your safety, as well as for the benefit of the animals.

Whiskeytown-Shasta-Trinity National Recreation Area

Northern California in the southern Klamath Mountains

Whiskeytown Lake, created as water was diverted from the Trinity River Basin to the Sacramento River, is the smallest of the Area's 3 impounded lakes. Its constant level in the summer makes it ideal for water activities, while the surrounding extensive backcountry can be explored by primitive road, by hiking or on horseback.

MAILING ADDRESS

Superintendent, Whiskeytown-Shasta-Trinity National Recreation Area, PO Box 188, Whiskeytown, CA 96095 **Telephone:** 916-241-6584

DIRECTIONS

The main Visitor Center is Overlook Information Station, at the intersection of CA 299 and Kennedy Memorial Drive.

VISITOR ACTIVITIES

• Whiskeytown Lake is excellent for most water-related activities, including swimming, scuba diving, water skiing, boating and fishing. • Picnicking, backcountry, hunting, interpretive programs and horseback riding are also popular. • Facilities include a museum at Shasta, a self-guiding trail, picnic area, bathhouse, boat ramp and rentals, 3.7 miles (5.9 km) of front country hiking trails and horse trails. • Visitors should inquire at Overlook Information Station or Headquarters for information about the Recreation Area and programs. • The Recreation Area is open all year, but swimming beaches close at 11 p.m. during the summer.

PERMITS, FEES & LIMITATIONS

• No entrance fee. • Free backcountry permits are required and available at Headquarters. • A goldpanning permit is required and costs $1. • Vehicles are restricted to designated roads.

ACCESSIBILITY

Most of the Recreation Area is accessible, including a new fishing access at Oak Bottom Beach.

CAMPING & LODGING

• Reservations are available for camping through MISTIX at 1-800-365-CAMP. Fees vary according to seasons and vehicles. • Other overnight accommodations are available in Redding, CA, 8 miles (12.9 km) east of Overlook Information Station.

FOOD & SUPPLIES

• Food and supplies are available at Oak Bottom Marina and the Whiskeytown Store, one-quarter mile (.4 km) off CA 299, during the summer season. • Food and supplies are also available in Redding.

FIRST AID/ HOSPITAL

• First aid is available in the Recreation Area. • The nearest hospital is in Redding.

GENERAL INFORMATION

The most prominent landmark of the region is the 6,209-foot (1,892.5 m) Shasta Bally, rising in the midst of rolling woodlands and clear-flowing streams. The summit may be reached on foot and by 4-wheel drive auto.

Yosemite National Park

Yosemite National Park, California   See Climatable No. 9

Yosemite National Park ranges from 2,000 feet (609.6 m) to more than 13,000 feet above sea level (3,962 m). It offers 3 major scenic features - alpine wilderness, groves of Giant Sequoias and Yosemite Valley - set aside in 1890 to preserve a portion of the Sierra Nevada mountains.

MAILING ADDRESS

Superintendent, PO Box 577, Yosemite National Park, CA 95389 **Telephone:** 209-372-0200

DIRECTIONS

Follow Rt. 140 and 120 eastbound from Merced and Manteca; Rt. 41 northbound from Fresno; and Rt. 120 westbound from Lee Vining (closed in winter).

VISITOR ACTIVITIES

• Hiking, climbing, horseback riding, fishing, swimming, rafting, boating (no motors), alpine and cross-country skiing, backpacking, bus tours, walks, talks, cultural demonstrations, self-guiding tours, interpretive exhibits and natural history seminars. • Facilities include picnic areas, Visitor Centers, showers, laundry, repair garage, service stations, alpine and nordic ski schools, a mountaineering school, recreational equipment rental and scheduled transportation. • There are 800 miles (1,290.3 km) of trails. • The Park is open year-round. • The Mariposa Grove Road is open all year except for intermittent winter closures. Tuolumne Grove, Glacier Point Road and Tioga Road are closed from mid-November to late May, weather permitting.

PERMITS, FEES & LIMITATIONS

• The daily vehicle **entrance** fee is $5. • Backcountry wilderness permits are available by written application to the Backcountry Office between March 1 and May 31, or in person at Wawona, Yosemite Valley, Big Oak Flat

Entrance or Tuolumne Meadows. • Fishing licenses are available in person only. • All vehicles are required to stay on surfaced roads. • Commercial vehicles are allowed only on Park business. Commercial buses require authorization from the NPS concessions management office.

ACCESSIBILITY

Facilities and activities are accessible upon request.

CAMPING & LODGING

• Camping is available year-round on a first-come, first-served basis.
• Reservations for the 5 Yosemite Valley campgrounds are available 8 weeks in advance by writing or calling MISTIX, PO Box 85705, San Diego, CA 92186-5705, 1-800-367-2267 (US), 1-619-452-8787 (International).
• Group campsites are available during the summer and must be reserved in advance. The Yosemite Valley Group Camp can be reserved up to 12 weeks in advance through MISTIX. • Other overnight accommodations are available in the Park at Yosemite Valley, White Wolf, Wawona, Tuolumne Meadows and at 5 High Sierra camps. Reservations are advised at all times.
• Additional accommodations are available nearby in Lee Vining, Groveland, El Portal, Oakhurst, Fish Camp and Mariposa.

FOOD & SUPPLIES

• Meals are served and food and supplies are available in the Park at Yosemite Valley, Wawona, White Wolf, Tuolumne Meadows and the High Sierra camps. • Food and supplies are also available in the nearby communities.

FIRST AID/ HOSPITAL

• Yosemite Medical Group provides 24-hour emergency outpatient care.
• Hospitals are located in Merced, Fresno, Sonora, Bridgeport and Mariposa.

Colorado

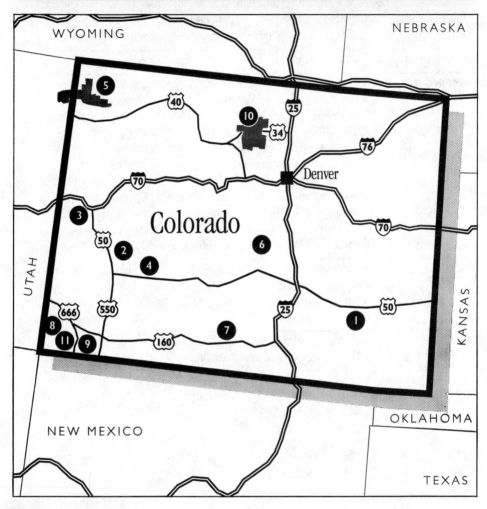

1　Bent's Old Fort National Historic Site

2　Black Canyon of the Gunnison National Monument

3　Colorado National Monument

4　Curecanti National Recreation Area

5　Dinosaur National Monument

6　Florissant Fossil Beds National Monument

7　Great Sand Dunes National Monument

8　Hovenweep National Monument

9　Mesa Verde National Park

10　Rocky Mountain National Park

11　Yucca House National Monument

Bent's Old Fort National Historic Site

La Junta, Colorado

Bent's Old Fort on the Arkansas River in southeastern Colorado was once the frontier hub from which American trade and influence extended. It played a significant role in the opening of the Southwest. It has been reconstructed as accurately as possible to its appearance in 1845-46 when its owners, Charles and William Bent and Ceran St. Vrain, were at the zenith of their commercial and political power.

MAILING ADDRESS

Superintendent, Bent's Old Fort National Historic Site, 35110 Highway 194 East, La Junta, CO 81050-9523 **Telephone: 719-384-2596**

DIRECTIONS

The Site is 8 miles (12.9 km) east of La Junta and 15 miles (24.1 km) west of Las Animas on CO 194.

VISITOR ACTIVITIES

• Interpretive and audiovisual program, guided tours, living history programs, demonstrations and special events. • Facilities include parking, restrooms and picnic area. • The Site is open daily from **8 a.m. to 4:30 p.m.**, from September through May; and from **8 a.m. to 6 p.m.**, Memorial Day through Labor Day except Thanksgiving, Dec. 25 and Jan. 1.

PERMITS, FEES & LIMITATIONS

• The entrance fee is $3 per vehicle or $2 per person. • Vehicles are restricted to the parking lot.

ACCESSIBILITY

Two accessible parking spaces are available; there is a paved trail from the parking area to the Fort and transportation is also available from the parking area to the Fort. A closed-captioned film is available, restrooms and water fountains are accessible and special tours are available upon request.

CAMPING & LODGING

Lodging is available in La Junta.

FOOD & SUPPLIES

Food and supplies are available in La Junta.

FIRST AID/ HOSPITAL

• First aid is available within the Site. • The nearest hospital is in La Junta.

GENERAL INFORMATION

• For your safety - Watch your step on the steep stairways. Do not let children climb on the walls or run on the upper gallery since there are no handrails. • Please do not bother/disturb the animals.

Colorado

Black Canyon of the Gunnison National Monument

Montrose, Colorado

Carved by the Gunnison River, Black Canyon's dark gray walls of schist and gneiss are penetrated only by slanting rays of sunlight. The canyon and its rims are home to a variety of wildlife, including black bear, golden eagles and the endangered peregrine falcon.

MAILING ADDRESS

Superintendent, Black Canyon of the Gunnison National Monument, 2233 E. Main, Suite A, Montrose, CO 81401 **Telephone:** 303-249-7036

DIRECTIONS

The South Rim is 15 miles (24.1 km) east of Montrose via Hwys. 50 and 347. The North Rim is 11 miles (17.7 km) south of Crawford off Hwy. 92 - 6 miles (9.6 km) of road is gravel.

VISITOR ACTIVITIES

• Hiking, fishing, wildlife watching, cross-country skiing, guided walks, lectures, evening campfire programs and interpretive exhibits. • The Monument is open year-round. • The Visitor Center is open from 8 a.m. to 7 p.m. in summer; reduced services in the spring and fall; closed in the winter. • The North Rim is closed in winter. • Facilities include the Visitor Center (offering information, exhibits and a bookstore), the Rim House, canyon overlooks, nature and hiking trails, and picnic areas. • A steep, 14% switchback road provides access to the Gunnison River at East Portal.

PERMITS, FEES & LIMITATIONS

• There is a $4 per vehicle or $2 per person **entrance fee.** There is no entrance fee at the North Rim. Frequent visitors may purchase an annual pass for $10. • All vehicles and bicycles must stay on established roads. • Leashed pets are permitted at overlooks, but are prohibited in the inner-canyon. • Backcountry permits are required for hiking and camping in the inner-canyon/wilderness. • Wood fires are prohibited in the inner-canyon.

ACCESSIBILITY

There are accessible camp sites on the South Rim and accessible restrooms at the Visitor Center.

CAMPING & LODGING

• Overnight camping is available at the South Rim's 102 sites and the North Rim's 13 sites for $7 per night. No reservations are taken. Inner-canyon camping requires a free permit, which is available at the Visitor Center. • Motels are available in several nearby communities, including Montrose, Delta, Hotchkiss, Crawford and Paonia.

FOOD & SUPPLIES

• Montrose and Delta offer a variety of groceries, sporting goods and other supplies. • Markets are also available in Hotchkiss, Crawford and Paonia.

FIRST AID/ HOSPITAL

• Limited first aid is available in the Monument (only in season). • The nearest hospital to the South Rim is in Montrose and to the North Rim is in Delta, 60 miles (96.7 km).

GENERAL INFORMATION

• Inner-canyon hiking is extremely strenuous, but several moderate to easy rim trails are available - ask a Ranger. • The best time to view wildlife is in the early morning. • In summer, interpretive activities are posted on the bulletin boards. • **For your safety** - Use caution and keep an eye on children, especially near overlooks, since not all have protective guardrails.

Colorado National Monument

Fruita, Colorado

Colorado National Monument preserves one of the grand landscapes of the American West with its 32 square miles (51.6 km) of bold, big and brilliantly colored towering masses of naturally sculpted rock.

MAILING ADDRESS

Superintendent, Colorado National Monument, Fruita, CO 81521
Telephone: 303-858-3617

DIRECTIONS

Take CO 340 from Fruita, 2.5 miles (4 km), or Grand Junction, 4 miles (6.4 km). Fruita and Grand Junction are accessible via I-70 and US 6 and 50.

VISITOR ACTIVITIES

• Exhibits, audiovisual programs, auto tours, interpretive talks, nature walks, campfire programs, picnicking, backcountry, hiking, climbing, horseback riding, cycling and cross-country skiing. • Facilities include a Visitor Center, parking, picnic areas, hiking trails and a self-guiding nature trail beginning at the Visitor Center. • The Visitor Center is open from 8 a.m. to 4:30 p.m., with reduced hours on Dec. 25. • Snow may limit access.

PERMITS, FEES & LIMITATIONS

• Permits are required for some special uses and events, and are recommended for backcountry camping. • No off-road vehicle use, including mountain bikes.

ACCESSIBILITY

Restrooms, the Visitor Center, 3 out of 16 overlooks along the 23-mile (37 km) scenic drive, Devil's Kitchen picnic area and Saddlehorn Campground are accessible.

CAMPING & LODGING

• Saddlehorn Campground offers 80 sites at $7 a night for up to 7 people. No reservations. • Backcountry camping is allowed except near roads and developed areas - subject to some restrictions. • Other overnight accommodations are available in nearby communities.

FOOD & SUPPLIES

Food and supplies are available in nearby communities.

FIRST AID/ HOSPITAL

• First aid is available in the Monument. • The nearest hospitals are in Fruita and Grand Junction.

GENERAL INFORMATION

• Do not touch, feed or harm the animals. • Do not hike or climb alone.
• Register for difficult and technical climbs.

Curecanti National Recreation Area
Gunnison, Colorado

C urecanti National Recreation Area's stark landscape has been transformed from a semi-arid locale into a lake-based recreation mecca by 3 dams on the Gunnison River that created 3 lakes surrounded by cliffs and rocky spires.

MAILING ADDRESS
Superintendent, Curecanti National Recreation Area, 102 Elk Creek, Gunnison, CO 81230 **Telephone:** 303-641-2337

DIRECTIONS
The Elk Creek Visitor Center is 16 miles (25.8 km) west of Gunnison via US 50 on Blue Mesa Lake. A Visitor Center and Narrow Gauge Railroad exhibit are at the Cimarron Area, 20 miles (32.2 km) east of Montrose.

VISITOR ACTIVITIES
• Boating, fishing, swimming, water skiing, windsurfing, campfire programs, picnicking, hunting, snowmobiling, naturalist activities, ice fishing, interpretive exhibits, and boat tours of Morrow Point Lake (call 303-641-0406 for information). • Facilities include parking, launching ramps, scenic overlooks, two marinas, showers, boat and slip rentals, a fish observation pond, restrooms, hiking trails, cross-country ski routes, amphitheater, telephones and snowmobile route. • The Recreation Area is open 24 hours a day year-round.

PERMITS, FEES & LIMITATIONS
• No entrance fee. • Fishing requires a Colorado fishing license available from the Colorado Division of Wildlife Office or local sporting goods stores. • Vehicles are restricted to designated roads.

ACCESSIBILITY
Parking, camping, visitor centers, restrooms and the amphitheater are accessible.

CAMPING & LODGING
• Camping is available on a first-come, first-served basis for $8 a night at Elk Creek, Lake Fork and Cimarron campgrounds, and for $7 a night at Red Creek, Dry Gulch, Ponderosa, East Portal and Stevens Creek campgrounds. Reservations are accepted for the East Elk Creek group camping area. • Backcountry camping is available at boat-in sites on Blue Mesa, Morrow Point and Crystal Lakes. • Other overnight accommodations are available nearby in Gunnison and the Montrose area.

FOOD & SUPPLIES
• Meals are served in the Recreation Area at the Elk Creek Marina. • Food and supplies are available at the Elk Creek and Lake Fork marinas. • Supplies are also available in Gunnison and Montrose.

FIRST AID/ HOSPITAL
• First aid is available in the Recreation Area. • The nearest hospitals are in Gunnison and Montrose.

GENERAL INFORMATION
• There are no designated areas for swimming and no lifeguards. • Watch out for precipitous shorelines, submerged rocks and cold water. • Summer afternoon winds are common.

Dinosaur National Monument
Dinosaur, Colorado

Preserved in the sands of an ancient river at Dinosaur National Monument is a time capsule from the world of dinosaurs. Thousands of bones and many complete skeletons have been removed from a single ridge and others remain exposed in the sandstone face.

MAILING ADDRESS

Superintendent, Dinosaur National Monument, PO Box 210, Dinosaur, CO 81610 **Telephone:** 303-374-2216

DIRECTIONS

To get to the Dinosaur Quarry Visitor Center, go 13 miles (20.9 km) east of Vernal, UT, to Jensen, UT, on US 40 and then 7 miles (11.2 km) north to the Quarry on UT 149. Headquarters is 2 miles (3.2 km) east of Dinosaur, CO, on US 40 and 37 miles (59.6 km) east of Vernal, UT on US 40.

VISITOR ACTIVITIES

• Dinosaur fossil displays, resource talks and programs (summers only), walking, hiking, picnicking, backcountry driving, fishing, white-water boating and wildflower viewing. • Facilities include nature trails, concession-operated boat trips, parking and restrooms at the Visitor Center, telephones, and boat ramp. • The Visitor Center is open from 8 a.m. to 4:30 p.m., from October through May; and from 8 a.m. to 7 p.m., Memorial Day through Labor Day. The Visitor Center is closed Thanksgiving, Dec. 25 and Jan. 1. • The backcountry and canyon road is closed due to snow in the winter. • All visitors must use a shuttlebus to the Quarry from Memorial Day to Labor Day.

PERMITS, FEES & LIMITATIONS

• There is a $5 **entrance fee** to enter the Monument on Quarry Road. • Permits are required for fishing, white-water boating, and backcountry hiking. • Some backcountry roads require a high clearance vehicle and are impassable when wet. Inquire at the Visitor Center.

ACCESSIBILITY

The Monument Headquarters Visitor Center is accessible. Dinosaur Quarry has limited accessibility. Ask about restrooms.

CAMPING & LODGING

• Camp sites are available on a first-come, first-served basis for $8 per night. • Backcountry camping permits are available by writing the Superintendent in advance or visiting any Ranger upon arrival. Drinking water in the backcountry is scarce. • Other overnight accommodations are available in Dinosaur, Rangely and Craig, CO; and in Vernal and Jensen, UT.

FOOD & SUPPLIES

Food and supplies are available in Dinosaur, Rangely and Craig, CO; and in Vernal and Jensen, UT.

FIRST AID/ HOSPITAL

• First aid is available in the Monument for emergencies. • The nearest hospitals are in Vernal, UT; and in Rangely, CO.

GENERAL INFORMATION

For your safety - Most of the accidents at Dinosaur occur while boating the rivers or while climbing or hiking in the rugged canyon areas. Check with a Ranger about your plans and local road conditions.

Colorado

Florissant Fossil Beds National Monument
Florissant, Colorado

A wealth of fossil insects, seeds and leaves are preserved in remarkable detail at Florissant Fossil Beds National Monument in addition to an unusual display of standing petrified Sequoia stumps.

MAILING ADDRESS

Superintendent, Florissant Fossil Beds National Monument, PO Box 185, Florissant, CO 80816 **Telephone:** 719-748-3253

DIRECTIONS

Take US Hwy. 24 west from Colorado Springs, 35 miles (56.4 km) to the town of Florissant. The Visitor Center is 2.5 miles (4 km) south of Florissant on Teller County Road #1.

VISITOR ACTIVITIES

• Interpretive exhibits, talks, walks, self-guiding trails, 12 miles (19.3 km) of hiking trails, picnic areas, and cross-country skiing. • Group tours and environmental education programs are available by reservation. • The Visitor Center is open daily from **8 a.m. to 4:30 p.m.**, with hours extended until 7 p.m. in the summer. Closed Thanksgiving, Dec. 25 and Jan. 1.

PERMITS, FEES & LIMITATIONS

• The **entrance fee** is $2 per person (no fee for children 16 and under or adults 62 and over). • Vehicles and mountain bikes are not permitted off designated roads.

ACCESSIBILITY

Parking, the Visitor Center, restrooms and 2 nature trails (with assistance) are accessible.

CAMPING & LODGING

• No camping or lodging is available in the Monument. • Camping is available in Pike National Forest.

FOOD & SUPPLIES

Food and supplies are available in the nearby towns of Florissant and Divide.

FIRST AID/ HOSPITAL

• First aid is available in the Monument. • The nearest hospital is in Colorado Springs.

GENERAL INFORMATION

• At 8,400 feet (27,559 m) elevation, visitors should be careful not to over exert themselves, use sunscreen and carry water on all hiking excursions. • Severe mountain weather occurs in winter with heavy snows. Lightning storms occur in the summer.

Great Sand Dunes National Monument
Mosca, Colorado

I n a corner of the remote high-mountain San Luis Valley in the Colorado Rockies, the Great Sand Dunes rise to heights of nearly 700 feet (213.4 m), forming the tallest sand dunes in North America. Covering 55 square miles

(88.7 km), the dunes provide many opportunities for hiking, wilderness camping and exploring.

MAILING ADDRESS

Great Sand Dunes National Monument, 11999 Highway 150, Mosca, CO 81146 **Telephone: 719-378-2312**

DIRECTIONS

The Visitor Center is on Hwy. 150, 38 miles (61.2 km) northeast of Alamosa, CO.

VISITOR ACTIVITIES

• Hiking, nature walks, dune climbing, picnicking, 4-wheel drive tours, snowshoeing, cross-country skiing, interpretive exhibits and naturalist activities from June through August. • Facilities include a Visitor Center, air pump, drinking water, picnic area, restrooms, fire grates, and 4-wheel drive road. • The Monument is open year-round. • The Visitor Center is closed on federal holidays in the winter.

PERMITS, FEES & LIMITATIONS

• The entrance fee is $4 per vehicle. Hikers, bikers and bus passengers are admitted for $2 a day. Entrance fees are collected from May through September. • Motor vehicles and their operators must be licensed. • The Medano Pass Primitive Road is restricted to 4-wheel drive vehicles and licensed trail bikes. • Off-road travel or driving on the dunes is prohibited.

ACCESSIBILITY

Parking at the Visitor Center, the Dunes, the campground and all restrooms is accessible.

CAMPING & LODGING

• There is an $8 a night fee for developed camp sites. No reservations are accepted. • Group camping may be arranged in advance by calling or writing. • Overnight accommodations are available in Alamosa; Salida, 90 miles (145.1 km); and Ft. Garland, 29 miles (46.7 km).

FOOD & SUPPLIES

Food and supplies are available 4 miles (6.4 km) south of the entrance station April through October.

FIRST AID/ HOSPITAL

• First aid is available in the Monument. • The nearest hospital is in Alamosa.

GENERAL INFORMATION

• Hiking on the dunes is most pleasant early and late in the day. Shoes should be worn or carried. • Most visitors begin their walk on the dunes from the picnic area. A walk to the top of the tallest dune and back requires about 1 1/2 hours.

Hovenweep National Monument

West of Cortez, Colorado

The desolate country north of the San Juan River contains mesas and small canyons where pre-Columbian Pueblo Indians once lived in pit houses and rooms in rows before adopting stone masonry in the 900s AD. After 1000 AD, they built multistoried dwellings. Hovenweep National Monument contains 6 groups of ruins.

MAILING ADDRESS

Superintendent, Hovenweep National Monument, McElmo Route, Cortez, CO 81321 Telephone: 303-529-4461

DIRECTIONS

The Monument is 45 miles (72.5 km) from Cortez. Travel south on US 666/160 to County Road 6 (the Airport Road), then follow Hovenweep signs. The route includes 15 miles (24.1 km) of graded gravel road.

VISITOR ACTIVITIES

• Self-guiding trails, picnicking and hiking. • Facilities include a Visitor Center, picnic area, trails and comfort station. • The Visitor Center is open daily from 8 a.m. to 5 p.m.

PERMITS, FEES & LIMITATIONS

• No entrance fee. • Vehicles, including bicycles, are restricted to roads.

ACCESSIBILITY

The Visitor Center, restrooms and picnic tables are accessible. The trails to the ruins are not accessible.

CAMPING & LODGING

Overnight camping is available for $6 a night. The campground is open all year, but there are limited facilities in the winter.

FOOD & SUPPLIES

Food and supplies are available at the Hatch Trading Post, the Ismay Trading Post and in Aneth.

FIRST AID/ HOSPITAL

The nearest hospital is in Cortez.

GENERAL INFORMATION

• During late May and June, biting gnats are abundant. • The trails are primitive, so wear sturdy hiking shoes. • Nearby points of interest include Mesa Verde National Park, Natural Bridges National Monument (see listings in this book) and the Anasazi Heritage Center.

Mesa Verde National Park

Mesa Verde National Park, Colorado   See Climatable No. 13

Mesa Verde National Park occupies part of a large plateau rising high above the Montezuma and Mancos Valleys. It preserves spectacular remains of the thousand-year-old Anasazi Indian culture, including their elaborate stone cities built in the sheltered recesses of the canyon walls.

MAILING ADDRESS

Superintendent, Mesa Verde National Park, Mesa Verde National Park, CO 81330 Telephone: 303-529-4465

DIRECTIONS

To get the most out of your visit, you should go first to the Far View Visitor Center (open only in summer from 8 a.m. to 5 p.m.) or the Chapin Mesa Museum (open from 8 a.m. to 6:30 p.m. in summer and 8 a.m. to 5 p.m. the rest of the year). The Park entrance is midway between Cortez and Mancos on US 160. It is 21 miles (33.8 km) from the entrance to the museum and the Chapin Mesa ruins area. The Far View Visitor Center is 15 miles (24.1 km) away.

VISITOR ACTIVITIES

• Photography, interpretive exhibits and lectures, picnicking, auto tours, guided tours, hiking and campfire programs (summer only.) • Facilities include gas stations, stores, showers, picnic areas, post office, laundry, hiking trails, and telephones. • Accommodations, facilities and services are available from mid-May to mid-October. Maximum interpretive services are offered from mid-June until Labor Day. • The Museum and Spruce Tree House cliff dwelling are open all year. Cliff Palace and Balcony House ruins are closed from about mid-October to mid-April. The Wetherill Mesa ruins are open from early June through Labor Day only.

PERMITS, FEES & LIMITATIONS

• The entrance fee is $5 per vehicle or $2 for bus passengers. • Vehicles are allowed only on roads, turnouts or parking areas. • The weight and length restrictions for Wetherill Mesa Road are 8,000 #GVW and 25 feet (82 m). • Hiking is restricted to 5 trails in the Park. • Bicycles are not allowed on Wetherill Mesa roads. Mountain bikes are not allowed on hiking trails.

ACCESSIBILITY

The scenic overlooks are accessible with assistance. The Chapin Mesa Archeological Museum has accessible restrooms and a ranger-assisted portable ramp. The Spruce Tree House and Step House ruins are accessible with assistance. Morefield Campground has accessible parking, restrooms, paved walks and graveled trails. The Visitor Center has parking and ramps. Wetherill Mesa has accessible restrooms.

CAMPING & LODGING

• Morefield Campground is open from mid-April through mid-October for tents and trailers. The fees are $8 per night for individual sites and $20 per night for organized groups or $1 per person, whichever is greater. The full hookup fee is $14.50 per day plus $2 per person for parties of 3 or more. No reservations accepted. Morefield has restrooms, and each site has a table, benches and grills. Souvenirs, a gas station, showers and laundry facilities are also available. • Lodging is available at Far View Lodge, which is closed in winter. It is advisable to make reservations with the Mesa Verde Co., PO Box 227, Mancos, CO 81328, phone 303-529-4421. • Other overnight accommodations are available in Cortez, 7 miles (11.2 km); and Mancos, 8 miles (12.9 km).

FOOD & SUPPLIES

• Meals are served in the Park at Morefield, Far View and Chapin Mesa. • Food and supplies are available at Morefield. • Food and supplies are also available in Cortez and Mancos.

FIRST AID/ HOSPITAL

• Emergency first aid is provided at the Chief Ranger's Office and the Morefield Campground Ranger Station. • The nearest hospital is in Cortez.

GENERAL INFORMATION

For your safety - Visits to cliff dwellings tend to be strenuous. Adequate footwear is recommended. Strenuous activity at the high elevations of the Park may adversely affect persons with heart or respiratory ailments. With the exception of Balcony House, all major cliff dwellings may be viewed from overlooks. Do not throw rocks or other objects from rim areas.

Rocky Mountain National Park

Estes Park, Colorado   See Climatable No. 14

The snow-mantled peaks of Rocky Mountain National Park rise above verdant subalpine valleys, glistening lakes and wildflower meadows that provide a home for a variety of wildlife, including Bighorn sheep - the Park's living symbol.

MAILING ADDRESS

Superintendent, Rocky Mountain National Park, Estes Park, CO 80517
Telephone: 303-586-2371 TDD: 303-586-8506

DIRECTIONS

The Park is accessible by Trail Ridge Road, which crosses the Continental Divide. Access from the east is via US 34/36 to Estes Park; and from the southwest via US 34 to Grand Lake. Trail Ridge Road is usually closed from mid-October until Memorial Day. Opening and closing dates vary with the weather.

VISITOR ACTIVITIES

• Interpretive programs, auto touring, picnicking, hiking, mountain climbing, fishing, horseback riding, cross-country skiing, snow-shoeing, snow-mobiling (west side only), and bird and animal watching. • Facilities include schedules for guided walks, campfire programs and other activities at Information Centers in summer. • More than 355.6 miles (573.5 km) of trails provide access to remote sections of the Park. • The Park is open year-round. The Park Headquarters/Visitor Center is closed Dec. 25.

PERMITS, FEES & LIMITATIONS

• Entrance fees are $5 per noncommercial vehicle and $3 per person for commercial vehicles or bus passengers. Children under 16 are admitted free. • A Colorado fishing license, available locally, is required. • Backcountry use permits for overnight stays are available from Park Headquarters or the Kawuneeche Visitor Center. • Vehicles must remain on established roads and parking areas. • No vehicles or combination rigs more than 50 feet (15.24 m) are allowed on Trail Ridge Road. Trailers more than 25 feet (7.62 m) are not allowed on Old Fall River Road.

ACCESSIBILITY

Braille and cassette tapes of publications are available at Visitor Centers. Parking, Visitor Center restrooms, comfort stations at Rock Cut and Rainbow Curve and trails at Sprague and Bear Lakes and along segments of the Colorado River are accessible. Campgrounds contain at least 1 fully accessible restroom. An accessible camp site is available by reservation for backcountry-type camping. Contact the Backcountry Office, Rocky Mountain National Park, CO 80517, phone 303-586-4459.

CAMPING & LODGING

• There are 5 road-side campgrounds: Moraine Park, Glacier Basin, Aspenglen, Longs Peak and Timber Creek. Sites are available for $7 on a first-come, first-served basis or $10 when reserved. Camping is limited to 3 days at Longs Peak and 7 days at the other campgrounds. Group sites at

Colorado

Glacier Basin can be reserved. Longs Peak is restricted to tent camping. Reservations for the Moraine Park and Glacier Basin campgrounds are available through MISTIX at 1-800-365-CAMP. • Privately owned campgrounds are available in the area. For more information, write to the Chamber of Commerce at either Estes Park, CO 80517 or Grand Lake, CO 80447. • Other overnight accommodations are available in Estes Park, 2 to 4 miles (3.2 to 6.4 km); and Grand Lake, 1 mile (1.6 km).

FOOD & SUPPLIES

Food and supplies are not obtainable in the Park. Food and supplies are available in Estes Park and Grand Lake.

FIRST AID/ HOSPITAL

• First aid is available in the Park or nearby in Estes Park and Grand Lake.
• The nearest hospital is in Granby, 14 miles (22.5 km) southwest of the Grand Lake Entrance.

GENERAL INFORMATION

• For your safety - Stay away from the edge of steep snow slopes and avoid sliding on snow or ice. Know and obey Park regulations. • Registration with a Park Ranger is required for all bivouac climbs. • Streams and waterfalls can be deceptively dangerous, especially in the spring. • Trail Ridge Road reaches elevations of more than 2 miles (3.2 km) above sea level and could be dangerous to persons with heart conditions and respiratory ailments.

Yucca House National Monument

Cortez, Colorado   See Climatable No. 36

This large prehistoric Indian pueblo ruin west of Mesa Verde is as yet unexcavated. **There are no visitor facilities or services.**

MAILING ADDRESS

Yucca House National Monument, c/o Mesa Verde National Park, Mesa Verde National Park, CO 81330 **Telephone: 303-529-4465**

DIRECTIONS

The lands surrounding Yucca House are privately owned. The approach road is almost impassable in wet weather. Visitors should seek directions from the Chief Ranger's Office, Mesa Verde National Park.

VISITOR ACTIVITIES

The ruins are not yet excavated, and there is little to see.

Connecticut

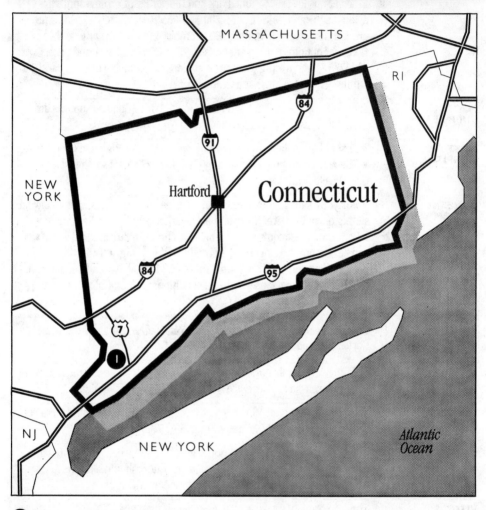

I Weir Farm National Historic Site

Weir Farm National Historic Site

Wilton and Ridgefield, Connecticut

J. Alden Weir, American impressionist painter, drew his inspiration from the quiet, rural landscape that surrounded his farm, home, and studio, and also from the artists who visited him.

MAILING ADDRESS
Weir Farm National Historic Site, 735 Nod Hill Road, Wilton, CT 06897
Telephone: 203-834-1896

DIRECTIONS
Take I-95 or I-84 to Route 7. From Route 7, take Route 102 west. Take the second left onto Old Branchville Road. At the stop sign, take a left onto Nod Hill Road. Weir Farm is seven-tenths of a mile (1.12 km) on the right.

VISITOR ACTIVITIES
• Interpretive talks, studio tours, changing exhibits, painting, sketching and walking trails. • The Visitor Center is open daily from **8:30 a.m. to 5 p.m.**, May through October (Monday through Friday in winter). • Call for an event and tour schedule, including art classes, lecture series and demonstrations.

PERMITS, FEES & LIMITATIONS
• No fees. • Vehicles are restricted to the parking area and paved roads.

ACCESSIBILITY
This is a new Site, and accessibility measures are not in place.

CAMPING & LODGING
Motels and inns are available in neighboring communities.

FOOD & SUPPLIES
Food and supplies are available in Wilton or Ridgefield.

FIRST AID/ HOSPITAL
The nearest hospital is in Danbury, 10 miles (16.1 km) north of the Site.

GENERAL INFORMATION
• For additional programming information, contact the Weir Farm Heritage Trust at 203-761-9945. • The Site's size and current visitor facilities are not suited for large bus tours.

District of Columbia

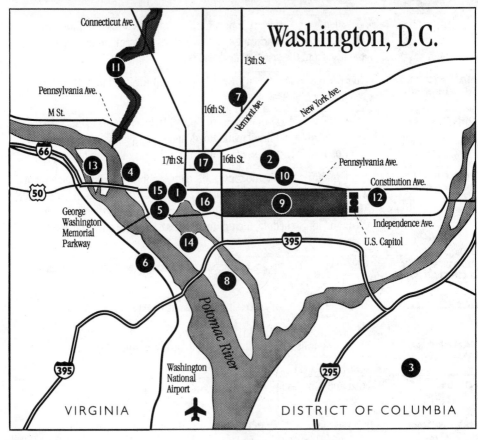

Washington, D.C.

Connecticut Ave.

13th St.

Pennsylvania Ave.

M St.

16th St.

New York Ave.

17th St.

16th St.

Pennsylvania Ave.

Constitution Ave.

George
Washington
Memorial
Parkway

Independence Ave.

U.S. Capitol

Potomac River

Washington
National
Airport

VIRGINIA

DISTRICT OF COLUMBIA

① Constitution Gardens

② Ford's Theatre National Historical Site

③ Frederick Douglas Memorial Home

④ John F. Kennedy Center for
   the Performing Arts

⑤ Lincoln Memorial

⑥ Lyndon Baines Johnson Memorial Grove
   on the Potomac

⑦ Mary McLeod Bethune Council House

⑧ National Capital Region

⑨ National Mall

⑩ Pennsylvania Avenue National Historic Site

⑪ Rock Creek Park

⑫ Sewall-Belmont House National Historic Site

⑬ Theodore Roosevelt Island

⑭ Thomas Jefferson Memorial

⑮ Vietnam Veterans Memorial

⑯ Washington Monument

⑰ The White House

District of Columbia

Constitution Gardens

Washington, DC   See Climatable No. 15

Constitution Gardens was constructed during the American Revolution Bicentennial on an island in a 7-acre lake as a memorial to the 56 Signers of the Declaration of Independence.

MAILING ADDRESS
Superintendent, National Capital Parks-Central, 900 Ohio Drive, SW, Washington, DC 20242 **Telephone:** 202-485-9880

DIRECTIONS
The Gardens are located between the Washington Monument and the Lincoln Memorial bordered by Constitution Avenue, 17th Street and the Reflecting Pool. The nearest Metro subway station is the Smithsonian, which is on the Blue and Orange lines.

VISITOR ACTIVITIES
Visitors can stroll through the Gardens and enjoy the area for its scenic beauty.

PERMITS, FEES & LIMITATIONS
Permits are required for special events and First Amendment activities.

ACCESSIBILITY
Parking is in the Washington Monument parking lot off of Constitution Avenue between 15th and 17th streets. There is a time limit of 2 hours for parking.

CAMPING & LODGING
There are numerous hotels and motels within the Washington, DC, area and in Maryland and Virginia.

FOOD & SUPPLIES
Food is available at each of the Smithsonian museums and at the Old Post Office Tower.

FIRST AID/ HOSPITAL
• First aid is available at the Lincoln Memorial. • The nearest hospital is George Washington University Hospital, 23rd and Pennsylvania Ave., NW.

GENERAL INFORMATION
• The Tourmobile has a stop at the base of the Washington Monument.
• Other parking facilities are along Constitution Avenue, and Madison and Jefferson Drive. Note the time limits in each area.

Ford's Theatre National Historic Site

Washington, DC

The theatre where President Abraham Lincoln was shot on the night of April 14, 1865, and the house across the street where he died early the next day are preserved as Ford's Theatre National Historic Site. The Site tells of the assassination events, reminds visitors of the troubling times this nation passed through and perpetuates the aspirations and hopes Lincoln had for the country.

District of Columbia

MAILING ADDRESS	Site Manager, Ford's Theatre National Historic Site, c/o NPS National Capital Region - Central, 900 Ohio Drive, SW, Washington, DC 20242 **Telephone:** 202-426-6924 **TDD:** 202-426-1749
DIRECTIONS	The Site is at 511 10th St., NW, between E and F streets in the heart of Washington. The House Where Lincoln Died is located across the street.
VISITOR ACTIVITIES	• Self-guided tours. • Fifteen-minute talks on the history of the assassination and the theatre are presented daily. • The Lincoln Museum is located in the theatre basement and includes a bookstore, restrooms and telephones. • The theatre itself is open to visitors except when it is closed for stage work, rehearsals or matinee performances. • No reservations are necessary, but it is recommended to call ahead to confirm theatre schedule.
PERMITS, FEES & LIMITATIONS	• Admission is free during National Park Service hours. • Admission to theatrical performances is by paid ticket only. Call the box office at 202-347-4833 for ticket information.
ACCESSIBILITY	The orchestra level of the theatre and the museum are accessible. The presidential box and the House Where Lincoln Died are not accessible. Call ahead to arrange for sign language and tours for the visually impaired. There is no reserved parking.
CAMPING & LODGING	Camping and lodging is available in the surrounding Washington area.
FOOD & SUPPLIES	There are numerous shops, restaurants and eateries nearby.
FIRST AID/ HOSPITAL	• Minor first aid is available. • Hospitals are located in Washington and vicinity.
GENERAL INFORMATION	• Pay parking is adjacent to the theatre. • Smithsonian museums, the F.B.I., the National Archives and the Washington Convention Center are located nearby.

Frederick Douglass National Historic Site

Washington, DC

Frederick Douglass, a former slave and one of the most commanding figures in America's battle for equal rights, lived at Cedar Hill, a beautiful Victorian home on the heights overlooking Anacostia with a view of the U.S. Capitol. Visitors can learn more at the Site about the man who was such an eloquent spokesman for oppressed people.

MAILING ADDRESS	Frederick Douglass National Historic Site, National Capital Parks - East, 1900 Anacostia Drive, SE, Washington, DC 20020 **Telephone:** 202-426-5961

District of Columbia

DIRECTIONS

Cross the 11th Street (Anacostia) Bridge to Good Hope Road, turn left on Good Hope Road to 14th Street and then right on 14th Street. Make a left onto W Street. The Home is on top of the hill at 14th and W streets, SE. Visitors arriving from the north or south on I-295 (Anacostia Freeway) should use the Pennsylvania Avenue East exit. Proceed east on Pennsylvania Avenue 2 blocks to Minnesota Avenue. Turn right on Minnesota to Good Hope Road. Turn right on Good Hope, proceed one-half block and turn left on 14th Street. Public transportation is available nearby.

VISITOR ACTIVITIES

• Guided house tours, interpretive talks and a film of Frederick Douglass' life is shown on the hour; tours are given on the half-hour. • Facilities include a parking area and Visitor Center. • The Site is open daily from 9 a.m. to 5 p.m., in the summer and from 9 a.m. to 4 p.m., in the fall and winter except Thanksgiving, Dec. 25 and Jan. 1.

PERMITS, FEES & LIMITATIONS

No permits or fees.

ACCESSIBILITY

The Site is accessible except for the second floor of the house.

CAMPING & LODGING

Overnight accommodations are available in Washington and vicinity.

FOOD & SUPPLIES

Food and supplies are available in Washington and vicinity.

FIRST AID/ HOSPITAL

• First aid is available at the Site. • Hospitals are located in Washington and vicinity.

GENERAL INFORMATION

For your safety - Be careful when climbing steps and walking on the hilly grounds.

John F. Kennedy Center for the Performing Arts

Washington, DC

Mandated by Congress to present and produce the finest performing arts from this country and abroad, the John F. Kennedy Center for the Performing Arts is a living memorial and cultural center where opera, ballet, film, drama, musical theater, chamber music or symphony orchestras are staged.

MAILING ADDRESS

General Manager, National Park Service, John F. Kennedy Center for the Performing Arts, 2700 F St., NW, Washington, DC 20566-0002 **Telephone:** 202-416-7910 **TDD:** 202-416-7920

DIRECTIONS

The Center is located at New Hampshire Avenue and F Street, NW, overlooking the Potomac River. The nearest subway station is Foggy Bottom/GWU.

District of Columbia

VISITOR ACTIVITIES	• Interpretive tours, exhibits and cultural events. • The Center is open year-round from **10 a.m. to midnight.** • Tours are conducted from **10 a.m. to 1 p.m.** daily. • Visitors should consult the Center's calendar of events, or call the Friends of the Kennedy Center at 202-416-8340, TDD 202-416-8524.
PERMITS, FEES & LIMITATIONS	• No permits are required. • Tickets are required for many of the performances and cultural events.
ACCESSIBILITY	The Center is accessible. Closed-loop handsets are available. ASL-interpreted events are on the schedule. Call the Friends of the Kennedy Center for more information.
CAMPING & LODGING	Overnight accommodations are available in Washington and the surrounding area.
FOOD & SUPPLIES	• Food and supplies are available in Washington and vicinity. • Restaurants are available on the Roof Terrace, and gift shops are located in the Hall of States and Motor Lobby A.
FIRST AID/ HOSPITAL	• First aid is available at the Center. • The nearest hospital is George Washington University Hospital, one-quarter mile (.4 km).

Lincoln Memorial

Washington, DC

Constructed as a tribute to the slain President who led the country through its greatest trial - the Civil War - the Abraham Lincoln Memorial in West Potomac Park features the famous statue that is 19 feet (5.8 m) tall, 19 feet wide and carved from 28 separate blocks of white Georgia marble.

MAILING ADDRESS	Superintendent, National Capital Parks-Central, 900 Ohio Drive, SW, Washington, DC 20242 **Telephone:** 202-485-9880
DIRECTIONS	The Lincoln Memorial is located off of Constitution Avenue and 23rd Street, NW, across from the Vietnam Veterans Memorial. The nearest Metro subway station is Foggy Bottom, 23rd and I Street, NW, on the Blue and Orange lines.
VISITOR ACTIVITIES	• Rangers are on duty from **8 a.m. to midnight** daily except Dec. 25. • Interpretive talks are given daily by Rangers. • A bookstore is on the Chamber level.
PERMITS, FEES & LIMITATIONS	Permits are required for special events and First Amendment activities.
ACCESSIBILITY	The Memorial has a ramp entrance to the lower level where there are restrooms, drinking fountains and an elevator to the Chamber level. Several parking spaces are available on the Memorial circle.

District of Columbia

CAMPING & LODGING
There are numerous hotels and motels within the Washington, DC, area and in Maryland and Virginia.

FOOD & SUPPLIES
Food and supplies are available in Washington and vicinity.

FIRST AID/ HOSPITAL
• First aid is available at the Ranger booth. • The nearest hospital is George Washington University Hospital, 23rd and Pennsylvania Avenue, NW.

GENERAL INFORMATION
• The Tourmobile and The Old Town Trolley provide service to the Lincoln Memorial and the Vietnam Veterans Memorial. • For further information, contact the Washington Convention and Visitor Association, 1575 I St., NW, Washington, DC, 20005.

Lyndon Baines Johnson Memorial Grove on the Potomac

Washington, DC

A living memorial to the 36th President, the park overlooks the Potomac River vista of the Capital and features 500 white pines and inscriptions on Texas granite.

MAILING ADDRESS
Superintendent, George Washington Memorial Parkway, c/o Turkey Run Park, McLean, VA 22101 **Telephone:** 703-285-2598

DIRECTIONS
The Grove is in Lady Bird Johnson Park on the George Washington Memorial Parkway west of I-95 and the 14th Street Bridge. Parking is at nearby Columbia Island Marina.

VISITOR ACTIVITIES
• Picnicking, strolling and fishing. • Facilities include restrooms, water, picnic tables and parking. • The Grove is open during daylight hours year-round.

PERMITS, FEES & LIMITATIONS
• No entrance fee. • Fishing permits are required. • Vehicles are restricted to parking lots.

ACCESSIBILITY
Parking, restrooms and trails are accessible.

CAMPING & LODGING
Overnight accommodations are available in Washington and vicinity.

FOOD & SUPPLIES
Food and supplies are available in the Washington area.

FIRST AID/ HOSPITAL
• First aid is not available within the Grove. • The nearest hospital is in Arlington, VA.

District of Columbia

Mary McLeod Bethune Council House National Historic Site

Washington, DC

This is the headquarters of the National Council of Negro Women established by Mary McLeod Bethune in 1935. The Site commemorates her leadership in African American women's rights movements from 1943-49 and her role as an educator, political activist and presidential advisor. The Site contains the largest body of original records related to the individual and collective achievements of African American women and is the only institution of its kind in the country.

MAILING ADDRESS
Bethune Museum and Archives, Inc., 1318 Vermont Ave., NW, Washington, DC 20005 **Telephone:** 202-332-1233

DIRECTIONS
The Site is in the Logan Circle Historic District between Thomas and Logan circles, NW. The nearest Metro subway station is McPherson Square (walk 4 blocks north).

VISITOR ACTIVITIES
• Five galleries display photographs, manuscripts, paintings and artifacts interpreting the history of Mary McLeod Bethune and African American women. • Audiovisual exhibits. • Site and gift shop hours are: Monday to Friday, 10 a.m. to 4:30 p.m. Summer hours are: Monday to Saturday, 10 a.m. to 4 p.m. • Write for a schedule of year-round concert, lecture and film series. • Archives are available to researchers by appointment.

PERMITS, FEES & LIMITATIONS
Fees for guided tours are $1 for adults; $.50 for ages 12-18; $.25 for ages 11 and under. There is no charge for school groups.

CAMPING & LODGING
Overnight accommodations are available in the Washington area.

FOOD & SUPPLIES
Food and supplies are available in the Washington area.

FIRST AID/ HOSPITAL
Medical services are available in the Washington area.

GENERAL INFORMATION
Rental use of facilities can be arranged by contacting the Site Coordinator.

National Capital Region

Washington, DC

The park system of the Nation's Capital comprises parks, parkways and reservations in the District of Columbia, including Battleground National Cemetery, the President's Parks, a variety of military fortifications, and green areas.

MAILING ADDRESS	National Capital Region Headquarters, 1100 Ohio Drive, SW, Washington, DC 20242 **Telephone:** 202-619-7222
DIRECTIONS	The Headquarters is located in East Potomac Park near the Jefferson Memorial. Take the Park Police/Potomac Park exit off of I-395.
VISITOR ACTIVITIES	• For information about or directions to any of the more than 300 park units in the Washington Metropolitan Area, call 202-619-7222. For a recorded message of daily events in the park areas, call 202-619-PARK. • The Headquarters building is open Monday through Friday from 8 a.m. to 4 p.m.
PERMITS, FEES & LIMITATIONS	Call Headquarters for more information.
ACCESSIBILITY	The Headquarters has parking, ramps and accessible restrooms.
CAMPING & LODGING	Overnight accommodations are available in Washington and the surrounding area.
FOOD & SUPPLIES	Food and supplies are available in Washington and vicinity.
FIRST AID/ HOSPITAL	Hospitals are available in Washington and vicinity.

National Mall

Washington, DC

This landscaped park extending from the Capitol to the Washington Monument was envisioned as a formal park in the L'Enfant Plan for the city of Washington in 1790.

MAILING ADDRESS	Superintendent, National Capital Parks-Central, 900 Ohio Drive, SW, Washington, DC 20242 **Telephone:** 202-426-6841
DIRECTIONS	Rows of stately elms mark the greensward from the US Capitol to the Washington Monument. The Mall includes many buildings of the Smithsonian Institution. For further information on the Smithsonian, contact Information and Reception Center, Smithsonian Institution, Washington, DC 20560, phone 202-357-2700. The Smithsonian Metro subway station is in the Mall.
VISITOR ACTIVITIES	Casual recreation.
PERMITS, FEES & LIMITATIONS	Permits are required for special events and First Amendment activities.

ACCESSIBILITY

There are several parking spaces designated on Jefferson and Madison Drive. Ramps are located on every corner and at every crosswalk. The Smithsonian Institution has a map showing the location of accessible entries to each museum. Maps are available at the Smithsonian Institute Information Center or write to Visitors Information and Associate Reception Center, 1000 Jefferson Drive, SW, Washington, DC, 20560.

CAMPING & LODGING

There are numerous hotels and motels within the Washington area and in Maryland and Virginia.

FOOD & SUPPLIES

Food services are available at each Smithsonian museum and at the Old Post Office Tower.

FIRST AID/ HOSPITAL

• First aid is available at the museums and theaters within the area.
• The nearest hospital is George Washington University Hospital, 23rd and Pennsylvania Avenue, NW.

Pennsylvania Avenue National Historic Site

Washington, DC

This site includes a portion of Pennsylvania Avenue and the area adjacent to it between the Capitol and the White House encompassing Ford's Theatre National Historic Site, several blocks of the Washington commercial district, the Old Post Office Tower and a number of federal buildings.

MAILING ADDRESS

Pennsylvania Avenue Development Corporation, 331 Pennsylvania Ave., NW, Suite 1220 North, Washington, DC 20004-1703 **Telephone:** 202-426-6720

DIRECTIONS

The Site includes the architecturally and historically significant area between the Capitol and The White House in Washington. There are Metro stations at Federal Triangle and Metro Center that serve the area.

VISITOR ACTIVITIES

• Walking tours, theatrical performances, shopping, ice skating and cafe in Pershing Park at 14th Street and Pennsylvania, noon-time activities in Western Plaza at 13th and Pennsylvania, tours of the National Archives, the F.B.I., the National Museum of American Art and the National Gallery of Art.
• Facilities include museums, theaters and stores. • The Site is always open.

PERMITS, FEES & LIMITATIONS

• There are fees for admission to performances at the theaters. • No trucks allowed.

CAMPING & LODGING

Overnight accommodations are available in Washington and vicinity.

FOOD & SUPPLIES

• There are numerous restaurants in the downtown area. • A grocery store is located at 12th and F streets, NW.

District of Columbia

FIRST AID/ HOSPITAL

• First aid is available at museums and theaters within the Site. • The nearest hospital is George Washington University Hospital, 23rd and Pennsylvania Avenue, NW.

GENERAL INFORMATION

Architour, a nonprofit educational organization, offers regularly scheduled tours of the Site. For information, call 202-265-6454.

Rock Creek Park

Washington, DC

Rock Creek Park is a ribbon of green that runs throughout Washington, DC, and offers opportunities for picnicking, hiking, biking, horseback riding, boating, and studying the area's history through Civil War forts and Pierce Mill, a restored gristmill where corn and wheat are still ground using water power.

MAILING ADDRESS

Superintendent, Rock Creek Park, Klingle Mansion, 3545 Williamsburg Lane, NW, Washington, DC 20008-1207 **Telephone:** 202-426-6832

DIRECTIONS

The main Visitor Center is located at Military Road, NW, and Glover Road, NW, about 1 mile (1.6 km) east of Connecticut Avenue, NW, or one-half mile (.8 km) west of 16th Street, NW.

VISITOR ACTIVITIES

• Nature walks and hikes, horseback riding, picnicking, golf, tennis, recreation fields, exercise trails, running and jogging, exhibit hall, demonstrations of grinding corn and wheat, various craft demonstrations, tennis classics, concerts, bird watching, kite flying and photography. • Facilities include a bookstore, restrooms, telephones, a planetarium at the Nature Center, an operating grist mill at Pierce Mill, the Art Barn, the Old Stone House and the Carter Barron Amphitheatre for summer events.

PERMITS, FEES & LIMITATIONS

• No entrance fee. • Rock Creek Horse Centre, near the Nature Center on Glover Road, offers horse rentals and riding instruction. • There is an 18-hole golf course with a greens fee, golf cart and golf club rental at 16th and Rittenhouse streets. • Reservations are required for the tennis courts.

ACCESSIBILITY

The Nature Center has accessible restrooms. The planetarium, exhibit hall, auditorium, first floor of the Old Stone House, the exercise course at 16th and Kennedy streets, the recreation area, Carter Barron Amphitheater and Picnic Groves #1, #6, #23 and #24 are accessible.

CAMPING & LODGING

• No camping is allowed in the Park. • Lodging is available in nearby motels and hotels in the Washington area.

FOOD & SUPPLIES

Food and supplies are available in Washington and vicinity.

FIRST AID/ HOSPITAL

• First aid is not available in the Park. • Obtain local assistance by dialing 911. • Nearby hospitals include George Washington University Hospital, Howard University Hospital and Sibley Hospital.

GENERAL INFORMATION

Wading and swimming are not recommended in the Park.

Sewall-Belmont House National Historic Site

Washington, DC

Affiliated area. Rebuilt after fire damage from the War of 1812, this red brick house is one of the oldest on Capitol Hill and has been the National Woman's Party headquarters since 1929. Sewall-Belmont House National Historic Site commemorates the party's founder and women's suffrage leader, Alice Paul, and associates.

MAILING ADDRESS

Sewall-Belmont House National Historic Site, 144 Constitution Ave., NE, Washington, DC 20002 **Telephone:** 202-546-3989

DIRECTIONS

The house is located near the US Capitol at 144 Constitution Ave., NE, at the corner of 2nd St., NE.

VISITOR ACTIVITIES

• Guided tours and exhibits featuring memorabilia of suffrage and equal rights campaigns, including busts and portraits of suffrage and equal rights leaders. • Antique furniture. • The tours are conducted Tuesday through Friday from 10 a.m. to 3 p.m., and Saturday, Sunday and holidays from 12 p.m. to 4 p.m. • The Site is closed Mondays, Thanksgiving, Dec. 25 and Jan. 1.

PERMITS, FEES & LIMITATIONS

No permits or fees.

ACCESSIBILITY

The Site is not accessible.

CAMPING & LODGING

• No camping or lodging is available within the Site. • Overnight accommodations are available in Washington and vicinity.

FOOD & SUPPLIES

Food and supplies are available nearby at Union Station and throughout the area.

FIRST AID/ HOSPITAL

• First aid is not available at the Site. • The nearest hospital is Capitol Hill Hospital, 7 blocks.

GENERAL INFORMATION

On-street parking can be scarce during the week, but there are plentiful spaces on weekends and holidays.

District of Columbia

Theodore Roosevelt Island

Washington, DC   See Climatable No. 38

Under President Theodore Roosevelt, the Government became the chief instrument in rescuing the public domain when more than 234 million acres were reserved for conservation. These contributions are memorialized on 88-acre Theodore Roosevelt Island in the Potomac River.

MAILING ADDRESS

Superintendent, George Washington Memorial Parkway, Turkey Run Park, McLean, VA 22101 **Telephone:** 703-285-2598

DIRECTIONS

The parking area is accessible from the northbound lane of the George Washington Memorial Parkway on the Virginia side of the Potomac River. A footbridge connects the Island to the Virginia shore. The Island is also accessible to pedestrians via the Metro station at Rosslyn and a 20-minute walk following city streets to the Key Bridge where the Mount Vernon Trail begins. Follow the trail to the Island entrance.

VISITOR ACTIVITIES

• Guided tours, hiking, fishing and wayside exhibits. • Facilities include restrooms, drinking water and hiking trails. • The Island is open year-round during daylight hours.

PERMITS, FEES & LIMITATIONS

• No entrance fee. • Fishing permits are required for persons older than 16. • Vehicles are not permitted on the Island.

ACCESSIBILITY

There is accessible parking. The restrooms are not accessible, and the trails have a gravel/dirt surface with difficult grades in some areas.

CAMPING & LODGING

• There is no camping or lodging on the Island. • Overnight accommodations are available nearby in Arlington, VA, and throughout the Washington area.

FOOD & SUPPLIES

Food and supplies are available in Arlington, VA, or the Washington area.

FIRST AID/ HOSPITAL

• First aid is available. • The nearest hospitals are in Arlington, VA, and Washington.

Thomas Jefferson Memorial

Washington, DC

This circular, colonnaded structure, in the classic style introduced to this country by Thomas Jefferson, memorializes the author of the Declaration of Independence and President from 1801-09 through interior walls presenting inscriptions from his writings and a heroic statue sculpted by Rudolph Evans.

MAILING ADDRESS	Superintendent, National Capital Parks-Central, 900 Ohio Drive, SW, Washington, DC 20242 **Telephone:** 202-485-9880
DIRECTIONS	The Memorial is on the south bank of the Tidal Basin near downtown Washington. From Virginia, take the George Washington Memorial Parkway to Memorial Bridge, cross the bridge, follow the signs on Independence Avenue to the Memorial. The nearest Metro subway station is the Smithsonian on the Blue and Orange lines.
VISITOR ACTIVITIES	• Interpretative talks are given daily by Rangers. • The Cherry Blossom Festival takes place about the first week of April with special walks and talks by Rangers at scheduled times.
PERMITS, FEES & LIMITATIONS	Permits are required for special events and First Amendment activities.
ACCESSIBILITY	There are parking spaces in the parking lot. An elevator in the lower lobby of the Memorial provides access to the Rotunda area.
CAMPING & LODGING	There are numerous hotels and motels in the Washington area and in Maryland and Virginia.
FOOD & SUPPLIES	Food and supplies are available in Washington and vicinity.
FIRST AID/ HOSPITAL	• First aid is available at the Ranger booth located at the Chamber level. • The nearest hospital is George Washington University Hospital, 23rd and Pennsylvania Avenue, NW.

Vietnam Veterans Memorial

Washington, DC

The mirrorlike surface of the Vietnam Veterans Memorial reflects the surrounding trees, lawns, monuments and people. The 58,132 names of the slain and missing are carved into the black granite walls, creating a quiet place to remember and honor all Vietnam veterans.

MAILING ADDRESS	Superintendent, National Capital Parks-Central, 900 Ohio Drive, SW, Washington, DC 20242 **Telephone:** 202-485-9880
DIRECTIONS	The Memorial is off of Constitution Avenue and 23rd Street, NW, Constitution Gardens and part of West Potomac Park. The nearest Metro subway station is Foggy Bottom, 23rd and I Street, NW, on the Blue and Orange lines.
VISITOR ACTIVITIES	• There are Rangers and volunteers who assist visitors in locating names, performing name rubbings and giving general information regarding the wall itself. • Rangers at the Memorial kiosk offer general directions and

provide computer printouts containing information such as date of birth, date of casualty, and branch of service of the soldiers whose names are on the wall.

PERMITS, FEES & LIMITATIONS

Permits are required for special events and First Amendment activities.

ACCESSIBILITY

The Memorial is accessible.

CAMPING & LODGING

There are numerous hotels and motels in the Washington area and in Maryland and Virginia.

FOOD & SUPPLIES

Food and supplies are available in Washington and vicinity.

FIRST AID/ HOSPITAL

• First aid is available at the Ranger booth right across from the Lincoln Memorial. • The nearest hospital is George Washington University Hospital, 23rd and Pennsylvania Avenue, NW.

GENERAL INFORMATION

• The Tourmobile and The Old Town Trolley provide service to the Lincoln Memorial and the Vietnam Veterans Memorial. • For further information, contact the Washington Convention and Visitor Association, 1575 I St., NW, Washington, DC, 20005.

Washington Monument

Washington, DC

The Washington Monument, a graceful and delicate obelisk rising more than 555 feet (169 m), was built in intervals between 1848 and 1885 and memorializes George Washington's achievements and unselfish devotion to principle and to country.

MAILING ADDRESS

Superintendent, National Capital Parks-Central, 900 Ohio Drive, SW, Washington, DC 20242 **Telephone:** 202-485-9880

DIRECTIONS

The Monument is on the National Mall between 15th and 17th streets and Independence and Constitution avenues. From Virginia, follow Rt. 50 East of I-395 North to Washington. The nearest Metro subway station is Smithsonian on the Blue and Orange lines.

VISITOR ACTIVITIES

• Visitors can ascend to the 500 foot (152.4 m) height of the Monument by elevator and view the city from 8 windows (2 on each side). • The Monument is staffed daily from 9 a.m. to 5 p.m., from September to March and from 8 a.m. to midnight from April through Labor Day. • Restrooms are at the Monument base.

PERMITS, FEES & LIMITATIONS

Permits are required for special events and First Amendment activities.

ACCESSIBILITY

The Monument is accessible with the use of the elevator and special viewers to use at the windows. Parking is in the Washington Monument parking lot off of Constitution Avenue between 15th and 17th streets. There is a 2-hour time limit in the parking lot.

CAMPING & LODGING

There are numerous hotels and motels within the Washington area and in Maryland and Virginia.

FOOD & SUPPLIES

• A snackbar and souvenir store are at the Monument base. • Other food establishments are at each Smithsonian museum and at the Old Post Office Tower.

FIRST AID/ HOSPITAL

• First aid is available at the Ranger Station. • The nearest hospital is George Washington University Hospital, 23rd and Pennsylvania Avenue, NW.

GENERAL INFORMATION

• The Tourmobile provides a stop at the Monument base. • Other parking is available along Constitution Avenue, and Madison and Jefferson Drive. Note the time limits in each area.

The White House

Washington, DC

Every President and First Family, except George Washington, has lived, entertained and conducted national and international meetings at The White House, the scene of many events in the country's history.

MAILING ADDRESS

The White House, c/o National Park Service, 1100 Ohio Drive, SW, Washington, DC 20242 **Telephone:** 202-755-7799

DIRECTIONS

The White House is at 1600 Pennsylvania Ave., NW, in downtown Washington, DC. Visitors enter through the East Gate from East Executive Park for scheduled tours.

VISITOR ACTIVITIES

• Free public tours year-round Tuesday through Saturday, **10 a.m. to noon.** No tickets required from Nov. 1 to Feb. 28. From March 1 to Oct. 1, tickets may be picked up on the Ellipse, the park area south of the White House grounds, beginning at **8 a.m.** on the day of the tour. These limited tickets are available until the supply is exhausted. One person may pick up tickets for their immediate family. During peak tourist season, it is advised to arrive early. For tour schedules, call 202-456-7041. • **Special events** open to the public include the Easter Egg Roll on Easter Monday, Spring and Fall Garden Tours and Candlelight Tours in late December. • The White House is closed to tours on Thanksgiving, Dec. 25 and Jan. 1 and for all official functions. • Some delays may occur due to official functions.

PERMITS, FEES & LIMITATIONS

• **No entrance fee.** Beware of people attempting to sell White House tours.
• No photography or strollers permitted inside The White House.

District of Columbia

ACCESSIBILITY

Wheelchair users and their immediate family (no more than 6) may enter at the entrance on Pennsylvania Avenue during the normal tour hours. No tour tickets are needed. Hearing or sight impaired visitors may make special arrangements with The White House Visitor Office at 202-456-2121.

CAMPING & LODGING

Camping and lodging is available in Washington and vicinity.

FOOD & SUPPLIES

Food and supplies are available within several blocks of The White House.

FIRST AID/ HOSPITAL

• Basic first aid is available at the Ranger Station on the Ellipse. • The nearest hospital is George Washington University Hospital, 23rd Street, NW.

GENERAL INFORMATION

For more information about The White House refer to *The President's House*, *The White House*, *An Historic Guide*, *The Living White House*, *The Presidents*, and *First Ladies of The White House*, published by The White House Historical Association, 740 Jackson Place, NW, Washington, DC 20506, 202-737-8292.

Florida

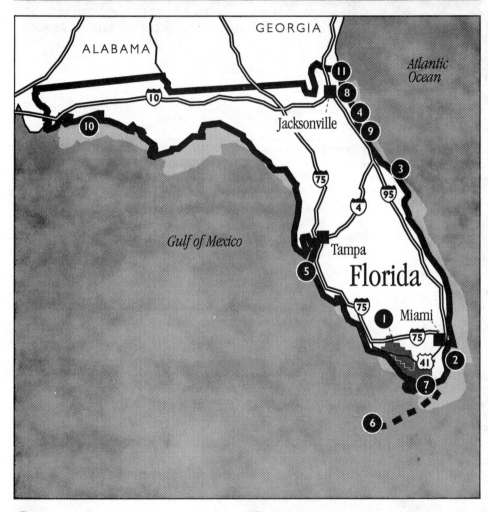

1. Big Cypress National Preserve
2. Biscayne National Park
3. Canaveral National Seashore
4. Castillo de San Marcos National Monument
5. De Soto National Memorial
6. Dry Tortugas National Park
7. Everglades National Park
8. Fort Caroline National Memorial
9. Fort Matanzas National Monument
10. Gulf Islands National Seashore
11. Timucuan Ecological and Historic Preserve

Big Cypress National Preserve

Ochopee, Florida

The land of Big Cypress National Preserve consists of sandy islands of slash pine, mixed hardwood hammocks (tree islands), wet prairies, dry prairies, marshes and estuarine mangrove forests. Bromeliads and orchids perch on the cypress and hammock trees, an occasional Florida panther leaves paw marks in wet marl and black bears claw crayfish from the sloughs.

MAILING ADDRESS	Superintendent, Big Cypress National Preserve, HCR 61, Box 110, Ochopee, FL 33943 **Telephone:** 813-695-4111
DIRECTIONS	The Preserve is 30 miles (48.3 km) west of Miami via US 41. The Visitor Center is 20 miles (32.2 km) into the Preserve on US 41.
VISITOR ACTIVITIES	• The Visitor Center is open daily, 8:30 a.m. to 4:30 p.m., except Dec. 25. • Thirty-one miles (50 km) of the Florida Trail pass through the Preserve. • Winter months (the dry season) are the best time to hike the trail. • Wading birds and wildlife.
PERMITS, FEES & LIMITATIONS	• Off-road vehicle permits are sold at the Visitor Center for $35. • For hunting and fishing permits, contact the Florida Game and Fresh Water Fish Commission, Tallahassee, FL 32301, phone 904-488-1960.
ACCESSIBILITY	Restrooms and picnic areas are accessible.
CAMPING & LODGING	• There are 9 frontcountry primitive campgrounds in the Preserve. • Backcountry camping is permitted. • Lodging is available in Everglades City, Miccosukee Indian Reservation, Naples and Miami.
FOOD & SUPPLIES	Food and supplies are available in Everglades City and the Miccosukee Indian Reservation.
FIRST AID/ HOSPITAL	• First aid is available at the Visitor Center. • Hospitals are in Naples and Miami.

Biscayne National Park

Homestead, Florida   See Climatable No. 17

A mainland mangrove shoreline, a warm shallow bay, many small keys and living coral reefs intermingle at Biscayne National Park, creating a vast, almost pristine wilderness and recreation area along the southeast edge of the Florida peninsula.

MAILING ADDRESS	Superintendent, Biscayne National Park, PO Box 1369, Homestead, FL 33090-1369 **Telephone:** 305-247-7275

DIRECTIONS

The Park's Convoy Point Visitor Center is 9 miles (14.5 km) east of Homestead on SW 328th Street (North Canal Drive). Boaters may enter the Park waters via the Intercoastal Waterway.

VISITOR ACTIVITIES

• Glass bottom boat sightseeing trips and snorkel/scuba trips to the coral reefs are provided by the Park's concessionaire at Convoy Point. Reservations are required. Call 305-247-2400. • The Convoy Point Visitor Center offers exhibits, slide presentations and information. • Canoe rentals are available. • Visitors with their own boat transportation may explore the waters, keys and reefs.

PERMITS, FEES & LIMITATIONS

• No entrance fee. • Because of damage caused by Hurricane Andrew, all Park islands, except the Elliott Key Harbor and Campground Complex, are closed to the public. These restrictions will be lifted as soon as possible.

ACCESSIBILITY

The Convoy Point Visitor Center and all Park restrooms are accessible. The concessionaire will provide any needed assistance for tour boats.

CAMPING & LODGING

• Tent camping sites are available on Elliott Key on a first-come, first-served basis. Campers must have their own boat transportation to the island. Fresh water, showers and restrooms are available. • Lodging is available in Homestead.

FOOD & SUPPLIES

Food and supplies are available in Homestead.

FIRST AID/ HOSPITAL

• First aid is available at the Convoy Point Visitor Center and from Rangers throughout the Park. • The nearest hospital is in Homestead.

GENERAL INFORMATION

• Work is continuing to complete construction and to repair hurricane damage at the Park. • The Park's new permanent Visitor Center at Convoy Point is scheduled for completion in late 1994.

Canaveral National Seashore

Titusville, Florida

More than 280 species of birds have been recorded and visitors can enjoy ocean beaches, fishing, boating, hunting and wildlife watching at Canaveral National Seashore.

MAILING ADDRESS

Superintendent, Canaveral National Seashore, 308 Julia St., Titusville, FL 32796 **Telephone:** 407-267-1110

DIRECTIONS

Located midway down the Florida east coast between Jacksonville and West Palm Beach, the Seashore is readily accessible via US 1 and I-95, I-4 and I-75. New Smyrna Beach provides access via FL A1A into the Seashore in the vicinity of Turtle Mound, a shell midden made by native Indians. Titusville offers access via FL 402 to Playalinda Beach on the Seashore's southern end.

In addition, the Intercoastal Waterway linking Florida with the North skirts the western edge of Mosquito Lagoon before entering the Indian River via the Haulover Canal.

VISITOR ACTIVITIES

• Bird watching, boating, swimming, surfing, sun bathing, shell collecting, surf fishing, wildlife observation, photography, wildland hiking, waterfowl hunting, picnicking and walking. • There are exhibits and slide programs at the Visitor Center. • The Seashore is open daily from 6 a.m. to 6 p.m. The Visitor Center is closed Dec. 25 and Jan. 1. • Restrooms are available at the beaches.

PERMITS, FEES & LIMITATIONS

• **No entrance fee.** • Backcountry camping and horse use are free. • Commercial shellfishing and Florida saltwater fishing license may be required. • Waterfowl hunting in authorized areas and seasons is regulated by the US Fish and Wildlife Service. • Pets and glass containers are not allowed on the beaches.

ACCESSIBILITY

The restrooms are accessible, and there is beach access at designated areas. There is a captioned slide program.

CAMPING & LODGING

• Backcountry camping is permitted on the North Beach and on the islands in the north end of Mosquito Lagoon. The area is closed when space vehicles are on the launch pad or during launchings. • Beach backcountry camping is closed from May 1 to Oct. 31. • Other overnight accommodations and private campgrounds are located in nearby communities.

FOOD & SUPPLIES

Food and supplies are available in Titusville, 12 miles (19.3 km) and in New Smyrna Beach, 10 miles (16.1 km).

FIRST AID/ HOSPITAL

• See a Ranger or go to the Ranger Station or Visitor Center for first aid. • The nearest hospitals are in Titusville and New Smyrna Beach.

GENERAL INFORMATION

• Swimming can be dangerous due to strong ocean currents. Lifeguards are not provided. • Visitors to inland areas should carry a repellent to protect themselves from mosquitoes and other biting insects. • Space operations at Kennedy Space Center require the closing of Playalinda Beach for safety and security prior to and during launches of the Space Shuttle. • The Space Center offers tours and exhibits and Merritt Island National Wildlife Refuge offers trails, exhibits, and a wildlife drive. • The climate is sub-tropical with short, mild winters and hot, humid summers. • Ocean temperatures vary from 55°F to 85°F during the year.

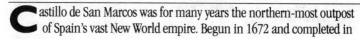

Castillo de San Marcos National Monument

St. Augustine, Florida

Castillo de San Marcos was for many years the northern-most outpost of Spain's vast New World empire. Begun in 1672 and completed in

1695, it is the oldest masonry fort, and the best-preserved example of a Spanish colonial fortification in the continental United States.

MAILING ADDRESS

Superintendent, Castillo de San Marcos National Monument, 1 Castillo Drive, East, St. Augustine, FL 32084 **Telephone:** 904-829-6505

DIRECTIONS

The Monument is at 1 Castillo Drive in downtown St. Augustine.

VISITOR ACTIVITIES

• Interpretive exhibits, Ranger talks, living history demonstrations and self-guiding tours. • Facilities include parking and restrooms. • The Monument is open from **8:45 a.m. to 4:45 p.m.**, except Dec. 25.

PERMITS, FEES & LIMITATIONS

• There is a $2 **entrance fee** for adults 17 and older. US Senior Citizens are admitted free.

CAMPING & LODGING

• There are no overnight accommodations within the Monument.
• Lodging is available in St. Augustine.

FOOD & SUPPLIES

Food and supplies are available in St. Augustine.

FIRST AID/ HOSPITAL

• First aid is available in the Monument. • There are 2 major hospitals in St. Augustine.

GENERAL INFORMATION

For your safety - Be aware of rough and uneven floors, fragile walls and steep drops.

De Soto National Memorial

Bradenton, Florida

Hernando De Soto landed on Florida's west coast in May 1539 to begin a quest for riches that would lead him and his army almost 4,000 miles (6451.6 km) through what is presently the southeastern United States. They were the first Europeans to explore deep into North America and to see the Mississippi River above its mouth.

MAILING ADDRESS

Superintendent, De Soto National Memorial, PO Box 15390, Bradenton, FL 34280-5390 **Telephone:** 813-792-0458/792-5094

DIRECTIONS

The Memorial is on the mouth of the Manatee River and Tampa Bay 5 miles (8 km) west of Bradenton on 75th Street, NW, 2 miles (3.2 km) north of SR 64W.

VISITOR ACTIVITIES

• Interpretive films, exhibits, a half-mile (.8 km) self-guided nature trail and fishing. • Living History Camp from mid-December through mid-April. • The Visitor Center is open daily from **8:45 a.m. to 5 p.m.**

PERMITS, FEES & LIMITATIONS

• No entrance fee. • Special films and programs are permitted with prior approval. • Permits are required for weddings and other special uses.

Florida

ACCESSIBILITY

The Visitor Center, parking, the nature trail, boardwalk and Living History Camp are accessible. There are accessible restrooms.

CAMPING & LODGING

Overnight accommodations are available in Bradenton.

FOOD & SUPPLIES

Food and supplies are available in Bradenton.

FIRST AID/ HOSPITAL

• First aid is available in the Memorial. • The nearest hospital is in Bradenton on 59th Street, 5 miles (8 km).

Dry Tortugas National Park

Key West, Florida

Almost 70 miles (112.9 km) west of Key West lies a cluster of seven coral reefs called the Dry Tortugas. These reefs along with surrounding shoals and waters make up Dry Tortugas National Park. Known for its famous bird and marine life, and its legends of pirates and sunken gold, Dry Tortugas National Park includes the largest of the 19th century American coastal forts.

MAILING ADDRESS

Site Supervisor, Dry Tortugas National Park, PO Box 6208, Key West, FL 33041 **Telephone:** 305-242-7700

DIRECTIONS

Boat or seaplane provide the only access to the park. Several boat and air taxi services offer trips to the Dry Tortugas from Key West and the Lower Keys, as well as from the Naples and Fort Meyers area of southwest Florida. Specific information about these services may be obtained from the Chambers of Commerce at 3330 Overseas Highway, Marathon, FL 33052, phone 305-743-5417; Old Mallory Square, Key West, FL 33040, phone 305-294-2587; and 1700 N. Tamiami Trail, Naples, FL 33940, phone 813-262-6141.

VISITOR ACTIVITIES

• Interpretive exhibits, self-guiding tours, Ranger-led activities, bird and wildlife watching, picnicking, salt water sport fishing, snorkeling, swimming and scuba diving. • Facilities include a Visitor Center, a picnic area, and salt water toilets. • Bush Key is closed to visitors from April to September to protect nesting Sooty and Noddy Terns. There is day use only on all keys except Garden Key.

PERMITS, FEES & LIMITATIONS

• No entrance fee. • A Florida salt water fishing license is required. • Personal watercraft, i.e., jetskis, are not permitted.

ACCESSIBILITY

Restrooms, picnic area and the first tier of Fort Jefferson are accessible.

CAMPING & LODGING

• Camping is permitted on Garden Key only in a small number of primitive camp sites that are available on a first-come, first-served basis. Groups of 10 or more must obtain a special permit in advance. • Other overnight accommodations are available in Key West, 70 miles (112.9 km).

FOOD & SUPPLIES

Food and supplies are available in Key West.

FIRST AID/ HOSPITAL

• First aid is available in the Park. • The nearest hospital is in Key West.

GENERAL INFORMATION

• The Park's central feature is Fort Jefferson, the largest brick and masonry fortification in the Western hemisphere. Construction was begun in 1846 but was never fully completed. • The cluster of 7 islands known as the Dry Tortugas and the 100 square miles (161.2 km) of pristine coral reefs and seagrass beds provide outstanding opportunities for viewing seabirds and marine life. • Created as Fort Jefferson National Monument by Presidential Proclamation Jan. 4, 1935 and reestablished as Dry Tortugas National Park Oct. 4, 1992. • Since the Park is isolated, visitors must provide for everything. All food, water and supplies must be brought from the mainland. All trash must be removed. • **For your safety** - Do not stand near wall edges. Mortar in the historic structures may be loose or weakened. Watch for uneven walking surfaces, spiral stairways, sudden drop-offs and darkened areas. Never swim alone. Be cautious in areas with strong currents. Cuts from coral and punctures from sea urchins may be painful and slow to heal.

Everglades National Park

Homestead, Florida   See Climatable No. 16

Everglades National Park's 1.4 million acres of marsh covered by scattered tall grasses provides a home to a rich mixture of plants and animals. The Park contains only part of the watery expanse for which it is named, but there are many opportunities to explore its mysteries and learn about its fragile nature.

MAILING ADDRESS

Superintendent, Everglades National Park, 40001 State Road 9336, Homestead, FL 33034-6133 **Telephone:** 305-242-7700

DIRECTIONS

The main Visitor Center is near the Park entrance, 12 miles (19.3 km) southwest of Homestead on Route 9336. Other Visitor Centers are in Royal Palm, Shark Valley, Flamingo and Everglades City.

VISITOR ACTIVITIES

• Boating, picnicking, wildlife and bird watching, photography, hiking, interpretive talks and exhibits, fishing, backcountry, canoeing, open-air tram and sightseeing boat rides. • Facilities include a bookstore, parking, restrooms and telephones at the Visitor Center, boat rentals and ramp, marina, nature trails, picnic areas, environmental study area and houseboat rentals. • Services are reduced at Flamingo during the summer. • The Park is open year-round.

PERMITS, FEES & LIMITATIONS

• The entrance fee is $5 per vehicle or $3 per person at the main entrance or $4 per vehicle and $3 per person at the Shark Valley entrance. Annual entrance permits are available for $15. • Shark Valley tram tours are concession fee-operated. • A Florida fishing license, available at local bait and tackle shops, is required for fresh water and salt water fishing. • Free backcountry permits are available at Everglades City and Flamingo Ranger stations. The May-October off-season has a self-registration system. • No off-road vehicles are permitted in the Park. No private vehicles are permitted on Shark Valley Road. All vehicles are restricted to designated roads.

ACCESSIBILITY

An access guide is available at visitor centers. Most walking trails and boat tours are accessible.

CAMPING & LODGING

• Individual camp sites are available on a first-come, first-served basis for $8 per night and $4 for walk-in tent sites from Nov. 1 to April 30. Camping is free the remainder of the year. • Group camp sites can be reserved by contacting Chief Ranger, ENP, 40001 State Road 9336, Homestead, FL 33034-6733. • Most backcountry camp sites are accessible by boat only. • There is a motor lodge at Flamingo. Reservations should be made well in advance by contacting Flamingo Lodge, Marina & Outpost, Flamingo, FL 33030, 813-695-3101. • Additional camping is available near Everglades City at Copeland, 7 miles (11.2 km) north on FL 29; and at Collier-Seminole State Park, 19 miles (30.6 km) west on US 41. • Other overnight accommodations are available in Homestead; Florida City, 12 miles (19.3 km); the Florida Keys, 40 miles (64.4 km) and Everglades City, 90 miles (144.1 km).

FOOD & SUPPLIES

• Meals are served at Flamingo. • Food and supplies are available at Flamingo Marina. • Food and supplies are also available in Homestead, Key Largo and Everglades City.

FIRST AID/ HOSPITAL

• First aid is available at Ranger stations. • The nearest hospital is in Homestead.

GENERAL INFORMATION

• Insect repellent is needed on all backcountry trails all year. • Mosquitoes and other biting insects make camping and backcountry use during the summer rainy season virtually unbearable by all but the most dedicated outdoorsperson. • Rates for overnight accommodations are considerably higher throughout South Florida during the winter season (Dec. 15 to April 15).

Fort Caroline National Memorial

Jacksonville, Florida

France's first attempt to stake a permanent claim in North America was begun in 1562 at La Caroline. The Fort's history is full of hardship and battles with the Spanish who were uneasy about a French settlement on the Florida coast that was so close to the routes used by their treasure ships.

MAILING ADDRESS

Superintendent, Fort Caroline National Memorial, 12713 Fort Caroline Road, Jacksonville, FL 32225 **Telephone:** 904-641-7155

DIRECTIONS

The Memorial is 13 miles (20.9 km) east of downtown Jacksonville. Take FL 10 to either Monument or St. Johns Bluff Road. Go north to Fort Caroline Road and then east to the Memorial entrance.

VISITOR ACTIVITIES

• The Visitor Center is open daily from 9 a.m. to 5 p.m., except Dec. 25.
• The Visitor Center includes exhibits, a sales area and an audiovisual room. • A one-quarter mile (.4 km) trail leads to the scaled model of Fort Caroline. A 1 mile (1.6 km) nature trail is also available. • Ranger programs are conducted on weekends.

PERMITS, FEES & LIMITATIONS

• No permits or fees. • Vehicles are restricted to designated roads.
• Picnicking is permitted only in designated areas.

ACCESSIBILITY

The Visitor Center and restrooms are accessible. An electric cart is available to provide assistance to the fort model.

CAMPING & LODGING

Overnight accommodations are available in Jacksonville.

FOOD & SUPPLIES

Food and supplies are available in Jacksonville.

FIRST AID/ HOSPITAL

• Basic first aid is available at the Memorial. • Doctors and hospitals are within 5 miles (8 km).

GENERAL INFORMATION

• Biting insects can be a problem. • Summers are hot and humid.

Fort Matanzas National Monument

Saint Augustine, Florida

Fort Matanzas, or Slaughters in English, marks the site where on Sept. 29 and Oct. 12, 1565, 200 to 300 soldiers from the French Fort Caroline were killed by the Spaniards in a battle for supremacy in the New World.

MAILING ADDRESS

Superintendent, Castillo de San Marcos National Monument, 1 Castillo Drive, St. Augustine, FL 32084 **Telephone:** 904-471-0116

DIRECTIONS

The Monument is 14 miles (22.5 km) south of St. Augustine. Take FL A1A on Anastasia Island. The Fort is accessible only by boat. A ferry crosses to Rattlesnake Island between 9 a.m. and 4:30 p.m. daily year-round, weather permitting.

VISITOR ACTIVITIES

• Interpretive walks and talks, ferry boat rides, fishing. • The grounds are open daily from 8:30 a.m. to 5:30 p.m. The Visitor Center is open from

9 a.m. to 5 p.m. • The Monument is closed Dec. 25.

PERMITS, FEES & LIMITATIONS

• No permits or fees. • Vehicles are restricted to designated roads.

ACCESSIBILITY

Restrooms and parking at Visitor Center, and a one-half mile (.8 km) nature trail boardwalk are accessible.

CAMPING & LODGING

• Lodging is available in St. Augustine Beach, 10 miles (16.1 km); or in St. Augustine, 15 miles (24.1 km). • Nearby campgrounds include Anastasia State Recreation Area, 12 miles (19.3 km); Flagler Beach State Recreation Area, 18 miles (29 km); and several private campgrounds.

FOOD & SUPPLIES

Food and supplies are available in St. Augustine Beach, 10 miles (16.1 km).

FIRST AID/ HOSPITAL

• First aid is available in the Monument. • The nearest hospital is in St. Augustine, 15 miles (24.1 km).

GENERAL INFORMATION

• For your safety - Do not swim in the treacherous waters near the inlet or climb on the Fort walls. Be wary of sharp oyster shells. • Other points of interest include historic sites in St. Augustine, 15 miles (24.1 km); and Marineland, 5 miles (8 km).

Gulf Islands National Seashore

Gulf Breeze, Florida/Ocean Springs, Mississippi

Clear blue waters, gentle sloping beaches, coastal marshes and interesting human history provide the perfect backdrop for recreation and relaxation at Gulf Islands National Seashore. The Seashore stretches from West Ship Island in Mississippi 150 miles (241.9 km) east to the far end of Santa Rosa Island in Florida.

MAILING ADDRESS

Superintendent, Gulf Islands National Seashore, 1801 Gulf Breeze Parkway, Gulf Breeze, FL 32561 **Telephone:** 904-934-2600, 601-875-0821

DIRECTIONS

Access to Ship Island in the Mississippi District is provided by concession boats from Gulfport, MS, March through October, and from Biloxi, MS, Memorial Day weekend through November. Consult the concessioner's printed schedule for frequency and times. Private boats may dock near Fort Massachusetts on West Ship Island during the day. Chartered or private boats provide access to Horn, Petit Bois and East Ship islands. Follow the signs on US 90 for the Seashore to Davis Bayou. Recommended routes for the main visitor areas within the Florida District are: Johnson Beach (Perdido Key) - Take FL 292 southwest from Pensacola; historic mainland forts and Naval Museum - Use the main entrance of Pensacola Naval Air Station off Barrancas (FL 295); Naval Live Oaks and the Fort Pickens and Santa Rosa

Areas - Take US 98 from downtown Pensacola across the Pensacola Bay Bridge.

VISITOR ACTIVITIES

• Interpretive exhibits, programs, trails, picnicking, hiking, sunbathing, swimming, boating, fishing, auto tours, scuba diving and guided fort tours.
• Facilities include picnic areas, bathhouses and outdoor showers, boat dock and ramp, laundry, boat charters, restrooms, visitor centers, souvenirs, bookstores, fishing piers, hiking and bicycling trails, playground, ball field, ball court and wilderness area.

PERMITS, FEES & LIMITATIONS

• The entrance fee is $4 per vehicle for a 7-day permit or $10 for an annual permit. • Vehicles are not permitted on sand dunes and beaches.
• Glass containers are prohibited on beaches. • No pets are allowed on beaches.

ACCESSIBILITY

An access guide is available at the Seashore visitor centers. Most day-use areas, the campground and visitor centers are accessible, including Fort Pickens and Fort Massachusetts.

CAMPING & LODGING

• Camping is available on a first-come, first-served basis for $10 per night for non-electric sites and $12 per night for electric sites. Long tent stakes for use in the sand and mosquito netting are musts. • Primitive camping is on East Ship, Horn and Petit Bois islands. • Other overnight accommodations are available in Gulfport, Biloxi, Ocean Springs and Pascagouls, MS; and in Pensacola, Pensacola Beach, Navarre Beach and Fort Walton Beach, FL.

FOOD & SUPPLIES

• Snacks are available at the Santa Rosa Area, the Perdido Key Area, the Fort Pickens Area, the Okaloosa Area and West Ship Island. • Food and supplies are available at the Fort Pickens Area campground store. • Food and supplies are also available in major urban centers along the entire 175-mile (280 km) overland route from Gulfport, MS, to Fort Walton Beach, FL; and from Ship Island, MS, to Santa Rosa Island, FL.

FIRST AID/ HOSPITAL

• First aid is available at Ranger stations. • The nearest hospitals are in Ocean Springs, MS, Highway 90, 5 miles (8 km); Pensacola, FL, Baptist Hospital, 12 miles (19.3 km); and in Gulf Breeze, FL, Gulf Breeze Hospital, 2 miles (3.2 km).

Timucuan Ecological and Historic Preserve

Jacksonville, Florida

Named for the Indians who once lived in the area perhaps for nearly 2,000 years, the Timucuan Ecological and Historic Preserve contains Atlantic coastal marshes, islands, tidal creeks and the estuaries of the St. Johns and Nassau rivers.

Florida

MAILING ADDRESS	Superintendent, Timucuan Ecological and Historic Preserve,13165 Mount Pleasant Road, Jacksonville, FL 32225 **Telephone:** 904-641-7155
DIRECTIONS	The Preserve encompasses most of the northeast section of Jacksonville. The National Park Service maintains operational areas at Kingsley Plantation, Fort Caroline and the Theodore Roosevelt Area. Please call for directions.
VISITOR ACTIVITIES	• Kingsley Plantation: The Visitor Center is open daily from **9 a.m. to 5 p.m.**, except Dec. 25. Ranger-conducted programs daily, exhibits, demonstration garden, self-guided walking tour of the grounds and historic structures. • Theodore Roosevelt Area: Open daily from **8 a.m. to dusk**. Hiking trails, birding, Ranger programs on weekends. • Fort Caroline: See separate listing in this book.
PERMITS, FEES & LIMITATIONS	• **No permits or fees.** • Vehicles are restricted to designated roads. • Follow State fishing and boating regulations.
ACCESSIBILITY	Parking area and some trails at Theodore Roosevelt Area are accessible. The grounds and some buildings at Kingsley Plantation are accessible.
CAMPING & LODGIN	No overnight accommodations are available in the Preserve. Lodging available in Jacksonville.
FOOD & SUPPLIES	Food and supplies are available in Jacksonville.
FIRST AID/ HOSPITAL	• Basic first aid is available at the Preserve. • Doctor's offices and hospitals in Jacksonville, 15 miles (24.1 km).

Georgia

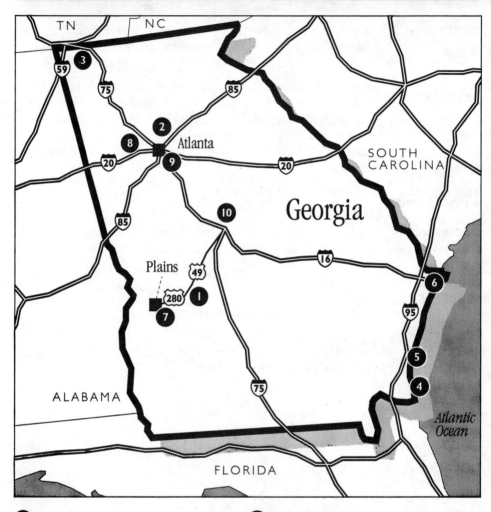

1 Andersonville National Historic Site

2 Chattahoochee River National Recreation Area

3 Chickamauga and Chattanooga National Military Park

4 Cumberland Island National Seashore

5 Fort Frederica National Monument

6 Fort Pulaski National Monument

7 Jimmy Carter National Historic Site

8 Kennnesaw Mountain National Battlefield Park

9 Martin Luther King Jr. National Historic Site

10 Ocmulgee National Monument

Georgia 143

Andersonville National Historic Site

Andersonville, Georgia

Andersonville, or Camp Sumter, was the largest of the Confederate military prisons established during the Civil War. More than 45,000 Union soldiers were confined in the camp during 14 months in which almost 13,000 died from disease, poor sanitation, malnutrition, overcrowding and exposure.

MAILING ADDRESS

Superintendent, Andersonville National Historic Site, Rt. 1, Box 80085, Andersonville, GA 31711 **Telephone:** 912-924-0343

DIRECTIONS

The Site is northeast of Americus, GA, on Route 49 in Macon County. I-75 south of Macon intersects Route 49 north of the Site. Routes 224 and 27 and US 280 at Cordele also connect I-75 with Route 49.

VISITOR ACTIVITIES

• Picnicking, auto tape tours, walking, commemorative monuments, interpretive exhibits, Visitor Center, Museum and POW Museum. • Facilities include parking and restrooms at the Visitor Center. • The Site is open daily from 8 a.m. to 5 p.m. with extended hours to 7 p.m. on Memorial Day.

PERMITS, FEES & LIMITATIONS

• No entrance fee. • Vehicles are restricted to the parking area and auto tour roads.

CAMPING & LODGING

Lodging is available in Americus, 10 miles (16.1 km); and in Montezuma, 10 miles (16.1 km).

FOOD & SUPPLIES

Food and supplies, while not available within the Site, are available in Andersonville, one-half mile (.8 km); Americus and Montezuma.

FIRST AID/ HOSPITAL

• First aid is available in the Site. • The nearest hospital is in Americus.

GENERAL INFORMATION

For your safety - Wear shoes to protect yourself from sandspurs that grow wild in the grass. Also be aware of snakes, poison ivy and fire ants (characterized by red sandy mounds), which have a painful sting. Do not climb on monuments, fences or earthworks.

Chattahoochee River National Recreation Area

Atlanta, Georgia

The 48-mile (77.4 km) stretch of the Chattahoochee River holds many opportunities to canoe, fish and hike the trails along the banks and also to learn about the area's rich natural and human history.

MAILING ADDRESS

Chattahoochee River National Recreation Area, 1978 Island Ford Parkway, Dunwoody, GA 30350 **Telephone:** 404-399-8070

Georgia

DIRECTIONS	Sixteen separate land units along a 48-mile (77.4 km) stretch of the Chattahoochee River, extending into northwest Atlanta, make up the Recreation Area.
VISITOR ACTIVITIES	• Fishing, picnicking, jogging, hiking, bird watching, photography, horseback riding and various river activities. • Facilities include watercraft rentals and bus shuttle service from mid-May through September. • The Recreation Area is open daily, except Dec. 25.
PERMITS, FEES & LIMITATIONS	• No entrance fee. • Vehicles are restricted to established roads and parking areas. • Glass containers are not permitted on the river.
ACCESSIBILITY	Some facilities and trails are accessible.
CAMPING & LODGING	Overnight accommodations are available in the Metro-Atlanta area.
FOOD & SUPPLIES	• Sandwiches, snacks and soft drinks are available within the Recreation Area. • Food and supplies are available in the nearby communities.
FIRST AID/ HOSPITAL	• First aid is available in the Recreation Area. • Hospitals are located close to most of the Recreation Area units.
GENERAL INFORMATION	• Please respect the river corridor and private property rights. • Only self-contained fires are permitted.

Chickamauga and Chattanooga National Military Park

Fort Oglethorpe, Georgia, and Lookout Mountain, Tennessee

On the fields and hills of Chickamauga and Chattanooga National Military Park, about 60,000 Union troops and 43,000 Confederates clashed during September 1863 in some of the hardest fighting of the Civil War. Visitors today can visit the separate areas and follow the battle that ended in the fall of Chattanooga.

MAILING ADDRESS	Superintendent, Chickamauga and Chattanooga National Military Park, PO Box 2128, Fort Oglethorpe, GA 30742 **Telephone:** 706-866-9241
DIRECTIONS	The Chickamauga Visitor Center is near Fort Oglethorpe on US 27 off of I-75 south of Chattanooga, TN. The Lookout Mountain Visitor Center is at the entrance to Point Park.
VISITOR ACTIVITIES	• Interpretive exhibits, auto tours, living history demonstrations, hiking and horseback riding. • A 26-minute multi-media presentation on the Battle of Chickamauga is available at Chickamauga Battlefield for $2.25 for adults, and $1 for children under 16 and seniors. • Facilities include park-

ing and restrooms at the Visitor Center, a museum and hiking trails. • The Park is open 24 hours a day, except for the Lookout Mountain Unit, which is closed at night. The Park is closed Dec. 25. Cravens House is closed from Dec. 1 to March 1.

PERMITS, FEES & LIMITATIONS

• The admission fee for Cravens House in the Lookout Mountain Unit is $2 per person. • No overnight parking is allowed.

ACCESSIBILITY

Chickamauga and Lookout Mountain visitor centers are accessible. There are designated parking spaces.

CAMPING & LODGING

Overnight accommodations are available in Fort Oglethorpe and Chattanooga.

FOOD & SUPPLIES

Food and supplies are available in Fort Oglethorpe and Chattanooga.

FIRST AID/ HOSPITAL

• First aid is available at Chickamauga and Point Park visitor centers.
• The nearest hospital is in Fort Oglethorpe several blocks from the Chickamauga Visitor Center.

Cumberland Island National Seashore

St. Marys, Georgia

Quiet forests, the gentle splash of water in salt marshes and the courting bellow of the alligator all are a part of Cumberland Island National Seashore, a complex ecological system of animal and plant communities on Georgia's largest and southernmost barrier island.

MAILING ADDRESS

Superintendent, Cumberland Island National Seashore, PO Box 806, St. Marys, GA 31558 **Telephone:** 912-882-4338

VISITOR ACTIVITIES

• Hiking, beachcombing, guided and self-guided tours, naturalist programs, fishing, swimming and backpacking.

PERMITS, FEES & LIMITATIONS

• No entrance fee. • Reservations are required for boat trips. • Fees for roundtrip ferry tickets are $10.07 for adults, $5.99 for children 12 and under and $7.95 for seniors 65 and older (includes tax).

ACCESSIBILITY

Restrooms are accessible. Assistance is needed to board boats.

CAMPING & LODGING

• Hand-carried tent camping only. Reservations are required. There is a 7-day camping limit. • Developed campground has picnic tables, food storage bins, grills, restrooms and showers. • Backcountry sites have no facilities other than drinking water.

FOOD & SUPPLIES

Food and supplies are available in St. Marys.

FIRST AID/ HOSPITAL

• Rangers have first aid and EMT training. • The nearest hospital is in St. Marys. • Medical helicopters have a 30-minute response time.

GENERAL INFORMATION

• Supplies should be purchased before leaving the mainland. • Preventing tick bites will also prevent Lyme Disease.

Fort Frederica National Monument

St. Simons Island, Georgia

Fort Frederica's ruins are a reminder of the struggle for empire between Spain and Great Britain. During this period, James Edward Oglethorpe founded the Georgia colony and built Fort Frederica on St. Simons Island where it flourished in the 1740s.

MAILING ADDRESS

Superintendent, Fort Frederica National Monument, Rt. 9, Box 286-C, St. Simons Island, GA 31522 **Telephone:** 912-638-3639

DIRECTIONS

Take the Brunswick-St. Simons (F.J. Torras) toll causeway that connects US 17 at Brunswick. The Monument is 12 miles (19.3 km) from Brunswick, GA, on St. Simons Island.

VISITOR ACTIVITIES

• Archaeological site includes interpretive exhibits and films, walking tours, taped walking tours and living history demonstrations during summer weekends. • A sales center offers books on the period and a wide variety of colonial reproductions. • The Monument is open daily from 8 a.m. to 5 p.m., except Dec. 25. The Visitor Center is open from 9 a.m. to 5 p.m., daily. Hours may be extended in the summer. Contact the Monument for more information.

PERMITS, FEES & LIMITATIONS

The entrance fee is $4 per vehicle and $2 per person for those entering on bicycle, bus or on foot.

ACCESSIBILITY

The Visitor Center, parking spaces, restrooms and theater are accessible. A wheelchair with wide tires for use on the grounds is available. A touch computer with open captioned film is available.

CAMPING & LODGING

• The closest campground is on Jekyll Island. • Many accommodations are available on St. Simons Island and the adjacent Sea Island.

FOOD & SUPPLIES

There are restaurants, grocery stores, hardware stores and clothing shops as well as convenience stores in St. Simons Island.

FIRST AID/ HOSPITAL

• First aid is available within the Monument. • A county emergency paramedic squad is nearby. • A full service hospital is located in Brunswick.

GENERAL INFORMATION

• Please do not walk on or touch the ruins. They are old, fragile and easily destroyed. • The water is deep and the banks are slippery. • For your safety - Do not take shelter under trees during high winds and thunderstorms. • Bring insect repellent in the late spring and early fall.

Fort Pulaski National Monument
East of Savannah, Georgia

Fort Pulaski was built on marshy Cockspur Island to guard the river approaches to Savannah. It was part of a coastal fortification system adopted by President James Madison after the War of 1812. Construction required $1 million, 25 million bricks and 18 years to complete. The fort was conquered during the Civil War before it could be occupied by United States troops.

MAILING ADDRESS
Fort Pulaski National Monument, PO Box 30757, Savannah, GA 31410-0757 **Telephone:** 912-786-5787

DIRECTIONS
The Fort is located on US Highway 80, 15 miles (24.1 km) east of Savannah, GA.

VISITOR ACTIVITIES
• The Monument encompasses more than 5,000 acres. Ranger talks and demonstrations are conducted on weekends throughout the year and daily during the summer. • Visitor activities include a museum and audiovisual program located in the Visitor Center, self-guided tours, picnicking, bird watching, fishing and a one-quarter mile (.4 km) marked nature trail. Other trails allow further exploration of the island. • The Monument is open daily from 8:30 a.m. to 5:15 p.m., except Dec. 25. Hours may be extended in the summer.

PERMITS, FEES & LIMITATIONS
There is an **entrance fee** of $2 per person with a maximum of $4 per family. Children ages 16 and younger and adults 62 and older are admitted free.

ACCESSIBILITY
Most facilities are accessible. Please call for details.

CAMPING & LODGING
Overnight accommodations are available in the nearby communities of Tybee Island and Savannah.

FOOD & SUPPLIES
Food and supplies are available in Tybee Island and Savannah.

FIRST AID/ HOSPITAL
• Basic first aid is available in the Monument. • The closest hospitals, Memorial Medical Center and Candler General, are in Savannah, 20 miles (32.2 km).

GENERAL INFORMATION
• The Fort was built for war. Stay off the mounds and top walls. Don't run on the terreplein (upper level). • Mosquitoes, horseflies and gnats are present. Use a repellent and wear protective clothing. • Watch your step in the Fort and stay on the trails. • Poisonous snakes, alligators and other animals are wild and protected.

Jimmy Carter National Historic Site

Plains, Georgia

Jimmy Carter National Historic Site includes President Carter's residence, boyhood home and high school. The Site exemplifies the rural southern culture of Plains, GA, which revolves around farming, church and school, which largely influenced the 39th President.

MAILING ADDRESS

Superintendent, Jimmy Carter National Historic Site, c/o Route 1, Box 800, Andersonville, GA 31711 **Telephone:** 912-924-0343

DIRECTIONS

The Site is 10 miles (16.1 km) west of Americus, GA, on US 280 in the town of Plains. Interstate access is the I-75 exit onto US 280 at Cordele, GA, or the I-85 exit onto US 280 at Columbus, GA.

VISITOR ACTIVITIES

• Driving tape tour, walking and self-guided tours and picnicking.
• Facilities include a Visitor Center, the Boyhood Home, the Carter Home (homes are closed to the public) and restrooms. • The Site is open daily from 9 a.m. to 5 p.m., except Dec. 25.

PERMITS, FEES & LIMITATIONS

No entrance fee.

CAMPING & LODGING

• There is a bed and breakfast in Plains and in Americus. • Camping is available nearby.

FOOD & SUPPLIES

• There are restaurants and a small grocery store in Plains. • Food and supplies are also available in Americus.

FIRST AID/ HOSPITAL

• First aid is available at the Railroad Depot in the Site. • The nearest hospital is in Americus.

Kennesaw Mountain National Battlefield Park

Kennesaw, Georgia

Kennesaw Mountain National Battlefield Park was established to commemorate Gen. William T. Sherman's 1864 Atlanta Campaign. It is one of the sites where Sherman's Union troops fought the Confederates under Gen. Joseph E. Johnston in the battles that led to the fall of Atlanta and the devastating March to the Sea.

MAILING ADDRESS

Superintendent, Kennesaw Mountain National Battlefield Park, 900 Kennesaw Mountain Drive, Kennesaw, GA 30144-4854 **Telephone:** 404-427-4686

DIRECTIONS

The Park is 3 miles (4.8 km) north of Marietta, GA. Take exit 116 off of I-75 and follow the signs for 4 miles (6.4 km) to the Park.

Georgia

VISITOR ACTIVITIES

• Exhibits and audiovisual programs, brochures including some foreign language versions available at the Visitor Center. • Interpretive programs are available on weekends in the summer. Other activities include walking and self-guided auto tours, hiking and picnicking. • The Park is open daily from 8:30 a.m. to 5 p.m., except Dec. 25. • For further information, call the Park.

PERMITS, FEES & LIMITATIONS

• There are no fees, but donations are appreciated. • All vehicles, including bicycles, are restricted to designated roads.

ACCESSIBILITY

Accessible features include a short trail to Cheatham Hill and a captioned slide program which is available upon request.

CAMPING & LODGING

Accommodations are available in Marietta, Kennesaw and Atlanta.

FOOD & SUPPLIES

Food and supplies are available in Marietta, Kennesaw and Atlanta.

FIRST AID/ HOSPITAL

• Minimal first aid is available in the Park. • A hospital is located in Marietta.

GENERAL INFORMATION

The weather is usually moderate year-round. Daytime temperatures are usually in the 40°F range in winter and 90°F range in summer.

Martin Luther King, Jr. National Historic Site

Atlanta, Georgia

Martin Luther King, Jr., National Historic Site preserves the birthplace and boyhood surroundings of the nation's foremost civil rights leader. The Site provides a feel for the close-knit community nick-named "Sweet Auburn."

MAILING ADDRESS

Martin Luther King, Jr. National Historic Site, 526 Auburn Ave., NE, Atlanta, GA 30312 **Telephone:** 404-331-5190

DIRECTIONS

On southbound I-75/85, exit at Butler Street. On northbound I-75/85, exit at Edgewood/Auburn Avenue. Turn east on Auburn Avenue and proceed .6 miles (1 km) to the Site.

VISITOR ACTIVITIES

• At present, the Park Service owns 19 historical structures within the Site. Twelve have been restored to their 1930 appearance with plans for restoration for the remaining structures. Several are used for administrative purposes while the rest are rented for residential purposes. • Ranger-guided tours of the Birth Home are conducted every half hour daily except Dec. 25 and Jan. 1. Tours are limited to 15 people on a first-come, first-served basis. The first tour begins at 10 a.m. and the last tour begins at 5 p.m.

• Additional activities are provided on a seasonal basis by the National Park Service and by private organizations at key sites, including Ebenezer Baptist Church, Martin Luther King, Jr. Center for Nonviolent Social Change, Inc., and the African-American Panoramic Experience (APEX).

PERMITS, FEES & LIMITATIONS

No fees.

ACCESSIBILITY

The first floor of the Birth Home is accessible. A photo album shows the second floor. An interpretive video is shown at the Visitor Contact Station and is captioned for the hearing impaired. The Site's official brochure is available in braille and on cassette tape. The King Center and Ebenezer Baptist Church are accessible, including restrooms.

CAMPING & LODGING

Overnight accommodations are available in the surrounding community.

FOOD & SUPPLIES

• Food and supplies are available in the Site along Edgewood and Auburn avenues. • Food and supplies are also available nearby in downtown Atlanta and the Little 5 Points area.

FIRST AID/ HOSPITAL

• First aid is not available within the Site. • The nearest hospital is Georgia Baptist Medical Center, one-half mile (.8 km) north of the Site on Boulevard Avenue.

Ocmulgee National Monument

Macon, Georgia

From Ice-Age hunters to the Creeks of historic times, there is evidence of 10,000 years of human habitation at Ocmulgee National Monument. The site features a distinctive culture of skillful farming people known as Mississippians who lived on the site between AD 900 and 1100.

MAILING ADDRESS

Ocmulgee National Monument, 1207 Emery Hwy., Macon, GA 31201
Telephone: 912-752-8257

DIRECTIONS

The Monument is located on US 80 (Emery Hwy.) on the east edge of Macon. Take exit 4 on I-16, follow US 80, 2 miles (3.2 km) to the Monument entrance.

VISITOR ACTIVITIES

• Museum, self-guiding brochure, walking trails, auto tour, picnic area and fishing. • A 12-minute movie is shown regularly. • Special events are planned throughout the year. A schedule is available. • The Monument is open from 9 a.m. to 5 p.m., daily except Dec. 25 and Jan. 1.

PERMITS, FEES & LIMITATIONS

• No entrance fee. • Park and drive in designated areas only.

Georgia

ACCESSIBILITY

The museum, restrooms, films and water fountains are accessible. Earthlodge is accessible with assistance.

CAMPING & LODGING

Overnight accommodations are available in Macon.

FOOD & SUPPLIES

Food and supplies are available in Macon.

FIRST AID/ HOSPITAL

• First aid is available at the museum. • The nearest hospital is in Macon.

GENERAL INFORMATION

• Spring and fall are the best seasons to visit. Summers are hot and insects are abundant. • Numerous other cultural attractions can be found in Macon and nearby communities.

Hawaii

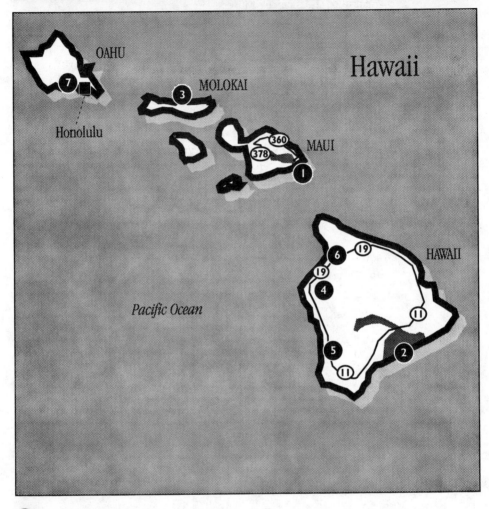

OAHU

Hawaii

MOLOKAI

Honolulu

MAUI

Pacific Ocean

HAWAII

1. Haleakala National Park
2. Hawaii Volcanoes National Park
3. Kalaupapa National Historic Site
4. Kaloko-Honokohau National Historical Park
5. Pu'uhonua o Honaunau National Historical Park
6. Puukohola Heiau National Historic Site
7. U.S.S. Arizona Memorial

Haleakala National Park

Makawao, Maui, Hawaii

Haleakala National Park includes Haleakala Crater, now a cool, cone-studded remnant of a once-active volcano, and the Kipahulu coastal area, a lush, green section of the park featuring a chain of unusually placid pools connected by a waterfall or cascade.

MAILING ADDRESS

Haleakala National Park, PO Box 369, Makawao, HI 96768 **Telephone:** 808-572-9306

DIRECTIONS

The Park extends from the 10,023-foot (3,055 m) summit of Mt. Haleakala down the southeast flank to the Kipahulu coast near Hana. These two sections of the Park are not directly connected by road, but are accessible from the town of Kahului. To reach the **summit area** from Kahului, take the Hana Highway (#36) to Haleakala Highway (#37). Turn right at this juncture and continue, traveling through the town of Pukalani to the Kula Highway junction. Veer left onto Haleakala Highway (#377) and continue onto Haleakala Road (#378). Veer left at this juncture onto 378, which leads directly into the Park. Driving time to the summit is about 1 1/2 hours. To reach the **Kipahulu (coastal) area** from Kahului, take the Hana Highway (#36/360/31) and continue through the town of Paia (the last town to purchase supplies before Hana). Continue from the town of Hana to the Kipahulu Ranger Station. It is 64 miles (103.2 km) from Kahului to Hana and 10 miles (16.1 km) from Hana to Kipahulu. Allow 3 to 4 hours travel time due to the narrow and windy road.

VISITOR ACTIVITIES

• Summit area: interpretive talks, guided hikes, exhibits, wilderness hiking, car-access nature trails, picnicking, bird watching, and sunrise and sunset viewing. Facilities include a nature trail at Hosmer's Grove, restrooms and bookstore at Headquarters and the Haleakala Visitor Center on the rim.
• Coastal area: interpretive talks, guided hikes, cultural demonstrations (see Ranger Station bulletin board), exhibits, hiking, picnicking, swimming and archaeological sites. Facilities include the Ranger Station, a bookstore and restrooms. • The Park is always open. • The Headquarters building is open daily from 7:30 a.m. to 4 p.m. The Haleakala Visitor Center is open from sunrise to 3 p.m. The Ranger Station is open from 9 a.m. to 5 p.m., daily.

PERMITS, FEES & LIMITATIONS

• The entrance fee is $4 per vehicle or $2 per person for the summit area. There is no entrance fee for the coastal area. • Hiking and horseback riding only on wilderness trails in the summit area. Horses and horseback riding are not allowed in the coastal area. • No pets or open fires are permitted in wilderness area or on trails in the summit area. Pets must be leashed at all times in the coastal area. • Free permits for wilderness camping in the summit area are available at Headquarters. No permit needed in the coastal area. • No water is available in the coastal area of the Park.

Hawaii

ACCESSIBILITY

There are accessible restrooms at Hosmer Grove, Headquarters and the Visitor Center in the summit area, and at the Ranger Station and campground in the coastal area. There is parking and ramp access at Headquarters, the Visitor Center and the Summit building in the summit area. There is ramp access at the Ranger Station.

CAMPING & LODGING

• In the summit area, wilderness camping at 2 locations is limited to 25 people total, 12 people per group. All campground space and permits are available from Headquarters from 7:30 a.m. to 3 p.m on a first-come, first-served basis on the day of use. There is a 3-night limit per month. There is car-access camping at Hosmer Grove with a 3-night limit per month with no fee or permit required. Space is limited at Hosmer Grove to 50 people, 12 people per group. • Kipahulu Campground in the coastal area is limited to 100 people, 12 people per group. Tent spaces are available on a first-come, first-served basis on the day of use. There is a 3-night limit with no fee or permit required. Camping is allowed in the designated campground only. • Wilderness cabins are available in the summit area by reservation only. There is a lottery for cabin use 3 months prior to the month of intended stay. There is a fee for cabin use and a 3-night limit per month. For more information and to enter the lottery, write the Park, Attn: Cabins or call 808-572-9177 for recorded information. • There is no commercial lodging within the Park.

FOOD & SUPPLIES

The last towns to purchase supplies are Pukalani on the way to the summit, 17 miles (27.4 km); and Hana on the way to the coast, 10 miles (16.1 km).

FIRST AID/ HOSPITAL

• First aid is available in the Park. • The nearest hospital to the summit area is Maui Memorial Hospital and Kaiser Clinic in Kahului, 32 miles (51.6 km). Medical facilities closest to the coastal area include the Hana medical clinic, 10 miles (16.1 km).

GENERAL INFORMATION

• Viewing of and from the summit is typically clearer in the morning. Temperatures average 30 degrees colder than at sea level and are often below freezing in the winter. • All visitors to the summit area should be prepared for rain, wind, strong sunlight and cold temperatures. • Oxygen concentrations are low at the summit. Pregnant women and visitors with heart and respiratory conditions should consider this. • Hazardous road conditions may be encountered. Visitors can consult a recorded message at 808-572-7749. • Visitors to the Kipahulu section should be prepared for periodic rainy conditions at the coast as well as strong sunlight. • Trails can be muddy; stream swimming is treacherous. Visitors can consult a recorded message at 808-248-7375.

Hawaii

Hawaii Volcanoes National Park

Hawaii Volcanoes National Park, Hawaii   See Climatable No. 18

Hawaii Volcanoes National Park was created primarily to preserve the natural setting of Mauna Loa and Kilauea volcanic mountains. The Park contains lush rain forests, raw craters, and great areas devastated by lava flows and pumice from eruptions in the distant and recent past.

MAILING ADDRESS

Superintendent, Hawaii Volcanoes National Park, PO Box 52, Hawaii Volcanoes National Park, HI 96718 **Telephone: 808-967-7311**

DIRECTIONS

The Park is 30 miles (48 km) southwest of Hilo or 95 miles (153 km) southeast of Kailua-Kona off of Highway 11.

VISITOR ACTIVITIES

• Kilauea Visitor Center is open daily from **7:45 a.m. to 5 p.m.**, and offers an eruption movie, displays and a bookstore. • The Thomas A. Jaggar Museum, open daily from **8:30 a.m. to 5 p.m.**, has geological displays and a bookstore. • The Park is always open. • Car touring, hiking, backpacking, picnicking and bird watching. • Check at the Visitor Center for Ranger-guided programs and current volcanic activity (pre-recorded 24-hour eruption message: 808-967-7977).

PERMITS, FEES & LIMITATIONS

• The **entrance fee** is $5 per vehicle or $3 per person. Frequent visitors may purchase an annual pass for $15. • No off-road driving or parking. • No bicycles or dogs permitted on the trails or in the backcountry. • No wood collecting or open fires allowed. • Permits are required for all overnight backcountry trips and are available at the Visitor Center.

ACCESSIBILITY

The Visitor Center, Jaggar Museum, Volcano House Hotel and Volcano Art Center are accessible. Pullouts along Crater Rim Drive and Chain of Craters Road offer panoramic views and accessible paths. Manakani Palo Campground has accessible restrooms and moderately accessible camp sites. Check at the Visitor Center for accessible Ranger-guided programs.

CAMPING & LODGING

• Overnight camping is on a first-come, first-served basis at the Namakani Palo and Kipuka Nene campgrounds. • The Volcano House operates a hotel on the rim of Kilauea caldera, and there are cabins at Manakani Palo campground. Reservations are recommended. Write The Volcano House, PO Box 51, Hawaii Volcanoes National Park, HI, 96718, or call 808-967-7321.
• Bed and breakfast accommodations are located in the town of Volcano, 2 miles (3.2 km). • Hotels are available in the towns of Hilo, 30 miles (48.3 km), and Kailua-Kona, 95 miles (153.2 km).

FOOD & SUPPLIES

• There is a restaurant and snack shop at The Volcano House Hotel.
• A diner, groceries and supplies are available in Volcano. • Supermarkets, variety stores and equipment rentals are available in Hilo.

FIRST AID/ HOSPITAL

• First aid is available at the Visitor Center. • The nearest hospital is in Hilo.

GENERAL INFORMATION

• Volcanic fumes present in some areas of the Park may be a health hazard for people with heart or breathing problems, infants, young children and pregnant women. • Be prepared for unpredictable weather. • When hiking, stay on the marked trails, avoid cliffs, earthcracks and steam vents. Carry water and wear sturdy shoes, long pants, sunscreen and a hat. • Volcanic activity creates exceptional conditions and may necessitate the emergency closure of roads and trails. Heed the instructions of Rangers on duty and obey all closure signs.

Kalaupapa National Historical Park

Molokai, Hawaii

Kalaupapa National Historical Park is dedicated to the preservation of the history of Kalaupapa Settlement where nearly 8,000 people suffering from leprosy, a disease that has been shrouded in fear and ignorance for centuries, have been treated by legendary figures since 1866.

MAILING ADDRESS

Kalaupapa National Historical Park, Kalaupapa, HI 96742

DIRECTIONS

Kalaupapa is accessible by plane or by foot. There are no roads connecting Kalaupapa with the rest of Molokai. For information on current airfares to Kalaupapa, visitors need to contact 1 of 2 tour companies owned and operated by residents.

VISITOR ACTIVITIES

• Visitors may hike the Pali trail to Kalaupapa in 1 to 1 1/2 hours. • Guided tours over rough roads of the 10,726-acre Park are available at the Settlement. • Those who do not have time to visit the Settlement can find an excellent view of the peninsula at Palaau State Park.

PERMITS, FEES & LIMITATIONS

A permit is required to enter the settlement, and all visitors must be 16 or older. These regulations are enforced to protect the privacy and lifestyle of the residents. Permits must be obtained in advance from the Department of Health. This may be done through 1 of the 2 tour companies at Kalaupapa. For information on permits and tours, contact Damien Tours or Ike's Scenic Tours, c/o Kalaupapa Settlement, Kalaupapa, HI, 96742.

CAMPING & LODGING

Overnight stays are limited to guests of residents.

FOOD & SUPPLIES

• There are no restaurants or stores within the Park. • All supplies for the community are delivered by small plane on one of the daily commuter air carriers, on mule back down the Pali trail, or on 1 of 2 barges a year that arrive in July and September.

Kaloko-Honokohau National Historical Park

Honaunau, Hawaii

Kaloko-Honokohau National Historical Park was the site of important Hawaiian settlements before European explorers arrived. The Park includes coastal areas, 3 large fishponds, a house site and other archaeological remnants to help preserve the native culture of Hawaii.

MAILING ADDRESS
Kaloko-Honokohau National Historical Park, PO Box 129, Honaunau, HI 96726

DIRECTIONS
The Park is on the Kona coast of the Island of Hawaii. Printed fact sheets about the Park are available from the Pacific Area Office, National Park Service, 300 Ala Moana Blvd., Honolulu, HI, 96850. The Park is 4 miles (6.4 km) south of Keahole Airport and 2 miles (3.2 km) north of Kailua-Kona on Highway 11. There is .8 miles (.128 km) of unimproved entrance road.

VISITOR ACTIVITIES
• The Park contains a great number of Hawaiian archaeological sites and features. According to legend, the first Hawaiian king, Kamehameha I, is buried somewhere in the Park. • The Park also provides an important habitat for 3 endangered species of Hawaiian water birds. • The Park is open from 8 a.m. to 3:30 p.m., daily. The office is open from 7:30 a.m. to 4 p.m. Monday through Friday.

ACCESSIBILITY
All Park restrooms are accessible.

Pu'uhonua o Honaunau National Historical Park

Honaunau, Kona, Hawaii

Pu'uhonua o Honaunau, meaning the place of refuge of Honaunau, was a sanctuary that provided a second chance for people who had broken sacred laws in ancient Hawaii, noncombatants during battles, defeated warriors and others who needed absolution or a safe haven before returning to everyday life.

MAILING ADDRESS
Superintendent, Pu'uhonua o Honaunau National Historical Park, PO Box 129, Honaunau, Kona, HI 96726 **Telephone: 808-328-2326**

DIRECTIONS
The Park is 30 miles (48.3 km) south of Keahole Airport on HI 160. Take HI 19 to Kailua, then HI 11 to Honaunau, then HI 160 to the Park.

VISITOR ACTIVITIES
• Picnicking, snorkeling, swimming, walking tours, craft demonstrations, interpretive exhibits, hiking, and fishing. • Facilities include restrooms and parking at the Visitor Center and a picnic area. • The Park is open daily from 6 a.m. to midnight.

PERMITS, FEES & LIMITATIONS	• Permits are required for picnicking by groups of more than 30 people. • Vehicles are restricted to designated roads.
ACCESSIBILITY	A wheelchair is available on loan. Ask at the Visitor Center for the accessible route. Restrooms are accessible. Sign language capability among staff.
CAMPING & LODGING	Overnight accommodations are available in Captain Cook, HI, 10 miles (16.1 km).
FOOD & SUPPLIES	• Limited supplies are available on HI 11. • Grocery stores are in Captain Cook.
FIRST AID/ HOSPITAL	• First aid is available in the Park. • The nearest hospital is in Kona, 12 miles (19.3 km).
GENERAL INFORMATION	• For your safety - Be alert for unexpected high waves. Do not climb on the stone walls or on the framework of the house models. If you leave the trail, watch for falling coconuts and coconut fronds. Do not climb the coconut trees. • Visitors to the area can also see Pu'ukohola Heiau National Historic Site (see listing in this book).

Pu'ukohola Heiau National Historic Site

Kawaihae, Hawaii

High on a hill above the Pacific Ocean on the island of Hawaii sits Pu'ukohola Heiau, the last major religious structure of the ancient Hawaiian culture built in the islands by Kamehameha I in 1790-91 and dedicated to his family war god Ku-kaili-moku.

MAILING ADDRESS	Superintendent, Pu'ukohola Heiau National Historic Site, PO Box 44340, Kawaihae, HI 96743 **Telephone:** 808-882-7218
DIRECTIONS	The Park is on the northwestern shore of the Island of Hawaii in the district of south Kohala. The access road to the Visitor Center is off of Rt. 270, one-quarter mile (.4 km) north of the Rt. 270 and Hwy. 19 intersection.
VISITOR ACTIVITIES	• Hiking, guided and self-guided tours, exhibits and interpretive talks are provided at the Visitor Center. • Hawaiian arts and crafts demonstrations are available 1 day a week from January to September. • Special Hawaiian programs are presented to the public throughout the year. • An annual Hawaiian Cultural Festival in August commemorates the establishment of the Site. • The Visitor Center is open from **7:30 a.m. to 4 p.m.**
PERMITS, FEES & LIMITATIONS	• **No entrance fee.** • There is a $1 per person charge for any non-educational groups who request guided tours.
ACCESSIBILITY	The Visitor Center and restrooms are accessible. Most of the trails are not accessible. Alternate viewing areas of major temple sites are provided at the Visitor Center.

Hawaii

CAMPING & LODGING
- Camping, swimming and picnicking are allowed at nearby Samuel Spencer County Beach Park. • Lodging is available nearby in Waimea, 10 miles (16.1 km); Kohala Coast, 7 miles (11.2 km); or Kailua-Kona, 30 miles (48.3 km).

FOOD & SUPPLIES
- Stores and small restaurants are available in Kawaihae, 1 mile (1.6 km) north of the Park. • Major shopping centers and restaurants are located in Waimea, Kohala Coast and Kailua-Kona.

FIRST AID/ HOSPITAL
- The nearest hospital is in Honokaa, 29 miles (46.7 km). • Lucy Henriques Medical Center is in Waimea, 12 miles (19.3 km).

GENERAL INFORMATION
- For your safety - Stay on the designated trails and do not climb on the walls of the temple. • The trail from the Visitor Center is long, hot and rugged. If you are not physically fit and attired properly, do not attempt the hike. You may view the area from Spencer County Beach Park. • To prevent grass fires, do not smoke. • The beach in front of the Site is unsuitable for swimming due to silt and coral collections.

U.S.S. Arizona Memorial

Pearl Harbor, Hawaii

The U.S.S. Arizona Memorial grew out of wartime desire to establish a memorial to honor those who died in the attack on Pearl Harbor on Dec. 7, 1941. It is the final resting place for many of the ship's 1,177 crewmen who lost their lives that day.

MAILING ADDRESS
Superintendent, USS Arizona Memorial, 1 Arizona Memorial Place, Honolulu, HI 96818-3145 **Telephone: 808-422-2771**

DIRECTIONS
The Memorial is a one-half hour drive from Waikiki. Take H-1 west past the airport to the "Arizona Memorial/Stadium" Exit. One hour by bus No. 20 from Waikiki.

VISITOR ACTIVITIES
- Free tours including Ranger talk, a 23-minute film, and shuttle boat to and from the Memorial. • Periodic Pearl Harbor survivor talks. • Museum and exhibits. • The Visitor Center is open daily from 7:30 a.m. to 5 p.m., except Thanksgiving, Dec. 25 and Jan. 1. • Boat tours to the Memorial are conducted from 8 a.m. to 3 p.m.

PERMITS, FEES & LIMITATIONS
- No entrance fee. • Limited parking available.

ACCESSIBILITY
Visitor Center, restrooms, boats and the Memorial are accessible. A film script is available for the hearing impaired.

CAMPING & LODGING
There are hotels at the airport and in Waikiki.

Hawaii

FOOD & SUPPLIES	Restaurants are nearby.
FIRST AID/ HOSPITAL	• First aid is available in the Memorial. • There is a hospital nearby.
GENERAL INFORMATION	The U.S.S. Bowfin and World War II Fleet Submarine Museum is adjacent to the Memorial.

Idaho

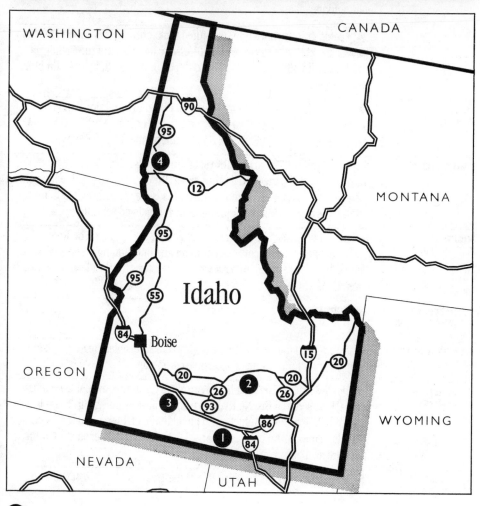

1 City of Rocks National Reserve

2 Craters of the Moon National Monument

3 Hagerman Fossil Beds National
   Monument

4 Nez Perce National Historical Park

City of Rocks National Reserve

Almo, Idaho

Scenic granite spires and sculptured rock formations dominate the landscape at City of Rocks National Reserve. Remnants of the California Trail are still visible, and recreational opportunities include rock climbing and camping.

MAILING ADDRESS
Manager, City of Rocks National Reserve, PO Box 169, Almo, ID 83312 Telephone: 208-824-5519 *or* Superintendent, National Park Service, 963 Blue Lakes Blvd., Twin Falls, ID 83301 Telephone: 208-733-8398

DIRECTIONS
Located 2 miles (3.2 km) southwest of Almo or 48 miles (77.4 km) south of Burley. Off of I-84, the road to Almo from Burley is paved. Roads within the Reserve are gravel, but are maintained. Roads are typically closed in midwinter due to snow. Please inquire locally for updated conditions.

VISITOR ACTIVITIES
• The Visitor Center is open daily from 8 a.m. to 5 p.m. • The Reserve includes hiking, technical rock climbing and outstanding scenery. • Write for a schedule of special events such as the Historic Trail Ride and the Dutch Oven Cook-Off.

PERMITS, FEES & LIMITATIONS
No entrance fee.

ACCESSIBILITY
Restrooms and the Visitor Center at Almo are accessible. Please check at the Visitor Center for a listing of accessible camp sites.

CAMPING & LODGING
• The Reserve has 100 established primitive camp sites available on a first-come, first-served basis. No RV hookups, facilities or dumping. There is a $5 camping fee per night/vehicle with an additional $4 per night for a second vehicle. A maximum of 8 people and 2 vehicles allowed per site. • Group sites are available for $20 per night.

FOOD & SUPPLIES
Basic supplies and gas are available at the Tracy Store and Post Office in Almo.

FIRST AID/ HOSPITAL
• A quick response unit is located in Almo. • The nearest hospital is in Burley, 50 miles (80.6 km). There is a 911 system.

GENERAL INFORMATION
• Limited water is available at the Reserve, fire wood is available for a fee at the Visitor Center in Almo. It is recommended that visitors bring their own wood. • Please stop by the Visitor Center for updated conditions on regulations, roads and weather.

Craters of the Moon National Monument
Southern Idaho

The fissure vents, volcanic cones and lava flows of the Great Rift Zone began erupting about 15,000 years ago and ceased 2,000 years ago. Geologists, however, predict that the landscape found at Craters of the Moon National Monument will erupt again.

MAILING ADDRESS
Superintendent, Craters of the Moon National Monument, PO Box 29, Arco, ID 83213 Telephone: 208-527-3257

DIRECTIONS
The Monument is 18 miles (29 km) southwest of Arco, ID, off of Hwys. 20/26/93.

VISITOR ACTIVITIES
• Hiking, picnicking, wildlife and bird watching, photography, interpretive talks and exhibits. • Groomed cross-country ski trails in the winter. • Visitor facilities include a museum, bookstore, restrooms and public telephones. • The Visitor Center is open from 8 a.m. to 6 p.m. in the summer and 8 a.m. to 4:30 p.m. the remainder of the year except for winter holidays.

PERMITS, FEES & LIMITATIONS
• The entrance fee is $4 per vehicle or $2 per person. • Backcountry permits are available. • No off-road driving is allowed. • Some areas are closed to the public.

ACCESSIBILITY
The Visitor Center and restrooms are accessible. There is a one-half mile (.8 km) trail at Devil's Orchard.

CAMPING & LODGING
• Camp sites are available for $8 per night. Individual camp sites can not be reserved. • Other overnight accommodations are available in Arco, 18 miles (29 km) outside the Monument.

FOOD & SUPPLIES
Food and supplies are available in Arco.

FIRST AID/ HOSPITAL
A hospital is located in Arco.

GENERAL INFORMATION
The Loop Drive is closed from November to April.

Hagerman Fossil Beds National Monument
Hagerman, Idaho

The carving action of the Snake River has exposed extraordinary fossils embedded in the banks of the river. Plans are underway to provide for continuing paleontological research and also for the display and interpretation of fossil specimens collected at the Monument.

MAILING ADDRESS
Hagerman Fossil Beds National Monument, PO Box 570, Hagerman, ID 83332 **Telephone:** 208-837-4793

DIRECTIONS
The Monument is 9 miles (14.5 km) south of Bliss, ID, on US 30.

VISITOR ACTIVITIES
• Scheduled tours, and exhibits. • Fishing with boats on the adjacent Lower Salmon Falls Reservoir and rafting on the Snake River.

PERMITS, FEES & LIMITATIONS
No fees.

ACCESSIBILITY
Interpretation waysides and overlooks are scheduled to be completed in 1994.

CAMPING & LODGING
There are local commercial campgrounds.

FOOD & SUPPLIES
Food and supplies are available in Hagerman.

FIRST AID/ HOSPITAL
The nearest hospitals are in Gooding, Jerome and Twin Falls.

Nez Perce National Historical Park

Spalding, Idaho

Today, 24 sites across the Idaho countryside commemorate the legends and history of the Nez Perce, explorers, fur traders, missionaries, soldiers, settlers and others who traveled and lived on this land.

MAILING ADDRESS
Superintendent, Nez Perce National Historical Park, PO Box 93, Spalding, ID 83551 **Telephone:** 208-843-2261

DIRECTIONS
The Visitor Center is in Spalding, 11 miles (17.7 km) east of Lewiston on Hwy. 95.

VISITOR ACTIVITIES
• Interpretive exhibits, a 23-minute movie, cultural demonstrations (summer only), Ranger programs (summer only), self-guiding walks, picnicking and fishing in Clearwater River adjacent to the Park. • The Visitor Center is open daily, except Thanksgiving, Dec. 25 and Jan. 1, from 8 a.m. to 4:30 p.m. in the off-season and 8 a.m. to 7 p.m. in the summer.

PERMITS, FEES & LIMITATIONS
• No entrance fee. • An Idaho fishing license is required.

ACCESSIBILITY
The restrooms and Visitor Center are accessible. The movie is shown in captioned video upon request. The TDD number is 208-843-2010.

CAMPING & LODGING
• Camping is available in Clearwater and Nez Perce national forests, 3 state parks and private campgrounds. • Other overnight accommodations are

available in Lewiston, Orofino, Kamiah and Grangeville, ID, or in Clarkston, WA.

FOOD & SUPPLIES

Food and supplies are available in the nearby communities.

FIRST AID/ HOSPITAL

The nearest hospital is in Lewiston, 12 miles (19.3 km).

Illinois

1 Chicago Portage National Historic Site

2 Illinois and Michigan Canal National Heritage Corridor

3 Lincoln Home National Historic Site

Chicago Portage National Historic Site

Lyons, Illinois

Affiliated area. A portion of the portage between the Great Lakes and the Mississippi, discovered by French explorers Jacques Marquette and Louis Joliet, is preserved by Chicago Portage National Historic Site. The portage was the crucial link between the Great Lakes and the continental interior.

MAILING ADDRESS	Director, Chicago Portage National Historic Site, c/o Forest Preserve District of Cook County, 536 N. Harlem Ave., River Forest, IL 60305 **Telephone:** 708-771-1335
DIRECTIONS	The Site is on the west side of Harlem Avenue (IL 43) one-half mile (.8 km) north of the Stevenson Expressway (I-55).
VISITOR ACTIVITIES	• Interpretive story board, monument (statue) of Marquette and Joliet, picnicking and occasional guided interpretive walks. Call for more information. • The Site is open from 9 a.m. to sunset and is closed in the winter.
PERMITS, FEES & LIMITATIONS	• No fees. • Vehicles are restricted to the parking area.
ACCESSIBILITY	The walkway around the monument is accessible.
CAMPING & LODGING	• There is no camping in the immediate area. • Lodging is available in the nearby communities of Lyons, Chicago, etc.
FOOD & SUPPLIES	Food and supplies are available in nearby communities.
FIRST AID/ HOSPITAL	The nearest hospital is in La Grange, IL, 4 miles (6.4 km) west.

Illinois & Michigan Canal National Heritage Corridor

Northeastern Illinois

Affiliated area. Completed in 1848, this canal and the railroads that paralleled it were instrumental in opening up the west and in the growth of Chicago. Today, it is the core of a system of parks and recreational activities including numerous museums and historical sites that bring the canal's rich heritage to life.

MAILING ADDRESS	Executive Director, I&M Canal National Heritage Corridor, 15701 S. Independence Blvd., Lockport, IL 60441 **Telephone:** 815-740-2047
DIRECTIONS	All major Corridor visitor attractions are accessible via I-55 and I-80. There

are 4 Travelers Information Station transmitters (AM 530) that provide directions to various towns, visitor centers and other facilities.

VISITOR ACTIVITIES

Numerous special events and regularly scheduled interpretive programs are held year-round at the various parks, historical society museums and other visitor attractions throughout the Corridor. Contact the Executive Director for a list of activities.

PERMITS, FEES & LIMITATIONS

There are admission fees for some special events, though most of them are free.

ACCESSIBILITY

Most of the visitor facilities in the Corridor are accessible. A few historic structures are not completely accessible.

CAMPING & LODGING

• Several state and county parks, as well as private concessionaires, offer camping sites all year. • There are numerous motels within the Corridor that are close to major visitor attractions. Contact the Executive Director for more information.

FOOD & SUPPLIES

Food and supplies are easily obtainable in all the communities located within the Corridor.

FIRST AID/ HOSPITAL

The Corridor communities of Chicago, Joliet, Morris, Ottawa and Peru have medical facilities.

Lincoln Home National Historic Site

Springfield, Illinois

This house in Springfield that Abraham Lincoln bought in the spring of 1844 for his wife and son was the only home the Lincolns ever owned. They lived in it for 17 years as Lincoln built his law practice and began a political career that would lead him to the Presidency of the United States.

MAILING ADDRESS

Superintendent, Lincoln Home National Historic Site, 413 South Eighth St., Springfield, IL 62701-1905 **Telephone:** 217-492-4150

DIRECTIONS

The Site is in downtown Springfield. The Visitor Center is at 426 South Seventh St. Public parking is available at the Site or nearby.

VISITOR ACTIVITIES

• The Visitor Center offers information services, exhibits, films and special programs as well as restrooms and a gift shop. • Ranger led tours of the Lincoln Home and occasional tours of the historic neighborhood. • The Site is open daily, except Thanksgiving, Dec. 25 and Jan. 1, from **8:30 a.m. to 5 p.m.**, with extended hours spring through fall.

PERMITS, FEES & LIMITATIONS

• **No entrance fee.** • There is a $1.50 per hour fee for on-site parking. • Vehicles are not permitted into the restored 4-block Lincoln Home Neighborhood. • Free tickets, with a specific tour time, are required for admission to the Lincoln Home and are available at the Visitor Center. Waiting times vary depending on the season and time of day.

ACCESSIBILITY

The walkways and Visitor Center are accessible. The first floor of the Lincoln Home is accessible on a conducted tour. Arrangements must be made with a Ranger at the Visitor Center desk.

CAMPING & LODGING

• Lodging is available within downtown Springfield as well as outlying areas. • Camping is available at various locations in the Springfield area.

FOOD & SUPPLIES

There are a number of restaurants in the downtown Springfield area.

FIRST AID/ HOSPITAL

• First aid is available within the Site. • The nearest hospital is 7 blocks north of the Site.

GENERAL INFORMATION

The Site includes a restored 19th century neighborhood, with historic wooden boardwalks that are uneven and slippery when wet. Use care when walking through the neighborhood and climbing the steep stairs of the Lincoln Home.

Indiana

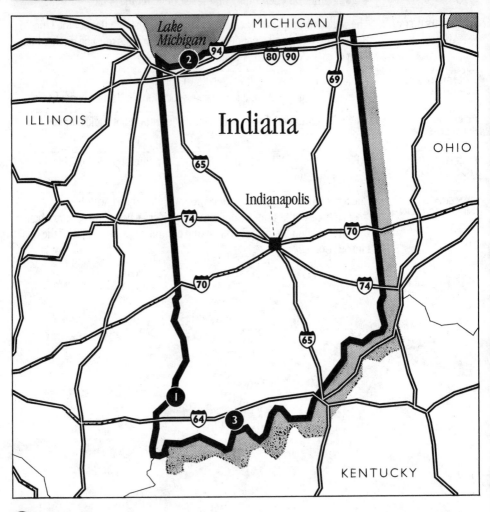

1 George Rogers Clark National Historical Park

2 Indiana Dunes National Lakeshore

3 Lincoln Boyhood National Memorial

Indiana

George Rogers Clark National Historical Park

Vincennes, Indiana

George Rogers Clark, one of the great figures of the American frontier, was an organizer of the Kentucky militia and commander of its defenses during the American Revolution. He was known as a skilled and fearless fighter who, aided at times by the French, added an area as large as the original 13 colonies to the United States.

MAILING ADDRESS	Superintendent, George Rogers Clark National Historical Park, 401 South Second St., Vincennes, IN 47591 **Telephone:** 812-882-1776
DIRECTIONS	Follow US 50 (east and west), which intersects with US 41 (north and south) at Vincennes. Take 6th Street on US 50 or the Willow Street Exit on US 41. The Park entrance is on Second Street.
VISITOR ACTIVITIES	• Interpretive exhibits, film, and living history weapon demonstrations and talks are available in the summer. • Facilities include the Memorial building, a Visitor Center and parking. • The Park is open daily, except Thanksgiving, Dec. 25 and Jan. 1, from 9 a.m. to 5 p.m. • The Park is subject to unscheduled closings in severe winter weather.
PERMITS, FEES & LIMITATIONS	• There is a $2 entrance fee at the Clark Memorial, April through November for persons 17 to 61 years old. • Motorcycles are not permitted on sidewalks.
CAMPING & LODGING	Overnight accommodations are available in Vincennes.
FOOD & SUPPLIES	Food and supplies are available in downtown Vincennes.
FIRST AID/ HOSPITAL	• First aid is available in the Park. • The nearest hospital is in Vincennes on 7th Street.

Indiana Dunes National Lakeshore

Porter, Indiana

Part of the shore and dunes at Lake Michigan have been preserved as a National Lakeshore. Visitors can swim, dune climb, hike and learn about the glacial advances and shrinking shoreline that formed the area.

MAILING ADDRESS	Superintendent, Indiana Dunes National Lakeshore, 1100 N. Mineral Springs Road, Porter, IN 46304 **Telephone:** 219-926-7561
DIRECTIONS	US 12 and 20, and IN 49 pass through the Lakeshore. I-94 and the Indiana Toll Road (I-80 and I-90) pass south of the Lakeshore and connect with roads that lead directly to the Lakeshore. The Dorothy Buell Memorial

Visitor Center is 3 miles (4.8 km) east of IN 49 on US 12 at the Kemil Road intersection.

VISITOR ACTIVITIES

• Swimming, hiking, biking, horseback riding, cross-country skiing, auto tours, photography, fishing, nature walks, interpretive talks, films and programs. • The Maple Sugar Time Festival is in March. The Duneland Harvest Festival is in September. • The Visitor Center is open daily, except Thanksgiving, Dec. 25 and Jan. 1, from 8 a.m. to 5 p.m., and until 6 p.m., in the summer.

PERMITS, FEES & LIMITATIONS

• No entrance fee. • An Indiana fishing license is available locally. • The parking fee at the West Beach area is $2.50 per vehicle. • Hunting and open fires (except in the campground) are prohibited. Grills and portable stoves using charcoal, gas or liquid fuels are permitted.

ACCESSIBILITY

Most visitor facilities, including parking lots, picnic areas, restrooms, fountains, the campground, beaches and some trails are accessible. A sand/snow chair is available for beach access throughout the year at West Beach. Contact the Visitor Center to arrange for its use at other beaches. Telecommunications Devices for the Deaf (TDD) are available at the Visitor Center, the Douglas Environmental Center, Headquarters and the Ranger Station.

CAMPING & LODGING

• Dunewood Campground, at Broadway and US 12, has 79 camp sites (54 conventional drive-in and 25 walk-in). There are no reservations and no hookups. The fees are: $10 per day for conventional sites and $8 per day for walk-in sites from April through October. The fees are reduced by half in the off-season and all year for Golden Age/Golden Access Passport holders. Reservations for camping are accepted at Indiana Dunes State Park in Chesterton, IN, 46304, 219-926-4520. • Lodging is available in Michigan City, 8 miles (12.9 km); Pines, 3 miles (4.8 km); Chesterton, 6 miles (9.6 km); Porter, 6 miles (9.6 km); and Gary, 20 miles (32.2 km).

FOOD & SUPPLIES

• Food concessions are available at the West Beach bathhouse and Mount Baldy in the summer. • Restaurants and grocery stores are located in the nearby communities.

FIRST AID/ HOSPITAL

• First aid stations are at the West Beach bathhouse and the Bailly Ranger Station. • The nearest hospitals are in Michigan City and Gary.

GENERAL INFORMATION

• Private property rights must be respected. • The South Shore Railroad, running between Chicago and South Bend, provides access to several facilities.

Lincoln Boyhood National Memorial
Lincoln City, Indiana

On this southern Indiana farm, Abraham Lincoln spent his youth and early manhood. He worked the land with his father, developed his love of reading and curiosity for knowledge, and sadly, lost his mother, Nancy Hanks Lincoln, when he was 9 years old.

MAILING ADDRESS

Superintendent, Lincoln Boyhood National Memorial, PO Box 1816, Lincoln City, IN 47552 **Telephone:** 812-937-4541

DIRECTIONS

The Memorial is on IN 162, 2 miles (3.2 km) east of Gentryville off of US 231, or 4 miles (6.4 km) south of Dale off of I-64.

VISITOR ACTIVITIES

• The Visitor Center houses memorial halls, a museum and film. • The burial site of Nancy Hanks Lincoln is at the Memorial. • The Lincoln Living Historical Farm has costumed interpretation. • There are walking trails and picnic areas. • The Visitor Center is open daily, except Thanksgiving, Dec. 25 and Jan. 1. Winter hours: 8 a.m. to 5 p.m. Summer hours: 8 a.m. to 6 p.m. • The Farm is open spring through fall from 8 a.m. to 5 p.m.

PERMITS, FEES & LIMITATIONS

• There is a $2 entrance fee with no more than $4 charged per family; no fee for educational groups and visitors younger than 17 or older than 61. • Vehicles are restricted to parking areas and paved roads.

ACCESSIBILITY

The Visitor Center and Farm are accessible. An access guide is available at the Visitor Center information desk.

CAMPING & LODGING

• Camping is available in an adjacent state park. • Lodging is available in nearby Dale and Huntingburg.

FOOD & SUPPLIES

Food and supplies are available in Dale and Santa Claus.

FIRST AID/ HOSPITAL

• First aid is available in the Memorial. • The nearest hospital is in Huntingburg, 15 miles (24.1 km).

GENERAL INFORMATION

• The Memorial is on the Lincoln Heritage Trail, an auto tour route that connects the sites relating to Lincoln's life in Kentucky, Indiana and Illinois. • **For your safety** - Stay on established trails. Beware of insects, poison ivy, snakes and farm animals. • Pets must be on a leash or carried.

Iowa

1 Effigy Mounds National Monument
2 Herbert Hoover National Historic Site

Effigy Mounds National Monument

McGregor, Iowa

Within Effigy Mounds National Monument's borders are 191 known prehistoric Indian burial mounds, 29 in the form of bear and bird effigies and the remainder conical or linear shaped.

MAILING ADDRESS

Superintendent, Effigy Mounds National Monument, Rural Route 1, Box 25 A, Harpers Ferry, IA 52146 **Telephone:** 319-873-3491

DIRECTIONS

The Monument is 3 miles (4.8 km) north of McGregor-Marquette on Hwy. 76.

VISITOR ACTIVITIES

• The Visitor Center contains a museum, interpretive exhibits, an auditorium, audiovisual presentations and a bookstore • There are 6 miles (9.6 km) of self-guiding trails. • Guided walks are offered 4 times daily in season with group tours offered by prior arrangement in the off season. • There are bird watching hikes, moonlight hikes and other special events in season. • The Visitor Center is open from 8 a.m. to 7 p.m., Memorial Day through Labor Day and from 8 a.m. to 5 p.m., the rest of the year.

PERMITS, FEES & LIMITATIONS

• There is a $2 per person **entrance fee** with a $4 maximum for families. No fee is charged for those 16 and younger or 62 and older. • Vehicles are restricted to the parking area.

ACCESSIBILITY

The Visitor Center, museum, auditorium and restrooms are accessible. The trails are steep but are accessible to some.

CAMPING & LODGING

• Camping is widely available within a 10-mile (16.1 km) radius at state and private campgrounds. • Lodging is available in Marquette-McGregor, IA, and Prairie du Chien, WI, 4 miles (6.4 km).

FOOD & SUPPLIES

Food and supplies are available in Marquette-McGregor and Prairie du Chien.

FIRST AID/ HOSPITAL

Medical facilities are available in Prairie du Chien.

GENERAL INFORMATION

• Summers are warm with moderate to high humidity. Winters can be very cold with temperatures to -30°F and snowy. • Summer safety tip - Watch out for stinging insects and poison ivy.

Herbert Hoover National Historic Site

West Branch, Iowa

Herbert Hoover - mining engineer, humanitarian, statesman and 31st President of the United States - was born Aug. 10, 1874, in a simple 2-room cottage in West Branch, IA. The National Historic Site includes the cottage and associated structures, a library/museum and the grave site where he and his wife are buried.

MAILING ADDRESS

Superintendent, Herbert Hoover National Historic Site, PO Box 607, West Branch, IA 52358 **Telephone:** 319-643-2541

DIRECTIONS

West Branch is 10 miles (16.1 km) east of Iowa City on I-80 and 40 miles (64.5 km) west of Davenport on I-80 at exit 254. The Visitor Center is on Parkside Drive at the intersection with Main Street.

VISITOR ACTIVITIES

• Interpretive talks and exhibits, picnicking, walking tours, walking trails, cross-country skiing and an operating blacksmith in the summer. • There is parking and restrooms at the Visitor Center. • The Visitor Center is open from 9 a.m. to 5 p.m., daily except Thanksgiving, Dec. 25 and Jan. 1.

PERMITS, FEES & LIMITATIONS

A $2 entrance fee admits adults to the Site and to the Hoover Presidential Library-Museum.

ACCESSIBILITY

Restrooms at the Visitor Center, parking and picnic tables are accessible. Ramps are provided for most historic buildings upon request.

CAMPING & LODGING

Overnight accommodations are available within a 15-mile (24.1 km) radius.

FOOD & SUPPLIES

A grocery store and pharmacy are located in West Branch.

FIRST AID/ HOSPITAL

• First aid is available in the Site. • The nearest hospital is in Iowa City via I-80. • There is a clinic 1 block from the Site.

GENERAL INFORMATION

Please note the historic walkway surfaces. Boardwalks are especially slippery in frost or wet weather.

Kansas

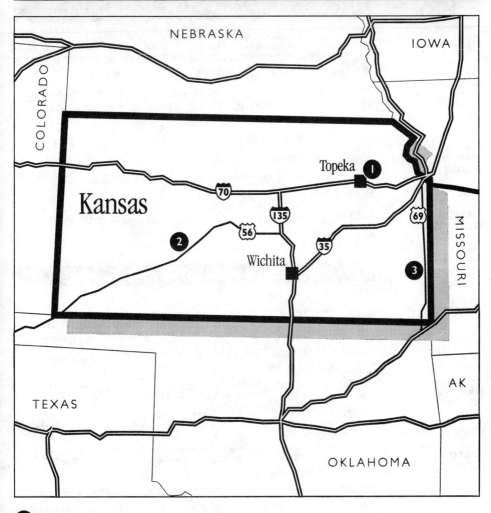

1. Brown v. Board of Education National Historic Site
2. Fort Larned National Historic Site
3. Fort Scott National Historic Site

Kansas

Brown v. Board of Education National Historic Site

Topeka, Kansas

Not open to the public. In 1954, the Supreme Court ruled that the separation of races in elementary schools violated the 14th Amendment to the United States Constitution, which guarantees all citizens equal protection under the law. The Site is under development to commemorate the end of segregation in public education and the case's role in the civil rights movement.

MAILING ADDRESS
Superintendent, Brown v. Board of Education National Historic Site, c/o NPS Midwest Regional Office, 1709 Jackson St., Omaha, NE 68102 **Telephone:** 402-221-3481

VISITOR ACTIVITIES
Although the Site is not open to the public yet, interpretive talks are available by advance arrangements.

Fort Larned National Historic Site

Larned, Kansas

The army established Fort Larned to counter Indian attacks on traders and emigrants using the Santa Fe Trail. The Fort became the principal guardian of the trail's commerce in the 1860s and a key post in the Indian War of 1868-69.

MAILING ADDRESS
Superintendent, Fort Larned National Historic Site, R.R. 3, Larned, KS 67550-9733 **Telephone:** 316-285-6911

DIRECTIONS
The Site is 6 miles (9.6 km) west of Larned on KS 156.

VISITOR ACTIVITIES
• The Visitor Center features a museum, a slide program, and a bookstore.
• Restored areas include a parade ground, barracks, officers' quarters, a hospital, shops, quartermaster storehouse, a school, commissary arsenal, and blockhouse/guardhouse. • Self-guided tours or write for a schedule of guided tours, living history and other special programs. • A history/nature trail offers an opportunity to observe prairie wildflowers and wildlife.
• Facilities include a picnic area. • The Site is open daily, except Thanksgiving, Dec. 25 and Jan. 1, from 8:30 a.m. to 5 p.m. Summer hours may be extended.

PERMITS, FEES & LIMITATIONS
There is a $2 entrance fee. Children 16 and younger and adults 62 and older admitted free.

ACCESSIBILITY
The Visitor Center is accessible. Accessibility to historic buildings varies. Call or write for current information.

CAMPING & LODGING	Overnight accommodations are available in Larned.
FOOD & SUPPLIES	• Only soft drinks are available in the Site. • Food and supplies are available in nearby communities.
FIRST AID/ HOSPITAL	• First aid is available in the Site. • The nearest hospital is in Larned.
GENERAL INFORMATION	The Site is on the Santa Fe National Historic Trail. Other Santa Fe Trail sites, including the Santa Fe Trail Center, are located nearby.

Fort Scott National Historic Site

Fort Scott, Kansas

From 1842-53, troops from Fort Scott helped to keep peace on the frontier between relocated Native Americans from the east, nomadic tribes and settlers. Their main duty entailed guarding caravans on the Santa Fe Trail and patrolling the far Indian country.

MAILING ADDRESS	Superintendent, Old Fort Boulevard, Fort Scott, KS 66701 **Telephone:** 316-223-0310
DIRECTIONS	The Site is near the intersection of US 69 and US 54 in the city of Fort Scott, which is 90 miles (145.1 km) south of Kansas City and 60 miles (96.7 km) northwest of Joplin, MO.
VISITOR ACTIVITIES	• Self-guided tours of reconstructed and restored historic buildings, including 33 furnished rooms. • Interpretive exhibits, living history demonstrations and special events as scheduled. • An introductory audiovisual program is available at the Visitor Center.
PERMITS, FEES & LIMITATIONS	The entrance fee is $2. Children 16 and younger and adults 62 and older admitted free.
ACCESSIBILITY	Parking, restrooms and first floors of historic structures are accessible. A 25-minute videotape tour of the Fort is available.
CAMPING & LODGING	• City park camping and a private campground are within 2 miles (3.2 km). • Nearby lodging includes motels and commercial bed and breakfasts.
FOOD & SUPPLIES	Restaurants and groceries are available in the city of Fort Scott.
FIRST AID/ HOSPITAL	• First aid is available in the Site. • The nearest hospital is in Fort Scott, 1 mile (1.6 km).
GENERAL INFORMATION	Additional points of interest in the area include a national cemetery, a restored Victorian downtown, trolley tours, the Ralph Richards Museum, Gunn Park and a Victorian homes auto tour.

Kentucky

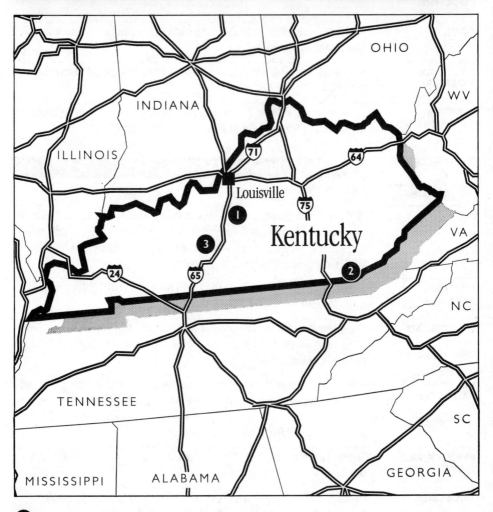

1 Abraham Lincoln Birthplace National Historic Site

2 Cumberland Gap National Historical Park

3 Mammoth Cave National Park

Abraham Lincoln Birthplace National Historic Site

Hodgenville, Kentucky

Abraham Lincoln was born in a humble log cabin on Sinking Spring Farm on Feb. 12, 1809. Today, Abraham Lincoln Birthplace National Historic Site includes a neo-classical marble and granite memorial that contains a 19th-century log cabin, symbolic of the one where Lincoln was born.

MAILING ADDRESS

Superintendent, Abraham Lincoln Birthplace National Historic Site, 2995 Lincoln Farm Road, Hodgenville, KY 42748 **Telephone:** 502-358-3137

DIRECTIONS

The Site is 3 miles (4.8 km) south of Hodgenville on US 31E and KY 61 and is 60 miles (96.7 km) south of Louisville.

VISITOR ACTIVITIES

• Interpretive talks, exhibits and films, hiking and picnicking. • Facilities include parking at the Visitor Center, parking and restrooms at the picnic area and an environmental study area. • The Site is open daily, except Dec. 25, from 8 a.m. to 6:45 p.m., from early June to Labor Day; from 8 a.m. to 5:45 p.m., in September, October, April and May; and from 8 a.m. to 4:45 p.m., the rest of the year.

PERMITS, FEES & LIMITATIONS

• No entrance fee. • Vehicles are restricted to designated roads.

ACCESSIBILITY

Restrooms, picnic grounds and the Memorial Building are accessible.

CAMPING & LODGING

Motels are adjacent to the Site.

FOOD & SUPPLIES

Food and supplies are available in Hodgenville.

FIRST AID/ HOSPITAL

• First aid is available in the site and nearby in Hodgenville. • The nearest hospital is in Elizabethtown, on KY 61, 12 miles (19.3 km).

GENERAL INFORMATION

For your safety - Watch for exposed roots and uneven ground along trails. Poison ivy and briars are abundant in woodland.

Cumberland Gap National Historical Park

Middlesboro, KY (also in Tennessee and Virginia)

Cumberland Gap National Historical Park marks the natural passage-way across the Appalachian Mountains for animals in search of food, Native Americans on their way to rich hunting grounds in Kentucky, and early settlers who followed Daniel Boone's Wilderness Trail into the new territory.

MAILING ADDRESS	Superintendent, Cumberland Gap National Historical Park, PO Box 1848, Middlesboro, KY 40965 **Telephone:** 606-248-2817
DIRECTIONS	Take US 25E from Kentucky or Tennessee or US 58 from Virginia. The Visitor Center is one-quarter mile (.4 km) south of Middlesboro on US 25E.
VISITOR ACTIVITIES	• Interpretive and audiovisual exhibits, hiking, picnicking, campfire programs, walking, music and craft demonstrations and a living history program. • 70 miles (112.9 km) of hiking trails. • Facilities include a bookstore with traditional Appalachian mountain crafts at the Visitor Center, restrooms, picnic areas, drinking water and a museum.
PERMITS, FEES & LIMITATIONS	Permits for backcountry camping are available at the Visitor Center.
ACCESSIBILITY	The Visitor Center, picnic tables, camp sites and a boardwalk to the Pinnacles Overlook are accessible.
CAMPING & LODGING	There is a 160-site campground with warm showers but no hookups for $8 a night for individuals and $1 a night per person for group sites.
FOOD & SUPPLIES	All services are available in the city nearby.
FIRST AID/ HOSPITAL	A hospital is in Middlesboro 2 miles (3.2 km) from Park Headquarters.
GENERAL INFORMATION	• For your safety - Never hike alone. Beware of snakes, poison ivy and poison oak. • Nearby points of interest include the June Tolliver House at Big Stone Gap, VA; Lincoln Memorial University in Harrogate, TN; Pine Mountain State Park, KY; and Dr. Thomas Walker State Park near Barbourville, KY. Directions and additional information are available at the Middlesboro Visitor Center.

Mammoth Cave National Park

Mammoth Cave, Kentucky   See Climatable No. 19

The Mammoth Cave system extends for more than 300 miles (483.8 km) of known passages, with more areas to be explored. It is the longest cave in the world and the main attraction of one of the greatest cave regions with its giant vertical shafts, underground rivers and rare animals, including eyeless fish, white spiders and blind beetles.

MAILING ADDRESS	Superintendent, Mammoth Cave National Park, Mammoth Cave, KY 42259 **Telephone:** 502-758-2328
DIRECTIONS	The Visitor Center is 9 miles (14.5 km) northwest of Park City off of I-65 via KY 255 and 70. It is 10 miles (16.1 km) west of Cave City off of I-65 via KY

Kentucky

70 and 255. Cave and surface tour information and ticket sales are available at the Visitor Center.

VISITOR ACTIVITIES

• Guided cave tours, guided nature walks and summer evening programs, self-guiding walking trails, picnicking, boating, fishing, backcountry hiking and Green River boat trips. • Cave tour reservations can be made by calling MISTIX at 1-800-967-2283. • For descriptions of tours, current schedules and prices, contact the Park or MISTIX.

PERMITS, FEES & LIMITATIONS

• No entrance fee. • Free permits for backcountry camping are available at the Visitor Center or the Park Headquarters Campground station. • There are fees for cave tours and Green River boat trips.

ACCESSIBILITY

The Visitor Center, Tour for the Mobility Impaired, Loop D of Headquarters Campground, the amphitheater and Heritage Trail are accessible. The picnic area, which is minimally accessible, does not have accessible restrooms.

CAMPING & LODGING

• The camping fee in the Headquarters Campground is $6 per night. Two remotely located campgrounds are free. There are no hookups. No reservations are accepted for these 3 campgrounds. Maple Springs Group Campground is available by reservation through the Chief Ranger's Office. • Mammoth Cave Hotel is open all year. For reservations, call 502-758-2225.

FOOD & SUPPLIES

• Meals are served in the Mammoth Cave Hotel dining room or coffee shop. • Supplies are available at the service center located next to the Headquarters Campground. The store is closed from Thanksgiving to Easter and is open only on weekends in the spring and fall.

FIRST AID/ HOSPITAL

• First aid is available in the Park. • The nearest hospital is Caverna Hospital at Horse Cave, US 31W, 15 miles (24.1 km).

GENERAL INFORMATION

• The temperature in the caves remains at 54°F, and the humidity can reach 100%. Bring a sweater or light jacket. In winter, warm clothing is advised. • Some cave tours are strenuous and require stooping, ascending and descending steps and walking over uneven terrain. Parts of the cave are wet and slippery, so wear sturdy walking shoes - not sandals. Be sure to select the tour that best meets your physical ability. • While driving, watch for deer. • Be aware of poisonous snakes and poison ivy.

Louisiana

ARKANSAS

MISSISSIPPI

Louisiana

TEXAS

Mississippi River

New Orleans

Gulf of Mexico

1 Jean Lafitte National Historical Park

2 Poverty Point National Monument

Jean Lafitte National Historical Park and Preserve

New Orleans, Louisiana

Jean Lafitte National Historical Park and Preserve contains Barataria, located south of New Orleans and featuring trails and canoe tours; Chalmette, the scene of the 1815 Battle of New Orleans; the French Quarter Unit, interpreting the ethnic population of the Delta; and the Acadian Cultural Center, which interprets Cajun culture and history.

MAILING ADDRESS

Superintendent, Jean Lafitte National Historical Park and Preserve, 419 Rue Decatur, New Orleans, LA 70130 **Telephone:** 504-589-3882

DIRECTIONS

The Park Headquarters is at 419 Rue Decatur in New Orlean's French Quarter. Additional visitor centers are: Acadian Cultural Center, Lafayette; Wetlands Acadian Cultural Center, Thibodaux; Prairie Acadian Cultural Center, Eunice; Barataria Preserve Unit, Marrero; Chalmette Unit, Chalmette; and the New Orleans Unit, New Orleans.

VISITOR ACTIVITIES

• Interpretive talks, exhibits, films, demonstrations and walks. • Visitor Center operations vary from unit to unit. Please call the Park Headquarters for detailed information. • The Park is closed on Dec. 25, and the Headquarters office and New Orleans Visitor Center are closed on Mardi Gras Day.

PERMITS, FEES & LIMITATIONS

• No permits or fees. • Vehicles are restricted to parking areas and designated roads.

ACCESSIBILITY

Visitor centers and most walks are accessible.

CAMPING & LODGING

Overnight accommodations are available in New Orleans.

FOOD & SUPPLIES

Food and supplies are available in New Orleans.

FIRST AID/ HOSPITAL

First aid and hospitals are available in New Orleans.

GENERAL INFORMATION

For information on each unit, call: Acadian Unit, 318-232-0789; Wetlands Acadian Cultural Center, 504-448-1375; Prairie Acadian Cultural Center, 318-457-8490; Barataria Preserve Unit, 504-589-2330; Chalmette Unit, 504-589-4430; and the New Orleans Unit, 504-589-2636.

Poverty Point National Monument

Epps, Louisiana

Poverty Point National Monument commemorates a culture that thrived during the first and second millennia, BC. Today, however, erosion and more than a century of agriculture have reduced what may have been the largest and most intricate geometrical earthwork in North America.

MAILING ADDRESS

Poverty Point National Monument, c/o Poverty Point State Commemorative Area, PO Box 248, Epps, LA 71237

DIRECTIONS

Located in northeastern Louisiana, the Monument consists of an existing state commemorative area and private land. The Monument will be established when the state transfers the commemorative area to the National Park Service.

VISITOR ACTIVITIES

No visitor facilities or services are provided by the National Park Service.

Maine

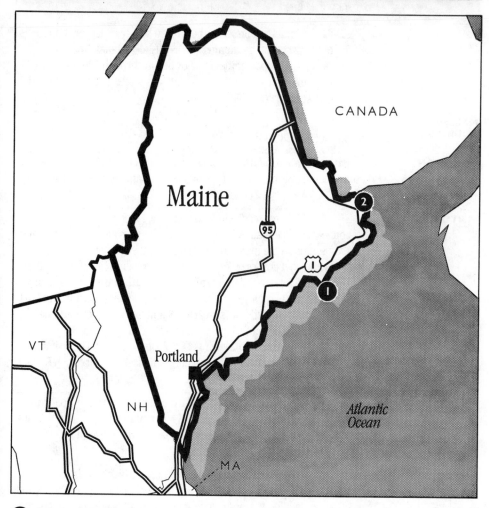

1 Acadia National Park

2 Saint Croix Island International Historic Site

Maine

Acadia National Park

Bar Harbor, Maine   See Climatable No. 20

Acadia National Park preserves the natural beauty of part of Maine's coast, its coastal mountains and its offshore islands. The Park provides numerous opportunities to enjoy beauty through 120 miles (193.5 km) of trails and 57 miles (91.9 km) of carriage roads, a network of woodland roads free of motor vehicles.

MAILING ADDRESS

Superintendent, Acadia National Park, Box 177, Bar Harbor, ME 04609 Telephone: 207-288-3338

DIRECTIONS

The Park is on ME 3, 47 miles (75.8 km) southeast of Bangor, ME. Schoodic Peninsula, the only part of the Park on the mainland, is accessible via ME 186.

VISITOR ACTIVITIES

• A 27-mile (43.5 km) scenic drive connects the lakes, mountains and the seashore. • Carriage roads are open to hikers, bicycles and horses. • Hiking trails, museums on the mainland and Little Cranberry Island, naturalist programs and boat cruises. • Facilities include beaches, campfire programs, audiovisual and interpretive programs, a cassette auto tape tour and picnic areas. • The Park is open year-round. The Visitor Center is open from May 1 to Oct. 31. Spring and fall hours are from 8 a.m. to 4:30 p.m. Summer hours are 8 a.m. to 6 p.m. Hours are subject to change. • The Park Headquarters closes on Thanksgiving, Dec. 25 and Jan. 1. • The Visitor Center, Nature Center, Museum and major portions of the Park Loop Road are not open in winter.

PERMITS, FEES & LIMITATIONS

• A $5 vehicle entrance fee is collected from May 1 to Nov. 1. • Boat cruise fares are $10 to $14 for adults and $7 to $9 for children under 12. • Vehicles are restricted to designated roads. No motorized vehicles, except for electric wheelchairs, are allowed on the carriage roads.

ACCESSIBILITY

Thompson Island, the Nature Center, Headquarters, Blackwoods and Seawall campgrounds, the Wendell Gilley Museum restrooms, gift shops and restaurant at Cadillac Mountain and Jordan Pond, slide presentations, some cruises and trails are accessible. Assistance may be needed to access the Visitor Center parking and restrooms.

CAMPING & LODGING

• Two campgrounds are available in the Park. Reservations are required at Blackwoods Campground from June 15 to Sept. 15. Call MISTIX at 1-800-365-2267. • Private campgrounds are available in the area. • Additional overnight accommodations are available in Bar Harbor, 3 miles (4.8 km); Northeast Harbor, ME, 14 miles (22.5 km); Ellsworth, ME, 20 miles (32.2 km); and Southwest Harbor, ME, 18 miles (29 km).

FOOD & SUPPLIES

• Meals are served in the Park seasonally. • Food and supplies are available in Bar Harbor, Northeast Harbor, Southwest Harbor and Ellsworth.

FIRST AID/ HOSPITAL

• First aid is available in the Park. • The nearest hospital is in Bar Harbor.

GENERAL INFORMATION

For your safety - Be particularly careful on the rugged shores of Acadia. Ledges and rocks below high tide are slippery. Watch out for storm waves, particularly in spring and autumn. Be aware of poison ivy or falling loose stones.

Saint Croix Island International Historic Site

Red Beach, Maine

In 1604, French settlers under Pierre de Gua, Sieur de Monts established a colony on Saint Croix Island that was abandoned the following year in favor of a better site but led to the founding of today's Province of Quebec where the language, culture and religion of royal France lives on.

MAILING ADDRESS

Superintendent, Saint Croix Island International Historic Site, c/o Acadia National Park, Box 177, Bar Harbor, ME 04609 **Telephone:** 207-288-3338

DIRECTIONS

The Site is 120 miles (193.5 km) north of Bar Harbor. It is 8 miles (12.9 km) south of Calais, ME, along US 1. Access to the island is by boat only. There is no ferry service to the island.

VISITOR ACTIVITIES

• Walking and picnicking. • There are no visitor facilities on the island. The mainland has a picnic area and pit toilet. No water is available. • A small interpretive shelter on the mainland explains the historic significance of the Site. • People with their own boats may visit the island anytime.

PERMITS, FEES & LIMITATIONS

• No entrance fee. • No vehicles are allowed on the island.

CAMPING & LODGING

Overnight accommodations are available in Calais.

FOOD & SUPPLIES

Food and supplies are available in Calais.

FIRST AID/ HOSPITAL

The nearest hospital is in Calais.

Maryland

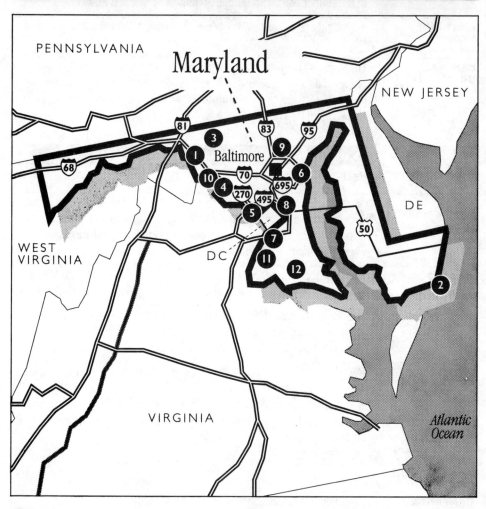

PENNSYLVANIA

Maryland

NEW JERSEY

81 **83** **95**

3 Baltimore **9**

1 **6**

68 **70** **695**

10 **4** **270** **495** **8** DE

WEST **5** **7** **50**

VIRGINIA DC **11**

12

VIRGINIA

Atlantic Ocean

---

1 Antietam National Battlefield

2 Assateague Island National Seashore

3 Catoctin Mountain Park

4 Chesapeake and Ohio Canal National Historical Park

5 Clara Barton National Historic Site

6 Fort McHenry National Monument and Historic Shrine

7 Fort Washington Park

8 Greenbelt Park

9 Hampton National Historic Site

10 Monocacy National Battlefield

11 Piscataway Park

12 Thomas Stone National Historic Site

Antietam National Battlefield
Sharpsburg, Maryland

When the fighting ended after the Battle of Antietam on Sept. 17, 1862, more men had been killed or wounded than on any other single day of the Civil War. Also, the war's course had been altered by Gen. Robert E. Lee's failure to carry the Confederate effort into the North.

MAILING ADDRESS
Antietam National Battlefield, PO Box 158, Sharpsburg, MD 21782-0158
Telephone: 301-432-5124

DIRECTIONS
The Visitor Center is 1 mile (1.6 km) north of Sharpsburg, MD, on Rt. 65.

VISITOR ACTIVITIES
• The Visitor Center is open daily, except Thanksgiving, Dec. 25 and Jan. 1, from 8:30 a.m. to 5 p.m., September through May, and from 8:30 a.m. to 6 p.m., June through August. • A 26-minute film is shown every hour on the hour, and an 18-minute slide program is shown every hour on the half hour. • Ranger-guided programs are offered throughout the summer. • The Visitor Center houses a museum. The battlefield can be toured by taking an 8-minute self-guided driving tour.

PERMITS, FEES & LIMITATIONS
The entrance fee is $2 per person, ages 17-61, and $4 per family.

ACCESSIBILITY
The Battlefield is accessible.

CAMPING & LODGING
Camping and lodging are available nearby.

FOOD & SUPPLIES
There are limited food and supplies available in Sharpsburg, but the larger community of Hagerstown, MD, is 10 miles (16.1 km) north.

FIRST AID/ HOSPITAL
First aid and a hospital are available in Hagerstown.

Assateague Island National Seashore
Maryland and Virginia

Assateague Island is a barrier island with a seashore heritage of wildlands, wildlife, and outdoor recreation opportunities that include birding, hiking, swimming, crabbing and wild ponies.

MAILING ADDRESS
Assateague Island National Seashore, 7206 National Seashore Lane, Berlin, MD 21811 Telephone: 410-641-1441, Maryland Visitor Center; 804-336-6577, Virginia Visitor Center

DIRECTIONS
Take US 50 East to State Route 611 South to the Maryland entrance. Take US 13 North or South to State Route 175 East to the Virginia entrance.

VISITOR ACTIVITIES

• Surf fishing, clamming, crabbing, canoeing, hiking, bird watching, swimming, interpretive programs in summer, hunting, pony round-up and auction on the last Wednesday and Thursday of July. • Visitor centers in both states feature exhibits, small aquariums and book stores. • There are nature trails and some bicycle paths in both states.

PERMITS, FEES & LIMITATIONS

• The entrance fee is $4 per vehicle for 7 days or $10 for an annual pass. • Off-road vehicles are permitted but require certain equipment and a $40 annual special use permit. • Pets are prohibited in the Virginia portion of Assateague and in Maryland's Assateague State Park. Dogs are allowed in other parts of Maryland, but are discouraged since there are many insects and hot, blowing sand is hard on their feet and eyes.

ACCESSIBILITY

Visitor centers, bath houses and some nature trails are accessible. A few camp sites, which are accessible, can be reserved.

CAMPING & LODGING

• Camp sites are available in Assateague State Park in Maryland for $18 a night or in the Seashore for $10 a night for more primitive camping. • There are commercial campgrounds in Chincoteague, VA. • Ocean City, MD, and Chincoteague, VA, provide a wide variety of motels and inns. • No concessionaires are available on the island.

FOOD & SUPPLIES

• Camping supplies and food are not available on the island. • Supplies can be purchased at several locations within 10 miles (16.1 km) at each state's Seashore entrance.

FIRST AID/ HOSPITAL

• First aid is provided by Rangers in Chincoteague or Ocean City. • Hospitals are in Berlin, MD, 8 miles (12.9 km) from the Maryland entrance; and in Salisbury, MD, 45 miles (72.5 km) from the Virginia entrance.

GENERAL INFORMATION

The Seashore has developed many brochures on backcountry camping, surf safety, and seashore recreation and wildlife.

Catoctin Mountain Park

Thurmont, Maryland

Read the story of a group of people and their effect on the land at Catoctin Mountain Park through old stone fences, logging roads, and a wealth of scenery, wildlife and historic buildings.

MAILING ADDRESS

Superintendent, Catoctin Mountain Park, 6602 Foxville Road, Thurmont, MD 21788 **Telephone:** 301-663-9330

DIRECTIONS

From Rt. 15, take Rt. 77 west for 3 miles (4.8 km).

VISITOR ACTIVITIES

Hiking, picnicking, Visitor Center, exhibits, interpretive programs, fishing, horseback riding trails (horses not available), rock climbing and cross-country skiing.

Maryland

PERMITS, FEES & LIMITATIONS

Permits are required for rock climbing and for use of the hike in Adirondack Shelter camp sites. Permits are available at no charge from the Visitor Center.

ACCESSIBILITY

Camp Greentop is accessible. The Chestnut picnic area has some tables designed for wheelchairs, accessible restrooms and the one-half-mile (.8 km) Spicebush Nature Trail. The trail features a paved surface, resting benches, and interpretive signs. Restrooms are accessible with assistance at Owens Creek Campground. Several rental cabins, showers and restrooms are accessible at Camp Misty Mount. The Visitor Center is accessible. Parking spaces are available at the Visitor Center, picnic areas and Owens Creek Campground. Most trail brochures are provided in large print upon request. Cunningham Falls State Park offers parking and an accessible trail to the Falls off of Rt. 77.

CAMPING & LODGING

• Owens Creek Campground is open from April 15 through the third Sunday in November. The fee is $6 per night per site. No reservations are accepted for individual sites. • Poplar Grove is a youth group only, tent camping area. Reservations are required. Contact the Park Visitor Center for an application. The fee is $10 per night per site. Each site can accommodate 25 people. • Camp Misty Mount is open from mid April through the end of October for individual cabin rentals. Cabin rental rates begin at $28 per night. Call 301-271-3140 for reservations and information. • Camp Greentop and Camp Round Meadow are large environmental education cabin camps available for rent by groups of 60 or more. They are reserved through applications taken between Dec. 1 and Dec. 15 for long-term groups, between Jan. 1 and Jan. 30 for spring weekend groups and between May 1 and May 30 for fall weekend groups. • Cunningham Falls State Park also has camping. Call 301-271-7574. • Motels are available in the town of Thurmont.

FOOD & SUPPLIES

• Cunningham Falls State Park has a concession at the William Houck Lake Area that is open from Memorial Day through Labor Day. • Other food and supplies are available in Thurmont.

FIRST AID/ HOSPITAL

Frederick and Hagerstown hospitals are within 20 miles (32.2 km).

GENERAL INFORMATION

Activities at Cunningham Falls State Park include camping, picnicking, hiking, swimming, boating and fishing. Big Hunting Creek offers fly fishing for trout. Regulations require a Maryland license, trout stamp, and "Catch and Release" of all trout.

Maryland

Chesapeake and Ohio Canal National Historical Park

Maryland and District of Columbia

The 184.5 miles (297.5 km) of the Chesapeake and Ohio Canal preserves history and nature. Its 74 lift locks raise it from near sea level to an elevation of 605 feet (184.4 m) providing quiet waters for canoeists, boaters and anglers. Its towpath offers a nearly level byway for hikers and bicyclists.

MAILING ADDRESS

Superintendent, C&O Canal National Historical Park, PO Box 4, Sharpsburg, MD 21782 **Telephone:** 301-739-4200 **Park Emergency:** 301-739-4206

DIRECTIONS

The Park Headquarters is 4 miles (6.4 km) west of Sharpsburg on MD 34. The Visitor Centers are: Great Falls Canal Tavern Museum, 11710 MacArthur Blvd., Potomac, MD 20854 301-299-3613; Hancock, MD, 326 E. Main St. 301-678-5463; and the Western Maryland Railroad Station Center, Canal Street, Cumberland, MD 301-739-4200.

VISITOR ACTIVITIES

• Hiking, biking, limited horseback riding, canoeing, boating, fishing, picnicking, conducted walks, and a canal museum at Great Falls, MD. • Mule-drawn boat rides at Georgetown and Great Falls Tavern are offered from mid-April through mid-October, weather permitting. Call 301-299-3613 or 202-472-4376 in advance. • Visitor facilities include picnic areas, boat rentals, boat ramps and bicycles. • The towpath is open year-round. The museum and visitor centers are closed Dec. 25.

PERMITS, FEES & LIMITATIONS

• There is a $4 per car or $2 per individual **entrance fee** for Great Falls. A $10 annual pass is available. • Parking is available in designated areas along the towpath. • A permit is required to camp at the Marsden Tract, 11.5 miles (18.5 km) from Georgetown. Permits may be obtained from the Park Ranger at Great Falls Tavern from 9 a.m. to 5 p.m., phone 301-299-3613.

ACCESSIBILITY

Accessible features include a water fountain at 30th Street, NW, in Georgetown; some ramps along the Canal Boat Towpath; a water fountain near the concession stand at Fletchers; one pit toilet at the Marsden Tract; downstairs at the Great Falls Tavern, restrooms, parking and the canal boat; and bridges to the Great Falls Overlook. The Canal Towpath is generally passable, but access is generally poor.

CAMPING & LODGING

• Primitive camping at Marsden Tract is available with a permit. • No reservations are required for "Hiker-Biker" camp sites. • Other overnight accommodations are available in major urban areas near I-70.

FOOD & SUPPLIES

• Fast food and drinks are available from concessionaires spring through fall at Great Falls, Swains Lock and Fletchers Boat House. • Fishing supplies are available from Swains Boat House and Fletchers Boat House. • Food and supplies are also available along the various adjacent access routes.

FIRST AID/ HOSPITAL

• First aid is available at all visitor centers and at the Park Headquarters.
• Hospitals are available along the route of the canal and in or near Potomac, Seneca, Poolesville, Brunswick, Sharpsburg, Williamsport, Hancock, Oldtown and Cumberland.

GENERAL INFORMATION

For your safety - Help prevent drowning by keeping your family or group together. Stay on the trail and out of the water.

Clara Barton National Historic Site

Glen Echo, Maryland

Clara Barton, humanitarian and founder of the American Red Cross, lived in Glen Echo, Maryland, for the last 15 years of her life. Visitors to her home, which is preserved as a National Historic Site, have the opportunity to examine Clara Barton's character apart from her public image.

MAILING ADDRESS

Clara Barton National Historic Site, 5801 Oxford Road, Glen Echo, MD 20812 **Telephone: 301-492-6245**

DIRECTIONS

Take MacArthur Boulevard from Washington, DC. From the Capital Beltway (I-495), use the Clara Barton Parkway to Glen Echo, MD. Follow signs for Glen Echo Park. Turn on Oxford Road to parking.

VISITOR ACTIVITIES

• Guided tours and exhibits. • Audiovisual programs available on Clara Barton and related topics. • The Site is open from 10 a.m. to 5 p.m., daily except Thanksgiving, Dec. 25 and Jan. 1. • A small picnic area is available for individual use. Groups of 10 or more must call ahead for a reservation.

PERMITS, FEES & LIMITATIONS

• No fees. • Vehicles are confined to the parking area. • Visitation to the historic structure is by guided tour only.

ACCESSIBILITY

Building accessible only on the first floor. There are no accessible restrooms.

CAMPING & LODGING

Overnight accommodations are available nearby in Glen Echo.

FOOD & SUPPLIES

Food and gasoline are available in Glen Echo.

FIRST AID/ HOSPITAL

• First aid is available within the Site or at the nearby Glen Echo Fire Department. • The nearest hospital is Sibley Hospital, Washington, DC, 4 miles (6.4 km).

Fort McHenry National Monument and Historic Shrine

Baltimore, Maryland

The resistance of a British naval attack against Fort McHenry in 1814 prevented the capture of Baltimore. The victory inspired Francis Scott Key to write "The Star-Spangled Banner" when a large flag was raised over the Fort after the 25-hour battle.

MAILING ADDRESS

Superintendent, Fort McHenry National Monument and Historic Shrine, Baltimore, MD 21230-5393 **Telephone:** 410-962-4299

DIRECTIONS

From I-95 northbound or southbound, take Exit 55 Key Highway/Fort McHenry and follow the blue and green signs on Key Highway to Lawrence Street. Turn left on Lawrence and left on Fort Avenue. Proceed to the Monument. From the Inner Harbor, take Light Street south to Key Highway. Turn left and follow the blue and green signs to Lawrence Street. Turn right on Lawrence and left on Fort Avenue. Proceed to the Monument.

VISITOR ACTIVITIES

• Interpretive exhibits and film, walking self-guided tours, picnicking, guided activities during the summer and by reservation for groups or on weekend afternoons in summer; and activities by the Fort McHenry Guard, a group of volunteers uniformed as 1814 defenders of Baltimore. • Facilities include parking and restrooms at the Visitor Center, a picnic area and a seawall walking/jogging path. • The Monument is open daily from **8 a.m. to 5 p.m.**, except Dec. 25 and Jan. 1. Call regarding extended summer hours.

PERMITS, FEES & LIMITATIONS

• There is a $2 per person **entrance** fee for persons ages 17 through 61.
• Vehicles are restricted to designated roads.

ACCESSIBILITY

Accessible parking and restrooms are available. Ramps are provided with the exception of the guardhouse at the Fort. There are written materials and an induction loop system in the Visitor Center auditorium for the hearing impaired. A 16-minute film is captioned for the hearing impaired. A raised relief map of the Fort with Braille text is provided for those with sight impairments.

CAMPING & LODGING

Lodging is available in Baltimore.

FOOD & SUPPLIES

Food and supplies are available in Baltimore.

FIRST AID/ HOSPITAL

• First aid is available within the Monument. • The nearest hospital is Harbor Hospital Center, Hanover Street, 2 miles (3.2 km).

GENERAL INFORMATION

For your safety - Do not climb on monuments, trees, cannons or the seawall. Stay away from the edge of the Fort walls.

Fort Washington Park

Fort Washington, Maryland

Fort Washington Park illustrates the significant development of changing military strategy and American history from 1808 to 1922. Military modifications are illustrated by the remains of several forts built during the days of wooden ships and the concrete batteries needed by larger cannon to combat armored ships.

MAILING ADDRESS

Fort Washington Park, Superintendent, National Capital Parks-East, 1900 Anacostia Drive, SE, Washington, DC 20020 **Telephone: 301-763-4600**

DIRECTIONS

Take Exit 3A from the Capital Beltway (I-95) to Rt. 210S (Indian Head Highway) 4 miles (6.4 km) to Fort Washington Road. Turn right and travel 3.5 miles (5.6 km) to the Park entrance.

VISITOR ACTIVITIES

• Fort tours and costumed living history presentations are available on Sundays. • Picnicking, fishing, bird watching and nature hikes. • The Visitor Center is open daily from **10 a.m. to 4:30 p.m.**, except Thanksgiving, Dec. 25 and Jan. 1. • There is a small museum exhibit and an 8-minute film on the Fort's history. • Phone or write for a schedule of events.

PERMITS, FEES & LIMITATIONS

The entrance fee is $4 per vehicle or $2 per person.

ACCESSIBILITY

Restrooms, picnic grounds, and the Visitor Center are accessible. Access is limited to the main parade ground at the old historic Fort.

CAMPING & LODGING

• No camping or lodging is available within the Park. • Motels are located at the Interstate interchange.

FOOD & SUPPLIES

• Food and supplies are not available within the Park. • Several restaurants and fast food establishments are 3.5 miles (5.6 km) east of the Park.

FIRST AID/ HOSPITAL

The nearest emergency medical facility is in Fort Washington, MD, 4.5 miles (7.2 km).

GENERAL INFORMATION

The Park has hot, humid summers and cold, wet winters.

Greenbelt Park

Greenbelt, Maryland

Greenbelt Park's 1,100 acres of woodland, 12 miles (19.3 km) from downtown Washington and 23 miles (37 km) from Baltimore, is an oasis of greenspace within an urban area. It provides a refuge for native plants and animals and facilities for camping, hiking and other outdoor recreation.

Maryland

MAILING ADDRESS
Superintendent, Greenbelt Park, 6565 Greenbelt Road, Greenbelt, MD 20770
Telephone: 301-344-3948

DIRECTIONS
From the Capital Beltway (I-95), take Exit 23 at Kenilworth Avenue (MD 201) and proceed south toward Bladensburg. Follow the signs to the Park.

VISITOR ACTIVITIES
• Picnicking, nature walks, horse trails (no horses available), biking and hiking.

PERMITS, FEES & LIMITATIONS
No entrance fee.

ACCESSIBILITY
Two accessible camp sites are available. The restrooms at Headquarters and the Sweetgum Picnic Area are accessible.

CAMPING & LODGING
A 174-site campground is open all year. Sites are available for $8 per night. No reservations are accepted, and there are no showers or hookups.

FOOD & SUPPLIES
Food and supplies are available in the city of Greenbelt.

FIRST AID/ HOSPITAL
The nearest hospital is in Lanham, MD, 5 miles (8 km).

Hampton National Historic Site

Towson, Maryland

Hampton National Historic Site includes one of the largest and most ornate Georgian mansions built in America during the post-Revolutionary period (1790) with its complex of outbuildings, English formal gardens and specimen trees.

MAILING ADDRESS
Superintendent, Hampton National Historic Site, 535 Hampton Lane, Towson, MD 21286 Telephone: 410-962-0688

DIRECTIONS
From Baltimore, follow the Jones Falls Expressway, the York Road (MD 45) or Charles Street north to Towson. In Towson, take Dulaney Valley Road (MD 146) across the Beltway (I-695) and immediately turn right onto Hampton Lane, which leads to the Site. The Site can also be reached from Beltway Exit 27, Providence Road. Take Exit 27B off Baltimore, Route 695. Turn right onto Hampton Lane and proceed three-quarters of a mile (1.2 km) to the Park.

VISITOR ACTIVITIES
• Tours of the mansion are offered every hour from 9 a.m. to 4 p.m.
• Self-guided tours of the grounds, stables, gardens and farm. • Facilities include parking, restrooms, a tea room and a gift shop. • The grounds are open daily from 9 a.m. to 5 p.m., except Thanksgiving, Dec. 25 and Jan. 1.

PERMITS, FEES & LIMITATIONS
No entrance fee.

ACCESSIBILITY

The Site is not accessible.

CAMPING & LODGING

Overnight accommodations are available in Towson, MD, 1 mile (1.6 km) south.

FOOD & SUPPLIES

• Meals are served in the tea room. • Food and supplies are available in Towson.

FIRST AID/ HOSPITAL

• First aid is available within the Site. • The nearest hospital is in Towson.

GENERAL INFORMATION

For your safety - Please be careful on the earthen ramps leading into the gardens. They are steeper than they appear. The cobblestone walks are slippery when wet.

Monocacy National Battlefield

Frederick, Maryland

In a battle here July 9, 1864, Confederate Gen. Jubal T. Early defeated Union forces commanded by Brig. Gen. Lew Wallace. Wallace's troops, however, delayed Early, enabling Union forces to marshal a successful defense of Washington, DC.

MAILING ADDRESS

Monocacy National Battlefield, 4801 Urbana Pike, Frederick, MD 21701-7307 **Telephone:** 301-662-3515

DIRECTIONS

The Visitor Center is about one-tenth of a mile (.16 km) south of the Monocacy River on Hwy. 355.

VISITOR ACTIVITIES

The Contact Station is open daily from 8 a.m. to 4:30 p.m., from Memorial Day to Labor Day and on Wednesdays and Sundays from Labor Day to Memorial Day except Thanksgiving, Dec. 25 and Jan. 1.

PERMITS, FEES & LIMITATIONS

No entrance fee.

ACCESSIBILITY

The Battlefield is accessible.

CAMPING & LODGING

Overnight accommodations are available in the local community.

FOOD & SUPPLIES

Food and supplies are available in the local community.

FIRST AID/ HOSPITAL

Medical facilities are available in Frederick.

GENERAL INFORMATION

No trails are available at this time.

Maryland

Piscataway Park

Accokeek, Maryland

Piscataway Park stretches for 6 miles (9.6 km) from Piscataway Creek to Marshall Hall on the Potomac River. It is part of an effort that began in 1952 to preserve the river view from Mount Vernon as it was in George Washington's day.

MAILING ADDRESS
Piscataway Park, Superintendent, National Capital Parks-East, 1900 Anacostia Drive, SE, Washington, DC 20020 **Telephone:** 301-763-4600

DIRECTIONS
Take Exit 3A from the Capital Beltway (I-95) to Rt. 210S (Indian Head Highway) 10 miles (16.1 km) to the intersection in Accokeek. Turn right onto Bryan's Point Road and go 4 miles (6.4 km) to the Potomac River.

VISITOR ACTIVITIES
• Picnicking, fishing, bird watching and farm tours. • Facilities include a picnic area, a boat dock and the National Colonial Farm. • The Park is open daily during daylight hours.

PERMITS, FEES & LIMITATIONS
• No entrance fee. • A fee is charged for tours of the National Colonial Farm.

CAMPING & LODGING
Overnight accommodations are available in suburban Maryland or metropolitan DC.

FOOD & SUPPLIES
Food and supplies are available in shopping centers along Rt. 210.

FIRST AID/ HOSPITAL
• First aid is not available in the Park. • The nearest hospital is in Washington, DC, Rt. 210 to Southern Avenue, 20 miles (32.2 km).

Thomas Stone National Historic Site

La Plata, Maryland

Habre-de-Venture, a Georgian mansion built in 1771 near Port Tobacco, Maryland, was the home of Thomas Stone, a Signer of the Declaration of Independence and delegate to the Continental Congress from 1775-78 and from 1783-84.

MAILING ADDRESS
Thomas Stone National Historic Site, c/o Superintendent, George Washington Birthplace National Monument, RR 1, Box 717, Washington's Birthplace, VA 22443 **Telephone:** 804-224-1732

DIRECTIONS
Follow Maryland Rts. 6 or 225 and Rose Hill Road. The Site is 6 miles (9.6 km) west of La Plata, MD.

VISITOR ACTIVITIES
Ranger-guided tours, self-guided tours, special events, and an audiovisual program.

Maryland

PERMITS, FEES & LIMITATIONS
• No fees. • No off-road travel is allowed.

ACCESSIBILITY
The Site is not accessible. Future plans include accessibility measures.

CAMPING & LODGING
Lodging is available in La Plata and other locations along the 301 corridor.

FOOD & SUPPLIES
Food and other supplies are available in La Plata.

FIRST AID/ HOSPITAL
First aid clinics and a hospital are available in La Plata.

GENERAL INFORMATION
• The house will be under reconstruction for several years. • For your safety - There are poisonous plants and ticks.

Massachusetts

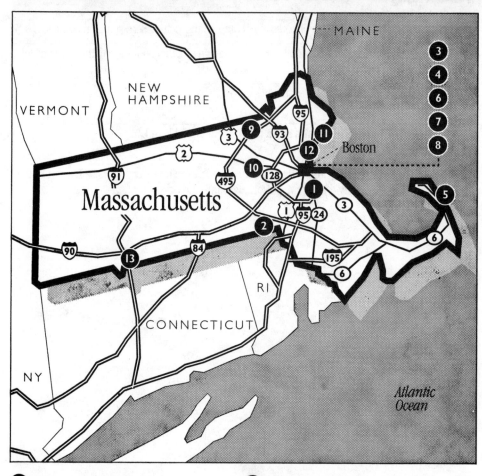

1 Adams National Historic Site

2 Blackstone River Valley National Heritage Corridor

3 Boston African American National Historic Site

4 Boston National Historical Park

5 Cape Cod National Seashore

6 Frederick Law Olmsted National Historic Site

7 John F. Kennedy National Historic Site

8 Longfellow National Historic Site

9 Lowell National Historical Park

10 Minute Man National Historical Park

11 Salem Maritime National Historic Site

12 Saugus Iron Works National Historic Site

13 Springfield Armory National Historic Site

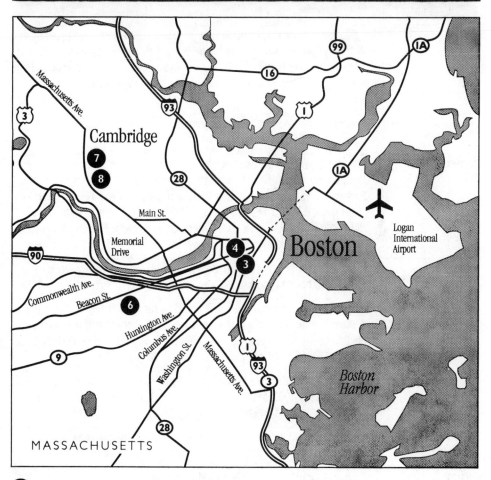

3 Boston African American National Historic Site

4 Boston National Historical Park

6 Frederick Law Olmsted National Historic Site

7 John F. Kennedy National Historic Site

8 Longfellow National Historic Site

Adams National Historic Site
Quincy, Massachusetts

A good claim can be made that the house continuously occupied by 4 generations of Adamses, beginning with John and Abigail Adams in 1788, is the most historic house in the United States since it never passed out of family hands and its furnishings have not had to be sought out or replaced.

MAILING ADDRESS

Superintendent, Adams National Historic Site, PO Box 531, Quincy, MA 02269-0531 **Telephone:** 617-773-1177

DIRECTIONS

The Site is 8 miles (12.9 km) south of Boston, MA. Take Route 93 (Southeast Expressway) south to Exit 8, Furnace Brook Parkway. From Furnace Brook Parkway, turn right onto Quarry Street at the second light. Follow Quarry Street to the end. Turn left onto Burgin Parkway. At the traffic light, turn right onto Dimmock Street then left on Hancock Street. The Visitor Center is on the right located in the Galleria at Presidents Place, 1250 Hancock St.

VISITOR ACTIVITIES

Interpretive programs through the 3 homes, an annual lecture series in June, special events and limited seasonal trolley service.

PERMITS, FEES & LIMITATIONS

• There is a $2 entrance fee valid for 7 days for visitors ages 17 through 61.
• Tours of 8 or more people require reservations. For reservations, contact the Division of Interpretation and Visitor Services, PO Box 531, Quincy, MA 02269-0531, 617-773-1177.

ACCESSIBILITY

The John Adams Birthplace, the John Quincy Adams Birthplace, the Visitor Center and the "Old House" are accessible. First floor only at Peacefield is accessible.

CAMPING & LODGING

• Lodging is readily available locally. • Camping is available nearby.

FOOD & SUPPLIES

Food and supplies are readily available locally.

FIRST AID/ HOSPITAL

• First aid is not available within the Site. • City Hospital is less than one-quarter mile (.4 km) from the Site.

GENERAL INFORMATION

• The Visitor Center provides visitor orientation, tour assignments and a fee collection station. Passes must be purchased at the Visitor Center before visiting homes. • Restrooms are only available at Visitor Center.

Blackstone River Valley National Heritage Corridor

Between Worcester, Massachusetts and Providence, Rhode Island

Affiliated area. The American Industrial Revolution had its roots here along 46 miles (74.1 km) of river and canals running from Worcester, MA, to Providence, RI, through the Blackstone Valley where the mills (including Slater Mill), villages and associated transportation networks tell the industrialization story.

MAILING ADDRESS
Blackstone River Valley National Heritage Corridor, 15 Mendon St., PO Box 730, Uxbridge, MA 01569 **Telephone:** 508-278-9400

DIRECTIONS
Take I-90 (Massachusetts Turnpike) to Worcester/Auburn, MA; or I-95 to Providence/Pawtucket, RI; or MA and RI Rts. 146 and 122 to connecting cities.

VISITOR ACTIVITIES
Auto touring, hiking, fishing, touring historic sites and natural areas, biking, bird watching, canoeing and picnicking.

PERMITS, FEES & LIMITATIONS
The Federal government does not own or manage land in the Blackstone River Valley.

ACCESSIBILITY
Varies at facilities and parks throughout the valley. Call for details.

CAMPING & LODGING
Hotels, motels and bed and breakfasts are throughout the Valley, especially in the Worcester, MA, and Providence, RI, areas.

FOOD & SUPPLIES
Restaurants and supply stores are throughout the Valley.

FIRST AID/ HOSPITAL
There are hospitals in Providence, Pawtucket, Woonsocket, Milford and Worcester.

GENERAL INFORMATION
The Blackstone River Valley National Heritage Corridor is a new type of National Park in which the Federal government does not own or manage land but works with numerous state, local and private partners to help protect historic and natural resources of the Valley.

Boston African American National Historic Site

Boston, Massachusetts

The Site contains 15 pre-Civil War African American history structures linked by the 1.6-mile (2.5 km) Black Heritage Trail. The meeting house is the oldest, standing, African American church in the United States. Augustus Saint-Gaudens' memorial to Robert Gould Shaw, the white officer who first led African American troops during the Civil War, stands on the trail.

MAILING ADDRESS	Site Manager, Boston African American National Historic Site, National Park Service, 46 Joy St., Boston, MA 02114 **Telephone:** 617-742-5415
DIRECTIONS	Since parking is difficult in downtown Boston, visitors are advised to park and take mass transit (MBTA Green or Red lines to the Park Street Station). If driving from the Massachusetts Turnpike, take the Prudential-Copley Square Exit to Stuart Street, then left onto Rt. 28 to the Boston Common. From Rt. 93, take Storrow Drive to Copley Square Exit. Turn left onto Beacon, right onto Arlington, left onto Boylston, left onto Charles Street (Rt. 28).
VISITOR ACTIVITIES	• Self-guided walking tours. • Guided tours are offered daily Memorial Day to Labor Day and by special request at other times. • Restrooms and information are located at the Site's Office. • The 1.6-mile (2.5 km) Black Heritage Trail connects the 14 sites. • The Site is open 5 days a week in the winter, spring and fall from 9 a.m. to 4 p.m., and in the summer from 9 a.m. to 5 p.m. The Site is closed Thanksgiving, Dec. 25 and Jan. 1.
PERMITS, FEES & LIMITATIONS	• No entrance fee. • Driving is difficult on Beacon Hill. • Historic homes on the Black Heritage Trail are not open to the public.
CAMPING & LODGING	A list of overnight accommodations available in Boston is offered at the Site Office.
FOOD & SUPPLIES	Food and supplies are available on Charles and Cambridge streets.
FIRST AID/ HOSPITAL	• First aid is not available in the Site. • Massachusetts General and Tufts University Clinic are located nearby in Boston.
GENERAL INFORMATION	The African Meeting House is open to the public on weekdays during the winter, spring and fall and daily during the summer.

Boston National Historical Park

Boston, Massachusetts

Learn about the revolutionary generation of Bostonians who blazed a trail from colonialism to independence by taking a walking tour. The 16 Boston National Historical Park sites are connected by the 2.5-mile (4 km) *Freedom Trail* that runs through downtown Boston and Charlestown.

MAILING ADDRESS	Superintendent, Boston National Historical Park, Charlestown Navy Yard, Boston, MA 02129 **Telephone:** 617-242-5644
DIRECTIONS	Visitors are advised not to drive in downtown Boston. Mass transit provides a good option. If driving, from Route 1 south and Route 93 north or south, follow the signs to the Charlestown Navy Yard (berth of the *U.S.S. Constitution*). Further directions into downtown Boston are available there.

VISITOR ACTIVITIES

• During the peak season (summer), the sites provide information in a variety of ways including tours, lectures, costumed interpretation, exhibits and publications. • National Park Service Rangers are at the Charlestown Navy Yard, Bunker Hill, Faneuil Hall and the downtown Visitor Center daily. • Rangers conduct 90-minute walking tours of the downtown portion of Boston's Freedom Trail daily from mid-April through November. • Rangers present historical talks at Faneuil Hall and the Bunker Hill Monument year-round. • At the Navy Yard, the US Navy conducts tours of the *U.S.S. Constitution* (Old Ironsides) daily from 9:30 a.m. to 3:50 p.m. Nearby, the USS Constitution Museum features exhibits and a gift shop. • Rangers conduct tours of the Navy Yard, Commandant's House and World War II Destroyer *U.S.S. Cassin Young* seasonally. • The Dorchester Heights Monument and grounds are currently undergoing preservation and rehabilitation. • Facilities include restrooms at the Visitor Center, Navy Yard and Faneuil Hall. • The Park is open in the summer from 9 a.m. to 6 p.m., and 9 a.m. to 5 p.m., in the winter or 10 a.m. to 5 p.m., depending on the site. The Park is closed Thanksgiving, Dec. 25 and Jan. 1.

PERMITS, FEES & LIMITATIONS

• Entrance fees are collected at the privately owned and operated sites by self-supporting associations working cooperatively with the Park. • Permits are required for special uses. • Commercial parking and limited free parking is available at the Navy Yard outside the Park. Commercial parking rates at fairly high costs are available in the city convenient to the Freedom Trail and public transportation.

ACCESSIBILITY

Restrooms at the Visitor Center, Faneuil Hall and Navy Yard are accessible. The USS Constitution Museum and a snack bar are accessible.

CAMPING & LODGING

Hotels and motels are located throughout the city.

FOOD & SUPPLIES

• A snack bar with inside and outside seating and counter service is available in the summer. • Food and supplies are available in Quincy Market, North End and Charlestown. There are many restaurants in the vicinity.

FIRST AID/ HOSPITAL

• First aid is available in the Park. • Hospitals near the sites include Massachusetts General, Bunker Hill Community Health Center, Tufts University and University Hospital.

Cape Cod National Seashore

South Wellfleet, Massachusetts

Each of the Cape Cod National Seashore sites within the 40-mile (64.5 km) section between Provincetown and Chatham reveals part of the Cape's rich history, including shifting sands and the area where the Pilgrims landed in 1620 before sailing to Plymouth.

MAILING ADDRESS	Superintendent, Cape Cod National Seashore, South Wellfleet, MA 02663 Telephone: 508-349-3785
DIRECTIONS	The 2 visitor centers are: Salt Pond Visitor Center (located on US Highway 6 in Eastham) and Province Lands Visitor Center (located on Race Point Road in Provincetown). Headquarters is at the Marconi Station Area in Wellfleet.
VISITOR ACTIVITIES	• Swimming, fishing, surfing, hiking, biking, picnicking, canoeing, shell-fishing, bird watching, photography, horseback riding, interpretive exhibits, ranger-guided programs and audiovisual exhibits. • The Salt Pond Visitor Center and Province Lands Visitor Center are open from 9 a.m. to 6 p.m., in the summer with reduced hours at other times. The visitor centers are closed from December through mid-April. • The Seashore is open from 6 a.m. to midnight daily.
PERMITS, FEES & LIMITATIONS	• The beach **entrance fee** is $5 per carload from late June through Labor Day. A seasonal pass is available for $15. • Oversand vehicle permits are $45, self-contained $75.
ACCESSIBILITY	Parking, restrooms, visitor centers and headquarters are accessible. The Coast Guard Beach and Herring Cove Beach are accessible. The Buttonbush Trail for the Blind is in Eastham. An accessibility folder is available upon request. Marconi Station and Fort Hill are good overlooks.
CAMPING & LODGING	• Various private campgrounds are available locally. Reservations are essential in summer. • Nickerson State Park is in nearby Brewster. Reservations are not accepted. • Lodging is available in nearby towns. For more information, contact the Cape Cod Chamber of Commerce, Hyannis, MA 02601.
FOOD & SUPPLIES	• Herring Cove Beach has a food concession in summer only. • Food and supplies must be bought outside the Seashore along Rt. 6 or in local towns.
FIRST AID/ HOSPITAL	• Emergency first aid only is available in the Seashore. • All towns have rescue squads. • The nearest hospital is in Hyannis, 30 miles (48.3 km).
GENERAL INFORMATION	For your safety - Do not take glass containers, rafts, rubber tubes, snorkels or masks to any beach. The ocean can be dangerous. Swim only where lifeguards are on duty. Watch out for ticks and poison ivy and painful sunburn.

Frederick Law Olmsted National Historic Site

Brookline, Massachusetts

Frederick Law Olmsted, best known as the creator of major urban parks, fathered the profession of landscape architecture in America. His home and office in Brookline have been preserved along with thousands of plans and photographs from 1860 to 1980, including his visions for Central Park and the U.S. Capitol grounds.

Massachusetts

MAILING ADDRESS

Frederick Law Olmsted National Historic Site, 99 Warren St., Brookline, MA 02146 **Telephone:** 617-566-1689

DIRECTIONS

From Rt. 128 (I-95), take exit for Rt. 9 East (Brookline/Boston), follow past the Brookline Reservoir and turn right on Warren Street to the Site (2 blocks) to the corner of Warren and Dudley streets. From the Southeast Expressway (I-93), go to Massachusetts Turnpike West and follow to Brighton-Harvard Street exit, stay on Harvard Street to Rt. 9 (Boylston Street), take a right, go 2 traffic lights west to Warren Street and turn left and follow to the Site.

VISITOR ACTIVITIES

• Guided tour of home, office and grounds. • Exhibits and video presentation. • Facilities include restrooms and a bookstore. • The Site is open Friday through Sunday from 10 a.m. to 4:30 p.m. Groups are admitted at other times by reservation. The Site is closed on Thanksgiving, Dec. 25 and Jan. 1.

PERMITS, FEES & LIMITATIONS

• No entrance fee. • There are special use fees by permit.

ACCESSIBILITY

There is a ramp to the visitor entrance, and the first floor of the house is accessible. There are multi-level room spaces in the office. There is no lift.

CAMPING & LODGING

Overnight accommodations are available nearby in Brookline/Boston.

FOOD & SUPPLIES

Food and supplies are available in Brookline/Boston.

GENERAL INFORMATION

• Parking is limited. • Nearby points of interest include the John F. Kennedy National Historic Site, the Longfellow National Historic Site, Boston National Historical Park (see entries in this book) and Boston Park System sites including the Arnold Arboretum of Harvard University designed by Olmsted, the Museum of Fine Arts and the John F. Kennedy Library and Museum.

John F. Kennedy National Historic Site

Brookline, Massachusetts

John Fitzgerald Kennedy National Historic Site preserves the house in the Boston suburbs of Brookline where the 35th President of the United States was born in 1917. It features a walking tour of the neighborhood that includes the house the Kennedys moved to in 1921, their church and the schools the future president attended.

MAILING ADDRESS

John F. Kennedy National Historic Site, 83 Beals St., Brookline, MA 02146 **Telephone:** 617-566-7937

DIRECTIONS

Take Allston/Brighton/Cambridge Exit from the Massachusetts Turnpike Extension. Proceed toward Allston along Cambridge Street and turn left onto Harvard Street. Turn left from Harvard Street onto Beals Street. The Site is also reached by public transportation.

VISITOR ACTIVITIES

• There is a Ranger-guided tour every hour. • Tours are available for school groups and other groups by reservation only. • The Site is open daily from 10 a.m. to 4:30 p.m., except Thanksgiving, Dec. 25 and Jan. 1.

PERMITS, FEES & LIMITATIONS

The entrance fee is $1 for adults. Ages 16 and younger and 62 and older are free.

ACCESSIBILITY

The Site is not accessible.

CAMPING & LODGING

Overnight accommodations are available nearby.

FOOD & SUPPLIES

Food and supplies are available 2 to 4 blocks away.

FIRST AID/ HOSPITAL

The nearest hospital is in Brookline, 1 mile (1.6 km).

Longfellow National Historic Site

Cambridge, Massachusetts

Poet Henry Wadsworth Longfellow lived here from 1837 to 1882 while teaching at Harvard. The house was also previously used by George Washington as his headquarters during the siege of Boston, 1775-76.

MAILING ADDRESS

Superintendent, Longfellow National Historic Site, 105 Brattle St., Cambridge, MA 02138 **Telephone:** 617-876-4491

DIRECTIONS

Cambridge is a historic city with old and new buildings of interest. For visitors unfamiliar with the area, the easiest way to see some of Cambridge's sights including the Longfellow House is to park in Boston under the Common and take the Red Line subway to Harvard Square. From there, walk to Brattle Street and continue down Brattle about .6 mile (1 km) to Longfellow House. Two colonial mansions, the William Brattle House and the John Vassall, Sr. House, are on the way. A return via Mason Street and Cambridge Common will lead visitors by a bronze plaque that marks the site of the "Washington Elm" where George Washington took command of the Continental Army.

VISITOR ACTIVITIES

• Ranger-guided tours are offered at 10:45 a.m., 11:45 a.m., 1 p.m., 2 p.m., 3 p.m. and 4 p.m. • Garden concerts are offered on alternate Sundays during the summer beginning in mid-June. • The Site is open daily from 10 a.m. to 4:30 p.m., except Thanksgiving, Dec. 25 and Jan. 1.

Massachusetts

PERMITS, FEES & LIMITATIONS

• The entrance fee is $2 for adults. There is no charge for persons 12 and younger or 62 and older. • No parking is available at the Site. Limited parking is .6 mile (1 km) away.

ACCESSIBILITY

On-site parking may be arranged in advance. Call 617-876-4491.

CAMPING & LODGING

Overnight accommodations are available in Cambridge, within walking distance, or in Boston, 7 miles (11.2 km).

FOOD & SUPPLIES

Food and supplies are available in Cambridge.

FIRST AID/ HOSPITAL

• First aid is not available at the Site. • The nearest hospital is in Mt. Auburn, .6 mile (1 km).

Lowell National Historical Park

Lowell, Massachusetts

The history of America's Industrial Revolution is commemorated at Lowell National Historical Park where exhibits and tours relate the story of the Northeast's transition from farm to factory, chronicle immigrant labor history and trace industrial technology.

MAILING ADDRESS

Superintendent, Lowell National Historical Park, 169 Merrimack St., Lowell, MA 01852 **Telephone:** 508-970-5000

DIRECTIONS

Take the Lowell Connector from either I-495 or US 3. Exit on Thorndike Street North and proceed about one-half mile (.8 km) to Dutton Street. Turn right on Dutton Street. Follow Dutton to the marked parking lot.

VISITOR ACTIVITIES

• The Park offers guided barge tours daily from July 1 to Columbus Day, aboard turn-of-the-century trolleys and foot tours (year-round). For reservations, call 508-970-5000. • Self-guided tours and exhibits are available year-round. • Facilities include a Visitor Center at 246 Market St., that is open daily from 9 a.m. to 5 p.m. • The "Working People Exhibit" at the Mogan Cultural Center is open Tuesday through Saturday from July 1 to Columbus Day and Wednesday through Sunday the rest of the year from 10 a.m. to 4 p.m. • Suffolk Mill Turbine Exhibit hours vary. • The Park is closed Thanksgiving, Dec. 25 and Jan. 1.

PERMITS, FEES & LIMITATIONS

• The fees for boat and trolley tours and the Boott Cotton Mills Museum are $3 for adults, $1 for ages 6 to 16, children under 5 are admitted free.
• There is a $1 discount for holders of Golden age, Golden Access and Golden Eagle passes.

ACCESSIBILITY

Accessible buildings within the Park include the Visitor Center, Mogan Cultural Center and the Boott Cotton Mills Museum. Tactile pedestrian maps, braille and large-print literature, cassette tapes of Park brochures and printed narrations of audiovisual programs are available upon request.

CAMPING & LODGING

Several hotels and bed and breakfasts are in the greater Lowell area. Call the Convention and Visitors Bureau at 1-800-443-3332 for more information.

FOOD & SUPPLIES

Many restaurants, diners and cafes are located near the Park. Pick up a dining guide at the Visitor Center.

FIRST AID/ HOSPITAL

• General first aid is available in the Park. • The nearest hospital is Saint's Memorial Hospital, one-quarter mile (.4 km).

Minute Man National Historical Park

Concord, Lincoln and Lexington, Massachusetts

What began as a struggle between British authorities and the people of Massachusetts escalated, on 20 miles (32.2 km) of winding road, into an all-out battle. Seventy-three British soldiers and 49 colonial militiamen died in this battle, which led to the American Revolution.

MAILING ADDRESS

Minute Man National Historical Park, PO Box 160, Concord, MA 01742
Telephone: 508-369-6993

DIRECTIONS

The North Bridge Visitor Center is off Liberty Street in Concord. The Battle Road Visitor Center is off Rt. 2A in Lexington. From I-95, take Exit 30B.

VISITOR ACTIVITIES

• Interpretive exhibits and film, walking tours, interpretive talks and living history demonstrations. • Sales and informational material are available. • Three hiking trails of 1 mile (1.6 km) or less are available. • The North Bridge Visitor Center is open year-round except Dec. 25 and Jan. 1. Call 508-369-6993 for hours and days of operation for other facilities.

PERMITS, FEES & LIMITATIONS

The only fee is $1 for tours of the Wayside.

ACCESSIBILITY

Visitor centers have accessible restrooms.

CAMPING & LODGING

Lodging is available in Concord and Lexington.

FOOD & SUPPLIES

Food and supplies are available in Concord and Lexington.

FIRST AID/ HOSPITAL

• First aid is available in the Park. • The nearest hospital is Emerson Hospital in Concord, 2 miles (3.2 km).

GENERAL INFORMATION

• Please respect the rights of private families living within the Park boundary. • Visitors to the area can also see historic sites relating to the lives of Henry David Thoreau, Louisa May Alcott and Ralph Waldo Emerson.

Salem Maritime National Historic Site

Salem, Massachusetts

In the 3 decades between the Revolutionary War and the War of 1812, Salem's name was synonymous with the overseas luxury trade. Its merchants took great risks to send ships on 1- or 2-year voyages in eastern seas to search for exotic goods.

MAILING ADDRESS
Superintendent, Salem Maritime National Historic Site, 174 Derby St., Salem, MA 01970 **Telephone:** 508-741-3648

DIRECTIONS
Salem is 20 miles (32.2 km) northeast of Boston. Follow I-95 North or US Rt. 1 North to Rt. 128 North to Exit 26 (Lowell Street) or Exit 25A (Rt. 114 East) to downtown Historic Salem. Follow the signs to the Visitor Center and parking facilities. Salem's public parking lots and meters are free on weekends and holidays.

VISITOR ACTIVITIES
• The Visitor Center offers information on the Site and numerous historical attractions in Salem and throughout Essex County that relate to the Site's themes of early settlement, maritime history and the textile and leather industry's history. • Follow the Heritage Walking Trail from the Visitor Center to the Site Orientation Center on the waterfront. • View a brief introductory program and dress up as a sailor. • Visit historic structures at your leisure or join a guided tour. • Check with a Ranger for the daily schedule and make reservations if needed. • Three centuries of historic homes and commercial structures make up this 9 acre Site, including Central, Hatches and Derby Wharves, Derby Wharf Lighthouse, the 1819 US Custom House, Public Store (bonded warehouse) and Scale Building. • Period homes include the Derby House (1760s), Narbonne-Hale House (1660s) and the Hawkes House (1800s), which serves as Headquarters. • Group tours and educational programs are offered, with advance notice, on a seasonal basis. • The Site is open year-round except for Thanksgiving, Dec. 25 and Jan. 1.

PERMITS, FEES & LIMITATIONS
• No entrance or program fees. • Permits are required for (limited) boat docking. Contact Headquarters to obtain information, regulations and permits.

ACCESSIBILITY
The Visitor Center, Orientation Center and restrooms are accessible. For additional information, please call ahead.

CAMPING & LODGING
RV and tent camping is available seasonally near the Site at Winter Island Maritime Park, 1 mile (1.6 km). Call 508-745-9430.

FOOD & SUPPLIES
Food and supplies are available within one-half mile (.8 km) of the Site.

FIRST AID/ HOSPITAL
• First aid is available within the Site. • The nearest hospital is 1.5 miles (2.4 km) from the Site.

GENERAL INFORMATION

The Site map/guide and Heritage Walking Trail map of Salem (including points of interest, accommodations and a calendar of events) are available by mail upon request.

Saugus Iron Works National Historic Site

Saugus, Massachusetts

This is the site of the first integrated ironworks in North America. It includes the reconstructed blast furnace, forge, rolling and slitting mill, and a 17th-century house to recreate the historic process of water wheels, bellows and forge hammer.

MAILING ADDRESS

Superintendent, Saugus Iron Works National Historic Site, 244 Central St., Saugus, MA 01906 **Telephone: 617-233-0050**

DIRECTIONS

The Site is 12 miles (19.3 km) north of Boston 1 mile (1.6 km) off of US Rt. 1. From Rt. 1 North or South, take Main Street, Saugus Exit. From I-95 North or South, take the Walnut Street Exit (Exit 43) in Lynnfield. Follow the brown National Park Service signs to the Iron Works.

VISITOR ACTIVITIES

• Interpretive tours, presentations and demonstrations of reconstructed iron works, film, museum, exhibits, historic house tour, 17th century herb garden, nature trail, picnicking and bookstore. • Call or write the Site for specialized school programs.

PERMITS, FEES & LIMITATIONS

• No fees. • Park in parking area only. • No open fires allowed in the picnic area.

ACCESSIBILITY

Reconstructed buildings are accessible using a special path. The Visitor Center, museum, restrooms and first floor of the Iron Works House are accessible.

CAMPING & LODGING

• Lodging is available along Rt. 1. • The closest camping is north of the Site on Rt. 114 in Harold Parker State Forest in Middleton.

FOOD & SUPPLIES

Food and supplies are available in Saugus Center and along US Rt. 1.

FIRST AID/ HOSPITAL

• First aid is available in the Site. • The nearest hospitals are in Melrose and Lynn.

GENERAL INFORMATION

For your safety - Be careful around the waterwheel pits and other historic structures. The slag can cause severe cuts. Wear closed shoes while on tour of the Site.

Springfield Armory National Historic Site
Springfield, Massachusetts

Gen. George Washington and his Chief of Artillery, Col. Henry Knox, chose Springfield as the site of the first United States arsenal in 1777. Centrally located and within easy reach of American troops, the arsenal was used to safely store weapons and ammunition away from the British.

MAILING ADDRESS

Springfield Armory National Historic Site, One Armory Square, Springfield, MA 01105-1229 **Telephone:** 413-734-8551

DIRECTIONS

The Site is in downtown Springfield just off State Street. Southbound on I-91, take Exit 5 - Broad Street. Turn left at the bottom of the off-ramp. Turn left again at the light. You will be traveling back north on Columbus Avenue parallel to I-91. Turn right on State Street. Turn left on Federal Street. Turn left into Springfield Technical Community College. Follow the road to the left to museum parking. Northbound on I-91, take Exit 4 - Broad Street. Continue straight at the bottom of the ramp. Turn right on State Street. Turn left on Federal Street. Turn left into Springfield Technical Community College. Follow the road to the left to museum parking.

VISITOR ACTIVITIES

• Film, videos, school programs, self-guided walking tour, exhibits of antique and modern machinery and firearms. • Special programs are announced throughout the year. • Special subjects and exhibits include women ordnance workers, handmade to assembly line, muskets to machine guns, life-saving guns, a top 10 of the world's greatest inventions and a small arms collection. • The Site is open from **10 a.m. to 5 p.m.**, daily, Memorial Day through Labor Day, and Mondays from Labor Day through Memorial Day. The Site is closed Thanksgiving, Dec. 25 and Jan. 1.

PERMITS, FEES & LIMITATIONS

No fees.

ACCESSIBILITY

The museum is accessible. The film is closed captioned for the hearing impaired.

CAMPING & LODGING

Lodging is available in the vicinity.

FOOD & SUPPLIES

Food and supplies are available in the vicinity.

FIRST AID/ HOSPITAL

• First aid is not available at the Site. • An emergency care facility is directly across from the museum.

Michigan

1 Father Marquette National Memorial and Museum

2 Isle Royale National Park

3 Keweenaw National Historical Park

4 Pictured Rocks National Lakeshore

5 Sleeping Bear Dunes National Lakeshore

Father Marquette National Memorial and Museum

St. Ignace, Michigan

Affiliated area. The Memorial pays tribute to the life and work of Father Jacques Marquette, French priest and explorer. It is near St. Ignace, MI, where he founded a Jesuit mission in 1671 and was buried in 1678.

MAILING ADDRESS	Straits State Park, 720 Church St., St. Ignace, MI 49781 **Telephone:** 906-643-9394 *or* 906-643-8620
DIRECTIONS	The Memorial is in Straits State Park near St. Ignace, MI.
VISITOR ACTIVITIES	Facilities include a Memorial structure, restrooms, picnic area, parking lots, trails, an overlook, kiosks and a museum-theater building and amphitheater.
PERMITS, FEES & LIMITATIONS	A Michigan State Park motor vehicle permit is required for entry to Straits State Park.
ACCESSIBILITY	The Memorial is accessible.
CAMPING & LODGING	Camping and lodging are located nearby.
FOOD & SUPPLIES	Food and supplies are available nearby.
FIRST AID/ HOSPITAL	Medical facilities are available nearby.

Isle Royale National Park

Houghton, Michigan   See Climatable No. 21

In Lake Superior's northwest corner is a wilderness island accessible only by boat or float-plane that contains wildlife, including wolves; unspoiled forests; numerous inland lakes; and 166 miles (267.7 km) of foot trails and rugged, scenic shores.

MAILING ADDRESS	Isle Royale National Park, 800 East Lakeshore Drive, Houghton, MI 49931-1895 **Telephone:** 906-482-0984
DIRECTIONS	Isle Royale is 15 miles (24.1 km) south of the Sibley Peninsula of Ontario, Canada; 22 miles (35.4 km) east of Grand Portage, MN; and 70 miles (112.9 km) north of Houghton in Michigan's Upper Peninsula. Although remotely located, Isle Royale is within 500 miles (806.4 km) of Chicago and 1,000 miles (1,612.9 km) of New York. It is accessible to all the large eastern and midwestern population centers of the United States and Canada. Transportation from the mainland to Isle Royale is by boat or float-plane.

Reservations are recommended. The National Park Service boat, Ranger III, departs from Houghton to Rock Harbor. Phone 906-482-0984. The Isle Royale Queen III departs from Copper Harbor to Rock Harbor. Phone 906-289-4437 (summer) or 906-482-4950 (winter).From Grand Portage, MN, to Windigo, Rock Harbor or areas in between, contact GPIR Transportation Lines, Inc., at 715-392-2100. Isle Royale Seaplane Service operates from Houghton to Rock Harbor or Windigo. Phone 906-482-8850.

VISITOR ACTIVITIES

• Boating (rentals at Windigo and Rock Harbor), boat tours, backpacking, hiking, scuba diving, wildlife viewing, canoeing, big lake kayaking and interpretive programs. • Facilities include boat tours, rental boats, canoes and motors, water taxi service, hiking trails, guided fishing trips and self-guiding trails. • Full service and facilities are available from mid-June to Aug. 31. There are limited services and facilities at other times. • The island is open from **April 16 to Nov. 1**.

PERMITS, FEES & LIMITATIONS

• No entrance fee.• Permits are required for camping, boating and scuba diving. Permits are available at Rock Harbor and Windigo. • There are a limited number of 3-sided campground shelters and group sites. • Fire-arms, pets and wheeled vehicles are prohibited. • Phone service is unavailable or extremely limited.

ACCESSIBILITY

Contact Isle Royale National Park for a brochure describing accessibility.

CAMPING & LODGING

• Camp sites cannot be reserved. There is no camping fee, but all campers must obtain a permit at Rock Harbor or Windigo. • Lodge and housekeeping facilities are available at Rock Harbor from late June through Labor Day. For reservations and rates, contact the Rock Harbor Lodge at 906-337-4993 (summer) or 502-773-2191 (winter).

FOOD & SUPPLIES

• First aid is available at the Ranger stations. • The nearest hospital is in Houghton, 73 miles (117.7 km) from Rock Harbor.

FIRST AID/ HOSPITAL

• Because Lake Superior is often rough, it is not recommended to cross the lake with boats of 20 feet (6.1 m) or less. However, boats that size or less can be transported on the Ranger III. • Fuel may be purchased at Rock Harbor or Windigo. • Lake Survey Chart 14976, "Isle Royale," is recommended for anyone navigating the Park's waters. Lake charts, topographic maps and publications on Isle Royale may be purchased from the Park's Natural History Association. Phone 906-482-7860.

Keweenaw National Historical Park

Calumet, Michigan

Keweenaw National Historical Park was established on Oct. 27, 1992 to commemorate the heritage of copper mining on the Keweenaw Peninsula - its mines, its machinery and its people - through its Quincy

Unit, home of the world's largest steam hoist, and the Calumet Unit, home of one of the most productive copper mines in world history.

MAILING ADDRESS

Keeweenaw National Historical Park, PO Box 471, Calumet, MI 49913-0471
Telephone: 906-337-3168

DIRECTIONS

Both of the Park's units are along US 41 just north of the twin towns of Houghton and Hancock on Michigan's Upper Peninsula. The Cooperating Sites are located throughout the peninsula using US 41 as the main connecting route.

VISITOR ACTIVITIES

• Important sites that tell the story of the Keweenaw Peninsula stretch for more than 100 miles (161.2 km) from Copper Harbor to Ontonagon.
• This new unit of the National Park Service is in the early stages of development. It will be several years before extensive visitor services, operated by the National Park Service, will be available. A number of major buildings will eventually be operated by the National Park Service in the Quincy and Calumet units. • There are a number of government and privately operated attractions that are cooperating with the National Park Service to tell the stories of Keweenaw. Brochures describing these sites are available from the Keweenaw Tourism Council at 1-800-338-7982 and at numerous businesses throughout Keweenaw. • A visit to the Cooperating Sites will provide a strong appreciation for the excitement, challenge and opportunity the mining industry created. The Cooperating Sites are the Quincy Mine Hoist and Underground Tours, Historic Calumet, Fort Wilkins State Park, Keweenaw County Historical Museum, Houghton County Historical Museum, Seaman Mineral Museum and Delaware Copper Mine.

PERMITS, FEES & LIMITATIONS

• Most of the Cooperating Sites have nominal **entrance fees.** • Most facilities are open daily during the summer. Hours and days of operation vary the remainder of the year. Contact the Keweenaw Tourism Council for more information.

ACCESSIBILITY

Most of the Cooperating Sites have some accessibility measures in place. Many of the sites have auxiliary materials for those with hearing and sight impairments. Most restaurants and several motels in Keweenaw are accessible.

CAMPING & LODGING

• Campgrounds are available in Fort Wilkins State Park in Copper Harbor; McLain State Park, 10 miles (16.1 km) from the Park; and in the City of Hancock. • Numerous hotels, cottages and bed and breakfasts are located in or near the Park. Contact the Keweenaw Tourism Council.

FOOD & SUPPLIES

• Food and supplies are available within the Quincy and Calumet units of the Park. • Many of the Cooperating Sites are near small communities with some services.

FIRST AID/ HOSPITAL

• The Cooperating Sites have limited first aid facilities. • Portage View Hospital is in Hancock, 1 mile (1.6 km) from the Quincy unit. Calumet General Hospital is just outside the Calumet unit.

GENERAL INFORMATION

• The Keweenaw is truly a 4-season recreation destination. Lake Superior dominates the weather. Summers are generally mild. Cooling breezes off of the lake make it advisable to keep a jacket or sweater handy. • Fall colors peak during the last part of September. • Lake Superior's warming effect continues through most of the winter. However, more snow falls on the Keweenaw than on any non-mountain location in the eastern half of the country. The long-term average is about 16 feet (4.9 m). Snowmobiling and cross-country skiing are popular and conditions are dependable.

Pictured Rocks National Lakeshore

Munising, Michigan

Cliffs, beaches, sand dunes, waterfalls and the forest of Lake Superior's shoreline are featured at Pictured Rocks National Lakeshore. The rocks for which the Park is named rise directly from the lake to heights of 50 (15.2 m) to 200 feet (61 m) and have been sculpted into caves, arches and formations that look like castles and fortresses.

MAILING ADDRESS

Superintendent, Picture Rocks National Lakeshore, PO Box 40, Munising, MI 49862 **Telephone:** 906-387-3700 *or* 906-387-2607

DIRECTIONS

The Lakeshore is accessible by car at Miners Castle, 7 miles (11.2 km) east of Munising on County Road H-58. The Munising Information Center, at the intersection of M-28 and H-58 in Munising, is operated jointly by the National Park Service and the US Forest Service. The Interpretive Center is at Munising Falls, 2.5 miles (4 km) east of Munising. The Headquarters building is at Sand Point, 2 miles (3.2 km) further. The Grand Sable Visitor Center is 1 mile (1.6 km) west of Grand Marais, and the Grand Marais Maritime Museum is in Grand Marais on Coast Guard Point.

VISITOR ACTIVITIES

• Besides the rock promontory called Miners Castle, the cliffs are visible from the Lakeshore Trail or by boat. • Commercially operated scenic cruises are conducted daily in the summer from the city dock in Munising. • Sightseeing, picnicking, scuba diving, sunbathing, hiking and photography. • Common throughout the area are inland lakes, ponds, streams, waterfalls and bogs, providing both educational and recreational opportunities for boating, fishing, hunting and swimming. • Winter activities include many miles of snowmobile trails and more than 23 miles (37 km) of groomed and maintained cross-country ski trails in Munising and Grand Marais. Snowshoeing and winter camping are also enjoyed. • There are nature walks and campfire programs in the summer. Consult a schedule at camping areas or Ranger stations. • The Interpretive Center is open daily in the summer; Headquarters is open Monday through Friday year-round, the Grand Sable Visitor Center is open daily in the summer and the Grand Marais Maritime Museum is open daily in the summer and intermittently the remainder of the year.

PERMITS, FEES & LIMITATIONS

• There is a fee for privately operated scenic boat cruises and for vehicle accessible campgrounds. • Backcountry camping permits are required and are available at visitor centers. • Vehicles and snowmobiles are restricted to designated roads. • Pets are not permitted in the backcountry and must be leashed in other areas.

ACCESSIBILITY

Restrooms, parking, grills, picnic tables and a half-mile (.8 km) nature trail at Sand Point are accessible. Accessible camp sites are available at the 3 campgrounds. They are held until 6 p.m. each day.

CAMPING & LODGING

• Camping areas are accessible by vehicle at Hurricane River, Little Beaver Lake and Twelvemile Beach. • Other overnight accommodations are available in Munising and Grand Marais.

FOOD & SUPPLIES

Food and supplies are not available in the Lakeshore. Food and supplies are available in Munising and Grand Marais.

FIRST AID/ HOSPITAL

• First aid is available in the Lakeshore. • The nearest hospital is in Munising.

GENERAL INFORMATION

• For your safety - Hikers should be especially cautious when near the steep cliffs of the Picture Rocks. Boaters should note that Lake Superior is always cold and frequently rough. • Summer visitors should be prepared for occasional cold, rainy weather and troublesome insects.

Sleeping Bear Dunes National Lakeshore

Empire, Michigan

Sleeping Bear Dunes National Lakeshore's diverse landscape includes massive coastal sand dunes, birch-lined streams, dense beech-maple forests and rugged bluffs towering as high as 460 feet (140 m) above Lake Michigan. Several miles offshore sit the tranquil and secluded Manitou Islands.

MAILING ADDRESS

Superintendent, Sleeping Bear Dunes National Lakeshore, PO Box 277, Empire, MI 49630 **Telephone:** 616-326-5134

DIRECTIONS

The Visitor Center and Headquarters are in a combined facility in Empire. The building is accessible by Hwy. M-22 from Leland and Frankfort, MI, and M-72 from Traverse City, MI.

VISITOR ACTIVITIES	• Bird and wildlife watching, fishing, hiking, interpretive programs, canoeing, swimming and cross-country skiing. • Facilities include a maritime museum, canoe rentals, beaches and trails. • The Lakeshore is open all year. The Visitor Center is open from **9 a.m. to 4 p.m.**, daily except Thanksgiving and Dec. 25. • The maritime museum is closed from November to April.
PERMITS, FEES & LIMITATIONS	• No entrance fee. • Michigan fishing and hunting licenses are required and are available at local outlets. • Free backcountry camping permits are required and available from Rangers.
ACCESSIBILITY	Accessible parking and restrooms are available at the museum, Visitor Center and Pierce Stocking Scenic Drive. Accessible restrooms are available at the Dune Climb and the Great Lakes Picnic Area. There are ramps to 2 overlooks at Lake Michigan, and the dunes overlook and North Bar Lake overlook are accessible. The Coast Guard station exhibit at the maritime museum is not accessible. The ferry and motorized tour of South Manitou Island is accessible with assistance. The Platte River and D.H. Day campgrounds have accessible camp sites and adjacent toilets. There is a large relief map and Ranger-led walks for the visually impaired. Guide dogs are allowed everywhere. The maritime museum has a captioned video and captioning is available for a slide program at the Visitor Center for the hearing impaired.
CAMPING & LODGING	• Camp sites are available for $10 per night at Platte River and $8 a night at D.H. Day campgrounds. No reservations are available. Campgrounds are open year-round with limited winter facilities (water only at Platte River). • Other overnight accommodations are available in Glen Arbor, 1 mile (1.6 km); Empire; Honor, 6 miles (9.6 km); and Frankfort, 12 miles (19.3 km).
FOOD & SUPPLIES	• Food and supplies are available within the Lakeshore at the Platte River campground area. • Food and supplies are also available just outside the Lakeshore and in Empire and Glen Arbor.
FIRST AID/ HOSPITAL	• First aid is available in the Lakeshore. • The nearest hospital is in Traverse City, 30 miles (48.3 km).
GENERAL INFORMATION	For your safety - Steep lakeshore bluffs are hazardous to climb and descend due to landslides and slumpage. On Lake Michigan, weather conditions can change drastically in a short time. If you are boating, be aware of the weather forecast and carry appropriate safety equipment. Avalanche conditions exist on steep, exposed slopes after heavy snows and/or strong winds. Hikers and cross-country skiers take caution.

Minnesota

1 Grand Portage National Monument
2 Pipestone National Monument
3 Voyageurs National Park

Minnesota

Grand Portage National Monument

Grand Portage, Minnesota

The reconstructed stockade area allows visitors to see Grand Portage National Monument as it would have been in the 1700s when it was the North West Company's fur trading headquarters on Lake Superior's western shore.

MAILING ADDRESS	Superintendent, Grand Portage National Monument, PO Box 668, Grand Marais, MN 55604 **Telephone:** 218-387-2788
DIRECTIONS	The Monument is off of US 61, 36 miles (58 km) northeast of Grand Marais, MN; 145 miles (233.8 km) from Duluth, MN; and 45 miles (72.5 km) southwest of Thunder Bay, Ontario. Headquarters is in Grand Marais.
VISITOR ACTIVITIES	• Guided tours, exhibits, demonstrations, audiovisual program, hiking, cross-country skiing, picnicking, wildlife and bird watching and photography. • Backcountry information may be obtained at the Monument. • The Monument is open daily from **8 a.m. to 5 p.m.**, from mid-May to mid-October. • Hiking trails include the half-mile (.8 km) Mt. Rose Trail and the 8.5-mile (13.7 km) Grand Portage, which is open year-round.
PERMITS, FEES & LIMITATIONS	• The **entrance fee** is $2 per person with a maximum of $5 per family (no fee for ages 16 or younger or 62 and older). • All vehicles are restricted to designated roads. • Backcountry permits are available from the Ranger Station at the Monument.
ACCESSIBILITY	Buildings, picnic grounds and restrooms are accessible.
CAMPING & LODGING	• No camping beyond primitive backcountry camping is available within the Monument; additional camping is available nearby. • Lodging is available at the nearby Lodge or at motels along the Lake Superior shore. Contact the Monument staff for a list of accommodations.
FOOD & SUPPLIES	Food and supplies are available in Grand Portage, Thunder Bay and Grand Marais.
FIRST AID/ HOSPITAL	• First aid is available at the Ranger Station. • The nearest hospital is in Grand Marais.
GENERAL INFORMATION	• The Grand Portage hike requires sturdy hiking shoes and a willingness to endure the discomforts of the trail, including mud, rocks, mosquitoes and flies. • A boat leaves daily from the dock for Isle Royale National Park, 22 miles (35.4 km) offshore.

Pipestone National Monument

Pipestone, Minnesota

Stone pipes were long known among the prehistoric peoples of North America. Digging at this Minnesota quarry for the red stone valued by carvers for its durability and relative softness probably began in the 17th century as this site became the preferred source for pipestone among the Plains tribes.

MAILING ADDRESS

Superintendent, Pipestone National Monument, PO Box 727, Pipestone, MN 56154 **Telephone:** 507-825-5464

DIRECTIONS

The 283-acre Monument is adjacent to the north side of the city of Pipestone in southwest Minnesota near Sioux Falls, SD. To Pipestone, follow US 75 and MN 23 and 30. A State Information Center is at Beaver Creek, directly off of I-90.

VISITOR ACTIVITIES

• Besides the interesting geology, history, archaeology, and pipestone crafts, the Monument offers an opportunity to observe and appreciate the natural environment. • Picnicking is available. • Facilities include interpretive exhibits, an audiovisual program, an Indian Cultural Center and souvenir sales. • The Visitor and Cultural centers are open from 8 a.m. to 6 p.m., Monday through Thursday, and from 8 a.m. to 8 p.m., Friday through Sunday from Memorial Day to Labor Day and from 8 a.m. to 5 p.m., the rest of the year. The Monument is closed Dec. 25 and Jan. 1.

PERMITS, FEES & LIMITATIONS

• The entrance fee is $2 per person; ages 16 and under and 62 and over admitted free. • No vehicles are allowed on trails.

ACCESSIBILITY

Parking, restrooms in the main building and at the picnic area, the trail, and Visitor Center exhibits are accessible.

CAMPING & LODGING

Overnight accommodations are available in Pipestone, 1 mile (1.6 km).

FOOD & SUPPLIES

Food and supplies are available in Pipestone.

FIRST AID/ HOSPITAL

• First aid is available in the Monument. • The nearest hospital is in Pipestone.

GENERAL INFORMATION

Visitors should visit Winnewisa Falls, one of the stops on the scenic trail.

Voyageurs National Park

International Falls, Minnesota   See Climatable No. 22

Upon arrival at one of the Park's 4 entry points, leave the car behind and set out on more than 30 lakes filling glacier-carved rock basins.

This is how the voyageurs traveled in the heyday of the fur trade in the late 18th and early 19th centuries.

MAILING ADDRESS

Superintendent, Voyageurs National Park, 3131 Highway 53, International Falls, MN 56649-8904 **Telephone: 218-283-9821**

DIRECTIONS

The periphery of the Park is easily approachable by surfaced roads from 4 points along US 53 when traveling from Duluth. County Rt. 23-24 from Orr leads to Crane Lake at the eastern end of the Park; County Rt. 129, or the Ash River Trail, provides access to Namakan Lake; County Rt. 122, south of International Falls, provides access to the south shore of Lake Kabetogama; and MN 11 from International Falls approaches the Park at Black Bay. There are no roads beyond the edge of the Park. Access is by power-boat, canoe, float-plane, hiking in summer and cross-country skiing in winter.

VISITOR ACTIVITIES

• Fishing, power boating, canoeing, hiking, swimming, cross-country skiing and snowmobiling. • Facilities include visitor centers, naturalist-guided boat, canoe and hiking tours, boat ramps, boat and canoe rentals, and fishing and boating guide services and outfitting. • There are about 25 miles (40.3 km) of trails. • The Park is open year-round. Access is limited during lake freeze-up and ice-out periods. Contact Headquarters for Visitor Center hours.

PERMITS, FEES & LIMITATIONS

• No entrance fee. • There are 6 miles (9.6 km) of road in the Park.

ACCESSIBILITY

Both visitor centers are accessible, including restrooms and parking. The Rainy Lake Visitor Center's trail is accessible for one-half mile (.8 km) of its 1-mile (1.6 km) length.

CAMPING & LODGING

• There are 120 primitive camp sites (accessible only by boat or float-plane) scattered throughout the Park, mostly on the major lakes. • Kettle Falls Hotel is located in the Park. • Other overnight accommodations are available in International Falls, Rainy Lake, Kabetogama, Crane Lake, Ash River and Orr.

FOOD & SUPPLIES

• Meals are served at the Kettle Falls Hotel. • Food and supplies are available in International Falls, Rainy Lake, Kabetogama, Ash River, Orr and Crane Lake.

FIRST AID/ HOSPITAL

• First aid is available from Park Rangers. • The nearest hospitals are in International Falls and Cook.

GENERAL INFORMATION

• Some of the land is privately owned, and there are many private cottages. Please respect the rights of property owners. • Boaters not familiar with the waters should obtain the services of a guide or use charts, both are available locally. • The large lakes can suddenly become rough. Keep informed about weather conditions. • Users of small boats and canoes should be particularly cautious and should be prepared to wait out rough water. • State boating regulations apply.

Mississippi

1 Brices Cross Roads National Battlefield Site

2 Natchez Trace Parkway

3 Natchez National Historical Park

4 Tupelo National Battlefield

5 Vicksburg National Military Park

Brices Cross Roads National Battlefield Site

Baldwyn, Mississippi

Brices Cross Roads National Battlefield Site commemorates a battle that was an unqualified victory for Gen. Nathan Bedford Forrest's Confederate troops but which failed in its final objective of disrupting Gen. William Tecumseh Sherman's supply route.

MAILING ADDRESS	Superintendent, Natchez Trace Parkway, RR 1, NT-143, Tupelo, MS 38801 **Telephone:** 601-680-4025
DIRECTIONS	The Site is 6 miles (9.6 km) west of Baldwyn on MS 370.
VISITOR ACTIVITIES	• The Site consists of 1 acre, but most of the scene of action is within view. • Folders are available at the Site. • Signs and markers provide interpretation. • Ten granite markers with bronze tablets describe the action that took place at specific locations and list the units involved.
PERMITS, FEES & LIMITATIONS	No entrance fee.
ACCESSIBILITY	The area is not accessible.
CAMPING & LODGING	Overnight accommodations are available in Baldwyn, Booneville and Tupelo.
FOOD & SUPPLIES	Food and supplies are available in Baldwyn, Booneville and Tupelo.
FIRST AID/ HOSPITAL	• First aid is not available at the Site. • Medical facilities are available in Baldwyn, Booneville and Tupelo.

Natchez National Historical Park

Natchez, Mississippi

European settlement of Natchez began with a French trading post in 1714. Control of the post passed to Spain in 1779 and then to the United States in 1798. In the decades before the Civil War, Natchez was a commercial, cultural and social center of the South's "cotton belt." Its power and wealth were unmatched by southern towns of comparable size.

MAILING ADDRESS	Superintendent, Natchez National Historical Park, PO Box 1208, Natchez, MS 39121 **Telephone:** 601-442-7047
DIRECTIONS	The Park is within the city limits of Natchez, MS, and consists of 2 sites. Melrose, an 1845 antebellum estate, is at 1 Melrose-Montebello Parkway off Sergeant Prentiss Drive (US 61 and 84). The William Johnson House complex, the circa 1841 home of free black William Johnson, is in downtown Natchez at 210 State St.

VISITOR ACTIVITIES	• Guided house tours, interpretive walks and programs, and school programs. • Facilities include restrooms, parking at Melrose and a cooperating association bookstore. • The Park is open daily from **8:30 a.m. to 5 p.m.**, except Dec. 25.
PERMITS, FEES & LIMITATIONS	There are fees for guided tours of Melrose mansion.
ACCESSIBILITY	Accessibility is limited, but improvements are planned.
CAMPING & LODGING	Overnight accommodations are available in Natchez.
FOOD & SUPPLIES	Food and supplies are available in Natchez.
FIRST AID/ HOSPITAL	• Basic first aid is available in the Park. • The nearest hospital is in Natchez, 1.5 miles (2.4 km).

Natchez Trace Parkway

Tupelo, Mississippi (Also in Alabama and Tennessee)

At first, Natchez Trace was probably a series of hunters' paths that slowly came to form a trail from Mississippi over the low hills into the valley of Tennessee. By 1810, the trace was an important wilderness road and the most heavily traveled pass/trail in the Old Southwest.

MAILING ADDRESS	Superintendent, Natchez Trace Parkway, RR 1, NT-143, Tupelo, MS 38801 Telephone: 601-680-4025
DIRECTIONS	The Tupelo Visitor Center is 5 miles (8 km) north of Tupelo at the intersection of Natchez Trace Parkway and Bus. US 45 North or at Parkway milepost 266.0.
VISITOR ACTIVITIES	• Hiking, walking, auto tours, swimming, boating, horseback riding, exhibits, biking, an interpretive film, fishing, running and jogging, Ranger talks and a crafts festival in the fall. • The only Visitor Center is in Tupelo at Parkway milepost 266.0. Several contact/information stations are at various locations. • The Parkway is open year-round, 24 hours a day. The Tupelo Visitor Center is open from **8 a.m. to 5 p.m.**, daily except Dec. 25.
PERMITS, FEES & LIMITATIONS	• No fees. • Hauling and commercial trucking are prohibited. • Camping is permitted only in authorized campgrounds.
ACCESSIBILITY	Most restrooms are accessible, as are all parking areas at Visitor/contact stations. Trails are not accessible.
CAMPING & LODGING	• Campgrounds are at Rocky Springs (22 sites), Jeff Busby (18 sites) and Meriwether Lewis (32 sites). There are no hookups and no fees. Camp sites

cannot be reserved; stays are limited to 15 days during the period of heavy visitation. • There is no other lodging within the Parkway.

FOOD & SUPPLIES

• Supplies are available at Jeff Busby Campground. • Food and supplies are available at Natchez, Port Gibson, Jackson, Tupelo, Cherokee and many other towns along the Parkway.

FIRST AID/ HOSPITAL

• First aid is available from Rangers. • Hospitals are in Natchez, Port Gibson, Jackson, Kosciusko, Tupelo, Florence, Columbia, Franklin, and other towns along the Parkway.

GENERAL INFORMATION

Summer weather is generally hot and humid. Winter is usually cold and damp with occasional warm periods. Spring and autumn are mild and warm.

Tupelo National Battlefield

Tupelo, Mississippi

The Battle of Tupelo, part of a larger strategy by Gen. William Tecumseh Sherman to protect the railroad that was his supply line, broke out on July 14, 1864 when Federal troops under Gen. A.J. Smith battled Confederates under Gen. Nathan Bedford Forrest. Both sides also battled the heat that ultimately forced the Federal's retreat.

MAILING ADDRESS

Superintendent, Natchez Trace Parkway, RR 1, NT-143, Tupelo, MS 38801 Telephone: 601-680-4025

DIRECTIONS

The 1-acre site is within the city limits of Tupelo, MS, on MS 6 about 1.3 miles (2.1 km) west of its intersection with US 45. It is 1 mile (1.6 km) east of the Natchez Trace Parkway.

VISITOR ACTIVITIES

• Folders are available on site. • Signs and markers provide interpretation. • Information about the area is available at the Tupelo Visitor Center of the Natchez Trace Parkway, Parkway milepost 266.0.

PERMITS, FEES & LIMITATIONS

No fees.

ACCESSIBILITY

The area is not accessible.

CAMPING & LODGING

Overnight accommodations are available in and near Tupelo.

FOOD & SUPPLIES

Food and supplies are available in Tupelo.

FIRST AID/ HOSPITAL

Medical services are available in Tupelo on South Gloucester Street, 2 miles (3.2 km).

Vicksburg National Military Park

Vicksburg, Mississippi

During the Civil War, control of a 1,000-mile (1,612.9 km) stretch of the Mississippi River from Illinois to the Gulf of Mexico was of vital importance to the Federal Government. In 1862, Gen. Ulysses S. Grant was put in charge of clearing Confederate resistance remaining at Port Hudson and the stronger, more important Vicksburg.

MAILING ADDRESS
Superintendent, Vicksburg National Military Park, 3201 Clay St., Vicksburg, MS 39180 **Telephone:** 601-636-0583

DIRECTIONS
The Park is just inside Vicksburg on historic US 80 within 1 mile (1.6 km) of I-20.

VISITOR ACTIVITIES
• Interpretive audiovisual programs and exhibits, auto tours, and guided and auto-tape tours. • Facilities include parking and restrooms at the Visitor Center. • The Tour Road opens daily at 7 a.m. and closes at sunset. The Visitor Center is open daily from **8:30 a.m. to 5 p.m.** The U.S.S. Cairo Museum is open daily from **8:30 a.m. to 5 p.m.** Summer hours and programs are conducted from **9:30 a.m. until 6 p.m.,** from June through mid-August. The Park is closed Dec. 25.

PERMITS, FEES & LIMITATIONS
There are fees.

ACCESSIBILITY
The Visitor Center, USS Cairo Museum, and main picnic area are accessible.

CAMPING & LODGING
Overnight accommodations are available in Vicksburg, within 1 block to 5 miles (8 km).

FOOD & SUPPLIES
Food and supplies are available in Vicksburg.

FIRST AID/ HOSPITAL
• First aid is available in the Park. • The nearest hospital is in Vicksburg, less than 1 mile (1.6 km) from the Visitor Center.

GENERAL INFORMATION
For your safety - Drive carefully on winding roads. Beware of poisonous plants, insects and reptiles. Do not climb on monuments or cannon.

Missouri

1 George Washington Carver National Monument

2 Harry S. Truman National Historic Site

3 Jefferson National Expansion Memorial

4 Ulysses S. Grant National Historic Site

5 Wilson's Creek National Battlefield

George Washington Carver National Monument

Diamond, Missouri

George Washington Carver, who was born a slave but who rose to prominence as an educator, botanist, agronomist, "cookstove chemist" and artist, has inspired generations of young African Americans. He helped the region break away from colonial status through his work to encourage farmers away from cotton to soybeans and peanuts.

MAILING ADDRESS
Superintendent, George Washington Carver National Monument, PO Box 38, Diamond, MO 64840 **Telephone:** 417-325-4151

DIRECTIONS
From either Neosho or Carthage, take US 71 Alternate to the town of Diamond. Go west 2 miles (3.2 km) on State Highway V and then south for 1 mile (1.6 km).

VISITOR ACTIVITIES
• Interpretive exhibits and film, guided tours and picnicking. • Facilities include a Visitor Center, parking and picnic areas. • The Monument is open daily from 8:30 a.m. to 5 p.m., with extended hours to 7 p.m., from Memorial Day to Labor Day. The Monument is closed Dec. 25.

PERMITS, FEES & LIMITATIONS
Permits and fees are required for some activities.

ACCESSIBILITY
The Carver Trail has slight inclines and is partially accessible. Drinking fountains, parking and displays are accessible. There are ramps and a subtitled film. An extra wheelchair is available.

CAMPING & LODGING
Overnight accommodations are available in Neosho, 10 miles (16.1 km); and Joplin, 14 miles (22.5 km).

FOOD & SUPPLIES
Food and supplies are available in Diamond.

FIRST AID/ HOSPITAL
• First aid is available in the Monument. • Hospitals are in Joplin and Neosho.

GENERAL INFORMATION
• Learn to identify and avoid poison ivy, which is found along the Carver Trail. • A prairie restoration project is in progress.

Harry S Truman National Historic Site

Independence, Missouri

The Gates house on Delaware Street in Independence, Missouri, began as the 19th century "mansion" belonging to the grandparents of Elizabeth Virginia Wallace, later to become Mrs. Harry Truman and the First Lady. During Truman's Presidency, it was the "Summer White House" before being purchased by the Trumans as their retirement home.

MAILING ADDRESS
Superintendent, Harry S Truman National Historic Site, 223 North Main St., Independence, MO 64050 **Telephone:** 816-254-2720

DIRECTIONS
Go east on Truman Road from I-435 or north on Noland Road from I-70. The Site is 2 blocks west on Truman Road from Noland Road.

VISITOR ACTIVITIES
• Tickets for guided tours are available only at the Truman Home Ticket and Information Center at the corner of Truman Road and Main Street adjacent to Independence Square. • Tickets are distributed on a first-come, first-served basis. Everyone older than 1 year must have a ticket. • There is no advanced registration for tickets or special group accommodation. • Walking tours are available daily in the summer season. • The ticket center is open daily from **8:30 a.m. to 5 p.m.**, except Thanksgiving, Dec. 25 and Jan. 1. • No home tours are given on Mondays from Labor Day to Memorial Day.

PERMITS, FEES & LIMITATIONS
The **entrance fee** is $2 per person (no fee for ages 16 and younger or 62 and older).

ACCESSIBILITY
Parking at the ticket center and Truman Home. Accessible restrooms only at the ticket center. The center is accessible. The Truman Home has a stair-trac step climbing device, and a wheelchair is available. A captioned slide program is available on request. Scripts are available in Spanish, German and Japanese. Large print scripts are also available.

CAMPING & LODGING
Lodging is available nearby.

FOOD & SUPPLIES
Food and supplies are available near the Ticket and Information Center.

FIRST AID/ HOSPITAL
• First aid is available in the Site. • The nearest hospital is 1 mile (1.6 km) west of the ticket center.

GENERAL INFORMATION
In the summer, tour tickets are frequently all distributed by 12:30 p.m. Arrive early in the day to avoid disappointment.

Jefferson National Expansion Memorial
St. Louis, Missouri

Jefferson National Expansion Memorial is a testament to Thomas Jefferson's vision of a continental United States. It includes exhibits, films and artifacts to help visitors understand westward expansion in the 19th century. The Memorial also contains the Gateway Arch, the mightiest free-standing arch ever built, to celebrate Jefferson's soaring mind.

Missouri

MAILING ADDRESS	Superintendent, Jefferson National Expansion Memorial, 11 North Fourth St., St. Louis, MO 63102 **Telephone:** 314-425-4465
DIRECTIONS	The Memorial is in the heart of downtown St. Louis on the Mississippi River.
VISITOR ACTIVITIES	• Interpretive exhibits, walking, photography, ascending the Arch and a film that details construction of the arch. • Facilities include the Old Courthouse, the Gateway Arch, the Museum of Westward Expansion, a new 70mm World Odyssey widescreen theater, a fee parking lot and restrooms. • The Memorial is open daily from 9 a.m. to 6 p.m., and 8 a.m. to 10 p.m., from Memorial Day through Labor Day. The Memorial is closed Thanksgiving, Dec. 25 and Jan. 1. • The Old Courthouse is open daily from 8 a.m. to 4:30 p.m., except Thanksgiving, Dec. 25 and Jan. 1.
PERMITS, FEES & LIMITATIONS	• The entrance fee is $2 per person and no more than $4 per family. • The fee for the elevator ride to the top of the Arch is $2.50 for adults and $.50 for children under 13. • Separate fees are charged for the 2 films.
ACCESSIBILITY	A 4-minute self-service video program is available in the Arch Visitor Center to provide current access information. A similar video is available at the Old Courthouse. Accessible restrooms are available in the Arch lobby and in the Museum.
CAMPING & LODGING	Overnight accommodations are available in St. Louis.
FOOD & SUPPLIES	Food and supplies are available in St. Louis.
FIRST AID/ HOSPITAL	• First aid is available in the Memorial. • The nearest hospital is in St. Louis, within 8 miles (12.9 km).
GENERAL INFORMATION	**For your safety** - Use caution on walkways, stairs and step-down wells. Be extra careful in the Old Courthouse, which has many steps and varying floor levels.

Ulysses S. Grant National Historic Site

St. Louis, Missouri

Open by appointment only. Ulysses S. Grant, commanding general of Federal forces during the Civil War and President of the United States, lived on this St. Louis County estate in the years before the war.

MAILING ADDRESS	Superintendent, Ulysses S. Grant National Historic Site, 7400 Grant Road, St. Louis, MO 63123 **Telephone:** 314-842-1867
VISITOR ACTIVITIES	While the National Park Service conducts architectural, engineering and historical research, the Site is currently open to formal groups by appointment only.

Wilson's Creek National Battlefield

Springfield, Missouri

Named for the stream that crosses the area, the Battle of Wilson's Creek was fought 10 miles (16.1 km) southwest of Springfield, MO, on Aug. 10, 1861. It was a bitter struggle between Union and Confederate forces for control of Missouri in the first year of the Civil War.

MAILING ADDRESS
Superintendent, Rt. 2, Box 75, Republic, MO 65738 **Telephone:** 417-732-2662

DIRECTIONS
The Battlefield is at the intersection of Rt. ZZ and Farm Road 182. From I-44, take Rt. MM south to Rt. ZZ south to intersection with Farm Road 182. From US 60/65, drive west on MO 14 to Rt. ZZ, south to the intersection with Farm Road 182.

VISITOR ACTIVITIES
• The Visitor Center contains a 13-minute film, an electric troop movement map, exhibits and a bookstore. • A 5-mile (8 km), self-guided tour road contains 8 stops, including historic Ray House and Bloody Hill. • Hiking trails and a picnic area are available. • The Visitor Center is open from 8 a.m. to 5 p.m., year-round. There are extended tour road hours in summer. The Battlefield is closed Dec. 25 and Jan. 1. • Interpretive programs include tours of Ray House and Bloody Hill, weapons firing demonstrations and living history demonstrations.

PERMITS, FEES & LIMITATIONS
• The entrance fee is $2 per adult, and $4 per carload/family. • Off-road vehicle use and relic collecting are prohibited. • Bicycles are restricted to a designated lane on the tour road.

ACCESSIBILITY
The Visitor Center is accessible. A donor wheelchair is available. Tour road stops are accessible. Hiking trails are not accessible.

CAMPING & LODGING
Overnight accommodations are available in Springfield, 10 miles (16.1 km).

FOOD & SUPPLIES
Food and supplies are available in Republic, 3 miles (4.8 km) or Springfield.

FIRST AID/ HOSPITAL
• First aid is available at the Battlefield. • There is an ambulance service from Republic to Springfield. • Hospitals are in Springfield.

GENERAL INFORMATION
• A schedule of interpretive programs is in the Visitor Center. • Hiking historic trails is encouraged, but beware of ticks and chiggers. • The water in Wilson's Creek is unhealthy. Do not fish, wade or drink. • Allow a minimum of 3 hours for a visit.

Montana

1 Big Hole National Battlefield

2 Bighorn Canyon National Recreation Area

3 Glacier National Park

4 Grant-Kohrs Ranch National Historic Site

5 Little Bighorn Battlefield National Monument

Montana

Big Hole National Battlefield

Wisdom, Montana

In the summer of 1877, 5 bands of Nez Perce Indians fleeing from United States Army troops fought at the site of Big Hole National Battlefield. The overwhelming loss of life at this battle was a tragic turning point in the Nez Perce War of 1877.

MAILING ADDRESS	Big Hole National Battlefield, PO Box 237, Wisdom, MT 59761 **Telephone:** 406-689-3155
DIRECTIONS	The Battlefield is 10 miles (16.1 km) west of Wisdom on MT 43.
VISITOR ACTIVITIES	Audiovisual and interpretive exhibits, self-guiding tours, picnicking, interpretive demonstrations and fishing.
PERMITS, FEES & LIMITATIONS	• The entrance fee from May to September is $2 per person or $4 per car. • A Montana fishing license is required to fish in the Battlefield area.
ACCESSIBILITY	Restrooms and the Visitor Center are accessible.
CAMPING & LODGING	• There are 2 motels in Wisdom. • The Battlefield is adjacent to Beaverhead National Forest, which does have campgrounds. Call the U.S. Forest Service at 406-689-3243.
FOOD & SUPPLIES	Food and supplies are available in Wisdom.
FIRST AID/ HOSPITAL	• First aid is available at the Battlefield. • The nearest hospital is in Hamilton, MT, 67 miles (108 km).
GENERAL INFORMATION	• For your safety - Animals native to the Battlefield are dangerous when startled or approached too closely. Always keep a safe distance. • Pets must be under physical control at all times.

Bighorn Canyon National Recreation Area

Fort Smith, MT (North Unit); Lovell, WY (South Unit)

Boating, fishing, waterskiing, swimming and sightseeing are the principal attractions at Bighorn Canyon National Recreation Area. The 71-mile-long (114.5 km) Bighorn Lake, created by Yellowtail Dam, provides a focus among the steep-sided canyons.

MAILING ADDRESS	Bighorn Canyon National Recreation Area, Box 458, Fort Smith, MT 59035 **Telephone:** 406-666-2412
DIRECTIONS	The North Unit of the Recreation Area is accessible via MT 313 from Hardin MT, 43 miles (69.3 km). The South Unit is accessible via WY 14A, Wyoming State Road 37, from Lovell, WY, 13 miles (20.9 km).

VISITOR ACTIVITIES

• All year-round water activities, including winter ice fishing and other recreational activities, sightseeing and weekend visitor programs in the summer. • The Area is known for a variety of sport fish such as walleye, trout, catfish, perch and others. • Visitor information and programs are available at the Bighorn Visitor Center, Lovell, WY; and the Fort Smith Visitor Center, Fort Smith, MT. • Marinas, open from Memorial Day through Labor Day, are on both ends of the lake. • Bighorn River guide services are available in Fort Smith, MT.

PERMITS, FEES & LIMITATIONS

No permits or fees.

ACCESSIBILITY

Visitor centers and public restrooms are accessible. Assistance is needed to use boat ramps and docks.

CAMPING & LODGING

• No reservations are needed for camp sites. • Boat-in camping facilities are located on the north and south ends of the lake. • Lodging adjacent to the Recreation Area is available at Fort Smith and Hardin, MT; and Lovell, WY.

FOOD & SUPPLIES

• Food services are provided at the Horseshoe Bend and Ok-A-Beh marinas. • Marinas provide camping and boating supplies. • Rental boats are available.

FIRST AID/ HOSPITAL

Medical facilities are available in Lovell, WY, 13 miles (20.9 km) and in Hardin, MT, 43 miles (69.3 km).

GENERAL INFORMATION

The average summer temperature is in the 80s°F. There are sub-zero temperatures and frequent snow in the winter.

Glacier National Park

West Glacier, Montana   See Climatable No. 23

With precipitous peaks ranging above 10,000 feet (3,048 m), the ruggedly beautiful Glacier National Park includes nearly 50 glaciers, many lakes and streams, a wide variety of wildflowers, and wildlife that includes grizzly bears.

MAILING ADDRESS

Superintendent, Glacier National Park, West Glacier, MT 59936 **Telephone:** 406-888-5441

DIRECTIONS

The Park is on US 2 and 89 and is near US 90 and 93.

VISITOR ACTIVITIES

• Hiking, backpacking, sightseeing, biking, horseback riding and tours, excursion boat cruises, non-fee fishing, cross-country skiing, snowshoeing, picnicking, interpretive exhibits and programs. • The St. Mary and Apgar Visitor Centers are open from mid-May through September. The Apgar Visitor Center is also open on Saturdays and Sundays from November through April. The Logan Pass Visitor Center is open from mid-June through September.

• Facilities include boat rentals, hiking trails, picnic areas, telephones, saddle horses, lake cruises and tour buses. • The Park is always open. Park offices are open Monday through Friday from 8 a.m. to 4:30 p.m. • Most of Going-to-the-Sun Road is closed in winter. The road into Swift Current Valley is plowed at times, but its status is weather dependent.

PERMITS, FEES & LIMITATIONS

• The entrance fee is $5 per vehicle or $3 per person. A $15 annual pass is available. Ages 16 and younger or 62 and older are admitted free. • Free permits are required for overnight stays in the backcountry. The permits are available at Apgar and St. Mary Visitor Centers and from Ranger Stations when staff is available. • Vehicles on Going-to-the-Sun Road between Avalanche Campground and the Sun Point parking area are limited to 20 feet (6.1 m) in length and 7.5 feet (2.3 m) in width (including mirrors). Trailers and over-length vehicles may be left at camp sites or parked at the Avalanche and Sun Point parking areas. Rental cars are available in surrounding communities, and a shuttle service is available. For details, call Rocky Mountains Transportation at 406-862-2539. Historic jammer bus tours are also available from Glacier Park, Inc., at 406-226-5551. • Bicycles are not allowed on portions of Going-to-the-Sun Road during peak travel times (June 15 through Labor Day). • Vehicles, including bicycles, are not allowed on trails or off the roads.

ACCESSIBILITY

Contact the visitor centers for information.

CAMPING & LODGING

• No reservations are available for camp sites. Arrive early for best choices. • There are 62 backcountry camp sites. A permit is required. • Other overnight accommodations in the Park are available from Glacier Park, Inc. From mid-May through October, write East Glacier Park, MT, 59434, or call 406-226-5551. From Oct. 15 to May 15, write Dial Tower, Station 1210, Phoenix, AZ 85077, or call 602-207-6000. Reservations are advised, and deposits are required. • The Park's 2 backcountry chalets, Granite Peak and Sperry, are temporarily closed until further notice. • Privately owned campgrounds are nearby. • Overnight accommodations outside the Park are available in St. Mary, West Glacier, East Glacier and Essex.

FOOD & SUPPLIES

• Apgar, Lake McDonald, Swiftcurrent, Rising Sun, and Two Medicine have campers' stores. • Meals are served at Apgar, Swiftcurrent, Rising Sun, Many Glacier and Lake McDonald hotels. • Food and supplies are also available nearby at St. Mary, West Glacier and East Glacier.

FIRST AID/ HOSPITAL

• First aid is available in the Park. • The nearest hospitals are in Cardston, Alberta, Canada, 35 miles (56.4 km); and in Whitefish, MT, 24 miles (38.7 km).

GENERAL INFORMATION

For your safety - Never climb alone. Register before and after each climb. Climbing is not encouraged because of unstable sedimentary rock. Avoid steep snowfields. Keep your distance from all animals and never try to approach or feed wildlife, especially bears.

Grant-Kohrs Ranch National Historic Site

Deer Lodge, Montana

Grant-Kohrs Ranch National Historic Site follows the development of the Northern Plains cattle industry from the 1850s, when Johnny Grant started the first cattle ranch in the Deer Lodge Valley. He later sold the ranch to Conrad Kohrs, and cattle still graze on the ranch's 266 acres.

MAILING ADDRESS	Grant-Kohrs Ranch National Historic Site, National Park Service, PO Box 790, Deer Lodge, MT 59722 **Telephone:** 406-846-2070
DIRECTIONS	The Site is three-quarters of a mile (1.2 km) off I-90 at the north edge of Deer Lodge. The ranch is accessible by either of the 2 Deer Lodge exits. The south Deer Lodge Exit will take visitors through the town to the ranch.
VISITOR ACTIVITIES	• Guided tours of the house, self-guiding walks and exhibits. • Special demonstrations of chuckwagon cooking, blacksmithing and ranching activities as staffing permits. • A Junior Rancher program is available for ages 4 through 12. • The Site is open year-round except Thanksgiving, Dec. 25 and Jan. 1. Minimum hours of operation are 10 a.m. to 4 p.m., with hours extended in the summer.
PERMITS, FEES & LIMITATIONS	The **entrance fee** is $2 per person, ages 17 and older, or $4 maximum per vehicle. Educational groups are admitted free.
ACCESSIBILITY	The Visitor Center and restrooms at the ranch are accessible. Ramps are available for the Draft Horse Barn and Blacksmith Shop. The ranch house and wagon collection are accessible. Bad weather may make packed dirt routes uncomfortable.
CAMPING & LODGING	Overnight accommodations are available nearby.
FOOD & SUPPLIES	• Picnicking is allowed along the Clark Fork River, but it is not convenient. • The Deer Lodge city park provides picnic facilities. • There are several restaurants in Deer Lodge.
FIRST AID/ HOSPITAL	A clinic and hospital are 1.5 miles (2.4 km) from the ranch.

Little Bighorn Battlefield National Monument

Crow Agency, Montana

Little Bighorn Battlefield National Monument memorializes one of the last armed efforts of the Northern Plains Indians, the Battle of the Little

Bighorn, where Lt. Col. George Armstrong Custer and close to 260 soldiers met defeat and death at the hands of several thousand Sioux and Cheyenne warriors.

MAILING ADDRESS	Superintendent, Little Bighorn Battlefield National Monument, PO Box 39, Crow Agency, MT 59022 **Telephone: 406-638-2621**
DIRECTIONS	The Monument lies within the Crow Indian Reservation in southeastern Montana. US 87 (I-90) passes 1 mile (1.6 km) to the west. US 212 connects the Monument with the Black Hills and Yellowstone National Park. The Crow Agency is 2 miles (3.2 km) north, and Hardin, MT, is 18 miles (29 km) north. The nearest cities are Billings, MT, 65 miles (104.8 km) northwest, and Sheridan, WY, 70 miles (112.9 km) south.
VISITOR ACTIVITIES	• Interpretive talks and exhibits at the Visitor Center, guided bus tours and hiking. • Facilities include parking and restrooms at the Visitor Center and interpretive markers. • The Visitor Center and Monument are open from 8 a.m. to 8 p.m., from Memorial Day through Labor Day, from **8 a.m. to 4:30 p.m.**, in the winter and from **8 a.m. to 6 p.m.**, in the fall and spring. The Monument is closed Thanksgiving, Dec. 25 and Jan. 1.
PERMITS, FEES & LIMITATIONS	• The entrance fee is $4 per vehicle; persons ages 62 and older are admitted free. • All vehicles are restricted to designated roads. • The tour road has an 8-ton (7,257 kg) limit. • No commercial buses are permitted beyond the Visitor Center.
ACCESSIBILITY	The Visitor Center is accessible, and reserved parking is available.
CAMPING & LODGING	Overnight accommodations are available in Hardin.
FOOD & SUPPLIES	Food and supplies are available in Hardin and Crow Agency.
FIRST AID/ HOSPITAL	• First aid is available in the Monument. • The nearest hospital is in Hardin.
GENERAL INFORMATION	For your safety - Beware of rattlesnakes. Stay on the paths while walking on the battlefield.

Nebraska

1. Agate Fossil Beds National Monument
2. Chimney Rock National Historic Site
3. Homestead National Monument of America
4. Scotts Bluff National Monument

Agate Fossil Beds National Monument

Harrison, Nebraska

Animal fossils in beds of sedimentary rock, formed about 19 million years ago by the compression of mud, clay and erosional materials deposited by water and wind, are concentrated under the grass-covered Carnegie and University hills at Agate Fossil Beds National Monument.

MAILING ADDRESS
Agate Fossil Beds National Monument, c/o Scotts Bluff National Monument, PO Box 27, Gering, NE **Telephone: 308-436-4340**

DIRECTIONS
The Monument is 34 miles (54.8 km) north of Mitchell, NE, via NE 29 and 3 miles (4.8 km) east on the County Road, or 22 miles (35.4 km) south of Harrison, NE, via NE 29 and 3 miles (4.8 km) east on the County Road.

VISITOR ACTIVITIES
• Picnicking, wildlife and bird watching, photography, hiking, interpretive talks and exhibits. • The Visitor Center is open from **8:30 a.m. to 5:30 p.m.**, year-round. • Trails are open from dawn to dusk. • Facilities include a bookstore, restrooms and telephones at the Visitor Center, 2 nature trails to in-site fossil exhibits and a picnic area.

PERMITS, FEES & LIMITATIONS
• **No permits or fees.** • Vehicles must stay on the paved road.

ACCESSIBILITY
The Museum/Visitor Center is accessible. The trails are not fully accessible.

CAMPING & LODGING
Camping is available in Crawford, NE, 50 miles (80.6 km) or in Scottsbluff, NE, 45 miles (72.5 km).

FOOD & SUPPLIES
Food and supplies are available in Harrison, NE, 25 miles (40.3 km), Mitchell, NE, 37 miles (59.6 km), Scottsbluff or Crawford.

FIRST AID/ HOSPITAL
Regional West Medical Center is in Scottsbluff, and there is a small hospital in Crawford.

GENERAL INFORMATION
For your safety - Watch for rattlesnakes and falling rocks while hiking the trails.

Chimney Rock National Historic Site

Bayard, Nebraska

Affiliated area. A spire of solitary grandeur, Chimney Rock stands 500 feet (152.4 m) above the nearby North Platte River. It served as a guide for trappers, traders and hundreds of covered wagon emigrants who viewed the column as a signal that the second half of their westward journey was beginning.

MAILING ADDRESS
Museum Director, Chimney Rock National Historic Site, Nebraska State Historical Society, Box 82554, Lincoln, NE **Telephone: 402-471-4758**

DIRECTIONS

The Site is 3.5 miles (5.6 km) southwest of Bayard on the south side of the North Platte River. From Bayard, US 26 intersects NE 92 at a point about 1.5 miles (2.4 km) from the Site. Gravel roads lead from NE 92 to within one-half mile (.8 km) of the Site. Travel from there is by foot only on an unimproved trail.

VISITOR ACTIVITIES

• Photography. • Facilities include an information trailer. A Visitor Center is expected to be completed in 1994. • The Site is open during daylight hours year-round. • Trailer #4 at the rest area on NE 92 operates from 9 a.m. to 6 p.m., from Memorial Day through Labor Day.

PERMITS, FEES & LIMITATIONS

• No permits or fees. • Vehicles are restricted to designated roads.

CAMPING & LODGING

Overnight accommodations are available in Bayard and Bridgeport, 12 miles (19.3 km) east.

FOOD & SUPPLIES

Food and supplies are available in Bayard.

FIRST AID/ HOSPITAL

• First aid is not available in the Site. • The nearest hospital is in Scottsbluff, 25 miles (40.3 km).

GENERAL INFORMATION

For your safety - Watch out for rattlesnakes, rough terrain and yucca plants. Boots and hiking clothes are essential.

Homestead National Monument of America

Beatrice, Nebraska

Homestead National Monument is located on the claim of Daniel Freeman, one of the first applicants to file for 160 acres under the Homestead Act of 1862. It is a memorial to the pioneers who braved the prairie frontier to build their homes and fortunes.

MAILING ADDRESS

Superintendent, Homestead National Monument of America, R.R. 3, Box #47, Beatrice, NE 68310 Telephone: 402-223-3514

DIRECTIONS

The Monument is in southeastern Nebraska 4.5 miles (7.2 km) northwest of Beatrice and 40 miles (64.5 km) south of Lincoln. Take NE 4 from Beatrice to the Monument.

VISITOR ACTIVITIES

• Interpretive exhibits, films, hiking, bird watching and cross-country skiing. • Walking tours and living history demonstrations during the summer. • Freeman School is open for limited hours during the summer, usually on the weekends. • Parking, restrooms and a picnic area are at the Visitor Center. Parking is available for larger vehicles and trailers. • The Monument is open daily from 8 a.m. to 6 p.m., from Memorial Day to

Labor Day and from 8:30 a.m. to 5 p.m., from Labor Day to Memorial Day. The Monument is closed Dec. 25.

PERMITS, FEES & LIMITATIONS

• No permits or fees. • Vehicles are restricted to the parking area and NE 4. • Motorcycles, bicycles, ATVs and snowmobiles are not allowed on the trails or grounds. • No pets are allowed on the trails.

ACCESSIBILITY

Parking, restrooms and the museum at the Visitor Center are accessible. Part of the trail system is in the tallgrass prairie.

CAMPING & LODGING

Lodging and city-operated camp sites are available nearby in Beatrice. No reservations are accepted for the camp sites. For more information, write the Beatrice Park and Recreation Department, City Auditorium, Beatrice, NE 68310, phone 402-228-3649.

FOOD & SUPPLIES

Food and supplies are available in Beatrice.

FIRST AID/ HOSPITAL

• First aid is available in the Monument. • Medical facilities are available in Beatrice.

GENERAL INFORMATION

• For your safety - Check carefully for ticks, which are most abundant from May through August. • No smoking on the trails.

Scott's Bluff National Monument

Gering, Nebraska

At one spot along the prairie pathway formed by the North Platte River Valley, an enormous bluff towered 800 feet (243.8 m) above the valley floor. It was a familiar sight first to Native Americans tracking buffalo herds and later to traders in caravans heading toward the Rockies.

MAILING ADDRESS

Superintendent, Scotts Bluff National Monument, PO Box 27, Gering, NE 69341 **Telephone: 308-436-4340**

DIRECTIONS

The Monument is 3 miles (4.8 km) west of Gering, NE, via NE 92. From US 26, follow NE 71 south for 5 miles (8 km) to NE 92. From I-80, go 45 miles (72.5 km) north on NE 71 to NE 92.

VISITOR ACTIVITIES

• Picnicking, wildlife and bird watching, photography, hiking, biking, interpretive talks and exhibits, and a living history program. • The Visitor Center is open from 8 a.m. to 5 p.m., from Labor Day to Memorial Day and from 8 a.m. to 6 p.m., during the summer. • The Summit Road is open from 8 a.m. to 4:30 p.m., from Labor Day to Memorial Day and from 8 a.m. to 5:30 p.m., during the summer. • The trails are open from dawn to dusk year-round. • Facilities include a bookstore, restrooms and telephones at the Visitor Center, 2 hiking trails, 1 bike trail and a picnic area.

Nebraska

PERMITS, FEES & LIMITATIONS	• The entrance fee is $4 per car or $2 per person for bus groups and motorcycles. • Vehicles must stay on paved roads.
ACCESSIBILITY	The Museum/Visitor Center is accessible. The trails are not fully accessible.
CAMPING & LODGING	Camping and lodging are available in Gering and Scottsbluff, 5 miles (8 km).
FOOD & SUPPLIES	Food and supplies are available in Gering and Scottsbluff.
FIRST AID/ HOSPITAL	• First aid is available in the Monument. • The nearest hospital is the Regional West Medical Center in Scottsbluff.
GENERAL INFORMATION	For your safety - Watch out for rattlesnakes. Remain on trails. Do not venture toward the cliff's edge. Watch for falling rocks.

Nevada

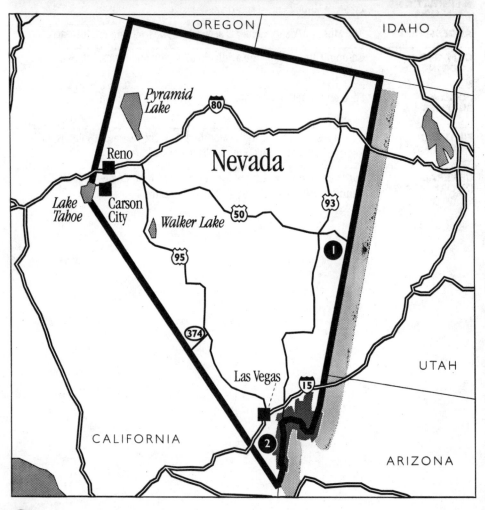

① Great Basin National Park

② Lake Mead National Recreation Area

Nevada · 249

Great Basin National Park

Baker, Nevada   See Climatable No. 24

The name Great Basin derives from a drainage peculiarity. Over most of the area, streams and rivers unable to find an outlet to the sea form shallow salt lakes, marshes and mud flats where the water then evaporates. Great Basin National Park also contains the 13,063-foot (3,981.6 m) Wheeler Peak, abundant wildlife and numerous limestone caverns, including beautiful Lehman Caves.

MAILING ADDRESS

Superintendent, Great Basin National Park, Baker, NV 89311 **Telephone:** 702-234-7331

DIRECTIONS

The Park Headquarters is 10 miles (16.1 km) from US 6-50 near the Nevada-Utah boundary via Nevada highways 487 and 488. From Salt Lake City, the Park is 230 miles (370.9 km) via I-15 and US 6-50. From Las Vegas, the Park is 286 miles (461.2 km) via I-15, US 93 and US 6-50. From Reno, the Park is 385 miles (620.9 km) via I-80 and US 50.

VISITOR ACTIVITIES

• Interpretive walks and talks, scenic drive, hiking, exhibits, audiovisual programs, picnicking, wildlife and bird watching, cave tours, photography, cross-country skiing, fishing, climbing and spelunking. • Ranger-led tours of Lehman Caves are conducted daily on a one-half mile (.8 km) paved trail with stairs. About 1 1/2 hours are required for the tour. The cave averages 50°F, so warm clothing is suggested. Tours are limited to 30 people. Children under 16 must be accompanied by an adult. • Facilities include a Visitor Center, hiking trails, cafe and gift shop, picnic area, public telephones, and a trailer dump station. • The Park is always open. The Visitor Center is open year-round from 8 a.m. to 5 p.m., except Thanksgiving, Dec. 25 and Jan. 1. • Cave tours are scheduled at least hourly in the summer. From October to May tours begin at 9 a.m., 11 a.m., 2 p.m. and 4 p.m. • The cafe and gift shop are closed from November through March. The Wheeler Peak scenic drive is inaccessible due to snow from October to May above the 7,500 foot (2,200 m) level.

PERMITS, FEES & LIMITATIONS

• The fees for Ranger-led cave tours are $4 for adults, $3 for children ages 6 to 15 and $2 for Golden Age and Access Passport holders. The tours are free for children under 6. • The dump station fee is $1. • Permits, available at the Visitor Center, are required for cave tours. • A spelunking permit is required for entry into any wild caves in the Park. • Voluntary registration for backcountry camping is available at the Visitor Center. • A Nevada fishing license and trout stamp are required to fish the Park streams. • Vehicles are restricted to designated roads and prohibited on trails.

ACCESSIBILITY

The Visitor Center and first room of the cave are accessible. Some camp sites are accessible and may be reserved.

Nevada

CAMPING & LODGING

• There are 4 campgrounds with sites available on a first-come, first-served basis. • Backcountry campers are asked to register at the Visitor Center upon arrival. Knowledge of cross-country hiking skills is recommended.
• Limited accommodations are available in the Baker area, 5 miles (8 km). Additional accommodations are available in Ely, NV, 70 miles (112.9 km), or in Delta, UT, 100 miles (161.2 km).

FOOD & SUPPLIES

• Food and supplies are available in Baker and Ely. • Visitors traveling from the east should be aware that Delta, UT, is the last stop for gas and supplies.

FIRST AID/ HOSPITAL

• First aid is available in the Park. • The nearest hospital is in Ely.

GENERAL INFORMATION

• Visitors should be aware of the high elevation - 7,000 to 13,000 feet (2,100 to 3,900 m). Those with heart conditions or difficulty breathing should adjust their activities accordingly. • On the cave tours, beware of low ceilings and wet walking surfaces. Use the handrails and stay with your group at all times. • **A special note** - Great Basin is one of America's newest National Parks, created by an Act of Congress on Oct. 27, 1986. A major planning effort is underway to determine levels of visitor use and development. As a result, facilities, permit requirements, and length of use limits may evolve. Stop at the Visitor Center for current information or contact the Park in advance.

Lake Mead National Recreation Area
Boulder City, Nevada

Completed in 1935, Hoover Dam created Lake Mead and Lake Mojave spanning 274 square miles (441.9 km) in one of the hottest, driest regions on Earth. The Recreation Area offers visitors the chance to enjoy water sports and activities as well as desert hikes and sightseeing.

MAILING ADDRESS

Superintendent, Lake Mead National Recreation Area, 601 Nevada Highway, Boulder City, NV 89005 **Telephone: 702-293-8906**

DIRECTIONS

The Alan Bible Visitor Center is near the southwest end of Lake Mead on US 93, 4 miles (6.4 km) east of Boulder City. The 1.5 million acre area stretches 140 miles (225.8 km) along the Colorado River between Nevada and Arizona.

VISITOR ACTIVITIES

• Swimming, fishing, boating, water skiing, dam tours, driving, backcountry hiking and hunting (in season only). • Facilities include a Visitor Center, cactus garden, interpretive programs, commercial raft and tour boat trips, boat rentals, marina and camp stores, boat mooring and marine supplies. • The Recreation Area never closes. • Most hiking is cross-country.

Ask a Ranger about good routes. Write for maps or approved roads. In summer, carry 2 or more quarts (1.9 l) of water per person.

PERMITS, FEES & LIMITATIONS

• An Arizona and/or a Nevada fishing license, available at most marinas, is required. • Off-road vehicle travel is prohibited.

ACCESSIBILITY

Many facilities are accessible.

CAMPING & LODGING

• Camp sites are available on a first-come, first-served basis for $8 a night for developed sites. Nearly all of the 9 developed areas have campgrounds equipped with individual sites, fire grates, tables, water, restrooms and sanitary disposal stations. There are utility hookups only at concessioner trailer courts. • Concession facilities are listed in a pamphlet available by mail from the Superintendent or at the Visitor Center. • Other overnight accommodations are available in Boulder City; Bullhead City, 6 miles (9.6 km); Henderson, 15 miles (24.1 km) and Las Vegas, 25 miles (40.3 km).

FOOD & SUPPLIES

• Fast food and restaurants are available in the Recreation Area. • Food and supplies are available in Boulder City, Searchlight, Bullhead City, Overton and Henderson.

FIRST AID/ HOSPITAL

• First aid is available in the Recreation Area. • The nearest hospital is in Boulder City.

GENERAL INFORMATION

• For your safety - For protection against the sun, wear a hat and tinted glasses. When swimming, be aware that distances to the islands, buoys and across coves are easily underestimated. Never swim alone or from an unanchored boat. • Always check the weather forecast and look for storm warning flags before boating or water skiing. Call 702-736-3854 for a current forecast. • Water skiers must wear a lifesaving device, and an observer must accompany the boat operator. • Waters below Hoover Day average in the low 50°sF, unsafe for swimming in Black Canyon. • Beware of oleander bushes found in all campgrounds - they are poisonous. Do not use any part of this plant for firewood or to roast marshmallows. For poison control, call 702-732-4989. • Do not let pets drink from the irrigation ditches.

New Hampshire

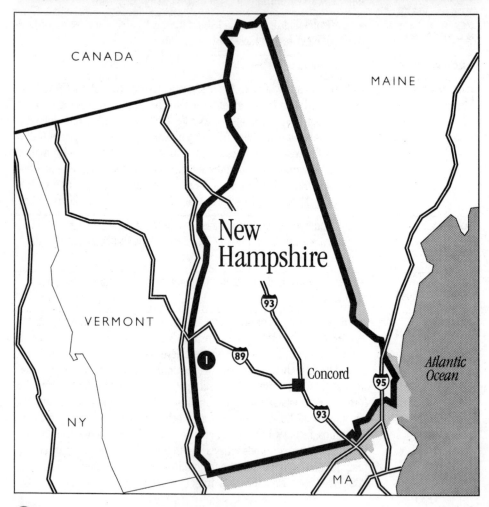

CANADA

MAINE

New
Hampshire

VERMONT

NY

Concord

Atlantic
Ocean

MA

I Saint-Gaudens National Historic Site

New Hampshire

Saint-Gaudens National Historic Site

Cornish, New Hampshire

Augustus Saint-Gaudens spent his most productive years as one of America's most popular and talented sculptors at "Huggins Folly," an ancient mansion crowning a bare New Hampshire hillside, which he transformed into an artists' retreat.

MAILING ADDRESS

Superintendent, Saint-Gaudens National Historic Site, RR 3, Box 73, Cornish, NH 03745 **Telephone:** 603-675-2175

DIRECTIONS

The Site is on NH 12A in Cornish, NH, 9 miles (14.5 km) north of Claremont, NH, and 2 miles (3.2 km) from Windsor, VT. Visitors traveling via I-91 should use the Ascutney or Hartland, VT, exits; via I-89 they should use the West Lebanon, NH, Exit (No. 20).

VISITOR ACTIVITIES

• Interpretive tours of house and grounds. • Saint-Gaudens' art works (100) are on permanent exhibit, picnicking, 2 nature trails, snowshoeing and cross-country skiing. • There is a Sunday concert series and changing art exhibits during the summer. • There is a sculptor-in-residence program at the Ravine Studio. • The Site is open from Memorial Day weekend through the end of October from **8:30 a.m. to 4:30 p.m.**, daily. The Site is closed to visitation from November through the end of May. • Facilities include parking, restrooms, picnic areas, museum, gardens and grounds.

PERMITS, FEES & LIMITATIONS

• The **entrance fee** is $2 per person. Those age 16 and younger are admitted free. • No snowmobiles or other off-road vehicles are allowed.

ACCESSIBILITY

An access map of the Site is available at the visitor kiosk in the parking lot. The historic house "Aspet" and the "Picture Gallery" are not accessible. Nature trails are not accessible.

CAMPING & LODGING

Overnight accommodations are available within a 15-mile (24.1 km) radius.

FOOD & SUPPLIES

Food and supplies are available in Windsor, VT, or Claremont, NH.

FIRST AID/ HOSPITAL

• Basic first aid is available within the Site. • The nearest hospital is 3 miles (4.8 km) away in Windsor.

GENERAL INFORMATION

Temperatures range from 65°F to 85°F in the summer.

New Jersey

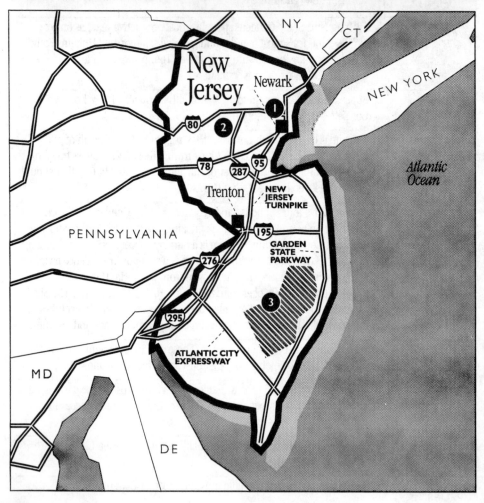

1 Edison National Historic Site

2 Morristown National Historical Park

3 Pinelands National Reserve

Edison National Historic Site

West Orange, New Jersey

Thomas Edison, who helped lead America from the age of steam to the age of electricity through his inventions, also developed this modern research lab in West Orange, NJ, where he worked from 1887 until his death in 1931.

MAILING ADDRESS	Superintendent, Edison National Historic Site, Main Street and Lakeside Avenue, West Orange, NJ 07052 **Telephone:** 201-736-0550
DIRECTIONS	The Site is west of the Garden State Parkway (Exit 145) off of I-280 (Exit 10 Westbound, Exit 9 Eastbound). Follow signs to the Site.
VISITOR ACTIVITIES	• Guided tours, exhibits, audiovisual programs, school programs and special events. • The Visitor Center is open daily from 9 a.m. to 5 p.m. • Interiors of Glenmont and Laboratory buildings may only be seen on guided tours. • Tours of the laboratory are given daily from 10:30 a.m. to 3:30 p.m. • Tours of Glenmont are given Wednesday through Sunday from 11 a.m. to 4 p.m. A pass for Glenmont is available at the Laboratory Visitor Center. Passes are distributed on a first-come, first-served basis. • The Site is closed Thanksgiving, Dec. 25 and Jan. 1.
PERMITS, FEES & LIMITATIONS	• The entrance fee is $2 per person for ages 17 to 61. Persons younger than 17 and older than 61 are admitted free. • Smoking, food and drink are not permitted on the Site. • Strollers and videocameras are not permitted on the tour. • Tour reservations are necessary for all non-family groups.
ACCESSIBILITY	With assistance, the Laboratory Complex is accessible. Glenmont is not accessible.
CAMPING & LODGING	Lodging is available nearby.
FOOD & SUPPLIES	Food and supplies are available in West Orange.
FIRST AID/ HOSPITAL	• First aid is available within the Site. • The nearest hospital is in Orange, 2 miles (3.2 km).
GENERAL INFORMATION	• Buildings are not air conditioned. Due to high heat and humidity in the summer, portions of the buildings may close. • Tours go between buildings. Inclement weather must be tolerated.

New Jersey

Morristown National Historical Park

Morristown, New Jersey

During 2 critical winters, Morristown sheltered the main encampment of the Continental Army. Gen. George Washington held his troops together and rebuilt his forces through the winter of 1777 and encountered one of the greatest tests of his leadership during the winter of 1779-80 when starvation and cold drove his men to mutiny.

MAILING ADDRESS

Superintendent, Morristown National Historical Park, Washington Place, Morristown, NJ 07960 Telephone: 201-539-2016

DIRECTIONS

The Park is most easily accessed by I-287. Southbound, use Exit 36 for Washington's Headquarters and the Museum. Use Exit 26B for the Jockey Hollow Area. Northbound, use Exit 36A for the Headquarters and Museum. Use the exit for N. Maple Avenue/Rt. 202 for the Jockey Hollow Area. Follow the brown signs.

VISITOR ACTIVITIES

• Guided tours of the Ford Mansion, interpretive talks, soldier life demonstrations, exhibits, movies, wayside exhibits and hiking. • Park roads are open from 8 a.m. to sunset daily. • The Museum and Visitor Center are open from 9 a.m. to 5 p.m. • The Ford Mansion is shown only by guided tours offered at 10 a.m., 11 a.m., 1 p.m., 2 p.m., 3 p.m. and 4 p.m. • The Wick House in Jockey Hollow is open from 9:30 a.m. to 4:30 p.m. • All Park buildings are closed on Thanksgiving, Dec. 25 and Jan. 1. • Some buildings are closed during the winter due to staff reductions.

PERMITS, FEES & LIMITATIONS

• The entrance fee for Washington's Headquarters and Museum is $2 for adults ages 17 to 61. • There is no entrance fee for the Jockey Hollow Area. • Vehicles and bicycles are permitted only on the paved roads and parking lots.

ACCESSIBILITY

The Visitor Center in Jockey Hollow and the Museum adjacent to Washington's Headquarters are accessible. Historic buildings are not accessible.

CAMPING & LODGING

• Within 30 to 40 miles (48.3 to 64.5 km), there are 6 state-run parks or forests that have camping facilities. • There are many motels in the surrounding area.

FOOD & SUPPLIES

Food and supplies are available in Morristown, Bernardsville and Mendham.

FIRST AID/ HOSPITAL

• First aid is available in the Park. • The nearest hospital is in Morristown, Madison Avenue, 1 mile (1.6 km) from Headquarters and 5 miles (8 km) from the Jockey Hollow Area.

GENERAL INFORMATION

Nearby points of interest include Edison National Historic Site (see listing in this book) and Great Swamp National Wildlife Refuge.

Pinelands National Reserve

Southern New Jersey

Affiliated area. Pinelands National Reserve is the largest essentially undeveloped tract on the Eastern seaboard. It is noted for its massive water resources with myriad marshes, bogs, ponds and the dwarfed pines from which it is named. Plant and animal diversity, especially rare and endangered species, and an ecosystem dependent upon periodic fires contributes to the area's character.

MAILING ADDRESS

The Pinelands Commission, PO Box 7, New Lisbon, NJ 08064

DIRECTIONS

The Reserve is, roughly, bounded by the New Jersey Turnpike and New Jersey Rt. 55 on the west, the Garden State Parkway on the east, I-95 on the north and the Delaware Bay on the south. The Reserve encompasses 1.1 million acres of Atlantic coastal plain in southern New Jersey (23 percent of the state's total land area), and includes portions of 56 municipalities and 7 counties - Atlantic, Burlington, Camden, Cape May, Cumberland, Gloucester and Ocean.

VISITOR ACTIVITIES

• Guides for activities within state parks, forests, wildlife management and natural areas, historic sites and marinas are available from the New Jersey Department of Environmental Protection and Energy. • For information on private facilities, contact the local chamber of commerce or the Division of Travel and Tourism, New Jersey Department of Commerce and Economic Development. • The Pinelands Commission has published a "Pinelands Guide" that contains a representative sample of places to visit and things to do.

PERMITS, FEES & LIMITATIONS

No entrance fee, but most state, municipal and private facilities require permits, charge fees and impose limitations.

ACCESSIBILITY

Totally or partially barrier-free facilities are provided. Specific facilities should be contacted in advance to determine the degree of accessibility.

CAMPING & LODGING

• Overnight, weekend and vacation camping accommodations are provided at most state forests and county parks. Reservations are required. Contact the New Jersey Department of Environmental Protection and Energy for more information. • Private lodging is available, primarily outside of the Reserve in the coastal and urbanized communities.

FOOD & SUPPLIES

Each of the communities within the Reserve have commercial establishments for food, beverages and supplies. These vary from small roadside farm stands and convenience stores to large supermarkets.

FIRST AID/ HOSPITAL

Each community is served by fire, police and emergency services.

GENERAL INFORMATION

• To obtain a map of New Jersey that will show the location of visitor opportunities, call 1-800-JERSEY-7. • The entire Reserve, two-thirds of which is privately owned, is governed by a land use management plan mandated by Congress and administered by a state agency - the Pinelands Commission. • The Reserve has been designated as an International Biosphere Reserve.

New Mexico

1	Aztec Ruins National Monument	**8**	Fort Union National Monument
2	Bandelier National Monument	**9**	Gila Cliff Dwellings National Monument
3	Capulin Volcano National Monument	**10**	Pecos National Historical Park
4	Carlsbad Caverns National Park	**11**	Petroglyph National Monument
5	Chaco Culture National Historical Park	**12**	Salinas Pueblo Missions National Monument
6	El Malpais National Monument	**13**	White Sands National Monument
7	El Morro National Monument	**14**	Zuni-Cibola National Historical Park

Aztec Ruins National Monument

Aztec, New Mexico

Because they thought the Aztecs of Mexico had originally built the structures, early settlers in the Animas River valley misnamed the site that includes a ruin of what was once a multi-story pueblo of about 400 rooms. The name persists today even though the Anasazi, ancestors of today's Pueblo Indians, built and occupied the community.

MAILING ADDRESS	Superintendent, Aztec Ruins National Monument, PO Box 640, Aztec, NM 87410 **Telephone:** 505-334-6174 (Voice or TDD)
DIRECTIONS	The Monument is north of the city of Aztec near the junction of US 550 and NM 544.
VISITOR ACTIVITIES	• There is a 400-yard (365.7 m) self-guiding trail through the West Ruin. • Interpretive exhibits and picnicking. • The Monument is open daily from 8 a.m. to 5 p.m., with hours extended to 6 p.m., from Memorial Day through Labor Day. The Monument is closed Dec. 25 and Jan. 1.
PERMITS, FEES & LIMITATIONS	The entrance fee is $2 per person. Ages 16 and younger admitted free.
ACCESSIBILITY	An access guide is available. Restrooms, the museum and sales area, parking, and sections of the trail are accessible.
CAMPING & LODGING	Overnight accommodations are available nearby in Aztec and Farmington, 18 miles (29 km).
FOOD & SUPPLIES	Food and supplies are available in Aztec and Farmington.
FIRST AID/ HOSPITAL	The nearest hospital is in Farmington.
GENERAL INFORMATION	• The trail is easy, but wear proper walking shoes. • Help preserve the Monument by staying off of fragile walls and on the trails.

Bandelier National Monument

Los Alamos, New Mexico

An area that is crossed only by trails, Bandelier National Monument is characterized by tan cliffs, forested mesas and deep gorges. It is of interest today to geologists and archaeologists because of its prehistoric Indian ruins, including cliff ruins that extend for 2 miles (3.2 km).

MAILING ADDRESS	Superintendent, Bandelier National Monument, Los Alamos, NM 87544 **Telephone:** 505-672-3861

A National Parks Portfolio

"It was the sublimest spectacle I ever witnessed, and I think the memory of it will remain with me always."

— Mark Twain at the Hawaii Volcanoes

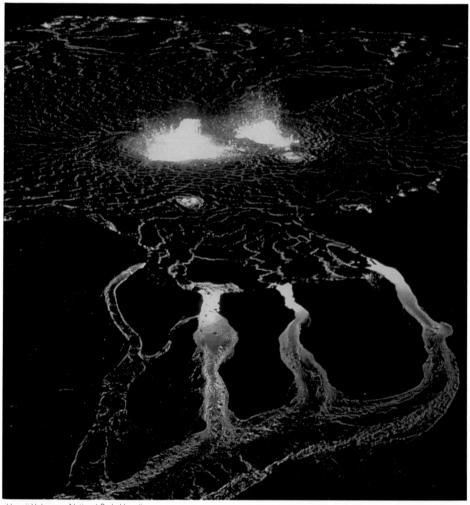

Hawaii Volcanoes National Park, Hawaii

Glacier National Park, Montana

Everglades National Park, Florida

Arches National Park, Utah

Shenandoah National Park, Virginia

Yosemite National Park, California

Virgin Islands National Park, St. John, Virgin Islands

Wind Cave National Park,
South Dakota

North Cascades National
Park, Washington

Mammoth Cave National Park, Kentucky

Bryce Canyon National Park, Utah

Petrified Forest National Park, Arizona

Glacier Bay National Park, Alaska

Carlsbad Caverns National Park, New Mexico

Glacier National Park, Montana

Grand Teton National Park, Wyoming

Kenai Fjords National Park,
Alaska

Yellowstone National Park, Wyoming

Glacier Bay National Park and Preserve, Alaska

Samoa National Park, American Samoa

Wind Cave National Park,
South Dakota

Yellowstone National Park,
Wyoming

Sequoia National Park, California

Canyonlands National Park, Utah

Voyageurs National Park, Minnesota

Everglades National Park, Florida

Great Smoky Mountains National Park, Tennessee

Grand Canyon National Park, Arizona

Wind Cave National Park, South Dakota

Canyonlands National Park,
Utah

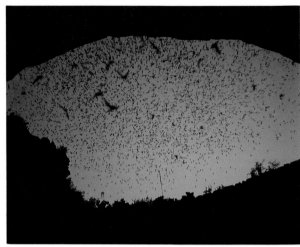

Carlsbad Caverns National Park, New Mexico

Mesa Verde National Park, Colorado

Rocky Mountain National Park, Colorado

Wrangell-St. Elias National Park and Preserve, Alaska

Haleakala National Park, Hawaii

Haleakala National Park, Hawaii

Yellowstone National Park, Wyoming

Lassen Volcanic National Park, California

Virgin Islands National Park, Virgin Islands

Mount Rainier National Park, Washington

Yosemite National Park, California

The National Park System

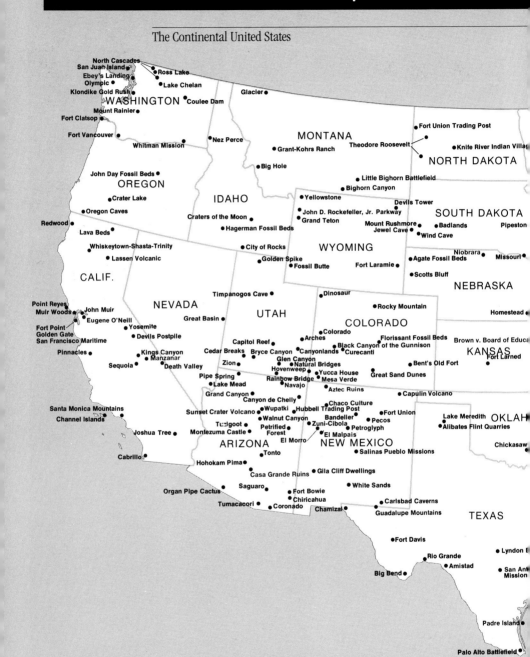

The Continental United States

North Cascades
San Juan Island
Ross Lake
Ebey's Landing
Olympic
Lake Chelan
Klondike Gold Rush
Glacier
WASHINGTON
Coulee Dam
Mount Rainier
Fort Clatsop
Fort Union Trading Post
Fort Vancouver
MONTANA
Nez Perce
Theodore Roosevelt
Whitman Mission
Knife River Indian Village
Grant-Kohrs Ranch
NORTH DAKOTA
John Day Fossil Beds
Big Hole
Little Bighorn Battlefield
OREGON
Bighorn Canyon
Crater Lake
IDAHO
Yellowstone
Devils Tower
Oregon Caves
John D. Rockefeller, Jr. Parkway
SOUTH DAKOTA
Redwood
Craters of the Moon
Grand Teton
Mount Rushmore
Badlands
Pipeston
Lava Beds
Hagerman Fossil Beds
Jewel Cave
Whiskeytown-Shasta-Trinity
City of Rocks
Wind Cave
Lassen Volcanic
WYOMING
Golden Spike
Niobrara
CALIF.
Fossil Butte
Fort Laramie
Agate Fossil Beds
Missouri
Scotts Bluff
NEBRASKA
Timpanogos Cave
Dinosaur
Point Reyes
Rocky Mountain
Homestead
Muir Woods
John Muir
NEVADA
Great Basin
Fort Point
Eugene O'Neill
UTAH
COLORADO
Golden Gate
Yosemite
Colorado
San Francisco Maritime
Devils Postpile
Florissant Fossil Beds
Brown v. Board of Educa
Pinnacles
Arches
Black Canyon of the Gunnison
KANSAS
Capitol Reef
Curecanti
Fort Larned
Cedar Breaks
Bryce Canyon
Canyonlands
Kings Canyon
Glen Canyon
Bent's Old Fort
Manzanar
Zion
Natural Bridges
Sequoia
Death Valley
Hovenweep
Yucca House
Great Sand Dunes
Pipe Spring
Rainbow Bridge
Mesa Verde
Lake Mead
Navajo
Grand Canyon
Aztec Ruins
Capulin Volcano
Canyon de Chelly
Chaco Culture
Santa Monica Mountains
Sunset Crater Volcano
Hubbell Trading Post
Fort Union
Lake Meredith
OKLAH
Channel Islands
Wupatki
Bandelier
Pecos
Alibates Flint Quarries
Walnut Canyon
Zuni-Cibola
Joshua Tree
Tuzigoot
Petrified
Petroglyph
Chickasaw
Montezuma Castle
Forest
El Malpais
ARIZONA
El Morro
NEW MEXICO
Cabrillo
Tonto
Hohokam Pima
Salinas Pueblo Missions
Casa Grande Ruins
Gila Cliff Dwellings
Saguaro
White Sands
Organ Pipe Cactus
Fort Bowie
TEXAS
Tumacacori
Chiricahua
Carlsbad Caverns
Coronado
Chamizal
Guadalupe Mountains
Fort Davis
Lyndon B
Rio Grande
San Ant
Amistad
Mission
Big Bend
Padre Island
Palo Alto Battlefield

Voyageurs
Grand Portage
Isle Royale
Keweenaw
NN.
e Islands
St. Croix
Pictured Rocks

Appalachian Trail
Saint Croix Island

MAINE
Acadia

VT.
Adams
Boston
Boston African-American
Frederick Law Olmsted
John Fitzgerald Kennedy
Longfellow
Minute Man

ississippi
Sleeping Bear Dunes
WISCONSIN

MICHIGAN

Mounds
t Hoover

VA

Perry's Victory
Cuyahoga Valley
Indiana Dunes

Theodore Roosevelt Inaugural

ILLINOIS
Lincoln Home

IND. OHIO

N.Y.
Marsh-Billings
Saint-Gaudens
Saratoga
N.H.
Salem Maritime
Lowell
Saugus Iron Works
Fort Stanwix
Martin Van Buren
Women's Rights
Springfield Armory
MASS.
CONN.
Del.
Roger Williams
Cape Cod

Upper Delaware
Delaware
Steamtown
Delaware Water Gap
Morristown
Weir Farm
Saint Paul's Church
Sagamore Hill
Edison
Fire Island

Eleanor Roosevelt
Home of Franklin D. Roosevelt
Vanderbilt Mansion

James A. Garfield
Hopewell Furnace
Valley Forge
Edgar Allan Poe
Thaddeus Kosciuszko

Allegheny Portage Railroad
Johnstown Flood
Fort Necessity
PA.
Eisenhower
Gettysburg
Catoctin
Independence
Hampton
Great Egg Harbor
MD.
Fort McHenry

Castle Clinton
Federal Hall
Gateway
General Grant
Hamilton Grange
Statue of Liberty
Theodore Roosevelt Birthplace

Friendship Hill
Antietam
Harpers Ferry
DEL.

Dayton Aviation Heritage
Hopewell Culture
William Howard Taft
Mamassas
Prince William Forest
Shenandoah
George Rogers Clark
Fredericksburg and Spotsylvania
Gauley River
New River Gorge
Bluestone
W. VA.
VA.
Richmond
Petersburg
Appomattox Court House
Booker T. Washington

Chesapeake and Ohio Canal
Thomas Stone
Assateague Island
George Washington Birthplace
Colonial
Maggie L. Walker

Arlington House
Clara Barton
Constitution Gardens
Ford's Theatre
Fort Washington
Frederick Douglass
George Washington Parkway
Greenbelt
John F. Kennedy Center
Lincoln Memorial
Lyndon Baines Johnson
Mary McLeod Bethune
Monocacy
National Capital Parks
National Mall
Pennsylvania Avenue
Piscataway
Potomac Heritage Trail
Rock Creek
Theodore Roosevelt Island
Thomas Jefferson Memorial
Vietnam Veterans Memorial
Washington Monument
White House
Wolf Trap Farm

Truman
erson National
sion Memorial
Ulysses S. Grant
Lincoln Boyhood
Abraham Lincoln Birthplace
KY.
SSOURI
Ozark
Wilson's Creek
ge Washington Carver
Fort Donelson
a Ridge
Buffalo
Smith ARK.
Brices Cross Roads
Hot Springs
rkansas Post
Natchez Trace Parkway
Natchez Trace Trail

Mammoth Cave
Big South Fork
Cumberland Gap
Obed
Stones River
TENN.
Carl Sandburg Home
Shiloh
Russell Cave
Little River Canyon
Ninety Six
Tupelo
Kennesaw Mountain
ALA.
Horseshoe Bend
Tuskegee Institute

Blue Ridge Parkway
Andrew Johnson
Guilford Courthouse
Great Smoky Mountains
N.C.
Chickamauga and Chattanooga
Cowpens
Kings Mountain
Chattahoochee River
Martin Luther King, Jr.
GEORGIA
Ocmulgee

Wright Brothers
Fort Raleigh
Cape Hatteras

Cape Lookout

Moores Creek

S.C.
Congaree Swamp
Charles Pinckney
Fort Sumter

MISS.
Poverty Point
Vicksburg
Jimmy Carter
Andersonville

LA.
Natchez

Thicket
Jean Lafitte
Gulf Islands

De Soto

Fort Pulaski
Fort Frederica
Cumberland Island
Timucuan
Fort Caroline
Castillo de San Marcos
Fort Matanzas

Canaveral

FLA.

Big Cypress
Everglades
Biscayne

Dry Tortugas

The National Park System

Alaska

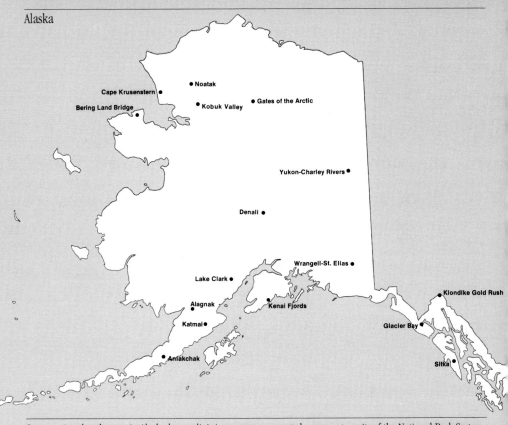

- Noatak
- Cape Krusenstern
- Bering Land Bridge
- Kobuk Valley
- Gates of the Arctic
- Yukon-Charley Rivers
- Denali
- Wrangell-St. Elias
- Lake Clark
- Klondike Gold Rush
- Alagnak
- Kenai Fjords
- Katmai
- Glacier Bay
- Aniakchak
- Sitka

Seven national park areas in Alaska have adjoining preserves, counted as separate units of the National Park System. They are: Aniakchak, Denali, Gates of the Arctic, Glacier Bay, Katmai, Lake Clark, and Wrangell-St. Elias.

Guam

- War in the Pacific

Hawaii

- USS *Arizona* Memorial
- Kalaupapa
- Haleakala
- Puukohola Heiau
- Kaloko-Honokohau
- Pu'uhonua o Honaunau
- Hawaii Volcanoes

Puerto Rico and the Virgin Islands

- Virgin Islands
- San Juan
- Salt River Bay
- Buck Island Reef
- Christiansted

American Samoa

- American Samoa

DIRECTIONS	The Monument is 46 miles (74.1 km) west of Santa Fe, NM, and is reached from Santa Fe north on US 285 to Pojoaque, then west on NM 502 to NM 4.
VISITOR ACTIVITIES	• Hiking, interpretive and audiovisual exhibits, self-guiding walking tours, picnicking and campfire programs nightly in the summer. • Printed trail guides of the ruins are available in French, Spanish, Japanese and German.
PERMITS, FEES & LIMITATIONS	• The entrance fee is $5 per car or $3 per person. • Dogs are permitted in parking areas and campground only; they must be on a leash. • No campfires are permitted in the backcountry. • Trailers are prohibited in Frijoles Canyon.
ACCESSIBILITY	There are accessible restrooms in the campground. The first part of the ruins trail (Visitor Center to main ruin) is accessible. A wheelchair is available on loan for use on the ruins trail.
CAMPING & LODGING	• Juniper Campground has 94 sites with no reservations accepted. Reservations for group camp sites are made through the Visitor Center. • Lodging is available in White Rock, 10 miles (16.1 km); and in Los Alamos, 13 miles (20.9 km).
FOOD & SUPPLIES	Food and supplies are available in Los Alamos, White Rock and Santa Fe.
FIRST AID/ HOSPITAL	• First aid is available in the Monument. • The nearest hospital is in Los Alamos.
GENERAL INFORMATION	Energy and endurance are required for longer hiking trips. You must be in good physical condition since trails lead into deep, steep-walled canyons of the rough and broken country. The altitude, about 7,000 feet (2,133 m), places an additional burden on the heart and lungs.

Capulin Volcano National Monument

Capulin, New Mexico

Capulin Mountain is the cone of a volcano that was active about 10,000 years ago. It consists chiefly of loose cinders, ash, and other rock debris that over time have stabilized and now host a great variety of vegetation and animal life.

MAILING ADDRESS	Superintendent, Capulin Volcano National Monument, PO Box 40, Capulin, NM 88414 **Telephone:** 505-278-2201
DIRECTIONS	Drive 3 miles (4.8 km) north of Capulin, NM, on Highway 325 to the Monument entrance. The Visitor Center is one-half mile (.8 km) east.
VISITOR ACTIVITIES	• Stop at the Monument Visitor Center for a look at exhibits and a 10-minute film depicting the birth of the volcano. • Walk the short nature

trail at the Visitor Center and enjoy a quiet meal at the picnic area just above the Visitor Center. • Drive the 2-mile (3.2 km) Crater Rim Road to the Crater Rim Parking Area and hike into the Crater itself. • The 1-mile (1.6 km) Crater Rim Trail offers outstanding vistas of a 200-square-mile (322.5 km) volcanic landscape. • The Monument closes at sunset.

PERMITS, FEES & LIMITATIONS

• The entrance fee is $4 per vehicle or $2 per person. • An entrance permit is required to drive up the volcano. • No pets allowed on trails.

ACCESSIBILITY

All Visitor Center facilities are accessible. Picnic area restrooms and 2 tables are accessible as is the nature trail. The film is captioned.

CAMPING & LODGING

• Tent and RV camping are available at the Capulin Camp in the village of Capulin. • There are campgrounds at Sugarite Canyon State Park, 35 miles (56.4 km) west; and at Clayton Lake State Park, 60 miles (96.7 km) east.

FOOD & SUPPLIES

• Convenience items are available at the Capulin Country Store in Capulin. • Larger stores are in Raton, NM, 30 miles (48.3 km) west; and in Clayton, NM, 50 miles (80.6 km) east.

FIRST AID/ HOSPITAL

• A 911 system and emergency medical services are available at the Monument. • A hospital is in Raton.

GENERAL INFORMATION

This striking landscape was first described by the Hayden Survey of 1869. Capulin Volcano has witnessed western commerce along the Santa Fe Trail, cast its shadow across thousands of Texas Longhorns on the Goodnight-Loving cattle drives, and now attracts thousands of visitors annually to this unspoiled region of the High Plains.

Carlsbad Caverns National Park

Carlsbad, New Mexico   See Climatable No. 32

Carlsbad Cavern is an incomparable realm of gigantic subterranean chambers, fantastic cave formations and extraordinary creatures, including the famous 300,000 Mexican free-tail bats in residence from the spring until October.

MAILING ADDRESS

Superintendent, Carlsbad Caverns National Park, 3225 National Parks Highway, Carlsbad, NM 88220 **Telephone:** 505-785-2232

DIRECTIONS

The Park is just off of US 62-180, 20 miles (32.2 km) from Carlsbad, NM, and 150 miles (241.9 km) from El Paso, TX. The Park Visitor Center is near the entrance to Carlsbad Cavern, which is 7 miles (11.2 km) from Whites City, NM.

VISITOR ACTIVITIES

• The cavern is self-guided most of the year. Visitors have the choice of doing the complete 3-mile (4.8 km) Blue Tour or the 1.25-mile (2 km) Red Tour. In the winter during the week, the first 1.5 miles (2.4 km) is a guided tour with the Red Tour remaining self-guided. On weekends in the winter, the tours are self-guided. • Guided tours to Slaughter Cave are offered twice daily from Memorial Day to Labor Day, and on weekends the rest of the year. • Bat flight programs are offered each evening from spring until fall at the cavern entrance. • Picnicking, photography, special programs and activities are offered as well.

PERMITS, FEES & LIMITATIONS

• The fees for Carlsbad Cavern are $5 for adults ages 16 to 62, $3 for children ages 6 to 15, and no charge for children under 6. • The fees for Slaughter Canyon Cave are $6 for adults ages 16 to 62 and $3 for children ages 6 to 15. No one under 6 is permitted. • Permits, available at the Visitor Center, are needed for backcountry camping.

ACCESSIBILITY

Most of the Red Tour is accessible. An access guide may be obtained at the Visitor Center desk outlining the route.

CAMPING & LODGING

Several campgrounds and other overnight accommodations are available nearby in Whites City and Carlsbad, NM.

FOOD & SUPPLIES

• A restaurant at the Visitor Center and an underground lunch room are available at the Park. • Supplies are available at Whites City and Carlsbad.

FIRST AID/ HOSPITAL

Rubber soled shoes and a light jacket or sweater are recommended for the cave tours and caverns.

Chaco Culture National Historical Park

Bloomfield, New Mexico

Despite long winters and short growing seasons, Chaco Canyon was a center of Anasazi Indian life 1,000 years ago. Great masonry towns connected with other towns by a network of roads are preserved today in the ruins at Chaco Culture National Historical Park.

MAILING ADDRESS

Superintendent, Chaco Culture National Historical Park, Star Route 4, Box 6500, Bloomfield, NM 87413 **Telephone:** 505-786-7014

DIRECTIONS

The Park is in northwestern New Mexico. From the north, turn off of NM 44 at Blanco Trading Post or Nageezi Trading Post, 7 miles (11.2 km) south of Blanco, and follow NM 57 for 29 miles (46.7 km) to Park Headquarters. The road is unpaved. From the south, turn north on NM 57 from I-40 at Thoreau and proceed 60 miles (96.7 km) to Chaco Canyon. A marked turnoff begins a 20-mile (32.2 km) stretch of unpaved road, NM 57, leading to the south entrance. The Visitor Center is just ahead. Inquire locally about road conditions in stormy weather.

VISITOR ACTIVITIES

• Guided tours and campfire talks in summer, exhibits, walking tours, picnicking and day hiking. • Five self-guiding trails lead visitors through several ruin complexes. Walking time for each is about 1 hour. There are 4 longer hikes as well. Inquire at the Visitor Center. • Facilities include restrooms, public telephones and drinking water at the Visitor Center. • The Visitor Center is open from **8 a.m. to 5 p.m.**, from Labor Day to Memorial Day with hours extended to **6 p.m.**, from Memorial Day to Labor Day. Ruins and trails are open from sunrise to sunset.

PERMITS, FEES & LIMITATIONS

• The **entrance fee** is $4 per vehicle or $2 per person. • Permits are required for the Park's 4 backcountry hiking trails. The permits are available at the Visitor Center or from a Ranger. • No overnight backpacking is allowed. • Trailers longer than 30 feet (9.1 m) are not permitted in the campground.

ACCESSIBILITY

An access guide is available at the Visitor Center. There are 2 accessible camp sites and accessible restrooms in the campground and at the ruins. Some trails are accessible with assistance.

CAMPING & LODGING

• No reservations are accepted for the camp sites, which are 1 mile (1.6 km) from the Visitor Center. Write to the Park for group camp site reservations. • Other overnight accommodations are available in Thoreau, 60 miles (96.7 km); Bloomfield, 60 miles (96.7 km); and in Farmington, 80 miles (129 km).

FOOD & SUPPLIES

Food and supplies are available at Blanco and Nageezi trading posts and in Crownpoint.

FIRST AID/ HOSPITAL

• First aid is available in the Park. • The nearest hospital is in Farmington.

GENERAL INFORMATION

• For your safety - Do not climb on the walls of the ruins, which are weak and dangerous. • No collecting of artifacts, plants or minerals. • Other points of interest in the vicinity are Mesa Verde National Park, 157 miles (253.2 km) north; El Morro National Monument, 96 miles (154.8 km) south, and Aztec Ruins National Monument, 58 miles (93.5 km) (see listings in this book).

El Malpais National Monument

Grants, New Mexico

El Malpais - "the badlands" in Spanish - is a spectacular volcanic area. The area was partially formed as recently as 1,000 years ago, featuring spatter cones, a 17 mile-long (27.4 km) lava tube system, and ice caves in an area rich in ancient Pueblo Indian history and diverse ecosystems.

MAILING ADDRESS

El Malpais National Monument, PO Box 939, Grants, NM 87020
Telephone: 505-287-3407

New Mexico

El Morro National Monument

Ramah, New Mexico

Rising some 200 feet (61 m) above the valley floor, El Morro is a massive mesa-point of sandstone. It was named for the Spanish conquistadors who used the site, with its large natural basin of rain and melted snow, as a camping spot in the 17th century.

MAILING ADDRESS	Superintendent, El Morro National Monument, Rt. 2, Box 43, Ramah, NM 87321 **Telephone:** 505-783-4226
DIRECTIONS	The Monument is 56 miles (90.3 km) southeast of Gallup via NM 602 and NM 53, and is 42 miles (67.7 km) west of Grants via NM 53.
VISITOR ACTIVITIES	• Hiking, picnicking, and interpretive programs by Rangers. • The Monument is open daily from **8 a.m. to 5 p.m.**, with hours extended to **7 p.m.** in summer. The Monument is closed Dec. 25. Mesa Top Trail is closed during heavy snow accumulation. • There are 2 miles (3.2 km) of hiking trails. The Mesa Top Trail rises 200 feet (61 km) via switchbacks - a natural trail over the mesa top.
PERMITS, FEES & LIMITATIONS	• The **entrance fee** per carload is $2 per person or $4. There is no charge for educational groups. • No off-road vehicles are allowed. Vehicles are restricted to Monument roads.
ACCESSIBILITY	Hiking trails are surfaced with minimum inclines on lower Inscription Rock Trail. An accessible camp site is available.
CAMPING & LODGING	• A 9-site primitive campground is available; no reservations accepted. The camping fee is $5 per night. • Lodging and other campgrounds are available in Grants, Gallup and Ramah.
FOOD & SUPPLIES	• Limited food and supplies are available 1 mile (1.6 km) east of the Park entrance and in Ramah. • Full services are available in Grants and Gallup.
FIRST AID/ HOSPITAL	The nearest hospitals are in Grants and Gallup.
GENERAL INFORMATION	• **For your safety** - Be cautious of soft terrain and high cliffs in this natural area. • Dogs must be kept on a leash. • Hiking shoes or shoes with traction are recommended for the trails. • Children must be accompanied by an adult as the Mesa Top Trail is a natural trail. • Advance notification is recommended to best accommodate groups.

Fort Union National Monument

Watrous, New Mexico

F ort Union, originally built in 1851 as the headquarters and supply depot for the Military Department of New Mexico, was the name given to 3 forts constructed near the Santa Fe Trail that culminated with the sprawling installation whose ruins visitors can see today.

MAILING ADDRESS

Superintendent, Fort Union National Monument, Watrous, NM 87753
Telephone: 505-425-8025

DIRECTIONS

The Monument is 8 miles (12.9 km) north of I-25 at the end of NM 161. Watrous, NM, is one-half mile (.8 km) south of the intersection of these 2 highways.

VISITOR ACTIVITIES

• Interpretive exhibits, living history demonstrations, walking tours and picnicking. • Facilities include restrooms and parking at the Visitor Center, a picnic area and a 1.5-mile (2.4 km) interpretive trail. • The Monument is open daily from **8 a.m. to 5 p.m.**, with longer hours in the summer. The Monument is closed Dec. 25 and Jan. 1.

PERMITS, FEES & LIMITATIONS

• The entrance fee is $3 per vehicle or $1 per person for ages 18 to 62.
• All vehicles must park at the Visitor Center. No vehicles are allowed on the historic trail.

ACCESSIBILITY

Parking and restrooms are accessible. A wheelchair is available for use on the trail.

CAMPING & LODGING

Overnight accommodations are available in Las Vegas, NM, 28 miles (45.1 km) southwest.

FOOD & SUPPLIES

Food and supplies are available in Las Vegas, NM.

FIRST AID/ HOSPITAL

• First aid is available in the Monument. • The nearest hospital is in Las Vegas, NM.

GENERAL INFORMATION

• For your safety - Do not climb on the walls or foundations of the ruins. Stay on the trail to avoid rattlesnakes in the high grass. • The first fort arsenal site is closed to the public.

Gila Cliff Dwellings National Monument

Silver City, New Mexico

G ila Cliff Dwellings National Monument offers a glimpse of the homes and lives of Native Americans who lived here from the 1280s through the early 1300s, as well as people from an earlier period who built pithouses, the earliest example from about AD 100 to 400.

MAILING ADDRESS	Gila Cliff Dwellings National Monument, Rt. 11, Box 100, Silver City, NM 88061 **Telephone:** 505-536-9461
DIRECTIONS	The Monument is 44 miles (70.9 km) from Silver City on NM 15. NM 15 is a narrow, winding, steep paved highway. Estimated travel time is 2 hours. Trailers more than 20 feet (6.1 m) long are recommended to use NM 180 (toward Deming) to NM 152 (toward San Lorenzo) to NM 35 (toward Lake Roberts) to NM 15 to bypass the narrowest, winding portion of NM 15.
VISITOR ACTIVITIES	• Self-guided interpretive trail, photography and exhibits at the Visitor Center and Contact Station. • The Visitor Center is open from 8 a.m. to 6 p.m., during the summer and from 9 a.m. to 4 p.m., in the winter. The Visitor Center is closed Dec. 25 and Jan. 1. • Other activities available in the adjacent Gila National Forest are picnicking, camping, wildlife and bird watching, hiking and fishing.
PERMITS, FEES & LIMITATIONS	• No fees. • Vehicles are restricted to the parking area and paved roads.
ACCESSIBILITY	The Visitor Center and Contact Station are accessible.
CAMPING & LODGING	• Camping is available in nearby Forest Service campgrounds. • Limited lodging is available at Gila Hot Springs, 3 miles (4.8 km) south of the Visitor Center.
FOOD & SUPPLIES	Food and supplies are available at Gila Hot Springs.
FIRST AID/ HOSPITAL	The nearest hospital is in Silver City.
GENERAL INFORMATION	• The trail to the cliff dwellings is 1 mile (1.6 km) and steep. Plan 1 hour for your visit. • Summer daytime temperatures vary between 80°F to 100°F and from 45°F to 55°F at night. Temperatures drop lower in the higher elevations.

Pecos National Historical Park

Pecos, New Mexico

Pecos National Historical Park contains the ruins of the ancient 15th-century Pueblo of Pecos, the remains of two Spanish missions built in the 17th and 18th centuries, and numerous archaeological sites in a landmark area on the Santa Fe Trail.

MAILING ADDRESS	Superintendent, Pecos National Historical Park, PO Drawer 418, Pecos, NM 87552 **Telephone:** 505-757-6414 or 757-6032
DIRECTIONS	The Park is 25 miles (40.3 km) southeast of Santa Fe via I-25 from the

interchanges at Glorieta, Exit 299, via the town of Pecos, 2 miles (3.2 km) south, and Rowe, Exit 307, 5 miles (8 km) north.

VISITOR ACTIVITIES

• The Visitor Center contains an exhibit room with 2,000 years of Pecos history and a 10-minute introductory film. • There is a 1.25 mile (2 km) self-guiding trail to the ruins of the pueblo and mission and a picnic area. • The Park is open daily, except Dec. 25, from **8 a.m. to 5 p.m.**, from Labor Day to Memorial Day; hours extended to **6 p.m.**, from Memorial Day to Labor Day.

PERMITS, FEES & LIMITATIONS

• The **entrance fee** is $4 per vehicle or $2 per person. • Vehicle use is restricted to parking areas and designated roads.

ACCESSIBILITY

Portions of the trail and restrooms are accessible. Parking is available at the Visitor Center and the picnic area.

CAMPING & LODGING

Camping is available in the Santa Fe National Forest, north of the village of Pecos on NM 63, and in other nearby areas. For further information, contact the Santa Fe National Forest, Pecos Ranger District, Box 429, Pecos, NM 87552, or call 505-757-6121.

FOOD & SUPPLIES

Food and supplies are available in Pecos, 2 miles (3.2 km); or in Santa Fe, 25 miles (40.3 km).

FIRST AID/ HOSPITAL

A medical clinic is in Pecos, and a hospital is in Santa Fe.

GENERAL INFORMATION

• Please do not climb or stand on walls of ruins. • Because the Park expansion is new, please check with a Ranger for the areas open to visitors.

Petroglyph National Monument

Albuquerque, New Mexico

More than 15,000 prehistoric and historic Native American and Hispanic petroglyphs and rock art carvings stretch 17 miles (27.4 km) along the volcanic escarpment on the west side of Albuquerque. The petroglyphs and associated archaeological sites relate a 12,000-year-long story of human use on Albuquerque's West Mesa.

MAILING ADDRESS

Petroglyph National Monument, 4735 Unser Blvd., NW, Albuquerque, NM 87120 **Telephone: 505-839-4429**

DIRECTIONS

From I-40, take the Unser Boulevard Exit (northbound on Unser). The Visitor Center is 2.5 miles (4 km) from I-40.

VISITOR ACTIVITIES

• Self-guided tours of the Boca Negra Unit are available daily, year-round. • Ranger-led tours into more remote canyons are available from Memorial Day through mid-October.

PERMITS, FEES & LIMITATIONS
The Boca Negra Unit (formerly Indian Petroglyph State Park) charges a $1 a vehicle **parking** fee ($2 a vehicle fee on weekends and holidays).

ACCESSIBILITY
The Visitor Center is accessible. The Boca Negra Unit is minimally accessible.

CAMPING & LODGING
Overnight accommodations are available throughout the greater Albuquerque area.

FOOD & SUPPLIES
Food and supplies are available throughout the greater Albuquerque area.

FIRST AID/ HOSPITAL
Albuquerque offers a full range of medical services.

GENERAL INFORMATION
As a new and developing National Park Service unit, many changes will occur over the next few years.

Salinas Pueblo Mission National Monument

Mountainair, New Mexico

Before they abandoned the area in the 1600s, Pueblo Indians forged a stable agricultural society in this area. They lived in apartment-like complexes in the Salinas Valley, an area that was a major trade center and one of the most populous parts of the Pueblo world by the 17th century.

MAILING ADDRESS
Superintendent, Salinas Pueblo Missions National Monument, PO Box 496, Mountainair, NM 87036 **Telephone:** 505-847-2585

DIRECTIONS
Follow I-25 south to Belen to NM 47 to US 60 east, 21 miles (33.8 km) to Mountainair.

VISITOR ACTIVITIES
• Interpretive exhibits, a 30-minute self-guiding walking tour at Abo, Quarai, and Gran Quivira ruins. • Facilities include a Visitor Center, restrooms, parking, and picnic areas. • The Headquarters in Mountainair is open from 8 a.m. to 5 p.m., daily. Abo, Quarai and Gran Quivira are open from 8 a.m. to 5 p.m., in the winter with hours extended to 6 p.m., in the summer. The Monument is closed Dec. 25 and Jan. 1.

PERMITS, FEES & LIMITATIONS
No entrance fee.

ACCESSIBILITY
Headquarters, the Visitor Center, parking, restrooms, and picnic area are accessible. At Quarai, the Visitor Center, parking and picnic area are accessible as well as the trail, weather permitting. At Gran Quivira, the Visitor Center, parking and picnic area are accessible. Abo is not accessible.

CAMPING & LODGING
• Lodging is available in Mountainair at the El Rancho Motel and Trails End Motel, 505-847-2577 and 505-847-2544, or the Shaffer Hotel (bed and

breakfast), 505-847-2888. • Camping is available at Manzano Mountain State Park, 13 miles (20.9 km) north of Mountainair.

FOOD & SUPPLIES

Food and supplies are available in Mountainair.

FIRST AID/ HOSPITAL

• First aid is available at Abo, Quarai, Gran Quivira and Headquarters.
• The nearest hospital is in Albuquerque, 75 miles (120.9 km).

White Sands National Monument

Alamogordo, NM

White Sands National Monument contains a significant portion of the world's largest gypsum dunefield, featuring glistening white dunes rising 60 feet (18 m) high and covering 275 square miles (443.5 km). Small animals have adapted to this area by developing light, protective coloration.

MAILING ADDRESS

White Sands National Monument, PO Box 1086, Holloman AFB, NM 88330-1086 Telephone: 505-479-6124

DIRECTIONS

The Visitor Center is 15 miles (24.1 km) southwest of Alamogordo on US 70-82.

VISITOR ACTIVITIES

• Guided walks, illustrated evening programs and star programs in summer, hiking, picnicking and backcountry. • Facilities include a museum, gift shop, picnic areas, grills, restrooms and drinking water only at the Visitor Center. • The Visitor Center is open from **8 a.m. to 7 p.m.**, in the summer and until **4:30 p.m.**, the rest of the year. The Monument is closed Dec. 25. The Dunes Drive is open in the summer from **6:30 a.m. to 10 p.m.**, and from 7 a.m. to 1/2 hour after sunset the remainder of the year.

PERMITS, FEES & LIMITATIONS

The entrance fees are $4 per vehicle or $2 per person.

ACCESSIBILITY

The Visitor Center and restrooms are accessible.

CAMPING & LODGING

• There are no campgrounds, but primitive backcountry camping is available with registration and clearance at Headquarters. • The nearest public camping facilities are in Lincoln National Forest, 35 miles (56.4 km) to the east and at Aguirre Springs, 30 miles (48.3 km) to the west. Information on National Forest camping is available from the Forest Supervisor, Lincoln National Forest, Alamogordo, NM 88310. For information on Aguirre Springs, write the District Manager, Bureau of Land Management, PO Box 1420, Las Cruces, NM 88001. • Several commercial campgrounds are open year-round in Alamogordo and Las Cruces. • Oliver Lee Memorial State

New Mexico

Park, 13 miles (20.9 km) south of Alamogordo has 44 sites, some with full hook-ups. Write Superintendent, Oliver Lee Memorial State Park, PO Box 1845, Alamogordo, NM 88310. • Other overnight accommodations are available in Alamogordo.

FOOD & SUPPLIES

• The gift shop has sandwiches, snack food and drinks. • Food and supplies are available in Alamogordo.

FIRST AID/ HOSPITAL

• First aid is available in the Monument. • The nearest hospital is in Alamogordo.

GENERAL INFORMATION

Due to testing on the surrounding White Sands Missile Range, Dunes Drive is occasionally closed for visitor safety. Closures average twice a week and last 2 hours.

Zuni-Cibola National Historical Park

Santa Fe, New Mexico

Not open to the public. Zuni-Cibola National Historical Park preserves and protects the historical, archaeological and cultural sites associated with the Zuni Tribe throughout its 1,700-year history, including its Anasazi, Mogollon and Hohokam roots, and the momentous encounter of the Zuni people with the 1540 Coronado Expedition.

MAILING ADDRESS

Zuni-Cibola National Historical Park, c/o Southwest Regional Office, National Park Service, PO Box 728, Santa Fe, NM 87504-0728 **Telephone:** 505-988-6892

VISITOR ACTIVITIES

Questions regarding Zuni sites and their use should be directed to the Governor, Pueblo of Zuni, PO Box 339, Zuni, NM 87327 **Telephone:** 505-782-4481, ext. 111

New York

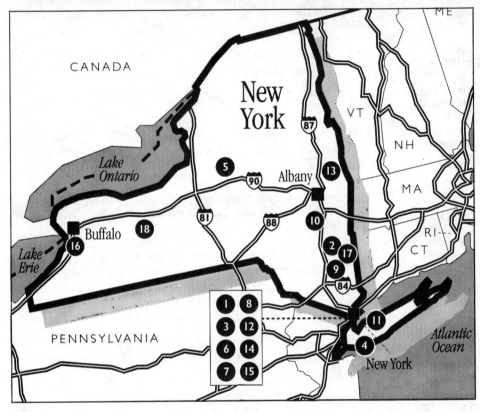

1 Castle Clinton National Monument

2 Eleanor Roosevelt National Historic Site

3 Federal Hall National Memorial

4 Fire Island National Seashore

5 Fort Stanwix National Monument

6 Gateway National Recreation Area

7 General Grant National Memorial

8 Hamilton Grange National Memorial

9 Home of Franklin Delano Roosevelt National Historic Site

10 Martin Van Buren National Historic Site

11 Sagamore Hill National Historic Site

12 Saint Paul's Church National Historic Site

13 Saratoga National Historical Park

14 Statue of Liberty National Monument

15 Theodore Roosevelt Birthplace National Historic Site

16 Theodore Roosevelt Inaugural National Historic Site

17 Vanderbilt Mansion National Historic Site

18 Women's Rights National Historical Park

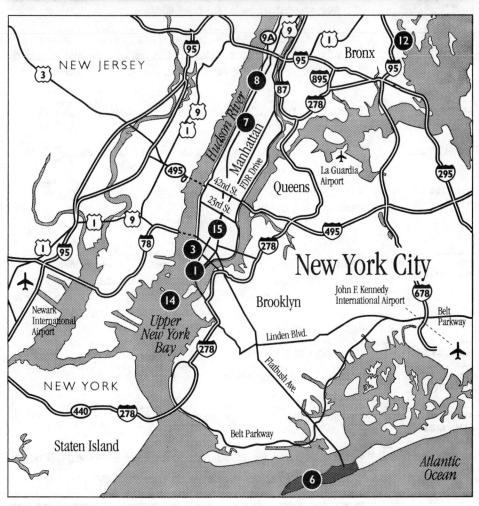

1 Castle Clinton National Monument

3 Federal Hall National Memorial

6 Gateway National Recreation Area

7 General Grant National Memorial

8 Hamilton Grange National Memorial

12 Saint Paul's Church National Historic Site

14 Statue of Liberty National Monument

15 Theodore Roosevelt Birthplace National Historic Site

Castle Clinton National Monument

New York, New York   See Climatable No. 25

Castle Clinton began as the South-west Battery in 1811, built during the "fortification fever" that swept New York after the British attack on the *Chesapeake*. It was later used for public entertainment, an immigrant landing depot and an aquarium.

MAILING ADDRESS

Superintendent, Manhattan Sites, 26 Wall St., New York, NY 10003
Telephone: 212-264-4456

DIRECTIONS

The Monument is in Battery Park at the southern tip of Manhattan. Public transportation is recommended.

VISITOR ACTIVITIES

• Interpretive exhibits, tours and school programs. • Facilities include a museum and restrooms. • The Monument is open daily from 8:30 a.m. to 5 p.m., except Dec. 25. Call Circle Line at 212-563-3590 for current ferry schedules.

PERMITS, FEES & LIMITATIONS

• Admission to Castle Clinton Museum is free. • The fees for round-trip tickets to the Statue of Liberty-Ellis Island are $6 for adults, $5 for seniors and $3 for children. • No vehicles are allowed in the Monument. • Permits are required for special uses, commercial photography and public gatherings. • Food and pets are prohibited.

ACCESSIBILITY

The museum and restrooms are accessible.

CAMPING & LODGING

Overnight accommodations are available in New York City.

FOOD & SUPPLIES

Food and supplies are available nearby.

FIRST AID/ HOSPITAL

• First aid is available in the Monument. • The nearest hospital is Beekman Downtown Hospital, one-half mile (.8 km).

Eleanor Roosevelt National Historic Site

Hyde Park, New York

Eleanor Roosevelt used Val-Kill Cottage as a retreat in her younger years and as her home in her later years where she entertained heads of state and had time to relax or work.

MAILING ADDRESS

Roosevelt-Vanderbilt National Historical Sites, 519 Albany Post Road, Hyde Park, NY 12538 Telephone: Information: 914-229-7821 Reservations: 914-229-9115

DIRECTIONS

The Site is 2 hours north of New York City and 2 miles (3.2 km) due east on US Rt. 9G from the home of FDR and Vanderbilt Mansion NHS.

VISITOR ACTIVITIES

• Guided tours of Mrs. Roosevelt's home. • The Site is open daily from May to October from 9 a.m. to 5 p.m., and on Saturdays and Sundays the remainder of the year. The Site is closed Thanksgiving, Dec. 25 and Jan. 1.

PERMITS, FEES & LIMITATIONS

• No entrance fee. • Groups of 10 or more must make reservations all year except Tuesdays and Wednesdays and from November through March.

ACCESSIBILITY

Restrooms are on the first floor.

CAMPING & LODGING

Overnight accommodations are available in Hyde Park.

FOOD & SUPPLIES

Food and supplies are available in Hyde Park.

FIRST AID/ HOSPITAL

First aid is available within the Site.

Federal Hall National Memorial

New York, New York

Throughout the 18th century, the corner of Wall Street and Nassau Street was the vital center of New York's greatest events, including one on March 4, 1789, when the government of the United States of America began to function.

MAILING ADDRESS

Superintendent, Manhattan Sites, Federal Hall National Memorial, 26 Wall St., New York, NY 10005 **Telephone:** 212-264-8711

DIRECTIONS

Public transportation is recommended. Federal Hall is accessible by subway from the Broad Street Station of the J, M and Z lines, the Wall Street stations of the 2, 3 and 4, 5 lines, the Rector Street Station of the N and R lines and the Fulton Street Station of the A line. New York City buses M1 and M6 stop at Wall Street and Broadway and the M15 bus stops at Wall Street and Water Street.

VISITOR ACTIVITIES

• Interpretive exhibits about George Washington, his inauguration, constitutional government and old Federal Hall. • Ten-minute and 30-minute films about George Washington and the inauguration are shown upon request. • Ranger-guided tours of the Memorial are available for large groups. • Ranger-guided Lower Manhattan historical walking tours are given every Friday at 2 p.m., April through October. • There are classical concerts every Wednesday in the rotunda at 12:30 p.m. • Write for a schedule of Friday afternoon movie programs (themes change monthly). • The Memorial is open from 9 a.m. to 5 p.m., Monday through Friday.

PERMITS, FEES & LIMITATIONS

• No entrance fee. • Permits are required for special uses, public gatherings and commercial photography and filmings. • Food or drink is prohibited inside the building.

ACCESSIBILITY

The 15 Pine Street entrance is accessible.

CAMPING & LODGING

Overnight accommodations are available throughout the New York City area.

FOOD & SUPPLIES

Food and supplies are available at nearby stores.

FIRST AID/ HOSPITAL

The nearest hospital is Beekman Downtown Hospital, one-quarter mile (.4 km).

GENERAL INFORMATION

A Ranger-staffed visitor information desk has information and free literature about New York City and specific points of interest, including the Statue of Liberty and Ellis Island, Castle Clinton National Monument (see listings in this book), the New York Stock Exchange, the Federal Reserve Bank, Fraunces Tavern, Trinity Church, St. Paul's Church, South Street Seaport and other tourist attractions.

Fire Island National Seashore

Patchogue, New York

For those willing to hike it, the 1,400 acres of wilderness protected at Fire Island National Seashore offers a view of the island as it must have been when the first Europeans saw it 400 years ago.

MAILING ADDRESS

Superintendent, Fire Island National Seashore, 120 Laurel St., Patchogue, NY 11772 **Telephone:** 516-289-4810

DIRECTIONS

Visitors may reach the island by automobile via bridges at the state and county parks. Except for these two points, Fire Island is roadless. Several mainland ferry lines operating from Bayshore, Sayville and Patchogue travel to the island. Sailors Haven and the Sunken Forest are served by the ferry terminal in Sayville, and Watch Hill is served by the ferry terminal at Patchogue. All 3 mainland villages are serviced by the Long Island Rail Road. Public ferries run from May 15 to Oct. 15.

VISITOR ACTIVITIES

• Fishing, clamming, swimming, walking, picnicking, guided nature walks and talks in summer, wildlife and bird watching, interpretive exhibits, hiking, boating and hunting. • The William Floyd Estate is a detached area of the Seashore on Washington Avenue in Mastic Beach on Long Island. This 612-acre estate was the home of a signer of the Declaration of Independence. There is a free guided tour of the house weekends from July 3 to Sept. 6 from 10 a.m. to 4:30 p.m. Grounds tours are self-guided. Group tours by appointment. For street directions, call 516-399-2030. • Nature trails are at Smith Point West, Watch Hill, Sailors Haven and Fire Island Lighthouse. • Facilities include marinas, guarded swimming beaches, Visitor Center, picnic areas, restrooms, bathhouse and telephones. • The Seashore is open every day year-round. Fire Island Lighthouse Visitor Center, Keepers Quarters and Tower close for the winter. • There is a 7-mile (11.2 km) sand trail from Smith Point to Watch Hill in the wilderness.

PERMITS, FEES & LIMITATIONS

• No entrance fee. • Permits for off-road vehicle travel for use from April 1 to June 13 and Sept. 15 to Dec. 31 are available at Smith Point only. • No pets allowed at the William Floyd Estate.

ACCESSIBILITY

Trails and facilities at Smith Point, Watch Hill, Sailors Haven and the Fire Island Lighthouse are accessible. There is an accessible boardwalk nature trail at Smith Point.

CAMPING & LODGING

• Reservations are required for the 25-site primitive campground at Watch Hill. • For information on other overnight accommodations on the island, call the Fire Island Tourism Bureau at 516-563-8448. • Motels are in most major communities on Long Island.

FOOD & SUPPLIES

• Snacks are available at Watch Hill and Sailors Haven. • Stores are at Watch Hill and Sailors Haven. • Food and supplies are also available on the mainland at Sayville, Patchogue and Bayshore.

FIRST AID/ HOSPITAL

• First aid is available in the Seashore. • The nearest hospitals are on the mainland at Patchogue and Bayshore.

GENERAL INFORMATION

• For your safety - Swim at protected beaches. Wear footgear on all boardwalks. Splinters are a common first aid problem. Watch for poison ivy, which abounds on the island. • Do not walk on the dunes; their fragile vegetation is easily destroyed. • Ticks are common in grass and underbrush and may carry disease.

Fort Stanwix National Monument

Rome, New York

A British fort originally built in 1758 to protect the Oneida Carry portage, Fort Stanwix was rebuilt by Americans in 1776 in time for a 1777 British siege that lasted from Aug. 3 to Aug. 22 when the British troops retreated into Canada. The fort has been almost entirely reconstructed to its 1777 appearance.

MAILING ADDRESS

Superintendent, Fort Stanwix National Monument, 112 East Park Street, Rome, NY 13440 **Telephone:** 315-336-2090

DIRECTIONS

The Monument is in downtown Rome, NY, which is accessible by car, bus train or plane. State routes 26, 46, 49, 69 and 365 pass within sight of the Fort. If you are traveling on the NY Thruway, take exits 32 or 33. A city parking garage is on N. James Street, within one-half block of the Monument's entrance.

VISITOR ACTIVITIES

• Interpretive films and exhibits, guided tours, living history program from May-September includes drill and occasional weapons-firing demonstrations. • The Monument is open daily from **9 a.m. to 5 p.m.**, from April 1 to Dec. 31 except Thanksgiving and Dec. 25. • The **entrance fee is** $2 per person ages 17 to 61. • There is no direct vehicle access to the Monument.

PERMITS, FEES & LIMITATIONS

The museum is fully accessible. Restrooms are accessible, and parking is available. A wheelchair is available upon request.

ACCESSIBILITY

Overnight accommodations are available in and around Rome.

FOOD & SUPPLIES

Food and supplies obtainable in Rome.

FIRST AID/ HOSPITAL

• First aid is available in the Monument. • The nearest hospital is Rome Memorial, 3 miles (4.8 km).

Gateway National Recreation Area

New York and New Jersey

At the entrance to the great New York/New Jersey estuary, 2 arms of land stretch across the water forming a natural gateway to the nation's greatest port and Gateway National Recreation Area - comprised of Sandy Hook, the Rockaway Peninsula, Staten Island and Jamaica Bay - offering the Jamaica Bay Wildlife Refuge, 3 forts, 2 historic airfields and the nation's oldest operating lighthouse.

MAILING ADDRESS

General Superintendent, Gateway National Recreation Area, Floyd Bennett Field, Brooklyn, NY 11234 **Telephone:** 718-338-3575

DIRECTIONS

The Recreation Area consists of 4 units. Three are in New York - the Jamaica Bay Unit in Brooklyn, Breezy Point Unit on the Rockaway Peninsula in Queens, and the Staten Island Unit on the Raritan Bay in Staten Island. The fourth area is the Sandy Hook Unit on a peninsula in the northeast corner of New Jersey in Monmouth County. Detailed mass transit and auto directions are available from Headquarters.

VISITOR ACTIVITIES

• Swimming, picnicking, sunbathing, sports, interpretive programs, biking, fishing, boating, bird watching, crabbing, horseback riding, miniature golf, tennis, kite and model aircraft flying and special events in the summer.
• Facilities include a marina, boathouse, beaches, sports facilities, restrooms, parking areas, wildlife refuge, bicycle trail and picnic areas. • The

Recreation Area is open daily year-round. Full services are provided from Memorial Day through Sept. 30 from 9 a.m. to 8:30 p.m. Jamaica Bay Wildlife Refuge is closed Dec. 25 and Jan. 1. The beach is closed in winter.

PERMITS, FEES & LIMITATIONS

• There are fees for boat launching and mooring facilities at Great Kills Park in the Staten Island Unit; for mooring facilities at Barren Island Marina and for parking at the Riis Park in the Breezy Point Unit; and for summer beach parking in the Sandy Hook Unit. • A fishing permit is required at some locations. • Permits are required for baseball, softball, tennis, soccer, archery, football and basketball facilities at Miller Field in the Staten Island Unit. Information and permits may be obtained by calling 718-351-6970 or by writing the Unit Manager, 26 Miller Field, Staten Island, NY 10306. • Off-road vehicles are not permitted on beaches and in certain natural areas.

CAMPING & LODGING

• Primitive camp sites are available for use by organized youth groups on a reservation basis. Reservations must be made through the Unit Manager's office at the Sandy Hook Unit, PO Box 530, Sandy Hook, NJ 07732 or by calling 908-872-0115; and at Floyd Bennett Field, 718-338-3706. • Other overnight accommodations outside the Recreation Area are available in Sandy Hook, Red Bank, Highlands, Staten Island, Jamaica Bay, Brooklyn, Queens and Breezy Point.

FOOD & SUPPLIES

• Fast food is available in all units, and a restaurant is at the Canarsie Pier. • Food and supplies are available outside of the Recreation Area at Sandy Hook, Red Bank, Highlands, Staten Island, Jamaica Bay, Queens, Brooklyn and Breezy Point.

FIRST AID/ HOSPITAL

• First aid is available in all units in the summer. • The nearest hospitals are: Sandy Hook - Patterson Army Hospital and River View Hospital; Staten Island - Staten Island Hospital; Jamaica Bay - Coney Island Hospital, Peninsula Hospital and Brookdale Hospital.

GENERAL INFORMATION

• For your safety - Swim only where lifeguards are on duty. The ocean can be dangerous. Be alert for riptides. Do not take glass containers, rafts, rubber tubes, snorkels or masks to any beach. Some of the areas have large patches of poison ivy. Consult Recreation Area personnel. • Write to the Area's Public Affairs Office, Floyd Bennett Field, Brooklyn, NY 11234 or call 718-338-3688 for a free copy of seasonal program guides.

General Grant National Memorial

New York, New York

Popularly known as Grant's Tomb, the General Grant National Memorial is the largest mausoleum in America, rising to 150 feet (45.7 m) from a bluff overlooking the Hudson River. It required hundreds of men working on the structure between 1891-97 and more than 8,000 tons of granite to complete.

MAILING ADDRESS
Superintendent, Manhattan Sites, 26 Wall St., New York, NY 10005
Telephone: 212-264-4456

DIRECTIONS
The Memorial is in Riverside Park near the intersection of Riverside Drive and West 122nd Street. Visitors can reach the area by IRT #1 subway to 116th or 125th Street or the 125th Street crosstown bus. Riverside Drive is also accessible from the Henry Hudson Parkway at several points. Parking is permitted near the Memorial.

VISITOR ACTIVITIES
• Interpretive talks and exhibits. • Facilities include exhibit rooms. • The Memorial is open Wednesday through Sunday from 9 a.m. to 5 p.m., except Wednesdays that follow Federal holidays on Mondays or Tuesdays. The Memorial is also closed on Thanksgiving, Dec. 25 and Jan. 1. Please call to verify days and hours of operation.

PERMITS, FEES & LIMITATIONS
No entrance fee.

CAMPING & LODGING
Overnight accommodations are available in New York City.

FOOD & SUPPLIES
Food and supplies are available several blocks away in Manhattan.

FIRST AID/ HOSPITAL
• First aid is available at the Memorial. • The nearest hospital is St. Luke's on Amsterdam Avenue, 10 blocks.

Hamilton Grange National Memorial

New York, New York

Closed for renovation. The many-sided complexity of Alexander Hamilton, revolutionary and politician, is illustrated by Hamilton Grange, the country home that Hamilton built as a quiet oasis for his family.

MAILING ADDRESS
Superintendent, Manhattan Sites, 26 Wall St., New York, NY 10005
Telephone: 212-264-4456

DIRECTIONS
The Memorial is at Convent Avenue and West 141st Street. Access by public transportation is recommended. Take the A, B, C or D subway to West 145th Street or the 8th Avenue IND express subway to West 145th. Visitors can also catch the Broadway Bus #4 to West 145th Street and Convent Avenue or the Convent Avenue #3 to 142nd Street.

VISITOR ACTIVITIES
The Memorial is closed for renovation. For information about the scheduled reopening date, call 212-264-4456.

Home of Franklin D. Roosevelt National Historic Site

Hyde Park, New York

Franklin D. Roosevelt, 32d President of the United States, was born and spent much of his life in the Hyde Park house where he and Eleanor raised their 5 children and entertained visiting dignitaries. It was in the office he called his "Summer White House" where FDR signed the agreement with British Prime Minister Winston Churchill that resulted in the world's first atomic bomb.

MAILING ADDRESS
Superintendent, Roosevelt-Vanderbilt National Historic Sites, 519 Albany Post Road, Hyde Park, NY 12538 **Telephone:** Information, 914-229-7821 Reservations, 914-229-9115

DIRECTIONS
The Site is on Rt. 9 in Hyde Park just north of Poughkeepsie and 2 hours north of New York City.

VISITOR ACTIVITIES
• House tours and exhibits in the Franklin D. Roosevelt Library. • Facilities include a bookstore, Tourist Information Center, parking, restrooms and library. • The Site is open daily from 9 a.m. to 5 p.m., except Tuesdays and Wednesdays from November through March, and Thanksgiving, Dec. 25 and Jan. 1.

PERMITS, FEES & LIMITATIONS
• The $4 entrance fee permits access to the Roosevelt Home and Library. Children ages 16 and younger are admitted free. • There is a $1 entry fee to the FDR Library for ages 62 and older. • Admittance to the Home is free for ages 62 and older.

ACCESSIBILITY
Parking and restroom are accessible. There are ramps with handrails.

CAMPING & LODGING
Overnight accommodations are available in Hyde Park and vicinity.

FOOD & SUPPLIES
Food and supplies are available in Hyde Park.

FIRST AID/ HOSPITAL
• First aid is available within the Site. • The nearest hospital is in Poughkeepsie, 6 miles (9.6 km).

GENERAL INFORMATION
For bus or large group reservations, please write in advance to Roosevelt-Vanderbilt National Historic Sites, 249 Albany Post Road, Hyde Park, NY 12538.

Martin Van Buren National Historic Site

Kinderhook, New York

Martin Van Buren bought the Lindenwald estate just south of Kinderhook for $14,000 in 1841. He made many improvements to turn it into his country seat where he could live out his post-White House years in the comfort and elegance he relished.

MAILING ADDRESS	Superintendent, Martin Van Buren National Historic Site, PO Box 545, Kinderhook, NY 12106 **Telephone:** 518-758-9689
DIRECTIONS	The Site is on Route 9H, 2 miles (3.2 km) south of the village of Kinderhook, NY. From Albany, NY: take 90 east; from MA Pike (Berkshire Spur) take 90 west; then south at Exit 12 (Rt. 9) 5 miles (8 km) to 9H; then 5 miles (8 km) to the Site. From the south: take 9 north to 9H north.
VISITOR ACTIVITIES	• Ranger guided tours (on the hour and one-half hour last for 45 minutes). • Special events (schedule sent upon request). • Interpretive audiovisual program and exhibits. • Visitor Center sales area. • Off site programs are available. • The Site is open daily from 9 a.m. to 5 p.m., from mid-April to Oct. 31; and Wednesday through Sunday from November to Dec. 5. • The grounds are open year-round. • The mansion is closed from Dec. 6 through mid-April and on Thanksgiving.
PERMITS, FEES & LIMITATIONS	The entrance fee is $2 for adults. There is no charge for ages 16 and younger or 62 and older.
ACCESSIBILITY	Wheelchair, closed caption on video and stereo amplifier listener are available. Parking in rear of the mansion.
CAMPING & LODGING	Overnight accommodations are available in the Kinderhook area.
FOOD & SUPPLIES	Food and supplies are available in Kinderhook.
FIRST AID/ HOSPITAL	• First aid is available within the Site. • The nearest hospital is in Hudson, NY, 12 miles (19.3 km) south.
GENERAL INFORMATION	• Group tours are required to make reservations. • Information is available for other sites in the area by telephone or mail.

Sagamore Hill National Historic Site

Oyster Bay, New York

For more than 30 years, Sagamore Hill was one of the most conspicuous homes in America as the activities of Theodore Roosevelt and his family were observed and discussed by correspondents who maintained a vigil at the "Summer White House" to cover the President and his visiting dignitaries.

MAILING ADDRESS	Superintendent, Sagamore Hill National Historic Site, 20 Sagamore Hill Road, Oyster Bay, NY 11771-1899 **Telephone: 516-922-4447**
DIRECTIONS	Sagamore Hill is on Cove Neck Road, 3 miles (4.8 km) east of Oyster Bay, NY. It can be reached by the Long Island Rail Road from New York City's Pennsylvania Station at 7th Avenue and 33rd Street. Taxis meet all trains. If traveling by car, take either Exit 41N from the Long Island Expressway or Exit 35 North from the Northern State Parkway to Rt. 106 Northbound. Follow Rt. 106 to Oyster Bay. Turn right at the third traffic light in Oyster Bay onto East Main Street. Follow the "Sagamore Hill" signs.
VISITOR ACTIVITIES	• Visitors can take self-guided tours of the Roosevelt home, the pet cemetery and the Old Orchard Home, containing exhibits relating to Theodore Roosevelt's political career, family life at Sagamore Hill and the lives of his 6 children. • There is a 26-minute film. • Facilities include souvenir and book sales, and parking. • The Site is open daily from **9:30 a.m. to 5 p.m.**, except Thanksgiving, Dec. 25 and Jan. 1.
PERMITS, FEES & LIMITATIONS	• The **entrance fee** is $2 for ages 17 to 61. • Vehicles are limited to the entrance road and parking area. • Pets must be leashed or carried.
ACCESSIBILITY	Restrooms and parking are accessible.
CAMPING & LODGING	Overnight accommodations are available in East Norwich and Oyster Bay.
FOOD & SUPPLIES	• A snack shop is open during the summer. • Food and supplies are also available in Oyster Bay.
FIRST AID/ HOSPITAL	• First aid is available within the Site. • The nearest hospital is in Glen Cove, 7 miles (11.2 km).
GENERAL INFORMATION	**For your safety** - Poison ivy and ticks are common in the area. Please stay on established paths and walkways. Heat exhaustion is common in the summer. Park fences are historic and unsafe for climbing.

Saint Paul's National Historic Site

Mount Vernon, New York

This 18th-century church is associated with the trial of John Peter Zenger and the fight for freedom of the press. The church was completed in 1787, and the Bill of Rights Museum occupies the former parish hall.

MAILING ADDRESS	Superintendent, Manhattan Sites, 26 Wall Street, New York, NY 10005 Telephone: 212-264-4456
DIRECTIONS	Take the New England Thruway north (Rt. 95) to the Conner Street Exit. Turn left, go up one light and take another left. Go straight, and the road becomes Rt. 22 (S. Columbus Avenue). Follow to St. Paul's, #897, on the right. From the Hutchinson River Parkway North, get off at US-1 Boston Post Road in Pelham Manor, NY. Turn left and go to Pelham Parkway. Turn right and follow to S. Columbus Avenue and turn left. Follow to the Site on the left.
VISITOR ACTIVITIES	• Walking tours of the church, museum and affiliated cemetery, which contains interesting 18th and 19th century markers and monuments. • Facilities include parking, restrooms and a museum shop. • The Site is open Tuesday through Friday from 9 a.m. to 5 p.m. by appointment, or on Saturdays from 12 p.m. to 4 p.m., without an appointment. The Site is closed on Saturdays prior to Federal holidays that fall on Mondays and on Thanksgiving, Dec. 25 and Jan. 1. • Groups of more than 5 people are asked to call in advance for Saturday tours.
PERMITS, FEES & LIMITATIONS	No entrance fee.
ACCESSIBILITY	The museum and restrooms are accessible. Limited parking is available. Access to other Site areas is under development. Call for details.
CAMPING & LODGING	Overnight accommodations are available in Mount Vernon, Bronx, New Rochelle or anywhere in metropolitan New York City.
FOOD & SUPPLIES	Food and supplies are available in Mount Vernon and vicinity.
FIRST AID/ HOSPITAL	• First aid is not available within the Site. • The nearest hospital is in Mount Vernon, 2 miles (3.2 km).

Saratoga National Historical Park

Stillwater, New York

A series of battles at Saratoga between American forces and British troops led by Gen. John Burgoyne began Sept. 19, 1777 and ended 3 weeks later with 1,000 British casualties, less than 500 American deaths and Burgoyne's surrender.

MAILING ADDRESS	Superintendent, Saratoga National Historical Park, 648 Rt. 32, Stillwater, NY 12170 Telephone: 518-664-9821
DIRECTIONS	The Park entrance is 30 miles (48.3 km) north of Albany, NY, on US 4 and

NY 32; Exit 12 off Northway (I-87). It is 15 miles (24.1 km) east of Saratoga Springs (take Rt. 29 East to Schuylerville, then Rt. 4 south to the Park entrance).

VISITOR ACTIVITIES

• Revolutionary War exhibits. • There is a 21-minute film shown every half hour. • The Visitor Center is open daily from 9 a.m. to 5 p.m. • There is a 9.5-mile (15.3 km) self-conducting tour through the Park also used for biking, and the 4.2-mile (6.7 km) Wilkinson Hiking Trail. • Cross-country skiing is available. • The Tour Road is open from April to November daily from 9 a.m. to 5 p.m., with extended hours in July and August. • The Visitor Center and Park are closed Thanksgiving, Dec. 25 and Jan. 1. • There are living history demonstrations in the summer.

PERMITS, FEES & LIMITATIONS

There is a $4 per vehicle or $2 per person **entrance fee**. A Park annual pass is available for $10. There is no fee for anyone under age 17 or over age 61.

ACCESSIBILITY

The Visitor Center has accessible parking and restrooms. The Park film is open captioned. Most tour stops are accessible. The hiking trail is not accessible.

CAMPING & LODGING

Overnight accommodations are available in nearby Stillwater, Schuylerville and Saratoga Springs.

FOOD & SUPPLIES

Food and supplies are available in Stillwater, Schuylerville and Saratoga Springs.

FIRST AID/ HOSPITAL

Medical services are available in Saratoga Springs, 15 miles (24.1 km) west.

GENERAL INFORMATION

Contact the Park for a summer special events calendar.

Statue of Liberty National Monument

New York, New York

The colossal figure of a woman striding with uplifted flame across the entrance to the New World is a symbol of America to most people. Along with the Statue of Liberty, an impressive museum honors the 12 million immigrants who entered America and a new life through Ellis Island, featuring 2 theaters, a learning center, a collection of artifacts donated by immigrants' descendants and the American Immigrant Wall of Honor, containing the names of 200,000 immigrants.

MAILING ADDRESS

Superintendent, Statue of Liberty National Monument, Liberty Island, New York, NY 10004 **Telephone:** 212-363-7770

DIRECTIONS

Liberty Island and Ellis Island are accessible only by ferry. Circle Line ferries leave Battery Park in Lower Manhattan and Liberty State Park in New Jersey. For schedules and group-rate information, call 212-269-5755.

VISITOR ACTIVITIES

• At the Statue of Liberty, visitors can reach the top of the pedestal by elevator or stairs. The public is not permitted access to the torch itself, but visitors can climb stairs to the statue's crown. • At Ellis Island, visitors can take advantage of guided tours, museum exhibits, a library and movie theaters. • Facilities include restrooms, public telephones, and souvenirs and books relating to the statue and to immigration. • The statue is open daily from 9 a.m. to 5 p.m., except Dec. 25 with extended hours in season. • Ellis Island is open daily from 9:30 a.m. to 6 p.m., except Dec. 25 with extended hours in season.

PERMITS, FEES & LIMITATIONS

• The round-trip concession boat fee is $6 for adults and $1.50 for children under 12. • No docking is permitted for private boats.

CAMPING & LODGING

Overnight accommodations are available in New York City and New Jersey.

FOOD & SUPPLIES

• Snacks are available at refreshment stands. • Food and supplies are available in New York and New Jersey.

FIRST AID/ HOSPITAL

• First aid is available. • The nearest hospital is in New York.

GENERAL INFORMATION

• Ascent to the statue's crown from the top of the pedestal is by spiral staircase only. The climb is equivalent to 22 stories, and those with physical difficulties are urged not to attempt it. • School groups should contact the school coordinator for pre-visit materials. Large groups should make reservations with the Circle Line Ferry, 212-269-5755.

Theodore Roosevelt Birthplace National Historic Site

New York, New York

Theodore Roosevelt - apostle of the "strenuous life," larger-than-life hero to millions of Americans and 26th President of the United States - was born on Oct. 27, 1858 in a typical New York brownstone on a quiet, tree-lined street where his family lived from 1854 until 1872.

MAILING ADDRESS

Superintendent, Manhattan Sites, 26 Wall St., New York, NY 10005
Telephone: 212-264-4456

DIRECTIONS

The Site may be reached from the 23rd Street or 14th Street stops of the #6 or N or R subways. Parking in the vicinity is scarce.

VISITOR ACTIVITIES

• Guided tours of Victorian-period rooms, museums, films and Saturday afternoon concerts. • Facilities include restrooms. • The Site is open Wednesday through Sunday from 9 a.m. to 5 p.m., except Federal holidays.

PERMITS, FEES & LIMITATIONS

The entrance fee is $1 for ages 17 to 61.

ACCESSIBILITY

The Site is not accessible.

CAMPING & LODGING

Overnight accommodations are available in New York City.

FOOD & SUPPLIES

Food and supplies are available in the neighborhood.

FIRST AID/ HOSPITAL

• First aid is available within the Site. • The nearest hospital is Cabrini Medical Center.

Theodore Roosevelt Inaugural National Historic Site

Buffalo, New York

An event of national significance and importance occurred on Sept. 14, 1901, in the home of Ansley and Mary Wilcox when their friend, Theodore Roosevelt, took the oath of office to become the 26th President of the United States just hours after the death of President William McKinley from an assassin's bullet.

MAILING ADDRESS

Superintendent, Theodore Roosevelt Inaugural National Historic Site, 641 Delaware Ave., Buffalo, NY 14202 **Telephone:** 716-884-0095

DIRECTIONS

The Site is 20 miles (32.2 km) south of Niagra Falls and 1 mile (1.6 km) north of downtown Buffalo.

VISITOR ACTIVITIES

• Guided house tours daily including a 12-minute slide presentation with interpretation and exhibits centering on events that occurred within the days of Roosevelt's inauguration, the Wilcox family and the turn of the century atmosphere surrounding the Victorian era. • The Site is open Monday through Friday from 9 a.m. to 5 p.m., year-round. From April to December the Site is also open Saturdays and Sundays from 12 p.m. to 5 p.m., and on Sundays from 12 p.m. to 5 p.m., from January through March. • There are self-guiding walking tours and several guided walking tours scheduled with a luncheon in the summer. • Various educational activities for groups of all ages are available upon reservation. • Yearly events include a lecture series in February, March and April, an Easter program for children, Summer Victorian Camp and a Teddy Bear Picnic, also for children, a Sept. 14 Inauguration Anniversary Luncheon and a Victorian Christmas Celebration.

PERMITS, FEES & LIMITATIONS

• House tour fees are $2 for adults and $1 for children with family rates available. • Walking tours are $5 per person. • Special group prices are available.

ACCESSIBILITY	A lower level and restroom are being completed that will be accessible. A captioned slide presentation is available. Touching baskets in the restored rooms and a Touching Museum are offered for the visually impaired.
CAMPING & LODGING	There are a few hotels and motels surrounding the Site, some within walking distance.
FOOD & SUPPLIES	Food and supplies are available throughout the Buffalo area.
FIRST AID/ HOSPITAL	• A first aid kit is available in the Site. • There are 2 hospitals within a 1-mile (1.6 km) radius.
GENERAL INFORMATION	There are several special events at various times during the year. Information provided upon request.

Vanderbilt Mansion National Historic Site

Hyde Park, New York

Once the country home of Frederick W. Vanderbilt, a grandson of Cornelius Vanderbilt who amassed the family fortune, the Vanderbilt Mansion is a magnificent example of the great estates built by wealthy financial and industrial leaders between 1880 and 1900.

MAILING ADDRESS	Superintendent, Roosevelt-Vanderbilt National Historic Sites, 519 Albany Post Road, Hyde Park, NY 12538 **Telephone:** Information, 914-229-7821 Reservations, 914-229-9115
DIRECTIONS	The Site is on US 9, 8 miles (12.9 km) north of Poughkeepsie, NY. Entrance to the grounds is through the main gate on US 9 North in Hyde Park. The Visitor Center is in the Pavilion near the mansion. The Site is 2 hours north of New York City on the east bank of the Hudson River.
VISITOR ACTIVITIES	• Tours are available beginning at the Visitor Center, interpretive exhibits and an audiovisual program. • Facilities include parking and restrooms. • The Site is open Thursday through Monday from 9 a.m. to 5 p.m., from November through March, and daily from April through October. The Site is closed Thanksgiving, Dec. 25 and Jan. 1.
PERMITS, FEES & LIMITATIONS	The entrance fee is $2. Ages 16 and under and 62 and over are admitted free.
ACCESSIBILITY	There is posted parking and an elevator in the mansion.
CAMPING & LODGING	Overnight accommodations are available in Hyde Park and vicinity.
FOOD & SUPPLIES	Food and supplies are available in Hyde Park.

| **FIRST AID/ HOSPITAL** | • First aid is available in the Site. • The nearest hospital is in Poughkeepsie, 6 miles (9.6 km). |

Women's Rights National Historical Park

Seneca Falls, New York

This Park commemorates women's struggle for equal rights. It includes the Wesleyan Methodist Chapel, the site of the first Women's Rights Convention in 1848, the Elizabeth Cady Stanton home, the M'Clintock House, where the Declaration of Rights and Sentiments was written, and other sites related to notable early women's rights activists.

MAILING ADDRESS

Women's Rights National Historical Park, PO Box 70, Seneca Falls, NY 13148 **Telephone:** 315-568-2991

DIRECTIONS

Take the New York State Thruway (I-90) to Exit 41 onto State Rt. 414 for 4 miles (6.4 km). Then go east on Rts. 5 and 20 for 2 miles (3.2 km). The Park is 1 hour from Rochester, Syracuse and Ithaca.

VISITOR ACTIVITIES

• The Visitor Center is at 136 Fall St., (Rts. 5 and 20) in downtown Seneca Falls. It includes exhibits on the first Women's Rights Convention, a 25-minute film, interactive videos, life-size statues of people who attended the convention and an orientation area. • The Visitor Center is open daily from 9 a.m. to 5 p.m., in the off-season with extended hours in the summer. • The Elizabeth Cady Stanton home is restored and open to the public for tours from 9 a.m. to 5 p.m., daily in the summer and 12 p.m. to 4 p.m., the rest of the year. • The Wesleyan Chapel, site of the first Women's Rights Convention, is open to the public. • Please write the Park for further information on interpretive activities. • The Park is closed Thanksgiving, Dec. 25 and Jan. 1.

PERMITS, FEES & LIMITATIONS

No entrance fee.

ACCESSIBILITY

The Visitor Center is accessible. Parking will be behind the Visitor Center.

CAMPING & LODGING

Overnight accommodations are available in the Seneca Falls-Waterloo area.

FOOD & SUPPLIES

Food and supplies are available in the Seneca Falls-Waterloo area.

FIRST AID/ HOSPITAL

The nearest hospital is in Geneva, 10 miles (16.1 km).

GENERAL INFORMATION

Other points of interest include the National Women's Hall of Fame, Seneca Falls Urban Cultural Park Visitor Center, Seneca Falls Historical Society and Montezuma National Wildlife Refuge, 5 miles (8 km).

North Carolina

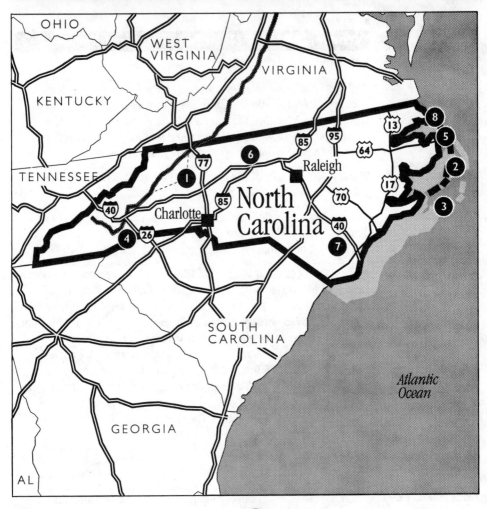

1. Blue Ridge Parkway
2. Cape Hatteras National Seashore
3. Cape Lookout National Seashore
4. Carl Sandburg Home National Historic Site
5. Fort Raleigh National Historic Site
6. Guilford Courthouse National Military Park
7. Moores Creek National Battlefield
8. Wright Brothers National Memorial

North Carolina   291

Blue Ridge Parkway

North Carolina and Virginia   See Climatable No. 26

The Blue Ridge Parkway follows the Appalachian Mountain chain for 469 miles (756.4 km) between the Shenandoah and Great Smoky Mountains National Parks. It provides seemingly endless views of many parallel ranges connected by cross ranges and scattered hills.

MAILING ADDRESS

Superintendent, Blue Ridge Parkway, 200 BB&T Building, Pack Square, Asheville, NC 28801 **Telephone:** 704-271-4779

DIRECTIONS

The Parkway intersects many US and state highways, including Interstates 64, 77, 40 and 26. Obtain by mail or in person at any Visitor Center a copy of the Blue Ridge Parkway Directory, which provides detailed maps and information.

VISITOR ACTIVITIES

• Auto tours, wildlife and wildflower watching, exhibits, picnicking, hiking, fishing, interpretive walks and talks, craft sales and demonstrations. • Facilities include gas, picnic areas, hiking trails, drinking water and restrooms. • The Parkway is open all year. Some sections may be closed in winter due to snow and ice. • The Minerals Museum near Spruce Pine, NC, and The Folk Art Center near Asheville, NC, are closed Thanksgiving, Dec. 25 and Jan. 1. • Campgrounds, picnic areas and other visitor facilities are open from May 1 through October. Limited camping facilities may be available in winter.

PERMITS, FEES & LIMITATIONS

• No entrance fee. • Commercial vehicles are not allowed on the Parkway unless they secure a special permit.

ACCESSIBILITY

Many facilities are accessible. Contact the Parkway Access Coordinator at 704-271-4789.

CAMPING & LODGING

• Parkway campgrounds are open from May through October, but limited camping facilities may be open in winter. Inquire in advance. The daily camping fee is $8. Sites in each campground are designated for trailers, but none are equipped for utility connections. Sanitary dumping facilities for trailers are provided. Camping is limited to 14 days and camp sites may not be reserved. • Lodging is available on the Parkway at Peaks of Otter Lodge, open all year and operated by Virginia Peaks of Otter Co., Box 489, Bedford, VA 24523, phone 703-586-1081. To reserve at Rocky Knob Cabins, open from June through Labor Day, write National Park Concessions, Inc., Meadows of Dan, VA 24120, or phone 703-593-3503. For Bluffs Lodge (in Doughton Park), which is open from May 1 to Oct. 31, write National Park Concessions, Inc., Rt. 1, Box 266, Laurel Springs, NC 28644, or phone 919-372-4499. For the Pisgah Inn, open from May 1 to Oct. 31, contact Parkway Inn, Inc., PO Drawer 749, Waynesville, NC 28786, phone 704-235-8228.

• Overnight accommodations are also available in most nearby communities. For further information, consult the Blue Ridge Parkway Directory.

FOOD & SUPPLIES

• Meals are served on the Parkway at Whetstone Ridge, Otter Creek, Peaks of Otter, Mabry Mill, Doughton Park, Crabtree Meadows and Mount Pisgah.
• Limited food and supplies are available on the Parkway at some Parkway gas stations and at campground stores. • Food and supplies are available nearby in most of the larger communities.

FIRST AID/ HOSPITAL

• First aid is available from Rangers. • Hospitals are in Roanoke, VA; Asheville, NC, and many other cities near the Parkway.

GENERAL INFORMATION

See listings in this book for Great Smoky Mountains National Park at the southern end of the Parkway and Shenandoah National Park to the north.

Cape Hatteras National Seashore

Manteo, North Carolina

Long stretches of beach, sand dunes, marshes and woodlands on North Carolina's Outer Banks have been set aside as Cape Hatteras National Seashore. Visitors are rewarded with the beauty and recreational opportunities created when the land and sea meet.

MAILING ADDRESS

Superintendent, Cape Hatteras National Seashore, Rt. 1, Box 675, Manteo, NC 27954 Telephone: 919-995-4474

DIRECTIONS

The north Seashore entrance is at the intersection of US 158, NC 12 and US 64-264 in the town of Nags Head. The southern entrance at Ocracoke is available through a toll ferry from Cedar Island. Call 919-928-3841 for reservations.

VISITOR ACTIVITIES

• The main Seashore Visitor Center is in Buxton, NC, on Hatteras Island.
• Visitor centers on Bodie Island and Ocracoke Island are open from Memorial Day to Columbus Day. • Swimming, fishing, boating, surfing, scheduled programs during the summer, interpretive exhibits, picnicking, bird watching and hiking. • The main Visitor Center is open from 9 a.m. to 5 p.m., daily except Dec. 25. • There is a special Ranger program for children in the summer.

PERMITS, FEES & LIMITATIONS

No entrance fee.

ACCESSIBILITY

Visitor Center parking lots, many scheduled programs and limited sites in all campgrounds are accessible. There are audio tours of visitor centers.

CAMPING & LODGING

• Cape Point and Oregon Inlet campgrounds are open from mid-April through October on a first-come, first-served basis. Ocracoke Campground is open from mid-April through October. Reservations are required from mid-May through mid-September through MISTIX, 1-800-365-CAMP. Frisco Campground is open from Memorial Day to Labor Day with no reservations accepted. • Lodging is available in nearby towns and villages. Write to the Dare County Tourist Bureau, Budleigh St., Manteo, NC 27954, or call 919-473-2138.

FOOD & SUPPLIES

Food and supplies are available in nearby towns and villages throughout the Seashore.

FIRST AID/ HOSPITAL

• First aid is available in the Seashore. • Physicians are available in Hatteras, Manteo and Nags Head. • The nearest hospital is in Elizabeth City, NC, 80 miles (129 km).

GENERAL INFORMATION

• Strong ocean currents make swimming dangerous, especially at inlets. • Sunscreen is strongly recommended. • Mosquitoes and other insects make repellent and netting a must. • Wear shoes to protect your feet when walking to the beach. • Pets must be restrained at all times. • Use extreme caution when bicycling the narrow Seashore roads and on NC 12. • Summer weather is very hot and humid - limit your physical activity and exposure. • Strong storms should not be taken lightly. Listen to weather forecasts and follow evacuation procedures.

Cape Lookout National Seashore

Harkers Island, North Carolina

The 55-mile-long (88.7 km) barrier islands of Cape Lookout National Seashore running from Ocracoke Inlet to Beaufort Inlet consist mostly of wide, bare beaches with low dunes, flat grasslands and large expanses of salt marsh along the sound. There is much to explore, including the village of Plymouth and Cape Lookout Bight lighthouse.

MAILING ADDRESS

Superintendent, Cape Lookout National Seashore, Harkers Island, NC 28531 Telephone: 919-728-2250

DIRECTIONS

The main Visitor Center is at Headquarters on the east end of Harkers Island, 25 miles (40.3 km) east of Beaufort/Morehead City, NC.

VISITOR ACTIVITIES

• Fishing, swimming, boating, shell collecting, photography and bird watching. • Interpretive programs are often given at the lighthouse and the Visitor Center during the summer. • The Visitor Center is open daily throughout the year except Dec. 25 and Jan. 1. • Hunting under state and Federal regulations is permitted.

PERMITS, FEES & LIMITATIONS

There are no entrance fees at the Seashore, but public access is provided by concessionaires who charge a modest fee for the ferry transportation.

ACCESSIBILITY

The new Visitor Center is fully accessible. New compost toilets on the Seashore are accessible, but there are no paved roads to the facilities.

CAMPING & LODGING	• Camping is permitted throughout the Seashore, but there are no organized campgrounds. • Concessionaires provide rustic cabins for a fee. • Motels and other lodging facilities are available on Harkers Island and in Beaufort and Morehead City.
FOOD & SUPPLIES	Food and supplies are available in Beaufort and Morehead City.
FIRST AID/ HOSPITAL	The nearest hospital is in Morehead City.
GENERAL INFORMATION	• Be prepared to carry everything needed, particularly food and water. • There is little shade or shelter on the islands. • Tents must be strong enough to withstand heavy winds. • Bring repellent to combat biting insects.

Carl Sandburg Home National Historic Site

Flat Rock, North Carolina

Connemara, a 240-acre farm in the Western North Carolina mountains, was home to Carl Sandburg, poet, author, lecturer and Abraham Lincoln biographer, for the last 22 years of his fascinating life.

MAILING ADDRESS	Superintendent, Carl Sandburg Home National Historic Site, 1928 Little River Road, Flat Rock, NC 28731 **Telephone: 704-643-4178**
DIRECTIONS	The Site is 3 miles (4.8 km) south of Hendersonville, NC. Turn off of US 25 onto Little River Road at the Flat Rock Playhouse. The Site is 26 miles (41.9 km) south of Asheville via I-26.
VISITOR ACTIVITIES	• Interpretive talks, exhibits and films, guided house tours, hiking and picnicking. • The Visitor Center is open daily, except Dec. 25, from 9 a.m. to 5 p.m. • Write for information about special programs and events.
PERMITS, FEES & LIMITATIONS	The house tour fee is $2 per person. No fee is charged for ages 16 and younger or 62 and older.
ACCESSIBILITY	The estate home is accessible to the second floor. The picnic area and restrooms are accessible. A captioned video tour of the house and grounds is available. A shuttle bus is available to get from the parking area to the home.
CAMPING & LODGING	Lodging is available in Hendersonville and Flat Rock.
FOOD & SUPPLIES	Food and supplies are available in Hendersonville and Flat Rock.
FIRST AID/ HOSPITAL	• First aid is available at the Site. • The nearest hospital is in Hendersonville.

North Carolina

GENERAL INFORMATION

For your safety - Be cautious on trails, around ponds and lakes, and while standing on the rock face atop Big Glassy Mountain. Stay on established walks and paths, do not climb fences, and be alert for poison ivy and snakes. Be wary of farm animals that can bite or kick.

Fort Raleigh National Historic Site

Manteo, North Carolina

Reconstructions, exhibits, live drama and talks give visitors a richer understanding of the people who supported the colony of settlers on Roanoke Island and of those who lived and died at the Site.

MAILING ADDRESS

Superintendent, Fort Raleigh National Historic Site, c/o Cape Hatteras National Seashore, Rt. 1, Box 675, Manteo, NC 27954 **Telephone:** 919-473-5772

DIRECTIONS

The Site is on US 64-264, 3 miles (4.8 km) north of Manteo, NC; 92 miles (148.3 km) southeast of Norfolk, VA; and 67 miles (108 km) southeast of Elizabeth City, NC.

VISITOR ACTIVITIES

• Interpretive exhibits and a 17-minute orientation film are available year-round in the Visitor Center. • Ranger-guided tours are available in the summer. • The "Lost Colony," a symphonic drama, is produced in the Waterside Theater in the summer. • The Elizabethan Gardens are adjacent to the Site and are maintained by the Garden Club of North Carolina, Inc. • Visitor facilities include a bookstore/gift shop, restrooms, parking and a picnic area. • The Site is open year-round, except Dec. 25, from 9 a.m. to 5 p.m., with hours extended to 8 p.m., in the summer.

PERMITS, FEES & LIMITATIONS

There are fees for the "Lost Colony" and the Elizabethan Gardens. The admission is set by those organizations.

ACCESSIBILITY

The Visitor Center parking lots, picnic area and historic trail to restored earthworks, exhibits, auditorium and most interpretive talks are accessible. Audio tours of the Visitor Center exhibits are available.

CAMPING & LODGING

• National Park Service campgrounds are in nearby Cape Hatteras National Seashore. • Private campgrounds are in adjacent communities. • Lodging is available in Manteo or on the Outer Banks, 14 to 18 miles (22.5 to 29 km).

FOOD & SUPPLIES

Food and supplies are available in Manteo.

FIRST AID/ HOSPITAL

• First aid is available at the Site or in Nags Head. • The nearest hospital is in Elizabeth City, NC, 80 miles (129 km).

GENERAL INFORMATION

Nearby points of interest include Cape Hatteras National Seashore and the Wright Brothers National Memorial (see listings in this book).

Guilford Courthouse National Military Park

Greensboro, North Carolina

The battle commemorated at Guilford Courthouse National Military Park was won by British troops led by Charles, Earl Cornwallis, on March 15, 1781. However, the decision by the Continental Army's Nathanael Greene to reconquer South Carolina and Cornwallis' plan to continue into Virginia precipitated the British surrender 7 months later.

MAILING ADDRESS

Superintendent, Guilford Courthouse National Military Park, PO Box 9806, Greensboro, NC 27429-0806 **Telephone: 919-288-1776**

DIRECTIONS

From US 220 (Battleground Avenue), turn east on New Garden Road and travel one-quarter mile (.4 km). The Visitor Center is near the New Garden Road entrance.

VISITOR ACTIVITIES

• The Visitor Center contains exhibits on the campaign and battle and a 20-minute film shown on the half-hour. • There is a self-guided auto tour over a 2.5-mile (4 km) road. • There is a bike lane on the tour road. • There are foot trails for hiking to historical points. Wayside exhibits interpret the battle. • The Visitor Center and Park are open daily, except Dec. 25 and Jan. 1, from 8:30 a.m. to 5 p.m. • Write for information on special events during the year. • Annual events include observance of the battle on March 15. • There are conducted programs during the summer.

PERMITS, FEES & LIMITATIONS

• No entrance fee. • There is a 1-hour parking limit at Tour Road stops.

ACCESSIBILITY

All facilities are accessible in the Visitor Center. The film is captioned. Parking is reserved at the Visitor Center and 7 tour stops. Foot trails are generally accessible.

CAMPING & LODGING

Camping and lodging is available in Greensboro.

FOOD & SUPPLIES

Food and supplies are available in Greensboro.

FIRST AID/ HOSPITAL

• First aid is available in the Park. • The nearest hospital is in Greensboro, 3 miles (4.8 km).

GENERAL INFORMATION

• Watch out for traffic on New Garden Road and Old Battleground Road. • The Park has 28 monuments honoring men and women of the Revolutionary period, including the Nathanael Greene Monument and the

Signers Monument, where 2 of North Carolina's 3 signers of the Declaration of Independence are buried. • Additional or after-hours parking is available at a lot on Old Battleground Road.

Moores Creek National Battlefield
Currie, North Carolina

Though the Revolutionary War battle of Moores Creek Bridge on Feb. 27, 1776 was a small one between loyalists and patriots of North Carolina, the implications were large. The victory demonstrated patriot strength in the countryside, discouraged British loyalist sentiment in the Carolinas and spurred revolutionary feeling throughout the colonies.

MAILING ADDRESS
Superintendent, Moores Creek National Battlefield, PO Box 69, Currie, NC 28435 **Telephone:** 919-283-5591

DIRECTIONS
The Battlefield is 20 miles (32.2 km) northwest of Wilmington, NC, via 421 and NC 210. From I-40, follow NC 210 west at the Rocky Point Exit.

VISITOR ACTIVITIES
• Exhibits, walking tours, picnicking, wildflower watching in season and bird watching all year. • Facilities include restrooms, a museum, trails and a picnic area. • 1-mile (1.6 km) History Trail and a one-third mile (.5 km) Tar Heel Trail depict the local Naval Stores industry during the Revolution. • The Battlefield is open daily from 9 a.m. to 5 p.m., and from 8 a.m. to 6 p.m., on Saturdays and Sundays from Memorial Day to Labor Day. The Battlefield is closed on Dec. 25 and Jan. 1.

PERMITS, FEES & LIMITATIONS
No entrance fee.

ACCESSIBILITY
The Visitor Center, parking, picnic area and restrooms are accessible.

CAMPING & LODGING
Overnight accommodations are available in Wilmington.

FOOD & SUPPLIES
Food and supplies are available in Currie, Atkinson, Burgaw and Wilmington.

GENERAL INFORMATION
• For your safety - When near the creek, please supervise children. Visitors should be aware of several species of poisonous snakes in the Park. • The historic reconstructed Moores Creek Bridge is for interpretation only. Please do not attempt to cross.

Wright Brothers National Memorial
Kill Devil Hills, North Carolina

On Dec. 17, 1903, a manned, heavier-than-air machine left the ground by its own power, moved forward under control without losing speed and landed on a point as high as that from which it started for the first time when Orville Wright piloted the flyer he and his brother Wilbur built on a stretch of beach near Kill Devil Hills.

MAILING ADDRESS

Superintendent, Wright Brothers National Memorial, c/o Cape Hatteras National Seashore, Rt. 1, Box 675, Manteo, NC 27954 Telephone: 919-441-7430

VISITOR ACTIVITIES

• Interpretive exhibits are available year-round, including reproductions of the Wright brothers' 1902 glider, the 1903 Flyer and camp buildings. • Orientation talks and walking tours. • Facilities include a bookstore, restrooms and telephones at the Visitor Center. • The Memorial is open daily, except Dec. 25, from 9 a.m. to 5 p.m., with hours extended to 6 p.m. in the summer.

PERMITS, FEES & LIMITATIONS

The entrance fee is $2 per person (16 and under and 62 and older free). An annual pass is available for $10.

ACCESSIBILITY

The Visitor Center parking lots, restrooms, the historic trail, exhibits and most interpretive talks are accessible. Audio tours of the Visitor Center exhibits are available.

CAMPING & LODGING

• National Park Service campgrounds are in nearby Cape Hatteras National Seashore. • Private campgrounds are in adjacent communities. • Lodging is available in Kitty Hawk, Kill Devil Hills and Nags Head, all within a 14-mile (22.5 km) radius.

FOOD & SUPPLIES

Food and supplies are available in adjacent communities.

FIRST AID/ HOSPITAL

• First aid is available in the Memorial or in Nags Head. • The nearest hospital is in Elizabeth City, NC, 66 miles (106.4 km).

GENERAL INFORMATION

• For your safety - Keep in mind that the generally windy conditions make the temperatures feel cooler than they actually are. Protect against sunburn, especially from spring through fall. • Nearby points of interest include Cape Hatteras National Seashore, 10 miles (16.1 km); and Fort Raleigh National Historic Site, 18 miles (29 km) (see listings in this book).

North Dakota

1 Fort Union Trading Post National Historic Site

2 International Peace Garden

3 Knife River Indian Villages National Historic Site

4 Theodore Roosevelt National Park
   North Unit
   South Unit

Fort Union Trading Post National Historic Site

Williston, North Dakota

John Jacob Astor's American Fur Co., built Fort Union in 1829 near the junction of the Missouri and Yellowstone rivers. In its heyday, the post was a busy place employing up to 100 people trading beaver furs and buffalo hides until the 1860s when the fort was dismantled by the Army for materials to complete Fort Buford.

MAILING ADDRESS

Superintendent, Fort Union Trading Post National Historic Site, RR 3, Box 71, Williston, ND 58801 **Telephone: 701-572-9083**

DIRECTIONS

The Site is on the Montana/North Dakota border and is reached via US 2 and ND 1804. It is 25 miles (40.3 km) southwest of Williston, ND, or 21 miles (33.8 km) northeast of Sidney, MT, via ND 58. The Site operates on Central Time.

VISITOR ACTIVITIES

• The Site is open daily from 8 a.m. to 8 p.m., in the summer and from 9 a.m. to 5:30 p.m., the rest of the year. • The Fort consists of a reconstructed palisade, stone bastions, flagstaff, Indian trade house and the Bourgeios House (Visitor Center). • Summer guided tours, living history program, exhibits, bookstore, wayside exhibits and a picnic area near the parking lot. • There is a 4-day fur trade rendezvous from Thursday through Sunday over the third weekend in June. • The Site is closed Thanksgiving, Dec. 25 and Jan. 1.

PERMITS, FEES & LIMITATIONS

• No entrance fee. • The Fort is a day-use site.

ACCESSIBILITY

All facilities are accessible. Parking is available. A shuttle cart to the parking area is available in summer.

CAMPING & LODGING

• The nearest overnight accommodations are in Sidney and Williston. • Primitive camping is available at Fort Buford State Historic Site, 2 miles (3.2 km). • The nearest National Park Service campground is at the North Unit of Theodore Roosevelt National Park, 70 miles (112.9 km).

FOOD & SUPPLIES

Food and supplies are available in Williston and Sidney.

FIRST AID/ HOSPITAL

The nearest hospital is in Williston.

International Peace Garden

Dunseith, North Dakota

Affiliated area. Peaceful relations between Canada and the United States are commemorated at the International Peace Garden. North Dakota holds the 888-acre U.S. portion for International Peace Garden, Inc., which administers the area for North Dakota and Manitoba.

MAILING ADDRESS

International Peace Garden, Inc., Rt. 1, Box 116, Dunseith, ND 58329
Telephone: 701-263-4390

DIRECTIONS

• Walking, picnicking, hiking, camping, canoeing, guided tours with advance arrangements as well as self-guided driving and walking tours. • The Garden is home of the International Music Camp and Legion Athletic Camp. • Formal gardens, arboretum, picnic areas, souvenir shops, bell tower, peace chapel and masonic auditorium. • The front entrance to the Garden is open all day, all year.

VISITOR ACTIVITIES

• The entrance fee is $7 per vehicle and $3 per person. A $12 season pass is available. • Vehicles are restricted to designated roads.

PERMITS, FEES & LIMITATIONS

The majority of facilities are accessible.

ACCESSIBILITY

• There are 20 camp sites available with electricity, water and cement pad for $10 a night; 6 sites with electricity for $8 a night; and 7 sites with no services for $6 a night. The campground has showers, dump stations, firewood and picnic tables. • Lodging is available in Boissevain, Manitoba (Hwy. 10) and Dunseith, ND (Hwy. 281).

CAMPING & LODGING

• Limited food supplies are available to campers at the U.S. and Canadian concessions. • The Errick Willis Pavilion features a Sunday smorgasbord and catering for bus groups, weddings, meetings, etc., with advance notice.

FOOD & SUPPLIES

The nearest hospitals are Bottineau Hospital, 30 miles (48.3 km); and Rolla Community Hospital, 30 miles (48.3 km).

FIRST AID/ HOSPITAL

• The main tourist season is mid-May through September. • Flowers in the formal garden are generally in full bloom and at their best color from mid-July through August.

Knife River Indian Villages National Historic Site

Stanton, North Dakota

The communities of Northern Plains Indians living in earth lodges in the Upper Missouri River Valley had been settled in the area for 700 years and had established a culture based on agriculture, raiding and hunting at the time of their contact with Europeans in 1738.

MAILING ADDRESS	Knife River Indian Villages National Historic Site, Box 9, Stanton, ND 58571 Telephone: 701-745-3309
DIRECTIONS	From I-94 at Bismarck, north on US 83 to ND 200 at Washburn, then 23 miles (37 km) west to Stanton, one-half mile (.8 km); US 31 north 35 miles (56.4 km) to Stanton and one-half mile (.8 km) north.
VISITOR ACTIVITIES	• Summer programs are conducted daily from June through August. They include guided tours to village sites, museum exhibits, a film, cultural demonstrations and guest speakers. • There are daily programs until Labor Day. • Special tours and programs are arranged upon request. • The Site is open daily, except Thanksgiving, Dec. 25 and Jan. 1, from **8 a.m. to 6 p.m.**, in the summer and **8 a.m. to 4:30 p.m.**, in the winter.
PERMITS, FEES & LIMITATIONS	• **No entrance fee.** • Vehicles are restricted to parking areas and designated roads.
ACCESSIBILITY	The Visitor Center, restrooms, picnic areas and village trails are accessible.
CAMPING & LODGING	Overnight accommodations are available nearby.
FOOD & SUPPLIES	Food and supplies are available nearby.
FIRST AID/ HOSPITAL	The nearest hospital is in Hazen, ND, 14 miles (22.5 km).

Theodore Roosevelt National Park

Medora, North Dakota   See Climatable No. 27

Theodore Roosevelt first came to the North Dakota badlands in September 1883. His subsequent trips to the cattle ranches he established where he lived the "strenuous life" he loved also helped sharpen and refine his interest in nature and conservation.

MAILING ADDRESS	Superintendent, Theodore Roosevelt National Park, Medora, ND 58645 Telephone: 701-623-4466
DIRECTIONS	The South Unit is along I-94, 17 miles (27.4 km) west of Belfield and 63 miles (101.6 km) east of Glendive. The main Visitor Center is at Medora at the entrance to this unit. The Painted Canyon Visitor Center is 7 miles (11.2 km) east of Medora on I-94. The entrance and Visitor Center to the North Unit is 15 miles (24.1 km) south of Watford City and 55 miles (88.7 km) north of Belfield on Hwy. 85.

North Dakota 303

VISITOR ACTIVITIES

• Interpretive exhibits, guided walks, campfire programs, auto tours, hiking, photography, backcountry, horseback riding, picnicking, wildlife and bird watching, and cabin tours. • The Park is open all year although some roads are closed during winter due to snow and ice. • The North and South unit visitor centers are open daily except Thanksgiving, Dec. 25 and Jan. 1. • Facilities include a bookstore and restrooms at the visitor centers, self-guiding nature trails, picnic areas and interpretive waysides along scenic drives.

PERMITS, FEES & LIMITATIONS

• The entrance fee is $4 per vehicle or $2 per person from May to September. Season passes are available for $10. • No off-road vehicles allowed. • Horses are not permitted in the campground or on nature trails. • Mountain bikes are restricted to paved roads. • Free backcountry permits are available at the North and South unit visitor centers. • No firewood is available in the campground and picnic area. Gathering of wood is prohibited.

ACCESSIBILITY

An access guide is available at visitor centers. All 3 visitor centers, Cottonwood and Squaw Creek campgrounds, the Maltese Cross Cabin, evening campfire programs, naturalist talks, some of the naturalist guided walks, sites in picnic areas, wayside exhibits and restrooms are accessible.

CAMPING & LODGING

• Camping is available in the South Unit at Cottonwood Campground and in the North Unit at Squaw Creek Campground for $7 per night from May to September. Camping is free the rest of the year. Both have tent and trailer sites. No reservations or hookups available. A dump station is in the North Unit. Group camp sites can be reserved by contacting the Park. • Lodging is available in nearby communities, including Medora.

FOOD & SUPPLIES

Food and supplies are available in nearby communities, including Medora, but are limited in winter.

FIRST AID/ HOSPITAL

• First aid is available at the visitor centers. • The nearest hospital to the South Unit is in Dickinson, 35 miles (56.4 km); and to the North Unit is in Watford City, 15 miles (24.1 km).

GENERAL INFORMATION

• For your safety - Wildlife is dangerous, so keep your distance. Drinking water should be obtained from approved water sources. Most backcountry water is not fit for human use. • The weather in the badlands can be very harsh with extremes in temperature and sudden violent storms. Prepare yourself for a variety of conditions.

Ohio

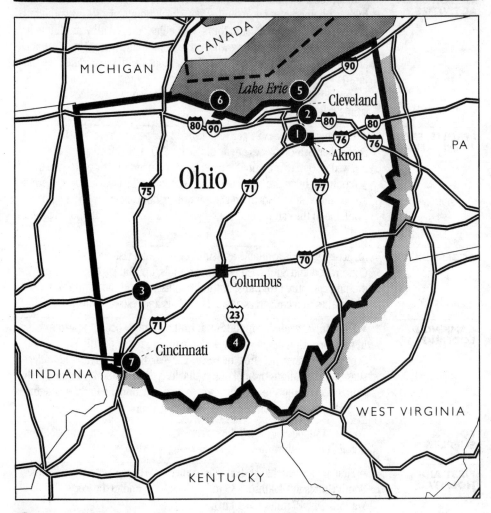

1. Cuyahoga Valley National Recreation Area
2. David Berger National Memorial
3. Dayton Aviation National Historical Park
4. Hopewell Culture National Historical Park
5. James A. Garfield National Historic Site
6. Perry's Victory and International Peace Memorial
7. William Howard Taft National Historic Site

Ohio

Cuyahoga Valley National Recreation Area

Brecksville, Ohio

The Cuyahoga Valley National Recreation Area preserves 33,000 acres of pastoral valley along 22 miles (35.4 km) of the Cuyahoga River between the cities of Cleveland and Akron. It includes river floodplain, steep and gentle valley walls forested by deciduous and evergreen woods, and numerous tributaries and their ravines.

MAILING ADDRESS	Cuyahoga Valley National Recreation Area, 15610 Vaughn Road, Brecksville, OH 44141 **Telephone:** 1-800-433-1986
DIRECTIONS	Headquarters is in Brecksville, OH, south of OH 82 on Riverview Road and east of OH 21 on Snowville Road.
VISITOR ACTIVITIES	• Hiking, biking, environmental education, interpretive programs and exhibits, cross-country skiing, special events, performing arts programs and sledding. • The Recreation Area is open daily from **8 a.m. to 11 p.m.**, but some areas close at dusk. The visitor centers are closed Thanksgiving, Dec. 25 and Jan. 1.
PERMITS, FEES & LIMITATIONS	• **No entrance fee.** • There is a $50 fee for reserving picnic shelters.
ACCESSIBILITY	Happy Days and Canal visitor centers are accessible. A 20-mile (32.2 km) trail, the Ohio and Erie Canal Towpath Trail, is accessible.
CAMPING & LODGING	• Lodging is available in the Recreation Area at the AYH Stanford Youth Hostel and the Inn at Brandywine Falls, a bed and breakfast. • Motels are available along OH 8, in Brecksville, Cleveland and Akron.
FOOD & SUPPLIES	Food and supplies are available in surrounding communities.
FIRST AID/ HOSPITAL	• First aid is available in the Recreation Area. • The nearest hospital is in Cuyahoga Falls, OH, 5 miles (8 km).

David Berger National Memorial

Cleveland Heights, Ohio

Affiliated area. This site honors the memory of the 11 Israeli athletes who were killed at the 1972 Olympic Games in Munich, Germany, one of which was David Berger, an American citizen.

MAILING ADDRESS	David Berger National Memorial, Jewish Community Center, 3505 Mayfield Road, Cleveland Heights, OH 44118 **Telephone:** 216-382-4000
DIRECTIONS	The Memorial is in the heart of Cleveland Heights in the northeast metropolitan Cleveland area.

VISITOR ACTIVITIES	Viewing the Memorial.
PERMITS, FEES & LIMITATIONS	No fees.
ACCESSIBILITY	The Memorial is accessible.
CAMPING & LODGING	A full range of services is available in Cleveland and vicinity.
FOOD & SUPPLIES	Food and supplies are available in Cleveland and vicinity.
FIRST AID/ HOSPITAL	Medical services are available in Cleveland and vicinity.

Dayton Aviation National Historical Park

Dayton, Ohio

Authorized on Oct. 16, 1992, the Park will preserve the area's aviation heritage associated with Orville and Wilbur Wright, their invention and development of aviation. The Park also commemorates the life and works of poet Paul Laurence Dunbar, an African American friend and classmate of the Wright brothers.

MAILING ADDRESS	Superintendent, Dayton Aviation Heritage National Historical Park, PO Box 9280, Wright Brothers Station, Dayton, OH 45409 **Telephone:** 513-223-0020
VISITOR ACTIVITIES	• **National Park Service facilities and services are not available.** Staff and visitor services to be developed beginning in 1994. • Park sites open to visitation are managed by cooperating partners at the Wright Cycle Company Shop, Wright Flyer III at Carillon Historical Park, Huffman Prairie Flying Field and Wright Brothers Memorial Hill at Wright-Patterson Air Force Base, and Paul Laurence Dunbar House State Memorial. There are limited schedules and seasons at all sites. Telephone the sites or call 513-223-0020 for more information. • The Aviation Trail driving tour includes 45 aviation-related sites throughout the community. A guidebook, available at area book stores, is required.
PERMITS, FEES & LIMITATIONS	There is a $1 per adult fee at Carillon Park and a $2.50 per adult fee at the Dunbar House. Other sites are free with donations accepted.
ACCESSIBILITY	Sites are not yet modified for accessibility. Special arrangements may be made locally.
CAMPING & LODGING	Camping and lodging are available in Dayton and vicinity.

FOOD & SUPPLIES

Food and supplies are available in Dayton and vicinity.

FIRST AID/ HOSPITAL

Medical services are available in Dayton and vicinity.

GENERAL INFORMATION

Contact the sites at: Wright Cycle Company Shop, 22 S. Williams St., 513-443-0793; Dunbar House State Memorial, 219 N. Paul Laurence Dunbar St., 513-224-7061; Carillon Historical Park, 2001 S. Patterson Blvd., 513-293-2841; and Huffman Prairie Flying Field and Wright Brothers Memorial Hill, Ohio Rt. 444, Wright-Patterson Air Force Base, 513-257-5886.

Hopewell Culture National Historical Park

Chillicothe, Ohio

Mound City, a unit of Hopewell Culture National Historical Park, was a village and burial site for people living along the Scioto River during the first 2 centuries AD. It includes 23 prehistoric earthworks originally constructed for defensive and religious purposes.

MAILING ADDRESS

Superintendent, Hopewell Culture National Historical Park, 16062 State Rt. 104, Chillicothe, OH 45601 **Telephone:** 614-774-1125

DIRECTIONS

The Visitor Center is on the west bank of the Scioto River on Ohio State Rt. 104, 2 miles (3.2 km) north of the US 35 intersection and 3 miles (4.8 km) north of Chillicothe, OH.

VISITOR ACTIVITIES

• Interpretive exhibits, walking, picnicking and special tours for organized groups with prior arrangements. • Self-guided interpretive trail. • Facilities include a Visitor Center, audiovisual programs, bookstore, picnic area and restrooms. • The Visitor Center is open from **8 a.m. to 5 p.m.**, daily except Thanksgiving, Dec. 25 and Jan. 1. Hours are extended from Memorial Day through Labor Day.

PERMITS, FEES & LIMITATIONS

The **entrance fee** is $2 per person or $4 per private vehicle.

ACCESSIBILITY

Most facilities and attractions are accessible.

CAMPING & LODGING

• There are several state park campgrounds and private campgrounds within a 30-mile (48.3 km) radius. • Motels are in Chillicothe. • For a list of accommodations, write the Superintendent.

FOOD & SUPPLIES

Food services are available in Chillicothe.

FIRST AID/ HOSPITAL

• First aid is available in the Park. • The nearest hospital is the Medical Center Hospital, 6 miles (9.6 km).

GENERAL INFORMATION

There are numerous historical and natural attractions nearby. These include prehistoric Indian sites administered by the Ohio Historical Society (Serpent Mound, Fort Ancient, Seip Mound, Fort Hill and Newark Earthworks); the Adena State Memorial; Ross County Historical Museum and several state parks. The popular outdoor drama "Tecumseh" is held from mid-June through early September. For more information, write the Superintendent of the Ross/Chillicothe Convention and Visitors Bureau, PO Box 73, Chillicothe, OH 45601, phone 614-775-4150.

James A. Garfield National Historic Site

Mentor, Ohio

The James A. Garfield National Historic Site preserves Lawnfield and other property associated with the life of the 20th President.

MAILING ADDRESS

Curator, James A. Garfield National Historic Site, 8095 Mentor Ave., Mentor, OH 44060 **Telephone:** 216-255-8722

DIRECTIONS

The Site is 25 miles (40.3 km) east of Cleveland off of I-90 on Mentor Avenue (Rt. 20).

VISITOR ACTIVITIES

• The home is open for tours. All outbuildings are closed to visitors. • The Visitor Center (Carriage Barn) should be open by fall 1994. • The Site is open Tuesday through Saturday from 10 a.m. to 5 p.m., and Sundays from 12 p.m. to 5 p.m., except for major holidays. • Various special events are held throughout the year. Call for details.

PERMITS, FEES & LIMITATIONS

• The entrance fee is $3 for adults, $2 for seniors and $1.50 for children ages 6 to 12. Children ages 5 and younger are admitted free. Group rates are available. • Vehicles are restricted to semi-paved areas.

ACCESSIBILITY

The Site will be fully accessible after restoration is completed in 1996 or 1997.

CAMPING & LODGING

Many motels are within 1 mile (1.6 km) of the Site.

FOOD & SUPPLIES

Many fast food and other restaurants are within one-half mile (.8 km) of the Site.

FIRST AID/ HOSPITAL

• Many medical facilities are within the immediate area. • Hospitals are in Painesville and Willoughby, less than 10 miles (16.1 km).

Perry's Victory and International Peace Memorial

Put-in-Bay, Ohio

Oliver Hazard Perry's victory over a British fleet in the War of 1812 contributed to a lasting peace. The victory helped persuade the British to cease hostilities and enabled the United States to claim the Northwest at the peace talks in Ghent a year later.

MAILING ADDRESS

Superintendent, Perry's Victory and International Peace Memorial, PO Box 549, Put-in-Bay, OH 43456 **Telephone:** 419-285-2184

DIRECTIONS

The Memorial is on South Bass Island, 3 miles (4.8 km) offshore from Catawba, OH, and 8 miles (12.9 km) from Port Clinton, OH, in Lake Erie. Ferry service is provided from Catawba and Port Clinton in season, and air service is provided from Port Clinton and Sandusky year-round.

VISITOR ACTIVITIES

• The tallest open-air observation deck in the National Park Service, 317 feet (96.6 m), is accessed by elevator. • Interpretive programs are held daily in season, including costumed demonstrations and musket firings on weekends. Special arrangements for demonstrations may be made by calling in advance. • A Visitor Center on street level includes exhibits on the Battle of Lake Erie and the construction of the monument, and a bookstore. • The Memorial is open from late April to late October daily from **10 a.m. to 5 p.m.**, in the spring and fall with hours extended to 7 **p.m.**, from mid-June to Labor Day.

PERMITS, FEES & LIMITATIONS

• The **entrance fee** is $2 per person for ages 17 to 61. • All youths must be properly chaperoned.

ACCESSIBILITY

The Visitor Center and restrooms are accessible.

CAMPING & LODGING

• South Bass Island State Park has 125, first-come, first-served camp sites. • The village of Put-in-Bay and surrounding South Bass Island have numerous motels and bed and breakfasts. Reservations are suggested. Contact the Put-in-Bay Chamber of Commerce.

FOOD & SUPPLIES

Restaurants, carry-outs and a grocery store are available in Put-in-Bay with more facilities available on the mainland.

FIRST AID/ HOSPITAL

• First aid is available in the Memorial and is tied to Put-in-Bay's EMS system. • The nearest hospital is in Port Clinton, 8 miles (12.9 km).

GENERAL INFORMATION

• South Bass Island has a variety of tourist attractions, including caves, a winery and numerous gift shops. Contact the Put-in-Bay Chamber of Commerce, PO Box 250, Put-in-Bay, OH 43456, for a complete visitor guide, including transportation schedules. • Vehicle transport to the island is limited. Island businesses provide a tour train, taxi and bus service, as well as bicycle and golf cart rentals.

William Howard Taft National Historic Site
Cincinnati, Ohio

William Howard Taft, the only person to serve as both President (1909-13) and Chief Justice of the United States (1921-30), was born and raised in this restored home that features 4 period rooms reflecting Taft family life in the 1860s.

MAILING ADDRESS

Superintendent, William Howard Taft National Historic Site, 2038 Auburn Ave., Cincinnati, OH 45219-3025 **Telephone:** 513-684-3262

DIRECTIONS

The Site is at 2038 Auburn Ave., 1 block north of the intersection of Auburn and Dorchester avenues. From I-71 North, take Exit 2 (Reading and Florence). Stay in the right lane; turn left at the first stoplight and proceed up the hill. Turn right on Auburn and go half a block to the home. From I-71 South, take Exit 3 (Taft Road) to Auburn Avenue.

VISITOR ACTIVITIES

• Interpretive tours of 4 restored rooms and self-guided exhibits. • Advance reservations are requested for groups of 25 or more. • A parking lot is available at the corner of Southern and Young streets. • The Site is open daily, except Thanksgiving, Dec. 25 and Jan. 1, from 10 a.m. to 4 p.m.

PERMITS, FEES & LIMITATIONS

No fees.

ACCESSIBILITY

A restroom and elevator are available. Call in advance for parking access at the Site.

CAMPING & LODGING

• Ohio State Park information for camping in the area is available from 1-800-BUCKEYE. • Hotels, motels and lodging are available in Cincinnati and vicinity.

FOOD & SUPPLIES

Food and supplies are available within one-half mile (.8 km) of the Site.

FIRST AID/ HOSPITAL

The Christ Hospital is 1 block north of the Site.

Oklahoma

1 Chickasaw National Recreation Area

Oklahoma

Chickasaw National Recreation Area

Sulphur, Oklahoma

Chickasaw National Recreation Area combines old and new and honors the Chickasaw Nation's contributions toward the preservation of startling natural features in this nearly level landscape that includes clear, cool streams and bromide and sulphur springs.

MAILING ADDRESS
Superintendent, Chickasaw National Recreation Area, PO Box 201, Sulphur, OK 73086 **Telephone:** 405-622-3165

DIRECTIONS
The Recreation Area is near Sulphur, OK, on US 177 and OK 7. It is accessible from Oklahoma City and Dallas/Ft. Worth via I-35.

VISITOR ACTIVITIES
• Interpretive exhibits, picnicking, swimming, boating, fishing, water skiing, biking, hiking, guided nature walks, wildlife and bird watching and photography. • The Recreation Area is always open. • Facilities include a bookstore, restrooms and telephones located at Travertine Nature Center, picnic areas, beaches, boat launches, trailer dump station, nature trails and a National Environmental Study Area. • Travertine Nature Center is closed on all holidays except Memorial Day, July 4th and Labor Day.

PERMITS, FEES & LIMITATIONS
• No entrance fee. • Permits are required for camping. • Golden Age and Access Passports available. • No off-road vehicles allowed. • No bicycles allowed on trails east of the Nature Center.

ACCESSIBILITY
Travertine Nature Center, fishing docks and most restrooms are accessible.

CAMPING & LODGING
• Camping is available on a first-come, first-served basis for $6 per night or $1 per person with 10-person minimum for group camping. Reservations are accepted for group camping by calling 405-622-6677. Hookups are not available. • Motels are located nearby in Sulphur.

FOOD & SUPPLIES
Food and supplies are available in Sulphur.

FIRST AID/ HOSPITAL
• First aid is available in the Recreation Area. • The nearest hospital is in Sulphur, 2 miles (3.2 km).

GENERAL INFORMATION
• Poisonous snakes and poison ivy are common. • Summers are hot and humid with sever thunderstorms common in May and June. • Tornadoes and thunderstorms are a threat April through June. Winters are generally mild.

Oregon

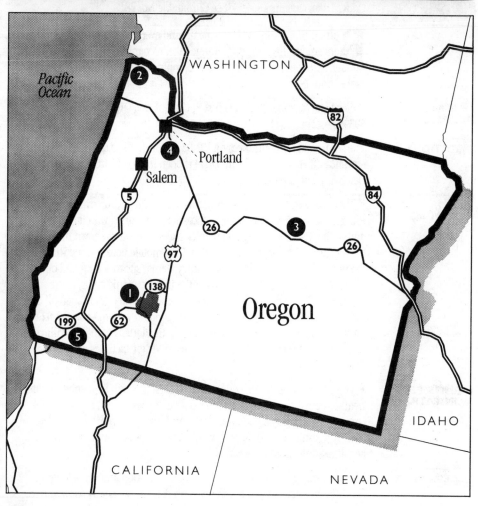

1 Crater Lake National Park

2 Fort Clatsop National Memorial

3 John Day Fossil Beds National Monument

4 McLoughlin House National Historic Site

5 Oregon Caves National Monument

Crater Lake National Park

Crater Lake, Oregon   See Climatable No. 28

Rolling mountains, volcanic peaks and evergreen forests surround this enormous, high Cascade Range lake, recognized worldwide as a scenic wonder. Activities include boat tours, camping and opportunities to learn more about geology.

MAILING ADDRESS

Crater Lake National Park, PO Box 7, Crater Lake, OR 97604 **Telephone:** 503-594-2211

DIRECTIONS

The south and west entrances on OR 62 are open all year. The north entrance off Hwy. 138 and Rim Drive is open from mid-June to early October, weather permitting.

VISITOR ACTIVITIES

• There are summer Ranger programs at Mazama Campground, daily Ranger talks, interpretive walks, concession boat tours, wildlife watching, auto tours, fishing, hiking and picnicking. • A movie is shown throughout the day at Steel Information Center. • Snowmobile access to the Rim and to the north side of the Park, cross-country skiing, snowshoeing and other winter recreational activities. • Facilities include picnic areas, restrooms and post office available through the summer. • The Park is open all day every day in the summer. In winter, the south and west road on OR 62 to Park Headquarters is open. The road from Headquarters to Rim Village closes at times during severe snowstorms. • Visitor facilities are closed Dec. 25.

PERMITS, FEES & LIMITATIONS

• The entrance fee is $5, collected from June through September or later if weather permits. • All vehicles are restricted to designated roads. • Back-country use permits are required for overnight stays. Information is available by writing the Park or at any visitor center. • Descent to the lake is permitted only on the Cleetwood Trail.

ACCESSIBILITY

The Steel Information Center, cafeteria and gift shop and some lodging facilities are accessible. Accessibility is hindered in winter by snow and ice.

CAMPING & LODGING

• Camp sites are available from late May through mid-October, weather permitting, for $11 per night. No reservations are accepted. • Reservations for Mazama Cabins, open during the summer, may be made by contacting Crater Lake Lodge, Inc., Crater Lake, OR 97604, phone 503-594-2511. • Other overnight accommodations are available in Medford, 80 miles (129 km); Klamath Falls, 54 miles (87 km); Union Creek and Fort Klamath.

FOOD & SUPPLIES

• Meals are served at the Rim Village cafeteria. • Some groceries are available at Mazama Village. • Food services, groceries and gasoline are available from mid-May through mid-October. • Food and supplies are also available at Fort Klamath and Union Creek.

FIRST AID/ HOSPITAL	• First aid is available in the Park. • An ambulance service is available in Chiloquin, OR. • The nearest hospitals are in Medford and Klamath Falls.
GENERAL INFORMATION	**For your safety** - Stay on trails, especially along the caldera rim. Footing can be treacherous on this volcanic rock and soil. Keep your distance from wildlife. Do not feed any wildlife.

Fort Clatsop National Memorial

Astoria, Oregon

From December 1805 until March 1806, members of the Lewis and Clark expedition wintered at Fort Clatsop, a log stockade 50 feet (15.2 m) square. The explorers built the Fort after their trail-blazing journey from the Mississippi River to the Pacific Ocean.

MAILING ADDRESS	Superintendent, Fort Clatsop National Memorial, Rt. 3, Box 604-FC, Astoria, OR 97103 **Telephone:** 503-861-2471
DIRECTIONS	The Memorial is 6 miles (9.6 km) southwest of Astoria, OR, just off US 101. Signs along US 101 and alternate 101 direct visitors to the Memorial.
VISITOR ACTIVITIES	• Interpretive exhibits, film and slide show programs, living history costumed demonstrations during the summer, hiking and picnicking. • A bookstore is operated by the Fort Clatsop Historical Association. • There are restrooms at the Visitor Center. • The Visitor Center and fort replica are open daily, except Dec. 25, from **8 a.m. to 5 p.m.**, in winter with hours extended to **6 p.m.**, in summer.
PERMITS, FEES & LIMITATIONS	• The **entrance fee** is $2 for ages 17 and older with a $4 per family maximum. Ages 62 and older are admitted free. • Vehicles are limited to roads and parking lots.
ACCESSIBILITY	Parking, restrooms, Visitor Center and audiovisual programs are accessible. The Fort and trails are generally accessible - ask for assistance. Captioned audiovisual programs are available.
CAMPING & LODGING	• Camping is available at Fort Stevens State Park, 8 miles (12.9 km). Reserve space by contacting Fort Stevens State Park, Hammond, OR 97121. • Lodging is available in the nearby towns of Astoria; Warrenton, 3 miles (4.8 km); and Seaside, 13 miles (20.9 km).
FOOD & SUPPLIES	Food and supplies are available in Warrenton, Astoria and Seaside.
FIRST AID/ HOSPITAL	• First aid is available in the Memorial. • The nearest hospital is in Astoria.

GENERAL INFORMATION

• For your safety - Caution is necessary within the fort replica where rooms are dark and floors uneven. Be careful at the canoe landing site since the banks can be slippery. • Other nearby Lewis and Clark sites are the Salt Works Site in Seaside; the trail over Tillamook Head to Cannon Beach; the Lewis and Clark camp site at McGowan, WA; and the Lewis and Clark Interpretive Center at Fort Canby State Park, Illwaco, WA.

John Day Fossil Beds National Monument

John Day, Oregon

John Day Fossil Beds National Monument preserves one of the most complete fossil records of the last 65 million years covering the Cenozoic Era, or the Age of Mammals, when mammals rose to become the dominant form of animal life and flowering plants became the dominant form of plant life.

MAILING ADDRESS

Superintendent, John Day Fossil Beds National Monument, 420 West Main St., John Day, OR 97845 **Telephone:** Office, 503-575-0721 Visitor Center, 503-987-2333

DIRECTIONS

The Monument is divided into 3 units. The main Visitor Center is 10 miles (16.1 km) west of Dayville, OR, at the Sheep Rock Unit. The Painted Hills Unit is 10 miles (16.1 km) west of Mitchell, OR. The Clarno Unit is 20 miles (32.2 km) west of Fossil, OR. The Headquarters is in John Day.

VISITOR ACTIVITIES

• A fossil museum and lab, film, exhibits and bookstore are available at the Visitor Center. • Each unit has overlooks, trails, exhibits, drinking water, restrooms and picnic tables. • Hiking, picnicking, fishing, biking, wildlife and wildflower watching. • Ranger conducted programs are offered. • Visitor Center hours vary with the seasons.

PERMITS, FEES & LIMITATIONS

• No entrance fee. • Vehicles are limited to parking areas and roads. • Climbing on geologic formations or collecting fossils is prohibited. • No hunting is allowed.

ACCESSIBILITY

An access guide is available at the Visitor Center or by mail. The Visitor Center is accessible. The TDD telephone number is 503-987-2334.

CAMPING & LODGING

• Several public and private campgrounds are nearby. • Lodging is available in John Day, Dayville, Mitchell and Fossil.

FOOD & SUPPLIES

Food and supplies are available in John Day, Dayville, Mitchell and Fossil.

FIRST AID/ HOSPITAL

• Monument staff can assist with minor first aid problems. • The nearest hospitals are in John Day, Prineville and Madras. • A clinic is in Fossil.

GENERAL INFORMATION

For your safety - Beware of deer crossing roads at dusk and night.

McLoughlin House National Historic Site

Oregon City, Oregon

Affiliated area. By the time his career directing the fur trade out of Fort Vancouver for the Hudson's Bay Company ended, John McLoughlin was famous for his efforts, intentional or not, in securing most of the Oregon Country territory for Americans, earning him the title "Father of Oregon."

MAILING ADDRESS

Superintendent, McLoughlin House National Historic Site, 713 Center St., Oregon City, OR 97045 **Telephone:** 503-656-5146

DIRECTIONS

The McLoughlin House is in McLoughlin Park between 7th and 8th streets less than 4 blocks east of Pacific Highway (US 99).

VISITOR ACTIVITIES

• Guided house tours. • The house is open Sundays from **1 p.m. to 4 p.m.**, and Tuesday through Saturday from **10 a.m. to 4 p.m.** The Site is closed in January and for holidays.

PERMITS, FEES & LIMITATIONS

The **entrance fees** are $2.50 for adults ages 17 to 61, $2 for ages 62 and older, and $1 for children ages 6 to 17. Children under 6 are admitted free with parents. Group rates for 12 or more are available.

CAMPING & LODGING

Overnight accommodations are available in Portland, 13 miles (20.9 km); and Oregon City, .6 mile (1 km).

FOOD & SUPPLIES

Food and supplies are available in Oregon City.

FIRST AID/ HOSPITAL

• First aid is not available in the Site. • The nearest hospital is in Oregon City, 2.5 miles (4 km).

GENERAL INFORMATION

• This affiliated area of the National Park System is owned and operated by the McLoughlin Memorial Association. • The Site is like a private home and has no facilities.

Oregon Caves National Monument

Cave Junction, Oregon

Groundwater dissolving marble bedrock formed the cave passages and intricate flowstone formations of the Siskiyou Mountains that are preserved at Oregon Caves National Monument and surrounded by virgin forests.

MAILING ADDRESS	Superintendent, Oregon Caves National Monument, 19000 Caves Highway, Cave Junction, OR 97523 **Telephone:** 503-592-2100
DIRECTIONS	The Monument is 20 miles (32.2 km) southeast of Cave Junction on OR 46. Travel either 50 miles (80.6 km) south of Grants Pass or 76 miles (122.5 km) north from Crescent City on US 199. The last 8 miles (12.9 km) of OR 46 are quite narrow and winding. Information is available on OR 46 just off US 199 at the Visitor Center.
VISITOR ACTIVITIES	• Cave tours (year-round daily except Dec. 25), hiking, wildlife and bird watching, picnicking and evening programs in the summer. • There are 5 miles (8 km) of trails in the Monument with many more in the surrounding Siskiyou National Forest. Several pleasant 1- to 4-hour walks through scenic virgin forest are available from May to November. • The Monument, encompassing a remnant old-growth Douglas/White Fir community, is a nature lover's paradise with more than 80 species of birds, 35 species of mammals and more than 110 species of plants. • Cave tour hours vary with the season. Summers are busy, so it's best to arrive in the morning.
PERMITS, FEES & LIMITATIONS	• No entrance fee. • Cave tours are provided by a private concessioner. Cave tour fees are $6.75 for adults and $3.75 for children ages 6 to 12. Special regulations apply to children under 6, and child-care services are available during cave tours for $3 per child. • Pets are permitted only in the parking areas. • Parking for RVs and trailers is extremely limited. Trailers are not recommended on the narrow and winding road to the Monument. There is parking/drop-off space for trailers at the Visitor Center in Cave Junction.
ACCESSIBILITY	The cave is not accessible except for the entrance room. Restrooms and a few picnic tables are accessible. Trails are not accessible.
CAMPING & LODGING	• The Siskiyou National Forest operates 2 campgrounds nearby from mid-June through the first week of September. Cave Creek Campground is 4 miles (6.4 km) from the Monument. No trailers are permitted. Greyback Campground is 8 miles (12.9 km) from the Monument. Trailers are permitted. Camp sites are on a first-come, first-served basis. There are no showers and only 1 site at Greyback has utility hookups (call 1-800-283-CAMP to reserve). • The Oregon Caves Chateau, an historic landmark, is the only lodging in the Monument. It is open from mid-June to Labor Day. Bed and breakfast-style lodging is available at the Chateau after Labor Day through mid-September. For information and reservations, write to Oregon Caves Chateau, PO Box 128, Cave Junction, OR 97523, phone 503-592-3400.
FOOD & SUPPLIES	• A coffee shop in the Chateau has limited hours year-round. A restaurant in the Chateau is open in the summer. • Groceries and supplies are available in Cave Junction.

**FIRST AID/
HOSPITAL**

• First aid is available in the Monument. • There is a doctor and clinic in Cave Junction. • The nearest hospital is in Grants Pass.

**GENERAL
INFORMATION**

• The tour route through the cave, about .6 mile (1 km), requires walking through narrow passages, bending in low places, climbing up and down about 500 steps and takes about 1 hour and 15 minutes. The tour is not recommended for persons with walking, breathing or heart problems. There is an emergency exit one-third of the way through the cave for those who do not wish to continue. • The cave temperature fluctuates around 41°F, and passageways may be wet and slippery, so wear proper clothing. • It is recommended that visitors, especially those with young children, stop at the Visitor Center for current information and waiting times before making the 45-minute drive to the Monument.

Pennsylvania

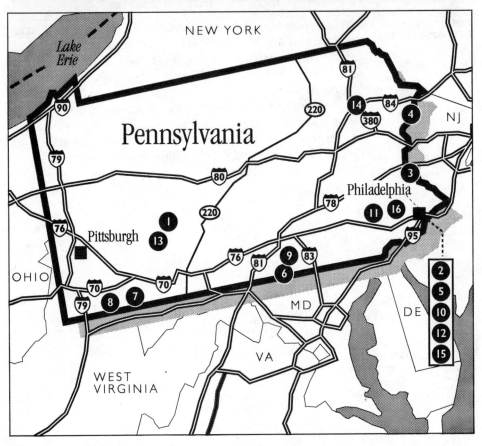

1. Allegheny Portage Railroad National Historic Site

2. Benjamin Franklin National Memorial

3. Delaware and Lehigh Navigation Canal National Heritage Corridor

4. Delaware Water Gap National Recreation Area

5. Edgar Allen Poe National Historic Site

6. Eisenhower National Historic Site

7. Fort Necessity National Battlefield

8. Friendship Hill National Historic Site

9. Gettysburg National Military Park

10. Gloria Dei (Old Swedes') Church National Historic Site

11. Hopewell Furnace National Historic Site

12. Independence National Historical Park

13. Johnstown Flood National Memorial

14. Steamtown National Historic Site

15. Thaddeus Kosciuszko National Memorial

16. Valley Forge National Historical Park

Allegheny Portage Railroad National Historic Site

Cresson, Pennsylvania

The railroad portage over the Allegheny Mountains, though only a short section of the Pennsylvania Main Line, was crucial to the enterprise since it joined the system's 2 great canals into an efficient artery between eastern and western Pennsylvania. The portage enabled passengers leaving Philadelphia in 1840 to reach Pittsburgh in 4 days instead of 23.

MAILING ADDRESS

Superintendent, Allegheny Portage Railroad National Historic Site, PO Box 189, Cresson, PA 16630 **Telephone: 814-886-6100**

DIRECTIONS

The Visitor Center is off the Gallitzin Exit of US 22 between Altoona and Cresson, PA.

VISITOR ACTIVITIES

• The Visitor Center is open daily, except Dec. 25 from **9 a.m. to 5 p.m.**, in winter with hours extended to **6 p.m.**, in summer. • Interpretive exhibits, models and a 20-minute film, which is shown every half hour. • Interpretive talks and costumed demonstrations near the Visitor Center and Lemon House, trails, hiking and picnicking. • Facilities include a bookstore, restrooms and telephones at the Visitor Center. Picnic facilities include water, tables, restrooms and grills. • Write for a schedule of special programs, including guided hikes and evening programs in the outdoor amphitheater.

PERMITS, FEES & LIMITATIONS

• No entrance fee. • Vehicles are restricted to parking lots and roads.

ACCESSIBILITY

The Visitor Center, Engine House Exhibit Shelter and restrooms are accessible. A boardwalk allows access to the remains of the Allegheny Portage Railroad.

CAMPING & LODGING

Overnight accommodations are available in Altoona, 12 miles (19.3 km); and in Ebensburg, 12 miles (19.3 km).

FOOD & SUPPLIES

Food and supplies are available in Gallitzin or Cresson.

FIRST AID/ HOSPITAL

• First aid is available in the Site or in Cresson. • The nearest hospital is in Altoona.

GENERAL INFORMATION

• Other historic railroad sites nearby include the Horseshoe Curve, the Gallitzin Tunnels and the Railroaders Memorial Museum in Altoona.
• Visitors can also visit the nearby Johnstown Flood National Memorial (see listing in this book), near St. Michael, PA.

Benjamin Franklin National Memorial
Philadelphia, Pennsylvania

Affiliated area. In the Rotunda of the Franklin Institute, the colossal seated figure of Benjamin Franklin by James Earle Fraser honors the inventor-statesman who filled a variety of positions in the country's early history.

MAILING ADDRESS	Executive Director, Benjamin Franklin National Memorial, 20th Street and Benjamin Franklin Parkway, Philadelphia, PA 19103 **Telephone:** 215-448-1329
DIRECTIONS	The Memorial is in the Franklin Institute Science Museum at 20th Street and Benjamin Franklin Parkway in Philadelphia.
VISITOR ACTIVITIES	• Exhibits of Franklin artifacts. • Facilities include parking and restrooms. • The Memorial is open from 9:30 a.m. to 4:30 p.m., weekdays; from 10 a.m. to 5 p.m., weekends; and from 10 a.m. to 5 p.m., daily in the summer. The Memorial is closed Thanksgiving, Dec. 24, Dec. 25, Jan. 1 and July 4.
PERMITS, FEES & LIMITATIONS	Admission to the Memorial is **free**. There is a separate admission fee for the adjacent Science Museum.
ACCESSIBILITY	The Science Museum is accessible. The Memorial is surrounded by stair entrances, but a ramp is available with prior notice.
CAMPING & LODGING	Overnight accommodations are available within walking distance in Philadelphia.
FOOD & SUPPLIES	• A snack bar is available in the Science Museum. • Food and supplies are available in Philadelphia.
FIRST AID/ HOSPITAL	• First aid is not available in the Memorial. • The nearest hospital is Hannemann Hospital, 9 blocks.
GENERAL INFORMATION	This affiliated area of the National Park System is owned and administered by The Franklin Institute.

Delaware and Lehigh Navigation Canal National Heritage Corridor
From Wilkes-Barre to Bristol, Pennsylvania

Affiliated area. These 2 19th-century canals and their associated early railroads opened up the rich anthracite coal fields of eastern Pennsylvania and fueled the Industrial Revolution.

Pennsylvania

MAILING ADDRESS	Delaware and Lehigh Navigation Canal National Heritage Corridor Commission, 10 East Church St., P-208, Bethlehem, PA 18018 **Telephone:** 215-861-9345
DIRECTIONS	The Corridor is 150 miles (241.9 km) long. It is best to contact the Corridor Commission to plan visits around seasonal celebrations, opportunities and activities.
VISITOR ACTIVITIES	Ethnic celebrations and festivals, ethnic church picnics, fairs, hiking, biking, cross-country skiing, birding, rafting, canoeing, tubing, 2 nationally known amusement parks, factory outlets, more than 100 nationally and regionally significant historic sites, 14 National Historic Landmarks, hundreds of National Register properties and districts, 2 National Natural Landmarks, 6 National Trails, 3 State Historical Parks, 7 State Parks, 2 State Scenic Rivers and 14 State Gamelands.
PERMITS, FEES & LIMITATIONS	Permits and fees vary from site to site.
ACCESSIBILITY	Accessibility varies from site to site.
CAMPING & LODGING	There is a variety of overnight accommodations.
FOOD & SUPPLIES	Food and supplies are available in the communities throughout the Corridor.
FIRST AID/ HOSPITAL	First aid and hospitals are not readily available in all areas.
GENERAL INFORMATION	For more information, call or write the various tourist promotion agencies serving the Corridor: Bucks County, Lehigh Valley and the Pocono Vacation Bureau.

Delaware Water Gap National Recreation Area

Bushkill, Pennsylvania and New Jersey

While the erosion and gradual uplift of the land apparent in Delaware Water Gap National Recreation Area is not unusual, the beauty of the landscape, with the breathtaking "S" curve twist in the Delaware River through Kittatinny Ridge, gives the gap its distinction.

MAILING ADDRESS	Superintendent, Delaware Water Gap National Recreation Area, Bushkill, PA 18324 **Telephone:** 717-588-2435
DIRECTIONS	From Pennsylvania, take I-84 east to Rt. 209 S (Exit 10) through Milford to the northern boundary of the Recreation Area. Take I-80 east past

Stroudsburg to 209 N (Exit 52) to the southern boundary. From New York City and New Jersey, take I-80 west to the Delaware Water Gap.

VISITOR ACTIVITIES

• Hiking, swimming, fishing, hunting, canoeing, boating, cross-country skiing, snowmobiling, ice fishing, pleasure driving, wildlife watching, picnicking, craft demonstrations, conducted walks, interpretive exhibits, rock climbing, sight-seeing, learning about nature and cultural history, and enjoying the solitude of a rural environment and change of pace. • The Recreation Area is open all day, every day. Some facilities are closed in winter. • A Recreation Area newspaper, published 3 times a year, is available upon request and lists current activities.

PERMITS, FEES & LIMITATIONS

Only commercial vehicles using Rt. 209 in Pennsylvania are charged a fee.

ACCESSIBILITY

Visitor centers have accessible parking, buildings and restrooms. Printed scripts are available for slide shows. There are accessible picnic sites at Kittatinny, Depew and Watergate in New Jersey and at Milford Beach, Childs Park, Toms Creek and Smithfield Beach in Pennsylvania. Write for an access guide.

CAMPING & LODGING

• Canoe camping is available in designated areas. There are 2 group campgrounds and 1 concession-operated family campground. • Lodging is available in Bushkill, Stroudsburg, Milford, Portland and Delaware Water Gap, PA; in Newton, Blairstown and Branchville, NJ; and in Port Jervis, NY.

FOOD & SUPPLIES

Food and supplies are available in Bushkill, Milford, Portland and Delaware Water Gap, PA; in Newton, NJ; and in Port Jervis, NY.

FIRST AID/ HOSPITAL

• First aid is available in the Recreation Area. • The nearest hospitals are in East Stroudsburg, PA; Newton, NJ; and Port Jervis, NY.

GENERAL INFORMATION

• Swim only at designated beaches. • No public transportation is available in the Recreation Area.

Edgar Allen Poe National Historic Site

Philadelphia, Pennsylvania

The life and work of Edgar Allan Poe, one of America's most gifted authors, are portrayed in a 3-building complex at 532 N. Seventh St., where he lived from 1843-44.

MAILING ADDRESS

Superintendent, Edgar Allan Poe National Historic Site, 313 Walnut St., Philadelphia, PA 19106 **Telephone:** 215-597-8974 **TDD:** 215-597-1785

DIRECTIONS

The Site is at 532 N. 7th St., 5 blocks from the Visitor Center at Independence National Historical Park.

VISITOR ACTIVITIES

• Exhibits, a slide presentation and Ranger-guided and self-guiding tours of the unfurnished home are offered daily. • The Site is open from 9 a.m. to 5 p.m., daily. • Facilities include a bookstore. • Children's activities include formal education programs, special workshops, a Junior Ranger Corps and a summer Magazine Club.

PERMITS, FEES & LIMITATIONS

No entrance fee.

ACCESSIBILITY

The first floor is accessible with some assistance.

CAMPING & LODGING

Commercial lodging is available nearby.

FOOD & SUPPLIES

Restaurants are located throughout the immediate area.

FIRST AID/ HOSPITAL

• First aid is available at the Site. • Five hospitals are within 2 miles (3.2 km) of the Site.

Eisenhower National Historic Site

Gettysburg, Pennsylvania

Built carefully around preserved features of a 200-year-old log cabin, the retirement home that Dwight and Mamie Eisenhower moved into in 1955 with its historical treasures has been protected for visitors as Eisenhower National Historic Site.

MAILING ADDRESS

Eisenhower National Historic Site, PO Box 1080, Gettysburg, PA 17325 Telephone: 717-334-1124 **TDD:** 717-334-1382

DIRECTIONS

All visits begin at the Eisenhower Tour Information Center in the lower level of the Gettysburg National Military Park Visitor Center on PA 134 (Taneytown Road) near its intersection with Business US 15 (Emmitsburg Road).

VISITOR ACTIVITIES

• A 10-minute orientation program, self-guided tours of the house and grounds, one-half mile (.8 km) self-guided walking tour of the farm and Ranger-conducted programs in season. • The Site is open daily from April to October and Wednesday through Sunday from November to March. The Site is closed Thanksgiving, Dec. 25, Jan. 1 and for 4 weeks in the winter. • Shuttles to the Site run from 9 a.m. to 4 p.m., and on a limited schedule in winter.

PERMITS, FEES & LIMITATIONS

• All visits to the Site are by shuttle bus. • Combined entrance and shuttle fees are $3.60 for adults, $1.60 for ages 13 to 16 and holders of Golden Age, Eagle and Access passes, and $1.05 for children ages 6 to 12.

ACCESSIBILITY

Visitors unable to board the shuttle bus may make arrangements to drive to the Site. Ask at the Eisenhower Tour Information Center. The first floor of the house is accessible with staff assistance. Accessible restrooms are available at the Visitor Center. Accessible portable restrooms are available at the Site. Free wheelchair loans are available. The orientation video is captioned, and a large print guide is available for the house tour.

CAMPING & LODGING

• Numerous motels and campgrounds are available in Gettysburg.
• Camping at adjacent Gettysburg National Military Park is available only for organized youth groups from April to November. Sites may be reserved by calling 717-334-0909.

FOOD & SUPPLIES

Many restaurants and stores are available in Gettysburg.

FIRST AID/ HOSPITAL

• First aid is available at the Site. • The Gettysburg Hospital is one-half mile (.8 km) from the Eisenhower Tour Information Center.

GENERAL INFORMATION

• A special event, An Eisenhower Christmas, is held every December. • For information on accommodations and attractions, write the Gettysburg Travel Council, 35 Carlisle St., Gettysburg, PA 17325.

Fort Necessity National Battlefield

Farmington, Pennsylvania

On July 3, 1754, the opening battle of the war that was known in America as the French and Indian War took place at a palisade fort built in 2 days by a young George Washington. He was forced to surrender here to an enemy for the first and only time in his military career.

MAILING ADDRESS

Superintendent, Fort Necessity National Battlefield, RD #2, Box 528, Farmington, PA 15437 **Telephone:** 412-329-5512

DIRECTIONS

The Battlefield is 11 miles (17.7 km) east of Uniontown, PA, on US 40.

VISITOR ACTIVITIES

• The Visitor Center contains exhibits, a 10-minute slide show and is staffed with a Ranger to provide information. The Visitor Center is open daily from 8:30 a.m. to 5 p.m., except Dec. 25. • From the Visitor Center, it is a short walk to the reconstructed Fort. The Fort is open daily from 8:30 a.m. to sunset except Dec. 25. • The Mount Washington Tavern is an historic tavern, furnished as a stagecoach stop from the early 19th century. In addition to the historic furnishings, it contains exhibits and is staffed with a Ranger. The Tavern is open daily from 8:30 a.m. to 5 p.m., except Dec. 25. • Jumonville Glen is open from mid-April through October and features self-guided trails. • Braddock's grave is open daily. • In the summer, there are daily musket firings, soldier talks and tours. Write for a calendar of special events and summer tours.

328

Pennsylvania

PERMITS, FEES & LIMITATIONS	The entrance fee is $2 for adults. Children 16 and under are admitted free. Seniors 62 and older who are U.S. citizens are admitted free. There is a maximum charge of $4 per family.
ACCESSIBILITY	All buildings are accessible.
CAMPING & LODGING	Camping and lodging are available within 5 miles (8.1 km) in Farmington and Chalk Hill.
FOOD & SUPPLIES	Food and supplies are available in Hopwood or Uniontown.
FIRST AID/ HOSPITAL	The nearest hospital is in Uniontown.
GENERAL INFORMATION	Fort Necessity has a Junior Ranger program for children ages 6 to 12. Upon completion, the children earn a sewn Fort Necessity patch.

Friendship Hill National Historic Site

New Geneva, Pennsylvania

Friendship Hill National Historic Site preserves the stone and brick home on the Monongahela River near Point Marion, PA, that belonged to Albert Gallatin, Secretary of the Treasury from 1801 to 1813 under Presidents Jefferson and Madison.

MAILING ADDRESS	Superintendent, Friendship Hill National Historic Site, RD 2, Box 149-A, Farmington, PA 15437 **Telephone:** 412-725-9190
DIRECTIONS	The Site is along PA 166 3 miles (4.8 km) north of Point Marion, PA, and mid-way between Uniontown, PA, and Morgantown, WV.
VISITOR ACTIVITIES	• The Gallatin House is open to the public. The exhibit room features a holographic presentation of Gallatin, his life and accomplishments. • A self-guiding audio tour is available for the historic sections of the house. • Ranger-led house tours are available in season. • The grave of Gallatin's first wife is a 20-minute, round-trip walk from the house. • Ten miles (16.1 km) of hiking trails offer wooded and meadow environments. Spring wildflower and fall foliage seasons are especially attractive along the trails.
PERMITS, FEES & LIMITATIONS	Establishment of a fee program is pending.
ACCESSIBILITY	The Gallatin House, restrooms and picnic area are accessible.
CAMPING & LODGING	Lodging is available in Uniontown, PA, 12 miles (19.3 km); and in Morgantown, WV, 10 miles (16.1 km).

FOOD & SUPPLIES

Food and supplies are available in Point Marion, PA; Smithfield, PA, 6 miles (9.6 km); and Masontown, PA, 6 miles (9.6 km).

FIRST AID/ HOSPITAL

Hospitals are in Morgantown, WV and Uniontown, PA.

Gettysburg National Military Park

Gettysburg, Pennsylvania

The battle that has come to be known as the "High Water Mark of the Confederacy" ended Gen. Robert E. Lee's hopes of launching an offensive operation in the North. There were more than 51,000 casualties, more than in any other battle fought in North America before or since.

MAILING ADDRESS

Superintendent, Gettysburg National Military Park, PO Box 1080, Gettysburg, PA 17325 **Telephone:** 717-334-1124

DIRECTIONS

Begin tours of the Park at the Visitor Center on PA 134 (Taneytown Road) near its intersection with Business US 15 (Emmitsburg Road).

VISITOR ACTIVITIES

• Auto tours, Ranger-conducted walks and talks, living history and campfire programs, hiking, biking, jogging and picnicking. • The Gettysburg Address is on loan from the Library of Congress and displayed during the summer.
• Facilities include visitor centers, restrooms and licensed battlefield guides.
• The Cyclorama Center is open from 9 a.m. to 5 p.m. The Visitor Center is open from 8 a.m. to 6 p.m., from mid-June to mid-August and until 5 p.m., the rest of the year. The Visitor Center and Cyclorama are closed Thanksgiving, Dec. 25 and Jan. 1.

PERMITS, FEES & LIMITATIONS

• There are fees for special programs. The electric map and Cyclorama are $2 for ages 17 to 61 and $1.50 for ages 62 and older. Children under 16 admitted free. • Battlefield guides charge $20 per car for a 2-hour tour. The charge for RVs is higher. • Park only in designated areas or along avenues, but not on the grass.

ACCESSIBILITY

The major program areas of the Visitor Center and Cyclorama are accessible, as are the restrooms. Parking areas are marked at each building. Free wheelchair loans are available while in the buildings. Various brochures and audio tapes with players provide information for those with hearing and sight impairments.

CAMPING & LODGING

• Camping is available only for organized youth groups. Group sites are available from mid-April to mid-October. Fee varies with group size. Call 717-334-0909. Groups may wish to make advanced reservations for bus tours with a licensed battlefield guide ($50). • Numerous motels are adjacent to the Park.

FOOD & SUPPLIES

Food and supplies are available in Gettysburg, 1 mile (1.6 km).

FIRST AID/ HOSPITAL	• First aid is available in the Park. • The nearest hospital is in Gettysburg.
GENERAL INFORMATION	For your safety - Do not climb on cannons and monuments. Parents should closely supervise children. Use extreme caution while driving Park roads. Bicycle riders should keep to the right with the flow of traffic and ride only on roads.

Gloria Dei (Old Swedes') Church National Historic Site

Philadelphia, Pennsylvania

Affiliated area. Gloria Dei Church is the second oldest Swedish church in the United States. It was founded in 1677, and the present structure, erected about 1700, is a splendid example of 17th-century Swedish church architecture.

MAILING ADDRESS	Superintendent, Independence National Historical Park, 313 Walnut St., Philadelphia, PA 19106 **Telephone:** 215-597-8974 (Voice and TDD)
DIRECTIONS	The Site is on the Delaware River at Columbus Boulevard and Christian Street. It is north of the Walt Whitman Bridge and south of the Ben Franklin Bridge on the east side of I-95.
VISITOR ACTIVITIES	• The church and grounds are open to the public. • Arrangements should be made in advance if a guided tour for a group is desired. • Facilities include restrooms, church and grounds. • The Site is open daily from 9 a.m. to 5 p.m.
PERMITS, FEES & LIMITATIONS	No entrance fee.
CAMPING & LODGING	Overnight accommodations are available in Philadelphia.
FOOD & SUPPLIES	Food and supplies are available in Philadelphia.
FIRST AID/ HOSPITAL	• First aid is not available in the Site. • The nearest hospital is in Philadelphia.
GENERAL INFORMATION	This affiliated area of the National Park System is owned and administered by the Corporation of Gloria Dei (Old Swedes') Church.

Hopewell Furnace National Historic Site
Elverson, Pennsylvania

From 1771 until 1883, Hopewell Furnace produced molded or cast iron products using iron ore, limestone and charcoal made from surrounding hard wood forests. Visitors can learn about the process and life in the village where the workers lived at the restored National Historic Site.

MAILING ADDRESS

Superintendent, Hopewell Furnace National Historic Site, 2 Mark Bird Lane, Elverson, PA 19520 **Telephone:** 215-582-8773 **TDD:** 215-582-2093

DIRECTIONS

The Site is 5 miles (8 km) south of Birdsboro on PA 345. It is 10 miles (16.1 km) from the Morgantown interchange on the PA Turnpike, via PA 23 East and 345 North.

VISITOR ACTIVITIES

• Interpretive programs and exhibits at the Visitor Center, living history programs in summer, hiking and self-guiding walking tours. • Parking and restrooms are at the Visitor Center. • Hiking trails join with those at adjacent French Creek State Park. • All facilities are open from 9 a.m. to 5 p.m., except Thanksgiving, Dec. 25 and Jan. 1. The restored village and parking lot close at 5 p.m.

PERMITS, FEES & LIMITATIONS

The entrance fee is $2 per person ages 17 to 61. Children ages 16 and under and U.S. citizens ages 62 or older are admitted free. A $5 family fee is available.

ACCESSIBILITY

The Visitor Center, general historic area and restrooms are accessible with assistance. A few historic structures are not accessible. The audiovisual programs at the Visitor Center are captioned for the hearing impaired. Large-print and braille guides are also available.

CAMPING & LODGING

• Camping facilities are available in the adjacent French Creek State Park, 215-582-9680. • Other overnight accommodations are available in Morgantown, 10 miles (16.1 km); Pottstown, 13 miles (20.9 km); and Reading, 15 miles (24.1 km).

FOOD & SUPPLIES

Food and supplies are available in Birdsboro and Elverson, 5 miles (8 km).

FIRST AID/ HOSPITAL

• First aid is available in the Site. • The nearest hospital is in Reading.

GENERAL INFORMATION

For your safety - Stay on established tour routes and do not climb on the unstable anthracite furnace ruins, fences and other historic structures. The sharp slag can cause severe, jagged cuts. Do not enter fenced areas or feed or handle livestock. Those allergic to bee and wasp stings should be cautious.

Independence National Historical Park

Philadelphia, Pennsylvania

Much of the nation's Colonial, Revolutionary and Federal-period heritage is preserved in Philadelphia and Independence National Historical Park, which includes a variety of sites such as Independence Hall, Carpenter's Hall, the Liberty Bell Pavilion and Christ Church.

MAILING ADDRESS

Superintendent, Independence National Historical Park, 313 Walnut St., Philadelphia, PA 19106 **Telephone:** 215-597-8974 **TDD:** 215-597-1785

DIRECTIONS

The Visitor Center is at Third and Chestnut streets in the heart of the city. Several parking garages are nearby (follow the signs). Rangers are available to answer questions at the center, where visitors can also obtain Park maps and additional city information. Most Park sites are within a few blocks of the Visitor Center.

VISITOR ACTIVITIES

• There are 24 separate sites. • Ranger-led and self-guided tours, exhibits, and special programs and films offered daily. • The Park is open daily from 9 a.m. to 5 p.m., with some extended summer hours. • There are bookstores at 5 locations, including the Visitor Center.

PERMITS, FEES & LIMITATIONS

No fees.

ACCESSIBILITY

An access guide is available at the Visitor Center. Most buildings are partially accessible. Captioned films are available on request.

CAMPING & LODGING

Commercial lodging is available nearby.

FOOD & SUPPLIES

Restaurants are located throughout the immediate area.

FIRST AID/ HOSPITAL

• First aid is available at each site. • Five hospitals are within 2 miles (3.2 km) of the Park.

GENERAL INFORMATION

To preserve our 18th century heritage, the National Park Service has retained narrow stairs and uneven walking surfaces. Please watch your step.

Johnstown Flood National Memorial

Saint Michael, Pennsylvania

Johnstown, a steel company town with a population of 30,000 in 1889, was built on a floodplain at the fork of the Little Conemaugh and Stony Creek rivers. When an old dam broke after a night of heavy rains on June 1, 1889, 20 million tons of water devastated the town and killed more than 2,200.

MAILING ADDRESS

Superintendent, Johnstown Flood National Memorial, PO Box 355, Saint Michael, PA 15951 **Telephone:** 814-495-4643

DIRECTIONS

The Memorial is 10 miles (16.1 km) northeast of Johnstown. Take US 219 to the Saint Michael/Sidman Exit. Head east on PA 869 1.5 miles (2.4 km) and turn left onto Lake Road at the Johnstown Flood National Memorial sign. Follow Lake Road 1.5 miles (2.4 km). The Visitor Center is on the right.

VISITOR ACTIVITIES

• The Visitor Center is open daily, except Dec. 25, from 9 a.m. to 5 p.m., with extended hours during the summer. • A 35-minute film is shown on the hour, exhibits, models and book sales. • Costumed presentations made during the summer. • Facilities include the Historic Unger House, South Fork Dam Abutment trails, picnic area, restrooms and nature trail. • There is a "Tales of the Great Flood" anniversary presentation at the end of May.

PERMITS, FEES & LIMITATIONS

No fees.

ACCESSIBILITY

The Visitor Center is fully accessible. Audio narration and audio boosters are available. The film is captioned. The North Abutment trail is paved. One picnic table is accessible. All restrooms are accessible.

CAMPING & LODGING

Overnight accommodations are available in nearby communities.

FOOD & SUPPLIES

Food and supplies are available in nearby communities.

FIRST AID/ HOSPITAL

• First aid is available in the Memorial. • Several hospitals and urgent care centers are available in Johnstown, 12 miles (19.3 km).

GENERAL INFORMATION

• Information is available on many nearby historic and cultural park sites, including the Saint Michael Historic District. • The closest National Park Service site is the Allegheny Portage Railroad National Historic Site (see listing in this book).

Steamtown National Historic Site

Scranton, Pennsylvania

The former Delaware, Lackawanna & Western Railroad yard, including the remains of the historic roundhouse, switchyard, associated buildings, 29 steam locomotives, and 78 passenger, freight and work cars, are being restored and preserved at Steamtown National Historic Site to interpret the story of early 20th-century steam railroading in America.

MAILING ADDRESS

Superintendent, Steamtown National Historic Site, 150 South Washington Ave., Scranton, PA 18503 **Telephone:** 717-961-2033

DIRECTIONS

From I-81, take Exit 52 (Central Scranton Expressway), continue to the third traffic light, turn left onto Washington Avenue, travel 1 1/2 blocks, turn right to the Site entrance.

VISITOR ACTIVITIES

• Regular interpretive tours are provided to the historic roundhouse and the locomotive shops. • From Memorial Day through the end of October, a live steam engine is used to operate a shuttle train within the yard and for interpretive tours to the nearby iron furnace. • Steam powered excursion trains are also scheduled to Moscow, PA, on Fridays, Saturdays, Sundays and holidays. • Additional interpretive programs are offered during the summer.

PERMITS, FEES & LIMITATIONS

The Site is undergoing construction and development. Access is provided to every possible location.

ACCESSIBILITY

Many motels, hotels and campgrounds are nearby.

CAMPING & LODGING

• There are vending machines in the Site. • Food and supplies are available in the surrounding Scranton area.

FOOD & SUPPLIES

• First aid is available in the Site. • Hospitals and emergency medical services are in the Scranton area.

FIRST AID/ HOSPITAL

Call the Site for more information.

Thaddeus Kosciuszko National Memorial

Philadelphia, Pennsylvania

The life and work of Thaddeus Kosciuszko, Polish-born patriot and hero of the American Revolution, are commemorated at 301 Pine St., Philadelphia. He is remembered for his efforts on behalf of the American fight for independence. This small townhouse where he rented a room during the winter of 1797-98 has been restored as a memorial to him.

MAILING ADDRESS

Superintendent, Thaddeus Kosciuszko National Memorial, 313 Walnut St., Philadelphia, PA 19106 **Telephone:** 215-597-8974 **TDD:** 215-597-1785

DIRECTIONS

Located at Third and Pine streets, the Site is 3 blocks from the Visitor Center at Independence National Historical Park.

VISITOR ACTIVITIES

• Exhibits and a slide presentation are available in English and Polish. • The Memorial is open daily from 9 a.m. to 5 p.m.

PERMITS, FEES & LIMITATIONS

No fees.

ACCESSIBILITY

The first floor is accessible with some assistance.

CAMPING & LODGING

Commercial lodging is available nearby.

FOOD & SUPPLIES

Restaurants are throughout the immediate area.

FIRST AID/ HOSPITAL

• First aid is available at the Memorial. • Five hospitals are within 2 miles (3.2 km) of the Memorial.

Valley Forge National Historical Park

Valley Forge, Pennsylvania

No battles were fought here, but during the winter of 1777-78 hundreds of American Revolutionary soldiers died at Valley Forge from sickness and disease caused by critical shortages of food, blankets and clothes needed to protect the men from the bitter cold.

MAILING ADDRESS

Superintendent, Valley Forge National Historical Park, Box 953, Valley Forge, PA 19481 **Telephone:** 215-783-1077

DIRECTIONS

The Park is 20 miles (32.2 km) west of Philadelphia. Entrances from major highways are well marked. Eastbound or westbound via the Pennsylvania Turnpike, take Exit 24 (Valley Forge). Stay in the right lane for the toll booth and immediately take the next right onto North Gulf Road. This will lead to the Visitor Center at the intersection of Valley Forge Road and PA 23. Westbound on the Schuykill Expressway (I-76) use the Goddard Boulevard Exit, turn right at the traffic light onto Goddard and then turn right again at the first traffic light onto North Gulph Road. This will lead to the Park. Travelers on US 202 should take the Rt. 422 West Exit and go 2 miles (3.2 km) to the Valley Forge Exit (PA 23 West), turn right at the exit and follow PA 23 to the Park entrance and Visitor Center.

VISITOR ACTIVITIES

• A 15-minute film, exhibits, self-guiding auto tour, picnicking, hiking, horseback riding trails, boating, fishing, biking, an auto tape tour from June through September, interpretation of historic homes, soldier life demonstrations and guided walks. • Facilities include parking, hiking and bike trails, bus tours, picnic areas and boat ramp. • The Park is open daily from 8:30 a.m. to 5 p.m., except Dec. 25.

PERMITS, FEES & LIMITATIONS

• The fee for Washington's Headquarters is $1 for ages 17 to 61. • Vehicles must stay on Park roads, which are narrow.

ACCESSIBILITY

Parking, restrooms, drinking fountains and telephones at the Visitor Center are accessible. Wayside exhibits and picnic area are accessible. A 10-mile (16.1 km) self-guided tour can be done by car. A wheelchair is available. There is a 6-mile (9.6 km) multi-use path. Hiking trails are uneven with natural earth terrain. An audiotape of the tour route is available for purchase, and there are some audio exhibits.

Pennsylvania

CAMPING & LODGING	Major hotels are within 5 miles (8 km) of the Park.
FOOD & SUPPLIES	• There is a snack bar in the Park. • Food and supplies are also available in King of Prussia.
FIRST AID/ HOSPITAL	• First aid is available in the Park. • The nearest hospital is in Phoenixville, 6 miles (9.6 km).

Rhode Island

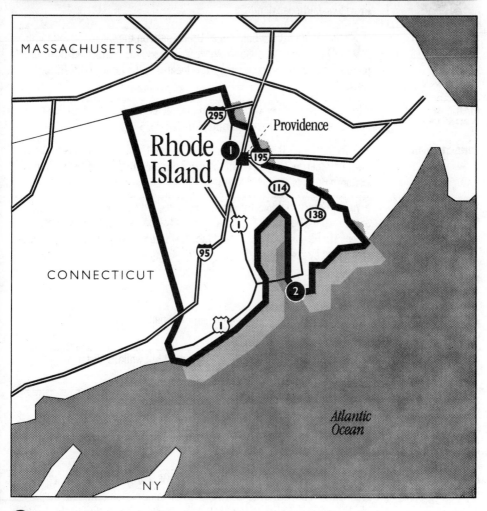

1 Roger Williams National Memorial

2 Touro Synagogue National Historic Site

Roger Williams National Memorial

Providence, Rhode Island

This Memorial is a landscaped urban park on the site of the founding of Providence in 1636 by Roger Williams, 17th-century advocate of religious freedom and democracy. It is located in the College Hill Historic District.

MAILING ADDRESS

Superintendent, Roger Williams National Memorial, 282 N. Main St., Providence, RI 02903 **Telephone:** 401-528-5385

DIRECTIONS

The Visitor Center is at the corner of Smith and North Main streets in downtown Providence, RI, just down the hill from the Rhode Island State House. Visitor parking is on Canal Street.

VISITOR ACTIVITIES

• Visitor Center includes interpretive exhibits, a slide show, bookstore and restrooms. • The Visitor Center is open daily from 8 a.m. to 4:30 p.m., except Thanksgiving, Dec. 25 and Jan. 1. • Interpretive programs for groups are offered by reservation.

PERMITS, FEES & LIMITATIONS

No fees.

ACCESSIBILITY

The Visitor Center, restrooms and Memorial paths are accessible. TDD is available.

CAMPING & LODGING

Hotels and historic bed and breakfasts are within walking distance.

FOOD & SUPPLIES

Food and supplies are available in Providence.

FIRST AID/ HOSPITAL

• First aid is available at the Visitor Center. • The nearest hospital is 1 mile (1.6 km) away.

GENERAL INFORMATION

Stop at the Visitor Center for a map and list of nearby sites in Historic Providence. The Memorial also serves as an information center for the Blackstone River Valley National Heritage Corridor (see listing in this book).

Touro Synagogue National Historic Site

Newport, Rhode Island

Affiliated area. For more than 2 centuries, this small synagogue on a quiet street in Newport, RI, has testified to the ideals of religious freedom. The Jewish settlers who first came to Roger Williams' colony as early as 1658 went on to build a permanent place to worship in 1763.

Rhode Island

MAILING ADDRESS	Touro Synagogue National Historic Site, 85 Touro St., Newport, RI 02840 Telephone: 401-847-4794
DIRECTIONS	The Site is in downtown Newport, RI, 1 1/2 blocks northeast of Washington Square and the Old Colony House.
VISITOR ACTIVITIES	• Register for guided tours, which begin on the hour and half hour. • The Site is open during the summer Sunday through Thursday from 10 a.m. to 5 p.m., and Friday from 10 a.m. to 3 p.m. It is open from 1 p.m. to 3 p.m., on Sundays the remainder of the year. Call for extended hours in spring and fall. Services are held at 7 p.m. on Fridays (6 p.m. in fall and winter) and at 9 a.m. on Saturdays.
PERMITS, FEES & LIMITATIONS	No fees.
ACCESSIBILITY	Access is difficult, but assistance is provided.
CAMPING & LODGING	Overnight accommodations are available in Newport.
FOOD & SUPPLIES	Food and supplies are available in Newport.
FIRST AID/ HOSPITAL	• First aid is not available in the Site. • Newport Hospital is 1 mile (1.6 km) away from the Site.

South Carolina

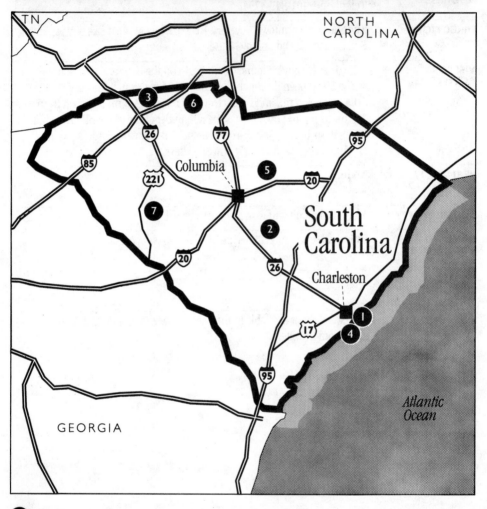

1. Charles Pinckney National Historic Site
2. Congaree Swamp National Monument
3. Cowpens National Battlefield
4. Fort Sumter National Monument
5. Historic Camden
6. Kings Mountain National Military Park
7. Ninety Six National Historic Site

South Carolina

Charles Pinckney National Historic Site

Mount Pleasant, South Carolina

Not open to the public. Charles Pinckney (1754-1824) was a statesman, Revolutionary War officer and a principal framer of the U.S. Constitution. He served 4 terms as governor of South Carolina and in the State Assembly. He also served in the U.S. Senate, House of Representatives and as President Jefferson's minister to Spain. His ancestral home, Snee Farm, once consisted of 715 acres, 28 of which are today preserved. Archaeological remains of brick foundations from the Pinckney era and an 1820s tidewater cottage are maintained on the Site.

MAILING ADDRESS	Charles Pinckney National Historic Site, c/o Superintendent, Fort Sumter National Monument, 1214 Middle St., Sullivan's Island, SC 29482 **Telephone:** 803-883-3123
DIRECTIONS	Follow US 17 north to Long Point Road one-quarter mile (.4 km) to the Site entrance. Travelers on I-526 should take the Long Point Road Exit eastbound and proceed 3 miles (4.8 km) to the entrance.
VISITOR ACTIVITIES	• The Site is expected to open in **May 1995.** • When the Site opens, self-guided tours of the grounds and house will be available.
PERMITS, FEES & LIMITATIONS	• No fees. • Vehicles restricted to parking areas.
ACCESSIBILITY	Trails, restrooms and the historic house will be accessible.
CAMPING & LODGING	Lodging is available in Mount Pleasant.
FOOD & SUPPLIES	Food and supplies are available in Mount Pleasant.
FIRST AID/ HOSPITAL	• First aid will be available at the Site. • The nearest hospital is in Mount Pleasant.
GENERAL INFORMATION	The Site is the last protected remnant of Snee Farm, the country estate of Charles Pinckney. In 1990, after a major private and public fund raising partnership, historic Snee Farm was conveyed to the National Park Service.

Congaree Swamp National Monument

Hopkins, South Carolina

Congaree Swamp National Monument boasts 90 tree species, including numerous state-record-sized trees and a few national champions, and abundant wildlife that includes the endangered red-cockaded woodpecker.

South Carolina.

MAILING ADDRESS	Superintendent, Congaree Swamp National Monument, 200 Caroline Sims Road, Hopkins, SC 29061 **Telephone:** 803-776-4396
DIRECTIONS	The Monument is off SC 48, 20 miles (32.2 km) southeast of Columbia, SC. SC 48 is well marked from its intersection with SC 478 eastward toward the Monument.
VISITOR ACTIVITIES	Twenty-five miles (40.3 km) of hiking trails, 2 boardwalks, canoeing, fishing, bird watching, photography, picnicking, guided nature walks and 2 self-guiding trails.
PERMITS, FEES & LIMITATIONS	• Free camping permits are available. • A fishing license is required by state regulations.
ACCESSIBILITY	The Visitor Station, restrooms and boardwalk are accessible.
CAMPING & LODGING	• Camping is allowed with a permit. • Group camping is available.
FOOD & SUPPLIES	Food and supplies are available in Columbia and surrounding communities.
FIRST AID/ HOSPITAL	• First aid is available in the Monument. • The nearest hospital is Baptist Hospital in Columbia.

Cowpens National Battlefield

Chesnee, South Carolina

Trace the Revolutionary battle that won permanent fame for Daniel Morgan's leadership as he led his troops to a complete victory over Banastre Tarleton's British Legion.

MAILING ADDRESS	Cowpens National Battlefield, PO Box 308, Chesnee, SC 29323 **Telephone:** 803-461-2828
DIRECTIONS	The Battlefield is 11 miles (17.7 km) west of I-85 and Gaffney on SC Scenic Foothills Highway 11, 2 miles (3.2 km) east of Chesnee, SC.
VISITOR ACTIVITIES	• Artifacts and exhibits, a fiber optic map of the battle, self-guided walking trail and an auto tour road. • A slide presentation, "Daybreak at the Cowpens," is shown on the hour. • The Battlefield is open daily, except Dec. 25 and Jan. 1, from 9 a.m. to 5 p.m.
PERMITS, FEES & LIMITATIONS	• The fee to view the slide presentation is $1 for adults and $.50 for children, tours and schools. • Commercial vehicles are not permitted on the tour road.
ACCESSIBILITY	The Visitor Center, picnic tables and main portion of the battlefield trail are accessible.

CAMPING & LODGING	Overnight accommodations are available in Gaffney.
FOOD & SUPPLIES	Food and supplies are available in Gaffney and Spartanburg.
FIRST AID/ HOSPITAL	• First aid is available in the Battlefield. • The nearest hospital is in Gaffney.
GENERAL INFORMATION	Call for a schedule of events and for more information.

Fort Sumter National Monument

Sullivan's Island, South Carolina

ort Sumter was one of a series of coastal fortifications built by the United States after the War of 1812. The first shots of the Civil War were fired here on April 12, 1861 as the Confederates conducted a 2-day bombardment that ended with the Union troops' withdrawal.

MAILING ADDRESS	Superintendent, Fort Sumter National Monument, 1214 Middle St., Sullivan's Island, SC 29482 **Telephone: 803-883-3123**
DIRECTIONS	Fort Sumter is in Charleston Harbor and can be reached only by boat. Tour boats leave from the city boat marina on Lockwood Drive, just south of US 17 in Charleston. For boat schedules, phone Fort Sumter Tours, 803-722-1691, or write 17 Lockwood Drive, Charleston, SC 29401. Fort Moultrie, administered with Fort Sumter, is on west Middle Street on Sullivan's Island. From US 17, take SC 703 to Middle Street. The Visitor Center is at Fort Moultrie.
VISITOR ACTIVITIES	• Interpretive exhibits, film and walking tours. • Facilities include restrooms at both forts and an observation deck at the Visitor Center. • The Monument is open daily, except Dec. 25, from 9 a.m. to 5 p.m., with hours extended to 6 p.m., in the summer.
PERMITS, FEES & LIMITATIONS	The tour boat fee to Fort Sumter is $9 for adults and $4.50 for children under 12. Children under 6 are free. There is no admission fee at Fort Moultrie.
ACCESSIBILITY	Fort Sumter has wheelchair lifts to all 3 levels. Fort Moultrie has parking and ramps that provide access to the Visitor Center.
CAMPING & LODGING	Hotels are in Charleston and Mount Pleasant, 5 miles (8 km).
FOOD & SUPPLIES	Food and supplies are available in Mount Pleasant, Sullivan's Island and vicinity.

South Carolina

FIRST AID/ HOSPITAL

• First aid is available in the Monument. • The nearest hospital is in Mount Pleasant.

GENERAL INFORMATION

For your safety - Be careful on uneven surfaces, stairs and near the chain barriers.

Historic Camden

Camden, South Carolina

Affiliated area. This early colonial village was established in the mid-1730s and was known as Fredricksburg Township until it was renamed in 1768 in honor of Charles Pratt, Lord Camden, a British Parliamentary champion of Colonial rights. It was one of the few frontier settlements where 2 Revolutionary War battles were fought.

MAILING ADDRESS

Director, Historic Camden, Highway 521 South, PO Box 710, Camden, SC 29020 Telephone: 803-432-9841

DIRECTIONS

Take I-20 east or west. Camden is 30 miles (48.3 km) northeast of Columbia, SC, a 4 1/2-hour drive from Atlanta, GA. Visitor Parking is off Broad Street.

VISITOR ACTIVITIES

• Guided and self-guided tours of 12 archaeological sites and historic homes. Tour headquarters and museum shop are in the Cunningham House off Broad Street. • A nature trail leads to Pine Tree Creek. • There is a picnic area. • Revolutionary War Field Days are held in November. Call for information. • The museum shop and office are open daily from 10 a.m. to 5 p.m. Tours are available daily except for Mondays and holidays. Guided tours are available Tuesday through Saturday from 10 a.m. to 4 p.m., and on Sundays from 1 p.m. to 4 p.m.

PERMITS, FEES & LIMITATIONS

• Admission is free to the museum shop, nature trail and picnic area.
• Tour fees are $4.50 for adults and $1.50 for students. Children under 6 are admitted free. Field trip and group rates are available.

ACCESSIBILITY

Limited access.

CAMPING & LODGING

• Historic Camden is within 30 miles (48.3 km) of 3 state parks with campgrounds. • Bed and breakfasts are available in Camden.

FOOD & SUPPLIES

Food and supplies are available in Camden and vicinity.

FIRST AID/ HOSPITAL

The nearest hospital is Kershaw County Memorial Hospital, 5 miles (8 km).

GENERAL INFORMATION

• Other than the Kershaw-Cornwallis House, few of the homes are open to the public regularly. Tours of private homes are offered by HisToury Inc.

Tours, PO Box 1746, Camden, SC 29020, phone 803-432-1723. • Development and administration of Historic Camden, an affiliated area of the National Park Service, are under the direction of the Camden Historical Commission.

Kings Mountain National Military Park

York and Cherokee, South Carolina

After a series of indecisive summer skirmishes, a mounted column of Carolinians and Virginians sought and found British Maj. Patrick Ferguson and his Loyalist battalion Oct. 7, 1780 at Kings Mountain. The Loyalists were soundly defeated at a crucial point during the American Revolution.

MAILING ADDRESS
Kings Mountain National Military Park, PO Box 40, Kings Mountain, NC 28086 **Telephone:** 803-936-7921

DIRECTIONS
The Park is reached from Charlotte, NC, by I-85; from Spartanburg, SC, by I-85; and from York, SC, by SC 161. The Park is on Hwy. 216 off of I-85, 10 miles (16.1 km) from Kings Mountain, NC, and 15 miles (24.1 km) southwest of Gastonia, NC, northeast of Gaffney, SC.

VISITOR ACTIVITIES
• Interpretive exhibits, self-guided tour, horse trail, hiking trail and an 18-minute film. • There are living history encampments 1 weekend in May and during the weekend nearest Oct. 7 annually. • Occasional special programs are announced. • The Park is closed Thanksgiving, Dec. 25 and Jan. 1.

PERMITS, FEES & LIMITATIONS
No fees.

ACCESSIBILITY
The Visitor Center, battlefield trail (steep in places), parking and restrooms are accessible. A script of the film and a contour map are available.

CAMPING & LODGING
• A small, primitive camp site is in the Park. Information and a brochure are available at the Visitor Center. • Camping is available in the adjacent Kings Mountain State Park. • Lodging is available in Kings Mountain, NC; Shelby, NC; Gaffney, SC; and York, SC.

FOOD & SUPPLIES
Food and supplies are available in Kings Mountain State Park in season and in the towns of Kings Mountain, NC; Blacksburg, SC; and Grover, NC.

FIRST AID/ HOSPITAL
• First aid is available in the Park. • Hospitals are in Kings Mountain, NC; Shelby, NC; and Rock Hill, SC.

Ninety Six National Historic Site

Ninety Six, South Carolina

Ninety Six was named by traders who thought the stopping place was 96 miles (154.8 km) from the Cherokee town of Keowee. By the Revolution, Ninety Six was a thriving village held by British loyalists until a siege by Nathanael Greene left it a smoking ruin.

MAILING ADDRESS

Superintendent, Ninety Six National Historic Site, PO Box 496, Ninety Six, SC 29666 Telephone: 803-543-4068

DIRECTIONS

The Site is 2 miles (3.2 km) south of Ninety Six, SC, off of SC 248.

VISITOR ACTIVITIES

• Interpretive exhibits, walking, horseback riding, hiking and fishing. • Facilities include parking and restrooms at the Visitor Center and an interpretive trail. • The Site is open daily except Dec. 25 and Jan. 1 from 8 a.m. to 5 p.m.

PERMITS, FEES & LIMITATIONS

• No fees. • Permits, available at the Visitor Center, are required for special uses such as group camping and collecting natural specimens. • No vehicles allowed in the Site.

ACCESSIBILITY

The Visitor Center and restrooms are accessible.

CAMPING & LODGING

Overnight accommodations are available in Greenwood, 10 miles (16.1 km).

FOOD & SUPPLIES

Food and supplies are available in Ninety Six.

FIRST AID/ HOSPITAL

• First aid is available in the Site. • The nearest hospital is in Greenwood.

South Dakota

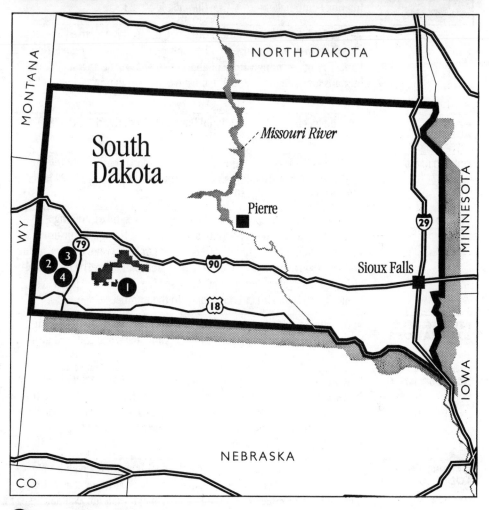

1. Badlands National Park
2. Jewel Cave National Monument
3. Mount Rushmore National Memorial
4. Wind Cave National Park

Badlands National Park

Interior, South Dakota   See Climatable No. 29

Out of the Dakota prairie, rain, wind and frost have carved the steep canyons, sharp ridges, gullies, spires and knobs of Badlands National Park. Though seemingly inhospitable at first glance, the area supported humans for more than 12,000 years and continues to provide habitat for many plants and animals.

MAILING ADDRESS
Superintendent, Badlands National Park, PO Box 6, Interior, SD 57750
Telephone: 605-433-5361

DIRECTIONS
The Ben Reifel Visitor Center is 2.75 miles (4.4 km) northeast of Interior on Rt. SH240. It is 28 miles (45.1 km) southwest of Kadoka and 29 miles (46.7 km) southeast of Wall on I-90.

VISITOR ACTIVITIES
• Ranger-conducted activities include nature walks, hikes, evening programs and fossil demonstrations in summer. • Hiking, scenic drives and wildlife watching. • Facilities include nature trails, 2 visitor centers, picnic areas and souvenirs. • The Park is open all day every day. The Ben Reifel Visitor Center is open daily except Thanksgiving, Dec. 25 and Jan. 1. The White River Visitor Center is open daily in the summer.

PERMITS, FEES & LIMITATIONS
• The entrance fee is $5 per vehicle or $3 per person. • Off-road driving is prohibited. • No open fires permitted. Cooking stoves and charcoal grills are allowed in campgrounds.

ACCESSIBILITY
Visitor centers and restrooms are accessible. Some camp sites and restrooms in Cedar Pass Campground are accessible. Fossil Exhibit and Window trails are accessible. The Park orientation video at Ben Reifel Visitor Center is captioned. Fossils, bones, rocks and plants are accessible and may be handled in the Touch Room.

CAMPING & LODGING
• Camping is available year-round for $8 per night. No reservations are accepted except for groups. • Write ahead or check at visitor centers for backcountry information. • Commercial campgrounds are available in Interior, Cactus Flat, Wall or Kadoka. • Reservations for lodging in the Park should be made with Cedar Pass Lodge at 605-433-5460. The Lodge is open from early May through early October. • Other overnight accommodations are available in Wall and Kadoka.

FOOD & SUPPLIES
• Meals are served at Cedar Pass Lodge from mid-April to late October. • Food and supplies are also available in Interior, Wall and Kadoka.

FIRST AID/ HOSPITAL
• First aid is available at Ranger Stations. • There are doctors in Wall, Kadoka and Rapid City. • The nearest hospital is in Philip, 35 miles (56.4 km) northeast of Cedar Pass.

GENERAL INFORMATION

• For your safety - Be alert for rattlesnakes. Water should be carried on longer hikes. Drinking water should come from approved sources. When afoot, keep a safe distance from buffalo. Climbing is discouraged on steep, barren slopes. • Other points of interest in the Black Hills include Jewel Cave, Wind Cave and Mount Rushmore (see listings in this book).

Jewel Cave National Monument

Custer, South Dakota   See Climatable No. 30

Buried beneath the Black Hills of South Dakota is the fascinating underground world of Jewel Cave with its chamber of glittering calcite crystals, its outstanding variety of colorful and strange cave formations and its 73 miles (117.7 km) of intricate maze-like passages.

MAILING ADDRESS

Superintendent, Jewel Cave National Monument, RR 1, Box 60AA, Custer, SD 57730 **Telephone:** 605-673-2288

DIRECTIONS

The Monument is accessible via US 16, which crosses the northern part of the Monument between Custer, SD, and Newcastle, WY. The Visitor Center is on US 16, 13 miles (20.9 km) west of Custer.

VISITOR ACTIVITIES

• Interpretive exhibits, cave tours and picnicking. • Facilities include information, a sales counter, picnic area, drinking water and restrooms. • The Visitor Center is open daily except Thanksgiving, Dec. 25 and Jan. 1. • Portions of the cave are open to the public. Interpretive tours are offered daily from May through September. Tours, if any, during the rest of the year are irregular. • Scenic tours are on a first-come, first-served basis. Reservations are required for spelunking tours.

PERMITS, FEES & LIMITATIONS

• The guide fee for tours is $4 for ages 16 and older, $2 for ages 6 to 15 and $2 for holders of Golden Age Passports. • The fee for spelunking tours is $8. • Vehicles restricted to roads and parking areas.

CAMPING & LODGING

• Commercial camping is available near Newcastle, WY, 25 miles (40.3 km); and Custer, SD, 13 miles (20.9 km). • Other overnight accommodations are also available in Newcastle and Custer.

FOOD & SUPPLIES

Food and supplies are available in Newcastle or Custer.

FIRST AID/ HOSPITAL

• First aid is available in the Monument. • Hospitals are in Custer and Newcastle.

GENERAL INFORMATION

• For your safety - Wear low-heeled shoes with non-slip soles while touring the cave. The tours are not recommended for those who have heart or respiratory ailments. • Due to the popularity of the tour, waits of up to 2 hours may be encountered during mid-day. • A light sweater or jacket is recommended on the cave tour. The cave temperature is 47°F all year. • Cave trails include numerous stairs.

Mount Rushmore National Memorial

Keystone, South Dakota   See Climatable No. 30

On the nearly indestructible granite face of Mount Rushmore, the heads of Presidents George Washington, Thomas Jefferson, Abraham Lincoln and Theodore Roosevelt are carved to symbolize the trials during the United States' first 150 years.

MAILING ADDRESS
Superintendent, Mount Rushmore National Memorial, PO Box 268, Keystone, SD 57751 **Telephone:** 605-574-2523

DIRECTIONS
The Visitor Center is 2 miles (3.2 km) southwest of Keystone on SD 244 and 25 miles (40.3 km) south of Rapid City on US 16.

VISITOR ACTIVITIES
• Evening programs in summer, interpretive exhibits, audiovisual programs, and wildlife and bird watching. • Facilities include a Visitor Center, restrooms, parking, floodlighted Memorial and gift shop. • The Visitor Center is open from 8 a.m. to 10 p.m., from Memorial Day through Labor Day and from 8 a.m. to 5 p.m., the remainder of the year. The Memorial is open, but the Visitor Center is closed on Dec. 25.

PERMITS, FEES & LIMITATIONS
• No fees. • No commercial vehicles are allowed in the Memorial. • Climbing of Mount Rushmore is prohibited.

ACCESSIBILITY
Accessible programs at the Visitor Center.

CAMPING & LODGING
• Many commercial, state park and U.S. Forest Service campgrounds are in Black Hills National Forest, Custer State Park and the towns of Rapid City, Rockerville, Keystone, Custer, Hill City and Hot Springs. Contact the U.S. Forest Service, Black Hills National Forest, PO Box 792, Custer, SD 57730, phone 605-673-2251; Custer State Park, Hermosa, SD 57744, phone 605-255-4515; or the South Dakota Division of Tourism, Pierre, SD 57501, phone 605-773-3301. • Other overnight accommodations are available in Keystone, 2 miles (3.2 km); and Hill City, 15 miles (24.1 km). For further information, contact the Chamber of Commerce, PO box 747, Rapid City, SD 57701, phone 605-343-1744.

FOOD & SUPPLIES
• Meals are served in the Memorial during the summer. Limited services are available the rest of the year. • Food and supplies are available in Keystone and Hill City.

FIRST AID/ HOSPITAL
• First aid is available in the Memorial. • The nearest hospital is in Rapid City.

GENERAL INFORMATION

• Stay on trails and stairs. • Visitors with heart or respiratory problems should be aware of the high elevation. • For information on tourist attractions in the Black Hills area, contact the South Dakota Division of Tourism, Pierre, SD 57501, phone 605-773-3301 or 1-800-843-1930.

Wind Cave National Park

Hot Springs, South Dakota   See Climatable No. 30

When first established, Wind Cave National Park's main goal was to protect the cave's underground geological wonders. Today, it is equally important to preserve the diverse mix of wildlife living in the Park's 28,292 acres of rolling grasslands, pine forests, hills and ravines.

MAILING ADDRESS

Superintendent, Wind Cave National Park, RR 1, Box 190 WCNP, Hot Springs, SD 57747 **Telephone:** 605-745-4600

DIRECTIONS

The Visitor Center is 11 miles (17.7 km) north of Hot Springs, SD, on US 385.

VISITOR ACTIVITIES

• Guided cave tours, candlelight and spelunking tours, evening campfire programs, cross-country hiking, wildlife viewing, interpretive exhibits and picnicking. • Facilities include a bookstore, restrooms and telephones at the Visitor Center. • Cave tours, consisting of a Garden of Eden Tour, a Natural Entrance Tour and a Fairgrounds Tour, are on a first-come, first served basis. • Reservations are recommended for candlelight and spelunking tours. Reservations are accepted beginning 1 month before the tour date. • The Park is always open. Cave tours are offered daily except Thanksgiving, Dec. 25 and Jan. 1. Cave tour schedule is limited during the off season.

PERMITS, FEES & LIMITATIONS

• No entrance fee. • Tour fees are: $2 for Garden of Eden; $4 for Natural Entrance; $5 for Fairgrounds; $5 for candlelight (ages 8 and older only permitted) and $8 for spelunking (ages 16 and older only permitted). Fees are half price for children ages 6 to 15 and holders of Golden Age and Golden Access passports. Children under 6 are free for the Garden of Eden, Natural Entrance and Fairgrounds tours. • A free permit, available at the Visitor Center, is required for backcountry camping.

CAMPING & LODGING

• No reservations are accepted for camp sites, which are open all year. The camping fee is $8 per night per site. Water and modern restrooms are available from May 15 to Sept. 15. • Lodging is available outside the Park in Hot Springs and Custer. • For further information, contact the South Dakota Division of Tourism, Pierre, SD 57501, phone 605-773-3301.

FOOD & SUPPLIES

• Lunch service is available at the Visitor Center from May through September. • Supplies are available in Hot Springs and Custer.

**FIRST AID/
HOSPITAL**

• First aid is available for major injuries in the Park. • The nearest hospital is in Hot Springs.

**GENERAL
INFORMATION**

• The cave is dimly lit, and the surface is uneven. Wear low-heeled walking shoes. A sweater or jacket is recommended. The cave temperature is 53°F all year. • Beware of bison. Prairie dogs can bite and their burrows harbor rattlesnakes. • Poison ivy abounds in the Park. • To avoid crowds, visit in the spring or fall.

Tennessee

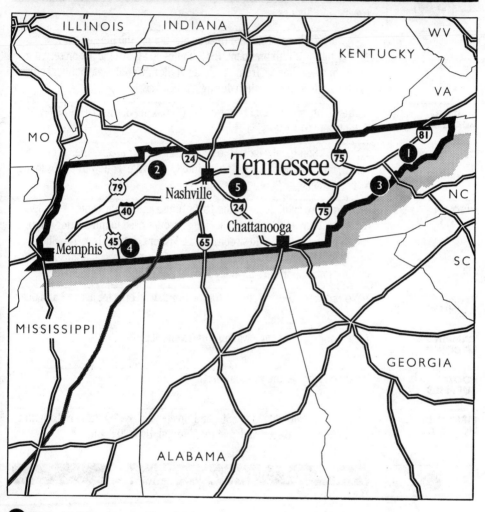

1. Andrew Johnson National Historic Site
2. Fort Donelson National Battlefield
3. Great Smoky Mountains National Park
4. Shiloh National Military Park
5. Stones River National Battlefield and Cemetery

Andrew Johnson National Historic Site

Greeneville, Tennessee

Andrew Johnson National Historic Site honors the life and work of the nation's 17th president. His 2 homes and grave site are preserved in the town where he rose from an obscure tailor through state political offices to ultimately lead the nation during a time of crisis.

MAILING ADDRESS	Andrew Johnson National Historic Site, PO Box 1088, Greeneville, TN 37744 Telephone: 615-638-3551
DIRECTIONS	From I-81 South, take Exit 23 to Rt. 11E north into Greeneville. From I-81 North, take Exit 36 to Rt. 172 south into Greeneville. Follow the signs to the Visitor Center.
VISITOR ACTIVITIES	• Interpretive exhibits are in the 1830s House and Visitor Center. • Ranger-led house tours of the Homestead. Large groups need to make prior arrangements before arrival. • Restrooms at the Visitor Center only. • The Site is open daily, except Dec. 25, from 9 a.m. to 5 p.m. • Special events include a celebration of Johnson's birthday Dec. 29 and Memorial Day activities.
PERMITS, FEES & LIMITATIONS	• No entrance fee. • Tour fee for the Homestead only for ages 18 and older.
CAMPING & LODGING	Motels and camping are available in Greeneville.
FOOD & SUPPLIES	Food and supplies are available in Greeneville.
FIRST AID/ HOSPITAL	• First aid is available in the Site and Greeneville. • Hospitals are Laughlin Memorial, Main Street, and Takoma Hospital, Hwy. 70 South.

Fort Donelson National Battlefield

Dover, Tennessee

The February 1862 fall of Fort Donelson, a 15-acre fort of 100 huts surrounded by 10-foot-high (3 m) walls of earth and logs, led the North to its first great victory and a new hero, Ulysses S. Grant, who became known as "Unconditional Surrender" Grant after the battle.

MAILING ADDRESS	Superintendent, Fort Donelson National Battlefield, PO Box 434, Dover, TN 37058 Telephone: Office, 615-232-5348; Visitor Center, 615-232-5706
DIRECTIONS	The Battlefield is 1 mile (1.6 km) west of Dover town square.
VISITOR ACTIVITIES	• Civil War museum, 10-minute slide program every hour and half hour and self-guided auto tour (rental tour tapes are available). • The Visitor

Center is open from 8 a.m. to 4:30 p.m., daily except Dec. 25.
• Interpretive talks and demonstrations are scheduled during the summer.

PERMITS, FEES & LIMITATIONS

• No fees. • A Tennessee fishing license is available in local stores. • Park only on pull-offs.

ACCESSIBILITY

The Visitor Center and Dover Hotel are accessible and have accessible restrooms.

CAMPING & LODGING

• Primitive camping for organized youth groups only within the Battlefield. Group leaders should contact the Battlefield. • Other overnight accommodations are available outside of the Battlefield in Dover; Paris Landing State Park, 16 miles (25.8 km); Clarksville and Paris, TN, 30 miles (48 km); and Murray, KY, 30 miles (48.3 km).

FOOD & SUPPLIES

Food and supplies are available in Dover.

FIRST AID/ HOSPITAL

• First aid is available in the Battlefield. • The nearest hospital is in Erin, TN, 20 miles (32.2 km).

GENERAL INFORMATION

For your safety - Be cautious near the Cumberland River. Watch for poison ivy and poisonous snakes. Hikers should walk facing traffic on Battlefield roads.

Great Smoky Mountains National Park

Gatlinburg, Tennessee (also North Carolina) See Climatable No. 26

The Park is a wildlands sanctuary preserving the world's finest examples of temperate deciduous forest with more than 1,500 types of flowering plants in an unspoiled setting similar to the one early pioneers found when they settled in the area.

MAILING ADDRESS

Superintendent, Great Smoky Mountains National Park, 107 Park Headquarters Road, Gatlinburg, TN 37738 **Telephone: 615-436-1220**

DIRECTIONS

The Park Headquarters and Sugarlands Visitor Center are on US 441, 2 miles (3.2 km) south of Gatlinburg, TN. The Oconaluftee Visitor Center is 2 miles (3.2 km) north of Cherokee, NC. There is also a Visitor Center in Cades Cove near Townsend, TN.

VISITOR ACTIVITIES

• Hiking, picnicking (available year-round), fishing, interpretive programs, nature walks, auto tours, horseback riding, and wildflower and bird watching. • A free copy of the Park's newspaper, "Smokies Guide," is available at visitor centers and contains current information on interpretive programs, facilities, activities and news items. • During winter, some picnic areas, campgrounds, roads and other facilities are closed. Main roads may close temporarily due to adverse weather conditions.

PERMITS, FEES & LIMITATIONS

• No entrance fee. • Backcountry camping permits are required and available at any Ranger Station or Visitor Center. • A Tennessee or North Carolina fishing permit, available locally, is required.

ACCESSIBILITY

Parking and restrooms at visitor centers, and Elkmont, Smokemont and Cades Cove campgrounds are accessible. Camp site reservations for an accessible site are available through the MISTIX system from May 15 to Oct. 31. There are level sites at Cataloochee and Big Creek campgrounds. An audio tape is available and literature for the hearing impaired is available at Sugarlands Visitor Center.

CAMPING & LODGING

• Three developed campgrounds (open year-round) are on the MISTIX reservation system from May 15 to Oct. 31. Reserved camp sites are available for $11 a night at Elkmont, Cades Cove and Smokemont by calling 1-800-365-CAMP. Seven other campgrounds are on a first-come, first-served basis and have sites available for $6 or $8 per night. There are no electrical or water hookups or showers. • There are more than 100 backcountry camp sites (some are rationed). Reservation-only backcountry shelters are at 13 points along the Appalachian Trail and at Mt. LeConte, Laurel Gap, Kephart Prong, Scott Gap and Rich Mountain. • Lodging is available at LeConte Lodge, accessible only by trail, which is open from late March to early November. Allow a half day to hike up a mountain trail to this secluded retreat. Reservations are necessary. Call or write LeConte Lodge, 250 Apple Valley Road, Sevierville, TN 37862, 615-429-5704.

FOOD & SUPPLIES

• Limited food and supplies are available in the Park. There is a small campground store at Cades Cove. • LeConte Lodge serves meals to overnight guests. • Gateway communities around the Park provide food services and supplies.

FIRST AID/ HOSPITAL

• First aid is available in the Park. • Numerous medical facilities, including clinics and hospitals, are near the Park.

GENERAL INFORMATION

For your safety - Hikers must be prepared to meet nature on its own terms. Don't travel alone, tell someone your schedule, have proper clothes and equipment, boil all drinking water and observe Park regulations. Stay on trails and keep off waterfalls and cliff faces. Bears and other animals may appear tame, but they are unpredictable and should not be approached or fed.

Shiloh National Military Park
Shiloh, Tennessee

When Gen. A.S. Johnston's Army of the Mississippi attacked Gen. U.S. Grant's Union Army of the Tennessee at its camps around Shiloh Church, the Confederates achieved complete surprise. The arrival of Northern reinforcements, however, forced a Confederate withdrawal the next day.

MAILING ADDRESS

Superintendent, Shiloh National Military Park, Rt. 1, Box 9, Shiloh, TN 38376 Telephone: 901-689-5275

DIRECTIONS

The Park is 10 miles (16.1 km) south of Savannah and Adamsville, TN, via US 64 and TN 22. It is 23 miles (37 km) north of Corinth, MS, via MS 2 and TN 22.

VISITOR ACTIVITIES

• Civil War exhibits, 25-minute orientation film shown on the hour and half hour, self-conducted auto tours (rental taped tours are available) and hiking or biking along a 9.5-mile (15.3 km) tour road. • The Visitor Center, open daily in winter from 8 a.m. to 5 p.m., with hours extended to 6 p.m., in summer, has a museum. • The battlefield is open from dawn to dusk year-round except Dec. 25. • Wayside audio stations are closed in winter. • Ranger interpretive programs are offered daily across the battlefield in summer and on weekends in summer and fall (weather permitting).

PERMITS, FEES & LIMITATIONS

• The **entrance fee** is $2 per person or $4 per family (no fee for ages 16 and younger or 62 and older). A yearly Park pass is available for $10. • Vehicles are restricted to parking areas and paved roads. • Pets must be on a leash under control of owners when outside vehicles.

ACCESSIBILITY

The Visitor Center, bookstore, auto tour route and National Cemetery are accessible.

CAMPING & LODGING

• Campgrounds are outside the Park in the community of Shiloh, 3 miles (4.8 km); and Pickwick Landing State Park and the TVA Public Use facility, Pickwick Landing, TN, 15 miles (24.1 km). • Lodging is available in Savannah, 12 miles (19.3 km); Adamsville, 10 miles (16.1 km); Selmer, 15 miles (24.1 km); Pickwick Landing State Park, TN, 15 miles (24.1 km); and in Corinth, MS, 23 miles (37 km).

FOOD & SUPPLIES

• Vending machines are behind the bookstore at Pittsburg Landing.
• Restaurants are available in surrounding communities.

FIRST AID/ HOSPITAL

• First aid is available in the Park. • The nearest hospital is in Savannah, TN.

GENERAL INFORMATION

• For your safety - All motorists, hikers and cyclists should use caution on Park roads. Be careful near steep river banks. • Write for additional information on Park activities and available area lodging.

Tennessee

Stones River National Battlefield and Cemetery

Murfreesboro, Tennessee

The fierce midwinter battle, which began the federal offensive to trisect the Confederacy, took place at Stones River National Battlefield Dec. 31, 1862 to Jan. 2, 1863. Stones River National Cemetery, with 6,831 interments and 2,562 unidentified, adjoins the Battlefield.

MAILING ADDRESS	Superintendent, Stones River National Battlefield, 3501 Old Nashville Highway, Murfreesboro, TN 37129-3095 **Telephone:** 615-893-9501 (TDD)
DIRECTIONS	The Battlefield is in the northwest corner of Murfreesboro, 27 miles (43.5 km) southeast of Nashville on US 41/70S.
VISITOR ACTIVITIES	• The Visitor Center contains a museum, slide program and publication sales. It is open from **8 a.m. to 5 p.m.**, daily except Dec. 25. • Drive or bike the tour road. A taped tour and brochure are available at the Visitor Center. • Interpretive trails and picnic table. • Write for a schedule of Ranger-led programs, living history demonstrations and cemetery lantern tours.
PERMITS, FEES & LIMITATIONS	• No fees. • Vehicles and bicycles are restricted to roads.
ACCESSIBILITY	Parking, restrooms and the Visitor Center are accessible. Trails are partially accessible. A captioned slide program is available on request. A braille guide is available.
CAMPING & LODGING	Camping and lodging are available in nearby communities.
FOOD & SUPPLIES	Food and supplies are available in Murfreesboro.
FIRST AID/ HOSPITAL	• First aid is available in the Battlefield. • Hospital and clinics are in Murfreesboro.
GENERAL INFORMATION	One of the oldest Civil War memorials, the Hazen Brigade Monument, is at Tour Stop 8.

Texas

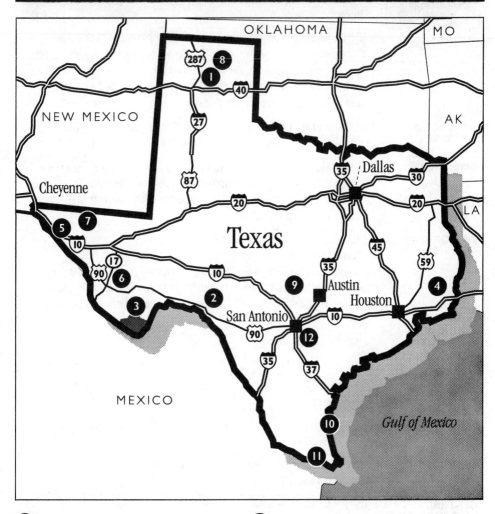

Alibates Flint Quarries National Monument

Fritch, Texas

Few prehistoric Native American archaeological sites in the Canadian River region of the Texas Panhandle are as dramatic as Alibates Flint Quarries. For 12,000 years, people quarried flint for tools here - dating back to Native Americans of the Ice Age Clovis Culture who used Alibates flint for spear points to hunt the Imperial Mammoth.

MAILING ADDRESS

Superintendent, Lake Meredith National Recreation Area, PO Box 1438, Fritch, TX 79036 **Telephone: 806-857-3151**

DIRECTIONS

On Rt. 136, 6 miles (9.6 km) south of Fritch, take Alibates Road 5 miles (8 km) to the Bates Canyon Information Station at Lake Meredith. Access to the Monument is available only by Ranger-guided tours from the Bates Canyon Information Station.

VISITOR ACTIVITIES

• Ranger-guided tours are offered twice daily from the Bates Canyon Information Station at Lake Meredith National Recreation Area.
• Interpretive exhibits. • The Information Center is open from 9:30 a.m. to 4:30 p.m., from Memorial Day through Labor Day. Tours are generally given at 10 a.m., and 2 p.m. Off-season tours are given by appointment only.

PERMITS, FEES & LIMITATIONS

• No fees. • No vehicles are permitted.

CAMPING & LODGING

Overnight accommodations are available in Fritch, Borger, Dumas and Amarillo.

FOOD & SUPPLIES

Food and supplies are available in Fritch, Borger, Dumas and Amarillo.

FIRST AID/ HOSPITAL

• First aid is not available in the Monument. • The nearest hospital is in Borger, 21 miles (33.8 km).

GENERAL INFORMATION

The Panhandle Plains Museum, on the campus of West Texas State University, has several exhibits of archaeological material from this region and a model of what a Plains Village structure might look like. The museum is in Canyon, TX, 16 miles (25.8 km) south of Amarillo.

Amistad National Recreation Area

Del Rio, Texas

Amistad, meaning "friendship" in Spanish, is an international Recreation Area on the United States/Mexico border. The Amistad Reservoir, created by the 6-mile-long (9.6 km) Amistad Dam on the Rio

Grande, offers outstanding recreational opportunities on waters of extraordinary blueness and clarity.

MAILING ADDRESS

Superintendent, Amistad National Recreation Area, PO Box 420367, Del Rio, TX 78842-0367 **Telephone:** 210-775-7491

DIRECTIONS

Headquarters and Information Center are just west of Del Rio on Hwy. 90. Ranger Stations are at Rough Canyon, off of Hwy. 277 North, and Diablo East and Pecos River, off of Hwy. 90.

VISITOR ACTIVITIES

• Boating, water skiing, swimming, fishing, scuba diving, camping on land and from boats, picnicking, wildlife and bird watching, and hunting during seasons. • Facilities include boat ramps, picnic areas, nature trails, archaeological sites, marinas, and boat and houseboat rentals. • The Information Center is open weekdays from 8 a.m. to 5 p.m., and weekends from 9 a.m. to 5 p.m. Ranger Stations are open intermittently. The Recreation Area is closed Thanksgiving, Dec. 25 and Jan. 1. • There are bookstores at Headquarters and Pecos River Ranger Station.

PERMITS, FEES & LIMITATIONS

• No fees. • A Texas fishing license is required for fishing on the U.S. side of the lake. A Mexican license is required to fish in Mexican waters. • A Texas hunting license is required for hunting. • Water skiers must wear an approved life-saving device and an observer must accompany the boat operator.

ACCESSIBILITY

Accessible restrooms are available at Headquarters, in the Rough Canyon, Diablo East and Pecos River areas, at the Blackbrush boat ramp and at Governor's Landing Campground. The Headquarters auditorium and Governor's Landing amphitheater are accessible.

CAMPING & LODGING

• Free camping is available at 4 campgrounds on Rt. 277 North, San Pedro Flats and Spur 406. Individual camp sites can not be reserved. No water or electricity. Group sites are available on Rt. 277 North, San Pedro Flats and Rock Quarry. They may be reserved up to 3 months in advance. • Backcountry shoreline camping by boat is permitted. • Commercial campgrounds and motels are in Del Rio.

FOOD & SUPPLIES

• Food and supplies are available at Lake Amistad Resort and Marina and the Rough Canyon Marina. • Restaurants and supplies are available nearby in Del Rio and Comstock.

FIRST AID/ HOSPITAL

• First aid is available at Headquarters and Ranger Stations. • The nearest hospital is in Del Rio, 7 miles (11.2 km).

GENERAL INFORMATION

For your safety - Strong winds can make boating hazardous - and in a very short time. Find a sheltered cove and wait until severe winds subside. It is not safe to stay on the lake in lightning storms. Winters are not usually severe, but extended exposure can induce hypothermia. Always watch the weather and dress accordingly. Call 210-775-2115 for a current National Weather Service forecast. The National Park Service provides free boat safety inspections. Check with any Ranger.

Big Bend National Park

Big Bend National Park, Texas   See Climatable No. 31

A land of desert and mountains cut through by the Rio Grande, Big Bend National Park is a study in contrasts. It is home to a desert amphibian, Couch's spadefoot toad; a mosquito fish that lives in just one pond in the Park; and a bird, the road-runner, that would rather run than fly.

MAILING ADDRESS

Superintendent, Big Bend National Park, Big Bend National Park, TX 79834 Telephone: 915-477-2251

DIRECTIONS

From San Antonio, it is 410 miles (661.2 km) to Park Headquarters at Panther Junction via US 90 to Marathon and south via US 385. From El Paso, it is 323 miles (520.9 km) to Panther Junction via I-10 to Van Horn, US 90 to Alpine and south via TX 118. It is 353 miles (569.3 km) via US 67 to Presidio and Texas Ranch Road 170 (the "Camino del Rio"). The Headquarters building is 27 miles (43.5 km) off Hwy. 385, 70 miles (112.9 km) south of Marathon or 25 miles (40.3 km) east of Study Butte.

VISITOR ACTIVITIES

• Interpretive programs, evening talks, hiking, horseback riding, picnicking, fishing, walking and auto tours, boating, biking and bird watching.
• Facilities include hiking trails, picnic tables, showers, service stations, telephones, post office, rental saddle horses and pack animals, laundry and restrooms. • The Park is always open. The information desk is open from 8 a.m. to 6 p.m., with extended hours during busy periods.

PERMITS, FEES & LIMITATIONS

• There is an **entrance fee**. • No off-road travel is permitted. • Trailers more than 20 feet (6 m) are not advised to try to enter the Basin or the 5-mile (8 km) continuous grade out of Castolon.

ACCESSIBILITY

There are some accessible facilities. Some trails are accessible.

CAMPING & LODGING

• Free camping is available. No reservations are accepted. • Information on backcountry camping is available at Headquarters. • Accommodations are also available in the Park at trailer parks and a lodge. For reservations at Chisos Mountain Lodge, contact National Park Concessions, Inc., Big Bend National Park, TX 79834, phone 915-477-2291. • Other overnight accommodations are available outside the Park in Terlingua, 23 miles (37 km); Lajitas, 39 miles (62.9 km); and Marathon, 70 miles (112.9 km).

FOOD & SUPPLIES

• Limited supplies are available at the Basin, Rio Grande Village, Castolon and Panther Junction in the Park. • Meals are served at Chisos Mountain Lodge. • Food and supplies are also available outside the Park in Alpine and Study Butte.

FIRST AID/ HOSPITAL

• First aid is available in the Park. • The nearest hospital is in Alpine, 108 miles (174.1 km).

GENERAL INFORMATION

• Be sure to obtain a pamphlet describing regulations and precautions, available at Headquarters. • Carry first aid supplies, including tweezers to extract cactus spines. • Carry drinking water on the trail and in the desert. • Check with a Park Ranger before traveling on any primitive roads. • Wear sturdy shoes and tough clothing while hiking and stay on trails.

Big Thicket National Preserve

Beaumont, Texas

What is extraordinary is not the rarity or abundance of the life forms at Big Thicket, known as an "American ark," but how many species coexist in the combination of virgin pine, cypress forest, hardwood forest, meadow and blackwater swamp.

MAILING ADDRESS

Superintendent, Big Thicket National Preserve, 3785 Milam, Beaumont, TX 77701 **Telephone:** 409-839-2689

DIRECTIONS

The Visitor Information Station is on the south end of the Turkey Creek Unit on FM 420, 7 miles (11.2 km) north of Kountze, TX, and 2.5 miles (4 km) east of US 69.

VISITOR ACTIVITIES

• Hiking and nature trails in 4 of the Preserve's units - Kirby Nature Trail, 1.5 miles (2.4 km), self-guiding; Turkey Creek Trail, 15 miles (24.1 km); Pitcher Plant, one-quarter mile (.4 km); Sundew Trail, 1 mile (1.6 km), self-guiding; Woodlands Trail, 6 miles (9.6 km); Beech Woods Trail, 1 mile (1.6 km); Beaver Slide Trail, 1.5 miles (2.4 km); and Big Sandy Horse Trail, 18 miles (29 km), no stable. • All-terrain bicycles are permitted on the horse trail. • Picnic sites, some with grills, in many of the units. • Power boating, canoeing and fishing. • Hunting by permit is authorized during the fall season. • Bird watching is popular during the spring and fall migrations. • Naturalist-led programs are arranged through special request by the Information Station at 409-246-2337.

PERMITS, FEES & LIMITATIONS

• No fees. • A free permit is required for backcountry camping. • A Texas license is required for fishing. • A state license and a free permit are required to hunt or trap. • Vehicles must stay on public roads. • No motorized vehicles are permitted on trails. • Pets must be on a leash or otherwise restrained and are not allowed on trails or in the backcountry.

ACCESSIBILITY

The Pitcher Plant and Sundew trails are accessible. Picnic tables, parking and restrooms are accessible at the Information Station and day-use areas.

CAMPING & LODGING

• Primitive backcountry camping is allowed in some units. Permits are free. Groups are limited to 8 people for up to 5 nights. Open fires are only permitted on sandbars in the Neches River. • Several private and public campgrounds are nearby offering tent and RV sites.

FOOD & SUPPLIES

Food and supplies are available in Beaumont, Kountze, Woodville and Silsbee.

FIRST AID/ HOSPITAL

• First aid is available in the Preserve. • Hospitals are in Beaumont, Woodville and Silsbee.

GENERAL INFORMATION

• Summers are hot and humid. Carry plenty of drinking water. Winters are cold and wet. Carry rain gear and dry clothing. • Be aware of poisonous snakes, poison ivy, chiggers, mosquitoes, fire ants, ticks and wasps. • The Preserve is fragmented. Respect private property.

Chamizal National Memorial

El Paso, Texas

A memorial to international cooperation and goodwill stands today on the Chamizal plain. Years of controversy and distrust surrounded attempts to settle border disputes between the United States and Mexico until it was decided in 1963 to build a concrete-lined channel for the Rio Grande.

MAILING ADDRESS

Superintendent, Chamizal National Memorial, 800 South San Marcial, El Paso, TX 79905 **Telephone:** 915-532-7273

DIRECTIONS

The Memorial is in south-central El Paso between Paisano and Delta on South San Marcial next to the Cordova Bridge. The entrance is on South San Marcial.

VISITOR ACTIVITIES

• Interpretive exhibits, arts, crafts, film presentations and theatrical performances. • Los Paisanos Art Gallery exhibits art from local and national artists, changing monthly. • The "Nuestra Herencia" mural depicts cultural interactions and Memorial themes. • Major events include the Classic Spanish Drama Festival in March, Regional Musics of Mexico in April, Concert Under the Stars every Sunday from June through August, Zarzuela Festival in August and the Border Folk Festival in October.

PERMITS, FEES & LIMITATIONS

• **No entrance fee.** • Permits are required for special uses. • Tickets are sold for some performances.

ACCESSIBILITY

All facilities and events are accessible.

CAMPING & LODGING

Hotels, motels and RV facilities are available in the greater El Paso area.

FOOD & SUPPLIES

A variety of stores and restaurants are available in the El Paso/Ciudad Juarez area.

FIRST AID/ HOSPITAL

Major hospitals and services are available throughout the city.

GENERAL INFORMATION

For current information on exhibits, concerts and performances, call 915-532-7273.

Fort Davis National Historic Site

Fort Davis, Texas

Today, the remnants of Fort Davis, a key post in the defense system of West Texas, are more extensive and impressive than any other southwestern fort. Troops who guarded immigrants, freighters and stagecoaches, and who contended with Comanche and Apache Indians, were based at the Fort.

MAILING ADDRESS

Superintendent, Fort Davis National Historic Site, PO Box 1456, Fort Davis, TX 79734 **Telephone: 915-426-3224**

DIRECTIONS

The Site can be reached from I-10 on the north and US 90 on the south by TX 18 and 118, and from US 90 on the west by TX 505, 166 and 17. Marfa is 21 miles (33.8 km) to the south.

VISITOR ACTIVITIES

• Interpretive exhibits, a 12-minute slide program, audio programs, and self-guiding tours of buildings and grounds. • From Memorial Day through Labor Day, several refurnished buildings are open with interpreters dressed in styles of the 1880s. • The Site is open daily, except Dec. 25, from 8 a.m. to 5 p.m., with hours extended to 6 p.m., in summer. • Facilities include parking, a bookstore and restrooms at the Visitor Center, hiking trails and a picnic area.

PERMITS, FEES & LIMITATIONS

The entrance fee is $4 per private vehicle or $2 per person.

ACCESSIBILITY

Parking, water fountain and restrooms are accessible. There is a paved ramp to the picnic area and paved ramps to buildings. A free electric cart is available at the Visitor Center. TTY-TDD available. Call 915-426-3224.

CAMPING & LODGING

Camping and lodging are available in Fort Davis and at adjacent Davis Mountain State Park.

FOOD & SUPPLIES

Food and supplies are available in Fort Davis.

**FIRST AID/
HOSPITAL**

• First aid is available at the Site. • Fort Davis Volunteer Ambulance Service
is available. • The nearest hospital is in Alpine, 26 miles (41.9 km).

**GENERAL
INFORMATION**

Carlsbad Caverns, Guadalupe Mountains and Big Bend National Parks are
within an easy drive (see listings in this book).

Guadalupe Mountains National Park

West Texas   See Climatable No. 32

Geologists from around the world come to Guadalupe Mountains
National Park to marvel at the mountains. They are part of one of the
finest examples of an ancient marine fossil reef that formed about 250
million years ago when a vast tropical ocean covered parts of Texas and New
Mexico.

**MAILING
ADDRESS**

Superintendent, Guadalupe Mountains National Park, HC 60, Box 400, Salt
Flat, TX 79847 **Telephone:** 915-828-3251

DIRECTIONS

The Park is on US 62/180, 55 miles (88.7 km) southwest of Carlsbad, NM,
and 110 miles (177.4 km) east of El Paso, TX. It is 65 miles (104.8 km)
north of Van Horn, TX, via SR 54.

**VISITOR
ACTIVITIES**

• Hiking and backpacking. • More than 80 miles (129 km) of hiking trails
in rugged mountainous terrain is available. • Horseback riding (no horse
rentals). • Guided tours and evening programs in summer. • A Natural
History Museum and bookstore are at Park Headquarters at Pine Springs.
• A History Museum is at historic Frijole Ranch. • A small Visitor Center
with exhibits is at McKittrick Canyon. • There is a 7-mile (11.2 km),
4-wheel drive road to historic Williams Ranch on the west side of the Park.
Obtain a key to locked gates at Pine Springs Visitor Center.

**PERMITS, FEES
& LIMITATIONS**

• No entrance fee. • A free permit, available at Pine Springs Visitor Center
or Dog Canyon Ranger Station, is required for overnight backcountry camping. • Vehicles are restricted to established roads. • No vehicles are permitted on Park trails. • Pets are not allowed in buildings, on trails or in the
backcountry. Pets are permitted in developed areas, but must be on a leash
or otherwise restrained. • Firearms are prohibited in the Park. • Fires, wood
or charcoal, are not permitted in the Park. Self-contained camp stoves may
be used.

ACCESSIBILITY

One RV site and restrooms at Pine Springs Campground are accessible. Pine
Springs Visitor Center is fully accessible. There is a one-third mile (.5 km)
accessible self-guiding nature trail from Pine Springs Visitor Center to the
ruins of Butterfield Stage station. The McKittrick Canyon Visitor Center and
restrooms are accessible. There are plans to make Frijole Ranch accessible.

CAMPING & LODGING

• Campgrounds at Pine Springs and Dog Canyon have sites available for $6 per night. Both have picnic tables, water and restrooms with flush toilets. Neither has showers or RV hookups. • There are 10 primitive backcountry campgrounds. • All individual camping is on a first-come, first-served basis. • Two group camp sites at Pine Springs may be reserved by calling 915-828-3251. • Lodging is available outside the Park in White's City, NM, 35 miles (56.4 km); Carlsbad, NM, 55 miles (88.7 km); Van Horn, TX, 65 miles (104.8 km); and El Paso, TX, 110 miles (177.4 km).

FOOD & SUPPLIES

• Food and supplies are available in White's City, Carlsbad, Van Horn and El Paso. • Gasoline is available in White's City, Van Horn and Dell City Junction, 29 miles (46.7 km).

FIRST AID/ HOSPITAL

• Limited first aid is available at Pine Springs and Dog Canyon.
• The nearest hospital is in Carlsbad, NM.

GENERAL INFORMATION

• For your safety - Check with a Park Ranger before hiking. Do not climb cliffs since rocks are unstable and unsuitable for technical climbing. Beware of cactus and spiny plants. Watch for and respect rattlesnakes during warm weather. • If backpacking, come prepared with sturdy boots, a tent, tough clothing, cold weather gear in winter, water repellent clothing for summer and winter and the capability to carry all the water you'll need - 1 gallon (4 l) per person per day is recommended - there is none available in the backcountry. • Anticipate storms and sudden weather changes. Violent winds are common in winter and spring. Thunderstorms are common in summer. Occasional freezing rain and snow in winter. Summer temperatures can be extreme. Winter temperatures are normally mild, but lows below freezing can be expected.

Lake Meredith National Recreation Area

Fritch, Texas

Contrasting spectacularly with its surroundings, Lake Meredith lies on the dry and windswept High Plains of the Texas Panhandle. It was created when Sanford Dam on the Canadian River flooded many natural breaks whose walls are crowned with white limestone caprock, scenic buttes, pinnacles and wind-eroded coves.

MAILING ADDRESS

Superintendent, Lake Meredith National Recreation Area, PO Box 1460, Fritch, TX 79036 Telephone: 806-857-3151

DIRECTIONS

The Headquarters is on Hwy. 136 in Fritch. Information about facilities at the various recreation sites is available here.

VISITOR ACTIVITIES

• Boating, water skiing, canoeing, fishing, picnicking, swimming, hunting, scuba diving, sailing, motorcycling and interpretive exhibits. • Facilities include a marina, restrooms, drinking water, beaches, launching ramps and picnic areas. • The Recreation Area never closes.

PERMITS, FEES & LIMITATIONS

• **No fees.** • Texas hunting and fishing licenses are available from the Texas Parks and Wildlife Department or at local sporting goods stores. • Boats are subject to Federal and state regulations.

CAMPING & LODGING

• No reservations are available for camp sites. Campers may stay up to 14 days. No camping is permitted in the launching areas or parking lots. • Information on backcountry camping is available from Headquarters. • Private campgrounds with hookups are available in nearby towns. • Other overnight accommodations are available in Fritch, Borger, Amarillo and Dumas.

FOOD & SUPPLIES

• Snacks are available at the Sanford-Yake Marina. • Limited picnic supplies are available at the marina. • Food and supplies are available outside the Recreation Area in Fritch, Sanford, Borger, Amarillo and Dumas.

FIRST AID/ HOSPITAL

• First aid is not available in the Recreation Area. • The nearest hospital is in Borger, 15 miles (24.1 km). Other hospitals are in Dumas, 20 miles (32.2 km) and Amarillo, 25-45 miles (40.3 to 72.5 km).

GENERAL INFORMATION

For your safety - Boaters should be familiar with Federal and state boating regulations, which can be obtained from Rangers or from Headquarters. Listen for storm warnings. Wait out storms in sheltered areas.

Lyndon B. Johnson National Historical Park

Johnson City and Stonewall, Texas

Lyndon Baines Johnson was a man who personified the many, often conflicting, moods of the Texas Hill Country where he grew up. He was the last President whose roots and early experience bridged the gap between the old America of local frontiers, crossroads and close neighbors, and the new America of world power, big cities and unknown neighbors.

MAILING ADDRESS

Superintendent, Lyndon B. Johnson National Historical Park, PO Box 329, Johnson City, TX 78636 **Telephone:** 210-868-7128

DIRECTIONS

Both units of the Park are on US 290, an east-west highway connecting Austin and Fredericksburg. North-south US 281 connects San Antonio with Wichita Falls. Johnson City is 50 miles (80.6 km) west of Austin and 60 miles (96.7 km) north of San Antonio. Stonewall is 15 miles (24.1 km) west of Johnson City.

VISITOR ACTIVITIES

• In Johnson City, there are tours of the Boyhood Home from **9 a.m. to 5 p.m.**, and self-guided tours of the Johnson Settlement. The Visitor Center is open from **8:45 a.m. to 5 p.m.** The Johnson City Unit is closed Dec. 25

and Jan. 1. • At the LBJ Ranch, bus tours are available from **10 a.m. to 4 p.m.** Tours depart from the Lyndon B. Johnson State Historical Park Visitor Center near Stonewall. Bus tours are 60 to 90 minutes long. Tours depart throughout the day on no set schedule. Tours may be abbreviated during periods of high heat and humidity or due to inclement weather. The LBJ Ranch Unit is closed Dec. 25.

PERMITS, FEES & LIMITATIONS

• No fees. • Access to the LBJ Ranch is by tour bus only. Access to the Johnson Settlement is by a one-half mile (.8 km) walking trail. • Pets are not permitted on tours.

ACCESSIBILITY

Most parking, restrooms, bus tours and interpretive tours are accessible.

CAMPING & LODGING

• Camping is available at local state, city and commercial campgrounds.
• Lodging is available in nearby motels and commercial bed and breakfasts.

FOOD & SUPPLIES

Food and supplies are available in Johnson City, Stonewall and other nearby towns.

FIRST AID/ HOSPITAL

• First aid is available in the Park. • The nearest hospital is in Fredericksburg, TX, 30 miles (48.3 km) west of Johnson City.

GENERAL INFORMATION

Advance reservations are recommended for large group tours. Groups of 15 or more arriving without reservations may experience long delays. Arrangements may be made by calling 210-868-7128.

Padre Island National Seashore

Corpus Christi, Texas

Located along the south Texas coast, this sparkling preserve embraces 80 miles (129 km) of white sand-and-shell beaches, picturesque windswept dunes, wild landscapes of grasslands, tidal flats teeming with shore life and warm offshore waters.

MAILING ADDRESS

Superintendent, Padre Island National Seashore, 9405 S. Padre Island Drive, Corpus Christi, TX 78418-5597 **Telephone: 512-937-2621**

DIRECTIONS

The only motor vehicle access to the Seashore is from the north end of the island. From Corpus Christi, take Hwy. 37 to Park Road 22. From Port Aransas and Mustang Island, take Park Road 53. The Visitor Center is 10 miles (16.1 km) south of the junction of Park Roads 22 and 53.

VISITOR ACTIVITIES

• Beach driving, fishing, swimming, wind surfing, sailing, boating, surfing, bird and wildlife watching, hiking, shelling, water skiing, interpretive programs and a self-guided nature trail. • The Seashore is open all day every day. • Malaquite Visitor Center is open from **9 a.m. to 4 p.m.**, with hours extended to **6 p.m.**, in summer. It includes interpretive exhibits and a bookstore. • Facilities at Malaquite Beach include restrooms, showers, telephones and a concessions store. • A boat ramp is available at Bird Island Basin.

PERMITS, FEES & LIMITATIONS

• The entrance fee is $4 per vehicle. An annual pass is available for $10.
• Vehicles are restricted to roads and the beach. Driving on the beach in front of the campground is prohibited. • Texas fishing license and salt water stamp are required for ages 17 to 65.

ACCESSIBILITY

The Malaquite Beach Visitor Center, Bath House and Padre Island Park Co., are fully accessible. Accessible restrooms are available throughout the Seashore.

CAMPING & LODGING

• Individual camp sites cannot be reserved. Overnight camping at Malaquite Beach Campground is $5 per night. Camp sites are paved. Rinse-off showers, flush toilets, picnic tables, fresh water and a dump station are provided. Tent camp sites are also available. Hookups are not available. • Open camping is permitted on 7.5 miles (12 km) of beach accessible by all 2-wheel drive vehicles and on 50 miles (80.6 km) of beach accessible by 4-wheel drive vehicles. • Hookups are available at Padre Balli County Park and Mustang Island State Park north of the Seashore boundary. For information, write Nueces County Parks, 10901 S. Padre Island Drive, Box 3G, Corpus Christi, TX 78418. • For information on lodging outside the Park, contact the Corpus Christi Chamber of Commerce, 1201 N. Shoreline, Corpus Christi, TX 78401, phone 512-882-6161.

FOOD & SUPPLIES

• The Padre Island Co., at the Malaquite Beach Visitor Center, provides snacks and beach supplies. • Supplies are available outside the Seashore in Corpus Christi and Port Aransas.

FIRST AID/ HOSPITAL

• First aid is available at the Gulf District Ranger Station and at the Malaquite Visitor Center. • The nearest hospital is in Corpus Christi, 32 miles (51.6 km).

GENERAL INFORMATION

• For your safety - Beware of the following hazards - overexposure to the sun, swimming alone, rattlesnakes, Portuguese man-of-war jellyfish, small stingrays and fishing lines. Always wear shoes when hiking. • Phone 512-949-8175 for a recorded informational message on beach conditions. • The Malaquite Beach Visitor Center phone number is 512-949-8068.

Palo Alto Battlefield National Historic Site

Brownsville, Texas

Not open to the public. The May 8, 1846 Battle of Palo Alto, the first battle of the 1846-48 Mexican-American War, was won by Gen. Zachary Taylor's 2,300-man U.S. Army of Occupation against 4,000 soldiers in Gen. Mariano Arista's Army of the North due to the vastly superior American artillery.

MAILING ADDRESS	Superintendent, Palo Alto Battlefield National Historic Site, PO Drawer 1832, Brownsville, TX 78522 **Telephone:** 210-548-2778
DIRECTIONS	The site is not yet open to the public, and there are no visitor facilities. There are a few monuments at the junction of FM 511 and FM 1847 that are on private land.
VISITOR ACTIVITIES	The Site was authorized on Nov. 10, 1978. The purpose of the Site and the authorized Site boundary were expanded on June 23, 1992. Arrangements are being made for a temporary administrative center. The Site legislation requires that the perspectives and historical data of Mexico and the U.S. will be used to interpret the battle and the Mexican-American War.
PERMITS, FEES & LIMITATIONS	None.
ACCESSIBILITY	Not accessible.
CAMPING & LODGING	Camping and lodging are available in Brownsville and the surrounding area.
FOOD & SUPPLIES	Food and supplies are available in the surrounding area.
FIRST AID/ HOSPITAL	Hospitals are in Brownsville.

San Antonio Missions National Historical Park

San Antonio, Texas

Four of the missions established along the San Antonio River in the 18th century, the greatest concentration of Catholic missions in North America, formed the foundation for the city of San Antonio and are preserved today in San Antonio Missions National Historical Park.

MAILING ADDRESS	San Antonio Missions National Historical Park, 2202 Roosevelt Ave., San Antonio, TX 78210 **Telephone:** 210-229-5701
DIRECTIONS	Visitors traveling north-south on I-37 should exit at West Southcross and proceed west on Southcross to Roosevelt Avenue. Turn left and follow Roosevelt to Mission San Jose. Visitors traveling on I-10 should exit on Probandt. Once on Probandt, follow the National Park Service signs to Mission Concepcion. Detailed information regarding routes to the other missions will be provided at Concepcion.
VISITOR ACTIVITIES	• Walking tours, interpretive talks and exhibits. • The Park is open daily, except Dec. 25 and Jan. 1, from 9 a.m. to 6 p.m., during Daylight Savings Time and 8 a.m. to 5 p.m., during Standard Time. • Facilities include parking, restrooms, a gift shop and a bookstore. • There is a .3-mile (.5 km) nature trail at Mission San Juan.

PERMITS, FEES & LIMITATIONS	No fees.
ACCESSIBILITY	Missions San Jose and Concepcion are accessible. At Missions San Juan and Espada the walks are graveled and challenging.
CAMPING & LODGING	Picnic, camping and lodging facilities are available nearby.
FOOD & SUPPLIES	A number of restaurants are nearby.
FIRST AID/ HOSPITAL	• First aid is available in the Park. • Various hospitals are in San Antonio.

Utah

1. Arches National Park
2. Bryce Canyon National Park
3. Canyonlands National Park
4. Capitol Reef National Park
5. Cedar Breaks National Monument
6. Golden Spike Historic Site
7. Natural Bridges National Monument
8. Rainbow Bridge National Monument
9. Timpanogos Cave National Monument
10. Zion National Park

Arches National Park

Moab, Utah　　　　See Climatable No. 33

Wind and water, extreme temperatures and underground salt movement are responsible for the sculptured rock scenery of Arches National Park, which boasts the greatest density of natural arches in the world.

MAILING ADDRESS	Superintendent, Arches National Park, PO Box 907, Moab, UT 84532 **Telephone: 801-259-8161**
DIRECTIONS	The Visitor Center is 5 miles (8 km) northwest of Moab on US 191.
VISITOR ACTIVITIES	• Interpretive exhibits, walks and talks, auto tours, wildlife watching, picnicking and backcountry. • Facilities include parking, restrooms and water at the Visitor Center, foot trails, a picnic area and self-guiding trails. • The Park is always open. • The Visitor Center is closed Dec. 25.
PERMITS, FEES & LIMITATIONS	• The entrance fee is $4 per private vehicle or $2 per person. A $10 annual pass is available. • Vehicles are restricted to established roads. Mountain bikes are considered vehicles. • Pets are not allowed on any trails. • Backcountry hikers must obtain a permit at the Visitor Center.
ACCESSIBILITY	Restrooms at the Visitor Center, and toilets in the campground, at Devils Garden Picnic Area and at the Windows Trailhead are accessible. An accessible short trail is at South Park Avenue. One accessible camp site at Devils Garden Campground is available on a first-come, first-served basis. The site is level with an accessible picnic table adjacent to accessible restrooms.
CAMPING & LODGING	• Individual camp sites, which cannot be reserved, are available for $7 per night. Group sites can be reserved. Write the Park for reservations. • Other overnight accommodations are available in Moab.
FOOD & SUPPLIES	Food and supplies are available in Moab.
FIRST AID/ HOSPITAL	• First aid is available in the Park. • The nearest hospital is in Moab.
GENERAL INFORMATION	For your safety - Carry plenty of water. Daytime temperatures can reach 110°F. Always hike or climb with others. Stay on trails. Climbing on sandstone can be hazardous.

Bryce Canyon National Park

Bryce Canyon, Utah   See Climatable No. 34

Intricate shapes and brilliant colors abound in Bryce Canyon National Park where erosion has created amazing formations out of 225 million- to 50 million-year-old rock, providing visitors with an awe-inspiring geology lesson.

MAILING ADDRESS
Superintendent, Bryce Canyon National Park, Bryce Canyon, UT 84717
Telephone: 801-834-5322

DIRECTIONS
The Park is in southwestern Utah within a 5-hour drive of 10 other units of the National Park System. Take UT 12 east from US 89. The Park entrance is 4 miles (6.4 km) off Rt. 12 on UT 63. UT 12 continues through Boulder to Capitol Reef National Park (see listing in this book).

VISITOR ACTIVITIES
• Information, a slide program, exhibits and publications sales at the Visitor Center. • Sightseeing, photography, wildlife watching, hiking and camping year-round. • Guided walks, horseback riding, van tours and evening camp-fire programs in the summer. • Cross-country skiing and snowshoeing in the winter. • Facilities include parking, restrooms at the Visitor Center and Sunset Point year-round (other areas seasonally), overlooks, trails, picnic areas. • Snowshoes are available for loan with security. • The Park is always open. The Visitor Center is open from 8 a.m. to 4:30 p.m., except Dec. 25, with extended hours in the spring, summer and fall. • The main Park road is open all year, but some spurs are closed in winter to permit cross-country ski access.

PERMITS, FEES & LIMITATIONS
• The entrance fee is $5 per vehicle or $2 per person. • Trailers are not permitted beyond Sunset Campground. They may be left at the Visitor Center. All vehicles more than 25 feet (7.6 m) are prohibited at Bryce/Paria points from noon to 5 p.m., from May to September. • Vehicles are restricted to paved roads and designated overlooks. • Free permits are required for backcountry camping.

ACCESSIBILITY
The Visitor Center, 2 camp sites at the north campground, the lodge, the general store, laundry and showers are accessible. The Sunset to Sunrise Point Trail is accessible with assistance near Sunrise. Overlooks are paved.

CAMPING & LODGING
• There are more than 200 camp sites available on a first-come, first-served basis for $6 per night. One loop is open for winter camping. • Required permits, information and maps for backcountry camping are available at the Sunrise Nature Center from Memorial Day to Labor Day. Permits are available at the Visitor Center the rest of the year. • Bryce Canyon Lodge has motel units and historical cabins available from mid-May through September. Reservations are available from TW Recreational Services,

451 Main, PO Box 400, Cedar City, UT 84720, phone 801-586-7686.
• Motels and campgrounds are along routes into the Park and in nearby communities.

FOOD & SUPPLIES

• Meals are served in the Bryce Canyon Lodge dining room. • Food and supplies are available at a general store in the Park and at stores and shops along routes into the Park and in nearby communities.

FIRST AID/ HOSPITAL

• First aid is available at the Visitor Center year-round and at the lodge in the summer. • The nearest hospital is in Panguitch, UT, 26 miles (41.6 km).

GENERAL INFORMATION

For your safety - Be aware of the extra needs at high altitudes where there is less oxygen. Know your physical limits. Summer storms are accompanied by lightning strikes in open areas and along rims. Animals are wild and should not be fed or handled.

Canyonlands National Park

Moab, Utah   See Climatable No. 33

Canyonlands National Park preserves an immense wilderness of rock at the heart of the Colorado Plateau where wind and water have cut flat layers of sedimentary rock into hundreds of colorful canyons, mesas, buttes, fins, arches and spires.

MAILING ADDRESS

Superintendent, Canyonlands National Park, 125 W. 200 South, Moab, UT 84532 **Telephone: 801-259-7164**

DIRECTIONS

The Park is divided into 3 districts. The Needles District is 80 miles (129 km) south of Moab and 50 miles (80.6 km) northwest of Monticello via US 191 and UT 211. Island in the Sky District is 35 miles (56.4 km) southwest of Moab via US 191 and UT 313. The Maze District is 140 miles (225.8 km) southwest of Moab via US 191, I-70 and UT 24. Access to the Maze is mostly over difficult 4-wheel drive roads.

VISITOR ACTIVITIES

• Hiking, 4-wheel driving, mountain biking, picnicking, boating, rafting, guided backcountry auto tours (by commercial outfitters) and interpretive exhibits, and programs. • Concession-operated tours and rentals are available in nearby towns. • Facilities include Ranger Stations, vault toilets, picnic areas and hiking trails. • Water is available seasonally in the Needles District, but nowhere else in the Park. • The Park is open all year. Park Headquarters in Moab and the Monticello Information Office are open from 8 a.m. to 4:30 p.m., weekdays, except holidays. Visitor centers are open daily, except Thanksgiving afternoon and Dec. 25, from 8 a.m. to 4:30 p.m., with extended hours from April through October.

PERMITS, FEES & LIMITATIONS

• The **entrance fee** is $4 per private vehicle or $2 per person. • Permits for backcountry use are issued in each district. • Boating permits are required.

Whitewater permits are available by application through the Chief Ranger's Office, and flatwater permits are available at any Ranger Station prior to launching. • Vehicles are restricted to established roads and 4-wheel drive routes. Bicycles are considered vehicles. Trail bikes must be "street-legal." Three- or 4-wheel ATV use is prohibited.

ACCESSIBILITY

Park offices in Moab and Monticello, and the Needles and Island in the Sky visitor centers are accessible with accessible restrooms nearby. Both camp-grounds have accessible restrooms. Grand View Point and Buck Canyon overlooks in Island in the Sky are accessible with assistance.

CAMPING & LODGING

• Individual camp sites are available on a first-come, first-served basis for $6 per night in the Needles District, collected from March through October when water is available. Campers must bring their own water for camping in Island in the Sky and Maze districts, and their own fuel for all districts. For group site reservations, available only in the Needles District, phone for information. • Backcountry camp sites are along the White Rim 4-wheel drive route in Island in the Sky District and should be reserved in advance by writing the White Rim Reservation Office, Canyonlands National Park, 125 W. 200 South, Moab, UT 84532. A $20 user fee is required when apply-ing. Other backcountry 4-wheel drive camp sites are available on a first-come, first-served basis. Backcountry permits are required. • Other overnight accommodations are available in Monticello, Moab, and Green River, 60 miles (96.7 km) from Moab.

FOOD & SUPPLIES

Food and supplies are available in Moab, Monticello, Green River and Hanksville.

FIRST AID/ HOSPITAL

• First aid is available in the Park. • Hospitals are in Moab and Monticello.

GENERAL INFORMATION

• Major changes may be implemented in the management of the Park's backcountry in 1994. Contact the Park for information. • Information about the Park is also available at the Moab Information Center, Center and Main streets, Moab, UT.

Capitol Reef National Park

Torrey, Utah   See Climatable No. 33

The Waterpocket Fold, a giant, sinuous wrinkle in the Earth's crust created 65 million years ago, stretches for 100 miles (161.2 km) with colorful cliffs, massive domes, soaring spires and stark monoliths, all protected with the free-flowing Fremont River by Capitol Reef National Park.

MAILING ADDRESS

Superintendent, Capitol Reef National Park, HC 70, Box 15, Torrey, UT 84775 Telephone: 801-425-3791

DIRECTIONS	The Visitor Center is 11 miles (17.7 km) east of Torrey on Hwy. 24, or 37 miles (59.6 km) west of Hanksville via Hwy. 24.
VISITOR ACTIVITIES	• Auto tours, interpretive exhibits and programs, picnicking, hiking and backcountry. • Facilities include a scenic drive, picnic areas, hiking trails and drinking water. • The Park is always open. The Visitor Center hours vary with the seasons. The Visitor Center is closed on Federal holidays from November through April.
PERMITS, FEES & LIMITATIONS	• The entrance fee is $4. • Permits for backcountry use are available at the Visitor Center. • Vehicles and mountain bikes are restricted to established roads.
ACCESSIBILITY	Accessible restrooms are 1 mile (1.6 km) south of the Visitor Center and on Loops B and C. The Visitor Center is partially accessible. One accessible camp site is available on Loop B of the Fruita Campground. It is reserved until 6 p.m. every night.
CAMPING & LODGING	• Individual camp sites are available on a first-come, first-served basis for $6 per night at Fruita Campground. Camping is free at Cedar Mesa and Cathedral Valley campgrounds. Access to Cedar Mesa is via a dirt trail that can be difficult at times. Access to Cathedral Valley is via a 4-wheel drive road. Group sites can be reserved in advance by writing the Park. • Camping is available in nearby communities and in the Dixie National Forest and Fishlake National Forest. • Lodging is available in nearby communities.
FOOD & SUPPLIES	Food and supplies are available in nearby communities.
FIRST AID/ HOSPITAL	• First aid is available in the Park. • A clinic is in Bicknell, 19 miles (30.6 km) west of the Visitor Center. • The nearest hospital is in Richvield, 72 miles (116.1 km).
GENERAL INFORMATION	• For your safety - Carry water even on short hikes. Most water in Capitol Reef is not safe for drinking. • Keep pets under physical restraint. • The elevation and desert climate make the area prone to temperature extremes. • Thunderstorms can bring flash floods from July through September.

Cedar Breaks National Monument

Cedar City, Utah

The great natural rock amphitheater of Cedar Breaks National Monument is a spectacle of gigantic dimensions. It is full of extraordinary forms wrapped in bold and brilliant colors created through millions of years of uplift and erosion.

MAILING ADDRESS	Cedar Breaks National Monument, PO Box 749, Cedar City, UT 84720 Telephone: 801-586-9451
DIRECTIONS	The Monument is 23 miles (37 km) east of Cedar City, UT, via UT 14.
VISITOR ACTIVITIES	• Monument roads and facilities are open from June through October. • Hiking, picnicking, interpretive activities, photography, wild flower watching, self-guided nature trails, skiing and snowmobiling. • The Visitor Center is open daily from 8 a.m. to 6 p.m., from June to September.
PERMITS, FEES & LIMITATIONS	The entrance fee is $4 per vehicle or $2 per person.
ACCESSIBILITY	Restrooms, camp sites, the picnic area, Visitor Center and overlooks are accessible.
CAMPING & LODGING	• A campground with 30 tent/trailer sites, available for $7 per night, is open from June to September. No reservations or group sites. • Other overnight accommodations are available outside the Monument in nearby communities.
FOOD & SUPPLIES	Food and supplies are available in nearby communities.
FIRST AID/ HOSPITAL	• First aid is available in the Monument. • The nearest hospital is in Cedar City.
GENERAL INFORMATION	• Elevations in the Monument exceed 10,000 feet (3,048 m). • Summer weather is cool with daytime temperatures in the 70s°F. Winter weather can be very cold with heavy snow. • The Utah Shakespearean Festival is held in Cedar City from late June through early September. The Festival includes the production of 6 plays in 2 theaters, including one of the closest replicas of an English Tutor Theatre in the world, seminars, tours and an authentic Renaissance Feaste.

Golden Spike National Historic Site

Brigham City, Utah

When the Central Pacific and Union Pacific railroad crews met on May 10, 1869 at Promontory Summit in Utah, a golden spike was symbolically tapped and a final iron spike was driven to connect the railroads into one transcontinental railroad linking East and West for the first time.

MAILING ADDRESS	Golden Spike National Historic Site, PO Box 897, Brigham City, UT 84302 Telephone: 801-471-2209

DIRECTIONS

The Site is 32 miles (51.6 km) west of Brigham City, UT, via Hwys. 13/83, or 30 miles (48.3 km) west of I-15 via Hwys. 13/83.

VISITOR ACTIVITIES

• Interpretive exhibits, audiovisual programs, interpretive history programs, picnicking, working replica steam locomotives, and auto tours and the Big Fill walk on an historic railroad grade. • The locomotives are exhibited from May to Oct. 3. • Facilities include a Visitor Center, parking, restrooms and a picnic area. • The Site is open daily, except Thanksgiving, Dec. 25 and Jan. 1, from 8 a.m. to 4:30 p.m., with hours extended to 6 p.m., in the summer.

PERMITS, FEES & LIMITATIONS

The entrance fee is $2 per adult up to $4 per private vehicle or $2 per person on buses.

ACCESSIBILITY

The Site is accessible.

CAMPING & LODGING

Overnight accommodations are available 30 miles (48.3 km) from the Site in Tremonton and Brigham City.

FOOD & SUPPLIES

• There are vending machines in the Site. • Food and supplies are available in nearby communities.

FIRST AID/ HOSPITAL

• First aid is available in the Site. • The nearest hospital is in Brigham City.

Natural Bridges National Monument

(near) Blanding, Utah

The 3 scenic treasures at Natural Bridges National Monument, Owachomo Bridge, Sipapu Bridge and Kachina Bridge, represent the 3 phases in a natural bridge's history as running water forms and then ultimately destroys these perforated rock walls.

MAILING ADDRESS

Superintendent, Natural Bridges National Monument, PO Box 1, Lake Powell, UT 84533 **Telephone:** 801-259-5174

DIRECTIONS

The Visitor Center is 40 miles (64.5 km) west of Blanding on UT 95. It is 44 miles (70.9 km) north of Mexican Hat on Rt. 261. It is 50 miles (80.6 km) east of Hite Marina on Lake Powell.

VISITOR ACTIVITIES

• Picnicking, auto tour of Bridge View Drive and hiking. • Facilities include a Visitor Center. • The Monument has interesting geological and archaeological aspects. • The Visitor Center is open daily, except Thanksgiving, Dec. 25 and Jan. 1, from 8 a.m. to 4:30 p.m.

PERMITS, FEES & LIMITATIONS

• The entrance fee is $4 per vehicle or $2 per person. • Trailers are limited to 21 feet (6.4 m) in the campground. • No backcountry camping is allowed.

ACCESSIBILITY

The Visitor Center, restrooms and several short trails are accessible.

Utah

CAMPING & LODGING

• There is a 13-site campground available on a first-come, first-served basis with no fee. • Other camping is available outside the Monument. • Lodging is available in Blanding, Mexican Hat and other surrounding communities.

FOOD & SUPPLIES

Food and supplies are available in Blanding, Mexican Hat and Fry Canyon (seasonally).

FIRST AID/ HOSPITAL

• First aid is available in the Monument. • Blanding Clinic is 40 miles (64.5 km) away. • The nearest hospital is San Juan County Hospital in Monticello, 65 miles (104.8 km).

GENERAL INFORMATION

Weather is best from late April through October.

Rainbow Bridge National Monument

Utah

Rainbow Bridge, the world's largest natural bridge, is considered a sacred place by the Navajo Indians and nestles among canyons carved by streams en route to the Colorado River. It arches to a height of 290 feet (88.4 m) with a span of 275 feet (83.8 m).

MAILING ADDRESS

Superintendent, c/o Glen Canyon National Recreation Area, Box 1507, Page, AZ 86040 **Telephone:** 602-645-8200

DIRECTIONS

Most people reach the Monument by tour boats, rented boats or private boats. From the Wahweap and Bullfrog marinas along the shores of Lake Powell in Glen Canyon National Recreation Area, the Monument is 50 miles (80.6 km). Rentals and tours can be arranged by contacting the concessioner, ARA Leisure Services, at 1-800-528-6154. A few visitors hike to Rainbow Bridge. It is a 15- or 13-mile (24.1 or 20.9 km) trip through the Navajo Nation. **Permits are required from the Navajo Nation.** Write to Navajo Nation, Recreational Resources Department, Box 308, Window Rock, AZ 86515, phone 602-871-6647 *or* 602-871-4941.

VISITOR ACTIVITIES

• Photography and walking. • There is a courtesy boat dock and restroom at Rainbow Bridge, but no water. • There is a short trail from the dock to Rainbow Bridge. • The Monument is always open. Rangers are available during summer and fall.

PERMITS, FEES & LIMITATIONS

No fees.

CAMPING & LODGING

• Camping is available outside the Monument in Glen Canyon National Recreation Area. • Other overnight accommodations are available in the Recreation Area and Page, AZ.

FOOD & SUPPLIES

Food and supplies are available at Dangling Rope Marina, 10 miles (16.1 km) by boat.

FIRST AID/ HOSPITAL

First aid is available at Dangling Rope Marina.

GENERAL INFORMATION

• Before beginning a trip, call the Navajo Nation at Window Rock at 602-871-6645 to check on the condition of the trail, whether or not the trading posts are open and areas where water and supplies are available. • Hikers should carry at least 1 gallon (4 l) of water a day per person in the summer. • Hikers may arrange one-way transportation by boat with the concessioner after hiking in.

Timpanogos Cave National Monument

American Fork, Utah

High on the steep rocky slopes of American Fork Canyon are 3 small limestone caves - Hansen Cave, Middle Cave and Timpanogos Cave - decorated with a dazzling display of sparkling crystal formations in a variety of fantastic shapes.

MAILING ADDRESS

Superintendent, Timpanogos Cave National Monument, RR 3, Box 200, American Fork, UT 84003 **Telephone:** 801-756-5239

DIRECTIONS

Exit I-15 North or South at Hwy. 92. Follow Hwy. 92 east 10 miles (16 km) to the Monument.

VISITOR ACTIVITIES

• Visitors follow a 1.5-mile (2.4 km) trail from the Visitor Center to the cave entrance rising 1,065 feet (324.6 m). • Guided tours through the cave. • Picnicking, fishing, exhibits and video program. • The caves are closed from Oct. 1 to May 1. Call ahead for opening and closing dates.

PERMITS, FEES & LIMITATIONS

Cave tour fees are $5 for ages 16 and older, $4 for ages 6 to 16 and $2.50 for holders of Golden Age Passports. Children under 6 admitted free. It is recommended that tickets for the cave tour be purchased in advance by writing or calling the Monument at least 2 weeks prior to a visit. Tickets may also be purchased at the Visitor Center up to the day of the tour if still available.

ACCESSIBILITY

The Visitor Center, concessions, restrooms and drinking fountain are accessible. Video programs are close captioned.

CAMPING & LODGING

• Camping is available in the surrounding Uinta National Forest. • A wide range of lodging is available in Salt Lake City and Provo, UT, 30 miles (48.4 km).

FOOD & SUPPLIES

Food and supplies are available within 7 miles (11.2 km) in American Fork, Alpine, Pleasant Grove and Highland.

FIRST AID/ HOSPITAL

• First aid is available in the Monument. • American Fork Hospital is 7 miles (11.2 km) from the Monument.

GENERAL INFORMATION

About 3 hours are required for the hike and tour of the cave. Tour group sizes are limited. Call 801-756-5239 to check on availability. A warm jacket or sweater and comfortable walking shoes are recommended.

Zion National Park

Springdale, Utah   See Climatable No. 35

Protected within Zion National Park's 229 square miles (369.3 km) is a spectacular cliff-and-canyon landscape and wilderness full of the unexpected, including the world's largest arch - Kolob Arch - with a span that measures 310 feet (94.5 m). Wildlife such as roadrunners, golden eagles and mountain lions also inhabit the Park.

MAILING ADDRESS

Superintendent, Zion National Park, Springdale, UT 84767 **Telephone:** 801-772-3256

DIRECTIONS

The Visitor Center at Kolob Canyons is accessible via Exit 40 from I-15. I-15 passes west of the Park and connects with UT 9 and 17 to the Park. US 89 passes east and connects with UT 9 to the Park. The Zion Canyon Visitor Center is a short distance from the Park's South Entrance.

VISITOR ACTIVITIES

• Interpretive films, exhibits and programs (schedules posted throughout the Park), driving, walking and hiking, mountain climbing, wading, biking, horseback trips, a 1 1/2-hour tram tour of major points of interest in the summer, and wildlife and bird watching. • Facilities include visitor centers, a Nature Center for children ages 6 to 12 from Memorial Day to Labor Day, water, fire grates, tables, a sanitary disposal station, telephones, picnic sites and religious services from May to September. • The Park is always open. Higher hiking trails are closed by snow in winter.

PERMITS, FEES & LIMITATIONS

• The entrance fee is $5 per vehicle or $3 per person on commercial vehicles. • There are size restrictions on vehicles traveling through the 1.1-mile (1.7 km) tunnel on the Zion-Mt. Carmel Highway. The tunnel height at the east entrance is 11 feet 4 inches (3.5 m). A fee may be required for escort service through the narrow tunnel. • Parking of large vehicles is regulated in parts of the Park in the summer. • Permits are required for all through Virgin River Narrows hikes. • Backcountry permits are required for overnight trips.

ACCESSIBILITY

The visitor centers and Zion Lodge are accessible. There are accessible camp sites in the South Campground. Many interpretive talks are accessible. The 1-mile (1.6 km) Gateway to the Narrows Trail, which begins at the north end of Zion Canyon Drive, is paved and accessible with assistance.

CAMPING & LODGING

• Camp sites are available on a first-come, first-served basis for $7 per night. Stays are limited to 14 days. • Zion Lodge is operated by the Utah

Parks Division of TWRS. Reservations for cabin and motel accommodations are available through TWRS, 451 North Main St., Cedar City, UT 84720, phone 801-586-7686. • Other overnight accommodations are available in surrounding communities.

FOOD & SUPPLIES

• Meals are served at Zion Lodge. • Food and supplies are available in Springdale.

FIRST AID/ HOSPITAL

• First aid is available in the Park. • A physician's assistant is available in Springdale in the summer, and a physician is in Hurricane, 24 miles (38.7 km). • Hospitals are in St. George, 45 miles (72.5 km); Cedar City, 60 miles (96.7 km); and Kanab, 42 miles (67.7 km).

GENERAL INFORMATION

For your safety - All hikers should take precautions. Obtain detailed information from a Park Ranger before attempting backcountry trails. Do not hike alone. Stay on established trails. Stay out of drainage areas during thunderstorms. Be alert for rockfalls and landslides.

Virginia

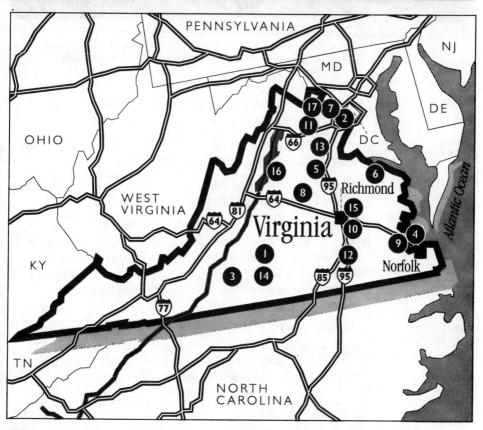

1 Appomattox Court House National Historical Park

2 Arlington House, The Robert E. Lee Memorial

3 Booker T. Washington National Monument

4 Colonial National Historical Park

5 Fredericksburg and Spotsylvania County Battlefields Memorial

6 George Washington Birthplace National Monument

7 George Washington Memorial Parkway

8 Green Springs Historic District

9 Jamestown National Historic Site

10 Maggie L. Walker National Historic Site

11 Manassas National Battlefield Park

12 Petersburg National Battlefield

13 Prince William Forest Park

14 Red Hill Patrick Henry National Memorial

15 Richmond National Battlefield Park

16 Shenandoah National Park

17 Wolf Trap Farm Park for the Performing Arts

Appomattox Court House National Historical Park

Appomattox, Virginia

Walk the old country lanes where Robert E. Lee, commanding general of the Army of Northern Virginia, surrendered his men to Ulysses S. Grant, general-in-chief of all United States forces, on April 9, 1865. Imagine the events that signaled the end of the Southern States' attempt to create a separate nation.

MAILING ADDRESS
Superintendent, Appomattox Court House National Historical Park, PO Box 218, Appomattox, VA 24522 **Telephone: 804-352-8987**

DIRECTIONS
The Visitor Center is in the reconstructed Court House building on VA 23, 3 miles (4.8 km) northeast of the town of Appomattox, VA.

VISITOR ACTIVITIES
• Walking tours (pamphlet available at the Visitor Center), audiovisual programs, interpretive exhibits, displays, a bookstore, and living history and Ranger talks in the summer. • The Visitor Center is open daily in winter from 8:30 a.m. to 5 p.m., and in summer from 9 a.m. to 5:30 p.m. The Visitor Center is closed on Federal holidays from November through February.

PERMITS, FEES & LIMITATIONS
• The entrance fee is $2 per person with a $5 maximum per vehicle. There is no charge for ages 16 and younger or 62 and older. • Vehicles are restricted to the parking area and paved roads. • Pets must be on a leash. • Picnicking is permitted in designated areas only.

ACCESSIBILITY
Parking areas, restrooms, drinking fountains and living history programs are accessible. Ramps, a braille map and folder, captioned slide program and large print brochures are available. Wheelchairs are available for use in the historic village.

CAMPING & LODGING
• Camping is available nearby at Holiday Lake State Park and at private campgrounds. • Lodging is available in the town of Appomattox.

FOOD & SUPPLIES
Restaurants, food and supplies are available in Appomattox.

FIRST AID/ HOSPITAL
• First aid is available in the Park. • There is a rescue squad in Appomattox. • The nearest hospital is in Lynchburg, 25 miles (40.3 km).

GENERAL INFORMATION
Allow at least 2 hours to visit the historical village.

Virginia

Arlington House, The Robert E. Lee Memorial

Arlington, Virginia

Today, the house that Robert E. Lee lived in for 30 years and that is uniquely associated with the families of Washington, Custis and Lee is a memorial to Lee, who gained the respect of Northerners and Southerners through his service in the Civil War.

MAILING ADDRESS

Arlington House, The Robert E. Lee Memorial, c/o National Park Service, George Washington Memorial Parkway, Turkey Run Park, McLean, VA 22101 **Telephone:** 703-557-0613

DIRECTIONS

The Memorial is accessible by shuttle bus or by a 10-minute walk from the Arlington National Cemetery Visitor Center/parking area. Access from Washington is via the Memorial Bridge. Access from Virginia is from the George Washington Memorial Parkway. The Memorial is also accessible by the Blue Line of the Metro subway system.

VISITOR ACTIVITIES

• Visitors tour the house with a self-guiding brochure. • National Park Service staff in period costume are stationed in the main areas to talk informally with visitors. • Guided tours are available by appointment for groups from September through May. • The Memorial is open from 9:30 a.m. to 6:30 p.m., from April through September and 9:30 a.m. to 4:30 p.m., from October through March. The Memorial is closed Dec. 25 and Jan. 1. • Robert E. Lee's birthday is recognized in January and the Lees' wedding anniversary is observed June 30 with special events.

PERMITS, FEES & LIMITATIONS

No fees.

ACCESSIBILITY

The first floor of the house and the museum are accessible. The house has a self-operated lift while the museum is accessible at ground level.

CAMPING & LODGING

Overnight accommodations are available in surrounding communities.

FOOD & SUPPLIES

Food and supplies are available in surrounding communities.

FIRST AID/ HOSPITAL

• First aid is available at the Memorial. • Hospitals are in Arlington and Washington, DC.

Booker T. Washington National Monument

Hardy, Virginia

Burroughs' tobacco farm, where Booker T. Washington was born in 1856, has been reconstructed and most of the Burroughs' original 207 acres have been set aside. Today, through demonstrations of farm life in pre-Civil War Virginia, visitors may get a feel for the leading African American educator's childhood.

MAILING ADDRESS

Superintendent, Booker T. Washington National Monument, Rt. 3, Box 310, Hardy, VA 24101 **Telephone:** 703-721-2094

DIRECTIONS

The Monument is 16 miles (25.8 km) northeast of Rocky Mount, VA, via VA 122 North; 20 miles (32.2 km) southeast of Roanoke, VA, via VA 116 South and 122 North; and 21 miles (33.8 km) south of Bedford, VA, via VA 122 South.

VISITOR ACTIVITIES

• Exhibits and audiovisual programs, self-guided historic and nature trails, craft demonstrations, picnicking and group tours by appointment. • Visitor facilities include African American book sales, period craft sales, restrooms and telephone at the Visitor Center, parking at the picnic area and an environmental study area. • The Monument is open daily, except Thanksgiving, Dec. 25 and Jan. 1, from 8:30 a.m. to 5 p.m. • Living history demonstrations are held from mid-June to Labor Day.

PERMITS, FEES & LIMITATIONS

The **entrance fee** is $2 per person. Ages 16 or younger and 62 or older are admitted free.

ACCESSIBILITY

Parking and Visitor Center are accessible. Restrooms and the historic trail have limited accessibility.

CAMPING & LODGING

• A commercial bed and breakfast is nearby. • Other overnight accommodations are available in Roanoke, Rocky Mount and Bedford. • For hotel and campground information, phone 703-721-2094 or write to the Monument.

FOOD & SUPPLIES

Food and supplies are available within a 10-mile (16.1 km) radius of the Monument or in Roanoke, Rocky Mount and Bedford.

FIRST AID/ HOSPITAL

• First aid is available in the Monument. • Hospitals are in Roanoke and Rocky Mount.

GENERAL INFORMATION

• **For your safety** - Keep your distance from the animals. Do not enter the pastures and pens. • Nearby points of interest include the Blue Ridge Parkway (see listing in this book), Fairy Stone State Park and Smith Mountain Lake.

Colonial National Historical Park

Jamestown and Yorktown, Virginia

The 23-mile (37 km) Colonial Parkway connects Jamestown National Historic Site with Yorktown Battlefield, the principal elements of Colonial National Historical Park, where visitors can learn about the lives of Virginia's earliest European settlers.

MAILING ADDRESS	Superintendent, Colonial National Historical Park, PO Box 210, Yorktown, VA 23690 **Telephone:** 804-898-3400
DIRECTIONS	Jamestown and Yorktown are off of major highways, Rt. 17 and I-64. The sites are accessible via the Colonial Parkway, which joins Jamestown, Williamsburg and Yorktown.
VISITOR ACTIVITIES	• Self-guided auto and walking tours, guided walking tours, interpretive exhibits, and living history and children's programs. • The Jamestown Entrance Station is open daily, except Dec. 25, from **8:30 a.m. to 4:30 p.m.**, with extended hours from April through October. The Yorktown Visitor Center is open daily from **8:30 a.m. to 5 p.m.**, with extended hours from April to October. Moore House, Nelson House and picnic areas are closed in winter.
PERMITS, FEES & LIMITATIONS	• The **entrance fee** at Jamestown is $8 per vehicle or $2 per person for ages 17 to 61. Educational groups are admitted free. There is **no fee** at Yorktown. • Drive and park only in designated areas. • There are no service stations. • The Colonial Parkway is closed to commercial traffic except buses with a permit. Bus permits are available at the Jamestown Entrance Station or Yorktown Visitor Center for $3.
ACCESSIBILITY	Parking, visitor centers and restrooms are accessible.
CAMPING & LODGING	• City and privately owned campgrounds are nearby. Contact the Park for further information. • Lodging is available in Yorktown and along Rt. 17 and in Williamsburg.
FOOD & SUPPLIES	Food and supplies are available nearby in Yorktown and Williamsburg.
FIRST AID/ HOSPITAL	• First aid is available in the Park. • Mary Immaculate Hospital in Newport News is 5 miles (8 km) from Yorktown. Williamsburg Community Hospital is 9.5 miles (15.3 km) from Jamestown.
GENERAL INFORMATION	For your safety - Stay on the paths. Do not walk or climb on ruins or earthworks. Do not go near the river.

Fredericksburg and Spotsylvania County Battlefields Memorial National Military Park

Fredericksburg, Virginia

Fredericksburg and Spotsylvania National Military Park commemorates 4 major actions of the American Civil War - the Battle of Fredericksburg, the Chancellorsville Campaign, the Battle of the Wilderness and the Battle of Spotsylvania Court House - and involves visitors in an absorbing historical experience.

MAILING ADDRESS	Fredericksburg and Spotsylvania County Battlefields Memorial National Military Park, 120 Chatham Lane, Fredericksburg, VA 22405 **Telephone:** 703-373-4461
DIRECTIONS	Fredericksburg Battlefield Visitor Center is at 1013 Lafayette Blvd., in Fredericksburg. Chancellorsville Battlefield Visitor Center is on Rt. 3, 8 miles (12.9 km) west of I-95.
VISITOR ACTIVITIES	• The visitor centers feature slide presentations and exhibits. They are open daily. • Chatham Manor, an 18th century plantation house, was used as a Union Army headquarters and field hospital. It is open daily. • Jackson Shrine, the house where Stonewall Jackson died, is open seasonally.
PERMITS, FEES & LIMITATIONS	No fees.
ACCESSIBILITY	Chancellorsville Battlefield Visitor Center is fully accessible. Fredericksburg Visitor Center is partially accessible.
CAMPING & LODGING	Camping and lodging are available in Fredericksburg.
FOOD & SUPPLIES	Food and supplies are available in Fredericksburg.
FIRST AID/ HOSPITAL	• First aid is available in the Park. • Mary Washington Hospital in Fredericksburg provides emergency care as do a variety of smaller medical centers.
GENERAL INFORMATION	In addition to the battlefields, Fredericksburg has a rich colonial history. For information about tours of houses, contact the Fredericksburg Visitor Center at 703-373-1776.

George Washington Birthplace National Monument

Washington's Birthplace, Virginia

George Washington Birthplace National Monument on the banks of Popes Creek, VA, evokes the spirit of the 18th-century tobacco farm where the national hero was born and spent his early years surrounded by farm buildings, groves of trees, livestock, gardens, fields of tobacco and wheat, and rivers and creeks.

MAILING ADDRESS	George Washington Birthplace National Monument, RR 1, Box 717, Washington's Birthplace, VA 22443 **Telephone:** 804-224-1732
DIRECTIONS	The Monument is on the Potomac River, 38 miles (61.2 km) east of Fredericksburg, VA, and is accessible via Rts. 3 and 204.

VISITOR ACTIVITIES

• Interpretive tours, films and exhibits. • Self-guided nature walks. • Picnicking and beach areas. • The Monument is open from **9 a.m. to 5 p.m.**, daily except Dec. 25 and Jan. 1.

PERMITS, FEES & LIMITATIONS

• The entrance fee is $2 per person ages 17 to 61. • No off-road travel allowed. • No overnight camping or parking permitted.

ACCESSIBILITY

Parking, restrooms, trails and buildings are accessible.

CAMPING & LODGING

• Camping is available at Westmoreland State Park, 6 miles (9.6 km). • Other overnight accommodations are available in nearby towns 15 to 40 miles (24.1 km to 64.5 km) away.

FOOD & SUPPLIES

Food and supplies are available in nearby towns.

FIRST AID/ HOSPITAL

• First aid is available in the Monument. • Medical clinics are in nearby towns. • A hospital is in Fredericksburg.

GENERAL INFORMATION

• For your safety - Do not feed or tease the animals or enter the pastures or pens. Poisonous plants are common in the area. • Other nearby sites include Stratford Hall, Birthplace of Robert E. Lee; and Westmoreland State Park.

George Washington Memorial Parkway

McLean, Virginia

George Washington Memorial Parkway preserves the natural scenery along the Potomac River and connects the historic sites from Mount Vernon past the nation's capital to the Great Falls of the Potomac to commemorate the life and achievements of the nation's first president.

MAILING ADDRESS

Superintendent, George Washington Memorial Parkway, Turkey Run Park, McLean, VA 22101 **Telephone: 703-285-2598**

DIRECTIONS

Access to the Parkway is from Exit 14 of the Capital Beltway (I-495) from Chain Bridge on Rt. 123, or from Washington via the 14th Street, Memorial or Theodore Roosevelt bridges.

VISITOR ACTIVITIES

• Areas assigned to the Parkway's administration, such as Great Falls Park, Arlington House, Clara Barton National Historic Site, Glen Echo Park and Theodore Roosevelt Island, offer opportunities for interpretive talks, exhibits, picnicking, hiking, climbing, biking and fishing. • Facilities include picnic tables, restrooms, parking, boat ramp and a bike/pedestrian trail. • The parks along the Parkway close at dark. Most parks close Dec. 25. The Glen Echo Carousel is closed from October to April.

PERMITS, FEES & LIMITATIONS

• There are user fees for 6 areas administered by the Parkway at Fort Hunt Park. Write or call for details. • Permits are required for fishing and picnicking at Fort Hunt Park from April to October. • Vehicles are restricted to paved roads.

ACCESSIBILITY

Areas under Parkway jurisdiction have various levels of accessibility.

CAMPING & LODGING

Overnight accommodations are available in the Washington, DC, metropolitan area.

FOOD & SUPPLIES

• Meals are served in Great Falls Park, Mount Vernon, Dangerfield Island and Lady Bird Johnson Park. • Food and supplies are available in nearby communities.

FIRST AID/ HOSPITAL

• First aid is available along the Parkway. • Hospitals are in the Virginia suburbs.

GENERAL INFORMATION

Other areas managed by the Parkway include the U.S. Navy Marine Memorial, Mount Vernon Pedestrian/Bike Trail, Riverside Park, Fort Marcy and Dyke Marsh.

Green Springs Historic District

Louisa County, Virginia

Affiliated area. This portion of Louisa County in Virginia's Piedmont is noted for its concentration of fine rural manor houses and related buildings in an unmarred landscape that extends over 14,000 acres.

MAILING ADDRESS

Green Springs National Historic Landmark District, PO Box 1838, Louisa, VA 23093 **Telephone:** 703-967-9671

DIRECTIONS

The District is 2 miles (3.2 km) north of I-64 at the junction with US 15. The District is bounded by US 15 and VA Rts. 22 and 613. There is no public land included.

VISITOR ACTIVITIES

A brochure of the District is available with a map at the National Park Service Office, 115 US 33 East, (Sage Building), Louisa, VA, to tour the District by auto. Phone 703-967-9671.

PERMITS, FEES & LIMITATIONS

• No fees. • Visitor access is from roads only. Please respect private property.

ACCESSIBILITY

Access is by vehicle only.

CAMPING & LODGING

Camping and lodging are available nearby.

FOOD & SUPPLIES

Food and supplies are available in nearby communities.

FIRST AID/ HOSPITAL

The nearest hospital is in Charlottesville, VA.

GENERAL INFORMATION

For other attractions in the Louisa County area, contact the Louisa County Tourism Council, PO Box 1494, Louisa, VA 23093, phone 703-894-4744.

Maggie L. Walker National Historic Site

Richmond, Virginia

This rowhouse at 110 1/2 E. Leigh St., Richmond, was the home of a former house slave's daughter who became a bank president and a leading figure in the Richmond African American community.

MAILING ADDRESS

Superintendent, c/o Richmond National Battlefield Park, 3215 E. Broad St., Richmond, VA 23223 **Telephone:** 804-780-1380

DIRECTIONS

The Site is at 110 E. Leigh St., in Richmond. Signs direct visitors from highways.

VISITOR ACTIVITIES

• Guided tours through the house museum. • A video on the life of Maggie Walker is shown on request. • Exhibits highlight her accomplishments and legacy. • The Site is open Wednesday through Sunday from 9 a.m. to 5 p.m., except Thanksgiving, Dec. 25 and Jan. 1. • Advance reservations for groups of 5 or more is required.

PERMITS, FEES & LIMITATIONS

No fees.

ACCESSIBILITY

The first floor of the house museum is accessible.

CAMPING & LODGING

Lodging is available in Richmond.

FOOD & SUPPLIES

Food and supplies are available in Richmond.

FIRST AID/ HOSPITAL

There are various medical facilities in Richmond.

Manassas National Battlefield Park

Manassas, Virginia

Manassas National Battlefield Park commemorates 2 clashes between Northern and Southern troops. Nearly 900 men lost their lives in July 1861, and another 3,300 died during a 3-day battle in August 1862, which brought the Confederacy to the height of its power.

MAILING ADDRESS

Superintendent, Manassas National Battlefield Park, 12521 Lee Highway, Manassas, VA 22110 **Telephone:** 703-361-1339

DIRECTIONS

The Park is 26 miles (41.9 km) southwest of Washington, DC. The Visitor Center is on Rt. 234 just north of I-66 at Exit 47B.

VISITOR ACTIVITIES

• Civil War exhibits, a 13-minute slide program is shown on the hour and half-hour and a 5-minute battlefield map program is continuously shown at the Visitor Center. • A 1-mile (1.6 km) self-guided walking tour of First Manassas and a 12-mile (19.3 km) self-guided auto tour of Second Manassas begin at the Visitor Center. • Conducted tours of both battles are available in season. • The Visitor Center is open daily from 8:30 a.m. to 5 p.m., except Dec. 25, with hours extended to 6 p.m., in the summer. The grounds are open from dawn to dusk, except Dec. 25.

PERMITS, FEES & LIMITATIONS

• The entrance fee is $2 per person for ages 17 to 61 with a $4 maximum per family. • Camping is prohibited.

ACCESSIBILITY

The Visitor Center exhibits, auditorium and restrooms are accessible. The slide show and battle map are captioned.

CAMPING & LODGING

Numerous campgrounds and motels are available near the Park.

FOOD & SUPPLIES

Restaurants and stores are along VA Rt. 234.

FIRST AID/ HOSPITAL

• Routine first aid is available at the Visitor Center. • The nearest hospital is in Manassas, 4 miles (6.4 km).

GENERAL INFORMATION

For your safety - Two heavily traveled roads divide the Park. Use extreme caution while driving these highways.

Petersburg National Battlefield

Petersburg, Virginia

Four railroad lines and key roadways made Petersburg important to Lt. Gen. Ulysses S. Grant's plan to capture Richmond during the Civil War. The plan led to a grim 10-month struggle as Grant's army gradually encircled Petersburg and cut the Confederates' supply lines.

MAILING ADDRESS

Superintendent, Petersburg National Battlefield, PO Box 549, Petersburg, VA 23804 Telephone: 804-732-3531

DIRECTIONS

The main Visitor Center is 2.5 miles (4 km) east of the center of Petersburg on State Rt. 36. The Five Forks Unit of the Battlefield is in Dinwiddie County, VA. From I-85, take the Dinwiddie Courthouse Exit, follow the signs to Courthouse Road, turn right on Courthouse Road (State Rt. 627) and proceed 5 miles (8 km) to Five Forks.

VISITOR ACTIVITIES

- A 17-minute map presentation is shown hourly at the Visitor Center.
- Demonstrations of mortar and cannon firings and soldier life in the summer. • Biking, picnicking, hiking and self-guiding auto tours.
- Facilities include bike trails, parking, restrooms and picnic areas.
- A Ranger is on duty at the Five Forks Visitor Contact Station in spring, summer and fall, and part-time in the winter. There are interpretive exhibits and brochures at the Station. • The Battlefield is open from 8 a.m. to dusk year-round. The main Visitor Center is open from 8 a.m. to 5 p.m., with hours extended to 7 p.m., in the summer. The Visitor Center is closed Dec. 25 and Jan. 1.

PERMITS, FEES & LIMITATIONS

There is a $2 per person or $4 per vehicle **entrance fee** at Petersburg. There is no fee at Five Forks.

ACCESSIBILITY

The Five Forks Contact Station is accessible.

CAMPING & LODGING

Camping and lodging are available in Petersburg and vicinity.

FOOD & SUPPLIES

Food and supplies are available in Petersburg and vicinity.

FIRST AID/ HOSPITAL

- First aid is available in the Battlefield. • The nearest hospital is in Petersburg.

GENERAL INFORMATION

Visitors to the area can also see the nearby Poplar Grove National Cemetery, which contains the graves of more than 6,000 soldiers. It is on VA 675, 3 miles (4.8 km) south of Petersburg.

Prince William Forest Park

Triangle, Virginia

The Piedmont forest of the Quantico Creek watershed serves as a sanctuary for plants and animals in rapidly developing Northern Virginia. It provides a home for a variety of wildlife and offers many opportunities for hiking, birdwatching and fishing.

MAILING ADDRESS

Superintendent, Prince William Forest Park, PO Box 209, Triangle, VA 22172 **Telephone:** 703-221-4706

DIRECTIONS

From Washington, DC, travel south on I-95 for 32 miles (51.6 km). Take Exit 150B or Rt. 619 West for one-quarter mile (.4 km). The Park entrance is on the right. The Visitor Center is straight ahead almost 1 mile (1.6 km).

VISITOR ACTIVITIES

- More than 37 miles (59.6 km) of hiking trails, fishing, picnicking, bicycle trail and off-road opportunities, bird watching, wildlife viewing, Ranger programs, films and bookstore. • The Park is open all year from dawn to dusk. The Visitor Center is closed on Dec. 25 and Jan. 1.

PERMITS, FEES & LIMITATIONS	• The entrance fee is $4 per vehicle or $2 per person. • Backcountry camping permits are available from the Visitor Center.
ACCESSIBILITY	The Visitor Center is accessible. Accessible camp sites are designated in Oak Ridge. The Pine Grove Nature Trail is paved.
CAMPING & LODGING	• Camping is available for $7 per night with no reservations accepted. The camping limit is 2 weeks per year. Group tent camping is $15 a night. Group and cabin camping is by reservation only. For all camp sites except cabins, call 703-221-7181. Group cabin campers should call 703-221-4706. • Other overnight accommodations are available in Triangle and Dumfries.
FOOD & SUPPLIES	Food and supplies are available in Triangle and Dumfries.
FIRST AID/ HOSPITAL	• The Park is on a 911 emergency system. • The nearest hospital is Potomac Hospital in Woodbridge, 9 miles (14.5 km).
GENERAL INFORMATION	• The Park offers good introduction to camping and experiencing the outdoors and cultural resources, such as the Civilian Conservation Corps facilities built in the 1930s. • Information on forest hazards, tips, orienteering and nearby attractions is available at the Visitor Center.

Red Hill Patrick Henry National Memorial

Brookneal, Virginia

Affiliated area. The law office and grave of the fiery Virginia legislator and orator are preserved at this small plantation, including a reconstruction of Patrick Henry's last home, several dependencies and a museum.

MAILING ADDRESS	Red Hill Patrick Henry National Memorial, Rt. 2, Box 127, Brookneal, VA 24528 **Telephone: 804-376-2044**
DIRECTIONS	The Memorial is 5 miles (8 km) east of Brookneal off of Rt. 40.
VISITOR ACTIVITIES	Video, museum, self-guided walking tour of restored law office and home, graveyard.
PERMITS, FEES & LIMITATIONS	The entrance fee is $3 for adults and $1 for students. Group rates are available.
ACCESSIBILITY	The Memorial is not accessible.
CAMPING & LODGING	Overnight accommodations are available in the vicinity.
FOOD & SUPPLIES	Food and supplies are available in the vicinity.

Richmond National Battlefield Park
Richmond, Virginia

Situated at the head of navigation on the James River and only 110 miles (177.4 km) from the Federal capital of Washington, the Confederate capital of Richmond was a military objective from the beginning of the Civil War. On April 3, 1865 the last of 7 major drives to capture the city succeeded.

MAILING ADDRESS
Superintendent, Richmond National Battlefield Park, 3215 East Broad St., Richmond, VA 23223 **Telephone:** 804-226-1981

DIRECTIONS
The Park Visitor Center is on the site of one of the Confederacy's largest hospitals at 3215 East Broad St., in the city of Richmond. Battlefield sites are in 3 counties surrounding Richmond - Henrico, Hanover and Chesterfield counties.

VISITOR ACTIVITIES
• Civil War exhibits, a 12-minute slide show and 30-minute film, self-guided auto tours (rental tapes are available) at the Visitor Center.
• Smaller orientation centers with exhibits are at Cold Harbor and Fort Harvison. These are staffed seasonally. • Hiking trails and interpretive waysides with audio stations augment visitors' experience and understanding. • Battlefield sites are open from dawn to dusk year-round. The Visitor Center is open from **9 a.m. to 5 p.m.**, except Thanksgiving, Dec. 25 and Jan. 1.

PERMITS, FEES & LIMITATIONS
• No fees. • Vehicles are restricted to parking areas and designated roads.

ACCESSIBILITY
The main Visitor Center, restrooms and picnic area are accessible.

CAMPING & LODGING
Lodging is available nearby.

FOOD & SUPPLIES
Food and supplies are available nearby.

FIRST AID/ HOSPITAL
Full medical services in Richmond and vicinity.

Shenandoah National Park
Luray, Virginia

Shenandoah National Park lies along a beautiful section of the Blue Ridge in an area that is successfully returning from agricultural overuse to its original natural beauty in the form of ridges and valleys that are more than 95 percent forested and laced with sparkling streams and waterfalls.

MAILING ADDRESS	Superintendent, Shenandoah National Park, Rt. 4, Box 348, Luray, VA 22835 Telephone: 703-999-2266
DIRECTIONS	The Park's Headquarters is 4 miles (6.4 km) west of Thornton Gap and 4 miles (6.4 km) east of Luray on US 211. Visitor centers are at Dickey Ridge and Big Meadows. Skyline Drive winds through hardwood forest along the crest of the Blue Ridge Mountains.
VISITOR ACTIVITIES	• Driving, horseback riding, picnicking, field trips, campfire programs and nature walks. • Pick up a Park newspaper from any Visitor Center, entrance station or concession lodge. • Facilities include gift shops, service stations, showers and laundry buildings, ice and wood sales, riding stables and self-guiding nature trails. • The Park is always open. Sections of the drive may be closed due to weather or for resource management. All facilities are available in the summer. Some are available in spring and fall.
PERMITS, FEES & LIMITATIONS	• The entrance fee is $5 per private vehicle or $3 per person. Ages 62 and older admitted free. • Vehicles are restricted to public roads. • Commercial trucking is restricted to Park business. Bicycles and other vehicles prohibited on trails. Chains and snow tires may be required in winter.
ACCESSIBILITY	Lodges, campgrounds, picnic grounds and most public buildings are accessible with parking and restrooms. A variety of interpretive activities and literature is also accessible. Further information is available by writing the Park.
CAMPING & LODGING	• Reservations are recommended for camping at Big Meadows May through October for $12 per night. Contact MISTIX, PO Box 85705, San Diego, CA 92138-5705, phone 1-800-365-CAMP. Three other campgrounds are on a first-come, first-served basis for $10 per night. Reservations are accepted for group camping at Dundo Campground. • For lodging information and reservations at lodges in the Park, contact ARA-Virginia Sky-Line Co., Box 727, Luray, VA 22835, phone 1-800-999-4714. • Other overnight accommodations are available in communities near the Park.
FOOD & SUPPLIES	• Meals are served in the Park at Elkwallow, Panorama, Skyland, Big Meadows and Loft Mountain. • Food and supplies are available in the Park at Elkwallow, Big Meadows, Lewis Mountain and Loft Mountain. • Food and supplies are available outside the Park in towns along Hwys. 340, 211 and 33.
FIRST AID/ HOSPITAL	• First aid is available in the Park. • Hospitals are in Front Royal, 6 miles (9.6 km); and Luray, 10 miles (16.1 km).
GENERAL INFORMATION	For your safety - Wear proper footwear when walking on trails. Most visitor injuries are caused by falls. Do your sightseeing from overlooks and trails. Do not feed or approach animals. Stay on trails.

Wolf Trap Farm Park for the Performing Arts

Vienna, Virginia

At this first National Park for the performing arts, Filene Center can accommodate an audience of 6,786, including 3,000 on a sloping lawn in a setting of rolling hills and woods. It features a stagehouse that is 13 stories high and a stage that is 125 feet wide by 60 feet deep (38.1 by 18.3 m).

MAILING ADDRESS	Director, Wolf Trap Farm Park, 1551 Trap Road, Vienna, VA 22182 **Telephone:** 703-255-1800
DIRECTIONS	From downtown Washington, DC, take the George Washington Memorial Parkway to the Capital Beltway (I-495) heading south into Virginia. Exit I-495 at Exit 11B (Tysons Corner-VA Rt. 123). Follow Rt. 123 briefly to Rt. 7 West (Leesburg Pike) and turn right. Travel west on Rt. 7 to Towlston Road. Turn left on Towlston Road at the Wolf Trap Farm Park sign. The Park entrance is 1 mile (1.6 km) from the turn and is well marked. Cars may also enter from the Dulles Toll Road up to 2 hours before performance time only. Take Exit 12B (from I-495) or Exit 67 (from Rt. 66) and follow to Exit 6 (Wolf Trap Exit).
VISITOR ACTIVITIES	• Performances ranging from ballet to pop, free performance previews, free children's programs, picnicking, walking tours of the Filene Center and interpretive programs. • The Park is closed on Dec. 25. • Visitor attractions are closed during fall, winter and early spring. • Children's programs are held during the summer.
PERMITS, FEES & LIMITATIONS	• Tickets are required for most performances. See a local newspaper or call the box office at 703-255-1860 for information on events. • Some permits may be required. • Parking is limited.
ACCESSIBILITY	Arrangements may be made in advance by calling 703-255-1820 (TDD). The Park will also provide hearing loops and wheelchairs upon request. Cart rides from the parking lots are provided in season.
CAMPING & LODGING	Overnight accommodations are available in the surrounding area.
FOOD & SUPPLIES	• Meals are available during the performance season only, prior to performances, in the Park. • Restaurants, food and supplies are available in the surrounding area.
FIRST AID/ HOSPITAL	• A physician is in attendance during the performing season. • The nearest hospital is Reston Hospital Center, Reston, VA.

Washington

1 Coulee Dam National Recreation Area

2 Ebey's Landing National Historical Reserve

3 Fort Vancouver National Historic Site

4 Lake Chelan National Recreation Area

5 Mount Rainier National Park

6 North Cascades National Park

7 Olympic National Park

8 Ross Lake National Recreation Area

9 San Juan Island National Historical Park

10 Whitman Mission National Historic Site

Coulee Dam National Recreation Area

Coulee Dam, Washington

The creation of this sprawling Recreation Area and the area's largest lake, Lake Roosevelt, began with the construction of Grand Coulee Dam in 1941. The Recreation Area now provides opportunities for boating, fishing, swimming, camping, hiking and tours of Fort Spokane and the dam.

MAILING ADDRESS

Coulee Dam National Recreation Area, 1008 Crest Drive, Coulee Dam, WA 99116 Telephone: 509-633-9441

DIRECTIONS

Information about access to the Recreation Area is available from the Headquarters in Coulee Dam.

VISITOR ACTIVITIES

• Water skiing, boating, swimming, bird watching, picnicking, audiovisual programs, interpretive talks and exhibits, fishing and hunting. • Facilities include picnic areas, boat ramps, boat and trailer dump stations, drinking water, bathhouse and ferry service. • Rental boats are available at Keller Ferry, Fort Spokane and Kettle Falls concessionaires. • The Recreation Area is always open. Visitor centers are open daily during the summer and inter-mittently the rest of the year. The Visitor Center at Grand Coulee Dam is closed Thanksgiving, Dec. 25 and Jan. 1. The recreation season is May through October.

PERMITS, FEES & LIMITATIONS

• **No entrance fee.** • Permits for fishing and hunting are available at local sporting goods stores. • Off-road vehicle use is prohibited.

ACCESSIBILITY

Most areas are accessible.

CAMPING & LODGING

• No reservations are accepted for camp sites, which are available for $8 per night at Kettle Falls, Evans, Fort Spokane, Spring Canyon, Keller Ferry, Hunters, Marcus Island, Gifford and Porcupine Bay. • For information about lodging outside the Recreation Area, contact the Chamber of Commerce, Grand Coulee, WA 99133, phone 509-633-0361.

FOOD & SUPPLIES

• Meals are served during the summer at Spring Canyon Campground and Seven Bays Marina. • Food and supplies are available at various marinas. • Food and supplies are available outside the Recreation Area in Grand Coulee, Coulee Dam, Colville, Kettle Falls and Northport.

FIRST AID/ HOSPITAL

• First aid is available in the Recreation Area. • Hospitals are in Grand Coulee, 5 miles (8 km), from the Spring Canyon Campground; Davenport, 25 miles (40.3 km), from Fort Spokane Campground; and Colville, 10 miles (16.1 km), from Kettle Falls Campground.

GENERAL INFORMATION

For your safety - Be alert to avoid floating logs and debris. Be sure to drown campfires. Check for drawdown levels on the lake.

Ebey's Landing National Historical Reserve
Whidbey Island, Washington

Ebey's Landing is the country's first Historical Reserve - a rural historic district established to preserve and protect an unbroken historical record from 19th century exploration and settlement in Puget Sound to the present. The Reserve includes historic farms on natural prairies, dramatic coastal beaches and bluffs, and stunning vistas of the Puget Sound and the Cascade and Olympic mountain ranges.

MAILING ADDRESS

Trust Board of Ebey's Landing National Historical Reserve, PO Box 774, Coupeville, WA 98239 **Telephone: 206-678-6084**

DIRECTIONS

There are several routes to the Reserve. One option is to drive onto Whidbey Island via Hwy. 20 by taking I-5 and following signs to Whidbey Island and then to Coupeville. Another option is to take the Keystone Ferry from Port Townsend, which is located on the Olympic Peninsula. The Keystone Ferry docks within the Reserve next to Fort Casey State Park, several miles from Coupeville. The Mukilteo Ferry, originating near Everett (north of Seattle), docks in Clinton on south Whidbey Island. Drive north for 30 miles (48.3 km) on Hwy. 525/20 after leaving the ferry and follow the signs to Coupeville. Another alternative is to fly into Oak Harbor, 10 miles (16.1 km) from Coupeville, via Harbor Airlines. Call 1-800-359-3220.

VISITOR ACTIVITIES

• Hiking, picnicking, bird and wildlife watching, scuba diving, fishing, kite flying, boating, photography and beach activities. • Visitors may visit a lighthouse, explore military forts and blockhouses, visit the historical museum in Coupeville, take a driving/bicycling tour of the Reserve or a walking tour of Coupeville's waterfront and historic structures.

PERMITS, FEES & LIMITATIONS

• No entrance fee. • Small fees may be charged at the historical museum or state parks. • Property outside of Reserve waysides, state park boundaries or town and county parks is privately owned. Respect these private lands and do not trespass.

ACCESSIBILITY

Select areas within the state parks and some of the Reserve's waysides are accessible. For more information, contact the Reserve's office.

CAMPING & LODGING

• Camp sites are available in the Reserve at Fort Ebey State Park, Fort Casey State Park or Rhododendron Park. Sites are available on a first-come, first-served basis for $8 a night at state parks. There are no hookups. • Camping is also available at Deception Pass and South Whidbey Island state parks on Whidbey Island. • Lodging is available in Coupeville and in the Whidbey Island towns of Oak Harbor, Freeland, Clinton and Langley.

FOOD & SUPPLIES

Food and supplies are available in Coupeville, Prairie Center and Oak Harbor.

FIRST AID/ HOSPITAL

A hospital is at 101 N. Main St., in Coupeville.

GENERAL INFORMATION

A free brochure is available at stores and public buildings, or may be requested by writing to the Reserve's Trust Board.

Fort Vancouver National Historic Site

Vancouver, Washington

The structures at Fort Vancouver National Historic Site are reconstructions based on archaeological discoveries and documentary material depicting the Fort when it was the Columbia Department headquarters for the Hudson's Bay Company's fur trading enterprise and the representative of Great Britain's business and governmental interests in the Oregon Country.

MAILING ADDRESS

Superintendent, Fort Vancouver National Historic Site, 612 E. Reserve St., Vancouver, WA 98661 **Telephone: 206-696-7655**

DIRECTIONS

To reach the Site, turn off I-5 at the East Mill Plain Boulevard interchange and follow the signs to the Visitor Center on East Evergreen Boulevard.

VISITOR ACTIVITIES

• Interpretive exhibits and tours of reconstructed buildings at the Fort site.
• Facilities include parking and restrooms at the Visitor Center and the Fort, and an information and sales desk. • The Site is open daily, except Thanksgiving, Dec. 25 and Jan. 1, from 9 a.m. to 5 p.m., with shortened hours during the winter. • Special events include Queen Victoria's Birthday in May, Brigade Encampment in July, Candle Lantern Tour in October and a Christmas Open House in December.

PERMITS, FEES & LIMITATIONS

The entrance fee is $2 per adult or $4 per family. Ages 16 or younger admitted free.

ACCESSIBILITY

The Visitor Center, 3 other buildings and restrooms at the Fort are accessible.

CAMPING & LODGING

Overnight accommodations are available in Vancouver.

FOOD & SUPPLIES

Food and supplies are available in Vancouver.

FIRST AID/ HOSPITAL

• First aid is available in the Site. • The nearest hospital is Vancouver Memorial Hospital, 2 miles (3.2 km).

GENERAL INFORMATION

For your safety - Watch your step at the Fort.

Lake Chelan National Recreation Area

Chelan, Washington   See Climatable No. 36

Lake Chelan rests in a glacially carved trough in the Cascade Range in northwestern Washington. At 1,500 feet (457.2 m), it is one of the nation's deepest lakes offering opportunities for boating and fishing.

MAILING ADDRESS

Superintendent, 2105 Highway 20, Sedro Woolley, WA 98284 **Telephone:** 206-856-5700

DIRECTIONS

The main access to Stehekin in the Recreation Area is by boat or float plane from the town of Chelan on Hwy. 97. There is no road access into Stehekin. Service is provided by Lake Chelan Boat Co., Chelan, WA 98816, phone 509-682-2224. Daily boat service is maintained from April 15 to Oct. 15. From Oct. 16 to April 14, boats go on Sundays, Mondays, Wednesdays and Fridays. There is no Sunday boat from Jan. 1 to Feb. 14. Air service is available for charter year-round, weather permitting, from Chelan Airways, Chelan, WA 98816, phone 509-682-5555.

VISITOR ACTIVITIES

• Interpretive exhibits, guided and self-guiding tours, picnicking, hiking, mountain climbing, horseback riding, boating, fishing, hunting and commercial river rafting. • Facilities include a picnic area, boat and bicycle rentals, a post office, commercial buses and shuttle bus service. • The Recreation Area is always open. Guided walks and programs are held from late June to early September. The shuttle bus operates from May 15 to Oct. 15.

PERMITS, FEES & LIMITATIONS

• No entrance fee. • The shuttle bus fee is $10. Reservations are necessary for the shuttle bus. Call 206-857-5700 for information on the shuttle bus and commercial buses operating out of Stehekin. • Backcountry permits are required and available at Ranger Stations at Stehekin, Chelan and Marblemount. • Special permits are required for livestock use.

CAMPING & LODGING

• Backcountry, cross-country and trail camping requires a permit. No permits required for boat camps. Reservations are required by mail. Write for more information to North Cascades National Park Service Complex, Wilderness District Office, 728 Ranger Station Road, Marblemount, WA 98267. • Lodge rooms and housekeeping facilities are available on a seasonal basis. Contact North Cascades Lodge, Stehekin, WA 98852, phone 509-682-4711. • Various private cabins are for rent in the Recreation Area. • Other overnight accommodations are available in Chelan.

FOOD & SUPPLIES

• Meals are served at North Cascades Lodge and other facilities. • Supplies are also available at North Cascades Lodge. • Food and supplies are available in Chelan.

**FIRST AID/
HOSPITAL**

• First aid is available at Ranger Stations. • The nearest hospital is in Chelan, 50 miles (80.6 km).

**GENERAL
INFORMATION**

• See the listings in this book for North Cascades National Park and Ross Lake National Recreation Area, the other 2 areas of the North Cascades National Park Service Complex. • **For your safety** - In the backcountry, hang all food out of the reach of bears. Stream crossings can be hazardous. Check conditions with a Ranger before starting out. Crossing snowfields may require special equipment.

Mount Rainier National Park

Ashford, Washington   See Climatable No. 37

Mount Rainier is a volcano born of fire and built up above the surrounding forests, glaciers and waterfalls by repeated eruptions and successive flows of lava. The deposited nutrient-rich ash and pumice layers in the soil support an abundance of wildflowers.

**MAILING
ADDRESS**

Superintendent, Mount Rainier National Park, Tahoma Woods, Star Route, Ashford, WA 98304 **Telephone:** 206-569-2211

DIRECTIONS

The Paradise Visitor Center is 74 miles (119.3 km) southeast of Tacoma on Rt. 7 to Elbe, then Rt. 706 to Longmire. It is 98 miles (158 km) southeast of Seattle and 87 miles (140.3 km) west of Yakima.

**VISITOR
ACTIVITIES**

• Backcountry hiking and mountain climbing, snowshoeing, cross-country skiing, picnicking, winter sports, interpretive programs and wildlife watching. • Facilities include exhibits at the visitor centers, restrooms, hiking trails, picnic areas, cross-country ski rentals and lessons, equipment rentals and nature trails. • The Park is always open. Many Park roads are closed from late November through June or July. • Conducted climbs are offered by Rainier Mountaineering, Inc., 201 St. Helens, Tacoma, WA 98042, phone 206-627-6242. From June to September, they are located in Paradise, WA 98398, phone 206-569-2227.

**PERMITS, FEES
& LIMITATIONS**

• The entrance fee is $5 per vehicle or $3 per person. • Permits for backcountry camping are required. They are available at Ranger stations and visitor centers. • Vehicles are restricted to public roads. No commercial vehicles (other than buses) allowed.

ACCESSIBILITY

Paradise Visitor Center is fully accessible. Other visitor centers have limited access. The Longmire Museum and lodges are accessible. Cougar Rock Campground has a limited access camp site and restroom. Self-guiding trails have limited access. Wheelchairs are available for short-time use at visitor centers.

**CAMPING &
LODGING**

- Camping in developed camp sites is available for $6 to $8 per night. Reservations are not accepted for individual sites. Group sites may be reserved by contacting the Chief Ranger's office at the Park address.
- Lodging is available at the National Park Inn at Longmire year-round and at Paradise Inn from late May through early October. For information, contact Mount Rainier Guest Service, Star Route, Ashford, WA 98304, phone 206-569-2275. • Other overnight accommodations are available in Ashford, Alder and Elbe.

**FOOD &
SUPPLIES**

- Meals are served in the Park at Longmire, Paradise Inn, Paradise Visitor Center and Sunrise. • Food and supplies are available at Longmire and Sunrise. • Food and supplies are available outside the Park in Ashford, Elbe, Packwood and Enumclaw.

**FIRST AID/
HOSPITAL**

- First aid is available in the Park. • Hospitals are in Enumclaw, 45 miles (72.5 km); Morton, 40 miles (64.5 km); and Puyallup, 40 miles (64.5 km).

**GENERAL
INFORMATION**

For your safety - In the backcountry, hike only in groups. Be prepared for sudden weather changes. Bring your own shelter.

North Cascades National Park

Sedro Wooley, Washington

North Cascades National Park contains some of America's most breathtakingly beautiful scenery - high jagged peaks, ridges, slopes, countless cascading waterfalls and about 318 glaciers - within its 505,000 acres.

**MAILING
ADDRESS**

Superintendent, North Cascades National Park, 2105 Highway 20, Sedro Woolley, WA 98284 Telephone: 206-856-5700

DIRECTIONS

Access to the North Cascades area from Burlington on the west and Twisp on the east follows WA 20 with branch routes to Baker Lake and Cascade River. Hiking access and roadside views of the northwest corner are available from WA 542 east from Bellingham.

**VISITOR
ACTIVITIES**

- Backcountry, viewing scenery, hiking, mountain climbing, horseback riding, fishing, auto tours, boating, wildlife and bird watching. • Facilities include launching ramps, hiking trails, horse and mule rentals nearby, and professional guide and packtrain services. • The Park is always open. Snow conditions prevent backcountry access in the winter. A portion of Hwy. 20, the North Cascades Highway, closes during the winter. • A new Visitor Center is open at Newhalem, WA, 206-386-4495.

**PERMITS, FEES
& LIMITATIONS**

- No entrance fee. • Vehicles are restricted to maintained roads.
- Adequate feed should be carried for horses. Grazing is not permitted in the

Park. A permit is required for livestock use. • Free permits for backcountry use are available at Park Offices or Ranger Stations and by mail through the Wilderness District Office in Marblemount. Call 206-873-4500 for permit information. • A state fishing license, available locally, is required.

ACCESSIBILITY

Sedro Woolley Headquarters, Visitor Center, restrooms, and some overlooks and campgrounds are accessible.

CAMPING & LODGING

• No reservations are available for camp sites. • For information on lodging in the Park, contact North Cascades Lodge, Stehekin, WA 98852. • The Chambers of Commerce for the counties and towns surrounding the Park have information on accommodations.

FOOD & SUPPLIES

Food and supplies are available in the Marblemount, Newhalem and Stehekin areas.

FIRST AID/ HOSPITAL

• First aid is available at Ranger stations. • The nearest hospital is in Sedro Woolley.

GENERAL INFORMATION

• See listings in this book for the other 2 units of the North Cascades group: Lake Chelan and Ross Lake. • **For your safety** - In the backcountry, hang food out of the reach of bears. Check stream conditions before starting trips. Crossing snowfields may require special equipment.

Olympic National Park

Port Angeles, Washington   See Climatable No. 38

Olympic National Park's mountain wilderness contains the finest remnant of Pacific Northwest rain forest, active glaciers, teeming wildlife - such as the rare Roosevelt elk and Olympic marmot - deep valleys, lush meadows and 57 miles (91.9 km) of wild, scenic ocean shore.

MAILING ADDRESS

Superintendent, Olympic National Park, 600 East Park Ave., Port Angeles, WA 98362 **Telephone:** 206-452-0330

DIRECTIONS

The Olympic Park Visitor Center is in Port Angeles. The Hoh Visitor Center is 32 miles (51.6 km) southeast of Forks.

VISITOR ACTIVITIES

• Interpretive and audiovisual programs, auto tours, bird and wildlife watching, picnicking, nature walks, hiking, mountain climbing, fishing, swimming, skiing and snowshoeing. • Interpretive tours are given July 1 through Labor Day. • The Park is always open. Holiday closings for buildings are Dec. 25 and Jan. 1. Visitor centers, including bookstores, restrooms and telephones, are open from 9 a.m. to 4 p.m., in winter with hours extended to 6 p.m., in summer. Roads in high elevations are usually open from June 1 to Oct. 1. High elevation trails are normally open from July 15 to Oct. 1.

PERMITS, FEES & LIMITATIONS

• The entrance fee is $4 per vehicle or $2 per person. An annual Park pass is available for $10. • Vehicles are restricted to roads. • Backcountry permits are available at all Ranger stations and most trailheads.

ACCESSIBILITY

An accessibility guide is available at visitor centers.

CAMPING & LODGING

• Camping in developed sites is $8 per night. Camping is limited to 14 days. Individual camp sites cannot be reserved. Group camp sites may be reserved by contacting Ranger stations. • Lodging is available and may be reserved by facility: Kalaloch Lodge, Inc., 206-962-2271; Log Cabin Resort, 206-928-3245; Lake Crescent Lodge, 206-928-3211; and Sol Duc Hot Springs Resort, 206-327-3583. • For information on accommodations near the Park, contact the Olympic Peninsula Resort and Hotel Association, Coleman Ferry Terminal, Seattle, WA 98104.

FOOD & SUPPLIES

• Meals are served in the Park at Hurricane Ridge, Sol Duc, Fairholm, Kalaloch and Lake Crescent. • There are small grocery stores at some lodges in the Park. • There are supermarkets outside the Park in Sequim, Port Angeles, Forks, Shelton and Aberdeen.

FIRST AID/ HOSPITAL

• First aid is available at most Ranger stations. • Hospitals are in Port Angeles, Forks, Shelton and Aberdeen-Hoquiam.

Ross Lake National Recreation Area

Sedro Woolley, Washington   See Climatable No. 36

Ross Lake National Recreation Area provides the corridor for the popular North Cascades Highway and includes the 12,000-acre Ross Lake, 910-acre Diablo Lake and 210-acre Gorge Lake, which provide water gateways to the more remote areas.

MAILING ADDRESS

Superintendent, Ross Lake National Recreation Area, 2105 Highway 20, Sedro Woolley, WA 98284 **Telephone:** 206-856-5700

DIRECTIONS

Access to the Recreation Area is via WA 20 from Burlington on the west and Winthrop on the east. The north end of Ross Lake is reached by a 38-mile (61.2 km) gravel road exiting from the Trans-Canada Highway near Hope, British Columbia. There is no road access from WA 20 to the south end of Ross Lake.

VISITOR ACTIVITIES

• Hiking, boating, canoeing, viewing scenery, rock climbing, wildlife and bird watching, auto tours, backcountry and horseback riding. • Facilities include boat rentals, launching ramps and wayside exhibits. • The Recreation Area is always open. Information offices are closed Thanksgiving, Dec. 25 and Jan. 1. Closings on other holidays vary. WA 20 and campgrounds except Goodell Creek are closed in winter.

PERMITS, FEES & LIMITATIONS

• No entrance fee. • Backcountry permits are available at all Ranger stations or by mail through the Wilderness District in Marblemount. Call 206-873-4500 for permit information. • A state fishing license is required. • There is a 1 vehicle limit at each camp site. Vehicles are restricted to maintained roads. • Grazing is not permitted. A special permit is required for livestock use.

ACCESSIBILITY

Call the Recreation Area for accessibility details.

CAMPING & LODGING

• No reservations are available for camp sites. Sites at Colonial Creek and Newhalem Creek campgrounds are $7 per night and $5 per night at Goodell Creek Campground. • For lodging information, contact the Ross Lake Resort, Rockport, WA 98283, phone 206-386-4437. • Overnight accommodations outside the Recreation Area are available in Marblemount, 8 miles (12.9 km); and Concrete, 28 miles (45.1 km).

FOOD & SUPPLIES

Food and supplies are available in Newhalem, Marblemount and Concrete.

FIRST AID/ HOSPITAL

• First aid is available in the Recreation Area. • The nearest hospital is in Sedro Woolley, 50 miles (80.6 km).

GENERAL INFORMATION

• See listings in this book for the 2 other units of the North Cascades group: Lake Chelan and North Cascades National Park. • Seattle City Light offers tours of hydro-electric projects. For information, contact the Skagit Tour desk at Seattle City Light, 1015 Third Ave., Seattle, WA, phone 206-684-3030. • **For your safety** - In the backcountry, hang all food out of the reach of bears. Check stream conditions with a Ranger before starting trips. Crossing snowfields may require special equipment.

San Juan Island National Historical Park

San Juan Island, Washington

San Juan Island in the summer of 1859 was an international tinderbox as military forces of Great Britain and the United States confronted each other in a crisis precipitated by the nations' dual claims to the island and the death of a Hudson's Bay Company pig at the hands of an American farmer.

MAILING ADDRESS

Superintendent, San Juan Island National Historical Park, PO Box 429, Friday Harbor, WA 98250 **Telephone:** 206-378-2240

DIRECTIONS

San Juan Island is reached by Washington State Ferries from Anacortes, WA, 83 miles (133.8 km) north of Seattle or from Sidney, British Columbia, 15 miles (24.1 km) north of Victoria. Regular commercial air service is also available. Park Headquarters and information center is in Friday Harbor at

125 Spring St. Other visitor contact stations are at American and British Camps.

VISITOR ACTIVITIES

• Hiking, picnicking, historical reenactments, interpretive walks and exhibits, and wildlife and bird watching. • Friday Harbor Visitor Center hours are 8 a.m. to 6 p.m., in summer and 8 a.m. to 4:30 p.m., in winter. American Camp Visitor Center hours are 8 a.m. to 6 p.m., in summer and 8 a.m. to 4:30 p.m., Thursday through Sunday in winter. British Camp buildings are open from mid-May through mid-September. Visitor centers are closed on Federal holidays from November through February. The Park is closed from 11 p.m. until sunrise.

PERMITS, FEES & LIMITATIONS

• No fees. • Horseback riding permits are available at Headquarters in Friday Harbor. British Camp is closed to horse use. • No off-road vehicles are permitted. • Small fires are allowed at Fourth of July Picnic Area below the driftwood line. Fires at South Beach are restricted to fire pits. No fires are allowed at British Camp. • Guss Island is closed to the public. • The tidelands along the historic waterfront at British Camp are closed to clamming.

ACCESSIBILITY

There are limited accessible trails and facilities. Contact the Park to arrange for special access needs.

CAMPING & LODGING

Overnight accommodations are available in Friday Harbor and around the island.

FOOD & SUPPLIES

Food and supplies are available in Friday Harbor.

FIRST AID/ HOSPITAL

• First aid is available in the Park. • A medical clinic is in Friday Harbor, 6 miles (9.6 km) from American Camp, 9 miles (14.5 km) from British Camp.

GENERAL INFORMATION

For your safety - Watch your step, especially at American Camp. Swimming is not advisable due to strong currents and cold water.

Whitman Mission National Historic Site

Walla Walla, Washington

In 1836, Marcus and Narcissa Whitman founded a mission among the Cayuse Indians at Waiilatpu, meaning "place of the people of the rye grass," where they worked to spread the Protestant faith and established an important station on the Oregon Trail for weary travelers.

MAILING ADDRESS

Superintendent, Whitman Mission National Historic Site, Rt. 2, Box 247, Walla Walla, WA 99362 Telephone: 509-529-2761

DIRECTIONS

The Site is 7 miles (11.3 km) west of Walla Walla on US 12.

Washington

VISITOR ACTIVITIES

• Interpretive exhibits, picnicking, self-guided walking tour with wayside exhibits and cultural demonstrations in the summer. • A 10-minute slide/sound presentation is shown every half hour on the hour and half hour in the Visitor Center. • The Visitor Center is open daily from **8 a.m. to 4:30 p.m.**, in the winter with hours extended to **6 p.m.**, in the summer. Site grounds are open until dusk. The Site is closed Thanksgiving, Dec. 25 and Jan. 1.

PERMITS, FEES & LIMITATIONS

The entrance fee is $2 per adult ages 17 to 61 with a maximum of $4 per family.

ACCESSIBILITY

A wheelchair is available for loan. A large type version of the Site brochure is available. Scripts for the 10-minute slide program and outdoor wayside exhibits are available.

CAMPING & LODGING

• Camping is available nearby at the Fort Walla Walla Campground.
• Lodging is available in Walla Walla.

FOOD & SUPPLIES

Food and supplies are available in Walla Walla and College Place.

FIRST AID/ HOSPITAL

Medical services are available in Walla Walla.

West Virginia

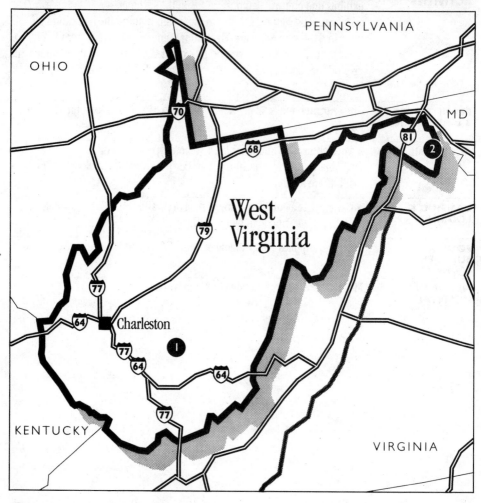

1 Gauley River National Recreation Area

2 Harpers Ferry National Historical Park

Gauley River National Recreation Area
Southern West Virginia

Gauley River National Recreation Area includes 25 miles (40.3 km) of free-flowing Gauley River and 6 miles (9.6 km) of the Meadow River that run through scenic gorges and valleys containing a wide variety of natural and cultural features. There are several Class VI rapids.

MAILING ADDRESS

Gauley River National Recreation Area, PO Box 246, Glen Jean, WV 25846
Telephone: 304-465-0508

DIRECTIONS

Access to the Recreation Area is via Rt. 129 at the Summersville Dam off of Rt. 19. Other access points include Carnifex Ferry Battlefield State Park off of Rt. 129 and the Swiss Road off of Rt. 39. The Recreation Area is between Summersville Dam and the town of Swiss, WV.

VISITOR ACTIVITIES

• Whitewater rafting, kayaking, hunting, fishing and trapping. • Hiking trails are accessible from Carnifex Ferry Battlefield State Park. • The main Gauley River rafting season consists of 5, 4-day weekends and 1, 2-day weekend from mid-September through mid-October. At this time, water is released from Summersville Dam to bring the lake to its winter level.

PERMITS, FEES & LIMITATIONS

• No fees. • Commercial rafting requires a license from the West Virginia Division of Natural Resources. • Private boaters need the skill to negotiate Class V plus rapids.

ACCESSIBILITY

Accessible facilities are available nearby at the state park and Summersville Dam.

CAMPING & LODGING

• Camping is available at Summersville Lake and at private campgrounds. • Lodging is available at Hawk's Nest and Babcock state parks; and at private hotels, motels and inns in Summersville, Glen Ferris, Fayetteville, Ansted, Lookout and Hico. Bed and breakfasts are available in many area towns.

FOOD & SUPPLIES

• Food and supplies are available seasonally from concessions at Summersville Lake. • There are stores in small towns nearby, including Mount Nebo, Gauley Bridge and Summersville.

FIRST AID/ HOSPITAL

Hospitals are in Summersville and Oak Hill.

GENERAL INFORMATION

• Most land along the Gauley River is privately owned. • A scenic overlook is in Carnifex Ferry Battlefield State Park. Battle reenactments take place annually at Carnifex Ferry, and a Civil War museum is open in the summer.

West Virginia

Harpers Ferry National Historical Park

Harpers Ferry, West Virginia

By mid-19th century, Harpers Ferry contained 3,000 inhabitants and had become an important arms-producing center and transportation link between east and west, but it was John Brown's 1859 raid and the Civil War that thrust the town into national prominence.

MAILING ADDRESS
Superintendent, Harpers Ferry National Historical Park, PO Box 65, Harpers Ferry, WV 25425 **Telephone:** 304-535-6223

DIRECTIONS
The Park is 65 miles (104.8 km) northwest of Washington, DC, and 20 miles (32.2 km) southwest of Frederick, MD, via US 340.

VISITOR ACTIVITIES
• Exhibits on each theme, hiking trails and self-guided walking tours.
• The Park is open daily, except Dec. 25, from **8 a.m. to 5 p.m.**, with hours extended to **6 p.m.**, in the summer. • Write for a schedule of events, such as living history demonstrations and special tours.

PERMITS, FEES & LIMITATIONS
• The entrance fee is $5 per vehicle or $3 per person. • Rock climbing registration is required for Maryland Heights.

ACCESSIBILITY
Restrooms, picnic areas, the Visitor Center, Information Center and some exhibits and trails are accessible. Transportation is available.

CAMPING & LODGING
Camping and lodging are available near the Park.

FOOD & SUPPLIES
Food and supplies are available in the towns of Harpers Ferry, Bolivar and Charles Town.

FIRST AID/ HOSPITAL
• First aid is available at the Ranger Station. • The nearest hospital is in Charles Town, 7 miles (11.2 km).

Wisconsin

1 Apostle Islands National Lakeshore
2 Ice Age National Scientific Reserve

Apostle Islands National Lakeshore

Bayfield, Wisconsin

These forested, sheltered islands on the world's most expansive freshwater lake, Lake Superior, offer numerous water and wilderness recreation pursuits in an area with a rich history.

MAILING ADDRESS
Superintendent, Apostle Islands National Lakeshore, Rt. 1, Box 4, Bayfield, WI 54814 **Telephone:** 715-779-3397

DIRECTIONS
The Headquarters Visitor Center is off of WI 13 in Bayfield, 23 miles (37 km) north of Ashland, WI, and 90 miles (145.1 km) east of Duluth, MN. Mainland visitor centers are accessible by car. Islands in the National Lakeshore are accessible by private boat and through the Apostle Islands Cruise Service and Apostle Islands Water Taxi, Inc.

VISITOR ACTIVITIES
• Sailing, boating, sea kayaking, hiking, picnicking, swimming, scuba diving, interpretive talks and tours, sport fishing and excursion boat trips.
• The Headquarters Visitor Center has exhibits and audiovisual programs. It is open daily, except Thanksgiving, Dec. 25 and Jan. 1, from 8 a.m. to 6 p.m., Memorial Day through Labor Day; daily from 8 a.m. to 5 p.m., Labor Day through the last weekend in October; and Monday to Friday from 8 a.m. to 4:30 p.m., the rest of the year. • Evening programs, nature walks and tours of historic commercial fisheries and lighthouses are conducted during the summer.

PERMITS, FEES & LIMITATIONS
• No entrance fee. • A free backcountry camping permit is required.
• A free dive permit is required for scuba diving. • Permits are available at visitor centers.

ACCESSIBILITY
The Headquarters Visitor Center in Bayfield is accessible. The Apostle Islands Cruise Service excursion boat is accessible. Visitors traveling through the islands by boat will find the visitor center at Stockton Island and the Manitou Fish Camp accessible.

CAMPING & LODGING
• Backcountry camping is available on 18 of 21 islands in the National Lakeshore. Permits are available on a first-come, first-served basis. Group camp sites may be reserved by calling 715-779-3397. Island camp sites are accessible by boat only. • Lodging is available in Bayfield, Washburn, Ashland, Cornucopia and on Madeline Island.

FOOD & SUPPLIES
Food and supplies are available nearby in Bayfield, Washburn, Cornucopia, Red Cliff, Ashland and on Madeline Island.

FIRST AID/ HOSPITAL
• First aid is available at Ranger stations. • The nearest hospital is in Ashland.

Wisconsin

GENERAL INFORMATION

• Summer temperatures average 75-80°F during the day and 55°F at night. Summer weather can change rapidly and become violent. • Small open boats are not recommended for inter-island use. • Winter temperatures of -20°F are not uncommon. Lake ice conditions vary. Extreme caution is required for crossing ice. • Biting insects are common from early May to mid-August. Black bears are found on several islands. Campers must keep camp sites clean and hang all food. • Wells are provided on some islands, but campers should be prepared to boil or filter lake water. • The Red Cliff Indian Reservation is 3 miles (4.8 km) north of Bayfield and is home to 600 Chippewa Indians. • Madeline Island, the largest Apostle Island, is not in the National Lakeshore. It can be reached by a 20-minute car ferry ride from Bayfield. Big Bay State Park and the Madeline Island Historical Museum are 2 of the island's attractions.

Ice Age National Scientific Reserve

Wisconsin

Affiliated area. The Ice Age National Scientific Reserve was established to preserve select glacial landforms and landscapes as evidence of the Wisconsinan glacial stage when much of the northern United States from the Atlantic coast to the Rocky Mountains was covered by ice as recently as 12,000 years ago. It is the first National Scientific Reserve.

MAILING ADDRESS

Wisconsin Department of Natural Resources, PO Box 7921, Madison, WI 53707 **Telephone:** 608-266-2181

DIRECTIONS

There are 9 separate units of the Reserve across the state from Lake Michigan on the east to the St. Croix River on the Minnesota-Wisconsin border. Five of the 9 units are operational - The Kettle Moraine State Forest, Devil's Lake, Mill Bluff, Interstate Parks and the Horicon Marsh Wildlife Area. Devil's Lake and Mill Bluff are accessible from I-90-94. Horicon is accessible from WI 33. Kettle Moraine is accessible from WI 67, which runs through the unit. Access to Interstate Unit is from US 8 and WI 35.

VISITOR ACTIVITIES

• Interpretive exhibits, auto tours, hiking, fishing, swimming, picnicking, wildlife watching, naturalist services and cross-country skiing. • Facilities include scenic drives, hiking trails, beaches, picnic areas, restrooms, ski trails, visitor centers at Kettle Moraine, Interstate and Chippawa Moraine, and a Nature Center at Devil's Lake. • Most parks are open from 6 a.m. to 11 p.m., daily. Naturalist activities are curtailed at Mill Bluff during the off-season, but are offered year-round at Kettle Moraine, Devil's Lake, Interstate, Horicon Marsh and Chippawa Moraine.

PERMITS, FEES & LIMITATIONS

• Vehicle use fees are $2 for 1 hour, $4 per day or $15 annually for Wisconsin residents, and $6 per day or $24 annually for non-residents.

• A Wisconsin fishing license, available locally or from the Department of Natural Resources, is required.

ACCESSIBILITY

Camping, picnicking, Kettle Moraine, Devil's Lake, Interstate and Mill Bluff are accessible.

CAMPING & LODGING

• Camping information is available by contacting Devil's Lake at 608-356-8301; Northern Kettle Moraine at 414-626-2116; Interstate at 715-483-3747; and Mill Bluff at 608-427-6692. • Overnight accommodations are available outside the Reserve in Baraboo, Campbellsport, St. Croix Falls, Horicon and other towns.

FOOD & SUPPLIES

• Food and supplies are available at Kettle Moraine and Devil's Lake. • Food and supplies are also available nearby in Baraboo, Campbellsport, St. Croix Falls, Horicon and other nearby towns.

FIRST AID/ HOSPITAL

• First aid is available in the Reserve. • Hospitals are in Fond du Lac, Baraboo, Campbellsport, St. Croix Falls and other nearby communities.

GENERAL INFORMATION

For your safety - When hiking, stay on designated trails. Swim only in authorized areas when lifeguards are on duty.

Wyoming

1 Devils Tower National Monument

2 Fort Laramie National Historic Site

3 Fossil Butte National Monument

4 Grand Teton National Park

5 John D. Rockefeller, Jr. Memorial Parkway

6 Yellowstone National Park

Wyoming

Devils Tower National Monument

Devils Tower, Wyoming

Once the core of an ancient volcano, Devils Tower rises 867 feet (264.3 m) from its base and is surrounded by the pine forests of the Black Hills and the grasslands of the rolling plains.

MAILING ADDRESS

Superintendent, Devils Tower National Monument, PO Box 8, Devils Tower, WY 82714 **Telephone:** 307-467-5283

DIRECTIONS

The Monument entrance, off of WY 24, is 7 miles (11.2 km) north of US 14; 28 miles (45.1 km) northwest of Sundance, WY; 33 miles (53.2 km) northeast of Moorcroft, WY; and 52 miles (83.8 km) southwest of Belle Fourche, SD. The Visitor Center is 3 miles (4.8 km) from the Monument's entrance and close to the Tower.

VISITOR ACTIVITIES

• Interpretive exhibits, photography, walking, hiking, mountain climbing, picnicking, fishing, and bird and wildlife watching. • Facilities include parking and restrooms at the Visitor Center, a picnic area and administration office. • The Monument is open all year. The Visitor Center is open from April through October.

PERMITS, FEES & LIMITATIONS

• The entrance fee is $4 per vehicle or $2 per person for ages 17 to 61. • Climbing permits are required. • Vehicles are restricted to designated roads.

ACCESSIBILITY

The restrooms in the picnic area are accessible. Campground Loop A and the administration building are accessible. Campground Loop B has 1 accessible camp site. Several other sites have picnic tables that are accessible. The Visitor Center is accessible, but the restrooms are not. Trails are steep and narrow.

CAMPING & LODGING

• No reservations are accepted for camp sites. Sites are available for $7 per night with a 14-day limit in the summer. • Other overnight accommodations are available outside the Monument in Sundance; Hulett, 11 miles (17.7 km); and Moorcroft.

FOOD & SUPPLIES

Food and supplies are available within 2 miles (3.2 km) of the campground.

FIRST AID/ HOSPITAL

• First aid is available in the Monument. • The nearest hospital is in Sundance.

GENERAL INFORMATION

For your safety - Be cautious of rattlesnakes. Stay clear of prairie dogs, which carry fleas and can bite.

Wyoming

Fort Laramie National Historic Site

Fort Laramie, Wyoming

As America expanded westward, this outpost in the Wyoming wilderness on the Laramie River near its confluence with the Platte played a crucial role in the transformation of the West, first as a fur-trading center, then as a military garrison along the Oregon Trail.

MAILING ADDRESS

Superintendent, Fort Laramie National Historic Site, Fort Laramie, WY 82212 **Telephone:** 307-837-2221

DIRECTIONS

The Site is 3 miles (4.8 km) southwest of the town of Fort Laramie, on Rt. 160.

VISITOR ACTIVITIES

• Visitor Center/Museum containing exhibits, a bookstore and an audiovisual program, is open daily from **8 a.m. to 4:30 p.m.**, except Thanksgiving, Dec. 25 and Jan. 1. From mid-May to late September, Visitor Center hours are extended to **7 p.m.** • The Fort grounds are open daily until dusk. • Self-guided tours of the parade ground in winter. • Summer interpretive program includes Fort tours, living history demonstrations, historic weapons demonstrations and special events. • A summer schedule of events is available May 1. • Picnic area is available.

PERMITS, FEES & LIMITATIONS

• The **entrance fee** is $1 per person or $4 per family (under age 16 or over age 62 admitted free). • Vehicles are confined to parking area and paved roads.

ACCESSIBILITY

The Visitor Center and the ground floors of all buildings are accessible. An accessible restroom is available in the Cavalry Barracks. Electric cart tours of the parade ground are sometimes available, staffing levels permitting - check at the Visitor Center.

CAMPING & LODGING

Campgrounds and motels are available in the nearby communities of Fort Laramie, 3 miles (4.8 km); Lingle, 10 miles (16.1 km); Guernsey, 13 miles (20.9 km); and Torrington, 20 miles (32.2 km).

FOOD & SUPPLIES

• Refreshments are available in the Enlisted Men's Bar during the summer. • Food and supplies are available in Fort Laramie, Guernsey, Lingle and Torrington.

FIRST AID/ HOSPITAL

• First aid is available at the Visitor Center. • The nearest hospital is in Torrington.

Fossil Butte National Monument

Kemmerer, Wyoming

Paleontologists and visitors alike can discover the past at Fossil Butte National Monument, which preserves a flat-topped rock that stands where the center of ancient Fossil Lake once was. The butte contains a remarkable number and broad spectrum of fish, insect and plant fossils.

MAILING ADDRESS
Superintendent, Fossil Butte National Monument, PO Box 592, Kemmerer, WY 83101 Telephone: 307-877-4455

DIRECTIONS
The Monument is in southwestern Wyoming, 14 miles (22.5 km) west of Kemmerer on US 30.

VISITOR ACTIVITIES
• Fossil exhibits, video programs, hiking, picnicking, and wildlife and bird watching. • A 2.5-mile (4 km) interpretive trail and a 1.5-mile (2.4 km) hiking trail. • The Visitor Center is open daily, except for winter holidays, from September to May from **8 a.m. to 4:30 p.m.**, and June to August from **8 a.m. to 7 p.m.** Park roads north of the Visitor Center are usually closed from November to early May. • Write for schedules of special events, guided hikes, walks and evening programs.

PERMITS, FEES & LIMITATIONS
• No fees. • All vehicles restricted to designated roads. • Rain or snow may make travel difficult or impossible. Check with park personnel at Visitor Center.

ACCESSIBILITY
Visitor Center, parking and restrooms are accessible. Picnic area has a boardwalk with a 5% grade.

CAMPING & LODGING
Overnight accommodations are available nearby in Kemmerer and Cokeville.

FOOD & SUPPLIES
Food and supplies are available nearby in Kemmerer and Cokeville.

FIRST AID/ HOSPITAL
• First aid available at the Monument. • The nearest hospital is in Kemmerer.

GENERAL INFORMATION
• The climate is semi-arid. • Bring water, a hat and comfortable hiking shoes.

Grand Teton National Park

Moose, Wyoming   See Climatable No. 39

The geologic forces and natural systems that interact to produce the inspiring scenery at Grand Teton National Park, which includes the Teton Range's jagged peaks mirrored in large lakes, also nurture a remarkable diversity of wildlife such as elk, moose, buffalo, bears, eagles and swans.

MAILING ADDRESS
Superintendent, Grand Teton National Park, PO Drawer 170, Moose, WY 83012 **Telephone:** 307-733-2880

DIRECTIONS
Park Headquarters and a Visitor Center are in Moose, 13 miles (21 km) north of Jackson on US 26, 89 and 191.

VISITOR ACTIVITIES
• Exhibits, Ranger-led activities, picnicking, backcountry hiking, mountain climbing, horseback riding, boating, fishing, biking, snowmobiling, cross-country skiing, and wildlife and bird watching. • Facilities include visitor centers, trails, picnic areas, boat rentals and ramps, a snowmobile route, cross-country ski trails, gasoline, a post office, religious services, restrooms and telephones. • The Park is always open. Moose Visitor Center is closed Dec. 25. Most facilities are closed during the winter. Colter Bay Visitor Center is closed from Oct. 3 through mid-May.

PERMITS, FEES & LIMITATIONS
• The entrance fee is $10 per vehicle or $4 per person, good for 1 week in Grand Teton and Yellowstone National Parks. • There is a $10 fee for motorboats and a $5 fee for non-motorized boats and snowmobiles. • Permits are required for backcountry camping, fishing (a state license), boating and oversnow travel. • Vehicles restricted to established roads. • Dogs are not permitted on hiking trails or in the backcountry. • Bicycles are prohibited on trails.

ACCESSIBILITY
Contact the Visitor Center for a brochure on accessibility.

CAMPING & LODGING
• No reservations are accepted for individual camp sites. Reservations for the trailer village with hookups at Colter Bay may be made by contacting the Grand Teton Lodge Co., PO Box 240, Moran, WY 83013, phone 307-543-2855. Group camp sites are reserved by writing the Chief Ranger between Jan. 1 and June 1. • Forest Service and commercial campgrounds are near the Park. • For lodging information and reservations in the Park, contact the Grand Teton Lodge Co., or Signal Mountain Lodge, Moran, WY 83103, phone 307-543-2831. • Lodging is available nearby in Jackson.

FOOD & SUPPLIES
• Meals are served at Dornans, Colter Bay, Jackson Lake, Jenny Lake and Signal Mountain lodges. • Food and supplies are available at Colter Bay Village, Jackson Lake Lodge, Jenny Lake, Signal Mountain, Moose and Kelly. • Food and supplies are also available nearby in Jackson.

FIRST AID/ HOSPITAL
• First aid is available at visitor centers, Ranger stations and Jackson Lake Lodge. • The nearest hospital is in Jackson.

GENERAL INFORMATION
• Autumn color is best the second or third week in September. • A recorded information service is available at 307-733-2220. • For state travel information, contact the Wyoming Travel Commission, Cheyenne, WY 82001, phone

307-777-7777. • **For your safety** - Register at Jenny Lake Ranger Station in summer and at Park Headquarters during other seasons before starting any off-trail hike or climb. Do not feed or touch any Park animal.

John D. Rockefeller, Jr. Memorial Parkway

Wyoming

Linking West Thumb in Yellowstone with the South Entrance of Grand Teton National Park, this scenic 82-mile (132.2 km) corridor commemorates John D. Rockefeller, Jr.'s role in the establishment of many parks, including Grand Teton.

MAILING ADDRESS	Superintendent, Grand Teton National Park, PO Drawer 170, Moose, WY 83012 **Telephone:** 307-733-2880
DIRECTIONS	The Parkway Ranger Station is just north of Flagg Ranch Village on US 89. Information on the Parkway is available through Dial-A-Park in Grand Teton at 307-733-2220.
VISITOR ACTIVITIES	• Information and self-guiding trails are provided through the Parkway. • River float trips, horseback riding, snowmobiling, boating, backcountry camping, fishing and cross-country skiing. • Facilities include gasoline at Flagg Ranch Village. Snow coach rides are available from Dec. 15 to March 15. • The Parkway is always open.
PERMITS, FEES & LIMITATIONS	• There is a $10 fee for motorboats and a $5 fee for non-motorized boats and snowmobiles. • Permits are required for snowmobiling, boating, backcountry camping and fishing (state license). • Vehicles are restricted to established roads.
CAMPING & LODGING	• Camping and lodging are available at Flagg Ranch Village in season. Contact the Village at 307-543-2861 for details. • Other overnight accommodations are available in Grand Teton National Park, Yellowstone National Park and Jackson, WY, 55 miles (88 km).
FOOD & SUPPLIES	• Meals are served and food and supplies are available at Flagg Ranch Village. • Food and supplies are also available during the summer in Grand Teton and Yellowstone National Parks.
FIRST AID/ HOSPITAL	• First aid is available at the Ranger Station and at Jackson Lake Lodge in Grand Teton National Park in the summer. • The nearest hospital is in Jackson.

Wyoming

Yellowstone National Park

Yellowstone National Park, Wyoming   See Climatable No. 39

Yellowstone would be a premier National Park for its scenery or its wildlife alone, including its famous geysers, American bison and elk, but its history also resonates with colorful tales of fur trappers - including Jim Bridger and Osborne Russell - and explorers and surveyors.

MAILING ADDRESS

National Park Service, PO box 168, Yellowstone National Park, WY 82190
Telephone: 307-344-7381

DIRECTIONS

The Park can be reached from the north by US 89; from the northeast by US 212; from the east through Cody via US 20, 14 and 16; from the south via the John D. Rockefeller, Jr. Memorial Parkway, US 89 and US 26; and from the west via West Yellowstone, US 191 and 20.

VISITOR ACTIVITIES

• Fishing, boating, driving, hiking, horseback riding, bird and wildlife watching, biking, stagecoach rides, boat and bus tours, snowmobiling, cross-country skiing, snowshoeing, and interpretive and campfire programs. • Facilities include roadside radio interpretation, interpretive display boards, amphitheaters, boat rentals, religious services, gasoline, horse rentals, laundries, photo shops, post offices, sewage dump stations, showers and tour buses. • The Park is always open. Park roads and entrances, except the North Entrance to Cooke City, MT, are ordinarily closed to auto traffic between Oct. 31 and May 1. • Thousands of visitors enter the Park in winter by oversnow vehicles. Heated snow coaches are operated by concessionaires. A variety of visitor centers, lodges and winter activities are available.

PERMITS, FEES & LIMITATIONS

• The entrance fee is $10 per vehicle or $4 per person, good for a week at Yellowstone and Grand Teton National Parks. • A $5 fee is charged for non-motorized boat permits, and a $10 fee is required for motorized boat permits. • Fees are also charged for horseback riding, stagecoach rides, and boat and bus tours. • Permits are required for fishing (state license), boating and backcountry camping. Permits are available at any Visitor Center or Ranger Station.

ACCESSIBILITY

Most facilities, including lodges, camping, visitor centers, picnic areas and restrooms, are accessible. Contact the Accessibility Coordinator, Office of the Superintendent, Yellowstone National Park, WY 82190, phone 307-344-7381, ext. 2135 for details.

CAMPING & LODGING

• There are 12 campgrounds in the Park. Reservations are accepted only at Bridge Bay Campground by MISTIX, 1-800-365-2267. Fees for camping range from free backcountry sites to $6-$10 per night for developed camp sites. • Reservations for hotels, lodges, cabins and a trailer park with utilities, which are open from mid-June through August, may be made by contacting TW Recreational Services, Inc., Yellowstone National Park, WY 82190-0165, phone 307-344-7311. • Other overnight accommodations are available outside the Park in Gardiner, Cooke City/Silver Gate, Livingston, Bozeman, West Yellowstone and Red Lodge, MT; and in Cody and Jackson, WY.

FOOD & SUPPLIES

• Meals are served in the Park at Lake, Canyon, Tower-Roosevelt, Mammoth Hot Springs, Old Faithful and Grant Village. Dinner reservations are required at the following hotel dining rooms: Grant Village, Old Faithful Inn, Canyon Lodge, Lake Yellowstone Hotel and Mammoth Hot Springs Hotel. Reservations may be made through any lodging desk or dining room host stand or by calling 307-344-7901 after the dining rooms open for the season. • Food and supplies are available at Lake, Fishing Bridge, Canyon, Tower-Roosevelt, Tower Fall, Mammoth Hot Springs, Grant Village and Old Faithful. • Food and supplies are available nearby at each community near the Park's 5 entrances.

FIRST AID/ HOSPITAL

• First aid is available in the Park. • Lake Medical, Mammoth Clinic and Old Faithful Clinic are open daily during business hours in the summer. 911 is available for emergency assistance. • A hospital is in Jackson.

GENERAL INFORMATION

• Write for pamphlets and a map and call 307-344-7381 for more information. • Five national forests providing recreational opportunities border Yellowstone.

American Samoa

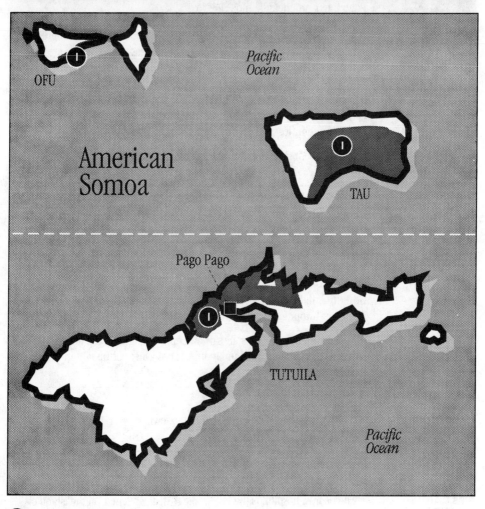

OFU

Pacific
Ocean

American
Somoa

TAU

Pago Pago

TUTUILA

Pacific
Ocean

The National Park of American Samoa

The National Park of American Samoa

Pago Pago, American Samoa

The National Park of American Samoa was authorized by Congress in 1988. It is not officially established until lease negotiations are completed. This will be the only National Park in the system where the land is leased from traditional owners. The proposed Park will protect the only paleotropical rainforest system in the U.S. The Park includes nearly 8,000 acres of rainforest on the islands of Tutuila and Ta'u and a pristine coral reef and magnificent white sand beach on the Island of Ofu.

MAILING ADDRESS	Superintendent, The National Park of American Samoa, Pago Pago, AS 96799
DIRECTIONS	American Samoa is the only U.S. territory south of the equator, 2,400 miles (3,870.9 km) south of Hawaii. Commercial flights are available from Hawaii.
VISITOR ACTIVITIES	• There are no Federal facilities. • Rainforest hiking, bird watching, flying fox (fruit bat) observation, snorkeling and cultural events. • For further information on activities, write the Office of Tourism, American Samoa Government, Pago Pago, AS 96799, or call 011-633-1091. (American Samoa is 1 hour earlier than Hawaii Standard Time).
PERMITS, FEES & LIMITATIONS	• No entrance fee. • Passports or other proof of citizenship are required for entry. • Hiking on private land requires landowner permission in certain locations.
ACCESSIBILITY	No Federal facilities.
CAMPING & LODGING	• Camping requires the permission of landowners. • Lodging adjacent to the Park is available on all islands.
FOOD & SUPPLIES	Food and supplies are available in nearby villages.
FIRST AID/ HOSPITAL	• The nearest hospital is the LBJ Tropical Medical Center on the island of Tutuila. • The islands of Ta'u and Ofu have no medical or emergency services.
GENERAL INFORMATION	American Samoa is only beginning to develop its tourism industry. Visitors should not expect U.S. mainland facility and service standards. Those willing to be flexible and culturally sensitive will find opportunities to interact with a rich and remarkably intact 3,000-year-old culture and experience first hand a unique tropical ecosystem.

Canada

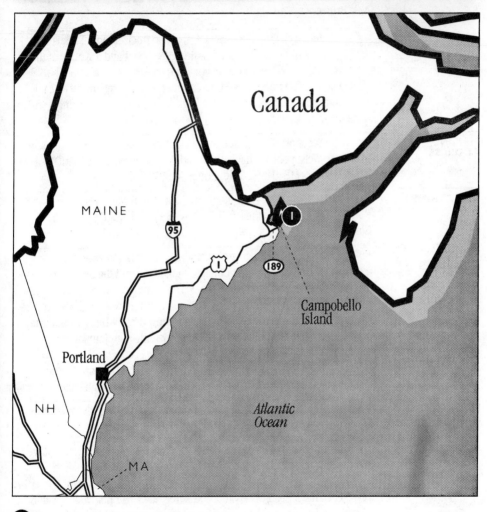

I Roosevelt Campobello International Park

Roosevelt Campobello International Park

New Brunswick, Canada

Affiliated area. The Roosevelt Campobello International Park is a memorial to President Franklin D. Roosevelt and a symbol of the close and neighborly relations between the peoples of Canada and the United States. The Park, once FDR's summer home, is set amidst coastal headlands, rocky shores, sphagnum bogs, fields and forests offering a variety of recreational opportunities.

MAILING ADDRESS

Executive Secretary, Roosevelt Campobello International Park Commission, PO Box 9, Welshpool, Campobello Island, New Brunswick, EOG 3HO *or* PO Box 97, Lubec, ME 04652 **Telephone: 506-752-2922**

DIRECTIONS

Follow ME 1 to Rt. 189. Cross Roosevelt Memorial Bridge to New Brunswick Rt. 774. The Park is on the left, 1.5 miles (2.4 km) beyond Canadian Customs.

VISITOR ACTIVITIES

• Visitor Center and Cottage area includes an orientation video, exhibits, a guided tour of the Roosevelt Cottage, a guided tour of the first floor of Hubbard Cottage and flower gardens. • The natural resource area includes hiking, picnicking, beachcombing, nature study, bird watching and scenic vistas. • The Park opens the Saturday following Victoria Day (the Saturday prior to U.S. Memorial Day), and remains open through Canadian Thanksgiving (U.S. Columbus Day). The Park is open from 10 a.m. to 6 p.m., A.D.T. (9 a.m. to 5 p.m., E.D.T.) daily. • The Hubbard Cottage is usually open, if there are no conferences, from July 1 through Labor Day.

PERMITS, FEES & LIMITATIONS

• No fees. • Cooking fires are permitted only in outdoor grills. • Vehicles are restricted to gravel roads.

ACCESSIBILITY

The Visitor Center and its restrooms, the first floor of the Roosevelt Cottage and the first floor of the Hubbard Cottage are accessible. A video of the second floor of the Roosevelt Cottage will be available in the Visitor Center in 1994. The Friar's Head Observation Deck, the Eagle Hill Bog Walkway and several picnic areas will be accessible in 1994.

CAMPING & LODGING

• Camping and hookups are available nearby at Herring Cove Provincial Park on Campobello. Cobscook Bay State Park in Edmunds, ME, has camping facilities. Camping is also available at private campgrounds on Campobello and in Lubec, ME. • Lodging is available at Welshpool and Wilson's Beach on Campobello and in Lubec.

FOOD & SUPPLIES

• There are several restaurants and take-outs on Campobello and in Lubec. • Food and supplies are available in Wilson's Beach and Lubec.

**FIRST AID/
HOSPITAL**

• First aid is available at the Welshpool Health Center, 2 miles (3.2 km); and at the Regional Medical Center in Lubec, 2 miles (3.2 km). • The nearest hospital is in Machias, ME, 30 miles (48.3 km).

**GENERAL
INFORMATION**

• The Park is administered by the Roosevelt Campobello International Park Commission, with equal representation from Canada and the United States. • Four turn-of-the-century cottages are utilized by the Commission as the Roosevelt Campobello International Park Conference Centre, hosting mostly governmental and academic conferences. • There is a 9-hole golf course at Herring Cove Provincial Park. • Local boat captains provide whale watching and scenic boat tours in season.

North Mariana Islands

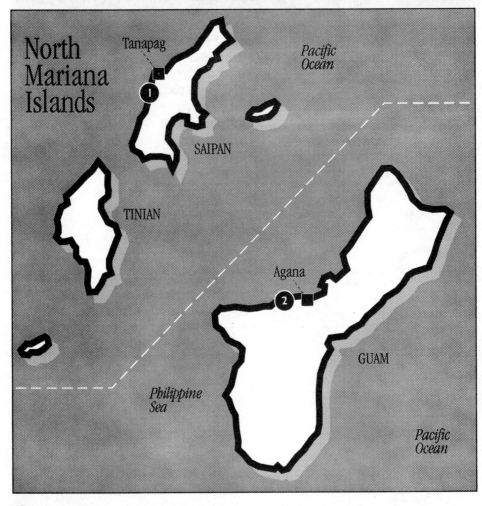

1 American Memorial Park

2 War in the Pacific National Historical Park

North Mariana Islands

American Memorial Park

Saipan, North Mariana Islands

Affiliated area. This site on Tanapag Harbor, Saipan, is designated as a recreational park and memorial honoring those who died in the Marianas Campaign of World War II.

MAILING ADDRESS	American Memorial Park, PO Box 198, CHRB, Saipan, MP 96950
DIRECTIONS	The Park lies just north of Garapan Village and consists of 133 acres of partially developed memorial and recreational facilities.
VISITOR ACTIVITIES	• Swimming, picnicking, boating and other recreation. • Facilities include picnic areas, a monument, tour boats, a launching ramp, jogging path, sports fields and beach. • The Park is always open.
PERMITS, FEES & LIMITATIONS	• No fees. • Vehicles are not allowed on the beach.
ACCESSIBILITY	No accessible facilities.
CAMPING & LODGING	Several hotels are within 1 mile (1.6 km) of the Park.
FOOD & SUPPLIES	Food and supplies are available in Garapan Village.
FIRST AID/ HOSPITAL	• First aid is available in the Park. • A hospital is adjacent to the Park.

War in the Pacific National Historical Park

Agana, Guam

The Pacific Theater of World War II involved vast distances, new strategy and 10 countries. War in the Pacific National Historical Park was established to honor the bravery and sacrifices of all people from all nations who fought in the Pacific Theater.

MAILING ADDRESS	Superintendent, War in the Pacific National Historical Park, Marine Drive, Asan PO Box FA, Agana, Guam 96910 **Telephone:** 671-477-9362 *or* 472-7240
DIRECTIONS	Guam is in the Western Pacific and is the southernmost island of the North Mariana Islands. Guam is 1,500 miles (2,419.3 km) south of Tokyo and 6,100 miles (9,838.7 km) west of San Francisco. The Park consists of 7 separate units, all located on the Philippine Sea (west) side of the island. The Visitor Information Center and Park Headquarters are on the beach side of

Marine Drive in the village of Asan. Guam is 15 hours ahead of Eastern Standard Time and does not observe Daylight Savings Time.

VISITOR ACTIVITIES

• Interpretive programs and exhibits at the Visitor Center, walking trails in 2 units and scuba diving in 2 units. • Facilities include restrooms in the Visitor Center and Southern Unit, beaches and picnic areas. • The Park is open from 7:30 a.m. to 3:30 p.m., Monday through Friday, and from 8:30 a.m. to 2 p.m., Saturdays and Sundays and Federal holidays. The Park is closed Thanksgiving, Dec. 25 and Jan. 1.

CAMPING & LODGING

Overnight accommodations are available in Tumon.

FOOD & SUPPLIES

Food and supplies are available in Agana and Tamuning.

FIRST AID/ HOSPITAL

• First aid is available in the Park. • The Naval Regional Medical Center and Guam Memorial Hospital are 1 mile (1.6 km) from the Park.

GENERAL INFORMATION

• The year-round average temperature is 80°F and the water temperature averages 81°F. • **For your safety** - Please stay off historic structures and guns. Do not disturb any historic ground features, such as foxholes and bomb craters. Do not enter the caves. Do not try to open sealed caves. Use caution when swimming, snorkeling or diving. There are several species of poisonous fish along the reefs. Do not disturb or remove any ammunition or military explosives on- or off-shore. • Do not trespass on private property.

Puerto Rico

Atlantic
Ocean

San Juan

Puerto Rico

Caribbean Sea

1 San Juan National Historic Site

Puerto Rico

San Juan Island National Historic Site
Old San Juan, Puerto Rico

Three massive fortifications, begun in the 16th century, protected Spain's empire in the New World and are today protected as San Juan National Historic Site. They stand as a representation of Spain's ancient power and a historic bond between the Americas.

MAILING ADDRESS

Superintendent, San Juan National Historic Site, Fort San Cristobal, Norzagaray Street, Old San Juan, Puerto Rico 00901 **Telephone:** 809-729-6960

DIRECTIONS

Headquarters is inside Fort San Cristobal just uphill from the northeast corner of Plaza Colon in Old San Juan. To reach Fort El Morro, follow Calle Norzagaray past San Cristobal until it ends one-half mile (.8 km) to the west. Park in the underground facility at Plaza Quintocentenaria and walk to the Fort.

VISITOR ACTIVITIES

• Exhibits, interpretive talks and tours on the hour, a 27-minute film is shown on the half hour, self-guiding tour maps for each fort are available in English and Spanish. • Facilities include bookstores, restrooms and public telephones. • Rental audio-tape tours of El Morro are available in English and Spanish from the bookstore. • Forts serve as visitor centers and are open from 9 a.m. to 5:30 p.m., daily except Dec. 25. • The Grounds of El Morro and ramparts along the City Walls are open from dawn to dusk. • Fort El Canuelo, on Isla de Cabras on the west shore of San Juan Bay, is **not open to the public.**

PERMITS, FEES & LIMITATIONS

• No entrance fee. • The grounds of El Morro are closed to vehicles. • Vehicles are restricted to parking areas and paved roads. Parking in Old San Juan is extremely limited.

ACCESSIBILITY

Entrances, main plazas, restrooms and museum exhibit areas at both forts are accessible. Many of the other areas of the forts are somewhat accessible by using the 200- to 300-year-old ramps originally intended for hauling cannon (steeper than current grade standards).

CAMPING & LODGING

Nearby lodging includes Hotel El Convento on Calle Cristo, Hotel Central on Plaza de Armas, and bed and breakfasts. Other accommodations are also available in sectors of San Juan, such as the Condado and Isla Verde.

FOOD & SUPPLIES

Restaurants and stores are throughout metropolitan San Juan.

FIRST AID/ HOSPITAL

The nearest hospital for English-speaking visitors is Ashford Presbyterian Hospital in the Condado sector, 3 miles (4.8 km).

GENERAL INFORMATION

• Visitors may examine some of the massive City Walls by walking along the harbor shoreline between El Morro and La Fortaleza, the home of the governors of Puerto Rico for more than 400 years. This early fortress/palace, begun in 1533, is also part of the area designated a World Heritage Site.

• Many other sites of historic interest, such as San Juan Cathedral or Casa Blanca, the home of the Ponce de Leon family, are within comfortable walking distance of the forts.

Virgin Islands

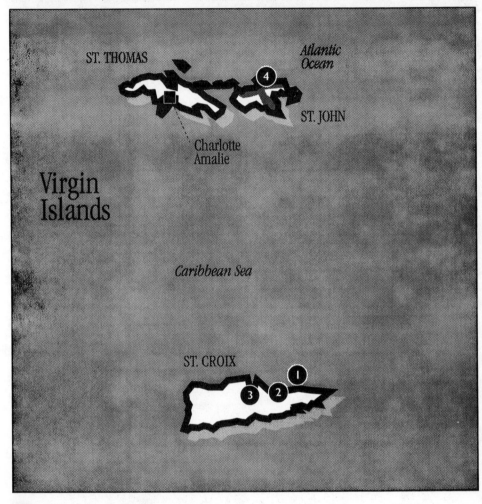

1. Buck Island Reef National Monument
2. Christiansted National Historic Site
3. Salt River Bay National Historical Park and Ecological Preserve
4. Virgin Islands National Park

Buck Island Reef National Monument

St. Croix, Virgin Islands

Swimming and snorkeling in the crystal-clear lagoon just off Buck Island near St. Croix is an ideal way to see one of the best Caribbean reefs firsthand for beginners and experts alike who are interested in an extraordinary array of underwater life as well as hiking through Buck Island's tropical vegetation.

MAILING ADDRESS	Superintendent, Christiansted National Historic Site, PO Box 160, Christiansted, St. Croix, Virgin Islands 00820 **Telephone: 809-773-1460**
DIRECTIONS	Access to the Monument is by concessionaires or private boat. Concession boats are available at Christiansted Wharf. The Monument is a 5.5-mile (8.8 km) sail from Christiansted.
VISITOR ACTIVITIES	• Swimming, snorkeling, boat trips, hiking, bird watching and picnicking. • Facilities include picnic tables, charcoal grills, a changing house, a sheltered picnic pavilion, restrooms and a nature trail. • The Monument is always open.
PERMITS, FEES & LIMITATIONS	• No entrance fee. • There are concession boat fees. • Boats should be maneuvered slowly through Monument waters. Water skiing and speeding are prohibited.
CAMPING & LODGING	• Camping is permitted on boats. • Overnight accommodations are available in Saint Croix.
FOOD & SUPPLIES	Food and supplies are available in St. Croix.
FIRST AID/ HOSPITAL	• First aid is available in the Monument. • A hospital is 6.5 miles (10.4 km) from downtown Christiansted.
GENERAL INFORMATION	For your safety - Avoid sunburn. Use caution in the water. Cuts from coral can inflict painful wounds. Spiny sea urchins are a particularly sharp hazard. Jellyfish, the Portuguese man-of-war and fire corals sting and burn. Treat all underwater creatures with respect. Practice snorkeling in shallow water before going to the reef.

Christiansted National Historic Site

Christiansted, Virgin Islands

Christiansted National Historic Site recognizes St. Croix Island's significance to New World history since it was the first territory now under the U.S. flag to have been discovered by Columbus. It played a part in the struggle for colonial empire and is an outstanding example of Danish colonial development.

MAILING ADDRESS

Superintendent, Christiansted National Historic Site, PO Box 160, Christiansted, Virgin Islands 00820 **Telephone:** 809-773-1460

DIRECTIONS

The Headquarters is in The Old Customs House in downtown Christiansted. Begin tours at the Fort.

VISITOR ACTIVITIES

• Self-guided walking tours and interpretive exhibits. • Facilities include restrooms and a museum. • The Site is open from 8 a.m. to 5 p.m., daily. The museum is open from 8 a.m. to 5 p.m., Monday through Friday, and from 9 a.m. to 5 p.m., Saturdays and Sundays.

PERMITS, FEES & LIMITATIONS

The **entrance fee** is $1 for ages 12 to 62 for the Fort and Steeple Building Museum.

CAMPING & LODGING

Overnight accommodations are available in the town of Christiansted.

FOOD & SUPPLIES

Food and supplies are available in the town of Christiansted.

FIRST AID/ HOSPITAL

• First aid is available in the Site. • The nearest hospital is in St. Croix, 6 miles (9.6 km).

GENERAL INFORMATION

For your safety - Beware of uneven walkways and stairs.

Salt River Bay National Historical Park and Ecological Preserve

St. Croix, Virgin Islands

Not open to the public. The Park/Preserve was established on Feb. 24, 1992 to protect nationally significant cultural and natural resources. The Park/Preserve contains cultural evidence of prehistoric settlement as well as evidence of 17th century European attempts to colonize the area. In addition to cultural resources, the Salt River Bay area includes prime examples of several types of tropical marine and terrestrial ecosystems, including a mangrove fringe forest, mangrove basin forest, salt pond and freshwater marsh. The Park/Preserve is home to 27 species of threatened or endangered plants and animals.

MAILING ADDRESS

Salt River Bay National Historical Park and Ecological Preserve, c/o Superintendent, Virgin Islands National Park, 6310 Estate Nazareth, Charlotte Amalie, St. Thomas, Virgin Islands 00802

Virgin Islands

Virgin Islands National Park

St. John, Virgin Islands   See Climatable No. 40

Just more than half of the small rugged volcanic island of St. John is protected as a natural paradise within Virgin Islands National Park where visitors can enjoy tropical forests, wildlife, wildflowers, breathtaking views and offshore coral reefs filled with a kaleidoscope of colorful fish and formations.

MAILING ADDRESS

Superintendent, Virgin Islands National Park, PO Box 710, St. John, Virgin Islands 00831 **Telephone:** Cruz Bay Visitor Center, 809-776-6201 Headquarters, 809-775-6238

DIRECTIONS

Headquarters is in Red Hook on St. Thomas. A Visitor Center is at Cruz Bay on St. John. Direct flights go to Charlotte Amalie, St. Thomas, or via San Juan. Taxis and buses run between Charlotte Amalie and Red Hook. A ferry operates hourly from 7 a.m. to 11 p.m. across Pillsbury Sound from Red Hook to Cruz Bay. Water taxi service is available after hours. A special boat for guests at Caneel Bay Plantation runs between Red Hook Visitor Station and Caneel Bay. There are package vehicle tours and scenic boat charters that leave St. Thomas with all transportation arranged for day trips. Taxi service and rental vehicles are available on St. John.

VISITOR ACTIVITIES

• Interpretive walks, talks and exhibits, hiking, guided snorkel trips, cultural demonstrations, picnicking, swimming, snorkeling, fishing, scuba diving, bird watching and auto tours. • Facilities include self-guiding walking and underwater trails, picnic areas, beaches and boat rentals. • The Park is always open. Headquarters is open from 8:30 a.m. to 5 p.m., daily. Cruz Bay Visitor Center is open from 8 a.m. to 4:30 p.m., daily.

PERMITS, FEES & LIMITATIONS

• No fees. • Persons returning to the U.S. mainland must go through Customs and Immigration at U.S. ports of entry. A special permit from the Department of Agriculture is required to exit with fruits, vegetables, plant cuttings and seeds. • The speed limit is 20 miles (32.2 km) per hour. Remember to drive on the left and sound your horn at blind curves.

ACCESSIBILITY

Check with Park staff about accessible beaches. Annaberg Sugar Mill is accessible with assistance. Some camp sites at Cinnamon Bay Campground are accessible. Ferries are accessible with assistance.

CAMPING & LODGING

• Cottage and tent site reservations must be made well in advance, but not more than 8 months prior to a visit. Primitive, unequipped camp sites may also be reserved. Contact Cinnamon Bay Campground, PO Box 720, St. John, Virgin Islands 00830, phone 809-776-6330. Or see a travel agent.
• Other overnight accommodations are available in St. Thomas.

FOOD & SUPPLIES	• Meals are served in the Park at Cruz Bay, Trunk Bay and Cinnamon Bay. • There are commissaries at Cinnamon Bay Campground, Cruz Bay and Coral Bay. • Food and supplies are also available in St. Thomas.
FIRST AID/ HOSPITAL	• First aid is available in the Park. • A clinic at Cruz Bay is open Monday through Friday from 7 a.m. to 11 p.m., and on Saturdays and Sundays from 8 a.m. to 11 p.m. Phone 809-776-6400. A nurse and doctor are on call 24 hours a day at 809-776-6471.
GENERAL INFORMATION	For your safety - Insect repellent may be useful because of mosquitoes and sand flies. While snorkeling and swimming, use lifeguard-posted beaches and avoid touching or standing on coral. Avoid sunburn. Avoid heavy surf and never swim alone. While hiking, avoid long, strenuous hikes in the middle of the day. Carry drinking water. Avoid eating unidentified plants. Stay on the trails. Do not climb on ruins. Wear sturdy shoes or boots. Tell someone of your plans, and do not hike alone.

National Trails System

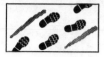

The National Trails System Act established 4 types of trails:

National Scenic Trails - continuous extended routes of outdoor recreation within protected corridors.

National Historic Trails - past routes of exploration, migration and military action. These are not necessarily continuous, but feature outstanding "high potential" trail sites and segments.

National Recreation Trails - existing federal, state or local trails recognized as components of the National Trails System.

Side and Connecting Trails - additional access routes to components of the National Trails System.

The 14 National Scenic and National Historic Trails managed by the National Park Service are included in the *Guide*. For more information, contact:

> National Trails System Branch
> National Park Service - 782
> PO Box 37127
> Washington, DC 20013-7127
> 202-343-3780

National Trails System

1. Appalachian National Scenic Trail
2. California National Historic Trail
3. Ice Age National Scenic Trail
4. Juan Bautista de Anza National Historic Trail
5. Lewis and Clark National Historic Trail
6. Mormon Pioneer National Historic Trail
7. Natchez Trace National Scenic Trail
8. North Country National Scenic Trail
9. Oregon National Historic Trail
10. Overmountain Victory National Historic Trail
11. Pony Express National Historic Trail
12. Potomac Heritage National Scenic Trail
13. Santa Fe National Historic Trail
14. Trail of Tears National Historic Trail

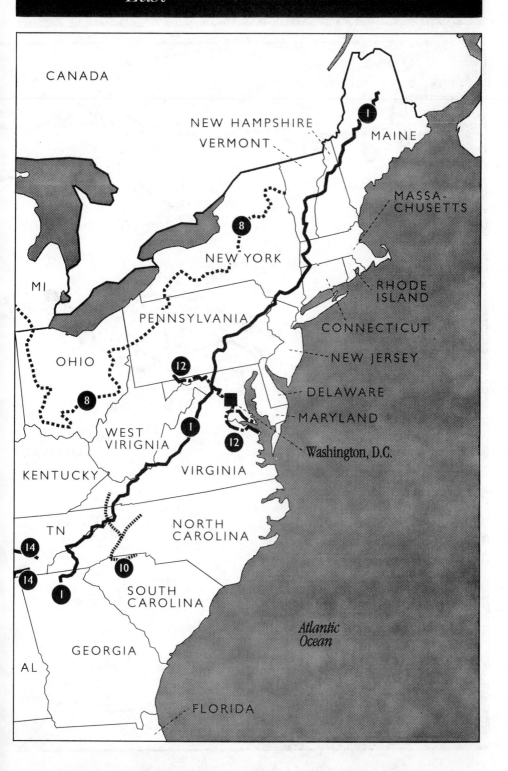

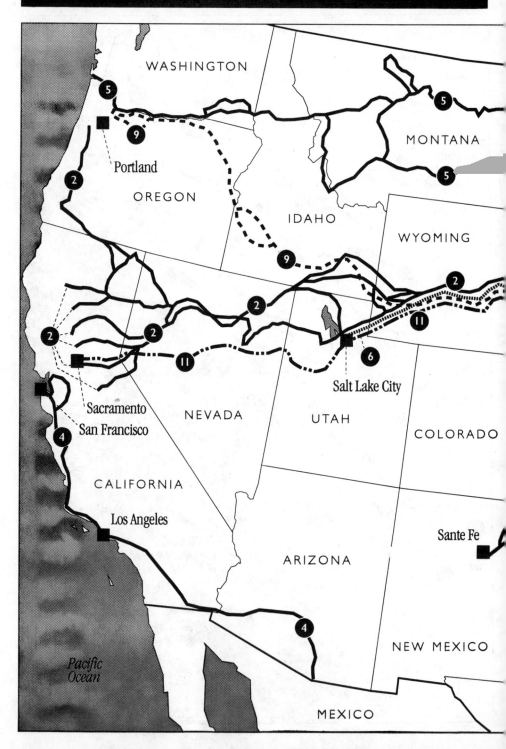

WASHINGTON

OREGON

Portland

IDAHO

MONTANA

WYOMING

NEVADA

UTAH

COLORADO

Salt Lake City

Sacramento

San Francisco

CALIFORNIA

Los Angeles

ARIZONA

Sante Fe

NEW MEXICO

Pacific
Ocean

MEXICO

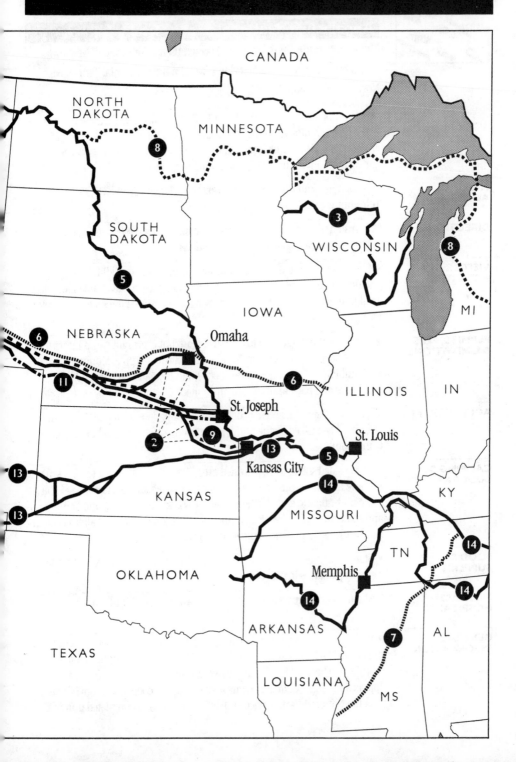

National Trails System

Appalachian National Scenic Trail

Maine, New Hampshire, Vermont, Massachusetts, Connecticut, New York, New Jersey, Pennsylvania, Maryland, West Virginia, Virginia, Tennessee, North Carolina and Georgia

The Appalachian National Scenic Trail is a 2,147-mile (3,462.9 km) footpath along the ridgecrests and across the major valleys of the Appalachian Mountains from Katahdin in the central Maine wilderness to Springer Mountain in a designated wilderness area in north Georgia.

MAILING ADDRESS	Appalachian Trail Conference, PO Box 807, Harpers Ferry, WV 25425-0807 Telephone: 304-535-6331
DIRECTIONS	The Trail has more than 500 access points. Contact the private, nonprofit Appalachian Trail Conference for directions.
VISITOR ACTIVITIES	• Short- and long-term hiking, backpacking, bird and wildlife watching, and other backcountry recreation. • Other activities are available along the Trail in 6 units of the National Park Service, 8 national forests and 60 state parks and forests.
PERMITS, FEES & LIMITATIONS	• Permits are not required to walk the Trail, but overnight camping permits are necessary in Shenandoah National Park, Great Smoky Mountains National Park (see listings in this book) and Baxter State Park in Maine. • Vehicles and pack animals are prohibited.
ACCESSIBILITY	There are no specific access provisions except at developed park sites, but the Trail has been hiked by the blind, persons on crutches and other persons with disabilities.
CAMPING & LODGING	• Three-sided shelters are provided every 10 to 12 miles (16.1 to 19.3 km). • There are numerous camp sites near or between shelter sites with fees at some mid-Atlantic and Northeast sites. • Lodges are in the White Mountains and some other areas. • Hostels and other overnight accommodations are in nearby towns. Conference guidebooks describe accommodations.
FOOD & SUPPLIES	• Stores are in nearby towns. • Long-distance hikers often mail food and resupply packages to post offices.
FIRST AID/ HOSPITAL	Medical services are available in larger towns near the Trail.
GENERAL INFORMATION	• Primary use is by weekend or short-term hikers. "Thru-hikers" generally start from the South in early spring and hike the entire length in 5 to 6 months. • The Trail is managed by volunteers in 32 local clubs under Appalachian Trail Conference auspices through a cooperative agreement with the National Park Service. • The Trail is the first completed unit of the

National Trails System 449

National Trails System established by Congress and the President on Oct. 2, 1968; initiated by volunteers in October 1921 and completed by volunteers on Aug. 14, 1937. More than 97% of the Trail is now on public land.

California National Historic Trail

From Independence and St. Joseph, Missouri, and Council Bluffs, Iowa, to California and Oregon

Including cutoffs, the California Trail contained more than 5,600 miles (9032.2 km) between Council Bluffs, IA, and St. Joseph and Independence, MO, at the starting points for the route of the greatest mass migration in American history.

MAILING ADDRESS
Regional Long Distance Trails Coordinator, Rocky Mountain Regional Office, RMR-PP, National Park Service, PO Box 25287, Denver, CO 80225

DIRECTIONS
Designated in 1992, the Trail is undergoing a major planning effort by the National Park Service and cooperating groups.

VISITOR ACTIVITIES
• The National Park Service, in cooperation with trail groups and governmental agencies, will begin to develop the Trail once planning is completed.
• Information on current Trail developments is available from the National Park Service, state and local tourism offices and appropriate trail organizations.

Ice Age National Scenic Trail

Wisconsin

Winding 1,000 miles (1,612.9 km) through Wisconsin, the Ice Age National Scenic Trail links together 6 of the 9 units of the Ice Age National Scientific Reserve (see listing in this book) through a chain of moraine hills created 10,000 years ago when glaciers retreated from North America.

MAILING ADDRESS
National Park Service, Ice Age National Scenic Trail, 700 Rayovac Drive, Suite 100, Madison, WI 53711 **Telephone:** 608-264-5610

DIRECTIONS
Currently, 450 miles (725.8 km) of the Trail are available for public use.

VISITOR ACTIVITIES
• Hiking, backpacking, nature study. • Some Trail segments are open to bicycling, cross-country skiing and limited snowmobiling. • Various facilities are provided by the managing authority for a particular segment.

PERMITS, FEES & LIMITATIONS
• Permits are required for a few Trail segments. • Excluding certain segments open to snowmobiles, use of motorized vehicles is prohibited.

ACCESSIBILITY

Restrooms, visitor centers and other facilities in some park and forest areas along the Trail are accessible. Few segments of the Trail are accessible.

CAMPING & LODGING

• Information on backcountry camping along the Trail is available by writing or calling the National Park Service. • There are fees for some developed campgrounds within national forests and state parks along the Trail. • Other overnight accommodations are available in communities along the Trail.

FOOD & SUPPLIES

Food and supplies are available in parks and communities along the Trail.

FIRST AID/ HOSPITAL

Medical services are available in communities along the Trail.

GENERAL INFORMATION

Additional information is available from the Ice Age Park and Trail Foundation, PO Box 423, Pewaukee, WI 53072-0423, phone 1-800-227-0046.

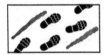

Juan Bautista de Anza National Historic Trail

Southwest Arizona and California to San Francisco

In 1775, a party of Spanish colonists led by Col. Juan Bautista de Anza set out from Mexico to establish an overland route to California. The 1,200-mile (1,935.4 km) Trail follows the trip that took them through the Southwest and up the California coast in 6 months to the Golden Gate where San Francisco now stands.

MAILING ADDRESS

National Park Service Western Regional Office, Division of Planning, Grants, and Environmental Quality, 600 Harrison St., Suite 600, San Francisco, CA 94107-1372 **Telephone:** 415-744-3932

DIRECTIONS

Established on Aug. 15, 1990, the Trail's use plan is projected for completion in March 1994. Precise management and route marking programs have not begun.

VISITOR ACTIVITIES

• Many sites along the Trail provide historical and commemorative information about de Anza and his expedition. • Portions of the historic route can be hiked, including 4.5 miles (7.2 km) between Tumacacori National Historical Park (see listing in this book) and Tubac Presidio State Historical Park just north of Nogales, AZ; the Santa Cruz River Park in Tucson, AZ; and several miles within Anza-Borrego Desert State Park in California.

Lewis and Clark National Historic Trail

Illinois, Missouri, Kansas, Nebraska, Iowa, South Dakota, North Dakota, Montana, Idaho, Oregon and Washington

The Trail commemorates the outbound and return route of the 1804-06 Lewis and Clark Expedition from the Mississippi River to the Pacific Ocean at the mouth of the Columbia River. The Trail includes 4,500 miles (7,258 km) of water routes, planned trails and marked highways.

MAILING ADDRESS

National Park Service, 700 Rayovac Drive, Suite 100, Madison, WI 53711
Telephone: 608-264-5610

DIRECTIONS

A general map and guide are available by writing to the National Park Service.

VISITOR ACTIVITIES

• Motor routes, foot trails and water trails connect historic and recreational sites along the 4,000-mile (6,451.6 km) Trail. • Sites are managed by cooperating Federal, state and local agencies, and private organizations. National Park Service areas that provide interpretive services include the Jefferson National Expansion Memorial, Knife River Indian Villages National Historic Site, Nez Perce National Historical Park and Fort Clatsop National Memorial (see listings in this book).

PERMITS, FEES & LIMITATIONS

Permits and fees vary according to location.

ACCESSIBILITY

Restrooms, visitor centers and other facilities are accessible at some park and forest areas along the Trail.

CAMPING & LODGING

Overnight accommodations vary according to location along the Trail.

FOOD & SUPPLIES

Food and supplies are available along the Trail.

FIRST AID/ HOSPITAL

Medical services are available along the Trail.

GENERAL INFORMATION

Information about specific sites on the Trail is available from the site's managing authority.

Mormon Pioneer National Historic Trail

Illinois, Iowa, Nebraska, Wyoming and Utah

Mormon emigration was one of the principal forces of settlement in the West. This 1,300-mile (2,096.7 km) trail follows the route over which Brigham Young led the Mormons from Nauvoo, IL, to the site of modern Salt Lake City, UT, in 1847 during their search for refuge from religious persecution.

MAILING ADDRESS	Manager, Mormon Pioneer National Historic Trail, National Park Service, RMR-PP, PO Box 25287, Denver, CO 80225 **Telephone:** 303-969-2830
DIRECTIONS	The Trail stretches from Nauvoo, IL, to Salt Lake City, UT. A Trail brochure with route information is available.
VISITOR ACTIVITIES	The Trail is a cooperative effort by many Federal, state and local agencies, cooperating groups and private landowners. Activities are numerous and varied. Contact the Trail Manager or the involved state tourism office for information.
PERMITS, FEES & LIMITATIONS	Some museums and parks along the Trail charge fees. Contact the Trail Manager for more information.
ACCESSIBILITY	Contact the Trail Manager for information.
CAMPING & LODGING	Contact the Trail Manager.
FOOD & SUPPLIES	Contact the Trail Manager.
FIRST AID/ HOSPITAL	Contact the Trail Manager.

Natchez Trace National Scenic Trail

Mississippi, Alabama and Tennessee

The Trail extends from Nashville, TN, to Natchez, MS, and parallels the existing Parkway that commemorates the historic Natchez Trace, an ancient path that began as a series of animal tracks and Native American trails and was later used by early explorers.

MAILING ADDRESS	Natchez Trace Parkway, RR1, NT-143, Tupelo, MS 38801 **Telephone:** 601-842-1572
DIRECTIONS	The Trail follows some existing portions of the old Natchez Trace that lie within the boundaries of the Natchez Trace Parkway (see listing in this book). Three principal segments of the Trace near Nashville, TN, and Jackson and Natchez, MS - totalling 110 miles (177.4 km) - have been identified for restoration and public trail use. Some of these segments are open to the public.
VISITOR ACTIVITIES	• The portions of the Trace open to the public will be limited to walking and horseback riding. • Bicycling is permitted the entire length of the Parkway. • Other activities are the same as for the Parkway.

National Trails System 453

North Country National Scenic Trail

New York, Pennsylvania, Ohio, Michigan, Wisconsin, Minnesota and North Dakota

The route of the North Country Trail extends 3,200 miles (5,161.2 km) from Crown Point, NY, to North Dakota traveling through the grandeur of the Adirondacks, Pennsylvania's hardwood forests, the farmland and canals of Ohio, the Great Lakes shorelines of Michigan, the glacier-carved lakes and streams of Wisconsin and Minnesota, and the vast plains of North Dakota.

MAILING ADDRESS
National Park Service, 700 Rayovac Drive, Madison, WI 53711 **Telephone:** 608-264-5610

DIRECTIONS
There are many points along the Trail that are accessible. Trail maps and brochures are available from the National Park Service.

VISITOR ACTIVITIES
• The Trail is primarily for hiking. Some segments are open to horseback riding and cross-country skiing. • When completed, the Trail will extend 3,200 miles (5,161.2 km) from Crown Point, NY, to Lake Sakakwea State Park on the Missouri River in North Dakota. About 1,400 miles (2,258 km) are currently available for public use. • The Trail is open at all times, except as limited by regulations governing individual parks and forests that the Trail passes through.

PERMITS, FEES & LIMITATIONS
Some permits are available for some segments.

ACCESSIBILITY
Some sections of the Trail are accessible. Restrooms and other facilities at developed areas in many Federal and state parks along the Trail are accessible.

CAMPING & LODGING
• Camping is permitted in backcountry sites or in developed campgrounds in forests and parks along the Trail. There are fees for some developed campgrounds. • A reservation system is used for some public and private campgrounds. • Backcountry cabins and lean-tos are available. • Other overnight accommodations are available in communities along the Trail.

FOOD & SUPPLIES
Food and supplies are available in some parks or communities along the Trail.

FIRST AID/ HOSPITAL
• No first aid is available in the parks along the Trail. • Medical services are available in some communities along the Trail.

GENERAL INFORMATION
Scenic, historic, natural and cultural sites are along the Trail.

Oregon National Historic Trail

Missouri, Kansas, Nebraska, Wyoming, Idaho, Oregon and Washington

As the harbinger of America's westward expansion, the Oregon Trail was the pathway to the Pacific for fur traders, gold seekers, missionaries and an estimated 300,000 emigrants who followed the route from the Midwest to Oregon on a journey that took more than 5 months to complete.

MAILING ADDRESS

Oregon-California Trails Association, PO Box 1019, Independence, MO 64051-0519 **Telephone:** 816-252-2276 *or* National Park Service, Pacific Northwest Regional Office, Oregon National Historic Trail, 909 First Ave., Seattle, WA 98101 **Telephone:** 206-553-5366

DIRECTIONS

General information and Trail brochures are available from the National Park Service Pacific Northwest Regional Office.

VISITOR ACTIVITIES

• The National Park Service Comprehensive Management and Use Plan describes the official Trail route, lists 125 historic sites and 7 cross-country segments, and makes recommendations for resource protection, trail management and marking. • Many of the sites and segments are on public lands and are open to visitors. Others are located on private lands - please check with landowners before entry. • For information about access and travel conditions along the cross-country segments, contact local offices of the Bureau of Land Management or the Forest Service. Agency addresses are listed in the Trail brochure.

Overmountain Victory National Historic Trail

Virginia, Tennessee, North Carolina and South Carolina

Overmountain Victory National Historic Trail is the 300-mile (483.8 km) path followed by a band of Revolutionary patriots through parts of Virginia, Tennessee and North Carolina to Kings Mountain, SC, where they defeated the British in 1780.

MAILING ADDRESS

National Park Service, Southeast Regional Office, Planning Division, 75 Spring St., SW, Atlanta, GA 30303 **Telephone:** 404-331-5465 *or* Overmountain Victory Trail Association, c/o Sycamore Shoals State Historic Area, Elizabethton, TN 37643

DIRECTIONS

The Trail may be accessed from the towns of Abingdon, VA; Elizabethton, TN; Elkin, North Wilkesboro, Lenoir, Morganton and Rutherfordton, NC; and Gaffney, SC. It crosses the Blue Ridge Parkway at Heffner Gap, NC, and the Appalachian National Scenic Trail (see listing in this book) at Yellow Mountain Gap. It passes through Cowpens National Battlefield and ends at Kings Mountain National Military Park (see listings in this book).

VISITOR ACTIVITIES	• The Trail is commemorated each fall by a 14-day reenactment with period costumes and equipment. Write OVTA, PO Box 632, Manassas Park, VA 22111 for more information. • Most of the Trail is marked on state highways. • Hiking opportunities are available at Sycamore Shoals State Historic Area, Carter County, TN; Roan Mountain State Park, Carter County, TN; Yellow Mountain Gap in the Cherokee National Forest, TN; North Cove/Linville Mountain in the Nantahala National Forest, NC; Minerals Museum/Heffner Gap along the Blue Ridge Parkway, NC; the W. Kerr Scott Reservoir, Wilkes County, NC; Cowpens National Battlefield, SC; and Kings Mountain National Military Park, SC.
PERMITS, FEES & LIMITATIONS	No fees.
ACCESSIBILITY	The visitor centers at Sycamore Shoals State Historic Area, Roan Mountain State Park, Minerals Museum, Cowpens National Battlefield and Kings Mountain National Military Park are accessible.
CAMPING & LODGING	• Camping is available at Roan Mountain State Park, Cherokee National Forest, W. Kerr Scott Reservoir and along the Blue Ridge Parkway. • Lodging is available at most major towns and cities along the route and at Roan Mountain State Park.
FOOD & SUPPLIES	Food and supplies are available in most major towns and cities along the Trail.
FIRST AID/ HOSPITAL	• First aid is available at state and Federal areas. • Medical services are available in most major towns and cities along the Trail.

Pony Express National Historic Trail

From St. Joseph, Missouri, to Sacramento, California

During its 18 months of operation between April 1860 and October 1861, the Pony Express delivered mail from St. Joseph, MO, to Sacramento, CA - a distance of 1,855 miles (2,991.9 km) - in just 10 days. The heroism and determination of Pony Express riders has inspired generations of Americans.

MAILING ADDRESS	Regional Long Distance Trails Coordinator, Rocky Mountain Regional Office, RMR-PP, National Park Service, PO Box 25287, Denver, CO 80225
DIRECTIONS	The Trail was designated by Congress in 1992 and is currently undergoing a major planning effort by the National Park Service and cooperating groups. The National Park Service, in cooperation with Trail groups and governmental agencies, will begin to develop the Trail once this planning effort is completed.

**VISITOR
ACTIVITIES**

Information on current Trail developments is available from the National
Park Service, state and local tourism offices and appropriate Trail organizations.

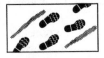

Potomac Heritage National Scenic Trail

Virginia, Maryland and Pennsylvania

The Trail begins at the mouth of the Potomac River and follows both
banks of the Potomac to the District of Columbia. For 184 miles
(296.7 km) it coincides with the Chesapeake and Ohio Canal Towpath, then
turns north, ending at Conemaugh Gorge.

**MAILING
ADDRESS**

Potomac Heritage National Scenic Trail, c/o National Capital Region-LUCE,
1100 Ohio Drive, SW, Washington, DC 20242 **Telephone:** 202-619-7025

DIRECTIONS

The Trail route has not been formally designated and is now generally
located on Federally and state managed trails. A planning effort is underway
that will result in a comprehensive management plan. The 700-mile
(1,129 km) Trail would extend through the Potomac River Valley linking
sites that commemorate a rich blend of historical events, natural scenes and
recreational opportunities.

**VISITOR
ACTIVITIES**

• The 17-mile (27.4 km) George Washington Memorial Parkway's Mount
Vernon Trail from Mount Vernon, VA, to Washington, DC, is a component of
the Potomac Heritage National Scenic Trail. See the Parkway listing in this
book for details. • The 184-mile (296.7 km) Chesapeake and Ohio Canal is
included as a segment of the Trail from Georgetown in the District of
Columbia to Cumberland, MD. See the Chesapeake and Ohio Canal
National Historical Park listing in this book for details. • The 70-mile
(112.9 km) Laurel Highlands National Recreation Trail in Pennsylvania is
also a ready-to-use component of the Trail. Contact State Parks,
Commonwealth of Pennsylvania, Department of Environmental Resources,
Harrisburg, PA 17100, for more information.

**GENERAL
INFORMATION**

By law, only those portions of the Trail already on Federal land may be
Federally owned.

Santa Fe National Historic Trail

Missouri, Kansas, Colorado, Oklahoma and New Mexico

After Mexican independence in 1821, U.S. and Mexican traders
developed the Santa Fe Trail from American Indian travel and trade
routes, and it quickly became a commercial and cultural link between the 2
countries.

MAILING ADDRESS

National Park Service, Southwest Region, Branch of Long Distance Trails, PO Box 728, Santa Fe, NM 87504-0728 **Telephone: 505-988-6888** *or* Santa Fe Trail Association, RR 3, Larned, KS 67550

DIRECTIONS

The 1,203-mile (1,940.3 km) route was established as a national historic trail by Congress in 1987. Much of the route may be traced from nearby highways. Moving east to west, major cities and highways include: Boonville and Independence, MO (via US 65 and 24); Kansas City, Council Grove, Larned, Dodge City and Cimarron, KS (via US 56); Lamarr, La Junta and Trinidad, CO (via US 50 and 350 along the Mountain Branch); Boise City, OK, and Clayton, NM (via US 56 along the Cimarron Cut-off); and Cimarron, Watrous, Las Vegas and Santa Fe, NM (along US 64 and NM 25).

VISITOR ACTIVITIES

• A few sites and segments are certified for public access. • Interpretive services are available at Fort Osage, MO; the National Frontier Trails Center in Independence, MO; Fort Larned National Historical Site (see listing in this book) and the Santa Fe Trail Center in Larned, KS; Bent's Old Fort National Historic Site (see listing in this book) in La Junta, CO; and Fort Union National Monument and Pecos National Historic Site (see listings in this book) in New Mexico. • Historic ruins may be accessed at various sites along the Trail, especially at Cimarron National Grassland in southwest Kansas and Comanche National Grassland in Colorado.

PERMITS, FEES & LIMITATIONS

• Federal, state and local parks and historic sites may charge entrance fees.
• Permission to enter private property is required.

ACCESSIBILITY

Many sites on private land are undeveloped. Most developed sites have some degree of accessibility and are working to improve access.

CAMPING & LODGING

Overnight accommodations are available in communities along the Trail.

FOOD & SUPPLIES

Food and supplies are available in communities along the Trail.

FIRST AID/ HOSPITAL

Medical services are available in communities along the Trail.

Trail of Tears National Historic Trail

Georgia, Tennessee, Alabama, Kentucky, North Carolina, Illinois, Missouri and Oklahoma

The Trail of Tears marks the routes used for the forced removal of more than 15,000 Cherokees from their ancestral lands in North Carolina, Tennessee, Georgia and Alabama to Oklahoma and Arkansas in a journey that lasted from June 1838 to March 1839.

National Trails System

MAILING ADDRESS	National Park Service Southwest Region, Branch of Long Distance Trails, PO Box 728, Santa Fe, NM 87504-0728 **Telephone: 505-988-6888**
DIRECTIONS	The Trail was established by Congress in 1987 and follows 2 routes: 1,226 miles (1,977.4 km) by water and 826 miles (1,332.2 km) by land. The water route begins at Ross's Landing in downtown Chattanooga, TN, and follows the Tennessee River all the way to the Ohio River, then down the Ohio to the Mississippi, and down the Mississippi past Memphis, TN, to the mouth of the Arkansas River, then up the Arkansas past Little Rock and Fort Smith, AR, to a point due south of Tahlequah, OK, where the Trail ends. The land route will be marked as an auto tour route connecting near the towns of Cleveland, Dayton, McMinnville and Nashville, TN; Hopkinsville, KY; Golconda and Vienna, IL; Cape Girardeau, Farmington, Rolla, Springfield and Cassville, MO, through Fayetteville, AR, on US 60 to Tahlequah, OK.
VISITOR ACTIVITIES	• Until the Trail's comprehensive management plan is implemented, exact development sites, themes and programs will not be determined. • Interpretive facilities associated with the Trail are available at the Museum of the Cherokee Indian, Cherokee, NC; Red Clay and Port Royal state historic areas, TN; Trail of Tears Park, Hopkinsville, KY; the New Echota State Historic Site, GA; Trail of Tears State Park, MO; and the Cherokee National Museum, Tahlequah, OK.
PERMITS, FEES & LIMITATIONS	• Some state and local parks have entrance fees. • Permission to enter private property is required.
ACCESSIBILITY	Most sites and Trail segments are undeveloped. State, local and private Trail sites are working to improve access.
CAMPING & LODGING	Overnight accommodations are available in communities and Federal, state and local recreation sites along the Trail.
FOOD & SUPPLIES	Food and supplies are available in communities along the Trail.
FIRST AID/ HOSPITAL	Medical services are available in communities along the Trail.

National Rivers

The National Rivers and National Wild and Scenic Rivers

The 15 National Rivers and National Wild and Scenic Rivers managed by the National Park Service are part of a system created to preserve certain rivers with outstanding natural, cultural or recreational features in a free-flowing condition. For more information, contact:

National Park Service
US Department of the Interior
Division of Park Planning and Protection
Room 3230
Washington, DC 20013-7127

Alagnak Wild River

Alaska

The Alagnak Wild River flows from Kukaklek Lake in Katmai National Preserve and offers 69 miles (111.2 km) of outstanding whitewater, opportunities to see abundant wildlife and sport fishing for 5 species of salmon.

MAILING ADDRESS
Alagnak Wild River, c/o Superintendent, Katmai National Park and Preserve, PO Box 7, King Salmon, AK 99613 **Telephone:** 907-246-3305

DIRECTIONS
The Wild River is accessible by scheduled airlines to King Salmon. Charter flights are available to Kukaklek Lake.

VISITOR ACTIVITIES
• Fishing and recreational river floating. • No visitor facilities.

PERMITS, FEES & LIMITATIONS
• No fees. • Backcountry permits are available by mail.

CAMPING & LODGING
• Wilderness camping is available. • Other overnight accommodations are available in King Salmon.

FOOD & SUPPLIES
Food and supplies are available in King Salmon.

FIRST AID/ HOSPITAL
• First aid is not available along the Wild River. • The nearest hospital is in Dillingham, AK.

GENERAL INFORMATION
• This is a wilderness area. • There is private property along the river.

Big South Fork National River and Recreation Area

Tennessee and Kentucky

Part of the Cumberland Plateau, the Big South Fork National River and Recreation Area was set aside so people could enjoy the rugged scenic area through white-water canoeing, rafting, kayaking, hiking and a variety of other activities.

MAILING ADDRESS	Superintendent, Big South Fork National River and Recreation Area, Rt. 3, Box 401, Oneida, TN 37841 **Telephone:** 615-569-3625
DIRECTIONS	I-75 and I-40 are the major access routes to the National River and Recreation Area. From I-75, proceed west via KY 80, 90 or 92, or TN 63 to US 27. Take US 27 to Oneida, TN. The Visitor Center is 12 miles (19.3 km) west of Oneida off of TN 297 in the Bandy Creek Campground. From I-40, proceed north via US 127 through Jamestown and then north on US 154 to TN 297. The Visitor Center is 12 miles (19.3 km) east.
VISITOR ACTIVITIES	• Canoeing, raft trips, hiking, horseback riding, mountain bike riding, interpretive walks, fishing, hunting, swimming and picnicking. • Facilities include exhibits at the Visitor Center and Blue Heron Mining Community, a stable, interpretive trails and horse trails.
PERMITS, FEES & LIMITATIONS	• No fees. • Free permits, available at the Bandy Creek Visitor Center, are suggested for backcountry users. • Vehicles are prohibited from the river gorge and limited to established roads.
ACCESSIBILITY	Restrooms, parking and developed facilities are accessible. Some paved trails provide access to overlooks.
CAMPING & LODGING	• Developed camping is available at Blue Heron and Bandy Creek campgrounds. Primitive camping (no water) is available at Alum Ford Campground. Backcountry camping is permitted. • Primitive lodging is available at Charit Creek Lodge by reservation. • Other overnight accommodations are available in local towns.
FOOD & SUPPLIES	Food and supplies are available in local towns.
FIRST AID/ HOSPITAL	• First aid is available in the National River and Recreation Area. • Hospitals are in Oneida and Jamestown, TN.
GENERAL INFORMATION	• **For your safety** - Paddling can be a dangerous sport on certain sections. Select a stream that matches your experience. Coast Guard-approved life jackets must be carried, and should be worn, on the river. Stay on designated hiking trails. Carry a first aid kit. • Steep grades and sharp turns are encountered on TN 297. Cars with trailers and RVs are advised to approach Bandy Creek Campground from Jamestown, TN.

Bluestone National Scenic River
West Virginia

T his scenic river preserves relatively unspoiled land in southwest West Virginia, contains natural and historic features of the Appalachian plateau, and offers excellent warm water fishing, hiking, boating and scenery in its lower 11 miles (17.7 km).

MAILING ADDRESS	Bluestone National Scenic River, PO Box 246, Glen Jean, WV 25846 Telephone: 304-465-0508
DIRECTIONS	Access is through Bluestone and Pipestem state parks off of Rt. 20. The National Scenic River is south of Hinton, WV, and northeast of Princeton, WV.
VISITOR ACTIVITIES	• Hiking, fishing, hunting, whitewater boating and photography. • Interpretive programs and guided hikes are scheduled regularly.
PERMITS, FEES & LIMITATIONS	• No fees. • Intermediate skill is required for whitewater, Class I and II. • Camping is prohibited. • No hunting or trapping is permitted in the upper 3.5 miles (5.6 km) of the Scenic River.
ACCESSIBILITY	Accessible facilities are available at Bluestone and Pipestem state parks.
CAMPING & LODGING	• Camping and lodging are available at Pipestem and Bluestone state parks. Mountain Creek Lodge, 1 of Pipestem's 2 lodges, is on the river and is accessible by tram from April through October. • Other overnight accommodations are available in surrounding towns.
FOOD & SUPPLIES	Food and supplies are available in the state parks and in area towns, including Athens, Hinton and Princeton.
FIRST AID/ HOSPITAL	• First aid is available at the state parks. • Summers County Hospital is in Hinton.
GENERAL INFORMATION	• A tram at Pipestem State Park provides access to the river. It is possible to transport boats on the tram. • **For your safety** - The hiking trail along the Bluestone River includes a ford of the Little Bluestone that can be dangerous or impassable at times.

Buffalo National River
Arkansas

D esignated as a National River in 1972, the Buffalo nestles in the Arkansas Ozarks and features white water, long quiet pools, bluffs that reach as high as 500 feet (152.4 m) above the river and many prehistoric and historic cultural sites as it winds its way from the Boston Mountains to its confluence with the White River.

MAILING ADDRESS	Superintendent, Buffalo National River, PO Box 1173, Harrison, AR 72602-1173 **Telephone:** 501-741-5443
DIRECTIONS	The Visitor Center is at Tyler Bend, 32 miles (51.6 km) south of Harrison on Hwy. 65. Information centers are at Buffalo Point off of Hwy. 14, at the Pruitt Ranger Station off of Hwy. 7 and at Headquarters on Walnut and Erie streets in Harrison.
VISITOR ACTIVITIES	• Canoeing, swimming, hiking, fishing, picnicking, interpretive exhibits, campfire programs, guided walks and canoe trips. • The National River is always open. Services are reduced in winter. • Facilities include exhibits, a bookstore, restrooms and telephones at information centers; picnic areas, hiking trails, canoe launch sites and canoe rentals.
PERMITS, FEES & LIMITATIONS	No entrance fee.
ACCESSIBILITY	Erbie, Tyler Bend and Buffalo Point Campgrounds have accessible camp sites and restrooms. Accessible camp sites are open until all other sites are filled. Buffalo Point Restaurant is accessible, but has no accessible restrooms.
CAMPING & LODGING	• Camping is available in 14 campgrounds. Sites are $7 per night for walk-ins or $10 per night for drive-ins at Buffalo Point Campground; and $7 per night at Tyler Bend Campground. All others are free and primitive. • For cabin rental information and reservations, contact Buffalo Point Concessions, HCR#66, Box 388, Yellville, AR 72687.
FOOD & SUPPLIES	• Meals are served at the Buffalo Point Restaurant from Memorial Day to Labor Day. • Food and supplies are available in local communities.
FIRST AID/ HOSPITAL	• First aid is available at Ranger stations. • The nearest hospital is in Harrison.
GENERAL INFORMATION	For your safety - Stay off of the bluffs, and keep alert to river conditions and avoid the river during high water times. Remove all ticks immediately

Delaware National Scenic River

Pennsylvania, New Jersey and New York

This river flows 41 miles (66.1 km) through the Delaware Water Gap National Recreation Area (see listing in this book) cutting a tight "S" curve through Kittatiny Ridge. The river provides beautiful landscape for sightseeing and geological study, as well as the Roebling Bridge and Zane Grey House and Museum historical sites.

MAILING ADDRESS	Superintendent, Delaware Water Gap National Recreation Area, Bushkill, PA 18324 **Telephone:** 717-588-2435

DIRECTIONS

For details on activities and other information, see the Delaware Water Gap National Recreation Area listing in this book.

Great Egg Harbor National Scenic and Recreational River

New Jersey

The Great Egg, 127 miles (204.8 km) of which was designated a National Scenic and Recreational River in 1992, is representative of rivers in southern New Jersey's famous "Pinelands," where the diversity and rarity of flora and fauna has led to establishment of the Pinelands National Reserve (see listing in this book). The Reserve is recognized as a unit of the South Atlantic Coastal Plain Biosphere Reserve under the United Nations Man and Biosphere Program.

MAILING ADDRESS

Great Egg Harbor National Scenic and Recreational River, c/o National Park Service, Mid-Atlantic Region, Room 260, Custom House, 2nd and Chestnut Streets, Philadelphia, PA 19106 **Telephone: 215-597-1582**

Mississippi National River and Recreation Area

Minnesota

For 72 miles (116.1 km), from Dayton to Hastings, MN, the Mississippi flows through a variety of landscapes passing cultural, historical and industrial features that relate the story of human activity in the area.

MAILING ADDRESS

Mississippi National River and Recreation Area, 175 5th St., East, Suite 418, Box 41, St. Paul, MN 55101-2901 **Telephone: 612-290-4160**

DIRECTIONS

Facilities and recreational opportunities are provided at numerous sites.

VISITOR ACTIVITIES

Boating, canoeing, fishing, swimming, hiking, biking, picnicking, nature study, visitor centers, historic sites, guided tours, self-guiding tours and boat tours.

PERMITS, FEES & LIMITATIONS

Fees and permits vary at parks along the river.

ACCESSIBILITY

Many facilities and programs are accessible.

CAMPING & LODGING

Overnight accommodations are available in the Twin Cities area.

FOOD & SUPPLIES

Food and supplies are available in the Twin Cities area.

FIRST AID/ HOSPITAL

Medical services are available in the Twin Cities area.

Missouri National Recreation River

Nebraska and South Dakota

The 2 separate segments - from Fort Randall Dam downstream to the backwaters of Lewis and Clark Lake, and from Gavins Point Dam downstream to Ponca State Park - of the Missouri National Recreation River are among the last free-flowing waters of the once "Mighty Mo." They still exhibit the river's dynamic character in their islands, bars, chutes and snags.

MAILING ADDRESS
Superintendent, Niobrara/Missouri National Scenic Riverways, PO Box 591, O'Neill, NE 68763 **Telephone:** 402-336-3970

DIRECTIONS
• **No National Park Service facilities.** • The U.S. Army Corps of Engineers, along with state and local agencies, provide access at various points on the river.

PERMITS, FEES & LIMITATIONS
There are **entrance fees** at Nebraska and South Dakota facilities.

CAMPING & LODGING
Overnight accommodations are available in state and local parks and nearby communities.

FOOD & SUPPLIES
Food and supplies are available in nearby communities.

FIRST AID/ HOSPITAL
Medical services are available in Yankton, SD; and Sioux City, IA.

GENERAL INFORMATION
For more information, contact the state tourism offices at 1-800-228-4307 in Nebraska and 1-800-843-1930 in South Dakota.

New River Gorge National River

West Virginia

Together, the New River and its gorge present an impressive display of natural forces while providing a home to many of West Virginia's rarest plants, and offering the most renowned fishing in the state and one of the finest whitewater experiences in the United States.

MAILING ADDRESS
New River Gorge National River, PO Box 246, Glen Jean, WV 25846 **Telephone:** 304-465-0508

DIRECTIONS
The Canyon Rim Visitor Center is on US 19 near Fayetteville at the New River Gorge Bridge. The Hinton Visitor Center is on WV 3 Bypass at Hinton, WV. The Grandview Visitor Center is 6 miles (9.6 km) off of I-64 on WV 9. The Glen Jean Bank Visitor Center is one-half mile (.8 km) off US 19 in Glen Jean.

National Rivers

VISITOR ACTIVITIES	• Interpretive programs, hikes, bird walks, whitewater rafting, canoeing, kayaking, fishing, hiking, bicycling, photography, sightseeing, picnicking and recreational climbing. • Slide programs are shown at Canyon Rim and Hinton visitor centers. • Facilities include restrooms, picnic areas, bookstores, telephones, boat launches, exhibits and informational bulletin boards. • Canyon Rim Visitor Center is open year-round. The other visitor centers are open seasonally.
PERMITS, FEES & LIMITATIONS	• No fees. • Ask at a Visitor Center for information on limitations and primitive camping. • Commercial rafting requires a West Virginia license from the Department of Natural Resources.
ACCESSIBILITY	The visitor centers and the boardwalk at Canyon Rim Visitor Center are accessible.
CAMPING & LODGING	• Primitive camping is available at Glade Creek, Sandstone Falls and other areas. Camping is also available at Babcock State Park within the National River boundaries. • Other private and state campgrounds are nearby. • Lodging is available in nearby communities.
FOOD & SUPPLIES	Food and supplies are available in Fayetteville, Oak Hill, Beckley, Hinton and smaller towns.
FIRST AID/ HOSPITAL	• First aid is available at visitor centers. • The Plateau Medical Center is in Oak Hill. Appalachian Regional and Raleigh General hospitals are in Beckley.
GENERAL INFORMATION	Nearby points of interest include an exhibition coal mine in Beckley; outdoor dramas performed by Theatre West Virginia at Grandview during the summer; the world's longest single arch steel bridge over the New River Gorge near Fayetteville; and Hawk's Nest, Babcock, Pipestem, Little Beaver and Bluestone state parks.

Niobrara National Scenic River

Nebraska and South Dakota

Perhaps the epitome of a prairie river, the Niobrara is known as a biological crossroads that, while primarily traversing private land, also flows by the Ft. Niobrara National Wildlife Refuge and land where the American Bison have been reintroduced.

MAILING ADDRESS	Superintendent, Niobrara/Missouri National Scenic Riverways, PO Box 591, O'Neill, NE 68763 **Telephone:** 402-336-3970
DIRECTIONS	The Scenic River is in north-central Nebraska and is reached via US 20 and US 83.

VISITOR ACTIVITIES	• No National Park Service facilities. • State and local facilities provide access at various points along the river.
PERMITS, FEES & LIMITATIONS	Smith Falls State Park has no admission fee.
CAMPING & LODGING	Camping and lodging is available in state and local parks and in nearby communities.
FOOD & SUPPLIES	Food and supplies are available in nearby communities.
FIRST AID/ HOSPITAL	Medical services are available in Valentine and Ainsworth, NE.
GENERAL INFORMATION	For canoeing information, contact the Valentine Chamber of Commerce, PO Box 201, Valentine, NE 69201, phone 1-800-658-4024. For additional information, contact the state tourism office at 1-800-228-4307.

Obed Wild and Scenic River

Tennessee

The Obed River and its 2 main tributaries, Clear Creek and Daddy's Creek, cut into the Cumberland Plateau of East Tennessee. The river provides some of the most rugged scenery in the southeast, featuring spectacular gorges as deep as 500 feet (152.4 m).

MAILING ADDRESS	Obed Wild and Scenic River, PO Box 429, Wartburg, TN 37887 **Telephone:** 615-346-6294
DIRECTIONS	Take US 27 or TN 62 to Wartburg, TN.
VISITOR ACTIVITIES	Swimming, fishing, hiking, picnicking and whitewater boating.
PERMITS, FEES & LIMITATIONS	No fees.
ACCESSIBILITY	The Visitor Center is accessible. Development is limited, making access within the Scenic River area difficult. There is minimal access by auto.
CAMPING & LODGING	• Camping is allowed along the river or at access sites. • Primitive camping facilities are available at Frozen Head State Park. Cumberland Mountain State Park has a developed campground. • Private campgrounds are along I-40 and in the Crossville area.
FOOD & SUPPLIES	Food and supplies are available in Wartburg, TN.

**FIRST AID/
HOSPITAL**

Medical services are available in Oak Ridge, Harriman and Crossville, TN.

**GENERAL
INFORMATION**

Whitewater boating depends on rainfall. The best boating is available from February to April. Commercial trips may be available. Call for water levels and float information.

Ozark National Scenic Riverways

Missouri

The first Riverways park created in 1964, Ozark National Scenic Riverways encompasses 134 miles (216.1 km) of the Current and Jacks Fork rivers and provides canoeing, tubing, fishing and swimming opportunities in clear, cold, blue water from nearly 100 springs. Ozark culture is also preserved throughout the area.

**MAILING
ADDRESS**

Superintendent, Ozark National Scenic Riverways, PO Box 490, Van Buren, MO 63965 **Telephone:** 314-323-4236

DIRECTIONS

The Riverways is 175 miles (282.2 km) south of St. Louis, MO, and 250 miles (403.2 km) southeast of Kansas City, MO. Developed areas are off of MO 19 at Akers Ferry, Pulltite and Round Spring. Alley Spring and Two Rivers can be reached via Hwy. 106 out of Eminence, MO. Big Spring is on Hwy. 103, 4 miles (6.4 km) from Van Buren, MO.

**VISITOR
ACTIVITIES**

• Canoeing, fishing, picnicking, float trips, tubing, boating, craft demonstrations, interpretive talks, cave tours, hunting, hiking and swimming. • Write for a list of canoe concessionaires. • Picnic pavilions are available by reservation. • Book sales and restrooms are available at Headquarters. • Winter float trips are available. • Interpretive activities are available in summer only.

**PERMITS, FEES
& LIMITATIONS**

No entrance fee.

ACCESSIBILITY

Many of the facilities are accessible with assistance. Accessible camp sites are available at some campgrounds. Write for detailed information.

**CAMPING &
LODGING**

• Camping in developed areas is available for $7 per night for family sites; $20 per night for 7 to 10 people in cluster sites with $2 per person added for 11 to 20 people; $30 for 7 to 15 people in group sites, $40 for 16 to 20 people, $50 for 21 to 25 people, $60 for 26 to 20 people and $90 for 31 to 45 people. Family and cluster sites are available on a first-come, first-served basis. Group site reservations are available through MISTIX at 1-800-365-2267. There is a 14-day camping limit. • No fees for gravel bar and primitive camp sites. • Rustic cabins are available at Big Spring. Reserve by writing

PO Box 602, Van Buren, MO 63965, or calling 314-323-4423. • Contact Alley Spring, HCR 3, Box 18, Eminence, MO, 65466, phone 314-226-3386 for motel information and reservations. • Other overnight accommodations are available in Salem, Mt. View, Eminence and Van Buren.

FOOD & SUPPLIES

• Meals are served at the Big Spring Lodge restaurant in season. • Camp stores are at Akers Ferry, Pulltite, Round Spring, Two Rivers and Alley Spring. • Supplies are available in Salem, Eminence, Van Buren, Ellington, Mt. View, Winona and Birch Tree.

FIRST AID/ HOSPITAL

• First aid is available at Ranger stations. • Hospitals are in Ellington, Salem and Mt. View.

GENERAL INFORMATION

For your safety - Life jackets or boat cushions must be carried for each person in a boat or canoe. Children under age 7 are required to wear a PFD. Non-swimmers and weak swimmers should wear life jackets at all times. Jumping or diving from bluffs is dangerous. Pick camp sites well above the river level. Flash flood warnings are issued when possible. Extinguish camp fires. Talk to a Ranger or concessioner about river conditions and hazards. Carry first aid kits, matches, billfolds and other valuables in waterproof containers. Check with a Ranger before entering caves.

Rio Grande Wild and Scenic River

Texas

This is a remote, undeveloped area administered by Big Bend National Park extending from Mariscal Canyon to the Terrell/Val Verde County line for 191.2 miles (308.3 km) along the American shore of the Rio Grande in the Chihuahuan Desert.

MAILING ADDRESS

Rio Grande Wild and Scenic River, c/o Superintendent, Big Bend National Park, TX 79834 **Telephone:** 915-477-2393

DIRECTIONS

See the listing in this book for Big Bend National Park for directions.

VISITOR ACTIVITIES

• Canoeing and rafting year-round. • Facilities include visitor centers at Persimmon Gap and Rio Grande Village, and an amphitheater at Rio Grande Village. There are no facilities in the Lower Canyons outside Big Bend National Park.

PERMITS, FEES & LIMITATIONS

• There is an **entrance fee** at Big Bend National Park. • A floating permit, available at Persimmon Gap Visitor Center and any Ranger Station, is required. • Vehicles are restricted to developed roads. • There is little or no access to the Lower Canyons.

CAMPING & LODGING

• Backcountry camping is permitted in the Lower Canyons. • See listing for Big Bend National Park for information on developed campgrounds and lodges.

FOOD & SUPPLIES	See listing for Big Bend National Park.
FIRST AID/ HOSPITAL	• First aid is available at Ranger stations. • The nearest hospital is in Alpine, TX, 100 miles (161.2 km).
GENERAL INFORMATION	• Floating the Lower Canyons requires 7 days. • There are no take-out points between La Linda, Mexico and Dryden Crossing, 83 miles (133.8 km). In an emergency, parties should be prepared to evacuate themselves. Rescue is difficult and patrols infrequent. • Within the Park, there are 2 canyons (Mariscal and Boquillas) that are relatively easy with numerous put-in points. • Write for equipment requirements.

Saint Croix National Scenic Riverway

Wisconsin and Minnesota

Free flowing and unpolluted, beautiful St. Croix River and its Namekagon tributary flow through some of the most scenic and least developed country in the upper midwest. Canoeists can be challenged by rapids, anglers can try for a variety of fish, and visitors in general can enjoy swimming, birdwatching and picnicking.

MAILING ADDRESS	Superintendent, Saint Croix National Scenic Riverway, PO Box 708, St. Croix Falls, WI 54024 **Telephone:** 715-483-3284
DIRECTIONS	Headquarters is at the corner of Hamilton and Massachusetts streets in St. Croix Falls.
VISITOR ACTIVITIES	• Fishing, canoeing, wildlife and bird watching, boating, hiking, hunting and cross-country skiing. • Exhibits and slide shows are featured at the visitor centers in Trego and St. Croix Falls. • A commercial-guided paddle boat is available in Taylors Falls, MN. Canoe rentals and shuttle services are available throughout the Riverway.
PERMITS, FEES & LIMITATIONS	No fees.
ACCESSIBILITY	Restrooms, exhibit area and auditorium at visitor centers are accessible. Toilets and picnic sites at Earl Park and some camp sites are accessible.
CAMPING & LODGING	• Camping is available at primitive, water accessible camp sites. Camping is limited to 1 night only at designated sites. No ORVs permitted. • State campgrounds nearby offer more services. • Lodging is available in nearby communities, including Hayward, Trego, Cable, Spooner, Pine City, Grantsburg, St. Croix Falls and Taylors Falls.
FOOD & SUPPLIES	Food and supplies are available in nearby communities.

FIRST AID/ HOSPITAL

Medical services are available in Hayward, Spooner, Grantsburg and St. Croix Falls, 10 miles (16.1 km).

GENERAL INFORMATION

• Canoe campers should have a life preserver for each person, an extra paddle, insect repellent, a small gasoline stove and drinking water.
• Firewood is scarce, and the cutting of trees or brush is prohibited.
• Drinking water is available at a few places along the river. • Deer ticks carry Lyme disease and are common along the river.

Upper Delaware Scenic and Recreation River

New York and Pennsylvania

The Upper Delaware Scenic and Recreation River is a 73.4-mile (118.3 km) stretch of free-flowing river between Hancock and Sparrow Bush, NY, along the Pennsylvania border in an area that is also home to the Roebling Bridge, believed to be the oldest existing wire cable suspension bridge.

MAILING ADDRESS

Upper Delaware Scenic and Recreation River, PO Box C, Narrowsburg, NY 12764 Telephone: 717-729-8251

VISITOR ACTIVITIES

• Canoeing, kayaking, rafting, tubing, sightseeing and fishing. • Facilities include an Information Center, 5 kiosks and the Roebling Bridge Contact Station, which are staffed in the summer. • The Zane Grey Museum, open daily from Memorial Day to Labor Day and on weekends in the spring and fall, contains exhibits, an audiovisual program, guided tours and a sales desk. • Boat rentals are available in the area.

PERMITS, FEES & LIMITATIONS

No fees.

ACCESSIBILITY

The Roebling Bridge, the Information Center and information kiosks are accessible.

CAMPING & LODGING

Overnight accommodations are available in the vicinity.

Special Interest Parks

These National Park sites are included for visitors with interests in a specific aspect of our country's history and culture. These categories may also suggest other sites for visitors to investigate.

African American History Sites

Booker T. Washington National Monument, VA
Boston African American National Historic Site, MA
Dayton Aviation National Historical Park, OH
Frederick Douglass National Historic Site, DC
George Washington Carver National Monument, MO
Maggie L. Walker National Historic Site, VA
Martin Luther King, Jr. National Historic Site, GA
Mary McLeod Bethune Council House National Historic Site, DC
Tuskegee Institute National Historic Site, AL

Archealogical and Paleontological Sites

Agate Fossil Beds National Monument, NE
Aztec Ruins National Monument, NM
Bandelier National Monument, NM
Canyon de Chelly National Monument, AZ
Casa Grande National Monument, AZ
Chaco Culture National Historical Park, NM
Dinosaur National Monument, CO
Florissant Fossil Beds National Monument, CO
Fossil Butte National Monument, WY
Gila Cliff Dwellings National Monument, NM
Hovenweep National Monument, CO
Mesa Verde National Park, CO
Montezuma Castle National Monument, AZ
Navajo National Monument, AZ
Petroglyph National Monument, NM
Tonto National Monument, AZ
Tuzigoot National Monument, AZ
Walnut Canyon National Monument, AZ
Wupatki National Monument, AZ
Yucca House National Monument, CO

Battlefields

Antietam National Battlefield, MD
Big Hole National Battlefield, MT
Brices Cross Roads National Battlefield Site, MS

Special Interest Parks

Chickamauga and Chattanooga National Military Park, GA
Colonial National Historical Park, VA
Cowpens National Battlefield, SC
Fort Donelson National Battlefield, TN
Fort Necessity National Battlefield, PA
Fredericksburg and Spotsylvania County Battlefields Memorial National Military Park, VA
Gettysburg National Military Park, PA
Guilford Courthouse National Military Park, NC
Horseshoe Bend National Military Park, AL
Jean Lafitte National Historical Park, LA
Kennesaw Mountain National Military Park, GA
Kings Mountain National Military Park, SC
Little Bighorn Battlefield National Monument, MT
Manassas National Battlefield Park, VA
Minute Man National Historical Park, MA
Monacacy National Battlefield, MD
Moores Creek National Battlefield, NC
Palo Alto Battlefield National Historic Site, TX
Pea Ridge National Military Park, AR
Petersburg National Battlefield, VA
Richmond National Battlefield Park, VA
Saratoga National Historical Park, NY
Shiloh National Military Park, TN
Stones River National Battlefield, TN
Tupelo National Battlefield, MS
Vicksburg National Military Park, MS
War in the Pacific National Historical Park, Guam
Wilson's Creek National Battlefield, MO

Hispanic Heritage Sites and Sites that Relate to America's Discovery

Amistad National Recreation Area, TX
Arkansas Post National Memorial, AR
Big Bend National Park, TX
Biscayne National Park, FL
Cabrillo National Monument, CA
Canyon de Chelly National Monument, AZ
Castillo de San Marcos National Monument, FL
Chamizal National Memorial, TX
Channel Islands National Park, CA
Christiansted National Historic Site, VI
Coronado National Memorial, AZ
Cumberland Island National Seashore, GA

De Soto National Memorial, FL
Dry Tortugas National Park, FL
El Morro National Monument, NM
Fort Caroline National Memorial, FL
Fort Frederica National Monument, GA
Fort Matanzas National Monument, FL
Fort Point National Historic Site, CA
Golden Gate National Recreation Area, CA
Gulf Islands National Seashore, FL
Jean Lafitte National Historical Park, LA
Jefferson National Expansion Memorial, MO
John Muir National Historic Site, CA
Natchez National Historical Park, MS
Natchez Trace Parkway, MS
Padre Island National Seashore, TX
Palo Alto Battlefield National Historic Site, TX
Pecos National Monument, NM
Point Reyes National Seashore, CA
Salinas Pueblo Missions National Monument, NM
San Antonio Missions National Historical Park, TX
San Juan National Historic Site, PR
Santa Monica Mountains National Recreation Area, CA
Sitka National Historical Park, AK
Timucuan Ecological and Historic Preserve, FL
Tumacacori National Monument, AZ
Wrangell-St. Elias National Park and Preserve, AK

Presidential History Sites

Abraham Lincoln Birthplace National Historic Site, KY
Adams National Historic Site, MA
Andrew Johnson National Historic Site, TN
Eisenhower National Historic Site, PA
Ford's Theatre National Historic Site, DC
General Grant National Memorial, NY
George Washington Birthplace National Monument, VA
Harry S. Truman National Historic Site, MO
Herbert Hoover National Historic Site, IA
Home of Franklin D. Roosevelt National Historic Site, NY
James A. Garfield National Historic Site, OH
Jimmy Carter National Historic Site, GA
John Fitzgerald Kennedy National Historic Site, MA
John F. Kennedy Center for the Performing Arts, DC
Lyndon Baines Johnson Memorial Grove on the Potomac, DC
Lyndon Baines Johnson National Historical Park, TX

Lincoln Boyhood Home National Monument, IN
Lincoln Home National Historic Site, IL
Lincoln Memorial, DC
Martin Van Buren National Historic Site, NY
Sagamore Hill National Historic Site, NY
Theodore Roosevelt Birthplace National Historic Site, NY
Theodore Roosevelt Inaugural National Historic Site, NY
Theodore Roosevelt Island National Memorial, DC
Theodore Roosevelt National Park, ND
Thomas Jefferson Memorial, DC
Ulysses S. Grant National Historic Site, MO
Washington Monument, DC
White House, DC
William Howard Taft National Historic Site, OH

Volcanoes, Caves and Hot Springs

Capulin Volcano National Monument, NM
Carlsbad Caverns National Park, NM
Crater Lake National Park, OR
Craters of the Moon National Monument, ID
Great Basin National Park, NV
Hawaii Volcanoes National Park, HI
Hot Springs National Park, AR
Jewel Cave National Monument, SD
Lassen Volcanic National Park, CA
Lava Beds National Monument, CA
Mammoth Cave National Park, KY
Oregon Caves National Monument, OR
Sunset Crater Volcano National Monument, AZ
Timpanogos Cave National Monument, UT
Wind Cave National Park, SD
Yellowstone National Park, WY

Women's History Sites

Clara Barton National Historic Site, MD
Eleanor Roosevelt National Historic Site, NY
Maggie L. Walker National Historic Site, VA
Mary McLeod Bethune Council House National Historic Site, DC
Whitman Mission National Historic Site, WA
Women's Rights National Historical Park, NY

Climatables™

Metric Conversion Chart

°F	°C	Clothing
110°F		
100°F	40°C	Light Clothes
90°F		
80°F	30°C	No Sweater
70°F	20°C	Sweater
60°F		
50°F	10°C	Light jacket
40°F		
30°F	0°C	Winter coat
20°F		
10°F	-10°C	Heavy winter coat
0°F	-20°C	Heavy winter clothes
-10°F		

Climatable No. 1

Katmai NP, Lake Clark NP, Alagnak Wild River

TEMPERATURE	J	F	M	A	M	J	J	A	S	O	N	D
Normal Daily Maximum	24	26	31	41	55	63	67	64	57	41	32	22
Normal Daily Minimum	3	4	8	22	32	40	45	45	38	25	15	5
Extreme High	54	54	56	63	78	86	90	88	75	66	53	53
Extreme Low	-42	-50	-50	-11	13	24	25	22	11	-5	-20	-48
Days Above 70°	0	0	0	0	1	4	10	4	0	0	0	0
Days Below 32°	29	26	29	25	16	3	2	2	5	24	27	28

PRECIPITATION	J	F	M	A	M	J	J	A	S	O	N	D
Normal	2.1	1.4	1.9	2.4	1.5	1.8	2.2	4.2	3.5	3.1	2.4	2.5
Maximum	3.0	3.0	2.4	3.0	3.0	3.9	4.9	11.2	6.6	6.4	3.4	3.6
Maximum 24 Hour	1.0	0.8	0.8	1.0	0.6	1.3	1.3	3.5	1.9	2.4	1.1	1.2
Maximum Snowfall	21	24	36	30	10	1	0	0	1	15	28	17
Days With Measurable Precip.	10	8	10	10	11	12	14	16	15	13	11	11
Average No. Thunderstorms	0	0	0	0	0	0	0	0	0	0	0	0

NOTES

• Wide variations in weather are experienced in the Parks due to differences in terrain and exposure to prevailing wind. • Precipitation is highest on the windward or eastern slopes and sharply decreases on the leeward sides.
• In the area of glaciers, total annual precipitation is 100" to 200".

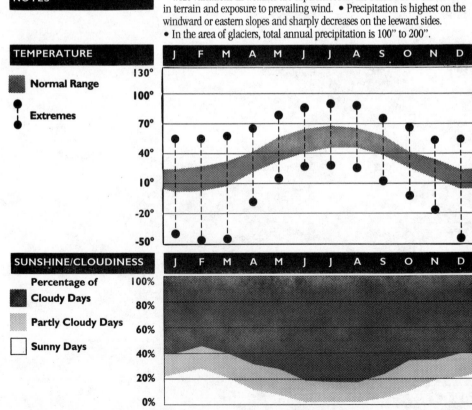

TEMPERATURE

Normal Range

Extremes

SUNSHINE/CLOUDINESS

Percentage of Cloudy Days

Partly Cloudy Days

Sunny Days

Wrangell-St. Elias NP, Aniakchak NM, Kenai Fjords NP

TEMPERATURE

	J	F	M	A	M	J	J	A	S	O	N	D
Normal Daily Maximum	29	31	35	42	49	57	61	60	54	44	35	30
Normal Daily Minimum	14	19	21	28	34	42	46	45	41	33	24	17
Extreme High	58	55	59	67	82	84	86	86	72	64	58	54
Extreme Low	-30	-21	-24	-9	6	29	32	30	20	-1	-8	-23
Days Above 70°	0	0	0	0	0	1	1	1	0	0	0	0
Days Below 32°	28	24	28	22	10	1	0	0	3	16	23	27

PRECIPITATION

	J	F	M	A	M	J	J	A	S	O	N	D
Normal	6.1	6.8	5.4	5.7	5.8	4.7	6.2	6.8	13.1	14.5	10.4	9.5
Maximum	15.8	19.0	12.4	12.2	13.6	13.2	17.8	18.3	27.7	26.6	30.6	19.8
Maximum 24 Hour	3.2	4.1	2.4	4.4	3.6	3.0	4.6	4.4	4.7	5.0	4.6	4.5
Maximum Snowfall	46	80	89	61	16	0	0	0	T	15	48	71
Days With Measurable Precip.	17	16	16	15	16	15	15	14	15	16	17	17
Average No. Thunderstorms	0	0	0	0	0	0	0	0	0	0	0	0

NOTES

- As evidenced by the glaciers, precipitation is greater at higher elevations.
- Record annual precipitation for Alaska of 332.29" was recorded on Montague Island in 1976. • At Thompson Pass just north of Valdez, a seasonal snowfall of 974.5" was recorded in 1952-53.

TEMPERATURE

Normal Range
Extremes

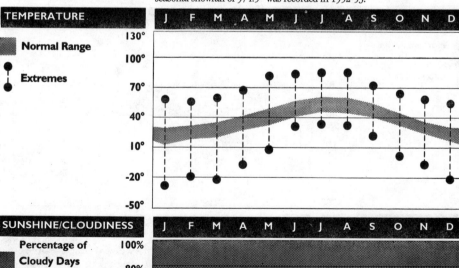

SUNSHINE/CLOUDINESS

Percentage of
Cloudy Days
Partly Cloudy Days
Sunny Days

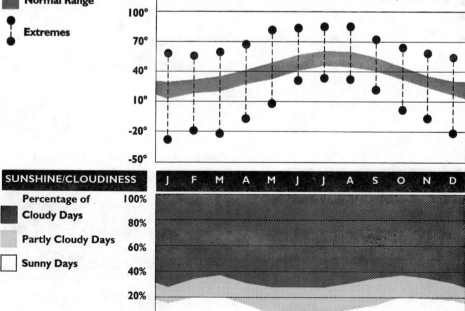

Climatable No. 3

Bering Land Bridge NP, Kobuk Valley NP, Noatak NP, Gates of the Arctic NP, Cape Krusenstern NM

TEMPERATURE	J	F	M	A	M	J	J	A	S	O	N	D
Normal Daily Maximum	-2	0	10	28	46	65	66	61	48	27	10	0
Normal Daily Minimum	-20	-17	-9	7	28	42	48	44	33	15	-2	-15
Extreme High	39	40	42	59	79	90	86	84	70	54	39	40
Extreme Low	-58	-64	-55	-44	-18	19	30	19	-1	-20	-50	-58
Days Above 70°	0	0	0	0	1	11	15	6	0	0	0	0
Days Below 32°	31	28	31	28	11	1	0	1	13	26	30	31

PRECIPITATION	J	F	M	A	M	J	J	A	S	O	N	D
Normal	0.7	0.6	0.8	0.8	0.9	1.2	2.7	2.7	2.5	0.9	1.2	0.8
Maximum	2.6	2.9	3.6	1.9	1.4	3.6	5.4	5.9	4.1	3.8	3.8	2.0
Maximum 24 Hour	0.9	0.6	0.8	1.0	0.9	1.2	2.0	2.1	1.4	0.9	0.7	0.5
Maximum Snowfall	24	14	22	18	12	2	0	1	7	18	29	22
Days With Measurable Precip.	8	7	8	6	6	8	11	14	12	10	10	9
Average No. Thunderstorms	0	0	0	0	0	1	2	0	0	0	0	0

NOTES

• The "Land of the Midnight Sun." The sun remains continuously above the horizon from the beginning of June until the middle of July. • On the Seward Peninsula, temperatures are more moderate and precipitation totals are less than in the remaining areas represented by this table.

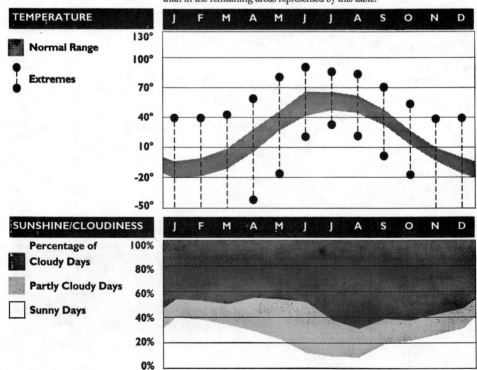

TEMPERATURE

■ Normal Range

● Extremes

Climatable No. 4

Denali NP, Yukon-Charley NPres

TEMPERATURE	J	F	M	A	M	J	J	A	S	O	N	D
Normal Daily Maximum	-2	8	20	37	55	68	70	63	51	30	11	0
Normal Daily Minimum	-20	-12	-6	14	30	42	46	41	32	15	-5	-15
Extreme High	51	51	53	65	90	93	94	86	78	63	52	45
Extreme Low	-60	-50	-47	-32	-8	19	23	19	3	-27	-51	-60
Days Above 70°	0	0	0	0	2	14	15	8	1	0	0	0
Days Below 32°	31	28	31	29	20	2	1	5	16	30	30	31

PRECIPITATION	J	F	M	A	M	J	J	A	S	O	N	D
Normal	0.6	0.5	0.5	0.4	0.8	2.0	2.2	2.0	1.3	0.9	0.6	0.5
Maximum	1.9	2.2	3.1	1.8	3.8	5.8	7.7	6.8	4.4	2.0	5.3	3.0
Maximum 24 Hour	1.0	1.2	1.9	1.6	2.7	2.1	3.3	2.6	1.8	0.9	1.6	1.3
Maximum Snowfall	30	40	41	21	14	3	0	4	16	35	69	36
Days With Measurable Precip.	6	5	5	5	7	10	13	13	10	10	9	7
Average No. Thunderstorms	0	0	0	0	0	2	2	1	0	0	0	0

NOTES

• In June, length of day ranges from 19 to 23 hours; in December, duration of daylight is 3 to 5 hours. • Yukon-Charley NPres has colder winters and warmer summers than Denali NP, but weather is more variable in Denali. • Alaska's record high temperature of 100°F was recorded at Fort Yukon in June 1915.

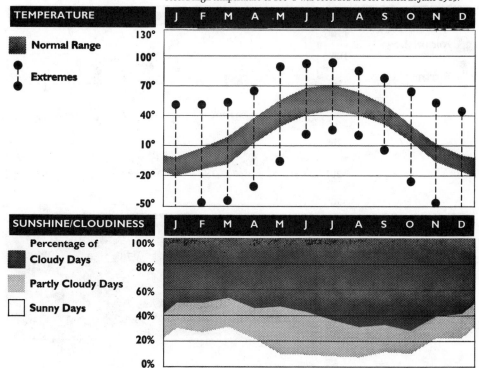

Climatable No. 5

Sitka NHP, Glacier Bay NP, Klondike Gold Rush NHP

TEMPERATURE	J	F	M	A	M	J	J	A	S	O	N	D
Normal Daily Maximum	32	38	41	48	55	62	63	62	57	48	41	35
Normal Daily Minimum	23	28	29	34	39	44	48	48	44	38	32	27
Extreme High	60	63	65	76	85	85	88	86	82	70	65	64
Extreme Low	-8	-4	-5	6	26	30	34	30	28	16	-1	-6
Days Above 70°	0	0	0	0	1	2	2	2	1	0	0	0
Days Below 32°	26	21	22	13	2	0	0	0	0	5	15	22

PRECIPITATION	J	F	M	A	M	J	J	A	S	O	N	D
Normal	5.1	5.8	5.0	4.4	4.4	2.9	4.9	7.7	11.7	12.8	9.4	7.2
Maximum	17.7	18.8	13.6	13.4	10.4	9.8	12.0	21.0	25.5	26.6	25.8	18.2
Maximum 24 Hour	3.8	2.7	3.2	2.2	3.1	2.0	2.1	4.2	6.4	4.9	4.3	3.2
Maximum Snowfall	44	24	32	12	1	0	0	0	T	19	26	40
Days With Measurable Precip.	17	18	17	17	16	13	17	18	22	25	23	21
Average No. Thunderstorms	0	0	0	0	0	0	0	0	0	0	0	0

NOTES

• Climate moderated by warm Alaska current flowing northward along the coast. • In higher elevation areas, temperatures are lower and precipitation is greater than shown in the table. • Wind speeds greater than 50 mph are often experienced in winter; watch the wind chill temperature.

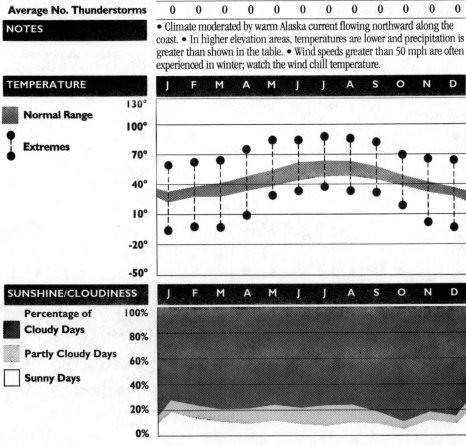

Climatable No. 6   481

Glen Canyon NRA, Grand Canyon NP

TEMPERATURE

	J	F	M	A	M	J	J	A	S	O	N	D
Normal Daily Maximum	42	48	59	69	79	88	94	91	85	68	54	44
Normal Daily Minimum	21	26	31	37	49	58	65	63	57	42	31	23
Extreme High	72	75	84	90	98	109	107	106	104	94	80	73
Extreme Low	-16	-14	-3	9	13	28	31	30	25	3	-1	-13
Days Above 90°	0	0	0	0	4	17	28	24	9	0	0	0
Days Below 32°	26	18	13	4	1	0	0	0	0	1	11	26

PRECIPITATION

	J	F	M	A	M	J	J	A	S	O	N	D
Normal	1.2	1.1	1.3	0.9	0.5	0.5	1.4	2.1	1.0	0.9	0.8	1.4
Maximum	NA	NA	NA	NA	NA	NA	NA	NA	NA	NA	NA	NA
Maximum 24 Hour	1.7	1.8	4.0	1.1	1.2	2.2	2.6	2.2	2.7	1.8	1.3	2.2
Maximum Snowfall	60	33	44	46	19	0	0	0	0	12	22	32
Days With Measurable Precip.	6	6	7	5	4	4	7	9	5	5	5	6
Average No. Thunderstorms	0	0	0	1	4	5	13	14	7	2	0	0

NOTES

• There is a strong temperature contrast between the floor and rim of the Grand Canyon. The summer climate of the Canyon floor is torrid. Temperatures can become dangerously high. The Canyon floor is considerably drier than the rim. • The Glen Canyon area is even drier than the Grand Canyon.

TEMPERATURE

Normal Range

Extremes

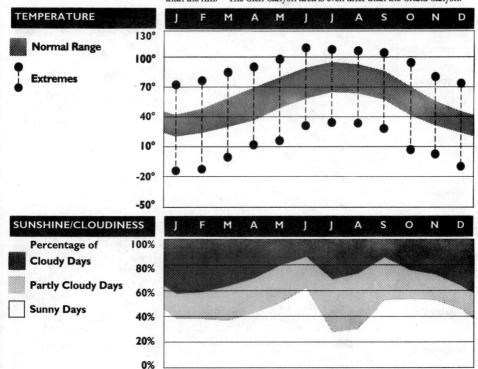

SUNSHINE/CLOUDINESS

Percentage of
Cloudy Days

Partly Cloudy Days

Sunny Days

Climatable No. 7

Hot Springs NP

TEMPERATURE	J	F	M	A	M	J	J	A	S	O	N	D
Normal Daily Maximum	54	58	66	76	83	91	95	95	89	78	67	55
Normal Daily Minimum	35	37	43	52	59	68	71	71	64	54	42	36
Extreme High	81	85	92	94	103	112	111	115	109	99	89	80
Extreme Low	-2	1	7	26	36	50	54	52	35	28	14	7
Days Above 90°	0	0	0	0	5	18	25	25	15	2	0	0
Days Below 32°	14	10	6	0	0	0	0	0	0	0	6	12

PRECIPITATION	J	F	M	A	M	J	J	A	S	O	N	D
Normal	5.3	4.8	5.2	5.9	6.1	4.3	4.2	3.2	3.8	3.5	4.6	4.6
Maximum	9.2	16.0	10.4	14.5	16.6	12.0	16.2	12.8	8.5	7.8	11.3	9.8
Maximum 24 Hour	5.5	5.5	4.6	6.2	8.0	4.4	8.4	4.1	5.4	3.8	5.5	3.4
Maximum Snowfall	15	11	4	0	0	0	0	0	0	0	4	10
Days With Measurable Precip.	10	9	10	10	10	9	9	8	9	7	8	9
Average No. Thunderstorms	3	3	8	8	9	10	12	9	5	3	3	2

NOTES

• Summers are warm and humid. • Summer rain falls as scattered showers and thunderstorms, often brief but locally heavy. • Winters are relatively mild; warm spells with temperatures in the 60s°F and 70s°F are not uncommon.

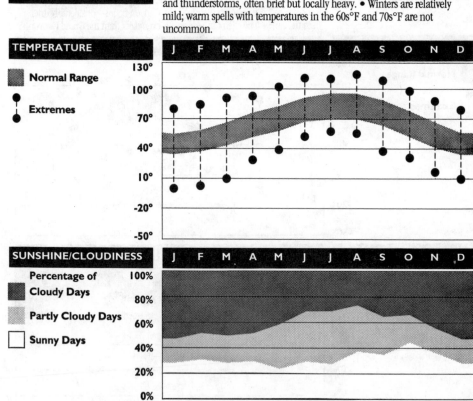

TEMPERATURE

Normal Range

Extremes

130°
100°
70°
40°
10°
-20°
-50°

SUNSHINE/CLOUDINESS

Percentage of Cloudy Days

Partly Cloudy Days

Sunny Days

100%
80%
60%
40%
20%
0%

Climatable No. 8

Cabrillo NM, Channel Islands NP, Santa Monica Mts. NRA

TEMPERATURE	J	F	M	A	M	J	J	A	S	O	N	D
Normal Daily Maximum	63	64	63	64	65	68	70	72	72	70	68	65
Normal Daily Minimum	47	48	49	51	55	58	61	62	61	56	51	47
Extreme High	85	87	91	88	94	93	91	89	104	99	100	89
Extreme Low	24	31	32	39	43	45	51	52	44	36	34	30
Days Above 90°	0	0	0	0	0	0	0	0	0	0	0	0
Days Below 32°	0	0	0	0	0	0	0	0	0	0	0	0

PRECIPITATION	J	F	M	A	M	J	J	A	S	O	N	D
Normal	3.3	3.0	2.1	1.0	0.2	0.0	0.0	0.2	0.1	0.2	1.7	1.9
Maximum	13.9	14.1	9.8	5.5	2.9	0.2	0.4	3.1	1.1	1.8	8.7	6.5
Maximum 24 Hour	5.3	4.2	4.1	2.1	1.5	1.1	0.4	2.8	1.9	0.9	4.2	5.3
Maximum Snowfall	0	0	0	0	0	0	0	0	0	0	0	0
Days With Measurable Precip.	6	6	6	3	1	0	0	0	1	2	4	5
Average No. Thunderstorms	0	0	0	0	0	0	0	0	0	0	0	0

NOTES

- Summer is very distinctly the dry season; little or no precipitation occurs.
- Spring and summer are characterized by morning low cloudiness and sunny afternoons. • In winter, fog can be expected one day in four. • In the spring, seas of 5' or higher are observed 30% to 40% of the time.

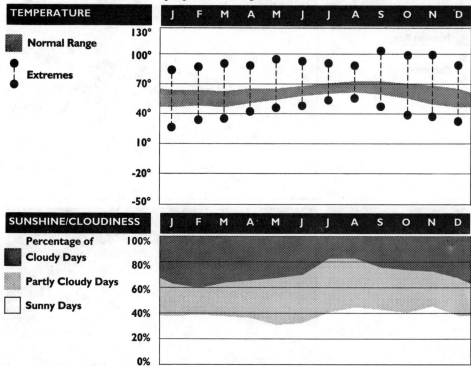

Yosemite NP, Devil's Postpile NM

TEMPERATURE	J	F	M	A	M	J	J	A	S	O	N	D
Normal Daily Maximum	47	55	59	66	73	82	90	90	85	74	58	46
Normal Daily Minimum	26	29	31	35	42	48	53	52	47	39	31	26
Extreme High	69	79	89	90	91	102	104	104	102	98	86	65
Extreme Low	7	10	10	20	26	30	38	32	28	21	16	-1
Days Above 90°	0	0	0	0	1	6	18	18	9	1	0	0
Days Below 32°	27	22	21	11	2	0	0	0	0	5	21	27

PRECIPITATION	J	F	M	A	M	J	J	A	S	O	N	D
Normal	6.6	5.0	4.6	3.5	1.5	0.6	0.4	0.3	0.7	1.4	4.7	6.9
Maximum	22.3	17.2	11.5	12.1	4.8	1.6	1.6	1.3	5.2	4.6	13.0	29.8
Maximum 24 Hour	5.8	4.6	2.9	2.9	1.9	1.0	1.0	0.7	3.2	2.3	3.4	6.9
Maximum Snowfall	49	89	67	81	7	0	0	0	0	T	21	51
Days With Measurable Precip.	12	10	11	9	6	3	1	1	2	5	9	11
Average No. Thunderstorms	0	0	1	2	3	4	5	3	2	0	0	0

NOTES

• Temperature and precipitation, especially snowfall, vary considerably with elevation, the higher elevation areas being cooler and wetter. • Summer evenings can be quite chilly.

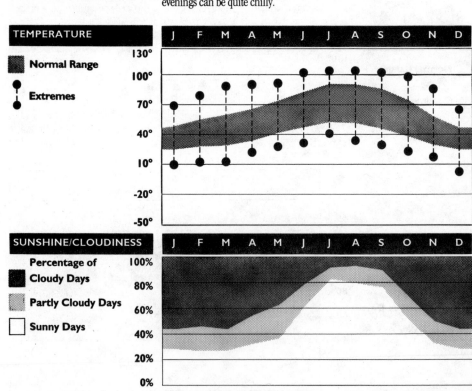

Climatable No. 10

Whiskeytown-Shasta-Trinity NRA, Lassen Volcanic NP

TEMPERATURE

	J	F	M	A	M	J	J	A	S	O	N	D
Normal Daily Maximum	43	49	53	60	70	78	87	86	80	67	53	45
Normal Daily Minimum	25	28	30	34	40	46	51	49	44	37	30	26
Extreme High	65	73	80	85	95	103	106	108	106	93	80	65
Extreme Low	-7	1	0	14	21	25	31	34	25	18	8	-11
Days Above 90°	0	0	0	0	1	7	19	17	7	1	0	0
Days Below 32°	26	22	21	12	4	1	0	0	2	7	19	26

PRECIPITATION

	J	F	M	A	M	J	J	A	S	O	N	D
Normal	3.7	2.2	1.8	0.9	0.8	0.8	0.4	0.6	0.6	1.2	2.3	3.8
Maximum	8.0	6.8	6.2	3.4	3.2	3.4	2.0	3.2	3.2	8.0	6.7	13.7
Maximum 24 Hour	3.0	2.1	2.1	1.1	1.1	1.1	1.2	1.3	1.4	2.8	2.6	4.6
Maximum Snowfall	48	23	22	10	2	0	0	0	3	1	33	28
Days With Measurable Precip.	11	9	10	7	4	2	1	1	2	5	9	10
Average No. Thunderstorms	0	1	1	1	2	2	1	1	1	1	0	0

NOTES

• Precipitation is a maximum in winter; heavy, persistent rains over periods of 7-10 days may be experienced. • Near Mt. Shasta, North America's record snowfall of 189" for a single snowstorm occurred. • Precipitation amounts are markedly less on the eastern slopes of the mountains.

TEMPERATURE

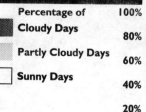

Normal Range

Extremes

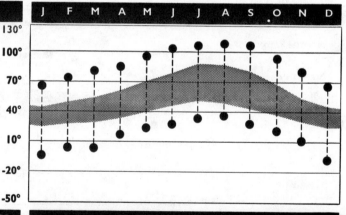

SUNSHINE/CLOUDINESS

Percentage of
Cloudy Days

Partly Cloudy Days

Sunny Days

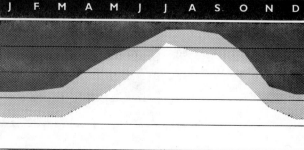

Climatable No. 11

Redwood NP, Lava Beds NM

TEMPERATURE	J	F	M	A	M	J	J	A	S	O	N	D
Normal Daily Maximum	53	55	55	57	60	62	64	64	65	62	58	54
Normal Daily Minimum	41	42	42	43	47	50	51	52	51	48	45	42
Extreme High	78	85	80	92	94	99	96	96	103	96	81	79
Extreme Low	21	26	29	32	32	39	39	42	39	32	29	18
Days Above 90°	0	0	0	0	0	0	0	0	1	0	0	0
Days Below 32°	2	1	1	0	0	0	0	0	0	0	0	2

PRECIPITATION	J	F	M	A	M	J	J	A	S	O	N	D
Normal	12.0	9.0	8.0	4.0	3.0	1.0	0.3	0.8	2.0	4.0	9.0	12.0
Maximum	20.0	16.0	15.0	11.5	8.0	4.0	2.5	6.0	7.0	13.0	18.0	19.0
Maximum 24 Hour	5.5	4.7	4.5	2.8	4.2	2.5	1.0	2.5	3.0	5.8	5.0	6.9
Maximum Snowfall	5	1	1	0	0	0	0	0	0	0	T	2
Days With Measurable Precip.	18	15	15	12	8	5	2	2	4	9	14	16
Average No. Thunderstorms	1	1	1	0	0	0	0	0	0	0	1	1

NOTES

• Usually more than 90% of the annual precipitation falls in the period of October through April; the total wintertime precipitation increases with distance north of Eureka.• With extended periods of heavy winter precipitation, some flooding can be expected along the Klamath River.

TEMPERATURE

Normal Range

Extremes

SUNSHINE/CLOUDINESS

Percentage of
Cloudy Days

Partly Cloudy Days

Sunny Days

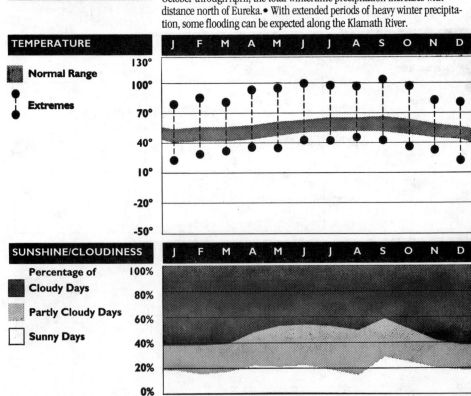

Sequoia & Kings Canyon NPs

TEMPERATURE

	J	F	M	A	M	J	J	A	S	O	N	D
Normal Daily Maximum	43	44	45	49	57	66	75	74	69	60	50	44
Normal Daily Minimum	24	25	25	29	36	44	50	49	45	38	30	26
Extreme High	65	70	72	75	82	87	90	86	87	79	72	70
Extreme Low	-5	-2	0	8	17	23	35	28	26	11	9	-4
Days Above 90°	0	0	0	0	0	0	0	0	0	0	0	0
Days Below 32°	28	24	26	20	10	1	0	0	1	7	20	26

PRECIPITATION

	J	F	M	A	M	J	J	A	S	O	N	D
Normal	8.8	6.4	6.0	4.5	1.5	0.5	0.1	0.1	0.6	1.3	4.9	7.8
Maximum	38.2	23.6	16.5	14.9	8.3	2.2	0.6	0.5	2.2	3.4	14.0	28.3
Maximum 24 Hour	7.5	6.8	4.6	4.0	5.1	1.2	0.4	0.4	1.4	2.7	3.9	10.1
Maximum Snowfall	101	154	168	143	31	8	0	0	4	11	57	80
Days With Measurable Precip.	10	9	10	8	5	2	1	1	2	3	7	10
Average No. Thunderstorms	0	0	0	2	2	2	1	1	2	0	0	0

NOTES

• The distinct summer dry season is typical of California. • Winter precipitation and snowfall can be extremely heavy along the western slopes of the Sierra Nevada Mountains.

TEMPERATURE

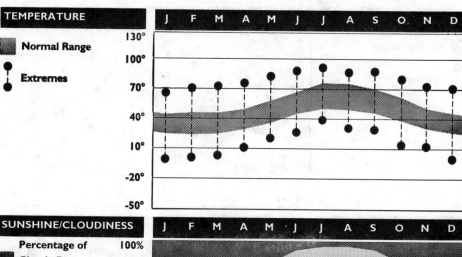

Normal Range

Extremes

SUNSHINE/CLOUDINESS

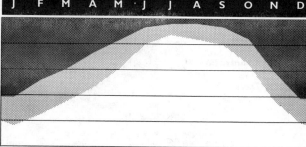

Percentage of Cloudy Days

Partly Cloudy Days

Sunny Days

Hovenweep NM, Yucca House NM, Mesa Verde NP

TEMPERATURE	J	F	M	A	M	J	J	A	S	O	N	D
Normal Daily Maximum	40	45	51	61	71	83	88	85	78	67	51	41
Normal Daily Minimum	16	20	25	32	41	50	57	55	48	37	26	18
Extreme High	62	66	76	80	91	100	101	99	100	85	72	67
Extreme Low	-27	-20	-3	8	17	28	40	36	24	11	-7	-22
Days Above 90°	0	0	0	0	0	6	14	7	1	0	0	0
Days Below 32°	30	26	26	16	4	0	0	0	1	9	24	30

PRECIPITATION	J	F	M	A	M	J	J	A	S	O	N	D
Normal	1.6	1.3	1.4	1.3	1.0	0.7	1.9	2.2	1.2	1.9	1.3	1.9
Maximum	5.5	4.3	3.8	3.7	3.4	2.1	5.9	4.8	4.3	7.4	2.5	5.0
Maximum 24 Hour	1.1	1.3	1.3	1.3	1.2	1.4	1.9	1.5	1.7	1.5	1.4	1.5
Maximum Snowfall	56	39	46	22	5	0	0	0	2	15	22	52
Days With Measurable Precip.	8	7	7	6	5	5	5	6	6	7	6	8
Average No. Thunderstorms	0	0	0	2	4	6	9	12	5	2	0	0

NOTES

• Precipitation is fairly evenly distributed throughout the year. There is a slight maximum of precipitation in winter while June tends to be the driest month.

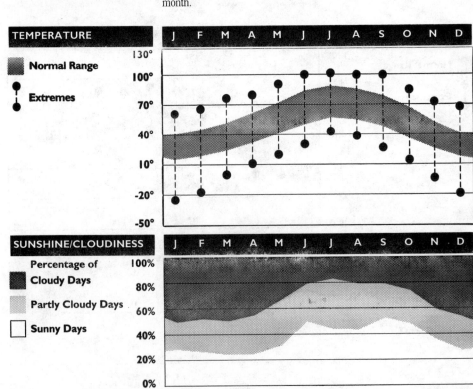

TEMPERATURE

Normal Range

Extremes

SUNSHINE/CLOUDINESS

Percentage of Cloudy Days

Partly Cloudy Days

Sunny Days

Climatable No. 14

Rocky Mountain NP

TEMPERATURE	J	F	M	A	M	J	J	A	S	O	N	D
Normal Daily Maximum	27	30	36	47	50	61	75	72	66	55	40	29
Normal Daily Minimum	1	2	8	21	30	36	42	41	33	25	15	6
Extreme High	47	55	57	69	76	88	86	83	81	71	58	47
Extreme Low	-46	-41	-30	-13	12	23	29	27	14	10	-20	-30
Days Above 90°	0	0	0	0	0	0	0	0	0	0	0	0
Days Below 32°	31	28	31	29	24	7	1	2	14	28	29	31

PRECIPITATION	J	F	M	A	M	J	J	A	S	O	N	D
Normal	1.1	0.9	1.1	1.0	1.3	1.4	1.5	1.0	1.3	0.9	0.8	1.2
Maximum	2.1	1.6	2.0	2.7	3.2	4.3	3.2	3.0	5.4	3.7	1.9	4.0
Maximum 24 Hour	0.8	0.6	0.7	0.6	1.4	1.0	0.9	0.8	1.2	1.4	0.6	1.3
Maximum Snowfall	29	32	26	23	12	T	T	T	38	39	22	32
Days With Measurable Precip.	7	5	7	7	7	9	9	9	7	6	5	6
Average No. Thunderstorms	0	0	0	2	8	10	16	14	6	1	0	0

NOTES

• Pleasantly cool summers and bitterly cold winters; below freezing temperatures have been observed in every month of the year. • Snow has fallen in every month of the year; near the National Park, a 24-hour snowfall of 76", the record for North America, was recorded.

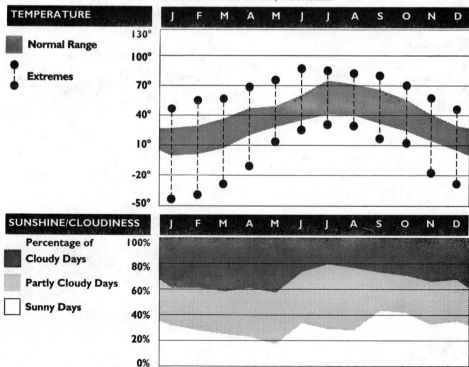

Climatable No. 15

District of Columbia and Vicinity

TEMPERATURE	J	F	M	A	M	J	J	A	S	O	N	D
Normal Daily Maximum	43	46	55	67	76	84	88	86	80	69	57	46
Normal Daily Minimum	28	29	37	46	56	65	70	69	62	50	40	31
Extreme High	79	82	89	95	97	101	103	101	101	94	86	75
Extreme Low	-5	4	11	24	34	47	55	49	39	29	16	1
Days Above 90°	0	0	0	0	2	8	13	10	4	0	0	0
Days Below 32°	23	19	8	1	0	0	0	0	0	0	4	16

PRECIPITATION	J	F	M	A	M	J	J	A	S	O	N	D
Normal	2.8	2.6	3.5	2.9	3.5	3.4	3.9	4.4	3.2	2.9	2.8	3.2
Maximum	7.1	5.7	7.4	6.9	10.7	11.5	11.1	14.3	12.4	8.2	6.7	6.5
Maximum 24 Hour	2.2	1.9	3.4	3.1	4.3	7.2	4.7	6.4	5.3	5.0	2.6	2.9
Maximum Snowfall	21	31	17	1	T	0	0	0	0	T	7	16
Days With Measurable Precip.	10	9	11	9	11	10	10	9	8	7	8	9
Average No. Thunderstorms	0	0	1	3	6	7	8	8	3	1	0	0

NOTES

• Summer days can be hot, humid and very oppressive. • Winters are cold, but rarely severe. The normal total seasonal snowfall is less than 18".
• Freezing temperatures normally occur until April 1.

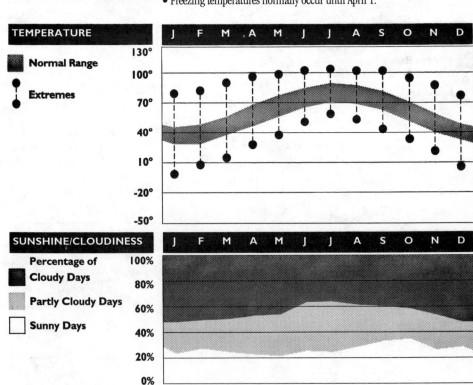

TEMPERATURE

- Normal Range
- Extremes

130° · 100° · 70° · 40° · 10° · -20° · -50°

SUNSHINE/CLOUDINESS

- Percentage of Cloudy Days
- Partly Cloudy Days
- Sunny Days

100% · 80% · 60% · 40% · 20% · 0%

Climatable No. 16

Big Cypress NP, Everglades NP

TEMPERATURE

	J	F	M	A	M	J	J	A	S	O	N.	D
Normal Daily Maximum	76	76	80	83	86	88	90	90	89	85	81	77
Normal Daily Minimum	56	57	61	65	69	73	75	75	74	70	63	58
Extreme High	88	89	92	96	98	98	99	98	99	95	90	88
Extreme Low	28	30	32	43	53	60	65	64	65	49	33	29
Days Above 90°	0	0	0	1	9	15	22	24	20	6	0	0
Days Below 32°	0	0	0	0	0	0	0	0	0	0	0	0

PRECIPITATION

	J	F	M	A	M	J	J	A	S	O	N	D
Normal	2.1	2.0	1.9	3.1	6.5	9.2	6.0	7.0	8.1	7.1	2.7	1.9
Maximum	6.8	8.1	10.6	17.3	18.5	23.5	17.4	16.9	24.4	21.1	13.2	6.4
Maximum 24 Hour	2.7	6.0	7.1	16.2	11.6	10.1	4.6	6.9	7.6	10.0	7.9	4.4
Maximum Snowfall	0	0	0	0	0	0	0	0	0	0	0	0
Days With Measurable Precip.	6	6	6	6	10	15	16	17	17	14	8	7
Average No. Thunderstorms	1	1	2	4	11	19	22	24	16	6	1	1

NOTES

• Summers are hot and humid; frequent daytime thunderstorms are often accompanied by rapid drops in temperature that persist for the remainder of the day. • Summer showers are typically short; rainfall generally extends over less than 10% of the day.

TEMPERATURE

Normal Range

Extremes

SUNSHINE/CLOUDINESS

Percentage of Cloudy Days

Partly Cloudy Days

Sunny Days

Climatable No. 17

Biscayne NP

TEMPERATURE

	J	F	M	A	M	J	J	A	S	O	N	D
Normal Daily Maximum	74	74	77	80	83	86	87	88	86	83	79	75
Normal Daily Minimum	63	63	66	71	74	76	78	78	77	74	69	64
Extreme High	86	88	91	94	95	97	98	98	96	93	90	85
Extreme Low	34	38	41	48	61	65	68	68	68	55	39	35
Days Above 90°	0	0	0	1	1	2	3	5	2	0	0	0
Days Below 32°	0	0	0	0	0	0	0	0	0	0	0	0

PRECIPITATION

	J	F	M	A	M	J	J	A	S	O	N	D
Normal	2.0	2.1	1.6	2.4	4.3	7.0	4.4	4.3	7.1	6.1	2.5	1.7
Maximum	6.3	7.3	4.3	10.4	11.7	18.9	8.0	14.0	16.0	18.0	10.9	7.8
Maximum 24 Hour	3.1	2.5	1.6	6.9	5.9	6.3	4.9	5.8	8.4	5.3	6.7	3.2
Maximum Snowfall	0	0	0	0	0	0	0	0	0	0	0	0
Days With Measurable Precip.	6	6	6	6	9	12	11	11	12	12	7	6
Average No. Thunderstorms	1	1	2	4	9	17	20	22	14	6	1	1

NOTES

• The intensity of the sunshine in summer can be distressing. • Daily summer showers are most frequent in the morning; in nearby island areas, they are most frequent in the afternoon. Total annual rainfall is significantly less along the coast. • No freezing temperatures have ever been recorded.

TEMPERATURE

Normal Range

Extremes

SUNSHINE/CLOUDINESS

Percentage of
Cloudy Days

Partly Cloudy Days

Sunny Days

Climatable No. 18   493

Hawaii Volcanoes NP

TEMPERATURE	J	F	M	A	M	J	J	A	S	O	N	D
Normal Daily Maximum	66	65	66	66	68	69	70	71	71	71	68	66
Normal Daily Minimum	50	50	50	52	53	54	55	55	54	54	53	51
Extreme High	77	81	77	76	83	83	85	81	85	80	79	75
Extreme Low	39	37	38	42	44	46	48	44	45	45	44	40
Days Above 90°	0	0	0	0	0	0	0	0	0	0	0	0
Days Below 32°	0	0	0	0	0	0	0	0	0	0	0	0

PRECIPITATION	J	F	M	A	M	J	J	A	S	O	N	D
Normal	12.1	10.3	11.9	10.9	8.0	4.2	4.9	7.2	4.5	6.5	12.9	12.3
Maximum	34.6	28.4	28.4	33.8	23.4	8.7	9.4	17.2	7.5	24.2	26.1	34.3
Maximum 24 Hour	10.5	4.8	5.2	7.4	4.8	3.6	3.7	11.0	4.2	10.0	11.7	9.4
Maximum Snowfall	0	0	0	0	0	0	0	0	0	0	0	0
Days With Measurable Precip.	17	18	24	25	25	24	27	26	23	24	23	21
Average No. Thunderstorms	1	1	2	1	1	0	0	0	0	1	1	1

NOTES

• Precipitation amounts are very sensitive to elevation and exposure to the trade winds. • Maximum precipitation on the windward slopes occurs at elevations between 2,000 and 4,000 feet. Near the peaks, rainfall is scarce, humidity is low, and below-freezing temperatures are common.

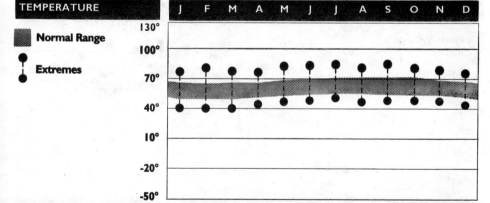

TEMPERATURE

Normal Range

Extremes

SUNSHINE/CLOUDINESS

Percentage of
Cloudy Days

Partly Cloudy Days

Sunny Days

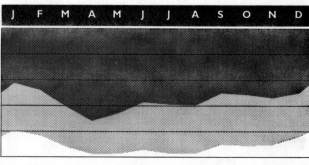

Climatable No. 19

Abraham Lincoln Birthplace NHS, Mammoth Cave NP

TEMPERATURE	J	F	M	A	M	J	J	A	S	O	N	D
Normal Daily Maximum	45	49	58	70	78	86	88	88	82	72	58	48
Normal Daily Minimum	25	26	35	45	52	60	64	62	56	44	36	28
Extreme High	76	82	86	90	94	105	108	102	106	97	85	80
Extreme Low	-20	-21	-8	21	27	37	44	43	31	19	1	-11
Days Above 90°	0	0	0	0	2	7	12	12	5	0	0	0
Days Below 32°	22	20	15	4	1	0	0	0	0	4	13	20

PRECIPITATION	J	F	M	A	M	J	J	A	S	O	N	D
Normal	4.2	3.8	5.1	4.4	4.5	4.6	4.7	3.4	3.6	2.6	4.0	4.5
Maximum	10.7	10.3	13.8	13.3	10.5	9.0	10.2	8.5	12.2	5.6	13.1	11.7
Maximum 24 Hour	3.9	3.2	4.3	5.0	4.2	3.6	4.0	3.7	4.8	3.2	6.7	3.1
Maximum Snowfall	22	15	24	2	0	0	0	0	0	0	15	11
Days With Measurable Precip.	11	11	13	12	12	10	10	9	8	8	10	11
Average No. Thunderstorms	2	2	6	8	10	12	15	10	5	3	2	1

NOTES

- In general, winters are moderately cold and summers are quite warm.
- The duration of periods of very cold weather in winter is usually short.
- On occasion, extended periods of hot, sultry weather are experienced in summer. • Autumn is the driest season.

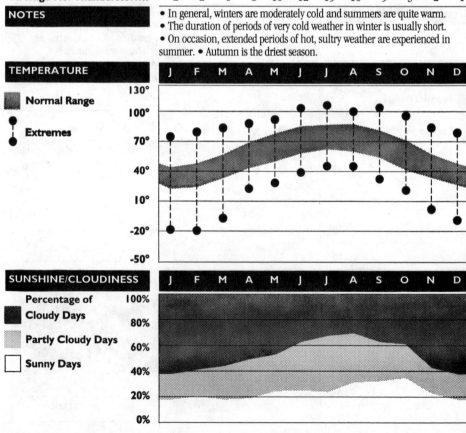

TEMPERATURE

Normal Range

Extremes

130°
100°
70°
40°
10°
-20°
-50°

SUNSHINE/CLOUDINESS

Percentage of
Cloudy Days

Partly Cloudy Days

Sunny Days

100%
80%
60%
40%
20%
0%

Climatable No. 20

Acadia NP, Roosevelt Campobello International Park,
Saint Croix Island NM

TEMPERATURE

	J	F	M	A	M	J	J	A	S	O	N	D.
Normal Daily Maximum	31	32	39	50	61	70	76	74	66	57	46	35
Normal Daily Minimum	15	16	24	34	42	50	54	54	49	42	33	20
Extreme High	57	54	63	82	88	93	96	94	92	81	71	61
Extreme Low	-16	-16	-3	10	25	35	41	35	30	21	6	-11
Days Above 90°	0	0	0	0	0	0	1	0	0	0	0	0
Days Below 32°	29	27	26	14	2	0	0	0	0	4	16	26

PRECIPITATION

	J	F	M	A	M	J	J	A	S	O	N	D
Normal	4.4	4.1	3.8	3.8	3.9	2.9	3.0	3.0	3.8	4.2	5.5	5.2
Maximum	12.0	9.9	10.7	8.1	11.0	8.2	7.2	6.1	6.0	9.2	9.6	10.3
Maximum 24 Hour	3.5	2.8	3.3	2.8	6.3	2.6	2.9	3.4	3.8	3.5	3.5	4.5
Maximum Snowfall	54	43	44	18	6	0	0	0	0	3	16	53
Days With Measurable Precip.	11	10	11	12	13	11	10	10	8	9	12	12
Average No. Thunderstorms	0	0	1	1	2	5	6	5	2	1	0	0

NOTES

- In winter, "northeasters" bring considerable rain, freezing rain, wet snow and high tides to these coastal areas; inland precipitation is mostly snow.
- Lies in the foggiest area of the US East Coast; heavy fog occurs on the average of 60 days a year. More than 1,500 hours per year are foggy.

TEMPERATURE

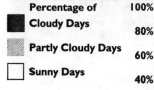

Normal Range

Extremes

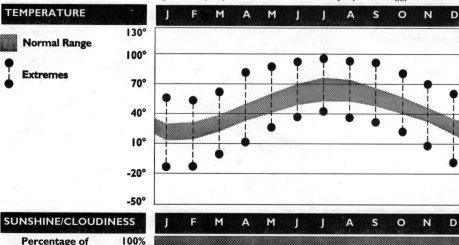

SUNSHINE/CLOUDINESS

Percentage of
Cloudy Days

Partly Cloudy Days

Sunny Days

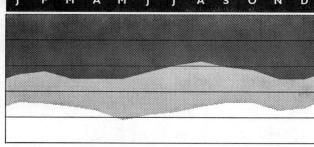

Climatable No. 21

Isle Royale NP

TEMPERATURE	J	F	M	A	M	J	J	A	S	O	N	D
Normal Daily Maximum	11	20	32	45	54	62	68	69	60	52	33	18
Normal Daily Minimum	-11	-5	9	25	36	43	50	54	47	39	17	-1
Extreme High	48	53	66	70	79	87	89	86	82	72	65	57
Extreme Low	-46	-44	-38	-5	19	32	37	34	29	12	-32	-41
Days Above 90°	0	0	0	0	0	0	0	0	0	0	0	0
Days Below 32°	31	28	30	22	8	0	0	0	1	6	28	31

PRECIPITATION	J	F	M	A	M	J	J	A	S	O	N	D
Normal	1.2	0.9	1.8	2.2	2.5	3.1	2.5	3.2	3.4	2.1	1.7	1.3
Maximum	4.7	2.4	5.1	5.8	7.7	8.0	8.5	10.3	6.6	7.5	5.0	3.7
Maximum 24 Hour	1.7	1.4	2.4	2.3	2.6	2.5	2.3	1.8	4.5	1.8	2.6	2.1
Maximum Snowfall	47	32	46	32	8	0	0	0	4	9	38	44
Days With Measurable Precip.	12	10	11	11	12	13	11	11	12	10	11	12
Average No. Thunderstorms	0	0	0	0	1	2	2	2	2	1	0	0

NOTES

• Summers are cool and winters are very cold; periods of warm summer temperatures rarely exceed 2 to 3 days in length • Day to day temperature changes are strongly moderated by the surrounding waters of Lake Superior, the coldest of the Great Lakes.

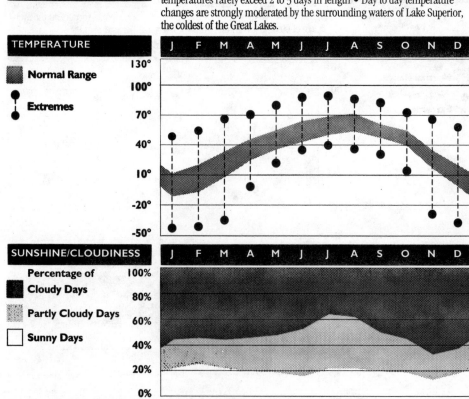

TEMPERATURE		
▓ **Normal Range**		
● **Extremes**		

130° 100° 70° 40° 10° -20° -50°

SUNSHINE/CLOUDINESS		
■ **Percentage of Cloudy Days**		
▒ **Partly Cloudy Days**		
☐ **Sunny Days**		

100% 80% 60% 40% 20% 0%

Climatable No. 22

Voyageurs NP

TEMPERATURE	J	F	M	A	M	J	J	A	S	O	N	D
Normal Daily Maximum	11	20	32	49	64	73	78	75	64	53	33	18
Normal Daily Minimum	-11	-5	9	27	39	49	54	51	42	33	17	-1
Extreme High	48	53	76	93	95	98	98	95	95	88	73	57
Extreme Low	-46	-44	-38	-14	11	23	35	30	20	7	-32	-41
Days Above 90°	0	0	0	0	0	1	2	1	0	0	0	0
Days Below 32°	31	28	30	22	8	0	0	0	5	15	28	31

PRECIPITATION	J	F	M	A	M	J	J	A	S	O	N	D
Normal	0.9	0.7	1.1	1.6	2.4	3.7	3.8	3.0	3.2	1.8	1.3	0.9
Maximum	3.0	1.8	3.1	3.3	6.7	8.2	9.5	11.3	7.4	4.8	3.5	1.7
Maximum 24 Hour	1.5	1.1	1.8	1.6	2.5	3.8	4.9	4.8	3.4	2.6	1.6	1.2
Maximum Snowfall	43	26	32	23	13	T	0	T	2	8	30	23
Days With Measurable Precip.	12	9	10	9	11	13	11	12	12	10	11	12
Average No. Thunderstorms	0	0	0	1	5	10	12	9	4	1	0	0

NOTES

• From December through February, the temperature falls below zero on most days and occasionally remains below zero for a week or more. • Winter can bring some heavy snowfalls with blizzard conditions and severely drifting snow.

TEMPERATURE

Normal Range

Extremes

SUNSHINE/CLOUDINESS

Percentage of Cloudy Days

Partly Cloudy Days

Sunny Days

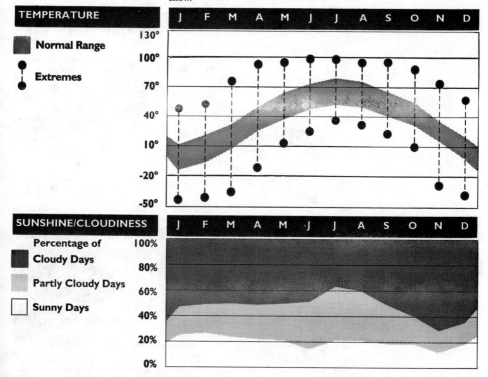

Climatable No. 23

Glacier NP

TEMPERATURE

	J	F	M	A	M	J	J	A	S	O	N	D
Normal Daily Maximum	27	33	39	52	63	69	79	77	66	55	39	32
Normal Daily Minimum	11	15	20	28	36	44	47	46	39	32	22	17
Extreme High	58	60	66	80	91	93	101	96	91	83	72	61
Extreme Low	-44	-40	-38	-12	1	24	30	30	11	-9	-33	-37
Days Above 90°	0	0	0	0	0	0	2	1	0	0	0	0
Days Below 32°	30	27	28	22	8	1	0	0	6	16	25	29

PRECIPITATION

	J	F	M	A	M	J	J	A	S	O	N	D
Normal	2.7	1.9	1.6	1.6	1.7	2.2	1.2	1.3	1.3	1.9	2.3	2.8
Maximum	4.7	2.5	3.4	4.5	5.3	9.2	5.7	4.9	3.2	2.3	2.9	3.0
Maximum 24 Hour	3.0	2.1	1.4	2.0	2.0	5.9	2.6	2.1	1.6	1.8	1.8	1.4
Maximum Snowfall	123	81	73	87	28	16	T	T	17	61	77	94
Days With Measurable Precip.	10	7	6	6	7	8	4	3	5	7	8	10
Average No. Thunderstorms	0	0	0	0	5	8	10	8	3	0	0	0

NOTES

• Annual precipitation varies within the Park from 20" to nearly 200" at the higher elevations of the windward slopes. The seasonal snowfall may exceed 1000" in some areas. Near the eastern border of the Park, the record 24-hour drop in temperature for the U.S. of 100°F was recorded.

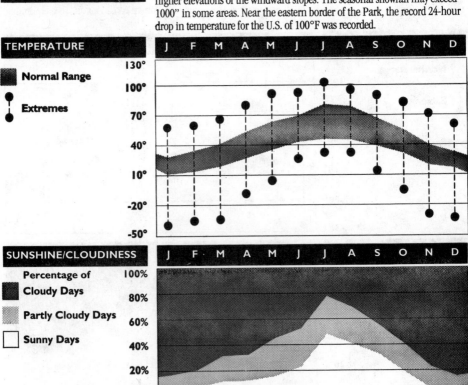

TEMPERATURE

- Normal Range
- Extremes

SUNSHINE/CLOUDINESS

- Percentage of **Cloudy Days**
- **Partly Cloudy Days**
- **Sunny Days**

Great Basin NP

TEMPERATURE

	J	F	M	A	M	J.	J	A	S	O	N	D
Normal Daily Maximum	41	44	48	56	66	76	86	83	75	62	49	42
Normal Daily Minimum	18	21	24	31	40	48	57	56	47	37	26	20
Extreme High	67	65	70	77	88	97	100	95	92	80	70	64
Extreme Low	-20	-12	0	10	13	25	39	32	21	6	-6	-13
Days Above 90°	0	0	0	0	0	1	7	3	0	0	0	0
Days Below 32°	29	25	26	18	7	1	0	0	2	10	23	29

PRECIPITATION

	J	F	M	A	M	J	J	A	S	O	N	D
Normal	0.9	1.0	1.4	1.3	1.1	0.9	0.9	1.1	0.9	1.0	1.2	1.2
Maximum	3.2	3.6	5.0	3.0	4.7	3.4	2.1	3.7	2.7	3.0	3.4	3.4
Maximum 24 Hour	2.2	1.6	1.5	1.6	1.6	1.4	1.1	0.8	2.4	1.1	1.5	1.6
Maximum Snowfall	34	39	52	35	23	8	0	0	2	42	48	46
Days With Measurable Precip.	7	7	8	8	7	5	6	5	4	5	5	6
Average No. Thunderstorms	0	0	0	1	5	7	12	12	4	1	0	0

NOTES

• This is a fairly arid area with a slight maximum of precipitation in the spring. • Thunderstorms are relatively infrequent and, for the most part, are not severe. • Local mountain and valley winds noticeably influence temperatures throughout the year.

TEMPERATURE

Normal Range

Extremes

SUNSHINE/CLOUDINESS

Percentage of
Cloudy Days

Partly Cloudy Days

Sunny Days

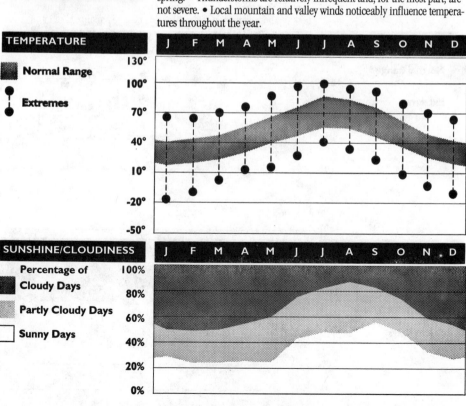

Climatable No. 25

New York City Sites, Statue of Liberty NM, St. Paul's NHS

TEMPERATURE	J	F	M	A	M	J	J	A	S	O	N	D
Normal Daily Maximum	38	40	49	61	72	80	85	84	76	66	54	42
Normal Daily Minimum	26	27	34	44	53	63	68	67	60	50	41	30
Extreme High	72	75	86	96	99	101	106	104	102	94	84	72
Extreme Low	-6	-15	3	12	32	44	52	50	39	28	5	-13
Days Above 90°	0	0	0	0	1	3	7	4	2	0	0	0
Days Below 32°	23	20	12	2	0	0	0	0	0	0	5	18

PRECIPITATION	J	F	M	A	M	J	J	A	S	O	N	D
Normal	3.2	3.1	4.2	3.8	3.8	3.2	3.8	4.0	3.7	3.4	4.2	3.8
Maximum	10.5	6.9	10.4	8.8	9.7	9.8	11.9	10.9	16.8	13.3	12.4	10.0
Maximum 24 Hour	3.9	3.0	4.2	4.2	4.9	4.7	3.6	5.8	8.3	11.2	8.1	3.2
Maximum Snowfall	27	28	30	14	T	0	0	0	0	1	19	30
Days With Measurable Precip.	11	10	12	11	11	10	11	10	8	8	9	10
Average No. Thunderstorms	0	0	1	2	4	6	7	7	3	1	1	0

NOTES

• City exhibits a very definite "heat island" effect; overnight temperatures are often distinctly warmer in both winter and summer as compared to surrounding suburban areas. • Some summer days can be very hot and humid; however, both warm and cold spells tend not to be prolonged.

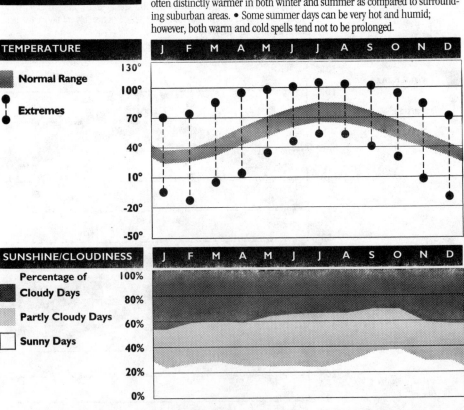

TEMPERATURE

Normal Range

Extremes

130°
100°
70°
40°
10°
-20°
-50°

SUNSHINE/CLOUDINESS

Percentage of
Cloudy Days

Partly Cloudy Days

Sunny Days

100%
80%
60%
40%
20%
0%

Climatable No. 26

Great Smoky Mountains NP, Blue Ridge Parkway, Appalachian NST

TEMPERATURE

	J	F	M	A	M	J	J	A	S	O	N	D
Normal Daily Maximum	48	51	60	70	76	82	84	84	78	70	59	51
Normal Daily Minimum	25	26	33	42	48	56	60	59	53	41	32	27
Extreme High	81	84	89	93	98	106	105	100	102	94	85	80
Extreme Low	-16	-16	-6	15	25	31	42	39	27	12	0	-12
Days Above 90°	0	0	0	0	1	5	8	7	3	0	0	0
Days Below 32°	22	20	17	7	1	0	0	0	0	6	17	22

PRECIPITATION

	J	F	M	A	M	J	J	A	S	O	N	D
Normal	4.5	4.2	5.6	4.5	4.4	4.6	5.1	4.5	3.7	3.0	3.7	4.2
Maximum	12.2	9.4	11.3	8.5	8.7	11.0	14.8	12.6	8.8	7.4	8.7	9.3
Maximum 24 Hour	3.4	3.3	4.5	3.3	3.1	4.6	4.4	3.6	3.0	3.7	2.8	3.1
Maximum Snowfall	26	19	25	2	0	0	0	0	0	8	7	15
Days With Measurable Precip.	11	10	12	10	12	11	11	11	9	8	10	10
Average No. Thunderstorms	1	1	4	6	10	12	13	11	4	1	1	1

NOTES

• Temperature and precipitation vary markedly with location depending on exposure and elevation. Precipitation is highest and temperature lowest along the ridge tops. • In winter, precipitation falls mostly as rain in the valleys and snow or rain on the ridges; snowfall amounts are quite variable.

TEMPERATURE

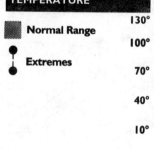

Normal Range

Extremes

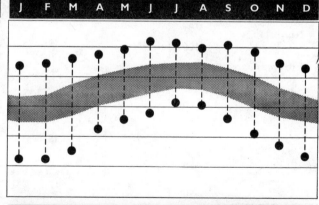

SUNSHINE/CLOUDINESS

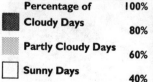

Percentage of
Cloudy Days

Partly Cloudy Days

Sunny Days

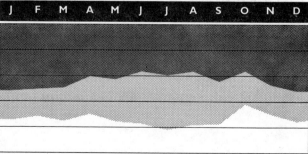

Climatable No. 27

Theodore Roosevelt NP

TEMPERATURE

	J	F	M	A	M	J	J	A	S	O	N	D
Normal Daily Maximum	20	27	36	54	67	76	84	82	70	58	39	27
Normal Daily Minimum	-2	6	15	30	42	50	56	54	43	32	18	6
Extreme High	58	66	78	94	106	104	109	107	104	94	79	67
Extreme Low	-40	-41	-28	-15	4	30	34	35	17	0	-24	-50
Days Above 90°	0	0	0	0	1	2	8	9	2	0	0	0
Days Below 32°	31	28	29	18	4	0	0	0	3	15	28	31

PRECIPITATION

	J	F	M	A	M	J	J	A	S	O	N	D
Normal	0.5	0.5	0.6	1.5	2.1	3.0	2.0	1.5	1.4	0.8	0.5	0.5
Maximum	1.4	1.5	2.5	4.8	7.4	7.7	6.2	5.6	6.2	3.6	1.6	1.4
Maximum 24 Hour	0.5	1.0	1.0	2.0	2.7	3.1	5.0	2.8	2.2	2.2	0.8	0.9
Maximum Snowfall	24	16	31	22	16	4	0	0	4	14	17	16
Days With Measurable Precip.	8	7	8	8	10	10	9	7	7	5	6	8
Average No. Thunderstorms	0	0	0	1	5	12	12	9	3	0	0	0

NOTES

• Winters are long and cold with periods of bitterly cold temperatures. Occasionally, blizzard conditions with dangerous wind chill temperatures can be expected. • Summers are punctuated with prolonged periods of high temperatures, though low humidity minimizes discomfort; nights are usually cool.

TEMPERATURE

- Normal Range
- Extremes

SUNSHINE/CLOUDINESS

- Percentage of Cloudy Days
- Partly Cloudy Days
- Sunny Days

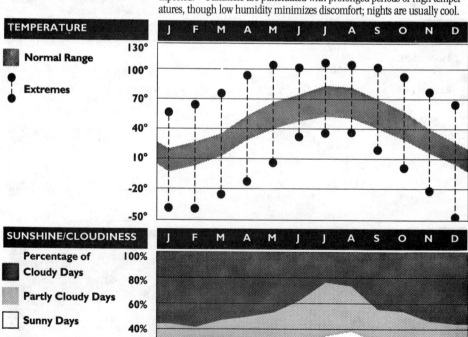

Climatable No. 28

Crater Lake NP

TEMPERATURE	J	F	M	A	M	J	J	A	S	O	N	D
Normal Daily Maximum	36	39	42	50	56	66	77	75	68	56	44	36
Normal Daily Minimum	17	18	20	24	30	35	40	39	34	29	24	19
Extreme High	58	66	69	82	86	98	97	101	96	87	72	58
Extreme Low	-26	-26	-15	0	5	11	18	15	9	0	-26	-30
Days Above 90°	0	0	0	0	0	0	2	1	0	0	0	0
Days Below 32°	31	28	30	27	20	11	5	6	13	22	26	30

PRECIPITATION	J	F	M	A	M	J	J	A	S	O	N	D
Normal	10.8	8.7	8.2	4.3	3.3	2.5	0.6	0.6	2.0	6.4	8.0	11.7
Maximum	20.9	19.7	15.2	11.6	8.7	9.2	2.9	5.3	6.9	19.1	17.2	38.5
Maximum 24 Hour	3.8	3.5	2.3	4.2	1.9	2.0	1.5	1.1	2.6	3.2	2.6	5.1
Maximum Snowfall	313	248	194	144	103	14	T	5	20	88	128	196
Days With Measurable Precip.	17	15	16	12	10	7	3	3	5	10	13	16
Average No. Thunderstorms	0	0	0	1	2	3	2	2	1	0	0	0

NOTES

• Freezing temperatures may be encountered throughout the year. • Prodigious amounts of snow fall in the Park, the greatest amounts on the western slopes; seasonal totals range between 275" and nearly 900". Snow depths can reach 20'. • Summers are sunny with only brief, infrequent showers.

TEMPERATURE

- Normal Range
- Extremes

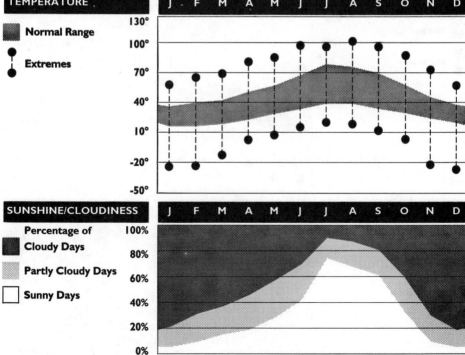

SUNSHINE/CLOUDINESS

- Percentage of Cloudy Days
- Partly Cloudy Days
- Sunny Days

Badlands NP

TEMPERATURE	J	F	M	A	M	J	J	A	S	O	N	D
Normal Daily Maximum	32	36	46	61	71	81	91	89	78	66	48	36
Normal Daily Minimum	6	9	19	32	42	53	59	56	46	33	20	10
Extreme High	75	74	88	92	105	114	116	113	108	98	81	77
Extreme Low	-42	-41	-28	-12	13	31	36	27	10	-7	-29	-41
Days Above 90°	0	0	0	0	1	6	17	16	5	0	0	0
Days Below 32°	30	27	27	16	4	0	0	0	2	14	27	30

PRECIPITATION	J	F	M	A	M	J	J	A	S	O	N	D
Normal	0.4	0.4	0.8	1.8	2.8	3.0	1.8	1.6	1.1	0.9	0.4	0.4
Maximum	3.1	1.8	2.7	5.5	6.9	9.5	6.5	7.8	3.9	4.0	2.7	1.8
Maximum 24 Hour	2.3	1.0	1.7	2.0	4.0	3.0	2.5	5.2	3.3	2.4	1.4	0.8
Maximum Snowfall	19	16	24	28	8	0	0	0	T	12	21	17
Days With Measurable Precip.	3	3	4	7	9	10	7	6	5	4	2	3
Average No. Thunderstorms	0	0	0	2	7	15	15	11	4	0	0	0

NOTES

• Summer days are quite hot, but low humidity keeps the heat from feeling oppressive. • Rainfall from late summer thunderstorms often evaporates before reaching the ground. • Winters are bitterly cold; temperatures of 20°F below zero can be expected several times each winter.

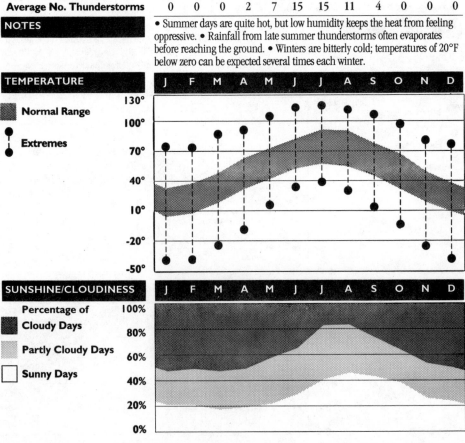

TEMPERATURE

Normal Range

Extremes

SUNSHINE/CLOUDINESS

Percentage of
Cloudy Days

Partly Cloudy Days

Sunny Days

Climatable No. 30

Mount Rushmore NM, Jewel Cave NM, Wind Cave NP

TEMPERATURE	J	F	M	A	M	J	J	A	S	O	N	D
Normal Daily Maximum	34	39	42	51	62	72	80	79	70	60	45	38
Normal Daily Minimum	6	10	15	25	34	43	49	46	37	27	16	10
Extreme High	64	68	70	80	90	97	100	96	97	85	76	68
Extreme Low	-43	-34	-30	-15	5	19	30	22	8	4	-25	-37
Days Above 90°	0	0	0	0	0	1	3	2	1	0	0	0
Days Below 32°	31	28	30	26	13	2	0	1	10	24	29	30

PRECIPITATION	J	F	M	A	M	J	J	A	S	O	N	D
Normal	0.4	0.5	0.9	1.9	3.1	3.5	3.0	2.0	1.2	0.7	0.5	0.5
Maximum	1.0	1.8	2.1	3.9	8.8	6.4	7.6	4.1	3.5	2.4	1.5	1.6
Maximum 24 Hour	0.5	0.6	1.0	2.0	4.0	3.4	2.0	2.4	1.3	1.6	0.4	0.6
Maximum Snowfall	26	29	38	49	26	13	0	0	15	22	27	46
Days With Measurable Precip.	7	7	9	9	12	12	9	8	7	5	6	6
Average No. Thunderstorms	0	0	0	2	7	15	15	11	4	0	0	0

NOTES

• Summer days range from warm to hot; nights are cool and comfortable.
• Sunny skies, the frequent occurrence of a warm, downslope wind or "chinook," and the tendency for cold, arctic air masses to stay east of the Black Hills, makes this region the warmest part of South Dakota in winter.

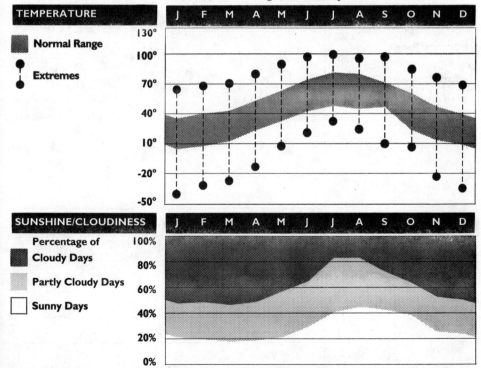

TEMPERATURE

Normal Range

Extremes

130°
100°
70°
40°
10°
-20°
-50°

J F M A M J J A S O N D

SUNSHINE/CLOUDINESS

Percentage of
Cloudy Days

Partly Cloudy Days

Sunny Days

100%
80%
60%
40%
20%
0%

J F M A M J J A S O N D

Climatable No. 31

Big Bend NP

TEMPERATURE	J	F	M	A	M	J	J	A	S	O	N	D
Normal Daily Maximum	59	64	70	78	85	90	88	87	83	76	67	61
Normal Daily Minimum	36	38	43	50	58	64	64	63	58	52	42	37
Extreme High	82	85	91	97	101	105	104	103	99	93	89	81
Extreme Low	-3	3	10	21	32	38	53	49	36	26	8	1
Days Above 90°	0	0	0	1	8	15	14	11	5	0	0	0
Days Below 32°	14	10	6	1	0	0	0	0	0	1	4	12

PRECIPITATION	J	F	M	A	M	J	J	A	S	O	N	D
Normal	0.8	0.4	0.3	0.6	1.5	2.3	2.9	2.4	1.9	1.4	0.4	0.6
Maximum	1.9	3.1	1.7	2.8	3.0	5.4	7.6	7.4	11.1	4.8	3.2	2.3
Maximum 24 Hour	1.3	1.3	0.8	1.2	1.7	2.6	3.3	2.9	2.4	4.3	1.4	1.1
Maximum Snowfall	26	7	2	2	0	0	0	0	0	T	4	9
Days With Measurable Precip.	4	3	2	2	2	3	8	8	5	4	3	4
Average No. Thunderstorms	0	0	1	1	3	5	13	11	4	2	0	0

NOTES

• Marked variations in weather are experienced over short distances due to changes in elevation and exposure. • Summer is the "rainy" season with showers and thunderstorms. Even more precipitation occurs on the high mountains, especially on the windward slopes.

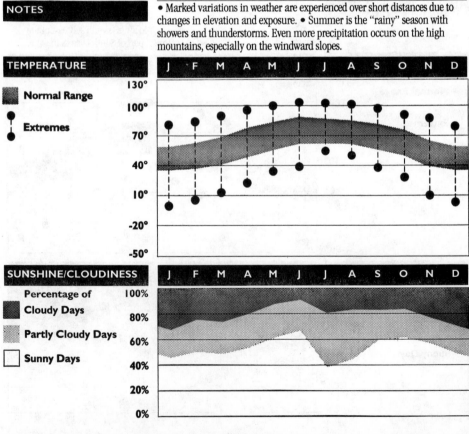

TEMPERATURE

Normal Range

Extremes

130°
100°
70°
40°
10°
-20°
-50°

SUNSHINE/CLOUDINESS

Percentage of
Cloudy Days

Partly Cloudy Days

Sunny Days

100%
80%
60%
40%
20%
0%

Climatable No. 32

Guadalupe Mountains NP, Carlsbad Caverns NP

TEMPERATURE	J	F	M	A	M	J	J	A	S	O	N	D
Normal Daily Maximum	57	60	68	78	86	93	92	91	86	77	66	58
Normal Daily Minimum	30	33	38	48	56	64	68	66	60	50	39	33
Extreme High	81	84	90	96	103	108	106	105	101	94	88	88
Extreme Low	-13	-10	9	21	30	47	50	50	33	23	14	3
Days Above 90°	0	0	0	2	10	23	24	22	11	1	0	0
Days Below 32°	18	15	8	1	0	0	0	0	0	1	6	16

PRECIPITATION	J	F	M	A	M	J	J	A	S	O	N	D
Normal	0.4	0.3	0.4	0.6	0.9	1.3	1.8	2.0	1.9	1.3	0.4	0.5
Maximum	2.4	2.0	3.6	5.8	10.9	4.0	6.0	5.7	12.3	5.1	1.6	2.6
Maximum 24 Hour	1.1	1.0	1.2	4.6	3.0	2.5	3.1	2.7	3.9	3.6	1.1	0.8
Maximum Snowfall	13	10	8	T	0	0	0	0	0	T	18	18
Days With Measurable Precip.	4	3	2	2	4	4	8	8	6	4	3	4
Average No. Thunderstorms	0	0	1	2	5	7	13	11	4	2	0	0

NOTES

• Spring is a comfortable season with mild sunny days and cool nights; an occasional dust storm can be expected. • Summer days are hot and nights are pleasantly cool. • In the high mountain areas, temperatures are 10 to 20 degrees colder and the precipitation is double that shown in the table.

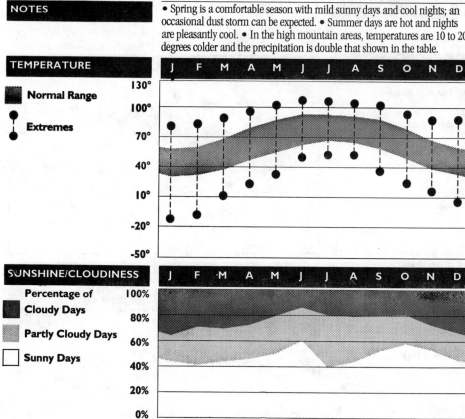

TEMPERATURE

Normal Range
Extremes

130°
100°
70°
40°
10°
-20°
-50°

SUNSHINE/CLOUDINESS

Percentage of
Cloudy Days
Partly Cloudy Days
Sunny Days

100%
80%
60%
40%
20%
0%

Climatable No. 33

Canyonlands NP, Capitol Reef NP, Arches NP

TEMPERATURE	J	F	M	A	M	J	J	A	S	O	N	D
Normal Daily Maximum	42	50	59	69	84	95	98	95	86	73	55	43
Normal Daily Minimum	17	24	31	40	49	58	65	64	54	42	29	20
Extreme High	67	75	85	91	101	109	111	108	108	94	80	68
Extreme Low	-28	-21	7	16	23	32	38	36	28	-6	-8	-15
Days Above 90°	0	0	0	0	6	20	30	26	12	0	0	0
Days Below 32°	30	22	17	6	0	0	0	0	0	5	20	29

PRECIPITATION	J	F	M	A	M	J	J	A	S	O	N	D
Normal	0.3	0.3	0.5	0.4	0.4	0.3	0.4	0.9	0.6	0.7	0.4	0.5
Maximum	2.2	1.8	3.2	2.7	1.9	2.1	2.2	3.0	2.4	3.8	1.9	2.1
Maximum 24 Hour	0.6	0.8	1.2	2.1	1.3	1.5	0.9	2.0	1.3	1.9	0.8	0.9
Maximum Snowfall	20	15	8	2	0	0	0	0	0	7	8	17
Days With Measurable Precip.	7	7	8	6	5	3	5	6	4	4	5	6
Average No. Thunderstorms	0	0	1	1	4	4	9	11	5	2	0	0

NOTES

• This is a fairly arid region, lying in the rain shadow of the mountains to the west. • Winters are quite cold, though below-zero temperatures are not common. On clear, still nights, cold air drainage keeps the valley bottoms significantly colder than the adjoining high elevation areas.

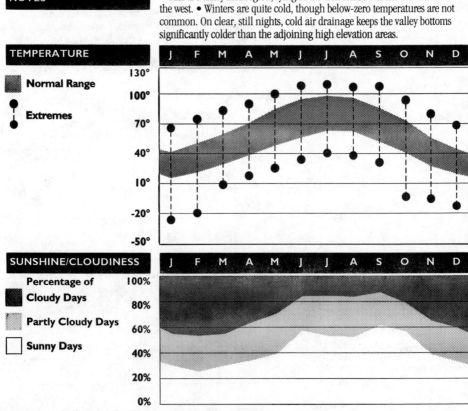

Bryce Canyon NP

TEMPERATURE	J	F	M	A	M	J	J	A	S	O	N	D
Normal Daily Maximum	39	41	46	56	66	76	83	80	74	63	51	42
Normal Daily Minimum	9	13	17	25	31	38	47	45	37	29	19	11
Extreme High	62	66	76	82	89	96	97	94	91	85	75	67
Extreme Low	-30	-29	-13	-5	5	20	25	23	17	-2	-20	-23
Days Above 90°	0	0	0	0	0	1	4	2	0	0	0	0
Days Below 32°	31	28	31	27	20	6	0	1	9	22	29	31

PRECIPITATION	J	F	M	A	M	J	J	A	S	O	N	D
Normal	1.7	1.4	1.4	1.2	0.8	0.6	1.4	2.2	1.4	1.4	1.2	1.6
Maximum	9.2	6.8	3.6	3.8	2.3	2.7	3.8	4.8	4.2	4.5	5.4	6.2
Maximum 24 Hour	2.3	1.5	1.1	1.8	1.2	1.7	1.8	3.8	3.4	1.7	1.5	3.2
Maximum Snowfall	63	75	75	62	18	6	T	T	4	22	22	49
Days With Measurable Precip.	7	7	8	6	5	3	5	6	4	4	5	6
Average No. Thunderstorms	0	0	0	1	5	6	14	19	7	2	0	0

NOTES

• Winters are very cold; below-zero readings occur often. • Snowfall amounts vary with elevation; near the rim of Bryce Canyon, winter snowfall averages more than 100". • Summers are delightfully cool with pleasant days and quite chilly nights. Temperatures reach 90°F on just a few days a year.

TEMPERATURE

Normal Range

Extremes

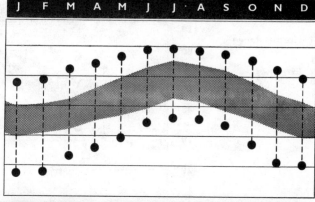

SUNSHINE/CLOUDINESS

Percentage of
Cloudy Days

Partly Cloudy Days

Sunny Days

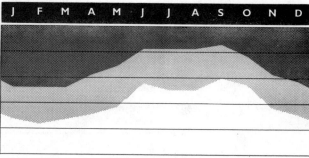

Climatable No. 35

Zion NP

TEMPERATURE

	J	F	M	A	M	J	J	A	S	O	N	D
Normal Daily Maximum	52	57	63	73	83	93	100	97	91	78	63	53
Normal Daily Minimum	29	31	36	43	52	60	68	66	60	49	37	30
Extreme High	71	78	86	94	102	114	115	111	110	97	83	71
Extreme Low	-2	4	12	23	22	40	51	50	33	23	13	6
Days Above 90°	0	0	0	1	8	21	30	28	18	3	0	0
Days Below 32°	19	14	10	3	0	0	0	0	0	1	9	18

PRECIPITATION

	J	F	M	A	M	J	J	A	S	O	N	D
Normal	1.6	1.6	1.7	1.3	0.7	0.6	0.8	1.6	0.8	1.0	1.2	1.5
Maximum	4.9	4.6	5.0	4.4	2.8	3.6	3.6	4.8	6.7	3.3	3.2	4.3
Maximum 24 Hour	1.6	1.3	0.9	1.2	1.8	2.2	1.1	1.6	1.4	1.3	1.3	2.0
Maximum Snowfall	26	18	14	3	T	0	0	0	T	1	5	21
Days With Measurable Precip.	7	7	8	6	5	3	5	6	4	4	5	6
Average No. Thunderstorms	0	0	0	1	4	5	14	15	5	2	0	0

NOTES

• Sharp changes in weather occur within the Park due to the rugged topography and range of elevations. • Seasonal snowfall averages 13", but much heavier snows accumulate in the high mountain areas. • Summer days are hot, but mountain breezes keep evenings cool especially in lower elevations.

TEMPERATURE

Normal Range

Extremes

SUNSHINE/CLOUDINESS

Percentage of
Cloudy Days

Partly Cloudy Days

Sunny Days

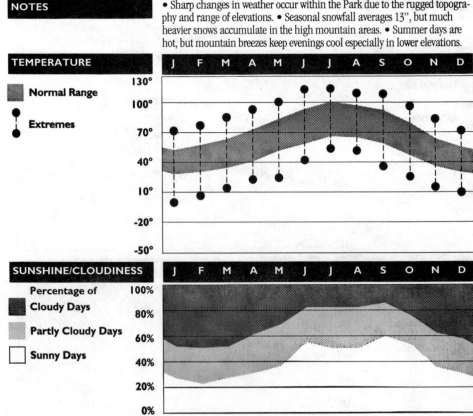

Climatable No. 36

Ross Lake NRA, Lake Chelan NRA

TEMPERATURE

	J	F	M	A	M	J	J	A	S	O	N	D
Normal Daily Maximum	37	42	48	57	66	70	78	77	70	58	45	40
Normal Daily Minimum	26	29	32	37	43	48	52	52	48	41	34	31
Extreme High	62	60	73	85	94	99	106	100	100	83	65	57
Extreme Low	-8	-10	3	24	29	35	38	37	35	21	5	8
Days Above 90°	0	0	0	0	1	1	3	3	1	0	0	0
Days Below 32°	23	19	16	4	0	0	0	0	0	1	11	19

PRECIPITATION

	J	F	M	A	M	J	J	A	S	O	N	D
Normal	10.3	8.6	6.8	4.4	2.5	2.1	1.2	1.3	3.5	8.0	10.5	12.3
Maximum	26.5	20.4	12.8	14.0	5.1	5.3	2.5	3.8	10.8	18.0	19.5	18.6
Maximum 24 Hour	4.1	6.2	3.0	3.3	1.6	1.4	1.8	1.9	2.5	6.5	4.0	3.8
Maximum Snowfall	81	69	34	10	0	0	0	0	0	1	25	78
Days With Measurable Precip.	19	17	18	15	12	10	8	9	12	16	20	21
Average No. Thunderstorms	0	0	0	0	1	2	1	2	1	0	0	0

NOTES

• The table typifies the lower western slopes of the North Cascades. • Temperatures are considerably colder and precipitation considerably greater in the high mountain areas to the east. In these areas, winter season snowfall ranges from 400" to 600"; snow depths can exceed 20'.

TEMPERATURE

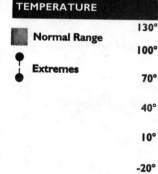

Normal Range

Extremes

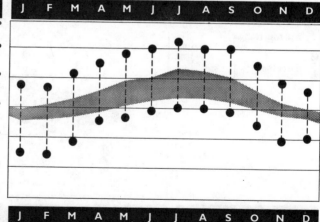

SUNSHINE/CLOUDINESS

Percentage of
Cloudy Days

Partly Cloudy Days

Sunny Days

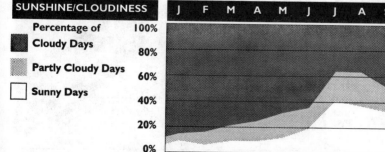

Climatable No. 37

Mount Rainier NP

TEMPERATURE	J	F	M	A	M	J	J	A	S	O	N	D
Normal Daily Maximum	34	38	43	51	59	64	74	75	68	57	42	34
Normal Daily Minimum	12	15	19	25	32	37	42	41	35	29	22	19
Extreme High	55	60	73	80	88	93	101	97	94	85	65	61
Extreme Low	-38	-35	-18	-3	13	22	27	24	18	-5	-12	-16
Days Above 90°	0	0	0	0	0	0	2	2	1	0	0	0
Days Below 32°	30	28	30	27	17	5	1	1	9	21	28	30

PRECIPITATION	J	F	M	A	M	J	J	A	S	O	N	D
Normal	14.6	10.2	8.9	6.3	4.0	3.8	1.6	2.9	4.6	7.7	12.1	15.9
Maximum	30.4	20.8	19.5	12.5	9.1	8.0	6.0	7.2	15.2	23.6	25.4	29.1
Maximum 24 Hour	5.7	4.8	3.3	5.4	2.2	2.8	2.3	2.5	4.5	5.3	7.9	7.9
Maximum Snowfall	193	182	155	107	46	9	6	T	27	65	138	164
Days With Measurable Precip.	22	20	21	19	16	15	9	11	13	16	20	23
Average No. Thunderstorms	0	0	0	0	1	2	1	2	1	0	0	0

NOTES

• The temperature data shown typify the moderate elevation areas; the precipitation data typify the higher elevations. • Winter season snowfall along the summit of the Cascades is 300"-500"; snow depths range from 10' to 25'. The record single snowfall for North America of 1,122" was set here.

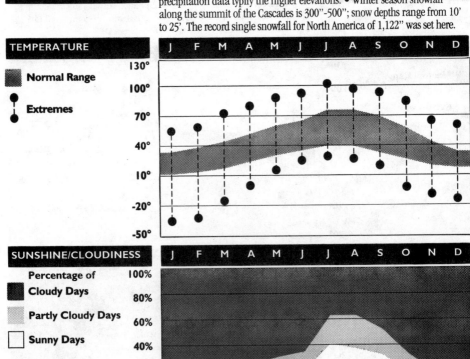

Climatable No. 38

Olympic NP

TEMPERATURE	J	F	M	A	M	J	J	A	S	O	N	D
Normal Daily Maximum	45	48	50	55	60	64	69	69	67	59	51	46
Normal Daily Minimum	33	35	34	37	42	46	49	50	47	42	37	35
Extreme High	65	72	70	79	90	96	95	99	92	81	69	64
Extreme Low	7	15	19	24	29	33	38	36	28	24	5	7
Days Above 90°	0	0	0	0	0	0	0	0	0	0	0	0
Days Below 32°	14	10	11	6	1	0	0	0	0	4	8	13

PRECIPITATION	J	F	M	A	M	J	J	A	S	O	N	D
Normal	15.1	12.1	11.3	7.1	4.7	3.1	2.3	2.8	5.3	10.5	13.9	16.3
Maximum	23.3	20.6	21.9	13.9	12.4	8.5	11.0	10.1	10.9	27.2	29.1	27.8
Maximum 24 Hour	8.3	5.1	4.2	2.8	3.5	2.0	6.4	3.1	4.1	5.5	5.4	6.8
Maximum Snowfall	40	13	10	3	T	T	0	0	T	T	16	12
Days With Measurable Precip.	22	20	21	20	16	14	12	11	13	18	22	23
Average No. Thunderstorms	0	0	1	0	0	0	0	0	1	1	1	1

NOTES

• The data shown are for the Pacific shore segment of the Park. In the high mountain areas of the Olympic Peninsula, temperatures are lower and total precipitation exceeds 200". • Winter is the rainy season; it rains often and moderately hard. Both gale force winds and fog are not unusual here.

TEMPERATURE

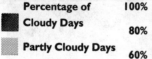

Normal Range

Extremes

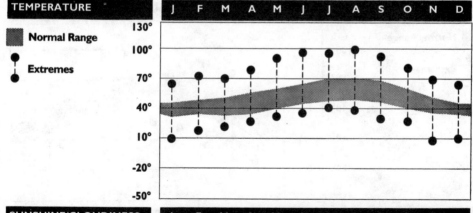

SUNSHINE/CLOUDINESS

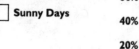

Percentage of Cloudy Days

Partly Cloudy Days

Sunny Days

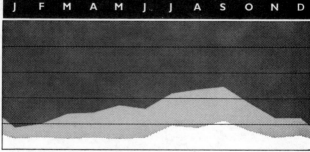

Climatable No. 39

Yellowstone NP, Grand Teton NP

TEMPERATURE	J	F	M	A	M	J	J	A	S	O	N	D
Normal Daily Maximum	26	32	38	48	60	70	80	78	68	56	38	28
Normal Daily Minimum	5	8	10	24	31	38	42	41	34	26	16	7
Extreme High	55	60	64	75	85	98	95	96	93	84	65	58
Extreme Low	-60	-63	-43	-28	0	18	24	18	7	-20	-36	-52
Days Above 90°	0	0	0	0	0	0	1	1	0	0	0	0
Days Below 32°	31	27	30	26	19	6	2	4	14	26	28	31

PRECIPITATION	J	F	M	A	M	J	J	A	S	O	N	D
Normal	1.4	0.8	1.1	1.3	1.9	2.2	1.2	1.4	1.3	1.0	1.1	1.2
Maximum	3.8	1.8	3.0	2.8	2.9	4.0	2.2	3.9	3.7	2.6	2.5	4.1
Maximum 24 Hour	0.9	0.7	1.2	0.9	1.2	0.9	0.9	0.9	1.5	0.7	0.9	1.7
Maximum Snowfall	42	30	32	24	14	6	6	2	8	18	23	31
Days With Measurable Precip.	14	12	12	10	10	10	7	8	8	9	10	13
Average No. Thunderstorms	0	0	0	1	5	11	14	12	2	0	0	0

NOTES

• The table characterizes the lower elevation areas of the Parks. Most of the park area is at higher elevations and, as such, temperatures will average at least 5 degrees colder. Precipitation will be much greater; the precipitation on the high windward slopes can be expected to be twice that shown here.

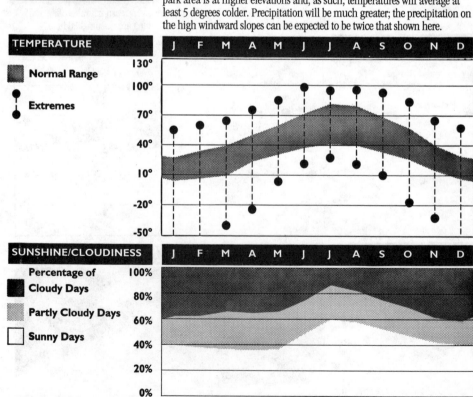

TEMPERATURE

Normal Range

Extremes

SUNSHINE/CLOUDINESS

Percentage of Cloudy Days

Partly Cloudy Days

Sunny Days

100%
80%
60%
40%
20%
0%

Climatable No. 40

Virgin Islands NP

TEMPERATURE	J	F	M	A	M	J	J	A	S	O	N	D
Normal Daily Maximum	82	83	84	85	86	87	88	88	88	87	86	84
Normal Daily Minimum	71	71	72	74	75	77	77	77	76	76	74	73
Extreme High	86	87	88	90	90	91	92	92	92	91	90	88
Extreme Low	63	65	66	65	69	69	71	67	71	68	67	64
Days Above 90°	0	0	0	0	0	2	6	8	4	1	0	0
Days Below 32°	0	0	0	0	0	0	0	0	0	0	0	0

PRECIPITATION	J	F	M	A	M	J	J	A	S	O	N	D
Normal	2.4	1.9	1.7	2.2	4.6	3.2	3.3	4.1	6.9	5.6	3.9	3.9
Maximum	NA	NA	NA	NA	NA	NA	NA	NA	NA	NA	NA	NA
Maximum 24 Hour	NA	NA	NA	NA	NA	NA	NA	NA	NA	NA	NA	NA
Maximum Snowfall	0	0	0	0	0	0	0	0	0	0	0	0
Days With Measurable Precip.	13	11	10	12	13	13	14	14	15	14	14	13
Average No. Thunderstorms	0	0	0	0	1	2	2	2	2	2	1	0

NOTES

• The dominant weather features are the consistent temperatures, the steady northeast trade winds, the daytime sea breezes and the afternoon showers.
• Tropical storms and disturbances can bring high winds and heavy rains, most commonly in the summer or fall.

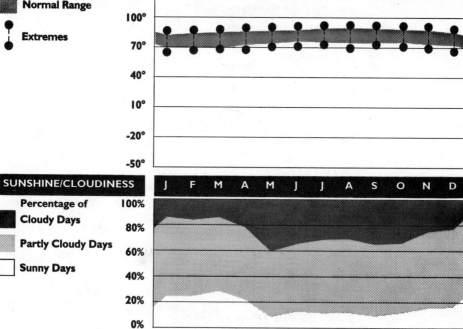

TEMPERATURE	
Normal Range	
Extremes	

SUNSHINE/CLOUDINESS	
Percentage of Cloudy Days	
Partly Cloudy Days	
Sunny Days	

Peak Visitation

The National Park Service maintains records of peak visitation indicating the relative times when sites have the most visitors. We have listed the month of peak visitation for each National Park area that is open to the public as an aid for travelers planning trips.

A

Abraham Lincoln Birthplace NHS *(July)*
Acadia NP *(August)*
Adams NHS *(July)*
Agate Fossil Beds NM *(July)*
Alagnak WR *(July)*
Alibates NM *(July)*
Allegheny Portage Railroad NHS *(July)*
Amistad NRA *(May)*
Andersonville NHS *(May)*
Andrew Johnson NHS *(May)*
Aniakchak NM *(September)*
Antietam NB *(September)*
Apostle Islands NL *(August)*
Appomattox Court House NHP *(July)*
Arches NP *(August)*
Arkansas Post NMEM *(May)*
Arlington Hse RELee NMEM *(July)*
Assateague Island NS *(August)*
Aztec Ruins NM *(August)*

B

Badlands NM *(August)*
Bandelier NM *(July)*
Bent's Old Fort NHS *(July)*
Bering Land Bridge NPRES *(August)*
Big Bend NP *(April)*
Big Cypress NPRES *(March)*
Big Hole NB *(July)*
Big Thicket NPRES *(May)*
Big South Fork NR and RA *(October)*
Bighorn Canyon NRA *(July)*
Biscayne NP *(August)*
Black Canyon of the Gunnison NM *(August)*
Blue Ridge Parkway *(August)*
Bluestone NSR *(August)*
Booker T. Washington NM *(August)*
Boston African American NHS *(July)*

Boston NHP *(August)*
Brices Cross Roads NBS *(August)*
Bryce Canyon NP *(August)*
Buck Island Reef NM *(February)*
Buffalo NR *(June)*

C

Cabrillo NM *(January)*
Canaveral NS *(July)*
Canyon de Chelly NM *(May)*
Canyonlands NP *(May)*
Cape Cod NS *(August)*
Cape Hatteras NS *(July)*
Cape Krusenstern NM *(September)*
Cape Lookout NS *(July)*
Capitol Reef NP *(May)*
Capulin Volcano NM *(July)*
Carl Sandburg Home NHS *(August)*
Carlsbad Caverns NP *(July)*
Casa Grande NM *(March)*
Castillo De San Marcos NM *(July)*
Castle Clinton NM *(August)*
Catoctin Mountain Park *(August)*
Cedar Breaks NM *(July)*
Chaco Culture NHP *(August)*
Chamizal NMEM *(July)*
Channel Islands NP *(August)*
Chattahoochee River NRA *(July)*
Chesapeake and Ohio Canal NHP *(July)*
Chickamauga and Chattanooga NMP *(July)*
Chickasaw NRA *(June)*
Chiricahua NM *(May)*
Christiansted NHS *(January)*
City of Rocks NRES *(July)*
Clara Barton NHS *(August)*
Colonial NHP *(July)*
Colorado NM *(August)*
Congaree Swamp NM *(May)*
Constitution Gardens *(July)*
Coronado NMEM *(April)*
Coulee Dam NRA *(August)*
Cowpens NM *(June)*
Crater Lake NP *(July)*
Craters of the Moon NM *(July)*
Cumberland Gap NHP *(July)*

Cumberland Island NS *(April)*
Curecanti NRA *(July)*
Cuyahoga Valley NRA *(July)*

D   DeSoto NMEM *(March)*
Death Valley NM *(April)*
Delaware NSR *(July)*
Delaware Water Gap NRA *(July)*
Denali NP *(August)*
Devils Postpile NM *(August)*
Devils Tower NM *(August)*
Dinosaur NM *(July)*
Dry Tortugas NP *(July)*

E   Ebey's Landing NHRES *(August)*
Edgar Allen Poe NHS *(August)*
Edison NHS *(August)*
Effigy Mounds NM *(July)*
Eisenhower NHS *(July)*
El Malpais NM *(July)*
El Morro NM *(August)*
Eleanor Roosevelt NHS *(October)*
Eugene O'Neill NHS *(April)*
Everglades NP *(March)*

F   Federal Hall NMEM *(July)*
Fire Island NS *(August)*
Florissant Fossil Beds NM *(August)*
Ford's Theatre NHS *(May)*
Fort Bowie NHS *(March)*
Fort Caroline NMEM *(July)*
Fort Clatsop NMEM *(August)*
Fort Davis NHS *(March)*
Fort Donelson NB *(February)*
Fort Frederica NM *(March)*
Fort Laramie NHS *(July)*
Fort Larned NHS *(August)*
Fort Matanzas NM *(July)*
Fort McHenry NM&HS *(June)*
Fort Necessity NB *(July)*
Fort Point NHS *(May)*
Fort Pulaski NM *(June)*
Fort Raleigh NHS *(August)*
Fort Scott NHS *(June)*

Fort Smith NHS *(July)*
Fort Stanwix NM *(July)*
Fort Sumter NM *(July)*
Fort Union NM *(July)*
Fort Union Trading Post NHS *(July)*
Fort Vancouver NHS *(July)*
Fort Washington Park *(May)*
Fossil Butte NM *(July)*
Frederick Douglass Home NHS *(February)*
Frederick Law Olmsted NHS *(August)*
Fredericksburg & Spotsylvania NMP *(August)*
Friendship Hill NHS *(August)*

G

Gates of the Arctic NP & PRES *(August)*
Gateway NRA *(July)*
Gauley River NRA *(September)*
General Grant NMEM *(May)*
George Washington Birthplace NM *(May)*
George Washington Carver NM *(July)*
George Washington Mem Pkwy *(July)*
George Rogers Clark NHP *(May)*
Gettsyburg NMP *(July)*
Gila Cliff Dwellings NM *(August)*
Glacier Bay NP & PRES *(August)*
Glacier NP *(July)*
Glen Canyon NRA *(August)*
Golden Gate NRA *(August)*
Golden Spike NHS *(July)*
Grand Canyon NP *(August)*
Grand Portage NM *(August)*
Grand Teton NP *(July)*
Grant-Kohrs Ranch NHS *(July)*
Great Basin NP *(August)*
Great Egg Harbor NS&RECR *(Information incomplete)*
Great Sand Dunes NM *(July)*
Great Smoky Mountains NP *(July)*
Greenbelt Park *(May)*
Guadalupe Mountains NP *(May)*
Guilford Courthouse NMP *(March)*
Gulf Islands NS *(June)*

H

Hagerman Fossil Beds NM *(Information incomplete)*
Haleakala NP *(July)*
Hamilton Grange NMEM *(August)*

Hampton NHS *(September)*
Harpers Ferry NHP *(May)*
Harry S Truman NHS *(July)*
Hawaii Volcanoes NP *(September)*
Herbert Hoover NHS *(July)*
Home of FDR NHS *(August)*
Homestead NM of America *(June)*
Hopewell Culture NHP *(August)*
Hopewell Furnace NHS *(August)*
Horseshoe Bend NMP *(April)*
Hot Springs NP *(July)*
Hovenweep NM *(July)*
Hubbell Trading Post NHS *(May)*

I

Independence NHP *(July)*
Indiana Dunes NL *(June)*
Isle Royale NP *(August)*

J

James A. Garfield NHS *(May)*
Jean Lafitte NHP *(March)*
Jefferson National Expansion Mem *(August)*
Jewel Cave NM *(July)*
Jimmy Carter NHS *(April)*
John D. Rockefeller Jr. Mem Pkwy *(July)*
John Day Fossil Beds NM *(July)*
John F. Kennedy NHS *(August)*
John F. Kennedy Center for the Performing Arts *(April)*
John Muir NHS *(April)*
Johnstown Flood NMEM *(July)*
Joshua Tree NM *(April)*

K

Katmai NP&PRES *(July)*
Kenai Fjords NP *(July)*
Kennesaw Mountain NBP *(April)*
Keweenaw NHP *(August)*
Kings Canyon NP *(August)*
Kings Mountain NMP *(July)*
Klondike Gold Rush NHP *(July)*
Knife River Indian Villages NHS *(July)*
Kobuk Valley NP *(July)*

L

Lake Clark NP & Pres *(August)*
Lake Chelan NRA *(August)*
Lake Mead NRA *(June)*

Lake Meredith NRA *(May)*
Lassen Volcanic NP *(September)*
Lava Beds NM *(August)*
Lincoln Boyhood NMEM *(August)*
Lincoln Home NHS *(July)*
Lincoln Memorial *(July)*
Little Bighorn Battlefield NM *(July)*
Longfellow NHS *(August)*
Lowell NHP *(July)*
Lyndon B. Johnson NHP *(March)*
Lyndon Baines Johnson Memorial Grove on the Potomac *(July)*

M

Maggie L. Walker NHS *(May)*
Mammoth Cave NP *(July)*
Manassas NBP *(May)*
Martin Luther King, Jr. NHS *(January)*
Martin Van Buren NHS *(July)*
Mary McLeod Bethune Council House NHS *(July)*
Mesa Verde NP *(July)*
Minute Man NHP *(July)*
Mississippi NR and RA *(Information incomplete)*
Missouri NRecR *(July)*
Monocacy NB *(July)*
Montezuma Castle NM *(April)*
Moores Creek NB *(July)*
Morristown NHP *(August)*
Mount Rainier NP *(August)*
Mount Rushmore NMEM *(July)*
Muir Woods NM *(August)*

N

Natchez NHP *(March)*
Natchez Trace NST *(Information incomplete)*
Natchez Trace Parkway *(July)*
National Capital Parks *(May)*
National Mall *(July)*
Natural Bridges NM *(June)*
Navajo NM *(August)*
New River Gorge NR *(July)*
Nez Perce NHP *(August)*
Ninety Six NHS *(April)*
Niobrara NSR *(July)*
Noatak NPRES *(August)*
North Cascades NP *(August)*

O

Obed W&SR *(July)*
Ocmulgee NM *(March)*
Olympic NP *(August)*
Oregon Caves NM *(August)*
Organ Pipe Cactus NM *(March)*
Ozark NSR *(July)*

P

Padre Island NS *(August)*
Palo Alto Battlefield NHS *(Information incomplete)*
Pea Ridge NMP *(July)*
Pecos NM *(August)*
Pennsylvania Avenue NHS *(July)*
Perry's Victory & IPMEM *(July)*
Petersburg NB *(March)*
Petrified Forest NP *(July)*
Petroglyph NM *(October)*
Pictured Rocks NL *(August)*
Pinnacles NM *(April)*
Pipe Spring NM *(June)*
Pipestone NM *(July)*
Piscataway Park *(May)*
Point Reyes NS *(July)*
Poverty Point NM *(Information incomplete)*
Prince William Forest Park *(May)*
Pu'uhonua o Honaunau NHP *(July)*
Puukohola Heiau NHS *(August)*

R

Rainbow Bridge NM *(August)*
Redwood NP *(July)*
Richmond NBP *(July)*
Rio Grande W&SR *(April)*
Rock Creek Park *(August)*
Rocky Mountain NP *(August)*
Roger Williams NMEM *(August)*
Ross Lake NRA *(August)*
Russel Cave NM *(July)*

S

Sagamore Hill NHS *(July)*
Saguaro NM *(February)*
Saint Croix NSRwy *(July)*
Saint-Gaudens NHS *(July)*
Saint Paul's Church NHS *(December)*
Salem Maritime NHS *(July)*

Salinas Pueblo Missions NM *(July)*
Samoa NP *(Information incomplete)*
San Antonio Missions NHP *(May)*
San Francisco Maritime NHP *(August)*
San Juan Island NHP *(August)*
San Juan NHS *(March)*
Santa Monica Mountains NRA *(May)*
Saratoga NHP *(August)*
Saugus Iron Works NHS *(August)*
Scott's Bluff NM *(June)*
Sequoia NP *(August)*
Shadow Mountain NRA *(July)*
Shenandoah NP *(August)*
Shiloh NMP *(April)*
Sitka NHP *(August)*
Sleeping Bear Dunes NL *(August)*
Springfield Armory NHS *(August)*
Statue of Liberty NM *(August)*
Steamtown NHS *(July)*
Stones River NB *(July)*
Sunset Crater NM *(July)*

T

Thaddeus Kosciuszko NMEM *(July)*
Theodore Roosevelt Birthplace NHS *(May)*
Theodore Roosevelt Inaugural NHS *(June)*
Theodore Roosevelt Island NMEM *(May)*
Theodore Roosevelt NP *(June)*
Thomas Jefferson Memorial *(April)*
Thomas Stone NHS *(June)*
Timpanogos Cave NM *(July)*
Timucuan Ecological and Historic Pres *(Information incomplete)*
Tonto NM *(March)*
Tumacacori NHP *(March)*
Tupelo NB *(August)*
Tuskegee Institute NHS *(September)*
Tuzigoot NM *(April)*

U

U.S.S. Arizona MEM *(July)*
Ulysses S. Grant NHS *(August)*
Upper Delaware NS&RecR *(July)*

V

Valley Forge NHP *(May)*
Vanderbilt Mansion NHS *(July)*
Vicksburg NMP *(August)*

Vietnam Veterans Memorial *(July)*
Virgin Islands NP *(April)*
Voyageurs NP *(June)*

W

Walnut Canyon NM *(August)*
War in the Pacific NHP *(Information incomplete)*
Washington Monument *(May)*
Weir Farm NHS *(May)*
Whiskeytown-Shasta-Trinity NRA *(August)*
White House *(April)*
White Sands NM *(July)*
Whitman Mission NHS *(June)*
William Howard Taft NHS *(May)*
Wilson's Creek NB *(June)*
Wind Cave NP *(August)*
Wolf Trap Farm Park for the Performing Arts *(July)*
Women's Rights NHP *(July)*
Wrangell-St. Elais NP & PRES *(August)*
Wright Brothers NMEM *(August)*
Wupatki NM *(July)*

Y

Yellowstone NP *(July)*
Yosemite NP *(August)*
Yukon Charley Rivers NPRES *(September)*

Z

Zion NP *(August)*

Index

D

Notes

Notes

Notes